MW00799603

Iran's Political Economy since the Revolution

More than three decades after the Iranian Revolution reconfigured the strategic landscape in the Middle East, scholars are still trying to decipher its aftereffects. Suzanne Maloney provides the first comprehensive overview of Iran's political economy since the 1979 revolution and offers detailed examinations of two aspects of the Iranian economy of direct interest to scholars and nonspecialist readers of Iran: the energy sector and the role of sanctions. Based on the author's research and experience as both a scholar and government adviser, the book features the evolution of the Islamic Republic from its revolutionary beginnings to a system whose legitimacy is grounded in its ability to deliver development and opportunity to its cititzenry. Moving chronologically from the early years under Khomeini, through the economic deprivations of the 1980s during the Iran-Iraq War, through liberalization under Khatami, to the present, Maloney offers fascinating insights into Iran's domestic politics and how economic policies have affected ideology, leadership priorities, and foreign relations.

Suzanne Maloney is a senior Fellow at the Brookings Institution Center for Middle East Policy.

Iran's Political Economy since the Revolution

SUZANNE MALONEY

Brookings Institution, Washington, D.C.

CAMBRIDGE
UNIVERSITY PRESS

University Printing House, Cambridge CB2 8BS, United Kingdom

One Liberty Plaza, 20th Floor, New York, NY 10006, USA

477 Williamstown Road, Port Melbourne, VIC 3207, Australia

4843/24, 2nd Floor, Ansari Road, Daryaganj, Delhi - 110002, India

79 Anson Road, #06-04/06, Singapore 079906

Cambridge University Press is part of the University of Cambridge.

It furthers the University's mission by disseminating knowledge in the pursuit of education, learning and research at the highest international levels of excellence.

www.cambridge.org
Information on this title: www.cambridge.org/9780521738149

First published 2015

A catalogue record for this publication is available from the British Library

Library of Congress Cataloging in Publication data
Maloney, Suzanne.
Iran's political economy since the revolution / Suzanne Maloney (Brookings Institution, Washington, DC).
pages cm
ISBN 978-0-521-50634-2 (Hardback) – ISBN 978-0-521-73814-9 (Paperback)
1. Iran–Economic policy. 2. Iran–Politics and government–1979-1997. 3. Iran–Politics and government–1997– 4. Iran–History–Revolution, 1979–Influence. 5. Energy industries–Iran. 6. Economic sanctions–Iran. 7. Iran-Iraq War, 1980–1988–Economic aspects. I. Title.
HC475.M314 2015
330.955–dc23
2014040461

ISBN 978-0-521-50634-2 Hardback
ISBN 978-0-521-73814-9 Paperback

Contents

I

Introduction

During the summer of 2012, the Islamic Republic of Iran was rocked by a crisis over chicken. As the world ratcheted up pressure on Iran in hopes of forcing its government to abandon its nuclear program, the fallout from the latest round of international sanctions rippled throughout the Iranian economy. The currency crashed, inflation spiked, and the primary engine of the country's wealth – its oil exports – plummeted by nearly 50 percent. Although sanctions, particularly those imposed by Washington, have been a prominent feature of the economic landscape here almost since the inception of the revolutionary state more than three decades earlier, no previous measures had delivered such an immediate, dramatic, or far-reaching blow.

In this charged environment, the skyrocketing price of chicken, which soared as high as three times its cost only a year earlier, emerged as a kind of shorthand for a newly urgent public debate over the economy, the government, and, by extension, the future of Iran. From the Friday prayers pulpit, the Iranian leadership's favored instrument of communication, clerics appealed to Iranians to abstain from chicken and eat more vege-tables instead, while others denounced the price spike as an enemy plot.[1]

---

[1] Grand Ayatollah Makarem Shirazi, one of Iran's most senior clerics, advised that "many people complain about the high price of chicken; but it is not a very important problem if they do not eat chicken. Most doctors have said that meat is not good for health and should be taken in small amounts." *Iranian Students News Agency* (ISNA), July 21, 2012. The comments prompted sufficient backlash that Makarem Shirazi was forced to issue a statement 10 days later clarifying that he had not issued a religious injunction prohibiting the eating of chicken. In Shiraz, the Friday prayer leader Ayatollah Imani denounced the high price of chicken as part of the "enemy's psychological warfare" on July 27, 2012.

The head of Iran's internal security forces took it upon himself to warn against broadcasting images of chicken on state-run television, for fear that the mere sight of *morgh polo* (chicken with rice, variations of which are a staple of the Iranian diet) would provoke class warfare. The issue inspired impassioned newspaper editorials, televised policy discussions, and, in classic Iranian fashion, endless jokes that circulated the country through routes both timeworn (word of mouth) and cutting-edge (Facebook and Twitter). The international media picked up the meme,[2] and as Iranians waited for hours in long lines for government-subsidized chicken, there was at least one case of a chicken-incited riot.[3] In an echo of President Mahmoud Ahmadinejad's 2005 campaign slogan, a newspaper affiliated with one of his rivals jabbed that Iranians "are still waiting for oil money to come to their table in order to purchase chicken!"[4]

The uproar seemed a suitably ironic denouement for a state whose founder, Ayatollah Ruhollah Khomeini, had explicitly touted the primacy of moral considerations over material ones. Even if "Iran's Islamic Revolution was not made over the price of melons," as Khomeini was reputed to have said, it briefly appeared that the revolution might be unmade over the price of chickens. For some outside observers[5] and Western policy makers, it was truly a case of chickens coming home to roost; the tragicomic implosion of the Iranian economy represented the potential vindication of the American strategy for thwarting Tehran's nuclear ambitions and offered long-awaited evidence that the Islamic Republic's manifold failings would ultimately prove the seeds of its own destruction.

---

[2] Najmeh Bozorgmehr, "Sanctions Threaten Weak Iranian Economy," *The Financial Times*, June 28, 2012; Marcus George and Yeganeh Torbati, "Iran's 'Chicken Crisis' Is Simmering Political Issue," *Reuters*, July 22, 2012, http://www.reuters.com/article/2012/07/22/iran-economy-chicken-idUSL6E8IJFYV20120722; Hossein Bastani and Ali Hamedani, "Growing Anger in Iran over Cost of Chicken as Sanctions Bite," *BBC Persian Service*, July 27, 2012, http://www.bbc.co.uk/news/world-middle-east-18999395; Meir Javedanfar, "Iran's Big Crisis: The Price of Chicken," *Bloomberg*, August 7, 2012, http://www.bloomberg.com/news/2012-08-07/iran-s-big-crisis-the-price-of-chicken.html

[3] Saeed Kamali Dehghan, "Reports of Street Protests in Iran Due to Soaring Price of Chicken," *The Guardian*, http://www.guardian.co.uk/world/iran-blog/2012/jul/23/street-protests-iran-chicken.

[4] "At an Iftar Banquet with the President a Criticism from University Students about the Government's Policies Was Raised," *Tehran-e Emrooz*, August 4, 2012.

[5] Avi Issacharoff, "Amid Sanctions, the Greatest Threat to Iran's Nuclear Program May Be the Price of Chicken," August 9, 2012, *Haaretz*, http://www.haaretz.com/blogs/east-side-story/amid-sanctions-the-greatest-threat-to-iran-s-nuclear-program-may-be-the-price-of-chicken.premium-1.457241; Joshua Foust, "The Annals of Chicken Politics, Iran Edition," TheAtlantic.com, July 31, 2012, http://www.theatlantic.com/international/archive/2012/07/the-annals-of-chicken-politics-iran-edition/260526/

However, behind the headlines, the reality of revolutionary Iran proved more multifaceted than the cursory media coverage might have suggested. Not for the first time, the country's course deviated from the presumptive script. In fact, the much-hyped "chicken revolution" did not transpire. A closer examination of the episode reveals a more complex array of causes, including but hardly limited to sanctions, and the regime's crisis management suggests something other than the inevitable demise of the Islamic Republic. First, the regime mounted a robust response to public hardship. Senior Iranian officials participated in crisis summitry to devise and implement damage control, and Iran's embattled institutions of civil society and representative rule – its newspapers and bloggers, its pork-barrel parliament – moved into high gear to press for improvements and highlight related problems. Despite the restrictions on its international trade and financial access, Tehran managed to procure imported chicken from allies, including Turkey and Brazil, and quickly sought to distribute it at a subsidized price. As they waited in the sort of ration lines that had not existed since the 1980–88 war with Iraq, Iranians continued to vent their outrage at the indignity of rising prices and low supplies. However, for the most part they remained unwilling to risk their lives or their livelihoods to translate their dissatisfaction into a direct challenge to the ruling system. Moreover, the chicken controversy did not have an immediately salutary effect on Iran's readiness to resolve the nuclear standoff.

To the disappointment of many, both inside Iran and beyond, the great Iranian chicken crisis of 2012 unfolded somewhat differently from initial expectations. Mitigation, improvisation, and the surprising capacity of Iran's postrevolutionary institutions enabled the Islamic Republic to survive yet another test of its endurance. This outcome does not contradict a core underlying reality of contemporary Iran: Sanctions have exacted a tremendous toll on a state whose political and economic development is already distorted by the epic turmoil and mismanagement of the postrevolutionary era. Even the most orthodox defenders of the Islamic Republic have been forced to alter their traditional blustering denial and acknowledge that the measures targeting Iran's access to the international financial system and its oil sector hit home. Sanctions have bound the horizons of the Islamic Republic, and for the foreseeable future, they will determine the opportunities of the Iranian people.

However, these sanctions have not played out in predictable fashion, and Iran's aborted chicken upheaval offers a reminder that the world has once again failed to anticipate the trajectory of the Islamic Republic's internal agonies. And it underscores the utility of developing a more nuanced understanding of Iran's political economy. As this episode demonstrates, the economy lies at the heart of the challenge facing Iranians as they survey their future, and for the world in seeking to influence the decisions of Iran's leaders. However, the formula for inducing moderation remains elusive, and the relationship between economic challenges and political change in Iran has proven more complicated than the crude logic of external economic pressure.

Despite Khomeini's dismissive rhetoric on the economy, which has been oversimplified and misconstrued in its frequent repetition,[6] the leaders of the Islamic Republic have always recognized the relevance of the price of melons. In the mobilization against the shah and its aftermath, Iran's revolutionaries deployed religious themes and institutions to seize the fulcrum of a disparate coalition that shared little other than their antipathy toward the shah. And yet, having waged a revolution in the name of religious righteousness and under the guise of theocratic imperatives, the postrevolutionary leadership has sought to govern largely through an appeal to the mundane and the distribution of the spoils. During the revolution's initial decade, the tensions within the relevant body of decision makers over the regime's economic approach produced epic battles among the leadership and nearly fractured the state. Over time, however, historical circumstances – in particular, the war with Iraq – compelled an uneasy consensus around economic liberalization and market forces. The evolution was also facilitated by the persistence of political competition, the exigencies of Iran's oil-based economy, and the legacy of popular demands for government accountability that dated back at least a century.

As the Islamic Republic has buttressed its ideological claims with economic ones, Tehran has subtly shifted the basis for its own legitimacy. The Islamic state's persistent reliance on populist promises was intended to buy off popular frustration, in the hopes that subsidies on consumer goods could supplant demands for greater political participation and social freedoms. This strategy backfired; instead, the regime has inadvertently cultivated a set of public expectations surrounding government performance, and its accountability to the people, that were never intended by its founders. The politics of populism and the rhetoric of redistribution have been far more powerful in shaping the popular

---

[6] Khomeini's reference to the significance of the price of melons is addressed in greater depth in Chapter 3.

imagination than the regime's appeals to anti-Americanism or the deployment of Shi'a ideology and institutions. By creating expectations of economic windfalls, greater egalitarianism, and an improvement in the plight of *mostazafan* (the oppressed), Iranian leaders effectively undercut the theocratic basis of their authority and bolstered a competing rationale – one that is based upon its citizens' expectations of a government that will deliver a better life.

In theory, at least, the shift in the basis of the Iranian regime, as articulated in both the rhetoric and the policies of its government, should entail a commensurate moderation of revolutionary radicalism, and even generate greater traction for international diplomacy toward Tehran. After all, a government whose legitimacy is increasingly contingent upon satisfying popular expectations of development is correspondingly more vulnerable to economic pressures and faces more immediate incentives to maintain durable, constructive relationships with the international community as part of a viable framework for trade and growth. And yet precisely the opposite has transpired in Iran's Islamic Republic. Even as the economy assumed a higher priority for the leadership and even as they found accord on areas of economic policy that had previously caused contention, the regime retained its predilection for provocation, continuing to subsidize terror abroad and investing in a nuclear infrastructure that unnerved the world. Here, too, the explanation for the puzzle of Iran's persistent obstructionism, despite the manifest costs to its growth and development, lies in a closer examination of its political economy – specifically, the empowerment of bifurcated authority, reliance on oil revenues, deeply rooted mistrust of foreign interest in Iranian resources, and the epic changes in world trade and economic growth that have occurred independently of Iran's own development.

THE CONTEXT: IRAN'S POSTREVOLUTIONARY POLITICAL ECONOMY

Three decades of rule by a revolutionary Islamic regime has generated outcomes that do not conform to the ideological imperatives of its founders – or, for the matter, the too-often cartoonish depiction of the Western imagination. Contemporary Iran is neither sequestered from the relentless forces of economic and cultural globalization, nor mired in the traditionalism that represents the ideal of some of its founders and the image relentlessly projected by the media. It is neither the glorious triumph of Islamic governance and economic management trumpeted by its leadership, nor fully the basket case, perpetually on the brink of collapse as a result of leadership fissures and fiscal strains, that American politicians repeatedly invoke.

Much of the difficulty in interpreting Iran's economic exigencies stems from the inherent ambiguities. First, Iran is both *rich and poor*: It is a tremendously wealthy country, a fact that often is downplayed in the policy debates around Iran's internal dramas and external pressures. Iran is a latent economic powerhouse and, with responsible governance, could play an important role in generating growth and prosperity in the Middle East. The country's most obvious advantages are its natural resources: Iran boasts the second largest reserves of gas and the third largest reserves of conventional oil in the world, earning $70 billion from oil exports in 2010 even as international sanctions began to constrain its energy exports. Beyond the petroleum sector, however, its temperate climate and strategic location along the crossroads of Asia and Europe have created a diverse economic base that predates the oil boom and remains a valuable juncture for transcontinental trade. Its human resources are equally impressive, with a well-educated labor force. Iran's long history as an integrated nation-state entails a familiarity with central government and stable borders long before most of its neighboring fellow oil producers. Even today, despite decades of sanctions, conflict, and internal mismanagement, Tehran credibly claims at least $100 billion in foreign reserves – a hefty war chest for enduring the epic international pressure that the regime faces today.

Still, in the face of these powerful advantages and a recent period of record high oil prices, Iran's position in the international economy has absolutely declined over the course of the past three decades. As Figure 1.1 suggests, Iran's national income shrank by half in the first decade of the revolution and rebounded during the reform era only to begin a descent anew with the global economic slowdown and the intensification of international pressure since 2010. High oil prices have boosted Iran's GDP, but growth remains erratic and anemic, even in the wake of the heftiest influx of oil revenues since the revolution during the past decade. Iran's relative position in the world economy has plunged as other developing economies – particularly those in Asia – have taken off.[7] This reflects the impact of several powerful, detrimental trends, particularly the post-revolutionary predilection for a dominant role for the state in the economy

---

[7] Hadi Salehi Esfahani and M. Hashem Pesaran, "The Iranian Economy in the Twentieth Century: A Global Perspective," *Iranian Studies* 42:2 (April 2009), p. 196.

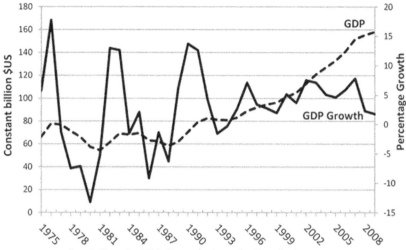

FIGURE I.I Iran's Erratic GDP Growth since the Revolution

and the decades of disruptions in Iran's trade relations and foreign investment wrought by economic sanctions, ideological imperatives, the inherent volatility of reliance on resource revenues, and the persistence of internal and regional conflicts.

Second, the Islamic Republic has proven both *developmental and predatory* in its stewardship of the national economy. Even the rosiest depiction of its socioeconomic benefits underscores how little of the original intentions of the revolution's participants was achieved by the state that emerged in its aftermath. Long-term trends suggest that the Islamic Republic has not manifestly altered the profoundly unequal patterns of wealth distribution that prevailed prior to the revolution.[8] Iran's repressive political climate and poor governance have negated much of the benefit of its infrastructure investments, as wider dispersion of educational resources and markedly higher literacy rates have corresponded to a steady decline in productivity.[9] The heavy hand of the state and parastatal firms has resulted in an enduring erosion of the manufacturing sector, with notable declines in productivity that have persisted

[8] Djavad Salehi-Isfahani, "Poverty, Inequality, and Populist Politics in Iran," *The Journal of Economic Inequality* 15:1 (March 2009), pp. 18–23.
[9] Mohammad Reza Farzanegan, "Education Spending and Productivity in Iran: Where Have All the Education Expenditures Gone?" Economic Research Forum 17th annual conference paper, March 20–22, 2011.

long after the original dislocations of the revolution and war.[10] States such as South Korea and Turkey, whose economies and growth trajectories were roughly similar to that of Iran prior to the oil boom and the revolution, have left the Islamic Republic in their dust on nearly any meaningful comparisons of growth, productivity, and per capita income. Socially, the legal framework erected during the Pahlavi period that facilitated female participation in the economy and advanced women's rights to divorce and child custody were jettisoned after the revolution despite persistent opposition by the world.

However, focusing solely on the problematic elements of the Islamic Republic's economic policies would foster an incomplete and skewed portrayal of the past thirty-five years. Despite its demonstrable failings with respect to economic management, its proclivity for alienating potential investors and trade relationships – and despite the dramatic declines in per capita GDP during the first fifteen years of the revolutionary regime – poverty in Iran today has become less widespread than it was before the revolution.[11] Infrastructure for the support of health, education, and social welfare has permeated the country on a dramatically wider basis, and the positive impacts on Iranian society are incontestable. Literacy rates among young Iranians are nearly universal, and overall female literacy had risen from 24 percent in 1976 to 77 percent by 2006.[12] Infant mortality has dropped by more than 75 percent, from 107 deaths out of every 1,000 live births in 1975 to 25.9/1,000 in 2009, and average life expectancy expanded from fifty-seven years to seventy-two years in the same time frame.[13]

Higher education has increased by more than tenfold (223 institutions at the time of the revolution to 2,471 in 2012).[14] Women represent a majority in both undergraduate and graduate university programs. Their representation in most areas of social and economic life reveals a broader societal transformation in gender roles, in spite of – and in some cases, because of – postrevolutionary setbacks for women's legal rights and social status. Moreover, this phenomenon is

[10] Farshid Mojaver, "Sources of Economic Growth and Stagnation in Iran," *The Journal of International Trade & Economic Development* 18:2 (June 2009), p. 292.
[11] For the most persuasive analysis of the trends that contributed to this shift, see Djavad Salehi-Isfahani, "Poverty, Inequality, and Populist Politics in Iran," *Journal of Economic Inequality* 7:1 (March 2009), pp. 5–28.
[12] UNESCO.   [13] World Development Indicators, World Bank.
[14] Ahmadinejad address, broadcast on state television, July 26, 2012, as recorded and translated by BBC Monitoring Middle East, July 28, 2012.

not limited to statistical estimates of income and affordability; most measures of social development attest to the dramatic expansion in the dispersion of infrastructure and in educational attainments. The vast majority of Iranians today have access to health care and education, at standards that are highly imperfect but that nonetheless represent a marked improvement upon the circumstances that existed prior to the revolution.

Finally, Iran is *integrated but isolated*. Manifold obstacles have impeded Iran's interactions with the international community: its leaders' early autarkic predilections, its clashes with its neighbors, inhospitable conditions for investment and tourism, and of course the increasing reach of international economic sanctions. Iranian leaders publicly reveled in the relative insulation of their economy as the contraction of U.S. credit markets helped spark a global recession in 2008.[15] Iran's exclusion extends well beyond its economy to its political and cultural connections to the world. As U.S. policy makers boast with veracity, Tehran today has few friends on the international stage; the Islamic regime is routinely condemned in nearly universal fashion in international organizations. Its singular regional ally, Syria, is enmeshed in a civil war and has been shunned by the rest of the Arab world. The revolution's tentative international opening during the 1990s, which saw its reformist president feted throughout Europe, within the decade reverted to reliance on fraternity of pariahs, such as Cuba, Venezuela, and Byelorussia. Iran's loneliness extends to its population, who face steep hurdles in traveling internationally thanks to financial sanctions and visa restrictions. At home, clerical leaders continue to inveigh against the evils of globalization, and the regime has waged an effective, if ultimately futile, battle to restrict the nation's access to information by banning satellite dishes, jamming foreign broadcasting, and heavily restricting Internet access.

Still, even today under the most robust external economic pressure that has ever been aligned against Tehran, the country remains inextricably intertwined in the international economy. Moreover, Iran today remains very much subject to a variety of global forces with respect to its culture, politics, and economy. Despite the sanctions' specificity

---

[15] "The Governor of the Central Bank: Do Not Worry about the Impact of Global Financial Crisis on Iran's Economy," *Hezbollah*, October 31, 2008, p. 4; "US Economic Crisis Can Be Opportunity for Iran, MP," *IRNA*, October 12, 2008; Ahmad Reza Pursanei, "Calm of Iran's Economy amid Global Crisis," *Javan*, October 15, 2008; "Presidential Aide: Iran Less Affected by Global Crisis," Fars News Agency, November 5, 2008.

in targeting individual Iranian officials and institutions for their roles in proliferation, terrorism, and human rights abuses, Tehran has managed to maintain at least the pretense of continuing engagement with the world. In August 2012, the Islamic Republic hosted the summit of the Non-Aligned Movement and succeeded in luring several world leaders to participate in the pageantry, including the newly elected Egyptian president, the Indian prime minister, and the secretary-general of the United Nations. Iranian leaders reliably participate in similar diplomatic symbolism, jetting to conclaves of the Organization of the Islamic Conference and the Shanghai Conference Organization and seizing the podium at the United Nations. The purpose of these ceremonies is clear – to assert Iran's historic aspiration to a leading role in the regional and broader international arenas.

This interconnection to the world beyond Iran extends throughout the population. A well-educated, high-income diaspora that has expanded since the revolution and continues to travel to and from Iran has lent much of the population a direct window on the worlds of Los Angeles, Toronto, and Melbourne. Moreover, the restrictions imposed by their own government as well as by the international sanctions have proven frequently porous, enabling Iranians to gain access to nearly any product of the international marketplace via the indefatigable black market. Most important to the association of ordinary Iranians to the wider world has been the information revolution. Iranians' access to the Internet has increased steadily – even, at least as far as official statistics show, after the 2009 crackdown – to more than 27 million,[16] and the Student Basij Organization has asserted that at least 17 million Iranians are registered users of Facebook.[17] Seventy-two percent of all Iranians have a cell phone.[18] The broad trends are clear – the more that political dynamics have conspired to isolate the Iranian regime, the more that its leadership and its population have become inextricably tied to an increasingly globalized world.

AIMS OF THE BOOK

Rich and poor, developmental and predatory, integrated and isolated – these are the paradoxes of Iran's political economy. And, by extension,

---

[16] World Development Indicators, World Bank.
[17] "Some 17 million Iranians are members of Facebook," *Ete'mad*, October 5, 2011, p. 1.
[18] World Development Indicators, World Bank.

these contradictions underscore the world's challenges in trying to influence its government's policy and future trajectory. These paradoxes highlight the analytical challenges of contemporary Iran: It is a complicated state, presiding over a political class and a nation that seem to be persistently in flux, and its ideological and institutional framework is riven by interlocking contradictions. This book sets out to investigate these paradoxes further, with three main objectives at heart. The first is to provide a comprehensive overview of the economic policy decisions and debates that have had such a formative impact on the Iranian state, society, and the political evolution of the Islamic Republic. During the past twenty-five years, as the Islamic Republic began to crack open its doors to researchers and journalists after a decade of revolution and war, the media, academic, and policy communities in the United States and Europe have generated a valuable literature that has helped greatly in elucidating a state that has suffers from too much presumed familiarity and too little real understanding.

Still, the forces that have sustained the revolution and the current leadership constantly seem to surprise the world, in large part because our approach to contemporary Iran remains curiously unrefined. Traditional policy analysis and historical overviews of the postrevolutionary regime have tended to underestimate the significance of economic issues and constraints. Instead, the narrative of the incipient Islamic Republic, and the subsequent identities adopted by the revolutionary state, has almost invariably been oriented through the lens of ideology – the harsh religiosity of Khomeini himself, the shrewd opportunism of the post-Khomeini years, the reformists' gradualism and embrace of tentative liberalization, the brash obstinacy embodied by President Mahmoud Ahmadinejad, and the uncertain opening presented by his successor, Hassan Rouhani.

In this way, conventional analysis emphasizes the primacy of the particular ideological preferences of the dominant Iranian political faction in determining domestic and foreign policy. The Iranian economy is generally treated as an afterthought to the central dimensions of Iran's politics, which are presumed to be primarily ideological, factional, and even personalistic. Many of the most valuable narratives of Iran's internal dynamics and foreign policy that have been produced since the revolution contain only glancing reference to monumental developments in the various elements of its trade, energy, or fiscal policies. And yet the dynamics of Iran's political economy have frequently proved essential in shaping the options and the evolution of the postrevolutionary state.

This tendency toward a selective analysis of Iran should not be surprising, as the record is largely conveyed by journalists, historians, and political scientists rather than economists. More generally, this focus on ideology as the paramount explanatory factor represents the legacy of a revolution in which the engagement of theological concepts and clerical leaders represented the most novel and compelling dimensions. Finally, analysts have tended to shortchange the impact of economics because Iran's leadership has frequently disdained its significance. From Khomeini's withering reference to the price of melons to Ahmadinejad's boasts that the Islamic Republic could survive oil prices as low as five dollars a barrel, Tehran has endeavored to depict its statecraft as transcending the mundane science of the economy.

Such rhetoric is pure propaganda and helps foster an artificial and incomplete understanding of the functioning of the Islamic Republic. Focusing on the ideological dimensions of Iran's evolution provides only a one-dimensional understanding of a multifaceted narrative. The evolution of Iran's revolutionary state is more readily explicable – and possibly even predictable – when the analysis incorporates the significance of economic resources and the centrality of political struggles over economic resources and policy. In fact, the revolution that was not about economics forged an environment in which the economy has been a central flashpoint for political contention. It was economics, not ideology, that initiated the most consequential political fissures within the Islamic Republic, empowering institutions such as the Majlis, constraining Khomeini's authority, and ultimately empowering the political currents that have fueled Iranian opposition movements. Economics forced Iran to abandon its early autarkic approach to the world and court major regional powers through mercantilist diplomacy. Most recently, the countervailing forces of international sanctions, elite implication in the system's crony capitalist underpinnings, and the state's capacity to buy off popular discontent have forged Tehran's revived efforts to negotiate an end to the costly standoff with the international community over the nuclear program.

Beyond integrating an appreciation for the economic aspects of Iran's political dynamics, the book seeks to delineate the factors that have generated such an unexpected and contradictory set of outcomes. Understanding the role of the economy in shaping Iran's political debates may add value to our understanding of Iranian policies, but it is equally if not more important to discern why the economy constitutes such a pivotal element of internal dynamics and external behavior. This study will emphasize four major aspects that have shaped Iran's political economy since the revolution.

The first of these is *the legacy of Iran's political and economic development* prior to the 1979 revolution. Any observer of Iran appreciates the relevance of the economy in shaping the evolution of the state and the political dynamics. In fact, the rich historical work on Iran's prerevolutionary history is rife with details of the salience of economic grievances in prior periods of political turmoil. In each of Iran's most significant turning points of the century that preceded the Islamic Revolution – the Tobacco Revolt, the Constitutional Revolution, the oil nationalization crisis – financial pressures intensified and expedited the political challenge to the status quo. This pattern extends through the 1979 revolution and beyond.

Iranian history has generated deeply engrained popular demands for government accountability and performance, which have manifested in repeated upheavals and efforts to constrain the authority of the Iranian state throughout the modern era. Economic grievances – in particular the inflationary pressures that have had their roots at least in part in erratic monetary policy – have served as the backdrop for each of Iran's prior periods of political ferment during the past century. This legacy is counterbalanced by the revolution's emphasis, via both rhetoric and institutions, of social justice – a powerful unifying theme that remains deeply resonant in the populist promises of every revolutionary leader, from Khomeini to Ahmadinejad. Moreover, not only have these preferences and predispositions imprinted themselves upon the Iranian approach to economic policies, in many cases the institutions of the prerevolutionary era survived the upheaval and the establishment of a new regime intact.

Iran's historical legacy is only one piece of the puzzle. The second factor that has had profound influence on the course of Iran's economic decision making is the postrevolutionary political context, whose foremost features include *the persistence of factional conflict and the bifurcation of authority* via dual and dueling institutions. Iran's ruling system is the product of its revolution – a competing, multipronged beast that incorporates a wide array of aims, interests, and actors. The divisions among the revolutionary coalition and the lack of consensus surrounding the postrevolutionary order resulted in a framework for the new state that precariously balances the sacred and the secular through a uniquely bifurcated framework of authority.

These conditions have proven mutually reinforcing – the fratricidal partisanship among the Iranian leadership has been channeled through and exacerbated by an elaborate array of parallel institutions that stretch throughout the political, economic, and social life of Iran. Iran's dual sovereignty and intense factionalism have had a direct and deleterious impact on the country's economic structure and policies, resulting in an even fiercer competition for access to the state and its prerogatives, additional barriers to fiscal and legal transparency, the proliferation of parallel institutions, and a long-standing philosophical rift over economic policy.

The third factor in shaping Iran's postrevolutionary political economy is oil, and *the state's control of massive revenues derived from resource exports*. Simply put, oil has underwritten the Islamic Republic's endurance even as it has increased Iran's vulnerability to the vicissitudes of international markets and the coercive efforts of its adversaries. Ironically, despite the revolutionaries' rhetorical disdain toward oil markets and world capitalism, Iran has been more dependent on oil revenues since 1979 than under the monarchy.[19] The advantages of Iran's resource bounty to the postrevolutionary state are in many respects obvious: Oil revenues reconstituted the institutions of the state after the revolutionary disruption and sustained the extension of central authority and the massive exigencies of the longest land war since the Korean conflict. This same income stream has enabled Iran's postrevolutionary leadership to retain a powerful base of support at home, through persistent overspending and reliance on distributive economic policies, and to use its resources and oil revenues to extend its influence across the region and to far corners of the globe.

However, Iran's postrevolutionary experience also offers a cautionary tale about the toxic impact of resource wealth on long-term growth, as well as on the development of democratic institutions. One need only compare the dramatic divergence between economic growth in Iran and the economies of Malaysia, South Korea, and Turkey since the 1960s; in the absence of abundant endowments of petroleum, each of these governments was forced to develop its manufacturing sector, attract foreign investment and its attendant influx of technology transfer, and establish better governance and more efficient use of available capital and resources. And despite its leadership's persistent blustering threats to use the "oil weapon," Tehran has never achieved any real leverage in this respect. Instead, the Islamic Republic has repeatedly found itself on the

---

[19] Massour Karshenas and Hassan Hakimian, "Oil, Economic Diversification and the Democratic Process in Iran," *Iranian Studies* 38:1 (March 2005), p. 74.

receiving end of crises provoked by market shifts and price volatility, as well as physical and financial attacks on its export capabilities that have battered its bottom line and regime resilience.

The fourth recurrent theme that runs throughout this analysis of the Islamic Republic's political economy is *Iran's tormented relationship with the world*. One of the hallmarks of Iranian history is a deep ambivalence and suspicion toward world powers and the global economy. The religious rhetoric deployed to galvanize opposition to the monarchy, and later during the war, helped to elevate and entrench this sense of antagonism toward the international community. However, the Islamic Republic has never pursued or achieved anything close to true autarky. And even if it had, the world was not prepared to disengage from Iran, as made clear by a war, a steady stream of refugees, and an array of other developments around the globe that have forced Iran into the world in diverse and persistent fashion as described previously. Still, there is a fundamental dichotomy in Iran's approach to the world, a resentment coexistent with a sense of imperative that has cultivated an array of contradictions in Iran's foreign and economic policies.

Iran's complex and contentious relationship with the world is particularly relevant today, as the policies of the Islamic Republic have become a major focus of international concern and initiative. The world's interest in Iran informs the final purpose of this book, which is to offer guideposts for understanding the future trajectory of the Islamic Republic, based on the historical analysis of the forces that have generated the current context, and to assess the policies of both Tehran and its critics for generating stability and prosperity in the Islamic Republic and across the region. Iran's flailing economy is frequently perceived as the Achilles' heel of the theocratic government, and nearly every effort that Washington has undertaken to persuade or coerce its leadership has had economics at its heart. For more than three decades, Western analyses and policy makers have periodically predicted that the economic pressures besetting the regime would finally cause its collapse. However, each of these predictions has proven inaccurate, or at least premature. As this analysis will demonstrate, the relationship between economic constraints and policy change or moderation exists, but it is neither linear nor immediate.

This book does not purport to offer a formula for achieving the most effective influence on Iran's policies. No analyst can offer a conclusive prediction on the precise array of pressure that would induce change in

Iran's ruling system or that would produce a reversal of its posture on the nuclear program and negotiations with the West. Instead, throughout the book, and in particular in the chapter devoted to trade and sanctions, this study endeavors to ascertain how sanctions have played into the intense political and philosophical debates on the economy, and the evolution of the Islamic Republic's approach to its domestic and foreign policies. In this way, the study addresses the dilemmas that confound Washington and the rest of the international community about the utility and limitations of economic pressure in reshaping Iran's decision making and its future trajectory.

STRUCTURE OF THE BOOK

It is tempting to view the Islamic Republic in isolation from its antecedents. At first glance, the theocratic state appears to represent such a sharp break from its conspicuously modernizing predecessor. However, a thorough consideration of Iran's prerevolutionary and postrevolutionary economy reveals profound elements of continuity, both in institutions – many of which were simply reconstituted in marginally altered form after the revolution – and in attitudes.

History matters as well in shaping the narrative and creating a sense of shared interests among disparate groups, even where a closer examination suggests that the narrative is not entirely accurate or that those interests actually frequently diverged. The legacy of European concession hunting and the role of foreign powers in determining the well-being of ordinary Iranians continue to weigh heavily on Iran's perception of diplomacy and trade today. The salience of Iranian history requires that this book, despite its primary focus on the postrevolutionary era, begin as any serious analysis of contemporary Iran must, with an examination in Chapter 2 of the long history of the Iranian state and the evolution of the economic and political conditions. Chapter 3 considers the revolution and its immediate aftermath, making the case that the opposition's success in ousting the shah was facilitated by its fusion of long-standing economic grievances, the desire for greater accountability and broadly held resentments against world powers for their role in shaping Iran's domestic politics and its economy.

Chapter 4 examines the war with Iraq, focusing on the formulation of economic policy and the mobilization of the economy under the auspices of state control to support the war effort. From the outset, the war violently transformed the Iranian economy and shaped the consolidation and development of the Islamic state. Over the course of the war, a bitter partisan divide crystallized within the regime over economic philosophy and programs, one that resulted in dramatic consequences for the structure of the Islamic Republic and the evolution of an increasingly disruptive clash among its political elites.

Chapter 5 focuses on the eight-year presidency of Ali Akbar Hashemi Rafsanjani, when the economy truly took center stage within the priorities of the revolutionary state via Rafsanjani's efforts to rebuild and reconfigure Iran's economy in the aftermath of the war and Khomeini's death. However, the Rafsanjani era did not generate a sustainable Thermidor, or moderation of Iran's revolutionary furies; in fact, the turn toward economic pragmatism was undercut at every turn by the persistence of ideologically motivated adventurism abroad and the renewal of repression at home.

Chapter 6 addresses the reform movement's unsuccessful efforts to undertake political reform, sociocultural liberalization, and a diplomatic charm offensive as a platform for stabilizing the postrevolutionary system. While economic issues were certainly on the agenda – in fact, perhaps the most significant accomplishments of the Mohammad Khatami era include a number of stepping-stone economic reforms – the reformists never conceived of the economy as the primary arena for political contestation, but rather saw it as inherently contingent upon achieving their broader political and social agenda.

Chapter 7 tackles more recent history, assessing the revival of radical populism during the Ahmadinejad administration and Iran's regression into a deeper and more dangerous isolation from the international community. Ahmadinejad's skillful deployment of economic frustrations catapulted him to office, and yet, combined with his antagonistic tendencies and rhetoric, the wanton spending, and other questionable fiscal and monetary policies undertaken during his eight-year presidency, achieved little real progress for the average Iranian or the country's economy.

The concluding chapters delve into greater detail on specific issues of fundamental relevance for the Iranian economy and the political options and opportunities of the current system. Chapter 8 examines Iran's lifeblood – its energy resources, and the patterns of development that have sustained the Islamic Republic but potentially mortgaged its future prospects. Chapter 9 focuses specifically on the issues of Iran's international economic relations, particularly examining the shifting patterns of trade and foreign investment in Iran and the implications of the evolving sanctions regime on the political course of the regime. Finally, Chapter 10 concludes with Rouhani's 2013 election and a look ahead, drawing lessons from the examination of Iran's political economy for Tehran, Washington, and the international community.

It may seem almost perverse to suggest that this study offers the basis for real optimism about Iran's future. However, just as this book argues for subordinating ideology in understanding Iranian politics, the analysis of Iran's postrevolutionary political economy suggests that one of the most important components of a representative and responsible government has already been achieved within Iran: the incorporation and institutionalization of claims for government accountability under the Islamic Republic. Iran's future remains subject to profound uncertainty, and the rationalizing imperative of sanctions may be undercut, at least temporarily, by the regime's well-honed capacity for crisis management and populist posturing. Still, when a revolutionary theocracy scrambles to address a crisis over the price of chicken, the mantle of the Prophet has given way to the mandate of the pocketbook.

2

The Prelude: The Political Economy
of Prerevolutionary Iran

Iran has a storied history as a nation-state, dating back at least as far as 559 BCE, when Cyrus the Great launched the conquests that would amass a vast Persian empire stretching from northern India to Greece. This history remains as fiercely cherished by Iranians as it is contested within their political and cultural life. As a result, there is a natural temptation to reach back through the millennia to situate the issues and dynamics of modern Iran within their broader historical context. While scholars have done valuable work on the economic patterns of early Iranian history,[1] the late nineteenth and twentieth centuries offer the most relevant starting point for this study.

This is when the contours of the modern Iranian state became manifest, thanks to repeated social uprisings, the centralizing force of an assertive new monarchy, and the country's integration into an emerging international petroleum industry. Over the same period, a powerful narrative emerged in Iran fusing economic grievances with resentment toward foreign intrusions and perceptions that the state had betrayed the country's values. These dynamics would crescendo in 1979, and they continue to shape Iran's evolution today. This history matters not because Iranians invoke it so frequently and with such passion, but because this context forged state and market institutions, ideological perspectives, and grievances.

This chapter reviews the key episodes and developments in shaping Iran's prerevolutionary political and economic context and sketches the

---

[1] Chief among these are Charles Issawi, *The Economic History of Iran* (Chicago: University of Chicago Press, 1972); and Ann K. Lambton, Landlord and Peasant in Persia: A Study of Land Tenure and Land Revenue Administration (London: I.B. Tauris, 1991).

backdrop that helped set the stage for the massive upheaval of the revolution and the adoption of a dualistic approach to development under the post-revolutionary regime. Such a historical perspective offers a richer understanding of the historical legacy that confronted the Islamic Republic and the salience of economic issues during the theocracy's reign.

THE QAJAR LEGACY

At the dawn of the twentieth century, the country now known as Iran seemed more historical relic than nation-state. Its territory was controlled by a Turkic-speaking dynasty, the Qajars, which seized authority a century earlier. The Qajars were but a shadow of the great Persian empires, including the Achemenids (559–330 BCE), the Sassanians (224–651 CE), and the Safavids (1501–1722), which had extended Iranian influence and transformed its territory.

The Qajar monarchs succeeded in reunifying the country at a critical moment and retaining the basic contours of Persian authority but failed to meet their most compelling internal challenge – establishing the basis for an effectively centralized government and economic development. Under their reign, most of the state's modern functions were anemic or ceded to nonstate actors, such as clerical responsibility for education and legal matters.[2] For most other purposes, including the raising of revenues and military contingents, the Qajars relied on informal mechanisms of power, such as co-opting tribal leaders, landowners, and other local leaders. The limitations on Qajar authority had a self-reinforcing quality; their heavy reliance on local notables left much of their territory beyond the central government's control, prompting the state to seek alternative revenues and thereby further eroding their fragile hold on power by devolving landownership and facilitating foreign interventions.

During this period, Persia's economy was small-scale and predominantly agricultural. Population size and prosperity had never recovered from the tumultuous aftermath of the Safavid Empire's demise and other nineteenth century disruptions, including the shifting regional trade routes.[3] Most of the state's resources had been generated through the sale of provincial tax concessions, but these proved insufficient to maintain

---

[2] For a thorough review of clergy-state relations during the Qajar period, see Hamid Algar, *Religion and State in Iran 1785–1906* (Berkeley: University of California Press, 1969).

[3] M. H. Malek, "Capitalism in Nineteenth-Century Iran," *Middle Eastern Studies* 27:1 (January 1991), pp. 67–78; Gavin Hambly, "An Introduction to the Economic Organization of Early Qājār Iran," *Iran* 2 (1964), pp. 69–81.

the Qajars' burgeoning royal infrastructure and expanding ambitions. While there were several intervals of reformist experimentation, the efforts were hesitant and inconsistent and failed to keep pace with the forces buffeting the country. By the turn of the century, a slow-motion process of imperial implosion was in process.

This period of ineffectual central leadership coincided with the encroachment of foreign powers into Persian politics, economy, and territory – a concern that became the focal point for the Qajars' internal rivals. Their suzerainty was eroded by the loss of the country's northern Caucasian territories in disastrous military adventures with Russia and the ceding of Herat to British assertions of influence in South Asia. A series of agreements with Moscow and London relinquished considerable authority over foreign policy and valuable economic prerogatives. Tax and tariff preferences codified in the Treaties of Golestan (1813) and Turkmenchai (1828) with the Russians, and the Treaty of Paris (1857) with the British began drawing Iran into the world economy in a profoundly disadvantageous fashion.[4]

Predictably, as Persian trade with Russia and Britain expanded, the composition of its commerce shifted in favor of exporting agricultural raw materials and importing finished foreign goods such as textiles. Tehran quickly became much more dependent on those two trade partners than it had been at the start of the nineteenth century. By the turn of the twentieth century, for the first time Persia would find itself dependent on imported wheat, a vulnerability that would continue to haunt future governments.[5] Shifting trade patterns smothered the country's nascent industrial capacity, and the intrusion of advantaged foreign firms deterred the establishment of independent domestic banks.[6] These imbalances also contributed to a balance of payments crisis, as expanding trade volumes were offset by declining prices of cash crops.[7]

Compounding matters was the 1870–1 famine, which devastated Iranian agriculture and produced famine conditions throughout the country, spiraling wheat prices and corresponding inflation, massive internal

[4] Ahmad Seyf, "Foreign Firms and Local Merchants in Nineteenth-Century Iran," *Middle Eastern Studies* 36:4 (October 2000), pp. 137–55; Ahmad Ashraf, "Historical Obstacles to the Development of a Bourgeoisie in Iran," *Iranian Studies* 2:2/3 (Spring–Summer, 1969), pp. 54–79;

[5] Gad G. Gilbar, "The Opening Up of Qajar Iran: Some Economic and Social Aspects." Bulletin of the School of Oriental and African Studies 49:1 (1986), p. 79.

[6] Ashraf (1969), p. 68.

[7] John Foran, "The Concept of Dependent Development as a Key to the Political Economy of Qajar Iran (1800–1925)," Iranian Studies 22:2/3 (1989), pp. 9–18.

displacement, pandemics, and widespread insecurity and social instability. The famine and its consequences changed patterns of land use and ownership, and its ripple effects depressed Iran's broader economic landscape.[8] The ineffectiveness of the Qajar state as well as the local governors exacerbated the crisis.

Exposure to the international economy was not purely a losing proposition for Iranians. Many merchants and craftsmen profited from expanding trade; international demand spurred new industries such as carpet weaving; and agricultural shifts helped bind the country's primary population centers. The historical literature features some debate over whether European penetration helped or hurt Persian living standards, but at least some segments of the population were better off as a result of the changes.[9]

The political consequences of the country's increasing integration into the world economy also cut in multiple directions. Thanks to Persia's porous borders and the mobility of Iranians (particularly minority ethnic groups such as Azeris), the lure of work opportunities in Russia – including in the nascent oil industry – drew hundreds of thousands of Iranians to Baku and other Caucasian and Central Asia cities. Nearly a quarter of the workers in the Baku oil installations were Iranians, while others found opportunities in mining, fishing, and construction. Subject to deportation and arduous working conditions, these expatriate Iranians were ripe for the influence of revolutionary movements sweeping Russia and its southern provinces.[10] Other emigrants made their way across the Levant and South Asia, and through their commercial and cultural connections with their homeland, including newspapers and educational institutions, they helped to introduce new ideas and connect Iran's experience with a broader debate about state modernization.

The real problem for the Qajar state was not the intrusion of foreign powers, but rather the intersection of the two most significant nineteenth-century trends – a weak central government chronically short on cash and the growing rivalry between two ambitious imperial powers. Too weak and too poorly organized to enforce tax collection, the Qajars managed their mounting debts by selling off Crown lands and auctioning off monopoly rights to foreign interests. Over time, these revenue-raising mechanisms sparked organized opposition to the central government.

---

[8] See Okazaki 1986 for a detailed discussion of the famine and its consequences.

[9] For a range of perspectives on this question, see Gilbar (1986); Seyf (2000); Malek (1991).

[10] Z. Z. Abdullaev, "Promyshlennost i zarozhdenie rabochego klassa Irana v kontse XIX–nachale XX vv," from Issawi, ed., 1971, pp. 50–2.

The Qajars' dysfunctionality helped intensify an indigenous intellectual debate around modernization and nationalism. The first protests against European products began at least a half-century earlier, and in "petition after petition, year after year" Iranian merchants and tradesmen appealed to the monarchy to insulate the domestic economy from the influx of European imports.[11] Pressure from both powerful domestic constituencies as well as the Kremlin had forced the revocation of a shockingly expansive concession to Baron Julius de Reuter encompassing banking, customs, railways, minerals, canals, roads, telegraph lines, and factories in 1872, famously described by Lord Curzon as "the most complete surrender of the entire resources of a kingdom into foreign hands that has ever been dreamed of, much less accomplished, in history."[12]

However, that episode did not dissuade the shah from continuing to sell off prerogatives for valuable economic sectors and public services. Roadways and river shipping, telegraph linkages and banknote printing, ports, fishing rights, railways, and insurance all were hawked to eager British and Russian investors in the final decades of the nineteenth century. Oblivious to the mounting dissatisfaction, Nasser al-din Shah proceeded with yet another concession in 1890 – the sale to a British businessman of rights to tobacco distribution and export. The concession threatened merchants as well as clergy, whose endowments benefited from sales of tobacco grown on their lands. Protests, and eventually a loosely organized boycott, began in Tehran and eventually spread to Shiraz, Tabriz, Isfahan, and Mashhad.

Despite past frictions, the merchants quickly aligned themselves with leading clergy. Their leaflets and telegrams sought to broaden the issue beyond the concession to indict the Qajars' leadership. As one merchant wrote, "This government does not care about the people. ... It acts as it wishes and is accountable to no one."[13] Several merchants persuaded the leading Shi'a authority in Karbala to weigh in on the concession as a violation of Islamic law and principles and later publicized erroneous reports that a leading Tehran cleric had issued a fatwa endorsing a tobacco boycott.[14] With the apparent support of the religious establishment, the boycott movement gained steam, and the shah abrogated the tobacco concession in January 1892.

Ironically, the cancellation of the concession did not prompt greater efficiency or sounder state economic policies, but precisely the opposite. The shah was obliged to pay an indemnity to the British purchasers of the

---

[11] Malek (1991), p. 75.   [12] Abrahamian (1982), p. 55.   [13] Moaddel (1992), p. 459.
[14] Moaddel (1992), p. 464.

tobacco concession, and in order to obtain these funds as well as to replace the tobacco monopoly's anticipated revenues from the concession, Nasser al-din Shah sought the country's first foreign loan.[15] The decision to borrow £500,000 from a British-backed bank opened the floodgates of foreign borrowing by the Qajar state, court, and other notables, hastening the process of imperial bankruptcy and collapse and inaugurating an almost uninterrupted Iranian dependency on easy cash and nonproductive income streams. Ironically, the lending institution was the Imperial Bank of Persia, an institution created to compensate the British and Baron de Reuter for the rescission of the 1870 concession. At the dawn of the twentieth century, the Persian state routinely operated in the red, with annual deficits of approximately $1 million. Within two decades, the waning Qajar dynasty owed the equivalent of £10.6 million, mostly to the British and the Russians.[16] Reliance on foreign sources of capital has remained a persistent dilemma for each of Iran's succeeding regimes.

The Tobacco Revolt and the political and economic trends that buffeted Iran during the preceding decades helped crystallize a number of important trends that continue to frame Iranian political culture and dynamics. It solidified the patterns of episodic cooperation and sense of shared interests among the merchant and clerical classes and helped intertwine economic grievances with suspicion of foreign influence and a sense of attack against religion and values. Their cooperation should not be overstated; clerical support in the Tobacco Revolt was not unanimous, particularly where the religious hierarchy was financially dependent on the central government. Still, the episode helped establish a powerful precedent for joint action among clerics and merchants. Moreover, it amplified the association among Iran's national identity and independence, its religious and cultural values, and the economic policies of the state.

The backlash to the Qajar concessions also sparked an enduring antipathy toward state intervention on the part of Iran's *bazaar*. In the absence of full-fledged colonial co-option, the Iranian *bazaar* had emerged as a more powerful, autonomous constituency than merchants in other parts of the region.[17] Iran's *bazaari*s felt their interests and influence were dramatically disadvantaged by the increasing involvement of Russia, Britain, and other foreign capitals with the Persian economy.

[15] Ramazani (1966), p. 70.
[16] Cyrus Ghani, *Iran and the Rise of Reza Shah: From Qajar Collapse to Pahlavi Power* (London: I. B. Tauris, 2000), p. 7.
[17] Nashat 1981, pp. 53–85.

Ironically, many *bazaari*s actually profited from the expansion of European penetration into Iran's economy, via both trade and their diversification into other sectors, particularly landownership, larger trading conglomerates, and even nascent industrial ventures.[18] Still, the continual ceding of economic privileges to foreign powers and the expanding reach of the state created real losses, a sense of dispossession, and pernicious resentment of the central government and the international community.

The endemic Iranian mistrust of foreign powers remains one of the most important legacies of this period. Qajar Iran was subjected to intense external machinations as the primary arena for competition between Russia and Britain. As one analyst notes, "Iran thus had all the disadvantages of being a colony without the few advantages," such as investment in industrial capacity, infrastructure, and bureaucratic development.[19] This suspicion of international intentions toward Iran manifested itself through opposition to foreign control over or access to Iranian resources and commerce.[20]

THE DAWN OF THE TWENTIETH CENTURY AND POPULAR PRESSURE FOR ACCOUNTABILITY

After the annulment of the Reuter concession, Persia's economic predicament deteriorated further. The underlying causes of the deficit that the concession was intended to fill, including mounting state debts and declining agricultural output, did not dissipate and were exacerbated in the 1890s by spiraling inflation related to a destructive feud over control of the Qajar monetary supply, a decline in the value of silver, and a global recession. In turn, the economic crisis further eroded the central government's authority, as provincial authorities began reneging on required tax remittances to Tehran.[21] The 1896 assassination of Nasser al-din Shah ushered in another brief experiment with reform that served as the prelude to the final collapse of Qajar authority and the first serious attempt to reshape the Persian state.

Nasser's son and successor, Muzaffar al-din Shah, exacerbated his father's challenge of a weak state infrastructure beset by heavy financial obligations and bereft of coherent leadership. Determined to find new

[18] Foran 1989, pp. 29, 36–7; Gilbar 1986, pp. 83–4.   [19] Bausani, p. 172.
[20] See Keddie 1971, p. 8, for more details on episodes beyond the Tobacco Revolt during the latter days of the Qajar dynasty and early twentieth century.
[21] Martin (1989), pp. 42–5.

revenue sources to finance (among other things) the new shah's foreign travels, Muzaffar's ministers increased borrowing from Britain and Russia, at times turning to one capital in order to pay off the other. The role of the great powers toward Persia during this period has generated considerable criticism, and it remains vivid in Iranian political culture today. But Muzaffar and his court were hardly passive actors. They sought to draw the two capitals into a bidding war for easy cash, to balance the state budget and enrich themselves, and they played upon British anxieties that parsimony toward Persia might leave their Indian interests vulnerable.[22]

The loans saved the Qajars from bankruptcy but had strings attached. Tehran ceded to Moscow final approval over any future loan negotiations as well as any reductions in customs duties. At the same time, Muzaffar's reform-minded court yielded to pressure to enlist outside expertise to supervise the state's newly revamped customs bureau, with Belgian officials taking control of the state's external revenue streams in 1898. Just as in the case of the previous round of reforms and revenue hunting, the new taxation and tariff regime proved both ineffective and unpopular. While the new taxes expanded government coffers, expenses more than kept pace, and by the end of 1905 the state deficit had grown to £800,000.[23]

Thanks to the new loans' terms, the new tariffs profoundly advantaged Russian economic interests in Iran, which expanded quickly and at the expense of Iranian industries and products such as cotton. The central government's tenuous control diminished further, as courtiers and provincial authorities engaged in rampant pillaging. The impact was felt across Iranian society: Merchants resented new taxes, craftsmen saw their sectors virtually wiped out by foreign competition, salaries for the palace guard as well as clerical subsidies were unpaid, and peasants faced sharp increases in the price of bread and sugar. Persia's nascent press gave voice to public outrage, and small protests erupted against state officials and their Belgian budget enforcer, Joseph Naus. Inspired by European ideas, emboldened by Russia's revolutionary ferment and its humiliating defeat by Japan as well as by Muzaffar's tentative reforms, Iran's educated elites began to reimagine the role of government and authority.

The empowerment of Europeans to implement more onerous taxes in more rigorous fashion proved to be an unintentionally incendiary

---

[22] Wilson (2002), p. 37.   [23] Afary (1996), p. 35.

decision, one that accelerated the end of Qajar rule and cemented a loosely organized coalition determined to curb the state's authority. Naus had emerged as the focal point for popular dissatisfaction over the corruption, insecurity, and poverty that the central government seemed unwilling or unable to reverse. In June 1905, 200 merchants and money-lenders shuttered their businesses to demand Naus's removal, marking the first salvo in the decade-long struggle known as the Constitutional Revolution.

The Crown attempted to placate the protesters by establishing an effectively powerless advisory committee of merchants, but this only strengthened the association between the economic grievances and elite pressure for greater state accountability. Next, Tehran sought to divert public frustration by implicating the *bazaar* in rising prices; however, once again, an attempt to mitigate the crisis only exacerbated it. The December 1905 beating of an elderly sugar merchant galvanized the *bazaaris*, who closed their shops in a show of solidarity and joined other opponents of the government to press for tangible concessions, including Naus's ouster and the establishment of a "house of justice."

The Constitutionalist movement reached its apex in June 1906, with another round of protests sparked by the arrest of opposition clerics, including one critic who had inveighed against the country's decline under Qajar stewardship: "In the past others looked on us as a great nation. Now, we are reduced to such a condition that our neighbors of the north and south already believe us to be their property and divide our country between themselves when they choose.... We have no guns, no army, no secure finances, no proper government, no commercial laws. In the whole of Iran we have not one factory of our own, because our government is a parasite.... All the backwardness is due to the autocracy and injustice and to the want of laws."[24]

The protests swelled as thousands of merchants, clerics, intellectuals, and others joined in a month-long sit-in at the British mission to Iran. Muzaffar finally conceded and in August 1906 formally announced the establishment of a constituent national assembly, or Majlis. It represented the advent of a new political era for Iran, one that enshrined – in principle more than in practice – the basic tenets of democracy: that the government should be based on written laws and that it should be accountable to its citizenry through representative institutions. The constitution signed in

[24] Abrahamian (1982), pp. 82–3.

December 1906, shortly before Muzzaffar's death, provided the framework for the Iranian parliamentary system until the 1979 revolution.

After this triumphal moment, five years of tortuous infighting ensued,
culminating in the Majlis's dismissal in 1911, midway through its
second term. The same problems that the constitution was intended to
ameliorate – fiscal imbalances and bureaucratic disarray, corruption,
foreign interference, and the eroding authority of the central government –
remained and in some cases had been exacerbated by instability. And yet
the towering achievement of the Constitutional movement remains intact
today, more than a century later – the parliament itself, and more importantly, the identification of elective institutions as the central mechanism
for protecting Iran's interests and resources from foreign predation and
venal leaders.

For the purposes of this study, several features of the Constitutional
movement and the brief period of representative government that
followed warrant comment. First is the salience of economic issues
throughout this monumental turning point in Iran's political evolution.
The Qajars' financial weakness and economic pressures generated the
unrest that forced the shah to accept the constitution and the parliament.
During the uprising, the economic crisis provided a crucial bridge across
disparate interests. The movement achieved its greatest traction in cities
where the economy was slowing[25] and drew its support from ordinary
Iranians, who identified the struggle as "a fight for lower prices for life
necessities," in part because of the deliberate insinuation by partisans that
constitutionalism would reduce bread prices.[26]

For this reason, many of the leading intellectuals associated with the
Constitutionalist movement viewed economic policy as a critical dimension of ensuring the success of their republican enterprise.[27] The two
parliaments that met during the Constitutionalist period gave legislators
final approval over treaties, concessions, and foreign loans. They also
initiated ambitious economic reforms, including the elimination of tax
farming, stiff reductions in subsidies to the court, and other measures
aimed at increasing revenues and decreasing expenses. However, many of
these reforms were never fully implemented as a result of social upheaval
and the state's limitations.

The Constitutional era state also began seeking technical assistance
from abroad, marking a shift from the prevailing mind-set of foreign

---

[25] Gilbar (1983), p. 197.   [26] Floor (1983), p. 212.   [27] Dadkhah (2003).

powers as the source of easy capital or rapacious intervention. In 1911, Tehran initiated an unofficial U.S. advisory mission to strengthen the state's capacity for collecting and managing its revenues. The American lawyer Morgan Shuster served briefly as the country's treasurer-general, launching aggressive tax collection improvements. His short-lived tenure left a residue of goodwill toward Washington – perhaps undeservedly so, given that the United States resisted efforts by the Majlis and Shuster to enlist American support[28] – and created a precedent for the subsequent half-century of U.S. assistance to Iranian governments.

The economic outcomes of the Constitutional movement were not unambiguously progressive or even constructive. The ambitious Majlis reforms were viewed as a direct threat to the interests of the Qajar throne as well as foreign powers, in particular Moscow, which found newfound room for maneuver in Persia thanks to a 1907 agreement with its old rival Britain to divide the country into spheres of influence. In June 1908, with Russian financial and logistical backing, Muhammad Ali Shah laid siege to the parliament building, sparking years of intermittent warfare between constitutionalists and royalists. The conflict gutted the parliament's governing capacity and entrenched problematic political tactics, such as the reliance on bribery and sponsored thuggery as means of gaining partisan advantage.

At the same time, Shuster's aggressive efforts to raise revenues intensified tensions with the Russians and their royalist allies, prompting Shuster's removal and ultimately the dismissal of the Majlis itself. Although the parliament was briefly reconvened three years later, both the assembly and the movement for a genuine constitutional monarchy had been dealt a near-fatal blow. During the World War I, Iran and its briefly revitalized central government succumbed to political impotence, foreign occupation, and tribal unrest.

The Constitutional movement also demonstrated the resonance of economic arguments against political liberalization in mobilizing political action by elites as well as the public. One of the most vocal opponents of constitutionalism, Sheikh Fazlallah Nuri, based his objections on the argument that the perfection of *shari'a* obviated the need for "man-made: laws. However, in order to galvanize broader support for his cause, Nuri deployed economic arguments as scare tactics, warning of wild and indiscriminate tax hikes. In 1907, he organized protests shouting, "We

---

[28] Ghaneabassiri (2002), pp. 155–61.

don't want constitutionalism, we want tea and rice."[29] Interestingly, Nuri had been a prominent challenger of Qajar concessionary policy and supported earlier fiscal reforms aimed at reducing state expenses and increasing the tax base, a stance that put him in conflict with the *bazaar*.[30]

As the distinguished historian Ervand Abrahamian notes, Nuri and other conservatives succeeded in confirming the skepticism toward constitutionalism that was already harbored by critical segments of the Iranian working class.[31] Nuri's tendency to indulge anti-Muslim prejudices and to equate Western influence and institutions with a threat to Iranian identity and sovereignty empowered a narrative conducive to authoritarian leadership and suspicious of economic liberalization, one that remains salient in Iran today. In this respect, Nuri – who was later executed for his role in the murders of constitutionalists – represents an important precursor to the clerical brand of paranoid populism that would become empowered by oil rents during the second half of the twentieth century and beyond. Indeed, Nuri would eventually be depicted by Ayatollah Khomeini as a heroic figure in an enduring struggle to defend Islam from the West.

The Constitutionalist era is often heralded simply for the emergence of representative government in Iran, but a review of the period offers a more textured interpretation of its political dynamics. Like the Tobacco Revolt, the Constitutional Revolution represented an attempt by actors across Iranian society to assert greater accountability over the state. Debates over the nature and sources of legitimacy and authority influenced the movement's leaders; however, their efforts also reflected the more prosaic motivations of resolving the persistent economic crisis and institutionalizing protections against arbitrary or preferential treatment by the state. And while there were multiple reasons for the demise of the constitutional order, the parliament's efforts to wrest greater financial control from foreign powers as well as long-standing royal constituencies ultimately unraveled the diverse coalition of merchants, clerics, and intellectuals who put the movement in power.

This episode, and its underlying tensions over modernization, centralization, and foreign influence, has had lasting impact on Iranian politics and economy. Many of the features of modern-day Iranian political culture can be traced to the Constitutional Revolution politics: the clerical-merchant-intellectual nexus of elite political coordination; the

---

[29] Martin (1987), p. 50.   [30] Martin (1987), pp. 39–53.   [31] Abrahamian (1985).

centrality of the principle of representative government for the modern Iranian polity; the shared antipathy toward foreign intervention in the country's political affairs; and, perhaps most importantly, unresolved resentments toward the great powers.

THE DAWN OF THE OIL ERA IN THE SHADOW OF WAR

The escalating unrest and foreign intervention that followed the abortive Constitutionalist movement also had a more immediate impact on Iran, facilitating British exploitation of Iran's petroleum resources. Ironically, the first prospecting for oil had been conducted by Baron Julius de Reuter, the initial recipient of the comprehensive 1870 concession; after its rescission, de Reuter maintained an active role in the Imperial Bank of Persia and other ventures there, including concessions for mineral rights in a small area near the port of Bushehr. De Reuter's exploration activities proved fruitless; his Iranian subsidiary was liquidated in 1894 and his concession lapsed five years later.

Still, a combination of foreign interest and bureaucratic desires for new revenue streams kept Persian oil in play. In 1901, the British engineer William Knox D'Arcy won Iran's first concession specifically for oil exploration. From the outset, the deal was embroiled in the strategic maneuvering of the great powers for influence in Persia. Russia dominated Iran's economy and "had nearly bought off the ruling elite" of Iran.[32] British officials helped broker D'Arcy's concession, using subterfuge and bribing several Qajar ministers,[33] in hopes of counterbalancing Moscow's growing sway. Eventually, the United Kingdom became the lead investor in Persian oil exploitation, which naturally (and deliberately) necessitated implicit security guarantees by the UK government to the company's operations. D'Arcy's initial offering deliberately excluded the northern provinces to head off anticipated Russian opposition to the deal. In return, Tehran was to receive 16 percent of net profits from any production.

D'Arcy's first fruitless drilling was focused on established seepages near Kermanshah along the Iraqi border. Confronted with brutal

---

[32] Ramazani (1966), p. 70.

[33] Chris Paine and Erica Schoenberger detail the British efforts to preclude Russian objections to the concession by transmitting the details of the proposal in Persian at a time when the Russian envoy's translator was traveling. Paine and Schoenberger, "Iranian Nationalism and the Great Powers: 1872–1954," *MERIP Reports* 37 (May 1975), p. 5; Ramazani (1966), pp. 71–72.

working conditions and rapidly declining capital, D'Arcy sought a loan from the British Admiralty in exchange for a contract to supply fuel oil for Britain's navy. London demurred but eventually helped arrange a deal with its existing fuel supplier, a Scottish firm known as Burmah Oil. Three years passed, with Qajar authority disintegrating and the country descending into upheaval, before the concession struck oil – a development that occurred after its parsimonious Scottish investors had decided to pull the plug on the operation. Established in 1909, the Anglo-Persian Oil Company (APOC) quickly emerged as a significant oil producer, permanently altering Iran's economy and its relations with the rest of the world.

APOC's early years featured grueling challenges in constructing industrial-scale facilities at Masjid-i Sulaiman. The area was a wasteland, used by nomadic tribes for grazing but inhospitable to a growing industry. All supplies were imported from abroad, with everything from workers' food to heavy drilling equipment hauled much of the way by mule-drawn wagons, over terrain so rough that the wheels required repairs halfway through the journey. The isolated location meant that many of the new company's employees were also imported, either from India or from Eastern Europe.[34] Khuzestan's lack of security or well-defined property rights required APOC to bargain with local tribal notables for protection. These deals set the stage for continuing British intervention – notably, after the outbreak of the World War I and German-inspired agitation among Baktiari tribesmen – and eventually put the tribes in conflict with the new central government under Reza Shah. The payments that helped ensure APOC's ability to proceed with its construction were deducted from Tehran's profit share under the concession.

Despite the difficulties, the infrastructure of a modern oil industry, including a refinery and export pipelines and pump stations, was slowly established in southwestern Iran. Still, financial challenges plagued APOC, and only after Winston Churchill, then-head of the British Admiralty, decided to convert the naval fleet from coal- to oil-powered fuel were the company's fortunes changed permanently. Churchill navigated tense domestic politics to secure a controlling interest for the British government in the company.[35] Tehran was not a party to this agreement and

---

[34] Alexander Melamid, "The Geographical Pattern of Iranian Oil Development," *Economic Geography* 35:3 (July 1959), p. 201.

[35] Sara Reguer, "Persian Oil and the First Lord: A Chapter in the Career of Winston Churchill," *Military Affairs* 46:3 (October 1982), pp. 134–8.

ultimately was treated by APOC and the British government as an after-thought in the oil sector's financial and operational framework.

Iran was a relatively minor player in the incipient world oil market, but APOC production comprised a disproportionately high share of British oil consumption until World War II,[36] and the company's revenues reaped at least £40 million for the British treasury during its first seven years. In contrast, the Iranian government received less than one-tenth that figure over the same period.[37] Moscow, and, belatedly Washington as well, attempted to gain a foothold in the lucrative Persian oil sector, but were outmaneuvered by the British.[38] Their exclusion did not last as the competition for access to Iranian resources intensified over the subsequent decades. The oil industry's birth and the British government's direct involvement had profound repercussions for Persia and the international economy. A country governed, barely, by a fading empire found itself in the crosshairs of the great power struggle, conditions that left a legacy of virulently anti-British sentiment, and resentment of the oil sectors' fiscal and operational framework.

BIRTH OF THE PAHLAVI MONARCHY

The Constitutional Revolution accelerated the Qajars' collapse, and the ensuing decade – which coincided with both World War I and the advent of Iran's oil industry – saw considerable instability. Despite its declared neutrality, the war entered Persia via Turkish incursions in the northwest and the 1907 Russian-British division of the country into spheres of influence and occupation. With battles raging throughout the country, the war imposed significant economic and political costs on Iran – further splintering the elite, jettisoning the parliament, and generating severe food shortages, epidemics, mass starvation, and internal displacement.[39]

In this context, the 1917 Russian revolution "looked little short of a miracle for Iran."[40] The new Soviet authorities renounced the 1907 Anglo-Russian agreement and quickly began withdrawing Russian troops. This promised some improvement in the country's circumstances, but a decade of domestic infighting, foreign occupation, and war had left

---

[36] Kent (1993), pp. 153–4.   [37] Fesharaki (1976), p. 9.

[38] For an overview of the earliest American efforts to obtain a Persian concession and the reasons for their failure, see Michael Rubin, "Stumbling through the 'Open Door': The U.S. in Persia and the Standard-Sinclair Oil Dispute, 1920–1925," *Iranian Studies* 28:3/4 (Summer–Autumn, 1995), pp. 203–29.

[39] Ghani (2000), p. 17.   [40] Katouzian (2009), p. 193.

little domestic political capacity for reasserting authority. The nominal Qajar leader, Ahmad Shah, was so ineffectual and unethical that he was induced to sell off the premiership by the British in exchange for a promise of a lifetime pension.[41] The British made use of this weakness in hopes of securing the periphery of its Indian colony, negotiating a 1919 agreement that further indebted the Qajar throne and accorded Britain vast influence in Persian affairs.

The new influx of capital offered a brief lifeline for the Qajar throne, but domestic agitation and foreign incursions had all but eroded its capacity. By 1921, when a general in the Russian-administered Cossack Brigade known as Reza Khan marched on Tehran, the old order collapsed with little resistance. In his initial role as army chief, Reza focused on reestablishing the authority of the central government and dramatically boosting the armed forces' funding. Over the next four years, Reza racked up impressive victories over rebellious tribes in Kurdistan, Khurasan, and Khuzestan. He also demonstrated a talent for exploiting the competition for power, and with the support of senior clerics and landlords as well as grudging British assistance, Reza assumed absolute leadership in 1925 and crowned himself the subsequent year.[42]

In an explicit about-face from his prior cooperation with liberal and socialist political parties, Reza courted senior *mujtahids* in Iran's emerging center of religious education in Qom, as well as Iraq-based clergy, although some remained skeptical about his intentions.[43] Similar efforts assuaged anxieties among the leading landowners, and his pledge to introduce modernity and prosperity in a troubled nation rallied a diverse array of supporters. A number of prominent politicians opposed Reza from the outset, including Mohammad Mosaddeq, who would return thirty years later to challenge Reza's son. After his coronation, Reza Shah dealt with dissenters harshly and paid little heed to his erstwhile supporters, as he embarked on a program to modernize and centralize Iran that inadvertently institutionalized opposition to the state.

Reza Shah adopted the family name Pahlavi from Iran's pre-Islamic past and eventually instituted the country's indigenous name, Iran, in place of Western-imposed Persia. He set about transforming the country just as deliberately – instituting mandatory military conscription and

---

[41] Ghani (2000), pp. 26–7.
[42] Mohammad H. Faghfoary, "The Ulama-State Relations in Iran: 1921–1941," *IJMES* 19:4 (November 1987), p. 416.
[43] Akhavi (1980), pp. 28–31.

social, judicial, educational, and economic reforms. Reza's state building was comprehensive and tenacious and extended from the very idea of the nation to the minutiae of his subjects' daily lives (he mandated the wearing of a particular style of hat). He personally promoted an effort to purify the Persian language of Arabic and foreign words.[44] His reforms reflected a deliberate effort to consolidate the country's political and economic structure under his personal control. With Mustafa Kemal Ataturk as his explicit model, Reza set out to achieve a modern state, which implied both secularization and centralization. From this foundation emerged the financial infrastructure, communications system, provincial organization, and educational and judicial structures under an integrated bureaucracy.

He also initiated change in the realm of women's status – outlawing public veiling (a regulation enforced violently) and expanding educational access; although these reforms were more symbolic than substantive, they underscored his growing authority.[45] Reza's policies – particularly government encroachments on the *madraseh* education and *shari'a* law – challenged existing institutions that were largely administered by the clergy and ensured their animosity. Beyond curtailing the clergy's formal authority, the new state institutions struck at clerical incomes and assets by transferring authority for property registration to the secular judicial system and by confiscating lands owned by religious endowments (*vaqf*).

Reza's centralization push required substantial resources. The country's financial situation had ameliorated, but Tehran was nowhere near solvent yet. A British inquiry into APOC's fiscal arrangements concluded that the company had profoundly underpaid the host government, failing to live up to even the relatively ungenerous terms of the original concession via a range of tactics to disguise and insulate its profits.[46] A settlement favorable to the company's interests was reached but was never ratified by Iran's parliament. With considerable volatility in the size of its annual royalty payment from APOC, Iranian frustrations with the oil concession mounted.

---

[44] Mehrdad Kia "Persian Nationalism and the Campaign for Language Purification," *Middle Eastern Studies* 34:2 (April 1998), pp. 9–36.

[45] Although Reza Shah introduced a secular civil code, he did not substantively alter the provisions based on Islamic law (*shari'a*) as they applied to women's personal status and family law. Thus, female access to divorce remained highly limited, as did rights to custody and employment. All in all, his policies regarding women were more restrained than those of his neighbors in Turkey or the Soviet Union.

[46] Paine and Schoenberger (1975), p. 12.

In 1929, agricultural prices collapsed as a result of the worldwide depression and newly instituted Soviet import restrictions. This jolted Iran and prompted Reza Shah to focus his attentions more firmly on the nation's economy. Given his Ataturk pretensions, it was hardly surprising that Reza Shah committed Iran to a state-centered program of economic development. In reality, his alternatives were limited: Domestic merchant capital had not recovered from the World War I and its aftermath, and foreign capital was not on offer.[47] With help from an another American financial adviser, the former U.S. State Department staffer Arthur Millspaugh, the fledging Iranian state sought to rationalize a haphazard financial bureaucracy and balance its accounts through new taxes, cancelling tax exemptions granted as political rewards to key constituencies, and a name-and-shame approach to tax delinquency.

Under Reza Shah, the state led Iran's nascent industrialization, establishing public enterprises in textiles, sugar, matches, cement, iron, and steel. By 1940, Iran boasted 260 factories, employing approximately forty-eight thousand workers, with the largest among these state-owned enterprises.[48] Together with increasing employment in the oil industry and traditional crafts, this formed the basis for the development of a modern middle class. The oil sector began to absorb tribal populations in the workforce, and the reach of the state (in the form of taxes, conscription, and security) began to extend to once largely autonomous parts of the country. A major component of Reza's modernization program entailed the construction of a north-south railway, a project that absorbed 37 percent of all government spending at its peak.[49] The railway did not itself transform the Iranian economy, but together with security and infrastructure improvements, a more integrated and efficient national economy emerged.

To support domestic industry, the government established exchange rate controls in 1930 and a monopoly over foreign trade in 1931 and built a system of state banks to extend commercial credit to the private sector. The foreign trade monopoly proved particularly lucrative, generating approximately 30 percent of government revenue and providing the wherewithal for industrial investments and infrastructure expansion. Reza Shah's budget was geared toward the construction of a potent state,

[47] Karshenas (1990), p. 70.   [48] Karshenas (1990), p. 76.

[49] Patrick Clawson, "Knitting Iran Together: The Land Transport Revolution, 1920–1940," *Iranian Studies* 26:3/4 (Summer–Autumn, 1993), p. 250.

with approximately three-quarters of all government expenditure between 1928 and 1933 plowed into the defense, finance, and interior ministries.

This disparity helped to exacerbate a decline in the country's agricultural base, contributing in the near term to inflation and in the longer term exacerbating the rural-urban divide. Reza Shah's tenure also began the process of dispossession of Iran's major landlords, who exerted powerful authority over the approximately 80 percent of the population who resided in rural areas.[50] New laws put landlords under the jurisdiction of the central government for the first time, but they did not substantially empower the peasantry, and if anything, the political and economic position of the rural poor and tenant farmers deteriorated. Not coincidentally, Reza himself emerged from this process as the country's largest landholder.

Oil revenues remained modest; still, they proved essential to Reza Shah's development efforts, mostly by enabling him to fund the centralization and professionalization of the army.[51] Resentment toward APOC lingered, reflecting a fundamental conviction among the court that Iran's chaotic condition at the concession's inception made it illegitimate.[52] Tehran and APOC began talks on revising the agreement in 1928, with the company seeking to extend the duration of its operations and the Iranians intent on reducing its prerogatives and establishing more ambitious revenue guarantees.

The talks went on for several years, led by Reza Shah's powerful Minister of Court Abdulhusayn Timurtash, an unabashed Russophile who had already proven sympathetic to Soviet efforts to gain a foothold in Iran's oil sector. The commercial and financial issues were significant, particularly for the cash-strapped Iranian monarchy, but there were formidable strategic implications at stake as well. Frictions over competing claims to Bahrain sank Iranian-British relations to a low ebb, while Moscow loomed large, in part as a result of Timurtash's assiduous exploitation of Soviet interest in Iran in an effort to play the great powers against one another to Iran's benefit.[53]

---

[50] Kian-Thiébaut (1998), p. 78.

[51] Zabih (1988), p. 3; Kazemi in Kedourie and Haim, eds. (1980), p. 220; Akhavi in Weiner and Banuazizi, eds. (1986), p. 200.

[52] Miron Rezun, "Reza Shah's Court Minister: Teymourtash," *International Journal of Middle East Studies* 12:2 (September 1980), pp. 127–8.

[53] Rezun (1980), p. 129; Peter J. Beck, "The Anglo-Persian Oil Dispute 1932–33," *Journal of Contemporary History* 9:4 (October 1974), pp. 123–51.

Still, the negotiations appeared to be making some headway in 1931 when APOC announced a significant drop in the net profits due to Tehran to a mere £306,872 as compared to £1,437,000 in 1929 and £1,288,312 in 1930. This abrupt decline was prompted by the confluence of expanding global oil supplies and declining demand as a result of the depression; still, the plunge exacerbated traditional Iranian suspicions of APOC. In November 1932 Reza Shah took the extraordinary step of canceling the concession outright, a move that met with public celebration and Majlis endorsement. The British were indignant; APOC demanded a retraction, while London frantically weighed its diplomatic and military options, including the prospects for occupying Iran's oil fields or retaliating with force.

Eventually, the matter was referred to the League of Nations, and the two sides worked out a new agreement in a matter of months. Tehran obtained a minimalist interpretation of its previous demands – a clarification of the accounting methods for calculating royalties, a very modest increase in its share of net profits, a guaranteed minimum payment, and other modifications in its favor including a much reduced concession territory. Still, Tehran's revenues continued to represent a minor share of APOC's profits and of the overall Iranian state budget (less than 17 percent of government revenues even at its peak.)[54] APOC achieved its fundamental objective, a thirty-two-year extension of the concession and the right to select the most attractive areas within the original concessionary area. Neither side fully prevailed, but on balance the agreement continued to favor APOC at Tehran's expense. The perpetuation of British control over Iran's oil production, and by extension its national income, reportedly left Reza Shah disconsolate.[55]

This episode serves as a powerful precursor to events two decades later and underscores the tensions that would reemerge during the 1951–4 oil crisis. The 1928–33 renegotiation of the APOC concession highlights the deep roots of Tehran's anti-British posture and the linkage between Iranian nationalism and the issue of resource control. While the British government mostly played a supporting role in the 1930s dispute, the close cooperation between APOC and its majority shareholder set the stage for much more substantial intervention by London and Washington in the nationalization a generation later. Finally, just as the 1951–4 oil crisis resulted in the elimination of a powerful nationalist rival to the

---

[54] Karshenas (1990), table 3.4, 82.   [55] Katouzian (1999), p. 36.

Pahlavi throne, so too did 1932–3 dispute; by the time of the settlement, Timurtash had been neutralized by Reza Shah, who saw his minister as the most potent threat to his authority and his family dynasty.

Overall, the balance sheet for Reza Shah's development efforts is mixed. The first Pahlavi shah launched industrial development and established mechanisms for private capital accumulation; however, this alone could not provide a durable economic foundation for Iran. Few if any of the government-owned enterprises were profitable or even self-sustaining, and the protectionist tariffs that reduced foreign competition also eroded efficiency. Projects were guided by political fiat rather than economic rationality, predictably favoring capital-intensive prestige projects and, occasionally, those that were wholly inappropriate or recklessly designed.[56] Industrialization was by necessity a top-down project, and the province of the shah's largesse, isolated from the traditional commercial bourgeoisie in the *bazaar*.

Iran changed dramatically over the subsequent sixty years, but Reza Shah's framework for economic development – rapid industrialization, infrastructure building, and a strong central state – remained largely intact until the 1979 revolution and in many ways beyond.[57] The main difference between Reza Shah's development program and that of his son was the source of public funding; initially, the state budget relied on trading monopolies and indirect taxation rather than the oil revenues that would come to dominate. Reza Shah's legacy has enjoyed a curious revival in contemporary Iran, where it appeals to a yearning for a strong secular leader, but the foundation he established was a somewhat illusory one. Reza weakened the parliament, dissolved and discredited the country's emerging political parties, and otherwise impeded the development of representative institutions or independent leaders. A generation of Iranian politicians, intellectuals, and activists, many of whom originally supported Reza Shah, was imprisoned, exiled, or executed, and the very product of his modernizing program, the educated middle class, became disaffected from the monarchy. Moreover, the processes that enabled Reza Shah to consolidate his authority over the nation – for example, his absolute control over the reins of power and his military victories over the tribes – facilitated personalistic rule; unlike his predecessors, he had

---

[56] Kamran Mofid, *Development Planning in Iran: From Monarchy to Islamic Republic* (Wisbech: Middle East and North African Studies Press, 1987), 15, 23–8.

[57] Looney (1982), p. 9.

no need for the consensus-driven process of elite consultation that had previously characterized governance in Iran.[58]

Reza Shah disrupted the traditional social links between the Iranian state and society and began a process of economic transformation that remained largely incomplete and superficial. Iran's traditional politics favored centralized monarchy; however, previous models of dynastic authority (Safavid and Qajar) "originated in religio-tribal movements which in some measure retained their primary tribal characteristics as time passed."[59] By contrast, Reza Shah forged a new context, grounded in the protonationalistic centralizing tendencies of a modern military rather than tribal affinities. As a result, the tribes' residual influence threatened his efforts to consolidate authority and was met with military repression. Some tribes were forcibly resettled, others manipulated into doing his fighting for him, and pressed from all sides, the tribal way of life deteriorated. Reza personally absorbed wide swaths of tribal lands to become one of the largest landowners in the country, reversing the previous half-century's pattern of land distribution from the Crown to empower the landlords.

Just as deliberately as he subdued tribal power, Reza Shah eroded the historic linkages between the Iranian state and the clergy. After negotiating a condominium with the leading *ulema* to ensure his ascent to power, he reversed course and embraced a secular state. He consciously sought to reduce clerical influence, and some of his policies – laws restricting religious dress, for example, and precluding the performance of Shi'a rituals – appeared designed to antagonize religious leaders. The secularization of the legal and educational systems deprived the clergy of their traditional status in society, and equally importantly of significant revenue earned through oversight of administrative issues, such as document notarization. His economic policies enriched a coterie of industrialists but hurt traditional craftsmen and merchants, who were historic allies of the clergy[60] – and began encroaching on the clergy's primary mechanism for securing their wealth, religious endowments.

Even policies that did not directly contravene their interests – such as the introduction of mass conscription – reinforced the shifts in the locus of

---

[58] Ervand Abrahamian, *Iran between Two Revolutions* (Princeton, NJ: Princeton University Press, 1987), 138.

[59] Akhavi in Banuazizi and Weiner, eds. (1986), p. 203.

[60] Abrahamian 1987, 150–2; H. E. Chehabi, *Iranian Politics and Religious Modernism: The Liberation Movement of Iran under the Shah and Khomeini* (London: I. B. Tauris, 1990), 92–4.

authority. This transformation is evidenced in the parliament's composition; clerical representation plummeted from approximately 40 percent
in 1926 to a negligible proportion a decade later.[61] Their successors were
predominantly men with university degrees, many from foreign institutions. The *hajji*s and *sayyid*s gave way to Ph.D and engineer – a process
that would reverse itself during the early postrevolutionary years, albeit
temporarily.[62] Altogether, Reza Shah's bureaucratization of state power
was mostly at the expense of the clergy, their social and economic position, and their dignity. Although senior clerics sought to minimize interaction and conflict with the regime, this period also saw the emergence of
an Islamically influenced opposition discourse that appealed to some
clerical leaders. Notably, opposition to the secularizing impact of the
shah's program was coupled with condemnations of his economic
policies – in particular the tax regime and government corruption.[63]

REZA'S EXILE AND THE INTERLUDE

The tenuousness of Reza Shah's state-building enterprise was exposed by
the rapidity of his eviction. His efforts to expand Iran's international
alliances beyond its traditional partners generated an incongruous affection for Hitler's Germany, an association that unwittingly placed his
country on the wrong side of yet another world war. Iran's initial neutrality proved insufficient to evade direct implication in the conflict after
the German invasion of the Soviet Union, and when Reza proved unwilling or unable to expel approximately two thousand German workers
from Iran, London and Moscow opted to move into Iran directly from
the north and the south. Reza's rapid departure was planned well in
advance of the decision to invade, with some consideration given by
London to the possibility of restoring the Qajar dynasty. In the end, the
Allies decided to test Reza's son and heir apparent, Mohammed Reza, on
the grounds that "the Crown Prince would offer the solution the least
distracting to Iran and Britain could always get rid of him quickly if he
proved unsuitable."[64]

---

[61] Akhavi (1980), p. 59.
[62] Reza Arasteh, "The Role of Intellectuals in Administrative Development and Social
Change in Modern Iran," *International Review of Education* 9:3 (1963), p. 329.
[63] Abrahamian (2008), p. 94.
[64] F. Eshraghi, "The Immediate Aftermath of Anglo-Soviet Occupation of Iran in August
1941," *Middle Eastern Studies* 20:3 (July 1984), p. 342.

When Reza sailed off to an ignominious exile on a British warship in September 1941, it is hardly surprising that Iran's politics and its economy were transformed. The young Swiss-educated Mohammad Reza Shah faced powerful challenges from domestic forces as well as those externally imposed. At twenty-two, his inheritance was unenviable – a regime "politically discredited by its failure to resist foreign armies" and a nation occupied by those same armies for the purposes of supporting a global war.[65] The British and Russians were joined in December 1942 by an American force that eventually reached thirty thousand troops, a presence that helped expand the U.S. relationship with Tehran.

The occupation generated severe economic disruptions, including hyperinflation, significant displacement, shortages in basic necessities, and widespread deterioration in the living standards of Iranians, as well as hoarding and profiteering. The sheer scope of the Allied war effort within Iran overwhelmed the local economy, as railways, ports, and roads were redirected toward transporting materiel to the Russian front. Most of Iran's domestic food production was diverted to Russia; existing food distribution networks were disrupted; and imports were restricted according to military priorities. Adding to the misery were massive internal displacement and sharp inflationary spikes caused by the Allies' rial-based spending; to pressure Tehran into expanding the monetary supply, the British used wheat imports as a "bargaining chip."[66] The legacy of Reza Shah's state-centric development policies meant that popular dissatisfaction was directed at the government as much as toward the Allies.[67] To help devise more effective responses to the economic pressures, Tehran prevailed upon Washington to resume its advisory mission, prompting the brief return of the former State Department staffer Arthur Millspaugh to the helm of Iran's finance ministry. Through these undertakings, American-Iranian cooperation began to assume greater significance for both governments.

Ironically, during the wartime hardship, Iranian politics were more encouraging. The sudden power vacuum paved the way for the reemergence of groups long repressed by Reza Shah. Publications flourished, and "involvement in politics and political radicalism became prestigious,

---

[65] Fred Halliday, *Iran Dictatorship and Development* (New York: Penguin Books, 1979), 24.

[66] Stephen L. McFarland, "Anatomy of an Iranian Political Crowd: The Tehran Bread Riot of December 1942," *International Journal of Middle East Studies* 17:1 (February 1985), p. 57.

[67] McFarland (1985), p. 53.

fashionable and sometimes rewarding."[68] The havoc wrought by the invasion and occupation played a direct role in radicalizing many sectors of the population. Several nationalist and leftist opposition groups were born during this period and remained significant actors through, and even after, the Islamic Revolution, including the National Front and the Tudeh (or Masses) Party. Led by the veteran politician Mosaddeq, the National Front initially lacked a specific platform, but its adherents generally encompassed Iran's middle classes and espoused a distinctly nationalist orientation. The Tudeh began as a classic liberal, nationalist opposition grouping, committed to expanding rights for labor and women, constitutional democracy, and land redistribution. Leadership splits and the active intervention of the superpowers quickly transformed the Tudeh into a Soviet-dominated subsidiary organization.

During this period, oil politics began to assume greater significance for both Iranians and the great powers. Encouraged by influential Iranian politicians, American oil companies began to assert their interests in expanding access to Middle Eastern resources, which were dominated by the British. The Soviets began to intensify pressure on Tehran for rights to its northern provinces. For their part, Iranian politicians began to appreciate their own oil interests more carefully, out of trepidation toward Moscow and an increasing awareness of the improved investment terms that more recent oil producers, such as Venezuela, had achieved. In 1944, Tehran announced a moratorium on any new foreign oil concessions, a decision subsequently endorsed by the Majlis.

The increasing centrality of oil politics for Iran and the great powers, together with emergence of a left-wing Iranian opposition with Soviet ties, helped catapult the country into the epicenter of the budding Cold War rivalry between Washington and Moscow. With Soviet troops refusing to leave Iran's northern provinces, the December 1945 declaration of autonomous socialist republics in Azerbaijan and Kurdistan shook the country and spawned the first major postwar crisis of the international system. Washington's increasing trepidation about Soviet expansionism meant that the United States for the first time assumed a direct diplomatic interest in the dispute, including referral to the UN Security Council. For Tehran, the matter took on even greater urgency after the announcement of a tripartite commission comprising America, Britain, and the Soviet

[68] Kian-Thiébaut (1998), p. 95.

Union, which Iranians interpreted as a harbinger of "impending doom – the state again being carved up into foreign spheres of influence."[69]

These fears facilitated the return of Iran's veteran prime minister, Ahmad Sultan Qavam, with authority to negotiate a resolution to the crisis. Ever the shrewd operator, Qavam undertook goodwill gestures, including efforts to draw the Tudeh back into the political fold of the monarchy. Under the shadow of increasingly pointed warnings from Washington and London, Qavam managed to persuade the Soviets to withdraw in exchange for an oil concession.[70] In May 1946, the Soviets withdrew, and Qavam bided his time before reversing course several months later with a crackdown on the Left. The Azeri autonomous republic quickly collapsed, thanks in part to its disastrous economic policies, and preparation for impending parliamentary elections provided Qavam with a rationale for dispatching central government troops to the wayward northern capitals. When the proposed Soviet oil concession was presented to the newly elected fifteenth parliament in October 1947, it was rejected out of hand.

The crisis forced a new American assertiveness against the prospect of Russian expansionism, foreshadowing the emergence of containment strategy.[71] Even as President Roosevelt was assuring his British counterpart that "we are not making sheep's eyes at your oil fields in Iraq and Iran,"[72] Washington was in fact beginning to appreciate Iran's strategic importance and the significance of its oil resources. The U.S. role – which previously had been limited to occasional technical assistance – intensified, beginning with development planning and advisory missions for Iran's military and security forces, and eventually encompassing an extensive assistance program.

---

[69] Ervand Abrahamian, "Factionalism in Iran: Political Groups in the 14th Parliament (1944–46)," *Middle Eastern Studies* 14:1 (January 1978), p. 50.

[70] This tactic of utilizing the quarrelsome tendencies of the Majlis as a decoy to evade international pressure would be deployed again, including by the Islamic Republic in its negotiations with European powers over the nuclear issue. For example, in 2004, Tehran agreed to accept the terms of the Additional Protocol to the Nuclear Nonproliferation Agreement with presumably full recognition that this agreement would never receive ratification from a conservative-controlled parliament.

[71] For a full account of the dispute and Qavam's bluff, which created the appearance of linkage between Soviet withdrawal and an oil concession, see Abrahamian (1987), and George Lenczowski, *Russia and the West in Iran, 1918–1948* (Ithaca, NY: Cornell University Press, 1949).

[72] James A. Bill, *The Eagle and the Lion: The Tragedy of American Iranian Relations* (New Haven, CT: Yale University Press, 1988), p. 28.

The tussle with the Soviets also precipitated a showdown over oil resources with the primary contender for their control, the British. In rejecting the Soviet oil concession, Iran's parliament also mandated government redress of "all cases where the rights of the people have been violated in respect of the natural wealth of the country, including its underground resources, with special reference to southern oil."[73] This represented a shot across the bow at the British and the company that by then had been renamed the Anglo-Iranian Oil Company (AIOC). The brewing conflict reshaped Iran's domestic politics and its relationship with Washington and the world. In this respect, while Moscow's bid for a toehold in northern Iran failed, its policies inadvertently helped to galvanize Iranian resource nationalism, prompting the British ambassador to Tehran to describe the outcome as "something of a victory" for the Soviets.[74]

After the Soviet withdrawal, the young shah's position remained precarious. To his credit, Mohammed Reza sought to mitigate the country's economic challenges, launching institutions aimed at managing the economy (the High Economic Council, the national Plan Organization, and several banks). These steps established a strong central commitment to economic planning that survived the revolution; from its inception, however, the shah's economic institution building was undermined by the simmering political tension within the country, which contributed to frequent changes in government as well as political violence.[75]

Tehran also sought to redress the enduring frictions with the British and AIOC. AIOC sought to improve the terms of the 1933 deal in its own favor, proposing revisions in 1949 that stipulated a 50 percent increase in Tehran's royalties for production. The company's management considered the package generous, but it did not satisfy Tehran. In the context of broader changes in the industry, including the recent Venezuelan precedent of fifty-fifty profit sharing, the 1949 Supplemental Agreement was seen as an affront, both in its terms and in its absence of parliamentary involvement. Already, oil nationalization bills were circulating the

---

[73] L. P. Elwell-Sutton, *Persian Oil: A Study in Power Politics* (London: Lawrence and Wishart, 1955), p. 119.

[74] Louise Fawcett, *Iran and the Cold War: The Azerbaijan Crisis of 1946* (Cambridge: Cambridge University Press, 1992), p. 95.

[75] Between 1941 and 1951, Iran's government changed on at least eleven different occasions – an average of seven months per administration. See Fariborz Mokhtari, "Iran's 1953 Coup Revisited: Internal Dynamics versus External Intrigue," *Middle East Journal* 62:3 (Summer 2008): p. 462.

parliament. At a basic level, Iran's maximalist demands for genuine control over the oil sector were incompatible with AIOC's corporate interests and Britain's strategic interests in what remained London's largest overseas investment.[76]

This historical episode, which resulted in the nationalization of Iran's oil sector and culminated in the brief collapse of the Pahlavi throne and a U.S.-backed coup to reinstate the young shah, has long drawn interest. Even the Islamic Republic – whose leaders disdained Mosaddeq's secular orientation – has utilized this chapter for its own purposes, and their efforts to downplay Mosaddeq's significance have only burnished his status as an Iranian national hero. The basic outlines of the events that drove the young shah into Italian exile and eventually restored him to the throne are well known, and their domestic and international implications have been examined in great depth in both the English- and Persian-language literature.[77]

Still, it is interesting, given the evolution of American-Iranian relations, that the political machinations deployed against Mosaddeq by both his domestic rivals and his superpower adversaries dominate the historical narrative of this period. What has faded into memory, at least for many casual observers of Iran, is the embargo on Iran's oil exports that preceded the coup, and that arguably bears equal responsibility for Mosaddeq's unseating. This aspect of the Mosaddeq affair offers an interesting if imperfect parallel to more recent confrontations between the international community and Tehran.

Iranian furor over the 1949 agreement dragged on for another year, as the shah grappled with constitutional revisions, continuing internal violence (including attempts on the lives of both the shah and his prime minister), and internal tensions with an increasingly assertive Majlis. Oil began to emerge as the focal point of nationalism, fueling a nascent alliance among clerics, merchants, and left-leaning groups that would

---

[76] Mary Ann Heiss, "The United States, Great Britain, and the Creation of the Iranian Oil Consortium, 1953–1954," *International History Review* 16:3 (August 1994), p. 512.

[77] A small selection of the English-language work on the Mosaddeq period includes Christopher de Bellaigue, *Patriot of Persia: Muhammad Mossadegh and a Very British Coup* (London: Bodley Head, 2012); Mark J. Gasiorowski and Malcolm Byrne, *Mohammad Mosaddeq and the 1953 Coup in Iran* (Syracuse, NY: Syracuse University Press, 2004); James F. Goode, *The United States and Iran: In the Shadow of Mosaddeq* (New York: St. Martin's Press, 1997); Mostafa Elm, *Oil, Power, and Principle: Iran's Oil Nationalization and Its Aftermath* (Syracuse, NY: Syracuse University Press, 1992); and Homa Katouzian, *Musaddiq and the Struggle for Power in Iran* (New York: St. Martin's Press, 1990).

continue for decades. The parliament filibustered the new AIOC agreement in late 1949, and a year later, a Mosaddeq-chaired commission formally rejected it. The government grudgingly withdrew the agreement and promised to reopen negotiations, but the issue had exacerbated internal tensions among the Iranian political class.

On one side were liberal nationalists such as Mosaddeq, aligned with a powerful contingent of radical clerics who mobilized mosques and organized large street demonstrations in support of nationalization. Their campaign echoed themes that had persisted since the Tobacco Revolt – that Iran could not be truly independent until it controlled its own resources. Conversely, the establishment and the court, including the young shah, saw the deal – and more broadly, British protection – as vital for the monarchy and Iran's development. For traditionalists such as Prime Minister General Ali Razmara, nationalization constituted "the greatest of treasons" because "under the present conditions Iran does not possess the industrial capacity to take the oil out and sell it on the world markets.... Gentlemen, you cannot yet manage a cement factory with your own personnel."[78] Mosaddeq responded that Iranians "do not consider legitimate a government that yields to such slave-like baseness."[79] His reproof would be echoed fourteen years later by Ayatollah Khomeini, who invoked Razmara's statement in denouncing the monarchy's infatuation with and subordination to Europe.[80]

Following the agreement's rejection, Tehran began pressing its case for nationalization, insisting that tanker captains recognize the newly established national oil company as the rightful owner of their cargoes. Neither the British government nor AIOC had any intention of humoring Iranian ambitions. This transpired in an environment of increasing political instability, culminating in the March 1951 assassination of the prime minister and oil workers' unrest. Razmara's assassination by radical leftists vaulted the nationalization cause forward; a week after his death, the parliament passed the Oil Nationalization Act and ushered in a momentous new era in Iran's history.

Mohammad Mosaddeq was named prime minister on April 30, 1951, and, with the exception of a brief interlude in July 1952, held office for the

---

[78] As quoted in Afkhami (2009), p. 121. Similar sentiments, with different wording, have been attributed to Razmara in other sources, including A. Milani (2011), p. 149.

[79] As quoted in Afkhami (2009), p. 121.

[80] Khomeini's speech on April 15, 1964, at the A'zam Mosque in Qom, as reprinted by the Islamic Republic of Iran World Broadcasting, http://www2.irib.ir/worldservice/imam/speech/14.htm

next twenty-eight months. His short tenure and abrupt removal loom large in Iran's history and its political economy. By framing the struggle for sovereignty in terms of access to and control over the country's resources, and specifically in opposition to the acquisitive self-interest of foreign powers, the crisis and the coup helped to fuse the connection between economic grievances and political mobilization that endures in Iran today, and contributed greatly to the inextricable link between energy and the quest for independence and government legitimacy. Thanks to Mosaddeq's legacy, Iranian economic policy remains predicated on this persistent struggle to assert the authority of the state over perceived threats from external actors.

The embargo began spontaneously, as AIOC's refusal to acknowledge the nationalization froze exports even before the law was enacted. In September 1951, the company warned that purchasing Iranian oil or any other assistance to Tehran's oil activities would elicit legal action. The following month AIOC pulled its personnel from Iran, and every alternative source of skilled oil workers refused Iranian appeals, except for Italy.[81] The British government upped the ante by freezing Tehran's UK-based assets, limiting its access to currency exchanges, and banning exports of key products including sugar and steel. London also flexed its military muscles, positioning warships in the Gulf to reinforce the company's threats against any Iranian customers.

British interests and perceptions of the crisis diverged from those of the other state emerging as a key stakeholder, the United States. Shutting down AIOC's Iranian production deprived London of approximately £100 million per year, as well as desperately needed crude and products. AIOC's Abadan refinery was the largest refinery in the world, and Britain's largest foreign investment, responsible for 6 percent of world oil production and nearly one-third of European imports of refined products.[82] Abadan was a vital strategic asset, responsible for the preponderance of British fuel oil and "a symbol which not even the most skeptical Arab could deny of British energy, British wealth, British efficiency, and British industrial might."[83] Moreover, Iran's nationalization

[81] May Ann Heiss, "International Boycott of Iranian Oil," in Gasiorowski and Byrne, eds., 183.
[82] W. Taylor Fain, *American Ascendance and British Retreat in the Persian Gulf Region* (New York: Palgrave Macmillan, 2008), footnote 91, pp. 218–19.
[83] Description of a British diplomat in Kuwait, as quoted in James A. Bill and William Roger Louis, eds., *Mosaddeq, Iranian Nationalism, and Oil* (London: I. B. Tauris, 1988), pp. 229–30.

would undermine the sanctity of all foreign contracts, inviting the demise of concessionary oil arrangements around the world and ushering in the inexorable decline of British power and the British Empire.[84]

In contrast to London's mercantile interests, American fears focused on the Tudeh and Soviet influence, and this meant that U.S. policy throughout the crisis diverged from that of its British ally. Whereas London wanted to squeeze Tehran, the Truman administration saw economic pressure as counterproductive and pointedly maintained U.S. economic ties with Iran while attempting to mediate. Even late in the crisis, President Eisenhower pressed the British to accept Iranian terms and briefly contemplated reviving direct assistance to a beleaguered Tehran.[85] Over time, however, Washington's perception of the stakes – and of Mosaddeq – evolved considerably. Concerns about security of supply receded, displaced by anxieties over whether the embargo had fatally weakened Mosaddeq and created inroads for the Tudeh. Frustration and skepticism replaced what began as a tentative U.S. embrace of Mosaddeq as a nationalist capable of impeding Soviet influence. American trepidation of the worst-case scenario – that nationalization would facilitate a Soviet beachhead in Iran – facilitated the intervention. The long-run outcome was arguably worse than American fears, as the U.S. role in the coup fostered an enduring resentment of Washington.

The complicated interplay among the three state actors and the company contributed to the stalemate. Mosaddeq encouraged U.S. concerns about Iran's economic vulnerabilities and Soviet influence in hopes of securing greater economic assistance from Washington, an approach that had unintended consequences. In addition, Mosaddeq and his allies gravely overestimated the country's leverage in international oil markets and its ability to continue production in the absence of its British partners; the Iranian supply was easily and quickly replaced by additional production in the worldwide market, and AIOC itself was reasonably equipped to ride out the standoff thanks to its considerable diversification and integration over its forty-year history. Iran's bargaining power effectively declined as AIOC ramped up production elsewhere, and Tehran bore the primary financial costs of the standoff.[86] Whereas other host governments

---

[84] Steve Marsh, "The United States, Iran and Operation 'Ajax': Inverting Interpretative Orthodoxy," *Middle Eastern Studies* 39:3 (July 2003), p. 8.

[85] Mark Gasiorowski, "The Coup d'Etat against Mosaddeq," in Gasiorowski and Byrne, eds. (2004), p. 232.

[86] By the end of the crisis, "there was such an abundance of oil that British officials especially doubted that it was in their interests to settle the Iranian oil dispute at that

had begun to wrest a greater share of profits from the producing companies through negotiations, Iran's more ambitious tactics generated costly retaliation. The experience taught Iranians "how dependent [their] country was on oil" and "the mistake was never repeated again."[87]

Scholars disagree on Mosaddeq's success in managing the economy during the embargo.[88] The prime minister himself argued at his trial that the coup was undertaken in part as a means of preventing Iran from achieving a sustainable nonoil economy.[89] His administration did avoid outright economic catastrophe, boosting nonoil exports and reviving growth despite the cutoff of its oil revenues. The impact of the crisis was mitigated in part by the economy's agricultural base and the low import dependence of Iran's manufacturing sector (textiles and carpet weaving, food processing, and tobacco).[90]

However, within the oil sector, the boycott proved nearly bulletproof. Without Western technocrats and labor, oil production slowed to a trickle, and Tehran exported approximately 100,000 tons of oil and products during the entire two-and-a-half-year crisis – the rough equivalent of a single day's exports prior to nationalization.[91] To offset the loss of oil income, the government sought new revenue sources, including more rigorous collection of customs duties, and instituted quotas and depreciated the rial to curb imports. Opium reemerged as a significant source of government revenues,[92] and the government offered national bonds that were eagerly purchased by Mosaddeq's supporters in the *bazaar*.[93] During the standoff's waning days, Mosaddeq also nationalized

time because re-integrating Iran's oil into world markets would potentially be very expensive." See Steve Marsh, "Thirty Years On: Iran's 'Silent Revolution,'" *Iranian Studies* 42:2 (April 2009), p. 221.

[87] Fereidun Fesharaki, *Development of the Iranian Oil Industry: International and Domestic Aspects* (New York: Praeger, 1976), p. 60.

[88] For the optimistic view, see Patrick Clawson and Cyrus Sassanpour, "Adjustment to Foreign Exchange Shock: Iran, 1951–53," *International Journal of the Middle East Studies* 19:1 (February 1987), pp. 1–23. For the pessimistic view of Mosaddeq's economic policies, see M. G. Majd, "The 1951–53 Oil Nationalization Dispute and the Iranian Economy: A Rejoinder," *Middle Eastern Studies* 31:3 (July 1995), pp. 449–59; and Kamran Dadkhah, "The Oil Nationalization Movement, the British Oil Boycott and the Iranian Economy 1951–53," in Elie Kedourie and Sylvia G. Haim, eds., *Essays on the Economic History of the Middle East* (London: Frank Cass, 1988), pp. 104–31.

[89] Katouzian (1999), p. 146.   [90] Clawson and Sassanpour (1987), p. 11.

[91] Clawson and Sassanpour (1987), p. 1.

[92] Bradley Hansen, "Learning to Tax: The Political Economy of the Opium Trade in Iran, 1921–1941," *Journal of Economic History* 61:1 (March 2001), p. 109.

[93] Keshavarzian (2007), p. 237.

a Soviet concession for the production and marketing of Iranian caviar, freezing operations in a joint-venture company that an Iranian parliamentarian described as a "nest of spies."[94]

Unfortunately, Tehran's ability to keep the economy limping along prolonged the crisis by contributing to Mosaddeq's overconfidence and playing into the tactical debate between Washington and London. British diplomats dismissed the possibility that Iran's economy would collapse, arguing that a state based largely on subsistence agriculture "does not 'collapse' economically. It sags."[95] Washington harbored more alarmist views, and fears that financial desperation would leave Tehran vulnerable to Soviet incursions motivated its advocacy for British concessions and increasing U.S. economic assistance.

Nationalization fused the relationship between national sovereignty and control of the country's oil resources. Mosaddeq appealed to President Truman that in "the half century of the former company's domination it has never been possible for the Iranian Government to make a free decision in its internal affairs and its foreign policy."[96] Defining the negotiating process in zero-sum terms meant that for Mosaddeq and the nationalists, backing down was tantamount to forfeiting Iranian sovereignty. Tehran's options were either "'real independence and happiness' (*sa'adat va istiqlal vaqa'i*), or 'surrender and submission' (*inqiyad va taslim*)."[97] This perception exacerbated Mosaddeq's innate mistrust of British intentions and dissuaded him from any compromise that might meet AIOC and British demands for compensation.

Eventually, the embargo and Mosaddeq's high-handed tactics toward his rivals eroded his delicate coalition of clerical, nationalist, and leftist allies, as well as his support on the streets. *Bazaari* merchants, who had been among the prime minister's most stalwart supporters, and an agitated labor movement turned against the prime minister on the basis of their economic concerns. Mosaddeq "had the courage to challenge but lacked the capacity to construct."[98] He tapped into a yearning for democracy and independence among Iranians but could not muster

[94] Clifton Daniel, "Iran Will Terminate Soviet Caviar Grant," *New York Times*, January 30, 1953, p. 1.
[95] Foreign Office correspondence, January 22, 1952. As quoted in Steve Marsh, *Anglo-American Relations and Cold War Oil: Crisis in Iran* (London: Palgrave Macmillan, 2003), p. 106.
[96] Rouhollah Ramazani, *Iran's Foreign Policy 1941–1975* (Charlottesville: University of Virginia Press, 1975), p. 440.
[97] Ramazani, (1975), p. 440.   [98] Bill (1988), p. 84.

either the institutions or the personal capacity to channel nascent nationalism into effective governance.

At the same time, Washington's perception of Iran's situation shifted considerably, in part thanks to the mercurial Mosaddeq. His rejection of successive British concessions, offered at least in part at Washington's behest, persuaded U.S. officials of the British view: that no settlement could be reached as long as the prime minister remained in office. And since the shah appeared wholly unwilling or unable to contain Mosaddeq, the onus fell on outside powers to avert the disaster of Soviet expansionism and the loss of the increasingly valuable strategic asset that Iran's oil resources represented. This assessment transformed Washington's preferred game plan from mediation to direct intervention, a change that emboldened Mosaddeq's internal opponents, many of whom were courted by London and Washington to advance their own aims.

In this way, the nationalization impasse gave way to the infamous coup, with the final mobilization facilitated by operatives and financial support from Washington and London. For the relatively small sum of $285,000, split almost evenly between Washington and London, crowds were rented and elites induced to agitate.[99] After a few tumultuous days, during which the initial plan appeared to implode and the shah decamped to Italy, Mosaddeq's brief reign was summarily ended, and the monarchy was reinstated and reinforced. The conventional historical narrative often overstates the importance of external interference. In fact, the seeds of Mosaddeq's demise existed independently of American or British support and were evident in the months of turmoil that led up to the coup and the defection of previously vital supporters such as Ayatollah Kashani.[100]

The coup proved a turning point for Iran, in both its internal political dynamics and its relationship with the world. Washington's involvement in Mosaddeq's ouster invested the Eisenhower Administration in his successor's fate, and the United States provided emergency aid to the new Iranian government – amounting to 60 percent of the national budget in 1954[101] – as well as crucial mediation in the still unresolved oil dispute. The generous American program of technical and financial

---

[99] Gasiorowski, "The Coup d'Etat against Mosaddeq," in Gasiorowski and Byrne, eds. (2004), p. 240.

[100] For an expansive discussion of the primacy of domestic factors in the cuop, see Darioush Bayandor, *Iran and the CIA: The Fall of Mosaddeq Revisited* (London: Palgrave Macmillan, 2010).

[101] Gasiorowski, *U.S. Foreign Policy and the Shah: Building a Client State in Iran* (Ithaca, NY: Cornell University Press, 1991), p. 101.

assistance enabled the shah to impose a higher degree of central control and reassemble the mechanisms of the state under his personal authority. Over the next decade, American economic and military aid leapt from a paltry $83.7 million during the three years preceding the coup to $1,048.7 million over the ensuing seven years, much of which was directed toward military and security needs.[102]

After Mosaddeq's removal, it took more than a year of contentious negotiations with the AIOC, London, and Washington to resolve the nationalization impasse. The end result was a multinational consortium with a minority share for a reconfigured AIOC – now christened as British Petroleum (BP)– and smaller stakes for several European and U.S. companies. Their participation was encouraged by the U.S. government[103] as well as their own interests in facilitating an "orderly re-entry" of Iran's oil to an already-saturated marketplace.[104] Iran secured a fifty-fifty split of profits from production but ceded effective control to the consortium and agreed to pay modest compensation to BP. These terms were substantially inferior to what Mosaddeq was offered and rejected. Tehran would continue to revisit the debate over the most appropriate role for international oil companies for the next two decades.

The consortium agreement did begin to funnel more oil revenues into the Iranian budget. Income from oil production accounted for approximately 41 percent of government revenue by 1960 and, along with the growing foreign assistance, began to cast a larger shadow on the overall national economy.[105] The establishment of Iran's storied economic planning office, the Plan and Budget Organization, linked oil revenues to developmental expenditures. Iran's expanding state income funded a

---

[102] Bernard Reich, "The United States and Iran: An Overview," in *Economic Consequences of the Revolution in Iran: A Compendium of Papers*, submitted to the Joint Economic Committee, Congress of the United States (Washington, DC: U.S. Government Printing Office, 1980), p. 18.

[103] In hopes of settling the Iranian standoff and staving off its continuing fears of Soviet incursions into Iran, Washington fought to ensure that U.S. firms were included in the consortium, including fiscal incentives and preferential treatment in the ongoing Justice Department investigation of oil industry collusion. See Theodore H. Moran, "Managing an Oligopoly of Would-Be Sovereigns: The Dynamics of Joint Control and Self-Control in the International Oil Industry Past, Present and Future," *International Organization* 41:4 (Autumn 1987), pp. 590–2; Burton I. Kaufman, "Oil and Antitrust: The Oil Cartel Case and the Cold War," *Business History Review* 51:1 (Spring 1977), pp. 35–56.

[104] Mira Wilkins, "The Oil Companies in Perspective," *Daedalus* 104:4 (Fall 1975), p. 165.

[105] Hootan Shambayati, "The Rentier State, Interest Groups, and the Paradox of Autonomy: State and Business in Turkey and Iran," *Comparative Politics* (April 1994), p. 317; Kian-Thiébaut (1998), p. 121.

major new government-directed industrialization effort, while the private
sector remained relegated to relatively small-scale consumer goods production.[106] Oil revenues also fueled the expansion of the state bureaucracy and armed forces, as well as the enhancement of Iran's military
capabilities. The expansion of public infrastructure and services meant
that, for the first time in Iran's history, the reach of the central government extended throughout the country.

This investment in state building produced many advances for Iran,
such as the Plan Organization, which became a powerful agent of economic policy and development. However, the empowerment of the central government also heralded its increasing authoritarianism. The
notorious internal intelligence service, Sazman-i Ittila'at va Amniyat-i
Keshvar, or SAVAK, was established during this period as part of a more
forceful effort to institutionalize the monarchy and enforce loyalty to it.
Politically, it was a period of regrouping by the shah and the circle of elites
that had associated themselves with the Pahlavi reign – "years of
groping," as characterized by one scholar of the period.[107] The redistributive policies of the brief Mosaddeq interregnum were abandoned,
replaced by an intensification of the patronage system surrounding the
court and the landed elites. American presence and support also grew
considerably, assuming a crucial role in guiding the monarchy through
the precarious transition. The relationship was deepened through a
1959 bilateral security agreement.

Thanks in part to American assistance, Iran's economy experienced a
modest recovery during the latter half of the 1950s, until rapidly
expanding demand, together with the growth in the monetary supply
produced by the 1957 devaluation, generated inflation and a balance of
payments crisis stemming from the import influx.[108] At the same time,
pressures caused by the entry of Soviet crude into Western oil markets and
general oversupply prompted oil companies to cut the "posted price,"

---

[106] In the late 1950s, revaluation of the rial subsidized substantial credit to the private
sector, while government subsidized banks, such as the Industrial Credit Bank and the
Industrial and Mining Bank of Iran, facilitated private capital accumulation, among
them providing approximately 30 percent of gross private investment in industry (a role
they would continue to play until the time of the revolution). Karshenas (1990), table
4.2, p. 102; Looney (1982), pp. 14–15; Parvin Alizade, "Industrial Development in Iran:
Recent Changes and Past Experiences," in *Iran's Economy after the Two Wars: Reconstruction and Development* (London: Institute of Developing Studies, 1992), p. 187.

[107] Marvin Zonis, *Majestic Failure: Fall of the Shah* (Chicago: University of Chicago Press,
1991), p. 107.

[108] Karshenas (1990), pp. 131–4.

meaning the first direct hit to the producing country's profits share. To address the slump, Tehran implemented an IMF stabilization program in 1960, cutting imports and investment. However, while excess capacity enabled industry and manufacturing to continue expanding, traditional sectors and the *bazaar* continued to experience declining wages. The decline stimulated political tensions and a new wave of political activism. The cycle of responses and counter-responses by the shah and the embryonic strands of popular opposition set the stage for the revolution two decades later.

THE 1960S: "REVOLUTION" AND REACTION

Intensifying financial pressures on both the state and the population meant that Iran in the early 1960s was again experiencing political upheaval and economic crisis. Labor strikes and demonstrations multiplied, and June 1960 parliamentary elections were annulled because of blatant fraud. With the new Kennedy administration advocating liberalization, the shah sought to co-opt his opposition by appointing Ali Amini, Iran's former U.S. ambassador and Mosaddeq era finance minister, as prime minister. While it was widely whispered that Washington foisted Amini upon the shah, there is little evidence of active U.S. intervention in the matter.[109]

Amini was an instrument rather than an ally of the shah, but his abbreviated stint as premier moved the monarchy from consolidation and crisis management toward an ambitious economic and social development agenda. During Amini's fourteen months in office, he undertook a number of reforms, including an anticorruption drive and the first serious attempt at land redistribution. However, the premier could not transcend his vulnerable position, in which he had the confidence of neither the shah nor the opposition. With popular agitation intensifying, Amini resigned in April 1962 after a dispute over military budget cuts.

His replacement, Assadollah Alam, was a close Pahlavi confidant charged with blunting the unrest provoked by the initial stab at land reform and launching a broader reform program that would become known as the White Revolution. The Amini era land reform measures were subsumed within the larger effort, which featured import-substitution industrialization; privatization of state-owned factories; the

---

[109] Akhavi (2009), pp. 213–14.

establishment of voting rights for women, profit-sharing schemes for workers, and a literacy corps; and nationalization of the forests. (The plan expanded in 1977 to incorporate thirteen tenets in the name of "The Revolution of the Shah and the People.") The "Revolution" was implemented through centrally coordinated Five-Year Plans, which were intended to jump-start a structural transformation of the economy.[110]

Although land reform predated the White Revolution, it represented a crucial plank in the overall program and the undertaking that had the broadest reach in a still predominantly rural country. It was intended to revive productivity and empower an independent peasantry as well as a new industrialized agricultural sector. These efforts involved the redistribution of a significant proportion of Iran's agricultural lands and eventually morphed into broader plans, implemented in multiple phases, for wholly transforming at least sixty-eight thousand villages and independent farms into a large-scale collective farm system.

Land reform confronted Iran's clergy with a particular challenge. Historically, Iran's religious leaders ranked among the country's largest landholders, via direct ownership as well as Islamic charities, through which wealth and property can be tithed to an endowment (*vaqf*) that in turn provides income for the maintenance of a religious shrine or facility.[111] Land reform was seen by many clerics as contravening guarantees under Islamic law for the protection and advancement of private property. Although there were other aspects of the White Revolution – including provisions related to women – that were at least as odious to the clerical leadership, land reform managed to mobilize vehement opposition by the different strands of the clergy, including its traditionally apolitical leader, Grand Ayatollah Mohammad Hussein Borujerdi, prior to his 1961 death.

The White Revolution became the centerpiece of the shah's domestic policy agenda, later intensified and accelerated by the influx of oil revenues. Its ambitious scope suited a leader who was personally more fixated on economic modernization than political development. This agenda also meshed well with Iran's intellectual and political elites, who were heavily influenced by the statist legacy of Marxist influence as well

---

[110] Protectionist restrictions were enacted on consumer goods imports, subsidized credit was offered to the private sector, and the shah undertook massive public investment in such capital-intensive industries as steel, aluminum, petrochemicals, and machinery, as well as encouraging foreign investment and maintenance of an overvalued exchange rate.

[111] Akhavi (1980), pp. 95–6.

as Western modernization theories.[112] In this sense, the White Revolution was very much an Iranian initiative, and the shah himself insisted on putting the issue before the population in a referendum, sparking some unease among his cabinet. Shaken by the brutal 1958 coup against Iraq's Hashemite monarchy, the shah became invested in the vision of what he described as "a social transformation unprecedented in Iran's three-thousand-year history."[113]

Nonetheless, many Iranians saw the initiative as integrally interconnected with the Crown's relationship with Washington. Its inception coincided with intensifying American concerns about regional stability and about the apparent vulnerabilities of an Iran continually in the throes of crisis. Its implementation corresponded with the rapid expansion of American presence in and support for Tehran, including pressure on the shah to bolster his regime via structural economic and political reforms. And while Washington played no direct role in devising the reforms, the perception of American responsibility was not wholly mistaken, since the shah himself embarked upon this course in part to ingratiate himself with Washington.[114]

These two aspects – the threat to the incomes of major constituencies, including the clergy, and the perception of the reform program as foreign inspired or even foreign controlled – galvanized amorphous dissatisfaction into something far more serious. The 1961 death of Iran's quietest senior cleric, Ayatollah Borujerdi, eroded the practical restraints on clerical activism, and interest in cooperation with the monarchy had slowly but steadily disintegrated. The public battle over the proposed reforms became transformed into a direct, and highly personalized, clash between the ambitions of the shah, who saw the White Revolution as the linchpin of his reign, and those of Khomeini, who was eager to stake his claim to clerical primacy. This confrontation foreshadowed the 1979 revolution – the emboldening of the opposition, the organizational links between the clergy and the *bazaar*, and the emergence of a powerful antimodernization narrative.

The White Revolution's formal promulgation met with fervent protests and demonstrations, particularly during the annual religious festivals of mourning, led by the religious and traditional merchant communities. Protests began mounting in Qom in October 1962 in response to new regulations extending suffrage to women, and within months Khomeini

---

[112] Milani, pp. 203–4.   [113] Akhavi (2009), p. 229.   [114] Zonis (1991), p. 72.

and other clerics urged a boycott of the referendum on the White Revolution. Opposition to the shah's reforms was not a purely clerical phenomenon: Students had been agitating for a year; the Tehran and Qom *bazaars* closed in protest; and the National Front tried to organize mass demonstrations. The government's response was swift and uncompromising; Front leaders were arrested, and the shah traveled to Qom to denounce his opponents as greedy and treasonous:

> They were always a stupid and reactionary bunch whose brains have not moved.... Black reaction understands nothing ... its brain has not moved for a thousand years. They think life is about getting something for nothing, eating and sleeping ... sponging on others and a parasitic existence ... those who lie about being patriotic and in practice turn their backs on the country are what I mean by black reaction ... it was they who formed a small and ludicrous gathering from a handful of bearded, stupid bazaaris to make noises ... they don't want to see this country develop.[115]

Only a few days later, the national referendum on the reforms passed in a suspiciously overwhelming landslide.[116] Instead of settling the issue, the vote only added fuel to the fire. During the Ramadan fast and the Nowruz holiday that followed, discord between the monarchy and the clerics intensified, culminating in the March 1963 storming of the Fayzieh seminary by paratroopers, who killed a number of students. In response, Khomeini declared that the shah "has dug his own grave and disgraced himself," and the stage was set for an epic confrontation between the two sides.[117]

That confrontation played out on Ashura, the commemoration of the martyrdom of Husayn, whose tormentors Khomeini openly compared with the shah. His speech was a deliberate provocation, undertaken in spite of ominous threats from SAVAK and in anticipation of repression. Khomeini's supporters also managed to win over the same gang leaders whom the monarchy had used as unofficial enforcers, their loyalty to the system undercut by the damage to their business interests exacted by police tactics in the *bazaar*.[118]

---

[115] Hamid Ruhani Ziyarati, *Nezhat-e Emam Khomeini*, vol. 1 (Tehran: 1981), p. 262. As quoted in Moin (1999), p. 88. It may be worth noting that Moin's rendition differs in wording, but not substance, from those published elsewhere, including Zonis (1971), p. 75. However, according to Moin, the news reporting on this speech was heavily edited precisely because the shah had deviated from his text in order to launch this diatribe.

[116] The formal count numbered 5,593,826 in favor and 4,115 opposed. Zonis (1971), pp. 75–6.

[117] Moin (1999), p. 95.   [118] Moin (1999), pp. 103–6.

This deployment of *bazaari* thugs to protect the Ashura protest march was just one element of a growing web of collaboration between the clerics and the *bazaar* that helped facilitate the revolution fifteen years later. The alliance between these two constituencies has received considerable attention but is frequently oversimplified.[119] Well before Khomeini moved to the fore, merchant opposition to Pahlavi policies had already become evident through a multiyear tax boycott, support for the National Front's electoral protests, and the teachers' strike. However, repression had neutralized the secular opposition groups, such as the Tudeh and the National Front. And while the White Revolution's launch coincided with labor unrest, the program had some appeal among workers and the rural peasantry, who hoped to benefit from land redistribution. The clerical community was best positioned to coordinate the protoopposition, with Khomeini its center of gravity.

Beyond forging an alliance with the *bazaar* and leftist opposition groups, the backlash to the White Revolution also enabled Khomeini to assert an alternative narrative rebutting the monarchy's claim to advancing the country. Some have suggested that Khomeini tactically refocused his rhetoric to emphasize economic concerns during the final months of the revolution in order to bridge the divisions within the antishah coalition and outmaneuver his leftist rivals by seizing their narrative. And yet his earliest political forays, including the 1963 sermons, hammered the issue of greed and corruption, presenting them in sharp contrast to their clerical opponents' rectitude and benevolence. Although his objections to the shah's reforms were wide-ranging, Khomeini saved special vitriol for the shah's economic policies, and the opening that they provided to the United States and Israel.

He wove economic grievances seamlessly into his broader denunciation of Pahlavi policies. "You don't know whether the situation will change one day nor whether those who surround you will remain your friends," Khomeini inveighed in his 1963 Ashura speech. "They are friends of the dollar. They have no religion, no loyalty."[120] He juxtaposed the monarchy's greed with a highly idealized defense of the clergy:

Now, these students of the religious sciences who spend the best and most active part of their lives in these narrow cells, and whose monthly income is somewhere between 40 and 100 tumans, are they parasites? And those to whom one source of income alone brings hundreds of millions of tumans are not parasites? People like

---

[119] Keshavarzian (2007), p. 239–40.   [120] Moin, p. 104.

Hajj Sheikh Abdol Karim, whose sons had nothing to eat on the night that he died; or the late Burujirdi, who was 600,000 tumans in debt when he parted from this world? And those who have filled foreign banks with the wealth produced by the oil of our poverty-stricken people, who have erected towering palaces but still will not leave the people in peace, wishing to fill their own pockets and those of Israel with our resources, they are not parasites? Let the world judge, let the nation judge who the parasites are![121]

Khomeini's arrest appeared to be an unambiguous victory for the shah – the culmination of his father's efforts to subdue a persistently intractable realm. However, it also represented the seeds of his destruction. A year later, the imam emerged again to confront the shah over the government's decision to extend diplomatic immunity to American military personnel. In Khomeini's sermons, this concession – which was concluded alongside a $200 million American loan for Iranian military purchases – symbolized a profound betrayal of Iranian sovereignty. For Khomeini, the material payoff compounded the insult of the privilege granted to Washington. "They have sold us, they have sold our independence," he inveighed, renouncing the parliamentarians as traitors. This time Khomeini went further than he had a year earlier, when he merely advised the shah "to learn from your mistakes." By 1964, the ayatollah had embraced revolution, arguing that "if the religious leaders have influence, they will not permit this nation to be the slaves of Britain one day, and America the next ... they will not permit Israel to take over the Iranian economy ... they will not permit such misuse to be made of the public treasury."[122]

That speech earned Khomeini a swift exile, first in Turkey, and then Najaf. Khomeini's departure removed an immediate threat to the monarchy. The clerical protests had electrified Iranian politics, but they had not generated a durable platform for coordinated action against the regime.[123] Still, the breach with the clergy forfeited a critical component of Iran's historic political equilibrium. Like Iran's secular-nationalist groups after the 1953 coup, the clerical establishment after 1963 was permanently alienated from the monarchy. Moreover, this episode catapulted Khomeini from his already lofty position as one of three acknowledged clerical leaders to another stratosphere. In the short term, the arrest provoked an unprecedented response of *ulema*-orchestrated unrest throughout the country, but over time it became clear that the episode invested Khomeini with the mantle of opposition leadership.

---

[121] Baktiari, p. 45.   [122] Moin, p. 123.   [123] Parsa, p. 2009.

The 1963 protests faded into memory for many Iranians, and meanwhile the country's fortunes soared. Even viewed independently of the increasing oil revenues, all indices demonstrate that Iran experienced vibrant and diversified expansion. National income expanded at a legendary rate during the 1960s and 1970s, nearly double that of its peer middle-income countries. Average annual growth rates between 1959 and 1972 were 9.8 percent – on par with the more recent experience of China. The nonoil sector expanded even more quickly than the overall economy, averaging 8.6 percent per year between 1963 and 1976.[124] Massive public investment and subsidized private capital funded a manufacturing boom that translated into an average annual growth rate of 14 percent, second only to South Korea during the period.[125]

It was a time of glittering growth in Iran, and not simply in economic terms. Primary education was made compulsory at the outset of the shah's rule and extended to intermediary schools in 1972. Thanks to this measure and the White Revolution's establishment of a "literacy corps" to extend educational services to rural areas, the number of primary school students increased from 286,000 in 1941/2 to 5.2 million in 1978/9, an eighteenfold expansion.[126] Adult literacy increased from 16 percent in 1960 to more than 36 percent in 1975.[127] Similar rates of educational expansion occurred at the university level. Women secured the right to vote and run in parliamentary elections, and their political participation helped advance a new family law bill. Passed in 1967, that law granted women the right to divorce, prevented husbands from unilaterally divorcing their spouse or taking a second wife, and enabled women's custody of children after divorce or death of a spouse. The middle class approached one-fourth of the labor force, composed of an estimated 700,000 salaried professionals and an additional 1 million families associated with the *bazaar* and small manufacturers.[128] These statistics matter and are too often subsumed within critiques of the

---

[124] Hadi Salehi Esfahani and M. Hashem Pesaran, "Iranian Economy in the Twentieth Century: A Global Perspective," *CWPE* 0815, March 2008, p. 7.

[125] Jahangir Amuzegar, *Iran's Economy under the Islamic Republic* (London: I. B. Tauris, 1993), pp. 5–6.

[126] David Menashri, *Education and the Making of Modern Iran* (Ithaca, NY: Cornell University Press, 1992), pp. 172–85.

[127] Mark Gasiorowski, *U.S. Foreign Policy and the Shah: Building a Client State in Iran* (Ithaca, NY: Cornell University Press, 1991), p. 135.

[128] Abrahamian (2008), p. 138.

monarchy's failings, particularly the lack of political freedoms. For millions of Iranians, the shah's development program generated tangible quality-of-life improvements, and expectations of upward mobility and future opportunities for their children that would surpass their own.

One of the White Revolution's major contributions was its expansion of Iran's private sector industrial base. Iran's auto sector is one of these success stories; starting from a string of auto repair shops in Mashhad, the Iran National Corporation was launched with support from a state bank in 1962. In the span of a decade, it had increased production from a handful of vehicles to nearly 100,000 units in 1978. Local content constituted a respectable 40 percent of all inputs to the industry by that time.[129] However, even in the early periods, prior to the massive increase in government revenues from the oil industry in 1973, the massive rate of public sector investment constrained opportunities for private capital, particularly in manufacturing.[130] The expansion of state banks and their generous provision of credit to the nascent private sector effectively muscled out two of the most important historical functions of the *bazaar*.[131] More broadly, the government's role as patron and distributor (of credit, import licenses, agencies) stunted the development of an industrial bourgeoisie, and the shah's heavy hand undercut the planning capacity of the burgeoning technocracy.[132]

Still, the shah's early successes at home fueled his interests in the world stage. Even as the White Revolution drew the United States and Iran into a closer embrace, the shah sought to improve relations with Moscow, to co-opt his leftist opposition with an eye toward ensuring Washington's continuing assistance. Several agreements boosted bilateral trade with Moscow, and in 1965 the two countries agreed to build a 10 billion cubic meters (bcm) capacity pipeline for gas exports to the Soviet Union. In return, Iran would receive Soviet military equipment and assistance in constructing steel and machine tool factories – projects that assumed an outsized place in the shah's vision of rapid industrialization. Similar

[129] Parvin Alizadeh, "Iran National Company," *Encyclopedia Iranica* Volume 13, Fascia 5, 2006, pp. 488–91.
[130] Mohammad A. Khatim, "Structure of the Public and Private Sector in Pre-Revolutionary Iran," in *The Economy of Islamic Iran between State and Market*, ed. Thierry Colville (Tehran: Institut Français de Recherche en Iran, 1994), p. 33.
[131] Nima Mazaheri, "An 'Informal' Revolution: State-Business Conflict and Institutional Change in Iran," *Middle Eastern Studies* 44:4 (July 2008): pp. 589–94.
[132] Vali Nasr, "Politics within the Late Pahlavi State: The Ministry of Economy and Industrial Policy, 1963–69," *IJMES* 32:1 (February 2000), pp. 97–122.

barter deals were struck with Eastern European countries, which provided credit for equipment and factories in exchange for Iranian consumer goods. These projects consciously fulfilled an economic and a strategic agenda – they advanced Iran's economic development while reinforcing Tehran's value to Washington.

OIL AND IRAN'S IMPERIAL AMBITIONS

The 1960s reforms began to reshape Iran's economy, but the shah's ambitions required more – specifically, an expansion in the national income. However, under the post-1953 oil sector arrangements, this remained beyond the monarch's reach. The consortium operators dictated production and price levels, which were based on a confidential formula that reflected corporate interests rather than those of the Iranian government.[133] Moreover, while the National Iranian Oil Company (NIOC), which was established as part of the nationalization, remained in existence, its actual responsibilities were highly circumscribed. For an Iranian leadership that remained frustrated with its limited authority over its own resources and revenues, the one obvious opportunity lay outside the geographical delineation of the consortium's mandate.

In 1957, the parliament passed a new oil law and quickly secured Tehran's real objective – luring non-consortium investors and assuming greater control over production and pricing. In this effort, the Iranian leadership had ready allies – U.S. firms and investors were seeking out Iranian opportunities as soon as the nationalization crisis ended.[134] Rather than an American or British oil company, however, the first real blow to the consortium monopoly over Iran's oil resources was by the Italian firm ENI, whose charismatic head, Enrico Mattei, was eager to break the British stranglehold on prime Middle Eastern reserves. The 1957 deal created Société Iranienne des Pétroles (SIRIP), the first-ever joint venture between an oil-producing country and a foreign firm. Iran received 75 percent of all future profits, shattering the prevailing fifty-fifty arrangement that Iran had fought so hard to achieve. Equally important for Tehran, the Iranian-Italian joint venture was subject to Iranian law, in

---

[133] For details on the process of determining Iranian production under the 1954 consortium arrangement, see Fereidun Fesharaki, *Development of the Iranian Oil Industry: International and Domestic Aspects* (New York: Praeger: 1976), pp. 54–5.

[134] See for example Robert L. Rosenberg, "Qom-1956: A Misadventure in Iranian Oil," *Business History Review* 49:1 (Spring 1975), pp. 81–104.

contrast to the consortium activities,[135] and incorporated provisions favoring domestic labor.

SIRIP was not commercially successful, but its establishment represented the most consequential shift in the Iranian oil sector since APOC's establishment. And it was even more significant for the industry; it left the prevailing fifty-fifty profit split "about as dead as the four minute mile," according to a British diplomat.[136] NIOC's subsequent tender drew interest from fifty-seven companies in nine countries, and over the next dozen years, Iran signed joint venture agreements with American, European, and Japanese oil firms.[137] In 1966, Tehran achieved even better terms through a service contract with the French company ERAP that apportioned all risk to the contractor. The ERAP deal served as a model for successor contracts, and equally importantly put the consortium itself on notice. At the same time, the shah pressed for production increases to meet his ever-growing revenue requirements by threatening "unilateral action" against the consortium in October 1966.[138]

Iran's economy continued to expand rapidly throughout this period, and organized political opposition withered after Khomeini's exile and the repression of the National Front and others. Yet below the surface, Tehran's progress did not eliminate the residual anger toward the monarchy and the changes under way. Indeed, even as the shah's prime minister, Hassanali Mansur, entered the parliament in January 1965 seeking approval for several new joint ventures, he was shot and killed by an assassin carrying a Quran and a photo of Khomeini, apparently in retaliation for Mansur's role in extending diplomatic immunity to U.S. soldiers in Iran.[139] This development, and other sporadic signs of turmoil including an assassination attempt against the shah himself three months later, did not dissuade the shah from pursuing increasingly ambitious development plans – all of which required more revenues.

It took time, and more aggressive action by Iran and other Middle Eastern oil producers, to seize full control over their own resources. The

---

[135] E. H. Wall, "The Iranian-Italian Oil Agreement of 1957," *International and Comparative Law Quarterly* 7:4 (October 1958), p. 738.

[136] Daniel Yergin, *The Prize: The Epic Quest for Oil, Money and Power* (New York: Simon & Schuster, 1991), p. 505.

[137] Fesharaki (1976), p. 71, pp. 74–5 (for a detailed chart of all nonconcessionary agreements).

[138] Dana Adams Schmidt, "Iran Is Pressing the West on Oil," *New York Times*, November 7, 1966, p. 75.

[139] A. Milani (2000), p. 171.

context was conducive – global demand for oil was increasing exponentially at an average rate of 7 percent per year during the latter half of the 1960s, and supply disruptions stemming from regional tensions and the assertions of nationalist producing governments added further upward pressures.[140] For years, oil producers carefully eyed precedents set by their competitors; for example, Iran's 1953 nationalization bid had been directly informed by the experience of Venezuela. Increasingly, producer governments sought to coordinate their positions through the nascent cartel, the Organization for Petroleum Exporting Countries (OPEC). With dramatic political and economic changes sweeping the industry, both producers and the companies themselves sought to negotiate in blocs in hopes of preserving their advantage. The oil companies hoped to insulate themselves from an escalatory contagion that meant that each agreement with a new host government only prompted expanding demands from another. The governments sought to redress the revenue balance conclusively and avoid disrupting the market for their oil.

Iran's involvement with OPEC dated back to its creation by Venezuelan and Saudi oil ministers after the oil companies' 1960 reduction in posted prices. Initially, the shah kept OPEC at arms' length, disinclined to risk his own position vis-à-vis the companies or Washington for an organization he described to President Lyndon B. Johnson in 1964 as an "instrument of Arab imperialism."[141] For this reason, Tehran struck an independent path in pressing the oil companies for increased revenues and production. The 1970 revisions to the consortium agreement increased Iran's profits share to 55 percent – an important breakthrough beyond the prevailing fifty-fifty standard but still substantially inferior to the terms that the government had received in its joint ventures and contracting deals. Not surprisingly, the specter of the nationalization crisis loomed large for Tehran. The shah invoked Mosaddeq in pejorative fashion when asserting himself vis-à-vis the oil companies, telling them in 1971 that "no one in Iran is cuddled up under a blanket or has shut himself off in a barricaded room."[142]

In 1971, the oil companies hammered out a tentative truce with Gulf oil producers, the Tehran Agreement, which set a 55 percent baseline for producers' share, raised oil prices by $0.35 per barrel, and instituted a new formula for subsequent price hikes. During this period, Iran's

---

[140] Jahangir Amuzegar, *Managing the Oil Wealth: OPEC's Windfalls and Pitfalls* (London: I. B. Tauris, 2001), p. 28.
[141] Yergin (1991), p. 534.   [142] Yergin (1991), p. 582.

production and revenues grew exponentially, from $791 million in oil revenues in 1970 to $2.6 billion in 1973.[143] Still, any equilibrium in the industry proved ephemeral. Further compromises were wrested from the companies, Libya and Iraq abruptly nationalized their concessions, and the Gulf States signed a "participation agreement" that for the first time affirmed their ownership of their oil resources.

Again, Tehran struck its own path; in January 1973, the shah announced to the nation that the consortium companies had not fulfilled the terms of the 1954 agreement. The result, inked in July 1973, was the St. Moritz Document, which refashioned the consortium into a service company under the auspices of full Iranian control and ownership. For the shah, the victory represented the wholesale reversal of his fortunes since his ignominious 1953 downfall. "Finally, I won out – 72 years of foreign control of the operation of our oil industry was ended," the shah wrote in his memoirs from his subsequent exile.[144] In retrospect, he also became bitterly convinced that his victory precipitated a foreign conspiracy to unseat him.

In the early 1970s, oil politics shifted the balance of power even more firmly in Tehran's favor. The October 1973 outbreak of yet another Middle Eastern war plunged the oil market into its greatest crisis ever. Arab governments announced a 70 percent price hike, to $5.11 per barrel, and deployed the first serious effort to use their newly established control over supply to extract political concessions from consumers. What began as phased cutbacks to the West quickly morphed into a full-fledged Arab oil embargo of the United States. In the ensuing panic, demand pushed prices as high as $22.00 per barrel. The shah opted not to join the embargo, instead exploiting the crisis to ratchet the price up even further.

During this period, Iran also began to assert its influence as the dominant regional power broker. In these aspirations, the shah had the support, albeit occasionally reluctant, of Washington. By virtue of the 1971 British withdrawal from the Gulf and the subsequent Nixon Doctrine, the United States was relying on local powers to maintain stability in this vital region, and Tehran was eager to take up the mantle. As Prime Minister Hoveyda pronounced on a U.S. visit in 1968, "In the troubled seas of the Middle East ... Iran stands on an island of stability and progress.... So if changing circumstances in the world impose upon us today added responsibility in working for the preservation of peace in the

---

[143] Gasiorowski (1991), p. 200.   [144] Pahlavi (1980), p. 96.

world at large, and especially in our own immediate area, we accept our share of these obligations willingly in the firm conviction that we possess the indubitable right, the economic capacity, and the political stability to do so."[145] These words would become apocryphal nine short years later, when U.S. President Jimmy Carter invoked similar themes at a 1978 New Year's banquet in Tehran.

The shah sought to project Iran's power in and beyond the Gulf. Close to home, he was even more assertive, occupying three small but strategic Gulf islands, engaging in escalating skirmishes with Iraq, funding a covert war in Iraqi Kurdistan, and sending troops to help defeat an Omani insurgency. The shah sought to use the oil influx to transform Iran's military capabilities and, by extension, Iran's strategic role. "Arms dealers joked that the shah devoured their manuals in much the same way as other men read *Playboy*."[146] The massive upsurge in military spending rippled across the economy; in little more than a decade, the population of Bandar Abbas multiplied by tenfold after it was selected as the headquarters of the shah's navy.[147] Iran's burgeoning revenues fueled and facilitated these endeavors, and the shah used diplomacy to further his regional ambitions and reinforce the economic boom. He saw national security and prosperity as two sides of the same coin. "What is the use of having an advanced industry in a country which could be brought to its knees when faced with any small asinine event?" the shah mused. "There is no economic power without military power."[148]

Ultimately, the shah's ambitions would crumble in the revolution's aftermath. The impressive statistics masked fundamental shortcomings. Increased government spending exacerbated inflation, as well as unemployment and slow growth in the nonoil sectors. Growth was profoundly uneven by sector and geography; although land reform and redistribution efforts were intended to "free" the peasantry from oppressively powerful absentee landlords, the general neglect and decline in the terms of trade for agriculture prompted massive migration from the rural areas to the cities, intensifying the rural labor shortage at the same time as

---

[145] *U.S. Department of State Bulletin* 59:1359 (December 13, 1968), pp. 659–62.

[146] Arjomand (2008), p. 124.

[147] Robert E. Looney, "The Role of Military Expenditures in Pre-Revolutionary Iran's Economic Decline," *Iranian Studies* 21(3–4): 1988, p. 54.

[148] Shahram Chubin, "Implications of the Military Buildup in Less Industrial States," in *Arms Transfers to the Third World: The Military Buildup in Less Developed Countries*, ed. V. Ra'anan (Boulder, CO: Westview Press, 1978), p. 268.

urban unemployment.[149] Increasing demand for foreign foods and shifts in patterns of agricultural consumption, consistent with the rapid urbanization and other societal changes, exacerbated Iran's persistent difficulty in meeting domestic demand.[150]

And then there was the spending. The national savings rate was effectively negative even before the 1972 oil boom and associated spending spree; throughout its reform program, Iran consumed nearly the equivalent of its total nonoil revenues – patterns that were only exacerbated by the explosion in national income after 1972.[151] Income inequality increased sharply during the 1970s, and such intense cash flows inevitably inflamed corruption.[152] Investment fever infected the bureaucracy; when queried why Iran's intelligence services did not foresee the revolution, a leading SAVAK general explained, "We have been doing real estate."[153] The influential Prime Minister Amir Abbas Hoveyda dismissed corruption as "the requisite by-products of development; don't worry, in the grand scheme of things, they amount to very little."[154]

These ambitions were undercut by their often-arbitrary nature and the lack of sustained follow-through. This was particularly true of the land reform program, which represented a major component of the shah's vision of a new Iran – as well as the intense opposition. And yet in practice, important components of the program were never systemically implemented; as late as 1976, large-scale farms constituted only 2.25 percent of Iran's agricultural lands and efforts were under way to roll back even these. However, the program and the government's failure to repudiate it formally when its implementation foundered contributed to rural distrust of the monarchy and eroded confidence in the sanctity of private property.[155] Food production increased, but not sufficiently to offset the population boom, and landlords benefited more than either sharecroppers, the intended beneficiaries, or the significant population of landless rural peasants, who were almost wholly disregarded in the plans.[156] Land reform altered the informal institutions governing rural

---

[149] H. Hakimian, *Labour Transfer and Economic Development: Theoretical Perspectives and Studies from Iran* (Hemel Hempstead: Harvester-Wheatsheaf, 1990).

[150] McLachlan (1986), pp. 157–8.   [151] Katouzian (1981), pp. 262–6.

[152] Salehi-Isfahani (2009), p. 19.   [153] Marvin Zonis, *Majestic Failure*, p. 90.

[154] As quoted in A. Milani (2000), p. 213.

[155] Fatemeh E. Moghadam, "An Historical Interpretation of the Iranian Revolution," *Cambridge Journal of Economics* 12 (1988), p. 409.

[156] Kaveh Ehsani, "Rural Society and Agricultural Development in Post-Revolution Iran: The First Two Decades," *Critique* 15:1 (Spring 2006): pp. 83–6.

agriculture, with a disproportionately negative impact on landless peasants (*khoshnesheen*), and helped spur the massive migration to the cities.[157] In addition, the measures put in place to address some of the negative consequences of the measure – such as the 1975 Anti–Land Speculation Law – compounded the dislocation and confusion about property rights. Housing for the millions of new city dwellers was at an acute shortage, and despite pledges to construct 1 million new housing units, the government managed to complete only 124,000.[158]

There were other problems. The shah's import-substitution program increased the country's oil dependence, while the heavily protected manufacturing sector was neither competitive nor inclined to seek overseas markets. As a result, the problems associated with Iranian industrial development were not those expected in a rentier economy – insufficient levels of investment or "Dutch Disease" – but rather something different and perhaps more thorny to resolve, low productivity of the investment.[159] The high import coefficient and the capital-intensive nature of the industrialization program meant that fewer than 5 percent of all the new jobs created between 1966 and 1976 were found in large urban manufacturing establishments.[160] While the manufacturing sector's share of employment rose modestly, absorbing some of the excess labor from agriculture, the construction and services sectors represented the true beneficiaries of Iran's growth – sectors that intensified rent seeking and generated mainly low-skill, low-security employment. Macroeconomically, the government became overwhelmingly dependent on oil revenues to finance its activities, and yet spending continued to outstrip revenues at such a pace as to have created a current accounts deficit of $2,617 million between 1963 and 1972.[161] The government resorted to foreign loans to meet its balance of payments demands, but the stratospheric increase in oil revenues in 1972 and 1973 resolved the dilemma, enabling the shah to disregard the fallout from his policies.

Nevertheless, while the oil boom rectified Iran's fiscal uncertainties, it also empowered shortsighted and insidious government economic policies. Halfway through the Fifth Five-Year Plan (which began in 1973),

---

[157] F. Moghadam (1988), p. 413.   [158] Clawson (2008), pp. 15–26.
[159] Massoud Karshenas and M. Hashem Pesaran, "Economic Reform and the Reconstruction of the Iranian Economy," *Middle East Journal* 49: 1 (Winter 1995), p. 94.
[160] Hakimian (1990), p. 158.
[161] M. H. Pesaran, "Economic Development and Revolutionary Upheavals in Iran" in *Iran: A Revolution in Turmoil*, ed. Haleh Afshar (Albany: State University of New York Press, 1990), p. 30.

the shah overrode the counsel of his economic advisers and doubled the plan's expenditures. As his advisers had predicted, this decision resulted in bottlenecks of stupendous proportions and triggered further inflationary pressures. Sectoral labor shortages also ensued as industrial job growth slowed, and efforts to substitute capital only created a spiraling demand for highly skilled expatriate personnel.[162] The capital-intensive nature and high import dependency of Iranian industry provided few of the forward or backward linkages that sound and balanced development requires.[163] Despite the prestige accorded heavy industry, the modern sectors of the nation's industrial plant were not particularly productive, and the modestly rising manufacturing output did not outperform traditional products (such as textiles, sugar, and tobacco) until after the oil price shock.[164] Even then, Iran's nonoil exports remained overwhelmingly concentrated in traditional sectors of agriculture, carpets, and textiles as late as 1977–8.[165] Many of the new jobs created were in the construction sector, and when the recession occurred, this sector was particularly hard hit.[166]

Culturally and financially jarring foreign enclaves expanded like sponges, soaking up vast sums for the salaries of skilled workers from outside Iran. The pace of activity meant that development took on an increasingly arbitrary tone: Neighborhoods were razed for roads; villages were relocated in the name of land reform. Tehran's handling of challenges that arose typically exacerbated the problems; for example, in 1975 the government purchased eight thousand trucks to alleviate supply ruptures but belatedly realized there was also a shortage of drivers. In response, the government authorized one thousand high-wage, low-skill expatriate workers and left the remaining vehicles to corrode in the desert.[167] This was emblematic of the logistical impediments of an overwhelmed transportation system, in which ships trying to dock at Khorramshahr faced a 160- to 225-day wait and the resulting costs,

---

[162] Hooshang Amirahmadi, *Revolution and Economic Transition The Iranian Experience* (Albany: State University of New York Press, 1990), p. 18.

[163] Alizade (1992), 212; Rostam M. Kavoussi, "Trade Policy and Industrialization in an Oil-Exporting Country: The Case of Iran," *Journal of Developing Areas* (July 1986): 468.

[164] Katouzian (1981), pp. 282–5.   [165] Katouzian (1981), pp. 325–6.

[166] James G. Scoville, "The Labor Market in Prerevolutionary Iran," *Economic Development and Cultural Change* 34:1 (October 1985), 149–53.

[167] Mohammad Amjad, *Iran from Royal Dictatorship to Theocracy* (New York: Greenwood Press, 1989), pp. 82–94.

which ran as high as $1 billion.[168] Other government efforts to address the muddle included measures such as a vicious antiprofiteering campaign and a 1975 industrial privatization scheme that further alienated merchants and sparked an "unprecedented" capital flight.[169]

Complicating the adjustment problems of the Iranian economy were the shah's often preposterous aims. He confidently boasted of plans to boost Iran's economy beyond that of Germany and France by the turn of the century, seemingly unaware that such growth was structurally impossible.[170] The shah's vision incorporated both messianic ambition and an obsession with modernization. He abhorred traditionalism; as he declared in his postrevolutionary memoirs, "I could not stop building supermarkets. I wanted a modern country."[171] He deferred his official coronation until 1967 on the grounds that "being king over a mostly poor, ill, and insecure people was no honor."[172] Whenever possible, he pressed to reinforce his preferred national myth of a country with an ancient history and an epic destiny, altering the official calendar to create the illusion of a continuous Pahlavi dynasty across millennia.

With retrospective wisdom, it may be tempting to depict or interpret the shah's ambition as degenerate or simply absurd. And yet despite the period's excesses and idiosyncrasies, the shah tapped into a deeply rooted, and surprisingly enduring, sense of Iranian ambition and prestige. Despite the postrevolutionary regime's hostility toward Iran's pre-Islamic traditions, Iranians remain profoundly attached to their national epic, which glorifies the ancient Persian Empire stretching from Central Asia to all of modern Turkey and into Egypt. The celebration of the Persian New Year (Nowruz) and the affection for Persian poetry testify to the widespread identification with a history as one of the world's great civilizations and a leading regional power.

Oil revenues enabled the Shah's messianic yet misguided development strategy, aimed at producing a "Great Society" to emulate the one he celebrated at Persepolis. Structurally hunchbacked yet oblivious to its weakness, the Iranian economy grew on the basis of distorted financial and political imperatives. The push did not occur without pushback; in 1974, disconcerted analysts within the Plan and Budget Organization

---

[168] Clawson (2008), pp. 15–26.   [169] Pesaran in Afshar, ed. (1990), p. 34.
[170] R. K. Karajnia, *The Mind of a Monarch* (London: George Allen and Unwin, 1977), p. 258; *Washington Post*, February 4, 1974, p. C5, as quoted in Kurzman (2004), p. 87.
[171] Mohammad Reza Pahlavi, *Answer to History* (New York: Stein & Day, 1980), p. 156.
[172] Afkhami (2009), pp. 247–8.

warned that a massive increase in government spending could have disastrous consequences for both the economy and the country's stability.[173] The shah dismissed these admonitions testily and insisted on spending all the anticipated oil revenues, a 287 percent increase.[174]

The flawed structure of the Iranian economy exacerbated an already tense political situation, but its soaring revenues and regional posture helped mask the instability. The shah had at his disposal a seemingly inexhaustible source of income that enabled feverish development and offered enviable leverage on the world stage. These funds precipitated rapid social change and dramatic economic growth, but also a political vacuum and broad dissatisfaction with the leadership. From this legacy, a powerful revolutionary movement found ample grounds for mobilization of society. However, the revolution could not so simply shed the environment that had molded it, and the factors within Iran's prerevolutionary political economy that facilitated the wholesale collapse of the Pahlavi order continued to constrain its successor.

[173] A. Milani (2000), p. 268.
[174] Hossein Razavi and Firouz Vakil, *The Political Environment of Economic Planning in Iran, 1971–1983* (Boulder, CO: Westview Press, 1984), p. 70.

3

The Economics of Upheaval, 1977–1980

More than forty years ago, Mohammad Reza Pahlavi, the self-proclaimed king of kings, presided over a grandiose celebration commemorating the purported twenty-five-hundred-year anniversary of the founding of the Persian Empire. The celebration convened in 1971 at Persepolis, in southwestern Iran, where the remains of this fabled capital – built by Darius, burned by Alexander the Great, and ravaged by time and travelers – frame the desert landscape. The walls showcase intricately carved friezes, depicting envoys from across the Achaemenian Empire offering tributes to the Persian king. There, in the shadow of the great gates and columns that had stood for two millennia, sixty-eight heads of state and hundreds of foreign dignitaries gathered in an air-conditioned tent city, dining on cuisine prepared by Maxim's of Paris and toasting their host with French champagne.

The expenses incurred for the party and the related infrastructure have been estimated at $35 to $300 million (and even higher), and everything except the carpets and the caviar was imported from abroad.[1] The crystal was Baccarat, the china Limoges and Haviland, the uniforms produced in France, and the tents in Switzerland. Iranian diplomats "used hard-knuckle politics" to lure prestigious guests, not so subtly hinting to

[1] Details of the celebration have been widely reported. This account is compiled from those given in James A. Bill, *The Eagle and The Lion the Tragedy of American-Iranian Relations* (New Haven, CT: Yale University Press, 1988), pp. 183–5; Dilip Hiro, *Iran under the Ayatollahs* (London: Routledge & Kegan Paul, 1985), pp. 56–7; Sandra Mackey, *The Iranians: Persia, Islam and the Soul of a Nation* (New York: E. Dutton, 1996), pp. 235–8; William Shawcross, *The Shah's Last Ride: The Fate of an Ally* (New York: Simon & Schuster, 1988), pp. 38–48.

foreign governments that future Iranian business was contingent on VIP presence.[2] As part of the lavish ceremonies, the shah addressed the tomb of Cyrus the Great, who had conquered a vast empire from Central Asia to modern Turkey and Egypt. Invoking this legacy, the shah declared, "Sleep happily, Cyrus, for we are awake."[3]

History would of course prove the shah's assertion painfully true. Iran was awake, and many Iranians were outraged by the royal excesses in Persepolis, which coincided with a severe drought and famine in several provinces, including the one where the festivities took place. University students held strikes; the *bazaar* closed in protest; urban violence escalated. And in Najaf, Iraq, another prominent Iranian stood before a different tomb, and he too summoned the imagery of Iranian history to herald the country's future. At the tomb of 'Ali, the cousin and son-in-law of the Prophet, who is revered among Shi'a, Ayatollah Ruhollah Khomeini vilified the imperial celebration and assailed the monarchy's legitimacy. Khomeini cataloged alleged offenses of the Pahlavi reign, arguing that monarchy contravened Islam and that the shah's rule was tyrannical and dominated by foreign masters. Khomeini concluded his sermon with an appeal for action, proclaiming:

Come to your senses; awaken Najaf! Let the voice of the oppressed people of Iran be heard throughout the world … Let them ask that this plundering and squandering be brought to an end, that they cease behaving toward our people in this way, that the huge budget of the government be spent on our wretched and hungry people. Let them request that the hungry be fed…I tell you plainly that a dark, dangerous future lies ahead and that it is your duty to resist and to serve Islam and the Muslim people.[4]

Khomeini's focus on the extravagance of the event was echoed by other Iranian political groups, as well as by some foreign observers. The shah and his defenders dismissed criticism as opportunistic and misguided. They pointed to the roads, schools, and other infrastructure constructed as part of the event's preparations; the private funding that defrayed some costs; and the celebration's promotion of Iranian culture.[5] They resented

---

[2] Milani (2011), p. 324.
[3] Homa Katouzian, *The Political Economy of Modern Iran, Despotism and Pseudo-Modernism, 1926–1979* (London: Macmillan, 1981), pp. 337–8.
[4] Khomeini's message on October 31, 1971, "The Incompatibility of Monarchy with Islam," from *Khomeini va Junbish*, pp. 36–53, as translated in Hamid Algar, *Islam and Revolution: Writings and Declarations of Imam Khomeini* (Berkeley: Mizan Press, 1980), pp. 203, 206–7.
[5] Afkhami (2009), pp. 412–15.

the scrutiny of the spending and the splendor as an unwarranted intrusion. "So what are the people complaining about?" the shah demanded. "That we are giving a couple of banquets for some 50 Heads of State? We can hardly offer them bread and radishes, can we? Thank heavens, the Imperial Court of Iran can still afford to pay for Maxim's services."[6]

The events at Persepolis did not precipitate Iran's revolution. However, they exemplified the lack of connection between the shah's development initiatives and their intended purpose, the consolidation of imperial authority. Within the decade, Khomeini's critique culminated in the collapse of the state that was celebrated amid such opulence in Persepolis. The ultimate success of the opposition reflected a variety of factors: namely, the monarchy's core weakness, Khomeini's personal charismatic leadership, and the opposition's organizational ingenuity.

While the movement that toppled the shah was broader, deeper, and far more sustained than prior Iranian upheaval, it shared much in common with the turmoil of 1896, 1905, 1953, and 1963 – in particular, a conviction among key political constituencies that the government had betrayed the nation, squandered its resources, and subjugated its population to foreign interests. And the conditions that prevailed in the revolution's aftermath – enduring upheaval, internal violence, deep divisions among the revolutionary coalition, and the exigencies of institution building – produced the paradoxical reconstruction of the Iranian state and the partition of central authority. This context ensured that economic issues assumed primary significance in the postrevolutionary politics and precipitated a competition for resources and influence that ultimately subsumed the initial philosophical differences over economic policy.

ECONOMICS AND THE REVOLUTION: IDEOLOGICAL FACTORS

The ideological foundations of the revolution and the subsequent state evolved organically from the contest among secular nationalists, leftists, and the monarchy. Post-1953 repression of existing political organizations left the Tudeh and National Front incapacitated and sidelined by the 1970s. Other groups emerged to fill the vacuum. Among these were Mehdi Bazargan's Liberation Movement of Iran (Nehzat-e Azad-e Iran); a spin-off from the National Front, the Nezhat-e Azad served as a nexus for Iran's rapidly changing social structure, fusing the middle class's rising

---

[6] *The Guardian/Le Monde*, October 16, 1971, as quoted in Bill (1988), p. 184.

expectations and political entitlement with Iran's traditional institutions, including the *bazaar*.[7] In addition, two Marxist guerrilla groups, the Sharikha-ye Fedayin-e Khalq and Mojahedin-e Khalq (MeK), emerged to advocate income redistribution and land reform. Violent tactics and clandestine structure limited their appeal, but also enabled some elements to survive the monarchy's crackdowns and undertake critical attacks on the security forces during the revolution.[8] These guerrilla organizations also collaborated uneasily with clerical opponents of the monarchy during the early 1970s, setting a pattern of distrustful cooperation that would make them prime actors in the revolution and prime suspects in its aftermath.

These new opposition groups emerged from the intellectual ferment of the 1960s and 1970s, which swept both Iran's clergy and lay thinkers and provided the basis for Islamic politicization honed to the Iranian experience. Islam offered a starkly different narrative from that of the monarchy, and it also proved a formidable motivational and organizational tool. Shi'ism emphasizes concepts of oppression, martyrdom, social equity, and legitimacy – themes that resonate with opposition discourse. In Iran, the emergence of Islamist political thought was interlinked with debates over modernization, and for this reason, both religious and secular intellectuals devoted much energy to articulating an alternative path. In this respect, the ideational foundations of the Islamic Republic were inherently concerned with modernity, much the same as prior periods of reformist thought had been elsewhere in the Muslim world.

Amid Iran's post-1963 political stasis, an important intellectual movement emerged, with diverse inceptions and characteristics but unified by anguish about Iran's circumstances and its relationship with the world. One of the exemplars was the writer Jalal Al-e Ahmad, whose book, *Gharbzadegi* (Weststruckness), chronicled an Iran that was overly fascinated with, and ultimately ignorant of, the technology of the West. Similarly, the sociologist Ali Shariati influenced the worldview of a generation of politically mobilized young Iranians. Arrested and imprisoned as a young academic, Shariati articulated traditional Shi'a themes in

---

[7] Chehabi (1990), p. 6.

[8] Misagh Parsa, *Social Origins of the Iranian Revolution* (New Brunswick, NJ: Rutgers University Press, 1989), pp. 182–5; Farideh Farhi, "Class Struggles, the State, and Revolution in Iran," in *Power and Stability in the Middle East*, ed. Berch Berberoglu (London: Zed Books, 1989), 102; Kian-Thiébaut (1998), pp. 169–88.

contemporary vocabulary with heavy Marxist influence. Shariati depicted a world divided between the oppressed (*mostazafin*) and the oppressors (*mostakhbarin*), arguing that true Islam was vested in the struggle of the oppressed. His rhetoric linked social and political grievances with the traditional sanctification of martyrdom and sacrifice. This worldview appealed to Iranians who felt dislocated by the profound socioeconomic transformations of the 1960s and 1970s, and it was assimilated and broadly applied to the official discourse of the revolution and the subsequent state. His embrace of a socially conscious interpretation of Shi'ism and his class-oriented appeals for a persistent struggle for justice and development helped galvanize opposition to the monarchy and fuse traditional religious idioms with a left-wing, anti-Western discourse.

One of the men who helped promote Shariati was Ayatollah Morteza Motahhari, who also played a formative role in shaping the economic discourse of the revolution. Motahhari was one of Khomeini's students and a favored protégé, so trusted that he was appointed as Khomeini's personal representative during his exile, including the collection of religious taxes. Motahhari's career was emblematic of the demographic and philosophical synthesis that these clerical intellectuals managed to achieve. During his early career, Motahhari read widely, including materials produced by the Tudeh, and he was capable of engaging leftists through their own vernacular. He flirted with the Fedayan-e Islam, and once established at Tehran University, he influenced many of the political actors who forged the new state and its economic policies.

Although his work was somewhat sympathetic toward the left, Motahhari endorsed a traditionally Shi'a interpretation of the state's role in the economy, in particular a robust defense of private property rights. He saw social justice as an integral dimension of an Islamic economy but argued that justice does not extend to egalitarianism. In addition, among Motahhari's key contributions was his call for strengthening the centralization of the clergy as a means of mitigating their financial reliance on traditional constituencies.[9] Ultimately, Motahhari shuttered the popular religious institution in Tehran where Shariati and others had made their fame and attacked Shariati's anticlerical views.[10] Motahhari maintained receptivity to nontraditional ideas, and his unfinished work on Islamic economics proved so controversial among the bastions of traditionalist

---

[9] Martin (2000), pp. 80–1.   [10] Dabashi (1993), p. 157.

interpretations – in the *bazaar* and the seminaries – that it was banned after his death.[11]

Other key ideologues who helped to shape the discourse of the opposition, and their thinking once in power, include a trio of influential clerics – coincidentally, none of whom survived the turmoil of the revolution and its early aftermath. Like his mentor Motahhari, Ayatollah Mohammad Beheshti, who emerged as one of the most influential players in the postrevolutionary power struggle, also defended private property as enjoined by the Quran, although he distinguished between legitimate and illegitimate sources of wealth and suggested a central role for the state in managing public goods.[12]

Another of Motahhari's contemporaries was Mahmoud Taleqani, who had actively opposed the monarchy since the late 1930s and helped found the Liberation Movement. Taleqani wrote widely on theology and political philosophy. His book *Islam and Ownership*, published in 1965, attempted to carve a niche for Islam as a viable alternative paradigm to either capitalism or communism. Taleqani held that Islamic values supersede either the class system or capitalist imperatives, but his stirring invocations on behalf of the oppressed were bounded by a rejection of government intervention. Taleqani's September 1979 death was seen by some observers as removing "an extremely popular man whom they [modernist Islamists] hoped would act as an effective counter-balance" against Khomeini.[13]

The Najaf-based Mohammad Baqr Sadr articulated a framework for an Islamic economy that was grounded in modernity and critical of the social implications of an unfettered free market. For Sadr, Islamic economics represented an ideal, whose study could serve as a "revolution for transforming a malevolent phenomenon to an auspicious one."[14] Sadr's epic work on the issue proposed a more substantial role for the state in the economy than Motahhari and his disciples, as well as an explicit government responsibility for advancing social justice – "a world of small farmers, merchants, and crafts workers, with a large and powerful state that intervenes extensively in the economy" to preserve Islamic values and prevent extremes of wealth and poverty.[15] His delineation of three

---

[11] Sohrab Behdad, "A Disputed Utopia: Islamic Economics in Revolutionary Iran," *Comparative Studies in Society and History* 36:4 (October 1994), p. 803.

[12] Abrahamian (1993), p. 43.   [13] Schirazi (1997), p. 51.   [14] Behdad (1995), p. 201.

[15] Behdad (1994), p. 790.

distinct categories of ownership – state, public, and private – fore-shadowed the contradictions in Iran's postrevolutionary economic order, with its cooperative sector and powerful parastatal organizations.

The intellectual discourse under the shah also featured an array of lay scholars and activists who tackled economic issues. Many, including Mehdi Bazargan, Habibullah Peyman, and Abolhassan Bani Sadr, sought to fuse Islamic teachings with socialist ideals in order to demonstrate that Islam offered practical solutions to Iran's dilemmas and to reinforce the quest for authenticity. In his writings, Bani Sadr was particularly expansive on the imperialist implications of a rentier economy centered around oil, arguing that "instead of an economy, [oil] creates a 'sucking machine' that increasingly and more extensively over time sucks up the oil, other resources and the fruits of the labor of the people, and exports these to the industrial states. The gap between the owners of the resource and its real users grows regularly wider. What remains is a bitterness in whose flames are consumed the children and the capabilities of the oil-producing nation."[16]

Ultimately, of course, the most influential ideologue of the post-revolutionary economy was Khomeini himself. Consistent with traditional Shi'a jurisprudence, which generally holds the sanctity of private property to be inviolable, Ayatollah Khomeini was a reliably staunch defender of property rights and the role of the private sector, views that were widely shared among the senior clergy.[17] This philosophical orientation was reinforced by the *ulema*'s strong alliance with the *bazaar*, whose financial support was crucial to the antishah movement and the nascent theocracy.[18] In his will, for example, Khomeini advises the government that

Islam provides for a balanced regime in which private property is recognized and repsected [sic] with proper limitations on the origins of property rights and consumption, such that, if it is properly implemented, the wheels of an healthy economy will begin turning and social justice, which is the necessary consequence of a healthy regime, will find reality ... Respect the legitimate and limited

---

[16] Abolhassan Bani Sadr, *Naft va Salteh* (Tehran, 1977), p. 21, as quoted in Shaul Bakhash, "The Politics of Oil and Revolution in Iran: A Staff Paper" (Washington, DC: Brookings Institution, 1982), pp. 4–5.

[17] Abrahamian (1993), pp. 39–40.

[18] Guilain Denoeux has analyzed the role of the *bazaar* during the prerevolutionary mobilization. Guilain Denoeux, *Urban Unrest in the Middle East: A Comparative Study of Informal Networks in Egypt, Iran, and Lebanon.* (Albany: State University of New York Press, 1993).

property rights. Give assurances to the people so that capital and constructive initiatives can have a chance to work and lead the country to self-sufficiency in small and large industries.[19]

In practice, however, Khomeini sought to coalesce the opposition's divergent factions by progressively framing a wider range of political issues – including the economy – in moral terms that resonated with both Islamist and secular leftist discourse. Thus, while his initial focal points, such as the education of women, tended to appeal to traditional segments of society, Khomeini widened his targets to include issues that evoked a strongly nationalistic theme of securing Iran's long-sought independence, such as a 1964 law guaranteeing the extraterritoriality of American personnel in Iran. These tactical shifts stirred the intellectual and middle-class echelons of Iranian society and foreshadowed his postrevolutionary posture.[20]

Increasingly, Iran's lower classes began to occupy a larger place in his appeal and remained a prominent element of his discourse even after the revolution as he repeatedly framed events through the perspective of the *mostazafin*, or dispossessed.[21] This rhetorical shift suggests Khomeini recognized the utility of appealing to this key constituency, even though the urban poor remained on the margins of antiregime activism.[22] The theme of social justice offered a powerful unifying concept among disparate social groups within the opposition, and it represented the most fruitful area of seeming conformity between Khomeini and his more liberal and more radical allies among the revolutionary coalition. There are, of course, crucial variations in their definitions of justice and their remedies, but such distinctions tended to be overlooked or underestimated in the euphoria of upheaval.[23]

The notion that the government ought to be promoting a more just social order was hardly new to the Islamic Republic; Mohammad

[19] Ruhollah Khomeini, *Iman Khomeini's Last Will and Testament* (Washington, DC: Interests Section of the Islamic Republic of Iran, Embassy of the Democratic and Popular Republic of Algeria, 1989), pp. 55–7.

[20] Roy Parviz Mottahedeh, "Iran's Foreign Devils," *Foreign Policy* 38 (Spring 1980): pp. 19–34.

[21] Bill (1988), p. 274.

[22] For an excellent overview of the role of the urban poor in reconfiguring the postrevolutionary economy, see Asef Bayat, *Street Politics: Poor People's Movements in Iran* (New York: Columbia University Press, 1997).

[23] Marvin Zonis, "The Rule of the Clerics in the Islamic Republic of Iran," *Annals of the American Academy of Political and Social Sciences* No. 482 (November 1985), p. 89.

Reza Shah saw himself as pursuing a similar goal, as did the more liberal-leaning of his various prime ministers.[24] However, Khomeini proffered a new moral economy for Iran that was intended to serve as an explicit rebuke to the frenzied commodification and commercialization of Iran in the Pahlavi period. He disparaged the shah's development program – his most vaunted accomplishment in the monarch's own narrative – as a failure and a fraud. "Muhammad Riza made loud claims about having 'A Mission to Serve the Country,' even writing a book with that title, and conducted a propaganda campaign about the alleged progress the nation had made," Khomeini said in a postrevolutionary interview. "Everyone knew those were lies. Everywhere in Iran there is still poverty and wretchedness; conditions for the common people are so miserable that they do not even have homes. The people that live right on top of our oil deposits are suffering from hunger and thirst and cannot even clothe themselves adequately."[25]

In addition, Khomeini linked the aspiration for a more just society and greater equity in the development of Iran's resources to the wealthy's obsession with the West. In his telling, the blame for Iran's poverty and oppression fell at the feet of Washington and its allies. The remedy – a truly independent Iranian government, able and willing to detach Iran from its Western orientation and alliances – would ameliorate its economic problems.

I once passed through the region of Ahvaz and its surrounding villages by train, and I remember seeing barefoot people – adults and children – rushing up to the train to beg for a mouthful of food. Vast oil resources lay beneath them, but the wealth of those resources produced went elsewhere – into the pockets of foreigners, particularly the Americans. In return, America gave us the military bases it constructed for itself in our territory. That is, it took the money it had paid for our oil and used it to build military bases for itself; this is one of the worst adversities it inflicted upon us. In addition, there were the burdensome contracts and agreements they imposed on us: none of them benefited our nation; on the contrary, they increased the domination of Iran by America. As a result of all this,

---

[24] Even Amir Abbas Hoveyda, the shah's long-standing prime minister, who was executed after the revolution, proclaimed in 1975 that Iran had transcended the failings of Western models of development, declaring, "In a world dominated by materialism ... we have chosen the path of idealism." Hoveyda, "The Future of Iran," in Jane W. Jacqz, ed., *Iran: Past, Present and Future* (New York: Aspen Institute for Humanistic Studies), 1976, p. 447.

[25] Khomeini's interview published in *Jumhuri-yi Islami*, January 2, 1980, as translated in Algar (1981), p. 335.

our people came to feel desperate ... The people were feeling desperate and waiting for some voice to be raised in protest so that they could join in.[26]

Others among the postrevolutionary leadership echoed similar themes. For the revolutionaries, economic grievances were undoubtedly subsidiary to their broader moral indictment of the Pahlavi monarchy. However, they were not irrelevant; rather, the economic issues were organically interwoven into a narrative of corruption and injustice that proved widely resonant and radically – even violently – motivational. According to the narrative of the revolution, the technocrats and elites of the Pahlavi era were guilty of "destroying the economy" by subjugating Iran to the whims and aims of the American imperialist agenda. In one of his final conversations with the former prime minister Amir Abbas Hoveyda before dispatching him to the firing squad, revolutionary prosecutor Sadeq Khalkhali lectured Hoveyda that "many things occurred against the interest of Iran and in favour of imperialism. You gave free oil to the Americans in Vietnam and supplied Israel with oil products and food during the war with the Arabs."[27]

This depiction of a foreign conspiracy centered on the exploitation of Iran's resources, both human and natural, in a way that echoed the Mosaddeq era debates and appealed to the leftist and nationalist elements of the revolutionary coalition:

Huge amounts of capital are being swallowed up; our public funds are being embezzled; our oil is being plundered; and our country is being turned into a market for expensive, unnecessary goods by the representatives of foreign companies, which makes it possible for foreign capitalists and their local agents to pocket the people's money. A number of foreign states carry off our oil after drawing it out of the ground, and the negligible sum they pay to the regime they have installed returns to their pockets by other routes. As for the small amount that goes into the treasury, God only knows what it is spent on.[28]

In this way, religious rhetoric helped temporarily to unite a disparate alliance behind a short-term goal of revolutionary mobilization but failed to generate a substantive discussion around a shared agenda for the future. Khomeini did not endeavor to persuade or win over his compatriots on behalf of a specific program or cause. Rather, he commanded a population on the basis of their faith to rise up against tyranny,

---

[26] Khomeini's interview published in *Jumhuri-yi Islami*, January 2, 1980, as translated in Algar (1981), p. 335.

[27] Moin (1999), p. 208.

[28] Khomeini, *Islamic Government* (Najaf, 1971), as translated in Algar (1981), p. 115.

despotism, and the corruption of Iran's patrimony. In this respect, economic grievances fueled a more fundamental critique – that of oppression or rule without justice (*zulm*)[29] – and facilitated the most radical response, revolution rather than compromise.

The centrality of political economy issues to the debates that dominated Iran's intellectual landscape in the 1960s and 1970s is not a purely academic concern. This discourse helped shape the impetus for revolutionary action and, perhaps more importantly, set the stage for the profound philosophical divide that emerged among the revolutionary coalition after the shah's departure. On one side were those who believed that the revolution had mandated a dramatic departure from past economic policy in order to advance social justice and address the needs of the poor, abjuring foreign capital and entanglements and pursuing independence through self-sufficiency. This perspective pervaded the main opposition groups, both Islamist and secular, as well as many younger revolutionaries.

Countering this stance were traditionalists, many of whom had links to the *bazaar* or large landholders and whose vision of an Islamist economy remained firmly grounded in an orthodox interpretation of Islamic law and philosophy. The crux of their argument centered on the Quranic invocations admonishing respect for private property and the encouragement of trade and industry. They were innately suspicious of state-centric economic policies on the grounds of political orientation – an aversion to Communism – as well as their own financial interests.

Towering above them, and mediating inelegantly among them, was Ayatollah Khomeini, whose ideological tendencies on economic issues proved malleable and subject to tactical adjustment based upon the needs of his primary objectives – the success of the revolutionary movement and the preservation of the Islamic order. By subordinating the existing divisions on questions of political economy, Khomeini's posture would only preserve and intensify them until the war, and his death, exhausted the contest.

Khomeini would later be described as disparaging economic concerns in provoking the revolution or shaping the priorities of the postrevolutionary state; his oft-cited aphorism on the price of melons is frequently deployed as evidence of his purist disinterest in temporal matters. But this is misleading; in the full rendition of Khomeini's account, economics is not irrelevant or disconnected, but rather, economic concerns and interests are inherently bound up in a more profound human quest that can only be satisfied by Islam.

[29] Akhavi (Albany: State University of New York Press, 1980), p. 95.

This movement, which from start to finish took about fifteen, sixteen years, and in which much labor and pain was given, much blood was given and young people were lost, homes were lost, families were destroyed, and especially during these last one to two years during which you all saw what transpired – it is our belief that this was all for Islam.

I cannot, and no intelligent person can, imagine that it could be said that we gave our blood so that melons would be less expensive, that we gave up our young men so that houses would be less expensive. No intelligent person gives up their child to get less expensive housing. People want everything that they have for their children, for their families. This logic is an invalid logic promoted perhaps by some self-serving individuals, putting in people's mouths the comments that we gave our blood so that some improvement would come to our agriculture; a person does not sacrifice himself so that something comes of his agriculture.

Why do they not speak of the very logic that the people, all throughout this time and especially recently, used as their logic? You all saw that every segment of society – women poured into the streets, young people poured into the streets, onto the roofs, into the alleys and neighborhoods, and everywhere their cry was that we want Islam and we want an Islamic Republic. It is for Islam that a person can give up his life. Our saints also gave up their lives for Islam, not for economics. Economic concerns are not worth such a thing – that a person would want an economic system and would sacrifice his life so that the economic situation would be improved! This is not sensible![30]

REVOLUTIONARY MOBILIZATION AND THE ECONOMY

To observers of Pahlavi Iran, the shah emerged victorious from each of his early struggles with competitors – the Tudeh and the communist Left in the 1940s, the liberal nationalists after 1953, and the clerics after 1963. Having crushed opponents of his agenda and exponentially expanded Iran's revenue base and regional primacy, the shah could credibly claim to be the most powerful Iranian monarch in two millennia. And yet while the post-1963 political environment had left the shah seemingly without any meaningful challenger to his control of his reign, it also planted the seeds of revolution. While the shah had massively enlarged the power of the state, he also divested it of any meaningful allies or bonds with society. The shah's repression of civil society and independent political action contributed to the mobilization of popular dissatisfaction under the sole rubric still available – religion.

---

[30] Mohammad Reza Akbari, ed., *Mavaz'-e Imam Khomeini*, vol. 1 (Payam-i 'Itrat, 1999), pp. 243–4.

Just as the shah reached what appeared to be the apex of his reign, he found himself confronted by intensified grievances, articulated by a citizenry whose expectations his policies had elevated but whose political participation his system blocked. When he began to permit some political liberalization, it served as an opportunity for articulating a wide range of popular demands, the first real platform for such an expression since the aborted uprisings of 1963. With this opening, the critique mushroomed through a disparate collection of organized groupings and informal networks, accelerated and intensified by the shah's tragic miscalculations, which set off a self-reinforcing cycle of incendiary violence and opposition. This mobilization reinforced antagonism toward the regime and consolidated that sentiment throughout Iranian society. However, its breadth also helped perpetuate competition among the revolutionary coalition and exacerbated the ideological and interest-based fissures that facilitated Iran's devolution into episodic civil war after the revolution.

The protests began in 1977 with activity among intellectuals and professionals, who responded to the shah's modest liberalization by publishing petitions and circulating letters on human rights. This opening created opportunities for political protest under the guise of cultural activities, such as the "ten nights" of poetry readings in 1977 or the Declaration of the Fifty-Eight, a scathing critique of the regime distributed by the professorial group in 1978. Attended both by university students and more traditional *bazaar* and working-class communities, these poetry readings resulted in the first salvo of opposition. Liberalization was intended to release some pressure and strengthen the monarchy; instead, the public expression of previously forbidden dissatisfaction with the status quo incited broader politicization, a cycle of demonstrations, and the mobilization of a nationwide revolutionary organization intrinsic to Iran's eighty thousand mosques and religious institutions.

The most important factor was Khomeini, whose focus on social justice helped coalesce disparate groups and whose strategic maximalism proved surprisingly successful in translating dissatisfaction into antigovernmental political action. By tradition, the clergy were apolitical; Ayatollah Boroujerdi's preferences and the monarchy's aggressive expansion encouraged their withdrawal from political activism, reinforced by the millenarian character of Shi'a doctrine.[31] However, mosques were the

---

[31] Beginning in 1501, the Safavid dynasty introduced Shi'ism to Iran and created bureaucratized religious institutions. In doing so they also sowed the seeds for the discrete development of a clerical hierarchy independent of state control. The millenarian

only alternative system of communication and organization with a nationwide base. Religious institutions offered some safe haven from government scrutiny and a natural venue for public gatherings, so anti-regime action began to be funneled increasingly through religious channels.

Moreover, despite the quietist tradition, the few clerics who remained politically active had assembled a potent opposition network. These men were primarily aligned with Ayatollah Khomeini, the legacy of his first confrontation with the shah and his forty years in Qom, where it is estimated that Khomeini taught approximately ten thousand seminarians. A nucleus of three hundred "constituted the central core of his under-ground clerical movement, which came to lead the Islamic revolution" and remain in power.[32]

Khomeini cultivated this network assiduously, politicking first on behalf of his mentor, Borujerdi, and then later his position among the grand ayatollahs.[33] His close associates continued agitating throughout his exile and made fragile inroads into coordination with other groups, such as the Mojahedin. This personal organization, though small at first, was more geographically dispersed than any remnants of political parties.[34] Khomeini's 1963 arrest and subsequent exile facilitated the network's expansion by making him almost invulnerable, even to the long arm of SAVAK, yet also enhancing his credibility.

Khomeini consistently recognized the importance of financial resources to his agenda. He appreciated the powerful historical precedents, includ-ing the role that the centralization of religious tax collection played in enabling the 1891 Tobacco Revolt.[35] And he understood that resources were needed to advance the revolution. Cultivating and expanding his

---

character of Shi'ism facilitated the clergy's withdrawal from politics after the decline of the early Safavid rulers and encouraged them to develop their own distinct hierocratic infrastructure with its own system for exercising authority. This did not, however, imply that Iran's religious leaders were apolitical; the doctrine of occultation innately consti-tutes a political judgment. By withholding any final religious imprimatur from temporal governance, Shi'a practice in Iran enshrines a "quality of permanent challenge within the Muslim community" while asserting the timelessness of divine supremacy. Mehdi Mozaffari, *Authority in Islam from Muhammad to Khomeini* (Armonk, NY: M. E. Sharpe, 1987), p. 37.

[32] Nikola B. Schahgaldian, "Iran after Khomeini," *Current History* (February 1990), p. 62.

[33] The homogeneity of the clerical establishment has become a standard assumption in analyses of the Iranian revolution from every perspective. However, this assumption disregards the degree to which the *ulema* clashed, over both personalities and politics, during the two decades of Khomeini's rise to power in absentia.

[34] Parsa (1989), p. 206.   [35] Dabashi, p. 169.

network required the collection and distribution of vast charitable alms and religious taxes given in Khomeini's name. In 1967, Khomeini declared that believers should direct their *sahm-e Imam* away from clerics who continued to support the Pahlavi state.[36] He also made efforts to recruit and retain his following, raising their stipends when he was under pressure during his Najaf exile.[37] Over the years, millions were raised, particularly in the final, intense push for the shah's ouster, either directed toward Khomeini and his allies or toward "strike funds" that were established to support workers who left jobs to protest. Although it is widely presumed and frequently asserted that much of this funding derived from the *bazaar*, no detailed accounting of the sources of Iran's revolutionary financing exists; nor is it known precisely how it was spent.[38]

During his long absence from Iran, Khomeini's works were distributed and he continued to communicate with Iranians through messages transmitted and replayed at local mosques, to overseas students, to clerics and seminary students who made pilgrimages to Karbala and Najaf. His network maintained "intensely personal commitments" to Khomeini.[39] When a government newspaper attacked Khomeini in January 1978, it sparked an opportunity to build on the ongoing mobilization of liberal intellectuals. During this period, he increased direct communication with Iran, sending forty-five messages between fall 1977 and January 1979 – more than a fourfold increase over the number of major addresses during his previous thirteen years in exile. In his final four months of exile, spent outside Paris after he was forced to leave Iraq, Khomeini gave 120 interviews, many to Western mass-audience publications, and this coverage – highlighting injustice under the shah – won him new appeal among the nonreligious segments of the Iranian population.[40]

---

[36] Dabashi, p. 432.   [37] Baqer Moin, p. 146.

[38] Marvin Zonis, "Iran: A Theory of Revolution from Accounts of the Revolution," *World Politics* 35:4 (July 1983), p. 593.

[39] Guilain Denoeux, *Urban Unrest in the Middle East: Comparative Study of Informal Networks in Egypt, Iran, and Lebanon* (Albany: State University of New York Press, 1993), pp. 183; Bakhash (1984), pp. 42–3.

[40] Bakhash (1984), p. 49. It is useful to point out here that postrevolutionary scholarship suggests that Khomeini's responses to interviewers' questions were in fact prepared in advance for him by four or five advisers, three of whom were not clerics, and that this plan was deliberately intended to meet the concerns raised by the Islamic component of the postrevolutionary state. See Afsaneh Najmabadi's discussion of Bani Sadr's memoirs (*Khianat be omid – Hope Betrayed*) in Najmabadi, "Mythifications of the Past and Illusions of the Future," in *The Islamic Revolution and the Islamic*

Precisely where the state failed – in organizing the populace and creating allegiance – the mosques that disseminated Khomeini's sermons succeeded, uniting divergent and historically opposed groups through religious institutions. This communication also ensured that religious forces assumed a predominant role in the political mobilization, catapulting Khomeini to its head. From his initial 1963 confrontation with the government, Khomeini proved to be a master politician, willing to exceed the bounds of acceptable dissent and able to propel others, particularly the restrained clerical establishment, to do the same. Rejecting conciliation in 1963 elevated him to folk hero status; likewise, in 1978, he spurned the nationalists' appeal for compromise. Ideological and tactical absolutism won Khomeini political preeminence, and this, more than theocratic rank, assured him of leadership. It also contributed to the revolutionary coalition's polarization after the monarchy collapsed.

Religious ceremonies and rituals offered logistical and motivational advantages as avenues for political protests. The 1977 death of Khomeini's son Mostafa under suspicious circumstances prompted mourning services across the country; an effort to quell potential protests by banning a second round of public remembrances was defied by seminary students protesting the publication of an inflammatory article about Khomeini. In turn, their fortieth-day ritual was marked across Iran by mass demonstrations and police violence, and in this way, the mourning ceremonies became a self-generating protest movement, as police firing on students resulted in further casualties and funerals-cum-demonstrations.

These commemorations as well as the passion plays and self-flagellation that take place on the anniversary of the martyrdom of Husayn – "the symbol of resistance against oppression" in Shi'a Islam[41] – delivered large, emotive crowds infused with a sense of injustice and divinely guided action. Annual religious feasts spawned impromptu rallies over political and economic grievances; the shah became personified as Yazid, the assassin of Husayn at Karbala, in Ashura processions focusing on contemporary repression and illegitimacy. The combination of religious ceremony and political action offered ready opportunities to organize and imbued political action with a sense of religious obligation. Occurring on the heels of intensified agitation among intellectuals and professionals, a budding opposition consensus began to form.

Republic, eds. Nikki R. Keddie and Eric Hooglund (Syracuse, NY: Syracuse University Press, 1986), pp. 153–4.
[41] Amjad (1989), p. 34.

Iran's traditional merchant community also played a central role in mobilizing and coordinating revolutionary activity.[42] As discussed in the previous chapter, closure of the *bazaar* had long served as a mechanism for conveying dissatisfaction with state policy, by virtue of the disruptive social and economic impact. In the 1970s, although the traditional commercial bourgeoisie remained the focal point for private capitalist activity, many merchants perceived the *bazaar* to be under siege from the monarchy's Westernization program.[43] The shah's antiprofiteering harangues directly targeted the traditional merchants,[44] as did the (largely unsuccessful) attempt to create an alternative industrial elite. The shah, with his typical dearth of political acumen, expressed antagonism for the *bazaar* – with which he should have shared the important common interest of economic prosperity – in both his policies and his words. "I could not stop building supermarkets. I wanted a modern country. Moving against the bazaars was typical of the political and social risks I had to take in the drive to modernization," the shah wrote effusively in his memoirs from exile.[45]

Demonstrating such governmental disdain for this segment of society, the modernization program cemented – at least temporarily – the alliance between the *bazaar* and clerical leaders. The *bazaar*, an essentially "conservative entity," provided financial backing and, in turn, the *ulema* furnished the partnership with the ideology of opposition to the state that excluded them both.[46] Merchants emerged as an active constituency early in 1977, and over subsequent months Tehran's main *bazaar* closed repeatedly in support of protesters. *Bazaari*s also provided crucial financial support for other striking groups, as well as for opposition mobilization, funding efforts to circulate Khomeini's messages.

---

[42] Arang Keshavarzian's study on the *bazaar* offers an important and nuanced appraisal of the role of this cohort on Iran's political and economic history. Keshavarzian, *Bazaar and State in Iran: The Politics of the Tehran Marketplace* (Cambridge: Cambridge University Press, 2007).

[43] Katouzian (1981), p. 278; Alizade (1992), p. 185; Tim McDaniel, *Autocracy, Modernization, and Revolution in Russia and Iran* (Princeton, NJ: Princeton University Press, 1991), pp. 103–4.

[44] According to one analyst, the spurt of commercial regulation during the 1970s resulted in "as many as a quarter of a million business affected, with 8,000 businessmen jailed, 23,000 deported, and 150,000 more cases pending the courts." See Norriss S. Hetherington, "Industrialization and Revolution in Iran: Forced Progress or Unmet Expectation?" *Middle East Journal* 36: 3 (Summer 1982), p. 362.

[45] Mohammad Reza Shah Pahlavi, *Answer to History* (New York: Stein & Day, 1980), p. 156.

[46] Amjad (1989), pp. 107–8.

However, while the *bazaar* was an important actor, it was hardly the only one. The other prerevolutionary economic élite, the country's powerful landlords, also had little invested in the shah's regime. Land reform, though never seriously endangering their interests, had managed to engender their permanent hostility. Loopholes and new industrial opportunities allowed most of the landowners to maintain or even advance their financial position. And while more land had been distributed to the peasantry, in fact the implementation – most small holdings remained below subsistence level or were distributed in noncontiguous parcels – did little to elevate the overall socioeconomic status of the rural poor.[47] Still, many landlords saw their traditional status threatened, and after the revolution, land reform remained a divisive issue within the new regime.

Beyond Iran's traditional elites, revolutionary sentiment also began to appeal to middle-class Iranians who might otherwise have been beneficiaries of the shah's modernization policies. As products of the monarchy's educational system, the new middle class might have been expected to align with him.[48] However, political restrictions, inflation, and the lack of job opportunities outside the state sector generated frustration and disillusionment. These disappointments intensified after the oil boom and the tumultuous economic conditions of the mid-1970s. Unrest at the universities had also flared sporadically throughout the 1970s, and in the atmosphere of global political ferment of this period, "politically conscious students rejected the West in its entirety."[49] The restrictions on political expression and the official backlash that followed the brief experiment in liberalization only further alienated the students.

The marginalization of another group – the large masses of urban poor – also contributed to the polarization of Iran's postrevolutionary

---

[47] Amjad (1989), pp. 82–5; Farhi in ed. Berberoglu (1989), p. 97; Farshad A. Araghi, "Land Reform Policies in Iran: Comment," *American Journal of Agricultural Economics* 71:4 (November 1989), pp. 1046–9.

[48] An American journalist married to an Iranian who lived in Iran during the 1960s wrote at the time about the unexpected emergence of a middle class, noting that "during all its many centuries Iran has been a nation of the very rich and the very poor. Now there is a struggling but ever-growing nucleus of genuine bourgeois. They are patently 'un-Persian' – people who cling to regularity and order, who buy insurance and avoid debt, wives who make their own clothes and do their own shopping and cooking; husbands who work from 8 till 4:30 regularly at the same job for years and who save up to buy a small car on time payments; people, in other words, who work toward improvement for the sake of their children and who want no revolutions." Annie Sinclair Mehdevi, "Iran Celebrates a 2,500[th] Birthday," *New York Times*, October 31, 1965.

[49] Kian-Thiébaut (1998), p. 193.

politics, and to the dispersal of power throughout a complex system of competing institutions. Although the national income had increased dramatically, individual wealth had not kept pace with the high inflation in the cost of living, and the massive influx into cities such as Tehran had spawned large sprawling slum cities. Millions of squatter migrants, though generally quietest for most of this century, were increasingly radicalized after 1963. The relative dearth of labor-intensive industries meant that those who fled rural poverty collected in the cities – "a mass of urban workers with no real skills and whose employment has been dependent on an ever-continuing construction boom and ever-growing demand for menial laborers."[50] Additionally, the presence of large segments of relatively unabsorbed newcomers to the cities tied urban centers of political activity to the periphery; "the movement of millions of people had connected these villages up into a network of political turmoil."[51]

And yet the "new poor," as Asef Bayat's perceptive study identifies them, did not fulfill a particularly active role in revolutionary mobilization or regime consolidation. Lacking formal vehicles, and historically disenfranchised, the urban poor were largely relegated to the sidelines of the upheaval.[52] They were, however, vulnerable to mobilization in cases when it satisfied their immediate needs and objectives, through mass institutions established during and after the revolution offering opportunities for upward mobility.[53] This situation strengthened the hand of extremists at either end of the political spectrum and facilitated the radicalization of public debate under the Islamic Republic.

During the monarchy's final eighteen months, labor activism emerged as a major factor. All labor unions, guilds, and professional associations were controlled by the state, as were the Chamber of Commerce and other business-oriented groups. Still, as the cycle of protest, reprisals, and commemorations began to accelerate, labor groups became politically engaged, with strikes shutting down most major industries for months. The labor actions began at large oil facilities and quickly engulfed Iran's core oil fields in Ahwaz, cutting production by one-third within weeks. These strikes and protests were accompanied by demands for better pay and living standards for workers. In addition, the demonstrations

---

[50] Abul Kasim Mansur, "The Crisis in Iran: Why the US Ignored a Quarter Century of Warning," *Armed Forces Journal* (January 1979), p. 26.

[51] Najmabadi (1987), p. 198.

[52] In addition to Bayat (1997), see Charles Kurzman, *The Unthinkable Revolution in Iran* (Cambridge, MA: Harvard University Press, 2004), pp. 100–2.

[53] A. Bayat (1997), pp. 159–60.

demanded legal reforms for worker protection as well as (or in some case, in lieu of) political reforms. In 1978, these labor-related demands far outstripped political demands – at least quantitatively – as a portion of overall union activity.[54]

Labor action during the revolution was not purely blue-collar activism. In fact, the strikes that had the greatest impact were those undertaken by civil servants. Government agencies formed individual strike committees and orchestrated their employees. The actions of Ministry of Power employees proved particularly instrumental; electricity blackouts exacerbated the chaos and uncertainty already afflicting the broader economy; and timing the actions to coincide with the state television's evening news broadcast underscored the shifting authority.[55] The Plan and Budget Organization (PBO) Employees Association sponsored lectures decrying the monarchy and in mid-1978 emerged as the coordinator for protests by government employees. Later that year, Khomeini appointed the PBO staffer Ali Akbar Moinfar as national strike coordinator; Moinfar would assume senior roles in the planning and petroleum sectors after the revolution.

Revolutionary sentiments also managed to afflict one of the bastions of Pahlavi rule, the military. The shah built a potent army and equipped it with the most modern weaponry. However, its leadership had been eroded by the shah's fears of rival power centers, while its enlisted ranks were readily susceptible to religious recruitment thanks to a deliberately suspicious deployment policy and a legacy of Tudeh influence and proved susceptible to religious recruitment.[56] As Khomeini began to assemble a shadow government, the Supreme Council of the Armed Forces unambiguously declared the neutrality of the armed forces and called all troops back to barracks. This decision, together with an earlier judgment to facilitate Khomeini's return and a subsequent revolt against the Imperial Guards incited by air force technicians (*homa faran*) at Tehran's Dushan Tapeh base, doomed the institution of the monarchy.

Several nascent institutions proved critical during the transition period – and remained relevant, empowered actors after the revolution. First and foremost were the organizations that evolved to fill gaps in the provision of social services to the rapidly expanding communities of urban poor. The monarchy had systemically expanded health and social

---

[54] Asef Bayat, Workers and Revolution in Iran. (London: Zed Books, 1987), pp. 86–7.
[55] Razavi and Vakil (1984), p. 105.
[56] William F. Hickman, *Ravaged and Reborn: The Iranian Army, 1982* (Washington, DC: Brookings Institution, 1982), pp. 6–7.

services through White Revolution programs as well as new institutions such as the 1974 founding of the Social Security Organization, but in their infancy they were not capable of meeting the needs of a hyperextending state and a rapidly urbanizing country. In this void, a variety of informal organizations, many associated with mosques and/or the *bazaar*, emerged to provide support.

By 1979 – as "the crisis of distribution had affected the regime's legitimacy" – the revolutionary coalition, with its strong base of neighborhood organizations, was able to ensure that "food was available everywhere in Iran at stable prices" and that the Paris-exiled Khomeini and his local representatives had access to telephone lines.[57] An array of "alternative supply systems" sprang to life, engaging a diverse array of *bazaar* merchants, public sector employees, students, and tradesmen.[58]

Khomeini and his adherents supplemented his personal network with a system of local, small-scale revolutionary committees (*komiteh*) that were organized in and through mosques. These institutions were "ideal instrumentalities of the revolution during a phase of the breakdown of central authority and the growing threat of anarchy," and their establishment encouraged and assisted the coordination of the diverse social composition of the revolution.[59] The *komiteh*s helped coordinate *bazaar* strikes, as well as student demonstrations and industrial actions. In this way, they provided organization and structure for the revolution. After the revolution, the *komiteh*s exacerbated the dualism of state structure and helped the politicized clergy to consolidate their power.

As the preceding analysis suggests, the revolution came about as a result of a complex array of factors, particularly the collapse of the monarchy's capacity to manage crises and co-opt elites, and the emergence of a skilled leader in Khomeini, who could mobilize a wide array of disaffected constituencies and align their interests under his leadership. While the economy exacerbated popular alienation, economic issues were not the primary driver for persuading millions of Iranians to risk their lives and livelihoods by taking to the streets. However, economic policy quickly emerged as the prism through which the ideological divisions among the postrevolutionary coalition would come into conflict. Equally

---

[57] Razi (1987), p. 459.   [58] Bayat (1997), pp. 52–3.
[59] Leonard Binder, "Iran's Unfinished Revolution: Possible Scenarios," in Joint Economic Committee of the Congress of the United States, *Economic Consequences of the Revolution in Iran* (Washington, DC: U.S. Government Printing Office, November 19, 1979), p. 27.

importantly, because of the invocation of economic themes during the revolutionary mobilization as well as the power struggle that succeeded it, economic progress and opportunity became the standard by which many Iranians gauged the success of the change. "They say we have not made revolution for economic betterment!" a factory worker in Azmayesh exclaimed in 1981. "What have we made it for, then? They say for Islam! But what does Islam mean then? We made it for the betterment of the conditions of our lives."[60]

POSTREVOLUTIONARY CONSOLIDATION IN THE SHADOW OF UNREST

Interpretations of the Islamic Revolution in Iran and the ensuing evolution of the state have reconciled the Iranian experience with the predicted pattern of postrevolutionary centralization. While conceding the novelty of its theocratic apparatus and nominally religious ideology, they have almost across the board reduced the implementation of the Islamic state in Iran to an unexceptional example of the inexorability of state consolidation of power. The expansion of the state bureaucracy, the intrusion of government into hitherto private realms of behavior, and the aggressive monopolization of power by the Islamists at the expense of other potential rivals and alternative perspectives support this view. Some analysts have interpreted this as part of a longer-term trend toward state centralization in Iran, which was merely perpetuated by the revolution.[61] Parallels are drawn between the Islamic Republic and other authoritarian states forged through revolution, particularly the Soviet Union.[62]

This perspective represents an oversimplified description of the Iranian political dynamic, disregarding an important consequence of the revolution: the reconfiguration of the state through explicitly ambiguous partition of authority and sovereignty. In the revolution's aftermath – and even in the wake of the Islamists' consolidation of authority – matters were rarely so simple, or so absolute. The Islamic Republic's establishment did not produce an unequivocally stronger and more centralized state. Rather, the revolution's centrifugal tendencies were distributed

---

[60] Assef Bayat, "Workers' Control after the Revolution," *MERIP Reports* (March/April 1983), p. 33.

[61] Farhad Kazemi, "Models of Iranian Politics, the Road to the Islamic Revolution, and the Challenge of Civil Society," *World Politics* 47 (July 1995), p. 572.

[62] Skocpol (1982), pp. 278–9; McDaniel (1991).

throughout a deliberately divided state structure, which owes its longevity to an intricate balancing act between theocracy and democracy. Sovereignty is explicitly divided between the power of the supreme leader, who holds ultimate and ostensibly divine authority, and the legitimizing force of the popular vote.

Revolution tends to intensify the continuous process of push and pull between the state and society. When the structure of authority dematerializes, even temporarily, social actors begin to assert themselves with renewed intensity and through innovative vehicles. Contenders for power must meet this challenge quickly. The most effective means of seizing control is by developing strong, viable institutions. In a competitive environment, all actors within a revolutionary coalition understand that the "first person to obtain decisive political control will gain the ability to define the procedures and institutions that dictate future political interactions ... in a way that bolsters their own personal power and gives them preferential access to society's economic resources."[63] In postrevolutionary Iran, all of the aspirants for postrevolutionary predominance sought to develop institutions and cultivate organizations that had sprung up independently in an attempt to outmaneuver their rivals. Although the Islamists ultimately won the day, four years of bitter contention among such a diverse coalition engendered a diffusion of power and authority throughout those institutions that constituted the state.

Predictably, the Islamic Revolution spawned myriad new organizations to consolidate authority as the shah's grip degenerated and challenges to the monarchy's control over society and the economy proliferated. Early in the upheaval, food cooperatives emerged in Tehran, in part in response to rising inflation and shortages of consumer products. The same period saw the birth of neighborhood committees that assumed responsibility for community infrastructure, such as water and power, and sponsor political meetings. And in the nation's factories and offices, "workers' councils" began to assert themselves, adopting militant stands, participating in labor mobilization, and generally contributing to the situation of economic paralysis under the final days of the shah. Despite its best efforts to sabotage these organizations through violence and intimidation, the monarchy was outnumbered

---

[63] Anthony Gill and Arang Keshavarzian, "State Building and Religious Resources: An Institutional Theory of Church-State Relations in Iran and Mexico," *Politics and Society* 27: 3 (1999): 431–65.

and overpowered. "The regime was witnessing the birth of a new civil order over which it had no control."[64]

Prior to the shah's ouster, Khomeini's public statements remained enticingly ambivalent about the future shape of the Iranian state. One analysis compares the "utopian" slogans of the French and Russian Revolutions, promising "liberty, equality, fraternity" and "bread, peace, and land," respectively, to the "primarily negative" rallying cry of the Islamic Revolution: Death to the Shah (*marg bar Shah*);[65] this is an indication of the extent to which the revolutionary coalition focused solely on a program of action to remove the shah and made little headway in establishing consensus on a vision for the future. Khomeini's rhetoric contributed to this process in other ways as well. As the leader of the revolution – the man whose words sent millions to the streets – he might have been expected to cultivate some grounds for a shared future. Instead, he narrated a deliberately vague agenda for revolution beyond the immediate and unconditional eradication of the monarchy. The following exchange between Khomeini and an Arab journalist, reproduced in Shaul Bakhash's history, is telling:

KHOMAINI: You think there is no program? Not at all. There is a program. Islam has a program. We also have a program. But the program is Islam and it is better and more progressive than the program implemented by the colonialists ...
INTERVIEWER: May we know the main guidelines?
KHOMAINI: Not yet. You must go, study and then grasp the main outlines. We will in the future announce all our political, economic and cultural policies.[66]

These undefined pronouncements – and other, perhaps more deliberately deceptive talk of democracy from his Paris exile[67] – contributed to aligning a wide swath of the Iranian population behind the Islamic

---

[64] A. Bayat (1997), pp. 53–5; Rahnema (1992), p. 69.
[65] Sreberny-Mohammadi and Mohammadi (1994), p. 118.
[66] Bakhash (1984), p. 48, as quoted from *Neda-ye Haqq: Majmu'eh-I az Payamha Mosahebeh-ha va Sokhranrani-ha-ye Imam Khomaini dar Paris* [The Voice of Truth: A Collection of the Messages, Interviews, and Speeches by Imam Khomeini in Paris] (Solon, Ohio: Muslim Student Societies in America, Europe, and Canada, 1357 [1979]), pp. 92–3.
[67] Khomeini agreed in a meeting with the National Front leader Karim Sanjabi to a future Iran that was both democratic and Islamic, but as Bakhash notes, Khomeini's "published views hardly suggested he understood the word democratic to mean a Western parliamentary democracy." Bakhash (1984), p. 72. Still, others accuse him of a premeditated obfuscation designed to win the support of the Iranian middle classes.

Revolution. During this period, Khomeini also cultivated the deference of a broader array of oppositionists, including Karim Sanjabi and Abolhassan Bani Sadr, a Parisian intellectual with a long history of radical politics and admiration for the ayatollah.

Although the Iranian state historically incorporated religious legitimacy and even theological institutions, there was no direct historical precedent for clerical rule. Khomeini's theory of Islamic governance – the guardianship of the religious jurist (*velayet-e faqih*) – rests on a novel and almost unprecedented reinterpretation of religious dogma, which remains contested by Shi'a theologians.

Khomeini's own conceptualization of the state was consciously desultory. He argued that an Islamic state exemplified the sanctity of Islamic society. Islam would be its purpose, its efficacy, its strength; the concepts of institutions or autonomy were irrelevant. Throughout his life, however, Khomeini's own views underwent a notable evolution, in a way that enhanced the role of the state. The first was his acceptance of a legitimate and just government in the absence of the Twelfth Imam, a doctrinal shift that encouraged new clerical activism and sanctioned religious rule by a clerical hierarchy for whom the Twelfth Imam's occultation precluded any true temporal authority.[68] With his articulation of the theory of *velayet-e faqih* and its later implementation via the Islamic Republic, Khomeini achieved those objectives, but in so doing, he also contributed to the erosion of the religious refutation of the hegemony of human institutions.

Until his actual return to Iran, Khomeini was "more concerned with the process of establishing such a state rather than with its institutional structure."[69] Physically and, to some extent, logistically disconnected by his exile from the daily dynamics of opposition mobilization, Khomeini managed the revolutionary enterprise through a small, handpicked group, including former students, acolytes, and long-standing representatives within Iran. Most of this select group would play crucial roles in the leadership of the state that emerged in the revolution's aftermath, including clerics such as Ali Akbar Hashemi Rafsanjani, Ayatollah Mohammad Reza Mahdavi Kani, and Ayatollah Mohammad Javad Bahonar, as well as leading figures in the Freedom Movement such as Ezzatollah Sahabi

---

[68] Hamid Hosseini, "From Buchanan to Khomeini: Can Neoclassical Economics Explain the 'Ideal' Islamic State of Iran's Despotic Ayatollah?" *American Journal of Economics and Sociology* 49: 2 (April 1990), p. 174.

[69] Binder (1980), p. 36.

and Mehdi Bazargan. Other key constituencies, including the *bazaar* and the military, were also represented among Khomeini's loose advisory council in exile, which was reborn as the Shura-ye Enqelab (Revolutionary Council) shortly before his return to Iran in January 1979. In his announcement of the new body, Khomeini asserted that its authority was validated by "religious right and based on the vote of confidence by an absolute majority of the people in me."[70]

In his speech on his February 1, 1979 arrival in Iran – the first time in fifteen years that he had set foot in his homeland – Khomeini described the departure of the shah as "the first step" but underscored what he saw as the uprising's unfinished business, proclaiming, "Our triumph will come when all forms of foreign control have been brought to an end and all roots of the monarchy have been plucked out of the soil of our land."[71] And yet his first act of leadership signaled Khomeini's underlying pragmatism and the patience with which he approached the challenge of establishing a new order. Even before the final collapse of monarchical authority, Khomeini had charged Bazargan with leading the transitional period that would be necessary to fashion a new system. This is notable not simply in the choice of personalities – Bazargan had a unique fusion of credentials, with both technocratic experience and religious-nationalist philosophy – but also in its reflection of Khomeini's priorities. The ascetic cleric implicitly recognized the exigency of preserving existing administrative structures in order to ensure the functioning of society and the economy. It presaged Khomeini's bureaucratic pragmatism; in his quest to eradicate the roots of the monarchy, there would be no razing of the bureaucracy, nor any clerical tolerance for a political void.

Unfortunately for Bazargan, the Provisional Government's formation set the stage for its eventual collapse. Bazargan's new role necessitated his departure from the Revolutionary Council and a reshuffling of that body's membership in favor of the clerics. "By the very act of appointing a titular head of government, Khomeini demonstrated that he himself remained the supreme authority" and reinforced the preeminence of the Revolutionary Council, which had been appointed by Khomeini and was accountable to no one but him.[72] During the subsequent nine months,

---

[70] Moin (1999), p. 197.
[71] "Declaration upon Arrival at Tehran," February 1, 1979, as translated in Algar (1981), p. 252.
[72] Baktiari (1996), p. 54.

the two institutions would engage in a fierce competition for influence in which the unelected Islamists would ultimately prove victorious. And the establishment of a modicum of central authority did little to stem the tide of chaos that had accompanied the revolution itself; instead, it accelerated and intensified the competition among the disparate groups within the antishah coalition.

The historical record leaves some uncertainty as to the intent of Khomeini and his allies regarding the position of the Provisional Government. Indeed, Khomeini's scathing attacks on Bazargan and Ali Khamenei's later admission that Bazargan won the position because "we had no one else, and at that time we ourselves lacked the ability"[73] suggest that the Provisional Government was designed to serve as a temporary "straw man" to deflect the moderates and prepare the ground for clerical rule. This argument forms part of a larger "longstanding implicit theme . . . to the effect that 'we' started the movement, while 'they' – the clergy – jumped on its bandwagon and 'hijacked' the revolution" that is characteristic of many of the secular groups that participated in the revolution.[74]

But while he initiated and authorized the Provisional Government, Khomeini also continued to empower the Revolutionary Council, which sought to extend its reach by formalizing newly established vehicles of mass mobilization, including the Pasdaran, or Islamic Revolutionary Guard Corps, and the paramilitary *komiteh*s. In addition, the council created new organs for consolidating its authority and achieving its vision of an Islamic social order, including the system of revolutionary courts and the (since-disbanded) Islamic Revolutionary Party. In some cases, these institutions cooperated with similarly tasked government bodies; in other cases, they competed with and superseded them.

The postrevolutionary government found itself vested with dual, and dueling, institutions of authority: an army spawned by the exigencies of opposition and those forces remnant from the ousted regime; an economy mobilized to combat central authority and the vestiges of a developmental state; and similar conditions in legal, educational, and cultural spheres. Both sets of institutions were crucial to the survival and legitimacy of the new regime; the paradox of sustaining both would prove to be a delicate balancing act for the theocratic government that emerged from the ashes

---

[73] Bazargan (1983), p. 28, as quoted in Bakhash (1984), p. 65.

[74] Afsaneh Najmabadi, "Mystifications of the Past and Illusions of the Future," in *The Islamic Revolution and the Islamic Republic*, eds. Nikki R. Keddie and Eric Hooglund (Syracuse, NY: Syracuse University Press, 1986), p. 149.

of the revolution. In many cases, a careful analysis of the process of transformation demonstrates the complicated and often contradictory genesis of institutional reconstruction.

The splintering of relations between the Islamists and the Provisional Government reflected the fundamental differences in their political approaches and their revolutionary activism. Bazargan and the Freedom Movement appealed for democratic rights through constitutional means, whereas many clerics maintained their collaboration with Marxist guerrilla groups and used rhetoric intended to resonate with the lower classes. The personality politics and relative ambitions favored the determined Islamists; as Bazargan acknowledged shortly before the culmination of the revolution, he did not see himself as "a bulldozer like Khomeini, I am a fragile automobile and I need a proper road on which to travel. You must pave the way for me."[75] Khomeini and the Islamists paved that road, and the liberals and their middle-class allies decisively lost the competition.

In understanding the postrevolutionary state and its political economy, the exigencies of competition and consolidation in the postrevolutionary interval represent crucial factors. These forces helped to generate competing institutions and splintered authority and cultivate adversarial relationships among the constituencies that had cooperated to oust the shah. Religious institutions, leadership, and ideology mediated among the competing factions and preserved a fragile coalition of merchants, landlords, and disaffected urbanites. In doing so, they prevented the ruptures that had enabled the shah to prevail in 1953 and 1963 (as well as 1975[76] and other lesser moments of potential revolt). Khomeini himself became the grand arbiter as well as the grand ayatollah, mediating among contending factions among the revolutionary coalition. This aspect of his style of leadership enabled him to retain flexibility and preserve and enhance his own authority as the ultimate decision maker. His mediation elevated his stature and amplified the finality of his decisions in those cases when he chose to intervene.

This approach helped the revolution to survive its birth; under leadership with less tactical acuity, the fundamental differences within the revolutionary coalition may have imploded the movement before it had achieved its goal. However, the profound differences within the coalition

---

[75] Moin (1999), 209.
[76] In 1975, clerical students rebelled with the blessing of Khomeini; however, apathy from the *bazaar* doomed the attempt.

and the competition that manifested itself through rival institutions also facilitated the perpetuation of an endemic schizophrenia within the post-revolutionary political élites. Unity did not exist among the parties that had coalesced to oust the shah, and the competition between them, combined with the explicit endorsement of violence by certain groups, accelerated the cycle of threat, response, and counterresponse. Each dimension of the situation – Khomeini's opaque leadership style, the asymmetry in the use of violent tactics, the empowerment of semisanc-tioned parallel organizations, and eventually the sense of siege generated by the standoff with Washington and the Iraqi invasion – intensified Iran's postrevolutionary disorder.

The chasms between the various parties pushed the debate to extremes and fractured the moderate intellectuals and organizations that might have served as bridges between them. Secular and socialist groups battled openly in streets against the religious governance and escalated a vicious terrorist campaign that targeted its leadership; the *ulema* themselves were riven by disputes over politics and personality; and the average Iranian found his entire world turned upside down – property confiscated, rela-tives and friends fled, businesses and universities ground to a halt as a result of violence and lack of any real authority. Comparatively – and relative to the coercive forces available to the shah – the revolution itself was relatively bloodless. But the turmoil that ensued as the revolutionary actors attempted to consolidate their gains was acute and often brutal.

Besides Khomeini and the liberal nationalists leading the Provisional Government, the other main contenders for power emanated from the secular. However, long-established groups such as the communist Tudeh operated from a significant disadvantage, having been almost completely crushed by SAVAK's zealous policing.[77] Determined not to repeat past mistakes, the remaining Tudeh leaders adhered closely to Khomeini's line throughout the revolution and its aftermath – acceding to *velayet-e faqih*, celebrating the seizure of the American Embassy, and pushing for radical economic policies such as expropriations and land reform. The Tudeh feared the political center – the moderate constitution-alists – more than the clerics, with whom they shared some common interests. Such a utilitarian strategy preserved their status as the clerical juggernaut eliminated all other elements of the revolutionary coalition,

---

[77] One researcher contends that the shah had executed or imprisoned more than 90 percent of the founders and original members of these two organizations by 1976. Amjad (1989), p. 107.

but eventually that alliance too would fray, and between mid-1981 and 1983, the Tudeh was essentially eliminated.

More radical groups, such as the Fedayin and the Mojahedin, were also tolerated after Khomeini's return, although both also fell victim to the Islamists' push for power and their own internal weaknesses. The Fedayin began agitating against Khomeini early on, boycotting the constitutional referendum, before it was itself splintered by tactical differences. In the north, Fedayin partisans helped encourage uprisings among Turkomen tribes and in Kurdistan, but both Fedayin factions found themselves under siege on the streets from semisanctioned gangs of *hezbollahi* youth and did not survive the postrevolutionary crackdown. The Mojahedin found greater success and longevity, yet this same stature contributed to their undoing. The relationship between the Mojahedin and the Islamists was always wary, thanks to significant philosophical differences and personality conflicts. Although they had long ties with key clerics and initially supported the Islamic Republic, the Mojahedin quickly evolved into the Islamists' most potent rival, drawing enthusiastic crowds to rallies and lectures. Their leadership became vocal opponents of clerical rule, even while they attempted to remain part of the system with reverent references to Khomeini. Eventually, they too were thoroughly – and brutally – eliminated after siding with Bani Sadr in his rupture from Khomeini.

Even among the clerics, there was little consensus about the path forward. The *ulema* have never been a monolithic segment of society, and at no time did their pluralism become more profound than at the moment of revolutionary triumph. As they were suddenly propelled to the center of political life, the clergy also found themselves more fully enmeshed than ever before in the rough-and-tumble of politics, intensifying competition among them. Their differences focused on fundamental issues of Shi'a doctrine, although personal ambitions and animosities played an important role as well. During Khomeini's long exile, many senior clerics walked a fine line between accommodation with the monarchy and outright opposition.[78] Many of these same men greeted his articulation of *velayet-e faqih* with hesitation, and most grand ayatollahs "maintained a distance and a degree of silence" from the new

---

[78] These included Ayatollahs Morteza Motahhari, Mohammad Husayn Beheshti, Mohammad Javad Bahonar, each of whom emerged as key figures in the early structure of Islamic government), as well as Grand Ayatollah Shariatmadari, who briefly stood against Khomeini's institutionalization of his own authority, but was eventually silenced.

government.[79] Some opposed the politicization of the clergy as a demotion of their proper spiritual role or an illegitimate usurpation of the place reserved in Shi'a doctrine for the occulted Mahdi. Others, including Ayatollahs Qomi, Shirazi, and Zanjani, emerged as vocal critics of the new order once its shape began to become clear. As a result of Khomeini's charisma and authority, he easily prevailed in the drafting of the Constitution, and those senior clerics who displayed ambivalence on this issue were either brought into line or cast out of the system of power.

There were many other serious divisions among the clerics who participated in the establishment of the postrevolutionary Islamic government. The most severe and enduring concerned the nature of the economy. A simplistic categorization of these early conflicts would distinguish those clerics who favored a vigorously Islamic government, with a strongly interventionist role for the state in the nation's cultural, social, and economic life in order to establish what they saw as a truly Islamic society, from those who challenged them, the traditionalist clergy, who interpreted Islamic law as restricting the state's role in the economy. There was an inexact but important correlation between those senior clerics with close personal ties to Khomeini and support for radical positions during the postrevolutionary regime's consolidation. These disputes intensified as the system and its challenges evolved, and their positions evolved as well.

Beyond the difficulties in achieving consensus among the incongruous and contentious actors within the revolutionary coalition, Iran's postrevolutionary leadership faced an array of imminent threats. Iran's ethnic heterogeneity[80] has long proven a critical factor in its politics, particularly during periods when the central government exhibits signs of instability or weakness. Historic aspirations for autonomy or independence among the Azeris, the Kurds, and other groups reasserted themselves as the revolution transpired, and ethnic mobilization facilitated the monarchy's

---

[79] Abbas Vali and Sami Zubaida, "Factionalism and Political Discourse in the Islamic Republic of Iran: the Case of the Hujjatiyeh Society," *Economy and Society* 14: 2 (May 1985), p. 140.

[80] Slightly more than half, or approximately 55 percent, of the population of Iran is ethnically Persian, and Azeri Turks constitute one-fourth of its citizenry. The Kurdish population is estimated between 8 and 10 percent, with Qashqais, Boir Ahmadis, Turkomans, Afshars, Bakhtiaris, Baluchis, Arabs, and Lurs filling out the rest. See Ali Banuazizi and Myron Weiner, "Introduction," in *The State, Religion, and Ethnic Politics: Iran, Afghanistan, and Pakistan*, eds. Banuazizi and Weiner (Syracuse, NY: Syracuse University Press, 1986), pp. 3–4.

demise by seizing military garrisons and armaments. Actions taken in the name of the revolution, however, also entailed an expectation of a greater stake in the postrevolutionary state through local autonomy.

The Kurdish case exemplifies the revolution's expansive impact on regional aspirations and ensuing instability. Although the Kurds quickly achieved de facto control of their province and had resisted the central government for a half-century, the Provisional Government rejected most of their demands for autonomy. Negotiations quickly erupted into full-scale warfare and a sporadic but aggressive insurgency that had to be met with force. Kurdish leaders boycotted the constitutional referendum and continued to press for greater regional autonomy, including religious freedom. The September 1980 Iraqi invasion complicated Kurdish loyal-ties and ignited hostility from both Tehran and Baghdad, each of which perceived its Kurds as potential collaborators. The invasion effectively concluded the Kurdish challenge, but during the new state's formative months, it instilled a sense of siege, escalated the propensity toward centralization and state domination, and accelerated the cycle of violence and repression.[81]

The Azeris, who compose Iran's largest ethnic minority, presented a more complicated challenge during the postrevolutionary consolidation. As are the Kurds, Iran's Azeris are distinguished by linguistic and ethnic differences, are heavily geographically concentrated within Iran, and have substantial cross-border populations and a history of resistance to the central state. In contrast to the Kurds, however, Azeris are predominantly Shi'a and thanks to a long history of integration and politicization are far better integrated within the leadership as well as merchant communities. This legacy of local leadership bred the inevitable conflict with the center.

The ethnic conflict was exacerbated by a competition for influence between Khomeini and Grand Ayatollah Mohammad Kazem Shariatmadari, a native Tabrizi who had maintained close ties with his region even though he was based in Qom. Though Shariatmadari and Khomeini studied together during their initial training and worked closely with one another during the unrest that resulted in Khomeini's exile, their paths and their philosophies markedly diverged thereafter. What began as a difference over strategy and theology – Shariatmadari favored compromise, quietism, and

[81] Charles MacDonald, "The Kurdish Challenge and Revolutionary Iran," *Journal of South Asian and Middle Eastern Studies* 13: 1–2 (Fall/Winter 1989): 52–69; Patricia J. Higgins, "Minority-State Relations in Contemporary Iran" in eds. Banuazizi and Weiner (1986), pp. 167–97.

the retreat of the clergy from day-to-day governance – devolved into a full-scale organizational rivalry, in which Shariatmadari was dramatically outmatched. His Muslim People's Republican Party remained regionally concentrated – a status that may have only heightened its threat in the eyes of an embattled central authority – and never managed to capture popular sympathy outside his native Azerbaijan. Khomeini dispatched military force and staged massive protests in Tabriz in support of his own authority, the office of the *velayat-e faqih*, and the new state, forcing the rival party to disband and Shariatmadari into increasing tighter straits. He was eventually stripped of his status as a grand ayatollah and *marja-ye taqlid*, implicated in a trumped-up plot against Khomeini himself, and placed under house arrest, where he died.

In addition to the uprisings in Kurdistan and Azerbaijan, during the six months that followed the revolution, the new regime faced tribal revolts in Mazandaran and Khuzestan and was compelled to call upon the regular military, with the dubious cooperation of the Revolutionary Guards, to subdue them. The situation in Khuzestan, southwestern Iran, was especially worrisome: The unrest pitted ethnic Arabs against Iranians in sustained violence in Khorramshahr, the center of the Iranian oil industry. This unrest increasingly absorbed an ideological dimension, as leftist groups with a long history of traction in the region actively cultivated uprisings among Iran's minorities in hopes of outmaneuvering their rivals. The linkage between leftist agitation and the bids by Kurds, Azeri, and Turkomen for greater autonomy after the revolution increased Tehran's apprehension toward these movements.

The revolution happened to coincide with a massive influx of Afghan refugees, eventually swelling as high as 3 million. The revolutionary disruptions, together with the religious sympathies of the revolutionary regime, contributed to a policy vacuum toward the refugee challenge and resulted in the absorption of most Afghan refugees within Iran's rapidly growing cities rather than in settlement camps. They were classified as "involuntary migrants" (*mohajeran*) rather than refugees (*panahande-gan*), a classification that provided legal resident status as well as some access to state benefits, including subsidized health care and food, but precluded other, more lucrative means of employment.[82] In addition, all foreign nationals were (and remain) barred from public sector employment in Iran, denying them access to much of the formal economy.

---

[82] Bahram Rajaee, "The Politics of Refugee Policy in Post-Revolutionary Iran," *Middle East Journal* 54:1 (Winter 2000), pp. 50, 57–8.

Many Afghans found low-skill, low-paying jobs to survive, but the situation was ripe for ethnic tensions and economic grievances.

The first fraying within the revolutionary coalition had a seemingly unlikely source: women. The spark was the issue of women's dress, which served for both sides as the harbinger of future social policy decisions. Khomeini's remarks in early March 1979 calling for enforcement of Islamic dress provoked protests after the news was reported, an event that happened to coincide with International Women's Day. Although some Iranian women willingly adopted conservative apparel associated with Islamic prescriptions for modest dress, many chafed at the prospect of its postrevolutionary compulsion. This represented the "first powerful challenge to Khomeini's authority,"[83] and it sufficiently spooked the clerics that they backed away from this mandate until they gained a tighter grip on power more than a year later.

Other social groups asserted themselves during the interregnum, and this spontaneous agitation must have appeared as anarchy to Iran's aspiring new leaders. Still active were the strike committees whose labor mobilization had shut down Iran's petroleum production and helped grind the monarchy to a halt; after the revolution, these *shuras* (councils) remained active and were predictably galvanized by the unrest and the opportunities it afforded. Their identification with the leftist groups, which was typically indirect, as well as their potential threat as an independent power base and a destabilizing force led the clerics to move quickly against the labor movement, first by attempting to co-opt it and later by neutralizing and dissolving it.[84]

Even segments of the military were clamoring for dramatic changes and in many cases, initiating these changes, such as the democratization of leadership, without official sanction; air force cadets held a sit-in in June 1979 in which eighteen thousand demanded the establishment of a classless army and excoriated the Provisional Government.[85] And while public sentiment favored a major reduction in the overall size of the military and/or its abolition in favor of some sort of "people's militia," many of the contending political groups, including those controlled by members of the *ulema*, had emerged from the revolutionary turmoil fully

---

[83] Moghissi (1994), pp. 140–3.
[84] Saeed Rahnema, "Work Councils in Iran: The Illusion of Worker Control," *Economic and Industrial Democracy* 13: 1 (February 1992), pp. 69–94.
[85] Bashiriyeh (1984), pp. 145–6.

armed with weapons unleashed in battles like that at Tehran's Dushan Tapeh air force base.[86]

The devolution of authority empowered individuals and organizations on the smallest scale: A single radical cleric could mobilize a network to force property expropriations; a single revolutionary *komiteh* could destabilize a neighborhood and unseat whatever authority had managed to be established. This was a potent threat; there were fifteen hundred *komiteh*s in Tehran alone when the Provisional Government was established. The confusion and competition that reigned during the crescendo of the revolution and the synthesis of the new regime provoked the emergence of paramilitary groups affiliated with the Islamic movement, vested with the sanction of Khomeini and of populist sentiment. Composed of longtime armed oppositionists from lower-middle-class backgrounds as well as more recent adherents,[87] they roamed the streets of Tehran, attacking leftist groups and provoking chaos. Khomeini sanctioned their transformation into an officially approved force to be called the Islamic Revolution Guard Corps in early May 1979.

Middle-class disenfranchisement played a significant role in the revolution, but these same groups appeared to recede from the political scene after its success. Some fled Iran as turmoil intensified, joining the "brain drain" that would become an endemic problem for the Islamic Republic. But many remained, some becoming radicalized and adhering to the leftist partisans in the postrevolutionary contest for influence. Others attempted to maintain the center, backing the National Front, the Freedom Movement, or several of the other moderate groups that remained active after the revolution. Divisions within and among these groups left them greatly outflanked by the clerics, and the secular middle found itself "trapped between the ideological radicalism of the left and the religious extremism of the right."[88]

THE NEW ORDER AND THE ECONOMY

In the immediate aftermath of the revolution, Iran experienced an ideological battle over its connection to the world economy, between the proponents of traditionalist interpretations of *shari'a* and statist ideas

---

[86] Nikola B. Schahgaldian, *The Iranian Military under the Islamic Republic* (Santa Monica, CA: RAND Corporation, 1987), pp. 18, 65; Hickman (1982), p. 10.

[87] Kenneth Katzman, *The Warriors of Islam: Iran's Revolutionary Guard* (Boulder, CO: Westview Press, 1993), p. 31.

[88] James A. Bill, "The Politics of Extremism in Iran," *Current History* (January 1982), p. 10.

propagated by leftist clerics and their supporters. Khomeini's successor described the transformation in a 2012 speech to students. "We chose a path which was based on some calculations we made. The Islamic Revolution made some big changes in this country. It changed a monarchy into a democracy. It changed dependence into independence. It changed a historical, chronic backwardness into progress.... The Islamic Revolution changed humiliation into self-confidence and a sense of dignity."[89]

The early phases of Iran's new order were dominated by improvisation, exigency, institutional upheaval, and political competition. Throughout the initial months, the economy was embroiled in chaos at least as severe and erratic as the political turmoil – in spite of a continued revenue flow that was more than sufficient to fund even the most ambitious plans of the new government. Massive dislocation of workers and projects contributed to the sense of uncertainty, and despite the efforts of the Provisional Government authorities to reimpose some degree of bureaucratic structure and systematic planning, the economy was in a process of wholesale collapse. The shah's grand schemes had been abandoned, construction ground to a halt, millions – perhaps as much as 30 percent of the country's labor force – had lost their jobs.[90]

Even in the midst of such intense institutional warfare, chaos on the streets, and ideological ferment, the emerging state was also subject to powerful forces of stability. Revolutionary leaders appreciated the urgency of reviving economic activity, and shortly after taking the helm, Khomeini urged labor groups to resume their work "for the sake of the revolution."[91] The new leadership left much of the economic infrastructure intact, as it was simply easier to resume or perpetuate the existing arrangements of the preceding system, particularly insofar as this facilitated the assertion of government control and the predominance of the Islamists in the power struggle.

Despite the self-referential utilization of Islamic rhetoric, the new regime only sporadically availed itself of existing Islamic institutions. Indeed Mohsen Nourbakhsh, who played a central role in Iran's economic management until his 2003 death, acknowledged that "there was

---

[89] Translation of Khamenei's August 6, 2012, speech before a university student gathering in Tehran, broadcast on IRIB Channel One on August 7, 2012, and translated and transcribed by BBC Monitoring, August 10, 2012.

[90] Youssef M. Ibrahim, "Iran Has Cash but Can't Spend It," *New York Times*, August 6, 1979, p. A1.

[91] Assef Bayat, "Workers' Control after the Revolution," *MERIP Reports* (March/April 1983), p. 20.

never any discussion of Islamic economics during that time."[92] Instead of channeling the windfall of expropriated assets into the traditional Islamic charities (*awqaf*) that had long served as repositories for public wealth in Muslim societies, the new state established parallel foundations outside the religious networks. Nor did the postrevolutionary regime seek complete monopolization of the state by the religious hierarchy; Khomeini always incorporated nonclergy in his inner circle and did not mandate religious credentials for political participation in the new state. Rather than relying wholly – or even primarily – on the clerical hierarchy to staff its bureaucracy, the Islamic Republic instead absorbed a vast cadre of lay people, mainly composed of students and aspiring technocrats from the lower middle class.[93]

The revolutionaries found themselves in the unexpected position of recapitulating some of the very policies they had so resented under the monarchy. With inflation running as high as 50 percent for basic foodstuffs and other goods, *bazaar* merchants became targets of resentment, and there were even calls for an antiprofiteering campaign led by Ayatollah Sadeq Khalkhali, the revolutionary prosecutor who led the hasty and brutal judicial retaliation against monarchists.[94] Labor leaders found themselves subject to a similar reversal by their former allies among the Islamic revolutionaries; their most ambitious demands, including a five-day, forty-hour workweek, were rejected by the government, and independent unions repeatedly found themselves repressed.[95] For the imam, the shah's departure invalidated any justification for labor actions, and he demanded that workers who continued to strike over unpaid wages and other economic concerns return to work immediately or be "regarded as opposition against the genuine Islamic Revolution."[96]

In addition, the postrevolutionary leadership maintained a civil taxation system to fund the state, rather than redirecting the religious taxes of *khoms* and *zakat*, which were left primarily in the hands of the clergy itself. This contradicted Khomeini's original treatise, in which he decried the need for extensive state infrastructure and anticipated relying solely on religious taxes.[97] He was not alone in this presumption; the first

---

[92] Bahman Ahmadi Amoee, *Iqtisad-i siysasi-i jumhuriya islami* [The Political Economy of the Islamic Republic] (Tehran: Gam-e No, 2003), p. 32.

[93] Olivier Roy, "The Crisis of Religious Legitimacy in Iran," *Middle East Journal* 53: 2 (Spring 1999), p. 204.

[94] John Kifner, "Unrest Grows in Iran As Prices Rise and Income from Oil Export Falls," *New York Times*, June 1, 1980, p. A1.

[95] Bayat (1987), 181.   [96] Bayat (1987), 109.   [97] Omid (1994), pp. 141–2.

postrevolutionary head of the Plan and Budget Organization, Ali Akbar Moinfar, "believed that government money was the Moslems' Treasury and had to be spent in an Islamic way."[98] And the emerging economic argument of the new Islamic state equated civil taxation with religious obligation. Ayatollah Ardebili, then-president of the revolutionary state's Supreme Court, asserted that "those who do not pay their taxes are like those who do not pay their *khoms*; their property is illicit, because property or wealth that evades tax payment does not belong to the owner but to the people, the martyrs, and the unfortunate rural dwellers."[99] However, a more traditional view among the senior clergy retained its discomfort with the notion of *velayet-e faqih* and continued to oppose paying taxes to any government in lieu of the return of the Mahdi. During the first decade of the Islamic Republic, the legitimacy of civil taxation remained a major point of contention between Khomeini and the senior clergy.[100]

The new regime saw some of its efforts to transform the economic framework of the country undermined by a newly empowered workforce; an attempt to change official work hours in the oil sector was quietly challenged and eventually abandoned.[101] Elsewhere, the exigencies of crisis management prompted other arrangements that became more entrenched over time, particularly as the revolutionary state was beset by other emergency situations such as the war. One of these patterns was the Islamic Republic's reliance on imported foodstuffs, a trend that began under the monarchy but contravened the new regime's commitment to self-sufficiency.[102] As the cost of food imports rose by as much as 300 percent in 1979, from $3 billion to an estimated $9 billion, the new leadership saw little choice. As a French banker involved with the transactions at the time remarked, "The easiest way to fuel a counterrevolution is to let the people experience hunger."[103]

---

[98] Razavi and Vaki (1984), 107.

[99] Fariba Adelkhah, *Being Modern in Iran* (London: 1988), p. 12.

[100] Shahrough Akhavi, "Elite Factionalism in the Islamic Republic of Iran," *Middle East Journal* 41:2 (Spring 1987), p. 190, p. 192.

[101] Edward Cowan, "Unrest Raises Doubts on Oil," *New York Times*, December 6, 1979, p. A1.

[102] Wheat imports increased by 103 percent between 1979 and 1981; red meat by 39 percent, according to Central Bank statistics quoted by Morady (1996), p. 14–15.

[103] Youssef M. Ibrahim, "Iran Has Cash but Can't Spend It," *New York Times*, August 6, 1979, p. A1.

Still, there were powerful ideological impulses in favor of economic transformation, and these – together with the power struggle and the chaotic environment – helped generate dramatic changes in other aspects of the economy. "Since the spirit of that time was in opposition to the capitalist economic structure, capitalist ideas and people who may have approved of them were perceived as outsiders [*gheyrkhodi*]," one economist who served with the Plan and Budget Organization has commented.[104] In pursuit of this new economic order, the long-standing relationship with Iran's oil consortium was annulled and oil production deliberately constrained, defense spending was slashed by as much as 60 percent,[105] and the overall state budget – and in particular, most of the shah's high-profile infrastructure projects – was drastically curtailed. The new leaders also launched a far-reaching land reform program and a massive absorption of the country's productive capacity under state control. However, by increasing unemployment and sharpening the abrupt fiscal contraction, the cumulative impact of these early moves only exacerbated the country's economic crisis.

An important factor in shaping the early reconstitution of the economy was the opacity of authority – a function of the competition between the Provisional Government and the Revolutionary Council. Government officials struggled to assert control over the economy as part of a broader quest to reinforce their role as the legitimate successor authority. The Plan and Budget Organization remained intact and, given its employees' role in coordinating the public sector strikes that helped precipitate the shah's downfall, it might have been expected to retain a central role in formulating economic policy. Instead, the Revolutionary Council adopted an activist posture that almost immediately outstripped the PBO and the government.

There was an ideological dimension to this competition; both in its appointments and its decrees, the Provisional Government mirrored the liberal nationalist orientation of its acting prime minister – many, like Bazargan, served in the shah's bureaucracy and distinguished themselves as opposition politicians. By contrast, their departure from the Revolutionary Council had prompted the appointment of six new members, including Habibollah Payman, Abolhassan Bani Sadr, and a young Mir Husayn Musavi – all of whom favored not simply a clerical-led

---

[104] Ahmadi Amoee (2003), pp. 250–1.
[105] Reuters, "Iran Slashes Budget Level," July 15, 1979.

government but policies that were populist, redistributionist, and interventionist in their approach.

Revolutionary Council leaders believed the right and responsibility of power lay with those who had ousted the shah, and sought to assert their authority forcefully. For example, when Ali Akbar Nateq Nuri, who became the council's deputy chair, sought the prosecution of anticlerical activists, Ayatollah Beheshti encouraged him to assume the role of judge himself. When Nateq Nuri initially demurred, saying, "I have never served as a judge; neither I nor my father nor grandfather have been judges," Beheshti responded, "My father was not the head of the Supreme Court either. There has been a revolution in this country; go and be a judge."[106]

While the Provisional Government could make a stronger technocratic claim than the Revolutionary Council, it was itself hardly a bastion of depoliticized expertise during this period. None of the early postrevolutionary PBO chiefs – Ali Akbar Moinfar, Ezzatollah Sahabi, and Musa Khayyer – was a trained economist; the first postrevolutionary national oil company chairman, Hassan Nazih, had no direct experience in the energy sector; and the same was true for many other senior officials during this period. Revolutionary credentials outweighed education and experience, and in some cases, familial connections to influential clerics or senior officials were prized as perceived insulation. These staffing decisions were not arbitrary; Moinfar led the strike coordination committee for the PBO, and Nazih's background as a human rights lawyer and personal relationship with Bazargan were seen as a gesture to oil sector workers, whose labor actions helped doom the monarchy and made them a dominant force in Iran's economy.[107]

Still, the growing fissures among the postrevolutionary leadership meant that the "men of trust," as Bazargan initially described Nazih, soon found themselves sidelined or worse.[108] Nazih's transgression involved resisting ideological purges of the oil sector and sparring explicitly with the clerics by denouncing Khomeini's emphasis on Islam's primacy. "If you think that we can put all political, economic and judicial

---

[106] Reza Khojasteh-Rahimi, "Ali Akbar Nateq Nuri Returns to Politics: The Secret Return," *Sharq*, December 25, 2003.

[107] In December 1978, the oil workers' syndicate announced, "We know that our strike was the decisive factor.... We control the country's economy." See *Kargaran Pishtaz-i Junbish-i Tudah-i* (Bahman, 1984), as cited in Mansoor Moaddel, "Class Struggle in Post-Revolutionary Iran," *IJMES* 23:3 (August 1991), p. 323.

[108] Youssef M. Ibrahim, "Iran Oil Chief's Job: Pacify the Workers," *New York Times*, March 13, 1979, p. D1.

problems into an Islamic mold," Nazih argued, "even the religious leaders know that this is neither possible nor beneficial."[109] Bolstered by Khomeini's authority and the incipient Islamic Republican Party, headed by his protégé Beheshti, the council eventually would win the day.

The competition for influence between the Provisional Government and the Revolutionary Council played out on the economy more than any other issue. Bazargan and his allies sought to fashion a new order that incorporated revolutionary demands for freedom and independence into institutions that bolstered the government. However, the innate temperance of the nationalist leadership left them disadvantaged in the cutthroat competition and the rapidly evolving new order. Bazargan acknowledged his handicap, arguing in May 1979 that "decision making roles are so numerous in our country that they have paralyzed much activity."[110]

Divisions over economic policy worked in favor of Khomeini and the Islamists, in part because the clerics' appeal spanned both ends of the ideological debate. The Revolutionary Council adopted an activist stance toward the country's immediate economic challenges and outstripped the technocrats' authority and relevance. This assertiveness ensured that the Revolutionary Council played the formative role during the interregnum in reshaping the Iranian state and society – and in advancing the eventual outcome of clerical preeminence. The Revolutionary Council's decrees helped forge the postrevolutionary economic framework and situated economic issues center stage in the power struggle that dominated the subsequent decade. Arguably, its early decisions have proven more durable – and equally problematic – than the constitution itself for the postrevolutionary political economy.

Among its more than sixty decrees and ordinances were measures that nationalized Iran's banks, facilitated widespread expropriations, reserved broad segments of the economy to the state, and created a nebulous category of semigovernmental organizations endowed with vast authority and assets. Notably, the first parliament established a review process intended to expose the council's actions to the scrutiny of elective institutions; however, the assessment commission was disbanded after a largely dormant four years.[111]

---

[109] John Kifner, "Iran's Oil Director Disputes Ayatollah on Primacy of Islam," *New York Times*, May 29, 1979, p. A1.
[110] Ibid.   [111] Schirazi (1998), p. 164.

In light of the opposition's critique of the shah's economic management, the successor state pursued policies that featured an even more central role for the government, assuming direct ownership and control of much of the expropriated resources through the National Iranian Industries Organization or the Industrial Development and Renovation Organization. By one analyst's calculation, the new regime absorbed direct command of 80 to 85 percent of Iran's major production units.[112] In the Islamic Republic's early years, the creation of new institutions and the redistribution of elite resources accompanied a dramatic program of nationalization of major sectors of the economy, including all private banks, insurance companies, all heavy industries (which included the mining and metals industries as well as plane, ship, and automobile manufacture plants), and all factories and organizations in debt.[113]

The council's assets grab should be seen in its proper context. Revolutionary turmoil and chaos had unhinged the existing socioeconomic order. As early as mid-1976, British government sources estimated that Iranians were expatriating approximately $1 billion per month, and at least twenty thousand had purchased homes in or near London.[114] This capital flight intensified dramatically as the monarchy collapsed, in volumes so high that it overwhelmed the banking system and prompted strikes by bank employees. Less than a year after the shah fled, Iran's GDP had fallen by 32 percent from only two years earlier.[115] A number of senior officials were arrested, tried, and executed; others were forced from their positions as a result of purges (*paksazi*, or cleansing). Altogether, an estimated 3 million Iranians simply fled the country during the revolutionary upheaval.[116] Those who departed were disproportionately wealthy and well educated, and capital flight during this period has been estimated in the range of $30 to $40 billion.[117]

[112] Anoushiravan Ehteshami, *After Khomeini: The Iranian Second Republic* (London: Routledge & Kegan Paul, 1995), p. 86.

[113] Mansoor Moaddel, *Class, Politics, and Ideology in the Iranian Revolution* (New York: Columbia University Press, 1993), pp. 252–3.

[114] Arjomand (1988), p. 111.

[115] Frederic L. Pryor, "The Political Economy of a Semi-Industrialized Theocratic State: The Islamic Republic of Iran," in *The Political Economy of Theocracy*, eds. Mario Ferrero and Ronald Wintrobe (London: Palgrave, 2009), p. 249.

[116] Akbar E. Torbat, "The Brain Drain from Iran to the United States," *Middle East Journal* 56:2 (Spring 2002), p. 276; Kanovsky (1997), p. 6, offers a similar range of 2 to 4 million.

[117] Torbat (2002), p. 290.

The former élites had become fully deprived of any popular support, as public clamor for expropriation actually in some cases preempted action by the central government. Radical labor mobilization, *komiteh* vengeance or acquisitiveness, revolutionary fatigue among embattled ownership, shifts in power and policy within the government itself: All these forces buffeted the vestiges of the private sector during the revolution's initial years, with an erratic tempo that paralyzed Iran's economy. Outcomes were frequently arbitrary, as a twist of fate determined the future of particular businesses and industrialists in the postrevolutionary upheaval, refuting any claim that the vast program of confiscations represented the product of deliberate planning or coordination.[118]

With respect to property ownership, as the scholar Mehrdad Haghayeghi has noted, the difficulty of the Provisional Government "was not due so much to the absence of authority, by to the excess of authority."[119] Labor strikes and fleeing owners ground production to a halt. The revolution's radicalization of the general public contributed to popular entitlement and lawlessness. University students took over several luxury hotels, protesting that dormitory space could not be found, while poor Tehranis simply moved themselves into the homes of the wealthy in the northern parts of Tehran and refused to leave.[120] They were provoked and organized by Islamic radicals, such as Muhammad Karrubi (brother of Mehdi, a leading Iranian politician), who created a network to identify, occupy, and distribute properties.

Many of those who benefited from the squatter expropriations were desperately poor, but there were also opportunists, profiteers, and powerful interrelationships between the clergy and the unofficial paramilitaries, each of whom sought to accelerate the transfer of power and outmaneuver the Provisional Government. The scholar Asef Bayat described the mood on the streets as a "moment of madness":

Landless peasants confiscated large agribusiness estates; hundreds of factories were taken over by workers; and the state offices began to be run by their employees. The revolutionary youth took the charge of the city police. Even the unemployed, who intrinsically lacked any institutions in which to function, took control of the streets by regulating the traffic. It was the time

---

[118] Bakhash (1984), pp. 180–5.
[119] Mehrdad Haghayeghi, "Agrarian Reform Problems in Post-Revolutionary Iran," *Middle Eastern Studies* 26:1 (January 1990), p. 36.
[120] For an excellent overview of the role of the urban poor in reconfiguring the postrevolutionary economy, see Bayat (1997).

of role-playing, of making a difference, of being counted, of taking revenge, of seizing the moment.[121]

In many cases, the motivations for nationalization transcended the presumptive intentions of acquisitiveness, retribution, or the philosophical preference for state expansion. In fact, many of the entities taken over by the revolutionary regime were in arrears to state banks, and nationalization offered a simple mechanism for negating their liabilities.[122] Many foreign firms had simply pulled out of Iran because of the inability to maintain security or staff during the revolutionary upheaval.[123] The seizures were justified on the basis that the wealth accumulated by the monarchy and its supporters was equivalent to the "spoils" of war, and as a result inherently illegitimate. "I don't want to use the word nationalization," explained Ali Akbar Moinfar, who was initially tasked with leading the Plan and Budget Organization, in June 1979. "I would rather say popular ownership and the transformation of industries into enterprises working for the interests of the people."[124]

Notably, however, to the extent that any of the expropriations were subject to a crude form of procedural attention, "the tribunals carefully avoided challenging the concept of private property," instead focusing on the alleged misdeeds of the prerevolutionary owners.[125] The process facilitated the new authorities' capriciousness to suit their interests; in some cases members of the same family, invested in the same sectors, received dramatically disproportionate treatment.[126] The assets of the shah and his closest supporters were treated differently; Khomeini ordered that royal resources should be kept distinct from state properties.[127] In other cases, the assets of the revolution's losing

---

[121] Asef Bayat, *Street Politics: Poor People's Movements in Iran* (New York: Columbia University Press, 1997), p. 61.

[122] Katouzian (1989), p. 56.

[123] Estimates at the time suggested approximately 15 percent of 500 U.S. firms had curtailed their operations in Iran entirely prior to the revolution. Vahe Petrossian, "Total takeover," *MEED*, July 13, 1979, p. 26.

[124] "Iran to Seize Some Industries," *AP*, June 20, 1979.   [125] Abrahmian (1993), p. 42.

[126] Arang Keshavarzian, "Regime Loyalty and Bazari Representation under the Islamic Republic of Iran: Dilemmas of the Society of Islamic Coalition," *IJMES* 41 (2009), p. 233.

[127] Ruhollah Khomeini, *Sahifeh-ye Nur* Volume 17 (Tehran: 1363/1984), p. 124, as quoted in Ali A. Saeidi, "The Accountability of Para-Governmental Organizations (Bonyads): the Case of Iranian Foundations," *Iranian Studies* 37:3 (September 2004), p. 484.

side were distributed as rewards to individuals as a means of building and reinforcing patronage networks.[128]

The scope of the government takeover was extensive. Appropriately, it began with the personal fortunes of the shah and his closest supporters, with the establishment of the Bonyad-e Mostazafan (Foundation for the Oppressed) in March 1979. Next, the council transferred the Chamber of Commerce and Guild Chamber to the relevant state ministries in May 1979. Then, in June 1979, the council nationalized twenty-three privately held banks (eleven owned by foreign firms); this order was followed by another in October 1979, extending the nationalization to the entire banking sector (thirty-six additional financial institutions). The order resulted in the consolidation of Iran's banking institutions into nine state-owned commercial and specialized banks and gave the Central Bank – and by extension, the central government – greater authority over their lending practices.[129] The banking system became the province of the Supreme Council of Money and Credit, which was established in February 1980 to create banking regulations consistent with Islamic law, including the prohibition of interest.

Later that month, the council ordered that the government had the right to assert ownership of any firm or organization with which it dealt and whose management had fled the country – a decree that resulted in the nationalization of approximately one thousand organizations of varying sizes and profitability. The prerevolutionary concentration of industrial and commercial enterprises in the hands of a relatively small array of individuals enabled this massive wealth transfer and predetermined the expansion of the state sector under the new order.[130] Meanwhile, national security concerns strengthened the nationalization impulse.

[128] For example, Ali Akbar Nateq Nuri has written of his role as a judge in the trial of members of the Forqan group, a prerevolutionary left-wing guerrilla movement. After their conviction, Nateq Nuri successfully appealed to Khomeini for permission to distribute the group's assets to the individuals who had helped capture them. "Thanks to arresting the Forghan/Forqan Group," Nuri writes, "these guys who had worked hard became homeowners." As quoted from Nuri's memoirs, pp. 188–9, in Reza Khojasteh-Rahimi: "Ali Akbar Nateq-Nuri Returns to Politics: The Secret Return," *Sharq*, December 25, 2003.

[129] Mehrdad Valibeigi, "Banking and Credit Rationing Under the Islamic Republic of Iran," p. 52.

[130] Approximately 150 families owned two-thirds of Iran's private financial and industrial establishments under the shah, and of that group, 10 families controlled 370 of the 473 largest firms. See Mehdi Mozaffari, "Why the Bazar Rebels," *Journal of Peace Research* 28:4 (November 1991), p. 384.

In July 1979, "strategic industries" such as metals, shipbuilding, aircraft manufacturing, and mining were absorbed by the government on the grounds of their vital importance to the state.[131] Eventually, the reach of the state extended well beyond the country's major industries, with August 1980 regulations empowering the government to assume control of small industries. The council's actions were paralleled by the Provisional Government's decisions, which structured an executive branch centered around an overwhelming state role in the economy. Four ministries were established to supervise various industries: the Ministry of Industry (which was charged with food processing, textiles, and pharmaceuticals), Ministry of Heavy Industry, Ministry of Mines and Metals, and Ministry of Petroleum.

The postrevolutionary shifts in ownership had varying consequences; for many sectors, the distinction between the narrow base of the monarchical elite and the direct absorption by state or semistate organizations after the revolution did not constitute a dramatic shift. Elsewhere, however, the state's insertion – and, in many cases, the corresponding eviction of foreign investors – was catastrophic. The pharmaceutical industry, for example, experienced a dramatic decline in investment and innovation, thanks to its nationalization as well as the associated departure of international companies and the introduction of a system centered on generic drugs.[132] While the long-term impact may have generated some net gains, since the prerevolutionary pharmaceutical sector was highly import-dependent, it also created shortages of vital medicines and the proliferation of shoddy substitutes at the hands of loosely regulated private pharmaceutical manufacturers and importers within Iran.[133] Elsewhere, expropriations alienated and impoverished many Iranians who might have otherwise made a constructive contribution to the revitalization of the economy in the fledging state. As one Iranian academic notes, the U.S.-Iran Claims Tribunal established after the hostage crisis ensured that

---

[131] Ali Rahnema and Farhad Nomani, *The Secular Miracle: Religion, Politics, and Economic Policy in Iran* (London: Zed Books, 1990), pp. 240–1.

[132] EIU-UNIDO (1995), xxxiii.

[133] See Vahid H. Nowshirvani and Robert Bildner, "Direct Foreign Investment in the Non-Oil Sectors of the Iranian Economy," *Iranian Studies* 6:2/3 (Spring–Summer 1973), p. 90. Medicine shortages have been widely documented in a variety of studies including Akbar Aghajanian, "Population Change in Iran, 1966–86: A Stalled Demographic Transition," *Population and Development Review* 17:4 (December 1991), p. 711, while the issue of counterfeit and substandard pharmaceuticals has repeatedly surfaced in the press. See "Iranmehr Hospital Scandal," *Iran News*, April 27, 2004, an editorial documenting the case of eleven deaths that resulted from tainted anesthesia.

"the Iranian government paid for each piece of confiscated foreign property," while "Iranian entrepreneurs received no comparable compensation."[134] Even decades later, outrage over the confiscations remains
intense within Iran; hints of the residual resentments play out on a routine
basis in the press, and in the attitudes of many Iranians toward the
presumptive beneficiaries of the postrevolutionary assets grab.[135]

Interestingly, the massive state appropriation of resources conflicted
with the preferences of important revolutionary constituencies. The
bazaar, which is frequently credited with financing opposition mobilization and whose allies featured prominently on the Revolutionary Council,
did not favor such an expansion of the public sector. And Khomeini spoke
out repeatedly against unlawful confiscation and the desirability of a
secure environment to attract the return of domestic capital. However,
with the revolution's triumph, the *bazaar* saw its opportunities expand
and its sinecures preserved – a situation that intensified the left-wing push
for state intervention in the economy during the 1980s.

The postrevolutionary economic transformation was not simply an
urban phenomenon. In addition to industrial takeovers, the revolutionary
state extended its reach across the countryside. The drive for more ambitious land reform represented the highest economic priority for several
groups, including the radical Left and the left-leaning clergy. Despite the
country's checkered experience with land reform, the issue remained a
vital one for a nation that remained predominantly rural. Moreover, the
same chaos that disrupted the urban and industrial economies also
wrought havoc in the provinces, where the power vacuum had prompted
a mass land grab. The multiplicity of authority and the lack of a confirmed legal framework exacerbated the confusion; individual clerics and
activists, revolutionary courts, *komiteh*s, and the advocacy of left-wing
parties such as the Fedayin incited annexations while others suppressed or
dissuaded them.

Peasants with small-scale subsistence plots endeavored to evict
their landlords; at the same time – and occasionally, in the same
place – wealthy landlords who lost property in the Pahlavi era land

---

[134] Akbar Karbassian, "Islamic Revolution and the management of the Iranian economy,"
Social Research 67:2 (Summer 2000), p. 623.
[135] See, for example, a letter from a distraught homeowner threatening suicide as a result of
bonyad attempts to claim his home. "Iran News Reviews Iranian Press, Television," *Iran
News*, January 5, 1998, p. 3; also see Adelkhah (2012), p. 29, for discussion of grudges
held against the Astan-e Qods foundation for its expansion at the expense of many local
families.

reform sought to reconstitute their prior holdings. An estimated eighty-eight of the ninety-three agricultural corporations that controlled much of the country's prime fertile land were fragmented amid the revolutionary upheaval.[136] The proliferation of revolutionary institutions and the fragmentation of interests and authority complicated the process, as did the role of leftist organizations that sought to incite conflict and land takeovers.

The Revolutionary Council first stepped into this loaded issue in 1979, with an edict empowering the government to confiscate abandoned land as well as *mavat* (barren) holdings. While this measure sidestepped the larger issue of land reform, it was interpreted as an encouragement to the radicals. Senior clerics such as Ayatollah Dastgheib in Shiraz agitated for official endorsement and facilitation of redistribution and exhorted peasant uprisings. The November 1979 fall of the Provisional Government paved the way for a more aggressive approach. In April 1980, the Revolutionary Council approved a land reform program with far-reaching implications for rural landholders. The law imposed unreasonably modest caps on landownership, effectively requiring the fragmentation of all but the smallest farms. A new administration for "the transfer and revitalization of land" was established to oversee the process, and during the subsequent eight months, the commissions approved the redistribution of 150,000 hectares of barren land and 35,000 hectares of arable land to the landless, with a shift of other lands to rural cooperatives.[137] However, the edict created sufficient backlash that in November 1980, Khomeini was forced to suspend its implementation.

DUAL, AND DUELING, AUTHORITY

The postrevolutionary consolidation vested much of the country's economic apparatus and the former elites' resources beyond the reach of state institutions. A new holding company for enterprises assumed by the state, the National Iranian Industries Organization (NIIO), was eventually established and affiliated with the Ministry of Industry, but the Industrial Development and Renovation Organization, which had been established in 1967, remained effectively autonomous until 1982.

---

[136] Ehsani (2006), p. 88.
[137] Mansour Moaddel, "Class Struggle in Post-Revolutionary Iran," *IJMES* 23:3 (August 1991), pp. 323–4.

In addition, the revolutionary state created nonprofit foundations, or *bonyads*, building upon a pattern begun by the shah, whose foundations (including the Pahlavi Foundation and the Foundation for Ferdousi's Shahnameh) served as vehicles for political, personal, or cultural goals. Their close identification with the monarchy resulted in their reconstitution in line with revolutionary objectives. Several were formally classified as public, nongovernmental organizations,[138] a telling reflection of the bifurcated nature of postrevolutionary authority. Over time, these foundations evolved into complex organizations with diverse commercial and industrial activities. Several were directed toward cultural issues, such as the cinema-oriented Farabi Foundation, the Sazman-e Tablighat-e Islami (Islamic Propaganda Organization), and the Bonyad-e Resalat (Foundation for Prophetic Mission), which publishes the influential conservative newspaper by the same name. However, the largest and most influential – the Bonyad-e Mostazafan va Janbazan (Foundation of the Oppressed and Self-Sacrificers) and Bonyad-e Shahid (Martyrs' Foundation) – were created to serve valued constituencies and entrusted with fulfilling the revolutionary mandate to promote social justice. Over time, the foundations became a large and consequential dimension of the supreme leader's political and economic influence, outside the scope of executive and legislative authority.

The Bonyad-e Mostazafan was established on March 5, 1979, by Khomeini's decree. The Bonyad immediately absorbed the Pahlavi Foundation and received a 1,000 million rial loan from the Central Bank in May 1979 per Revolutionary Council directive.[139] Like the shah, who used charity as both a political tool and an "economic weapon,"[140] the new regime vested the organization with extraordinary resources and political consequence; in addition to the Pahlavi Foundation holdings, the assets of the country's fifty-one largest industrialists were also nationalized during the early postrevolutionary period, and many were transferred to the *bonyads*.[141] Just as the shah used the Pahlavi Foundation to

---

[138] The charter of the Bonyad-e Shahid (Martyrs' Foundation), for example, describes it as "a public and non-governmental institution" with "legal status and financial and administrative independence." From "Majles: 11 Nov Session," *Resalat*, November 12, 1997, pp. 12–13, from FBIS-NES-98-051, February 20, 1998.

[139] Ali Rashidi, "De-Privatisation Process and the Iranian Economy after the Revolution of 1979," in *The Economy of Islamic Iran: Between State and Market*, ed. Thierry Colville (Tehran: Institut Français de Recherche en Iran, 1994), p. 47.

[140] Hiro (1985), pp. 131–2.

[141] For a description of the major industrial families under the shah and the process of nationalization, see Anoushiravan Ehteshami, *After Khomeini: The Iranian Second Republic* (London: Routledge & Kegan Paul, 1995), pp. 83–8.

assist favored constituencies, including the "families of police, military, and SAVAK personnel who were victims of confrontations with guerrillas,"[142] the Islamic Republic directed Mostazafan to support families of those killed by the shah's regime.

Its initial charter sketched these claims vaguely, conferring upon the Revolutionary Council the authority to seize all properties of the shah and his "affiliates, agents and associates." These assets were to be "duly utilized for the benefit of the needful people from all walks of life, in such development projects as housing, farming etc."[143] A report issued by the foundation in the 1990s described its first purpose as "the centralization, management, control and exploitation of all the remaining properties from the Pahlavi era and those related properties which had been transferred to the authority to the Bonyad," with a second and equally important duty to spend these incomes on behalf of the deprived.[144]

Mostazafan's establishment coincided with the Revolutionary Council's growing activism. During the new state's early months, the foundations strengthened the dichotomy among rival centers of authority in Iran and helped facilitate the eventual domination of radical factions over the moderates. Khomeini designed the Mostazafan to operate separately from or outside the scope of the formal government structure; its charter chastises that "the Government should be notified that such property does not concern it, but it shall be handled by the Islamic Revolution's Council."[145] In May 1980, after ordering an investigation into the foundation, Khomeini placed responsibility for its management with the prime minister's office. Mostazafan had other serious problems during this formative period. The organization had inherited much of Iran's productive capacity, but it also absorbed the brunt of the revolution's instability and liabilities. Correspondence reprinted in the Bonyad's subsequent publications suggests that these debts, and the ambiguities and insecurities surrounding them, required Khomeini's intervention to resolve.

---

[142] Naraghi (1994), p. 46.

[143] P. M. Moayed, Official Translator to the Ministry of Justice, "Charter of Imam Khomeini Authoring the Establishment of Mostazafan Foundation," certified July 18, 1991. Provided by foundation officials.

[144] *Gozaresh-e Jamea'-ye Amelkard-e Hasht Saleh-ye Bonyad-e Mostazafan va Janbazan-e Enqelab-e Islami, 1368–1376* [Report of all the Activities of Eight Years of the Islamic Revolution Bonyad and Janbazan Foundation, 1989/90–1997/98] (Tehran: Bonyad, 1998/99), p. 15.

[145] Moayed, "Charter."

Khomeini also established another important new revolutionary institution, the Imam's Relief Committee (Komiteh-ye Emdad; IRC), in March 1979. The Komiteh provides medical, educational, and social assistance to the rural poor, women, and orphaned children. Although it owns substantial property and land holdings and engages in economic activities, it also has relied heavily on direct transfers from the state.[146] Its activities have corresponded closely with Iranian foreign policy, including emergency relief supplies to Kosovo; disaster relief in Azerbaijan, Tajikistan, and Afghanistan; and humanitarian assistance to southern Lebanon.[147] At home, Komiteh-ye Emdad works extensively in rural Iran, with responsibility for support for some 4 million poor Iranians and educational funding for 650,000 primary and 15,000 university students.[148] The IRC was headed for many years by Habibollah Asgarowladi, secretary of the Islamic Coalition Association, a traditionalist faction with roots in the Tehran *bazaar*.

Several months after the creation of Mostazafan and the Komiteh-ye Emdad, the Jehad-e Sazandegi (Reconstruction Crusade) was established. The Jehad was tasked with spreading the fruits of an urban revolution to Iran's still largely rural population, and its creation coincided with the eruption of provincial tribal unrest. At its outset, the organization was staffed primarily by volunteers, much as its military counterpart the Revolutionary Guard was, and the Bazargan administration sought to maintain that status to preclude a turf battle with government ministries.[149] That containment effort failed; the Jehad's efforts to promote

---

[146] "Details of Subsidies Amounting to More Than 6,088bn Rials," *IRNA*, May 24, 1994, from *BBC Summary of World Broadcasts*, May 31, 1994; coverage of January 21, 1998 Majlis session, *Resalat*, January 22, 1998, p. 6, in FBIS-NES-98-076. See also Asghar Schirazi, *Islamic Development Policy: The Agrarian Question in Iran* (Boulder, CO: Lynn Rienner, 1993), pp. 163–4.

[147] "Azeri Deputy Premier Praises Iran's Humanitarian Aid," *IRNA*, March 12, 1997, in FBIS-NES-97-071; "Rally Demonstrators Give Donations to Afghanistan," *IRNA*, February 11, 1998, in FBIS-NES-98-042; "Tajik Minister Hails Iran's Social Welfare Scheme," *IRNA*, September 5,1997, in FBIS-SOV-97-248; "Joint Delegation Visit Southern Lebanon," *Iran News* (Internet edition), November 28, 1998; "Official on Hizballah, Syria, Peace Process," *Al-Nahar*, November 24, 1996, p. 11, in FBIS-NES-96-230; "Iran Launches Aid Campaign for Kosovo Refugees," *Iran News* (Internet edition), April 24, 1999; "Solidarity Day with Kosovar Muslims Observed Throughout Country," *Tehran Times* (Internet edition), May 15, 1999.

[148] "Rafsanjani Praises Participation in Majles Election," *IRNA*, March 9, 1996; "Over 4 Million People Get Pensions from Relief Committee," *IRNA*, November 19, 1996.

[149] Emad Ferdows, "The Reconstruction Crusade and Class Conflict in Iran," *MERIP Reports* 13 (March/April 193), p. 12. For a detailed review of the evolution of the Jehad, see Schirazi (1993).

economic development in the countryside and inculcate regime ideology were gauged successful, and it was elevated to a full government ministry in 1984, only exacerbating the system's bureaucratic redundancy.[150]

In addition, the Housing Foundation (Bonyad-e Maskan) was established to channel residential resources to the poor, particularly in light of a 1980–2 government freeze on property prices in Tehran. Predictably it became a vehicle for radical clerics who advocated redistributive policies and limits on private property. Bonyad-e Maskan was initially funded through religious taxes and eventually began receiving direct transfers from Mostazafan as well as through the national budget.[151] It was later partially absorbed within the government housing ministry, with an independent identity and budget,[152] its efforts redirected toward disaster relief and postwar reconstruction.[153]

The Bonyad-e Shahid was established in March 1980 to support veterans of the revolution and their families and eventually assumed responsibilities for war victims. Its funding derived from expropriated property and annual government subsidies.[154] Initially, Bonyad-e Shahid was headed by Mehdi Karrubi, a prominent leftist cleric, who was forced out over corruption allegations. The cultural and charitable wing of the Bonyad-e Shahid administered special rights for its constituencies, including prioritized university admission, employment consideration, and assistance with arranging marriages.[155] Like the other foundations, Bonyad-e Shahid expanded steadily, eventually

---

[150] "There Have Been Calls for Rural Improvements in Iran," *MEED*, July 6, 1985, p. 10.

[151] Sharbatoghlie (1991), p. 78.

[152] "Popular Participation, Most Important Factor in War-Torn Regions," *Tehran Times* (Internet edition), September 27, 1998; Hooshang Amirahmadi, "Iranian Recovery from Industrial Devastation during War with Iraq," in *The Long Road to Recovery: Community Responses to Industrial Disaster*, ed. James K. Mitchell (New York: United Nations University, 1996).

[153] Shaul Bakhash, *The Reign of the Ayatollahs: Iran and the Islamic Revolution* (New York: Basic Books, 1984), pp. 186–9; Jahangir Amuzegar, *Iran's Economy under the Islamic Republic* (London: I. B. Tauris, 1993), pp. 101–2.

[154] "Details of Subsidies Amounting to More than 6,088bn Rials," IRNA, May 24, 1994, from *BBC Summary of World Broadcasts*, May 31, 1994; "President Hashemi-Rafsanjani Presents 1376 Budget Bill to Majles," *Ettela'at*, November 24, 1996, pp. 2–3, in FBIS-NES-96-232, November 24, 1996.

[155] "Bonyad-e Šahid," in *Encyclopaedia Iranica*, ed. Ehsan Yarshater (Costa Mesa: Mazda Press), pp. 360–1; Amirahmadi in Esposito, ed. (1995), pp. 236–7; Iran Research Group, *Iran Yearbook 1989–1990* (Bonn: MB Medien & Bucher Verlagsgesellschaft mbH, 1989), pp. 10, 45–6.

absorbing hundreds of subsidiaries in industry, construction, agriculture, commerce, and services.

Although created with profuse and often contradictory purposes, these parastatals gradually generated self-interested agendas and mechanisms for achieving them. At the outset, they offered a convenient repository for the accumulated economic dilemmas of the new order. The creation of channels to absorb the deposed elite's resources was to facilitate the new leadership's efforts to restore economic order and outmaneuver leftist rivals. The *bonyad*s often worked hand in hand with the Revolutionary Guard, which aided in expropriations of landholdings and businesses.[156] The *bonyad*s' status left them largely unaccountable to the executive and legislative branches of the government; for most of the postrevolutionary period, public nongovernmental institutions were exempted from taxation and other transparency and accountability measures.

Reflecting the institutional dualism of this period, the foundations initially tended to replicate functions formally assigned to the central government. In some cases, they merged with ministries or evolved into independent government agencies for reasons involving logistical efficiency, political infighting, or both. For example, the Bonyad-e Umur Muhajirin-e Tahmili was eventually subsumed within the Ministry of Labor, and one of the cultural foundations, the Islamic Propaganda Organization, would gradually adopt direct government oversight.[157]

Many of these new organizations became valuable beachfronts in the power struggle between the clerical faction and its left-wing opponents. The scope of the state's authority was marginalized as the Revolutionary Council wrested control of organizations such as the Reconstruction Crusade from the Provisional Government. In addition, the "regular" institutions of government, including the military, underwent successive purges. Approximately 60 percent of the military had deserted in the earliest days of the revolution, and within the subsequent eighteen months, another eight to ten thousand officers had been dismissed.[158]

Similar developments reconfigured other public institutions. The *shura*s, or workers' councils, that emerged during the revolution

---

[156] Katzman, p. 41.

[157] Amirahmadi, in Esposito, ed., 1995, p. 235; "Majles Session: 30 Apr 96," *Resalat*, May 1, 1996, pp. 5, 13, in FBIS-NES-96-139-S, May 1, 1996.

[158] Gasiorowski, "The Nuzhih Plot and Iranian politics," *IJMES* 34:4 (November 2002), p. 647.

remained in force throughout 1979, enabling worker takeovers of factories and other enterprises. In August 1979, concerned that labor activism was advantaging the secular Left, the Islamists attacked the labor movement and purged antagonistic *shura*s and individual workers. Those *shura*s at odds with the Islamic Revolution Party were replaced by government-sponsored Islamic associations (*anjoman-e eslami*) and direct individual control was reestablished over companies.[159] The Plan and Budget Organization was effectively shuttered as a result of the *paksazi* (cleansing) process. The purges exacerbated the centrifugal tendencies of the new state and the primacy of politicization within the government bureaucracy by perpetuating a sense of institutional threat and mutual suspicion.

HOSTAGE CRISIS

In November 1979, the competition among state institutions claimed its most consequential victim: the Provisional Government itself. The end occurred courtesy of a crisis – the seizure of the American Embassy in Tehran by a student group calling itself "Students Following the Imam's Line." The students' protest was not coordinated with the Revolutionary Council in advance – they were reacting to the October 1979 admission of the exiled shah into the United States for medical treatment and, weeks later, the broadcast of a meeting between Bazargan and U.S. National Security Adviser Zbigniew Brzezinski. In the days that followed, Khomeini endorsed their move on the basis of "the overwhelming popularity of the act among the Iranian masses."[160] His blessing endowed the hostage taking with a sacral imprimatur and all the bureaucratic complexities of a major policy endeavor.

Over the subsequent 444 days, the hostage crisis transformed Iran's revolution at home and on the world stage. The embassy seizure ended the moderates' prospects and inflamed the power struggle among the revolutionary coalition. Khomeini's allies immediately recognized the tactical utility of the crisis as a means of securing their hold on power and tarnishing their rivals as imperialist lackeys.[161] Bazargan and the Provisional Government resigned in protest, and over

---

[159] Bayat (1987), pp. 100–1.   [160] Bill (1988), p. 295.

[161] See, for example, Khomeini's reported comments to Bani Sadr, "We keep the hostages, finish our internal work, then release them. This has united our people. Our opponents do not act against us." As quoted in Moin (2000), p. 228.

the ensuing weeks other rivals, such as Ayatollah Shariatmadari, were forcefully marginalized.

It also transformed Iran's place in the world, precipitating the first deployment of economic pressure against the revolutionary regime, discussed in greater detail in Chapter 9, and empowering a more radical approach toward the region. For many Iranians, the embassy seizure was another expression of the revolution's rejection of *zulm* (unjust rule), and Iranian leaders anticipated international acclaim and the support of underprivileged constituencies within the United States. On the first American visit of Iran's then-Prime Minister Mohammed Ali Rejai in September 1980, he was apparently unnerved to realize that the hostage seizure had not drawn greater sympathy to Iran's grievances.[162]

The initial round of American sanctions banned Iranian oil imports and quickly expanded to incorporate a freeze of Iranian assets held in U.S. financial institutions. Iranian leaders welcomed the measures and quickly reciprocated by prohibiting oil exports to Washington. From the outset, Khomeini proclaimed defiance and appeared to see economic pressure as a less urgent threat than the prospect of an American-orchestrated coup. "We fear neither economic boycott nor military intervention. What we fear is cultural dependence and imperialist universities that propel our young people into the service of communism."[163] After the U.S. oil embargo was launched, Khomeini responded that "the wheat and barley we grow in our own country" would sustain Iranians in the face of economic pressures – a stirring line that failed to account for the revolutionary state's increasing reliance on imported agricultural goods.[164]

Caught up in the fervor of the revolution's unlikely endurance, Iranian decision making around the hostage crisis was driven primarily by regime consolidation and ideological inculcation. Khomeini argued that "this action has many benefits" and promised that "taking hostages has increased our credibility … We will reach our objectives and we will get many concessions."[165] Prime Minister Rejai argued to the Majlis that the episode benefited Iran by signaling that the country would never again serve as Washington's compliant proxy.[166] This embrace of economic adversity – and even external economic pressure – as a prerequisite for

---

[162] Harold H. Saunders, "Beginning of the End," in Christopher et al. (1985), pp. 291–2.

[163] Khomeini, "The Meaning of the Cultural Revolution," *Kayhan-i Hava'i*, April 30, 1980, in Algar, trans. (1981), p. 299.

[164] John Kifner, "Iran Official Urges Foreign Envoys to Seek Shah's Extradition by U.S.," *New York Times*, November 13, 1979, p. 1

[165] Moin (2000), p. 228.   [166] Baktiari, p. 73.

securing Iran's independence and national prosperity remains a prominent feature of the postrevolutionary economy to this day.

The imposition of sanctions exacerbated the conspiratorial mind-set of the embattled revolutionaries, who were convinced that Washington was seeking to engineer the revolution's demise and reinstall the shah as in 1953. Economic pressure only reinforced Tehran's determination to stay the course, another historical pattern that would remain consistent throughout the subsequent three decades. "The Americans think Iran is their private property ... and that it should remain American property forever," Bani Sadr proclaimed. "If they can't have it today, they want to take over Iran tomorrow and they are using [the hostage crisis] to add on pressure in order to topple us from the inside. So we are going to live here and resist. We will live with the hostages."[167]

Iran's reciprocal freeze on oil exports to the U.S. reflected another frequently deployed tactic for dealing with sanctions – the imposition of countermeasures in hopes that the costs and inconvenience to the source would match or even eclipse those experienced by Iran. Then-Foreign Minister Sadegh Ghotbzadeh declared that "the United States is the loser in this," and Ayatollah Husayn Ali Montazeri, then a key Khomeini protégé, proclaimed that "the oil weapon will make the West tremble."[168] This proved overly optimistic. While the revolution had already hiked global oil prices, the U.S. import ban did not precipitate significant new price escalation, since Washington only imported approximately 4 percent of its oil from Iran. Beyond oil, evidence suggests that the eventual U.S. embargo enacted during the crisis only codified the status quo; revolutionary disruptions and political differences had already eliminated most bilateral trade.[169]

The economic dimensions of the hostage crisis continue to loom large on both sides: The crisis forged a new bipartisan consensus within Washington around the use of sanctions and elevated economic pressure as the primary U.S. policy lever. For Tehran, the episode forced the regime to embrace a new economic paradigm that incurred tangible costs as a result of its radicalism. This was the message that Richard Morefield, one of the diplomats held hostage, delivered to Massoumeh Ebtekar, the students' spokesperson who eventually went on to serve as the Islamic Republic's first female cabinet official, shortly before their release: "you were the first social revolution in history that didn't have to compromise

---

[167] Bowden (2006), p. 496.   [168] Kifner (November 13, 1979), p. 1.
[169] Steven Rattner, "Iran Shifting Trade from U.S.," *New York Times*, December 18, 1979.

from the very first moment for lack of money. When you took over, you had all the money you needed to make Iran back into part of the Fertile Crescent ... Anything was possible because you had the money, and you threw that away."[170]

THE LEGAL FRAMEWORK OF THE REVOLUTIONARY ECONOMY

Even as the hostage ordeal began, Iranians were already enmeshed in the process of drafting the legal framework of the new state. During his final days in exile, Khomeini began adapting his abstract theoretical writings to realities of the country from which he had been absent for fifteen years, and his decisions during this period established many of the Islamic Republic's most enduring leaders and institutions. After appointing the Revolutionary Council to oversee the transition, tapping Bazargan to head the Provisional Government, he tasked Hassan Habibi with devising a draft constitution. The retention of a constitution testifies to the power of Iran's historical legacy – even religious cadres assumed that the implementation of divine sovereignty should entail a written compact with the nation subject to popular approval.

Considerable ambiguity persisted over whether Khomeini intended an active role for the clergy in the postrevolutionary political life of the nation.[171] While provoking explicit misgivings from secular activists, Khomeini's first national political act – a referendum on the question of establishing an Islamic republic in Iran held on March 30–1, 1979 – did not decisively answer the question. In a single proposition ballot without alternative choices, the Iranian electorate approved the Islamic Republic

[170] Bowden (2006), p. 573.
[171] There are some who argue that Khomeini deliberately concealed his ambitions and intentions until after the success of the revolution and the establishment of the state. This contention tends to be based on several pieces of evidence: first, his promise to the National Front leader Karim Sanjabi to establish a "democratic and Islamic" government; second, his repeated disavowals of any plans to assume a formal government position in media interviews during the Neuphle-le-Château period of his exile. For a discussion of these issues and of the early construction of the Islamic state, see Shaul Bakhash, *The Reign of the Ayatollahs: Iran and the Islamic Revolution* (New York: Basic Books, 1984), pp. 71–91; Asghar Schirazi, *The Constitution of Iran Politics and the State in the Islamic Republic* (London: I. B. Tauris, 1997), pp. 22–57. Schirazi in particular takes a distinctly Machiavellian view of the statements and policies adopted by the clerical élite during this period. For another example of apprehensive interpretation of clerical motives, see also Cheryl Benard and Zalmay Khalilzad, *"The Government of God" – Iran's Islamic Republic* (New York: Columbia University Press, 1984), 103–13.

and gave the new state and its leadership an overwhelming mandate. Habibi's draft constitution was reworked by Bazargan's cabinet, which incorporated elements of Iran's 1906 Constitution and that of the French Fifth Republic. The end result proposed a liberal republican state with a powerful presidency and only a nominal role for Islamic precepts.[172]

The draft constitution, and the protracted conflict over the process of finalizing it, incited an intense national debate over the future state's composition and capabilities and exacerbated the ideational competition among the revolutionary coalition. In the end, separatist and secularist demands prompted increasingly exclusionary proposals from the Islamist and clerical groups, which then generated a backlash from the leftist groups; such spiraling factionalism swung August 1979 elections for the Assembly of Experts, a body established to finalize the draft, heavily in favor of Khomeini's camp. In this sense, a theocratic state was not a foregone conclusion; it was the direct product of the postrevolutionary power struggle.

The constitution produced by the Assembly of Experts in 1979 bears some striking similarities to the body of laws developed during the Constitutional Revolution seventy years earlier. It contained significant elements of representative democracy: an elected presidency and parliament, for example, as well as provisions for the competitive selection and popular oversight of the spiritual leadership. However, the final version also established *velayet-e faqih* as the new state's central institution, remanding of several basic elements of state sovereignty – including control of the armed forces and ultimate juridical authority – to this office. The *faqih* also serves as head of the state and the final arbiter of all domestic and international aspects of Iranian politics.

Velayet-e faqih has no direct precedent in the history of Islamic governance, although it is not entirely without doctrinal support from other theologians.[173] Traditional interpretations of Shi'a doctrine cite the theological premise of the Twelfth Imam's occultation as withholding ultimate legitimacy from temporal rule and obligating compliance with

---

[172] The draft constitution describes a state with no specific clerical offices, and a Council of Guardians composed of lay judges and tasked only with limited powers to review legislation for compliance with Islamic law. See Bakhash (1984), p. 74.

[173] As noted in Chapter 1, the concept of *velayet-e faqih* claimed deep roots in Shi'a jurisprudence; however, Khomeini operationalized that concept in a much different format than his predecessors anticipated. See Hamid Enayat, "Iran: Khumayni's Concept of the 'Guardianship of the Jurisconsult,'" in *Islam in the Political Process*, ed. James Piscatori (Cambridge: Cambridge University Press, 1983), pp. 160–3.

such rule, since *any* government in the imam's absence is unjust. This proposition permitted the parallel consolidation of mundane authority in the imperfect hands of the monarchy, and the assumption of "uncontested religious authority" by the clerical hierarchy, in such a way that neither was diminished nor precluded from intervening in the other's realm.[174] This concord was at times uneasy, but it endured and received relatively little canonical challenge.

That is, of course, until exile and the escalation of social tensions back at home initiated Khomeini's reinterpretation. His 1970 treatise, *Islamic Government*, elaborated on the foundations of his provocative reconceptualization of the link between religion and politics. In practice, the impetus for, and rationale behind, the office of the *faqih* derives immediately from the personal qualifications of Ayatollah Khomeini; its qualifications and responsibilities were constructed to suit his individual qualities, a distinction reflecting his exalted status and broad support during the revolution.[175] Khomeini's focus on individuals over institutions suggested that "the special qualities of leadership" superseded Islamic laws as the state's basis.[176] Given his age, the primacy of his position created considerable tension among Iranian leaders over the issue of succession. Ayatollah Taleqani is reported to have said of the clergy, "Now, based on their own measurements, they want to tailor-make the constitution like a suit of clothes."[177]

In hopes of durably institutionalizing the office of *faqih*, there were some early efforts to combine it with the presidency, which would have

---

[174] Said Amir Arjomand, *The Shadow of God and the Hidden Imam: Religion, Political Order, and Societal Change in Shi'ite Iran from the Beginning to 1980* (Chicago: University of Chicago Press, 1984), p. 229.

[175] Khomeini became universally addressed as "Imam," a title that can be broadly referent to piety, but that – within the clergy – tends to be reserved for the twelve leaders of the early Muslim community who inherited authority from the Prophet. Khomeini's assumption of that title suggested the blurring of that line, and the possible dilution of the precept of *intizar*, or anticipation of the Mahdi. Rebuking Khomeini on this point, Ayatollah Kazem Shariatmadari "warned the faithful that the long awaited twelfth Imam did not return to earth on a chartered Air France jumbo jet." Quote from Abbas Kelidar, "Ayatollah Khomeini's Concept of Islamic Government," in *Islam and Power*, eds. Ali Dessouki and Alexander S. Cudsi (Baltimore: Johns Hopkins University Press, 1981), p. 89. For remarks on the principle of *intizar* and *velayet-e faqih*, see Enayat in ed. Piscatori (1983), p. 174.

[176] Enayat in Piscatori, ed. (1983), p. 165.

[177] Bani Sadr attributes this retort to Ayatollah Taleqani, but of course Taleqani's premature death in 1979 precludes any independent confirmation of the accuracy of this provenance. From Abolhassan Bani Sadr, *Sad Maqaleh* [One Hundred Articles] (1980), p. 199, as quoted in Schirazi (1997), p. 46.

also established some electoral mechanism for its selection. Others lobbied to have the assembly's draft set aside altogether. Their case was furthered by the lack of active support for *velayet-e faqih* by other senior clerics and the opposition of several key members of Khomeini's circle.[178] However, these efforts to modify the institution or moderate its powers were obliterated by Khomeini's increasingly vocal advancement of the institution. After Bazargan's half-hearted effort to restart the process of drafting a constitution, Khomeini gave a thundering defense of his vision: "The *velayet-e faqih* is not something created by the Assembly of Experts. It is something that God has ordained."[179]

Such a statement – issued in Iran's highly politicized environment only days before the U.S. Embassy seizure – represented another of Khomeini's bold tactics, adopting an uncompromising position to outmaneuver his bickering rivals and secure his own vision. The Assembly of Experts' draft received an overwhelming endorsement in a national referendum.[180] The final version stripped the presidency of specific authority and ceded the dominant role in the new state to the *faqih*. In this way, the Constitution enshrined dual authority as one of the most basic principles of the Islamic Republic.

With respect to the economy, the Constitution contained language that offered powerful validation to radical leftist dogma. The document's framers sought to establish a distinctly Islamic – as opposed to capitalist or socialist – economy, but in the absence of any real debate or

---

[178] Khomeini's conceptualization of an Islamic state tended to win the most support from Iran's second-tier clerical élites, according to Akhavi (1980), p. 176, whereas many senior ayatollahs expressed both doctrinal and tactical reservations. In most cases, however, even these individuals remained silent rather than actively opposed to the revered Khomeini, although subsequent profound disputes over policy issues and Islamic laws (for example, in the case of the land reform legislation) drew them into more resolute opposition to the regime. Said Amir Arjomand cites early objections to *velayet-e faqih* from Grand Ayatollahs Kho'i, Qomi, and Shariat-madari, as well as Ayatollahs Baha' al-Din Mahallati, Sadeq Ruhani, Ahmad Zanjani, Ali Tehran, and Mortaza Ha'eri Yazdi. See Said Amir Arjomand, *The Turban for the Crown: The Islamic Revolution in Iran* (New York and Oxford: Oxford University Press, 1988), pp. 155–6.

[179] *International Herald Tribune*, October 24, 1979, as quoted in Bakhash (1984), p. 86.

[180] However, as Asghar Schirazi notes, 15,758,956 voters took part in the December 1979 constitutional referendum, substantially less than the 20,439,908 Iranians who cast ballots in the March polling to approve "an Islamic Republic" (out of a potential electorate of 21 million). This decline can be interpreted as the inevitable diminution of revolutionary mobilization, or the decline in Khomeini's sway in his first eight months of leadership (Schirazi's construal), or some combination thereof. See Schirazi (1997), p. 52.

consideration as to what that might entail, the theocracy's legal framework evolved to satisfy the revolutionary coalition's inchoate opposition to the West. However, in establishing the economy's legal framework, the clerical faction already appreciated that its primary competition derived not from Bazargan's Provisional Government and the liberal nationalists, but rather from the secular Left. Mohsen Nourbakhsh, one of the few economists who was awarded received a senior post in the new regime, commented that "the leftist groups were very active in both the universities and the press and their influence was apparent as the Revolutionary Council debated the constitution."[181]

This dynamic helped shaped a constitution replete with populist jargon and riven with contradictions on the economy. Consistent with the Revolutionary Council's far-reaching expropriation and nationalization program already under way, the Constitution sought to enshrine a redistributive economy. While economic issues are referenced throughout the document, chapter IV (articles 43 through 55) presented the fundamental configuration of the new economic order. Notably, the opening provisions reflect an idealized and aggrandized estimation of the postrevolutionary state: The government was charged with providing "basic necessities for all citizens," including employment, "with a view to attaining full employment." Extravagance, exploitation, and monopolies were prohibited. Moreover, the Constitution directed that the economy should facilitate individual engagement in "intellectual, political, and social activities leading to all-round development of his self, to take active part in leading the affairs of the country, improve his skills, and to make full use of his creativity."

The constitutional provision most relevant for Iran's postrevolutionary economic development is article 44, which divides the country's economic system into three distinct spheres: state, cooperative, and private sectors. Of the three, the state sector is by far the most expansive, comprising "all large-scale and mother industries, foreign trade, major minerals, banking, insurance, power generation, dams, and large-scale irrigation networks, radio and television, post, telegraph and telephone services, aviation, shipping, roads, railroads and the like." The Constitution also assigns the state control over "public wealth" – broadly described as "uncultivated or abandoned land, mineral deposits, seas, lakes, rivers and other public waterways, mountains, valleys, forests, marshlands, natural

---

[181] *Iqtisad-i siysasi-i jumhuriya islami*, p. 66.

forests, unenclosed pastures, legacies without heirs, property of undetermined ownership, and public property recovered from usurpers." Cooperatives were designated as producers and distributors, whereas the private sector was accorded – almost as an afterthought – "supplementary" activities in agriculture, industry, trade, and services. The interpretation and implementation of article 44 emerged as central elements in the debate over Iran's economic policy.

The constitutional framework included vague admonitions that the economy must be independent of "foreign domination" and must strive to eliminate "poverty and deprivation."[182] Article 44 also restricted the ability of foreign entities to invest in Iran. In addition, Article 81 prohibited the "granting of concessions to foreigners or the formation of companies or institutions dealing with commerce, industry, agriculture, service, or mineral extraction." Some have interpreted this article as precluding any foreign investment in the nation's economic activities, while others have argued that it limited foreigners to a minority stake in Iranian ventures.[183]

Despite the salience of leftist ideology within the revolutionary coalition, the revision of the draft Constitution fell to a defender of private property, Ayatollah Beheshti. Beheshti's prior writings argued that "legitimate" wealth warranted protection under Islamic law and tradition because it stemmed from human efforts; however, during his brief stint in power, Beheshti embraced more radical policies. Still, his influence and that of other traditionalist clerics who participated in the constitutional redrafting explain Articles 46 and 47, which contain mild guarantees for private property.

For the most part, however, the economy was an abstraction for the assembly and failed to engage their convictions with the same force as political and cultural decisions. "When the constitution was being worked out by the assembly of experts, I remember Bani-Sadr telling me that on far-reaching economic reforms you could easily get the mullahs' 'yes.' A friend of mine – he is now in prison – inserted an article in the constitution about the ecology, it was easy to convice [sic] the *mullah*s to put an article into the constitution to protect the environment. But you had to discuss for ten or twenty hours, to no conclusion, whether a man's shirt had to have long sleeves to be Islamically acceptable. These things

[182] Amuzegar 1993.   [183] Khajehpour in Esposito and Ramazani, eds. (2001), p. 95.

used to consume these people so much that major national problems were not seriously addressed, with devastating consequences."[184]

In addition to setting the legal parameters for postrevolutionary economic activity, the Constitution's text and the process for its approval impacted the economy by institutionalizing inherent tensions within the structure of the new state. The constitutional framework cemented ideological and turf battles between the parliament and the Council of Guardians (Shura-ye Negahban), a twelve-member body empowered to review all legislation for conformity with Islam *and* the Constitution. For revolutionary Iran's first decade, conflicts between these two legislative bodies over economic issues and state prerogatives stymied development and nearly paralyzed the state.

THE AFTERMATH OF PROVISIONALISM

The demise of Bazargan's government and Bani Sadr's January 1980 election as the Islamic Republic's first president may have been expected to quell the internecine conflict within the revolutionary coalition; instead, the transition only exacerbated the frictions. Bani Sadr saw his victory as a vindication of his intellect and charisma, and as a mandate for his sweeping transformation of the new government. The Islamic Republican Party – established to consolidate clerical authority – perceived the situation rather differently. Antagonism between the new president and the clerics who controlled the IRP, particularly Ayatollah Beheshti, was already high. Bani Sadr's leftist streak, manifested by his commitment to state control of the economy, aroused the suspicions of clerical traditionalists, particularly as he increased links with the Mojahedin and other leftist groups, while others were wary of his relative moderation on the U.S. Embassy crisis and his opposition to postrevolutionary purges. Mostly, however, it was Bani Sadr's transparent ambition and botched attempts at asserting his leadership that won him the enmity of other contenders within the increasingly narrow political élite.

Precluded by Khomeini from offering a cleric as a candidate, the IRP reluctantly supported Bani Sadr in the presidential election, although Beheshti assiduously promoted alternative candidates. Having lost this first contest, Beheshti organized to ensure that the Islamists retained tight control over other nascent institutions and managed to secure a dominant

---

[184] Ali Reza Nobari, "Ali Reza Nobari: 'We Started to Feel Cold Sweat on Our Brows,'" *MERIP Reports* 104: (March–April 1982), p. 16.

presence in parliament and push forward his handpicked candidate for prime minister, Mohammad Ali Reja'i. Bani Sadr sought in vain to buttress his position by cultivating a closer relationship with leftists as well as the armed forces. However, by publicizing his differences with the clerics, Bani Sadr found himself overpowered and outmaneuvered by Beheshti and the IRP. The party effectively controlled the cabinet, the Revolutionary Guard, the broadcasting services, as well as the judiciary and purge committees, which were carrying out a low-level campaign of terror. Seeking an institutional power base, Bani Sadr took an assertive stance on economic policies and managed to install key protégés in key economic posts, including Ali Reza Nobari at the helm of the Central Bank.

When he accepted Bazargan's resignation, Khomeini called upon the Revolutionary Council to assume overt responsibility and "perform these duties, particularly those relating to the cleansing of the government and the welfare of the poor and the homeless in a completely revolutionary and decisive manner."[185] This directive helped Bani Sadr advance one major element of the radicals' economic agenda, state control over foreign trade. His administration put forward a draft bill that would gradually nationalize all foreign trade. Although it received parliamentary approval in March 1980, the issue quickly stalled amid deep philosophical objections from the Guardians' Council, which advocated more traditional economic interpretation.

For Iran's leftists, state control over foreign trade represented an integral dimension of the revolutionary struggle. "Until the first item of the section 44 of the constitution is implemented, economic independence is impossible," MP Musavi Boujnordi argued in 1982.[186] As with other contested economic policies, such as land reform, the debate over foreign trade proved to be protracted and fierce. Both issues evoked fierce passions among their partisans and the complex historical legacy of a country still transitioning from decentralized feudalism to a modern nation-state. At their core, the two issues hinged on the fundamental limits of state authority and the legitimacy of private property, issues that continue to provoke debate within Iran.

---

[185] "Iran's Civil Government Out; Hostages Face Death Threat; Oil Exports Believed Halted," *New York Times*, November 7, 1979, p. A1.

[186] Musavi Boujnourdi, "Nationalization of Foreign Trade," *Iran Times*, November 20, 1982, p. 8.

As part of its assertion of greater economic control, the new regime also sought to exert direct influence in other arenas that had previously been subject to market forces, such as foreign exchange. Here, ideological preferences and suspicions were reinforced by the rapid deterioration of Iran's trade and diplomatic relations with Europe and America. The shah had created a unitary exchange system, with virtual parity between the rial's official rate and its free market price; the Islamic Republic opted to craft a multiple-rate system that would evolve significantly during the ensuing three decades. The revolutionaries saw the exchange rate as a useful tool of reinforcing government preferences for resource allocation; the multiple exchange rate regime was enacted with the goal of allocating resources to sectors of the economy viewed as more desirable or necessary by the government. For example, soon after the introduction of the multiple rate system, the goal of increasing Iran's nonoil exports spurred the granting of subsidized rates for foreign exchange receipts in that sector.

The initial break of the unitary exchange rate occurred shortly after the shah's departure, and by August 1980 it had fractured further. This began with a bonus for repatriation of foreign currency earned by Iranian workers abroad (first 115 rials per dollar, later 150, versus the official rate of 70.5 rials per dollar). Targeted exchange rates were created to facilitate particular transactions, such as the requirement that nonoil exporters sell foreign currency proceeds to the banking system at a rate 11 percent higher than the official one. Soon, a tiered system based on the state's priorities emerged; imports of goods and services deemed less essential were shifted to higher exchange rates.

The clerics' successful ascendance had a range of other social and economic implications. During this period, Iranian leaders undertook other steps that would have a formative influence on Iran's long-term economic conditions. These included the approach to women's legal rights and status, a central tenet of the religious forces' worldview. As a result, the Pahlavi era family code – which raised the legal age for marriage and assured women greater authority on divorce and polygamous marriage – was abrogated quickly after the shah's departure. In its place, the minimum age of marriage was lowered to nine for girls, and both polygamy and *siqeh*, or temporary marriage, were legalized without constraint.[187] Rigorous enforcement of Islamic dress code began by mid-1980, with the veil mandated for all public sector positions.

---

[187] Inequities in the family law, in particular, as well as other restrictions within the political system, are severely detrimental to women and are the focus of today's activism among

In addition to these changes, the revolutionaries effectively disbanded the shah's family planning initiatives. Consistent with Khomeini's preferences, the religious leadership extolled the virtues of early marriage and large families, inveighed against family planning as a Western conspiracy, and sought to influence young women's options in ways that directly impacted family size. And yet "the new regime did not formulate an explicit population policy" in its earliest years.[188] On the basis of his 1980 *fatwa* on contraception, the Ministry of Health assumed responsibility for family planning activities, and contraceptives remained both legal and free.[189] However, logistical constraints on access to birth control resulting from sanctions and the war, together with the regime's pronatalist policies, combined to generate Iran's postrevolutionary baby boom.

As the power struggle intensified, it prompted the revolutionaries to undertake more dramatic social policies to shore up their base. The most dramatic was the cultural revolution launched in April 1980. Iran's universities, which had become hubs of political activism, were shuttered for the subsequent four years. A semigovernmental organization, the Council for the Cultural Revolution, was established to devise new curricula in cooperation with organizations such as the Center for Cooperation of Seminaries and Universities (Daftar-e Hamkari-ye Hawzeh va Daneshgah). In the short term, the university closures helped elevate ideology and expedite the elimination of leftist groups that held sway among younger Iranians.

In the revolutionary narrative, the cultural revolution was necessary to secure Iran's emancipation and eventual prosperity. In launching this initiative, Khomeini's directive closing the universities stressed that their subordination to foreign interests had diminished their relevance.

We have had universities in our country for fifty years now, and throughout this period, the backbreaking expenditures that have been lavished upon them have been borne by our toiling masses. But we have been unable to attain self-sufficiency in any of the subjects taught in our universities. After fifty years of universities, when someone falls sick, many of our doctors will recommend

---

Iranian women. See Ziba Mir-Hosseini, *Marriage on Trial: A Study of Islamic Family Law: Iran and Morocco Compared* (London: I. B. Tauris, 1993).

[188] Homa Hoodfar, "Devices and desires: population policy and gender roles in the Islamic Republic," *Middle East Report* 190 (September–October 1994), p. 12.

[189] Marie Ladier-Fouladi, "Sociodemographic Changes in the Family and Their Impact on the Sociopolitical Behavior of Youth in Postrevolutionary Iran," in Nabavi (2012), p. 138.

that he go to England for treatment; we do not have doctors that can meet the needs of our people. We have had universities, but we are still dependent on the West for all that a nation needs.... To Islamize the universities means to make them autonomous, independent of West and independent of the East, so that we have an independent country with an independent university system and an independent culture.[190]

CONCLUSION

The paranoia that infected the revolutionary elites was well founded. Opposition to the clerics' nascent domination was beginning to coalesce in ways that directly threatened regime stability. The monarchy's final prime minister, Shahpour Bakhtiar, had assembled a potent infrastructure in exile courtesy of the Pahlavis, other wealthy Iranian exiles, and several Arab states. They joined to back a July 1980 plot organized by former military, Pahlavi officials, and the secular opposition, which might have succeeded had it not been discovered. The revelation of the Nuzhih plot prompted a new round of terror and the eviction of the National Front, one of the revolutionary state's residual ties to the modern middle class. The secular nationalists' struggle collapsed, and after a year, its leadership fled to the West.

Consider the early dilemmas that the Islamic Republic faced: tribal revolts in its provinces, social unrest in its cities, a vicious power struggle among the contenders for power, and eventually a war that sent a long-standing enemy into its cities. The challenges to its survival shaped the state that emerged, particularly its governing institutions and its patterns of authority. The vast philosophical and organizational disparities within the revolutionary coalition perpetuated competition after the shah's ouster, which in turn escalated extremist rhetoric and violence, sacrificing the center of Iranian politics as it invigorated its peripheries. The clergy's victory did not conclude this competition; it merely narrowed its scope. The power struggle remains one of the defining attributes of contemporary Iran.

The postrevolutionary regime has intensified pernicious patterns of state domination of Iran's economic life. The revolution's focus on social justice as a key unifying concept among the disparate interests opposing the shah directly linked its outcome to the welfare of the country's

---

[190] Khomeini, "The Meaning of the Cultural Revolution," *Kayhan-i Hava'i*, April 30, 1980, in Algar, trans. (1981), pp. 295–6, 299.

populace. Over time, the political logic of revolutionary consolidation, the power struggle, and the long, brutal war with Iraq steadily transformed the state's mandate from an ideological one to a material one, and Iran's abundant revenue stream enabled its leaders to embrace this agenda without appreciating the extent to which it would undercut their original source of legitimation.

Twenty years after the revolution, the supreme leader Ali Khamenei mused about the prerevolutionary economy, calling the growth and development achieved by the monarchy a "false solution [that] was adopted by the hireling and traitor Shah." He stressed that "the real solution, all in all, is that a nation should endeavor to stand on its own feet. It should think with its own brain, see things with its own eyes, choose with its own will, and choose only what is useful and beneficial for it."[191]

If this revolution had not occurred, if those thunderous screams had not moved everything in this country ... then God only knows what state our country would be in today. You can take a look at some of the backward countries in Asia or Africa and you can rest assured that we would be in a worse state than them despite our outstanding geographical, climactic and historical positions. This revolution responded to the cry of this country. It rescued this nation and ensured that it would not go over the precipice.[192]

By contrast, the shah until his death remained embittered and bewildered by the revolution's rejection of his vision. "The nation I had led to the threshold of progress, power, and self-confidence lay torn and bleeding. A worn, fanatic old man was repeatedly telling the Iranian people how mean, miserable, and poverty-stricken they were. The women's rights I had so painfully established on a basis of dignity and pride were ground into the dust of the Middle Ages. The many projects I had begun but been unable to complete lay fallow ... A litany of shattered dreams!"[193]

---

[191] Khamenei's speech, delivered on a visit to Gilan province, May 2, 2001, broadcast on Vision of the Islamic Republic of Iran Network 1, 1713 GMT 4 May 2001, FBIS-NES-2001-0505.

[192] Khamenei's speech, delivered on a visit to Gilan province, May 2, 2001, broadcast on Vision of the Islamic Republic of Iran Network 1, 1713 GMT 4 May 2001, FBIS-NES-2001-0505.

[193] Mohammad Reza Pahlavi, *Answer to History* (New York: Stein & Day, 1980), p. 18.

4

The Cost of the Sacred Defense, 1980–1989

Contemporaneous with the postrevolutionary power struggle, the new state faced a series of external threats. The obsessive fear of American intervention was confirmed by the botched April 1980 mission to rescue the hostages. And while Tehran initially maintained slightly better relations with Moscow, these too gradually eroded because of the Soviet occupation of Afghanistan and Iran's 1981–2 crackdown on the Tudeh Party. Closer to home, after an initial welcome elsewhere in the Muslim world, the new regime's honeymoon quickly ended; between the hostage crisis and Khomeini's provocative rhetoric, Iran's neighbors grew justifiably alarmed at Tehran's promise to "export the revolution." The Islamic Republic found itself profoundly isolated as a result of its own statements and policies, and isolation only heightened its leadership's paranoia and hostility toward the international system.

In September 1980, after months of deteriorating relations and low-level violence in Khuzestan and along the Shatt al-Arab naval passage, Saddam Hussein invaded Iran and began what would become the longest and bloodiest war between two states since the Korean conflict. At home, the revolutionary state remained caught in the throes of turmoil on the streets and increasingly violent competition within the establishment, exacerbated by the July 1980 failed coup attempt.

The Iraqi invasion changed everything for Iran. It was an existential conflict that required a Herculean effort to sustain – an exigency complicated by the state's isolation and its leaders' conviction that the invasion represented only the first front in an international conspiracy to extinguish the revolutionary regime. From the outset, the conflict violently transformed the Iranian economy – denying the new government key ports, devastating thousands of square miles of territory, leaving millions internally displaced, altering export routes, destroying refining and petrochemical facilities, and heightening fears about the new state's survival.

Yet, despite the exigencies of the war effort, the political competition initiated during (and left unresolved by) the revolution raged on. Fierce disputes among the various factions over the nature of the state and its economic policies only intensified. Throughout the 1980s, Iranian politicians remained locked in internecine ideological battles, in which matters of economic policy featured prominently as a proxy for broader differences among the revolutionary coalition. The economy also featured prominently in the campaign waged against Iran by Iraq's allies, whose enthusiasm for their chosen partisan was dwarfed by their eagerness to incapacitate Tehran.

Whenever the Islamic Republic's obituary is written, the war will stand as its most consequential chapter. The war facilitated the revolution's consolidation, the assertion of state authority in the economy and society, the forcible revival of an economy on the brink of collapse, as well as the intensification of ideological tensions that fractured the revolutionary coalition on economic policy. These debates revealed a basic schism within the Islamic Republic's leadership, long after the religious forces outflanked the secular elements of the postrevolutionary coalition – a divide between those who saw the revolution's imperatives as fundamentally redistributional and those who sought to preserve the traditional protections within Islamic law for private property and free markets.

During this period, the fundamental framework of the postrevolutionary economy was written into law, but so were the precursors of reform. During the war, the Islamic Republic's fundamental legitimacy became inherently interrelated with the regime's success in delivering economic opportunities. As Iran's revolution fought for its survival, its leaders were increasingly forced to contend with the economic implications of their policy choices and articulate their claim to a popular mandate in terms of development achievements in addition to religious dogma. Such a shift was a natural part of revolutionary consolidation, but the war expedited and amplified the rationalization process in ways that continue to shape the state's political economy.

THE OUTBREAK OF WAR

From the outset, Iran's revolutionaries saw their uprising as a transnational phenomenon, and their rhetoric and ambitions set them at odds with their neighbors, even those like Saddam Hussein whose relations with Tehran had long been strained by ideological, territorial, and coethnic disputes. The revolution quickly exacerbated these frictions. The Islamic Republic's provocations held particular resonance within Iraq – a Shi'a majority state led by a radical Sunni Arab nationalist, a land that had been Khomeini's home for most of his fifteen-year exile. Najaf's leading *ulema* welcomed Iran's religious revolution. Such ferment unnerved Iraq's ambitious, paranoid, and brutal leadership, who moved against their own Shi'a population and then trained their sights on the provocateurs themselves. Through mid-1980, Baghdad and Tehran traded epithets and stoked mutual resentments.

Whatever threat Baghdad may have perceived from Iran's nascent theocracy, the decision to strike Tehran also reflected Saddam's innate opportunism. Despite Iran's audacious rhetoric, the revolution rejected the shah's military posture and turned inward, and the postrevolutionary institutional collapse and expulsions intensified these trends. With Iran enmeshed in domestic disputes, its military capabilities withering under purges, Baghdad perceived a historic chance. Iran's chaos created an opening to permanently vanquishing its nemesis and seizing the helm of a region in flux. Beyond regional primacy, Saddam had a more immediate objective – redressing what he saw as an unsatisfactory maritime border between the two countries and absorbing southern Iran's oil-rich, Arab-populated territories.[1]

With his trademark recklessness and conceit, Saddam abrogated the 1975 treaty that had previously settled the Shatt's status, and on September 22, 1980, launched an air and ground assault into southwestern Iran. Iraqi forces quickly seized Khorramshahr and surrounded Khuzestan's major cities. In the initial assaults, Iran's acting oil minister was captured while visiting Iran's Abadan refinery to inspect the damages. In November, Saddam launched a second front in Kurdistan, already home to a bitter insurgency against the new regime.

The Iraqi incursion caught Tehran totally unaware. Iran's military was near collapse, and the new state had only the most tentative grip on its coercive forces. There were dozens of armed paramilitary groups, loosely

---

[1] Even as Iran sought to appeal to fellow Shi'a and subvert its neighbors, Iraq had an established campaign to instigate ethnic separatism in Khuzestan. See Ibrahim Anvari Tehrani, "Iraqi Attitudes and the 1975 Agreement," in *The Iran-Iraq War: The Politics of Aggression*, ed. Farhang Rajaee (Gainesville: University Press of Florida, 1993), pp. 19–21.

affiliated with individual clerics and organizations, and the leadership prioritized the political reliability of remaining units more than their capabilities.[2] Despite these handicaps, the Islamic Republic faced the challenge rather than simply collapse. A nation still recovering from revolution rallied around its new leaders, who in turn used the war to consolidate their power and to oust their remaining rivals.

For Iranian leaders, the invasion confirmed their paranoia and fulfilled their anticipation of an American military intervention to undo the revolution. "Iran has tried to sever all its relations with this Great Satan and it is for this reason that it now finds wars imposed upon it," Khomeini proclaimed after the first incursion. "America has urged Iraq to spill the blood of our young men, and it has compelled the countries that are subject to its influence to boycott us economically in the hope of defeating us. Unfortunately, most Asian countries are also hostile to us. Let the Muslim nations be aware that Iran is a country effectively at war with America, and that our martyrs – the brave young men of our army and the Revolutionary Guards – are defending Iran and the Islam we hold dear against America."[3]

The war's demands had unanticipated consequences for Iran's strategic posture that countered expectations that the fledgling revolution would be quickly extinguished. Iran's difficulties in obtaining spare parts meant that Tehran struggled to mount an effective campaign against Baghdad. At the time of the Iraqi invasion, Iran's tank fleet was only 30 percent operational, its helicopter force was grounded, and its officer corps had been devastated by purges and flight.[4] The revolutionaries' antipathy toward the West had prompted the cancellation of contracts that might have averted the shortages, including a British-built munitions complex near Isfahan that was almost completed when Tehran abandoned it. These deficits persisted throughout the conflict; as late as 1986, Iran had only a few dozen operational fighter aircraft.[5]

The imbalance in Iranian and Iraqi arms imports amplified over time; Iraqi arms purchases eclipsed Tehran's by as much as six to one.[6] Beyond

---

[2] Several months before the war's outbreak, Prime Minister Rajai declared that a "'*maktabi*' [Islamically oriented] army is preferable to a victorious army." *New York Times*, January 5, 1980.

[3] Khomeini, "Message to the Pilgrims," *Jumhuri-yi Islami*, September 13, 1980, from Algar (1981), p. 305.

[4] Chubin and Tripp (1988), p. 33.   [5] Cordesman (1987), p. 115.

[6] Shahram Chubin, "The Last Phase of the Iran-Iraq War: From Stalemate to Ceasefire," *Third World Quarterly* 11:2 (April 1989), p. 6

quantity, Iraq benefited from its ability to purchase integrated packages, whereas Tehran had to hunt down spare parts for U.S. weapons systems on the black market.[7] Delays, scams, additional layers of corruption, middlemen, and supply chains that were not interoperable raised the overall costs to Tehran exponentially. However, resupply demands compelled new Iranian trade ties, and eventually, corresponding political and security relationships – forcing Tehran to abandon its early autarkic delusions. Iran's military commanders gained a crash course in smuggling and began to develop a sophisticated conventional arms industry to compensate for their inability to import materiel.

The invasion's impact on Iran's domestic policies and politics was equally considerable. By mid-1981, Iraq occupied ten thousand square miles in Iranian territory, including Khorramshahr's key port, forcing the Islamic Republic to truck imports overland via Turkey and destroying much of Iran's refining and petrochemical facilities. Over time, 2 million Iranians fled their homes. The war and the internal power struggle heightened fears of political instability and exacerbated financial concerns initially prompted by rumors of the Islamization of the banking system, provoking a run on bank deposits.

Despite the war's toll, Iran's economy rebounded in the early years. In 1982, Khamenei proclaimed that "the country is in a very pleasant economic situation."[8] Oil production, while substantially lower than its 1976 height, rallied from 700,000 barrels per day (bpd) in November 1980 to 2.3 mbpd in 1983, and revolutionary disruptions had significantly escalated prices. The revolutionary regime paid off most of the Pahlavi era debts, and, through smuggling and ingenuity born of desperation, managed to create a robust domestic defense-industrial complex. Private merchants managed to thrive despite upheaval, restrictions, and government intervention. During the new regime's first three years, the private sector's share of imports increased over the previous three years, from 49 percent to 64 percent, as entrepreneurship revived itself.[9] Allies such as Commerce Minister Habibollah Asgharowladi helped merchants secure prominent roles in the new state-run distribution networks. Chaos and conflict helped generate dynamism, which in turn reinforced the commitment of Iran's more dogmatic ideologues to the revolutionary ideals of self-sufficiency and autonomy.

---

[7] Cordesman (1987), p. 27.

[8] R. W. Apple Jr., "Rebuilding Iran's Economy," *New York Times*, November 15, 1982.

[9] Mozaffari (1991),p. 386.

Still, even as industry rebounded, political skirmishes raged and the government had to contend with the war's massive disruptions. The desperate effort to ramp up production of war materiel further exacerbated existing inefficiencies, and the conflict intensified Iran's difficulties in obtaining needed imports. Car manufacturing declined, and even after Tehran found a new supplier for producing domestically assembled Peykans, financial problems resulted in repeated layoffs and production far below capacity.[10]

The war also helped justify the expansionary monetary policy initiated after the revolution, when the nationalization and merger of banks eroded public confidence in the sector. The Central Bank "provided liquidity to ensure its survival ... (even as) the sharp decline in oil prices increased the government's need to borrow from the banking system to finance its deficits."[11] By the same token, the war also encouraged a reliance on deficit financing that exacerbated inflation, government overspending, and public underinvestment.[12]

In late 1982, after mounting import bills and falling oil revenues eroded the country's foreign currency reserves, the government established the Foreign Exchange Allocation Commission, tasked with distributing the nation's limited foreign currency resources to sectors essential for wartime priorities. The state assumed far-reaching control over foreign trade, and four-fifths of imports of "essential" goods were allocated to public enterprises and the rest to approved, highly regulated private importers.[13] Most basic imports were rationed, an array of price controls were instituted, and certain items were banned as "nonessential" because of the limited foreign exchange reserves, though many were legalized after the 1988 cease-fire.

The elaborate rationing scheme extended to all food except fresh fruits and vegetables. This enabled Tehran to prevent the collapse of the state treasury. Instead, wartime rationing became a massive new government commitment. For consumers, this meant long lines, high prices, and an explicit relationship between the state and the distribution of material needs. By 1986, food subsidies alone constituted 5 percent of the state's budget and were increasing by 10 percent annually.[14] The wartime price

---

[10] Behzad Yaghmaian, "Recent Developments in the Political Economy of Iran: 'The Triangle Crisis,'" in Bina, ed., p. 175.

[11] Zangeneh, MEP 1998.

[12] Khajehpour in Esposito and Ramazani, eds. (2001), p. 95; Valibeigi, pp 62–3.

[13] Amuzegar (1993), pp. 142, pp. 162–3.   [14] Amirahmadi (1990), p 166.

supports proved one of the most toxic elements of the postrevolutionary political economy – a politically intractable issue despite broad consensus that the costs were unsustainable. The price of wheat, relative to the basket of typical consumer goods, declined by 90 percent between 1980 and 1993, contributing to the thirty kilogram per person increase in bread consumption during the revolution's first decade.[15]

The war also consolidated state control over the country's industrial sector to ensure production of spare parts and other military necessities. During the war, the wave of nationalizations expanded: Fifteen insurance companies in June 1981 and all heavy industries formally expropriated the following month. Iran's dualistic institutional structure contributed to the factional gridlock. The state takeover of the banking system moved forward as well, with the 1983 law on interest-free banking.

It was not simply the public sector that expanded under the fog of war; Iran's newly created parastatals exploited the permissive environment to entrench their roles. The Jihad-e Sazandegi, or Construction Crusade, swelled to encompass forty thousand to fifty thousand employees engaged in infrastructure development and construction. By 1984, the Jihad had built or repaired nearly half the country's prerevolutionary road capacity.[16] Within another few years, the Jihad began broad-based provision of water, electrification, and other infrastructure throughout rural Iran.[17] Several other *bonyad*s became active in the war effort,[18] including the Bonyad-e Umur Muhajirin-e Tahmili (Foundation for the Affairs of the Imposed War Refugees).

The war also persuaded Khomeini to expand the Bonyad-e Mostazafan's mandate to include responsibility for war casualties. This elevated the foundation's position within the social order, as the protector of those who had given their lives for the regime, and accelerated its consolidation and expansion. In early 1987, Khomeini ordered that all properties with uncertain ownership be placed under state control, instructing that these assets be distributed among the foundations and other revolutionary organs to benefit the war's victims.

The parastatals' expansion exacerbated growing problems for the new regime: institutional redundancy, competition, and waste. The wartime

[15] Karshenas and Pesaran (1995).
[16] Ahmad Sharbatoghlie, *Urbanization and Regional Disparities in Post-Revolutionary Iran* (Boulder, CO: Westview Press, 1991), pp. 75–6.
[17] Ehsani (2006), p. 89.
[18] Kevan Harris, "The Imam's Blue Boxes," *MER* 257 (Winter 2010), pp. 22–3.

ration system enhanced the role of *komiteh*s and local mosques, and judicial institutions and prisons proliferated. These same factors hindered sound government management of the challenges confronting it. An attempt to revive central planning crashed and burned in 1983, with the demise of legislation proposing a new five-year plan. The bill was deliberately crafted to appeal to revolutionary sensibilities but retained the ambitious development targets that characterized the prerevolutionary planning process.

Spiraling inflation fed perceptions that merchants were exploiting the turmoil and prompted a backlash directed toward the *bazaar* and more activist government efforts to manage prices and supply. Newspapers inveighed against capitalists and hoarders, a special court on guild affairs was established to enforce price controls, and as early as 1983, leaders such as Rafsanjani chided the *bazaar* merchants to adhere to government regulations on pricing.[19] In 1983, Commerce Minister Asgharowladi attempted to lift price controls on consumer goods including rice; the resulting spike in inflation prompted a quick policy reversal and Asgharowladi's resignation.[20] Also ousted from the cabinet was Labor Minister Ahmad Tavakkoli, after efforts to advance legislation restricting labor rights.

ENDING THE SIEGE: THE ALGIERS ACCORDS AND THE HOSTAGE DENOUEMENT

As the hostage crisis continued, what began as a moral and strategic cause for Tehran had become a financial and economic siege. The episode had already fulfilled one of its objectives: Islamists had attained the upper hand in the domestic power struggle. And the shah's July 1980 death meant that another goal was now permanently out of reach. Meanwhile, the magnitude of the country's economic challenges could not be ignored as the U.S. embargo and pricing disputes eroded anticipated oil revenues and forced drastic reductions in government spending.[21] Most importantly, the Iraqi invasion and the start of what would be a long war had already begun to reorder Iran's priorities. "Is the hostage issue more important than the slaughter and the crimes of Saddam's regime in our country?" Rafsanjani demanded in an effort to prod the Majlis to support negotiations. Ultimately, a consensus emerged, crassly described by the

---

[19] Keshavarzian (2007), pp. 161–2.   [20] Baktiari (1996), p. 93.
[21] Reuters, "Iran Reports Big Oil-Income Loss," *New York Times*, June 13, 1980.

individual who would lead Tehran's negotiations, "The hostages were like a fruit from which all the juice had been squeezed out."[22]

By September 1980, the standoff was ripe for denouement, and the remaining issues were mainly economic. Shortly before Saddam struck, Khomeini declared his conditions for ending the hostage siege, and three of his four demands concerned the shah's property, Iran's frozen assets, and its outstanding debts.[23] Correspondingly, the negotiations that produced the January 1981 Algiers Accords devoted considerable effort to accounting issues and the mechanics of settling the two countries' outstanding financial disputes.

One of the most important, and inventive, aspects of the hostage crisis was the carefully crafted sequencing of reciprocal arrangements that enabled the eventual agreement to overcome the profound mistrust between the two parties. Still, even after months of intricate discussions, the financial issues and logistical impediments created a series of last-minute snags that nearly scuttled the agreement altogether. In the final weeks, Tehran publicly rejected agreed-upon terms, instead demanding a $24 billion escrow fund to cover the return of the shah's personal assets. As then-Deputy Secretary of State Warren Christopher, who led the final talks, commented retrospectively, "implementation of the [financial] agreement involved multiple acts of faith on both sides. The Iranians entrusted enormous fund transfers to others. The banks, meanwhile, were willing to pay over $5.6 billion into an escrow account on the basis of a garbled payment instruction from Iran and an order from a lame-duck Secretary of the Treasury, despite the fact that Iran had refused to sign a technical annex to the escrow agreement."[24]

Somewhat surprisingly, although the war ultimately hastened Tehran's efforts to end the siege, the Iranians did not press Washington for arms or spare parts. U.S. officials anticipated just such a demand, and in fact had offered and were prepared to accept such a demand, at least in modest terms. This was not an oversight, but rather a deliberate decision by Iran's radicals. The IRP "saw an arms relationship [with Washington] as the thin end of the wedge, or a new umbilical cord which would drag Iran down again into a position of dependency, and more important, give

---

[22] Shaul Bakhash, *The Reign of Ayatollahs* (New York: Basic Books, 1990), p. 149.
[23] In addition to these three demands related to Iran's economy, Khomeini insisted upon a nonintervention pledge by Washington.
[24] Christopher, "Introduction," in Christopher et. al. (1985), p. 16.

the military real clout domestically."[25] Their real sense of threat was directed at the country's commander in chief, Bani Sadr, whose public revelations about this unfortunate omission precipitated his removal. This would not be the last time that the clerical leadership put factional advantage ahead of national interest to the detriment of the country's security and development.

In the final weeks of the ordeal, Iran's approach became even more erratic and opaque. Tehran's final proposal, put forward on January 15, 1981, was unexpectedly accommodating and included better financial terms than the Iranians had previously advanced, notably the decision to pay off all of its outstanding loans from U.S. banks, almost $5 billion. Washington interpreted this surprising shift as an indication of Iranian urgency to conclude the standoff; for Tehran, in fact, it reflected the intensifying power struggle between the clerics and the leftists. The leftists understood that Khomeini used the crisis to entrench his authority; they also appreciated the resolution would sideline them further.[26] That supposition was not inaccurate – within the next six months, Bani Sadr and his allies had been ousted.

Throughout the crisis, Washington was understandably anxious to prevent either the perception or the reality that the United States had effectively paid a ransom to Iran's revolutionaries for the release of its diplomats. In explaining the terms of the eventual deal, the State Department spokesperson emphasized, "Iran is not getting one dime of U.S. money ... the basic exchange is we're getting back what they took from us and giving back to them what we took from them."[27] Christopher later argued that the Algiers Accords succeeded in "preserving American honor by returning only frozen assets and thus not paying blackmail."[28] However it may be couched, it is undeniable that the release of the hostages and the resolution of the first, fierce American-Iranian skirmish were predicated upon a financial deal. The Tribunal met for the first time on July 1, 1980, at the Hague in the Netherlands, where it has continued to function until this day.[29]

---

[25] Chubin and Tripp (1988), p. 207.
[26] Robert Bennett, "U.S. Banks Deny Responsibility for Snag in Freeing of Hostages," *New York Times*, January 20, 1981, p. A1.
[27] Bowden (2006), p. 577.
[28] Warren Christopher and Richard M. Mosk, "The Iranian Hostage Crisis and the Iran-U.S. Claims Tribunal: Implications for International Dispute Resolution and Diplomacy," *Pepperdine Dispute Resolution Law Journal* 7:2 (2007), p. 173.
[29] See the discussion of sanctions in *Chapter 9* for additional details on the Tribunal.

Several aspects of the Algiers Accords remain controversial both within Iran and in the United States. Many Iranian politicians expressed dissatisfaction with the deal's failure to repatriate all the frozen assets, as per the parliament's November 1980 directive. Iran's chief negotiator, Behzad Nabavi, was criticized for having sacrificed $12 to $40 billion.[30]

CONFLICT ON THE HOME FRONT: A LEADERSHIP AT WAR WITH ITSELF

Meanwhile, internal violence remained a devastating factor throughout the war's early years; much of this stemmed from the ongoing purges against left-wing groups. With both sides continuously raising the stakes, government institutions literally warred with one another through early 1981, while gangs of *hezbollahi*s and revolutionary tribunals unleashed vicious attacks and the state strained to mount a defense against the Iraqi invasion.

Bani Sadr waged a pitched battle for influence from his January 1980 election to the weak presidency, only to find his assiduous self-promotion blocked or undermined by the IRP and its Majlis supporters. Unable to gain parliamentary support for his preferred prime ministerial nominee, Bani Sadr was forced to accept Mohammad Ali Raja'i, whom he derided as incompetent. Even at this early stage, the infighting directly impacted economic decision making; the Majlis tried to take away Bani Sadr's discretionary budget and denied his Central Bank governor permission to represent the country at the annual International Monetary Fund conference in Washington.[31]

The war briefly seemed to give Bani Sadr a new lease on life. Although the Constitution gave the supreme leader command over the country's armed forces, Khomeini delegated that authority to Bani Sadr, who threw himself into the part with gusto and frequent trips to the front. However, clerical machinations soon impinged upon this role, with the establishment of the Supreme Defense Council enabling the clerics – and the Revolutionary Guard – to usurp the mantle of leadership of the war effort. As his influence waned, Bani Sadr increasingly aligned himself with the Mojahedin-e Khalq, the only serious threat to the Islamists' monopolization. The protracted power struggle within the system became

---

[30] Baktiari (1996), p. 156.   [31] Bakhash (1986), p. 130; Baktiari (1996), p. 74.

increasingly costly, and on June 11, 1981, Bani Sadr was officially deemed an enemy of the state.

Once again, rather than subduing the conflict, the elimination of yet another of the clerics' rivals only escalated Iran's turmoil. Bani Sadr quickly went underground and then fled Iran, provoking a cataclysmic round of violence that decimated the new state's leadership as well as the remaining opposition parties. Within days after the president's dismissal, the Mojhideen accelerated the postrevolutionary civil war. On June 27, 1981, Ali Khamenei was the victim of an assassination attempt. The subsequent day, a bomb blast ripped through an IRP meeting, killing Ayatollah Beheshti and dozens of other senior politico-clergymen, including four cabinet ministers and twenty-seven Majlis representatives.

These developments provoked a crisis of epic proportions within the clerical élite; the revolution's survival was at stake, as was its leaders' security. They responded with a brutal purge, including more than two thousand executions, which only escalated the violence. A number of officials, including key elements of the new government's economic team, chose to flee, including the first postrevolutionary oil minister and Central Bank governor. The government had begun to recover when another explosion on August 30 took the lives of Reja'i, who had been elected to replace Bani Sadr as president, and Prime Minister Mohammad Javad Bahonar. Many other key figures were killed over the ensuing months, including a key IRP leader, Hassan Ayat; Ayatollah Madani, Khomeini's representative in Tabriz; and the Provisional Government's defense minister, Mostafa Chamram. As terrorism culled leading figures in the revolutionary movement, the war also began to take its toll, with casualties including the head of the armed forces and the sitting defense minister, who were killed in an October 1981 plane crash.

The deaths of Ayatollahs Beheshti and Bahonar, as well as the untimely natural death of Ayatollah Taleqani and the 1979 assassination of Ayatollah Motahhari – another "cleric who might have played a moderating and mediating role" – deprived the Islamic Republic of an array of political actors who were both powerful and pragmatic.[32] Their loss through these acts of violent sabotage not only deprived the leadership of alternative views, but helped to spin the regime into a cycle of increasingly extremist and authoritarian policies, enforced through progressively more violent tactics.

---

[32] James A. Bill, "Power and Religion in Revolutionary Iran," *Middle East Journal* 36:1 (Winter 1982), pp. 37–8.

Into this fluid and fearful situation, three individuals stepped to the fore to guide the country through the war – Ali Khamenei, who quickly won the nascent regime's third presidential election in less than two years; Ali Akbar Hashemi Rafsanjani, who assumed the speakership of the parliament; and Mir Husayn Musavi, a layman who won the parliament's nod for prime minister after Khamenei's first two choices were rejected. Each of these three individuals carved out an important role, representing influential constituencies, on the central questions of the postrevolutionary political economy, and their internecine conflicts helped define the shape of Iran's economy, the tenor of its political culture, and the transformation of the revolutionary mandate.

The political conflict at the top trickled down to Iran's streets. Throughout the war's early years, a severe interpretation of Shi'a doctrine was enforced. "There is no music, no decent television, no good restaurants," an Iranian businessman lamented to a Western reporter in 1982. "I'm not a politician, I'm not a terrorist, I'm not anything. But if I talk about meat prices or pop music or American films, I'm making a political comment and I'm in trouble. I feel as if the life is being slowly squeezed out of me. We had a good country and we were happy people. Now it's all gone, ruined. We'll end up even more dependent on the West, because these people will never be able to run an economy successfully."[33]

A NEW PHASE IN THE WAR, AND IN THE POWER STRUGGLE

Despite unmistakable signals and explicit warnings, Tehran was caught off guard by the initial Iraqi incursion. During the next eight years, the campaign mutated from a defensive to an offensive one, requiring the Islamic government to undertake a complex military, economic, diplomatic, and political program of regime consolidation and state development. In the immediate aftermath of the invasion, however, the task was much simpler and the stakes were even higher – the very survival of Iran as an independent nation.

Tehran began its counterattack by January 1981 and quickly scored impressive gains – liberating Abadan in the spring, and then launching a series of assaults to evict the remaining Iraqi troops. In fierce battles near Dezful and Khorramshahr in mid-1982, Iran succeeded in expelling the invaders and liberating most of the seized oil fields. Various efforts

---

[33] R. W. Apple, "Islamic Iran: Fighting to Be Free of the West," *New York Times*, November 22, 1982.

to mediate the conflict had gained little traction; the two combatants continued to articulate maximalist demands and appeared determined to continue the conflict until absolute victory. The regional and international climate no doubt facilitated the perpetuation of the standoff; Tehran's decision to move into Iraq was emboldened by the Israeli invasion of southern Lebanon, while Baghdad's setbacks prompted more activist U.S. support to Saddam. For their part, Iranian leaders were convinced that Saddam was unredeemable and that peace required his elimination. The next six years would be spent in a doomed effort to prevail on Iraqi territory, a campaign that consolidated the revolution and then left the state in tatters.

From the outset, Iranian leaders had articulated expectations for compensation in their war demands, ranked at the top of the revolutionary state's priorities alongside demands for Saddam Hussein's removal. However, as the conflict shifted in Tehran's favor, Saddam began evincing interest in a cease-fire, and his regional backers sought to facilitate the effort with additional assistance to Baghdad as well as financial feelers to Tehran. In June 1982 – only days after successful Iraqi strikes on Iran's oil export facilities – the newly formed Gulf Cooperation Council proposed a cease-fire, offering a reported $25 billion in reparations to Tehran in exchange for stopping its advances.

The Iranian response was typically opaque. A foreign ministry official visiting Dubai declared that the war had already inflicted a $150 billion toll on Tehran and insisted that Saddam – rather than a third party – assume responsibility for reparations.[34] Khomeini's son Ahmad later wrote that his father opposed the decision to reject the offer and argued that spurning it meant "this war will never end."[35] At the time, however, there was little evidence of such pragmatism from anyone within the power structure; all of the Islamic Republic's senior officials publicly endorsed the shift from defensive to offensive posture.

Khomeini also sought to persuade the country that the revolution's achievements, and the Islamic Republic's establishment, justified the war's human and economic sacrifice, arguing that "the counter-revolutionaries are trying to dishearten the Muslim people of Iran by spreading rumours about shortages of commodities. This is meant to strike a blow against

---

[34] Fred H. Lawson, "Using Positive Sanctions to End International Conflicts: Iran and the Arab Gulf Countries," *Journal of Peace Research* 20:4 (December 1983), p. 314.

[35] Ahmad Khomeini, *Majmu'eh-ye Asar-e Yadgar-e Imam*, Volume 1 (Tehran: 1996), p. 717, as quoted in Moin (1999), p. 249.

your honour. They think that you have lost your dear ones and your young ones for material things and that you served Islam simply for the purpose of filling your stomach."[36]

But even as Khomeini was deriding the presumptive popular desires for "material things," the revolution that he spearheaded turned its focus precisely to these issues, as the power struggle morphed from one centered on the theocratic schism among the postrevolutionary coalition to one in which economic policy decisions emerged as the fiercest areas of contention among the revolutionary élite. The rivalry between the parliament and the executive branch unleashed a new phase in the postrevolutionary power struggle – one that no longer concerned the religious character of the regime, but instead divided the Islamists into fiercely opposing blocs. These factions, loosely conceived as traditional conservatives and radical leftists, shared a belief in the revolution's religious mandate but differed in their interpretation of that objective.

The parliament, which was dominated by radicals in its first two postrevolutionary terms, served as the setting for the fiercest of these debates. This institution took the lead in implementing revolutionary slogans and exploring the underlying contradictions between the ideals of social justice and the constraints of Islamic jurisprudence. The centrality of the Majlis to the forging of a new political economy for Iran is not coincidental; it reflects the institution's legacy, forged during prior periods of domestic debate over economic issues, including the Constitutional Revolution and the oil nationalization.

Beyond the historical parallels, the parliament's pivotal role in shaping economic policy throughout the Islamic Republic's first decade inadvertently helped generate both liberalizing and pragmatic imperatives within the nascent state. As the MPs' push for social justice ran up against the constraints of unelected organizations with a more conservative orientation, the same individuals who once adopted defiantly radical and anti-Western views began to appreciate the utility of democratic values and representative institutions. At the same time, years of deadlock as a result of doctrinal differences on economic policy exhausted some of the most fervent passions among the leadership and facilitated the subsequent embrace of market reforms and greater openness to the world that became evident during the Rafsanjani presidency.

---

[36] Khomeini, *Sahifeh-ye Nur*, Volume 14 (Tehran: 1982), p. 63, as quoted in Moin (1999), p. 254.

During the revolution's early years, these passions helped instigate a fierce contest between these two factions over four core issues of economic policy. The resolution of each of these contests helped clarify and transform the decision-making process and the scope of state authority within Iran. The first concerned the ambitious land reform program that was initiated and then frozen by the Revolutionary Council in 1980. This remained a deeply controversial issue, not simply in the countryside but among the revolutionary élites themselves. Ultimately, the divisions precluded any possibility of rehabilitating the prerevolutionary landlords and exacerbated the existing tensions within the revolutionary coalition. In October 1980, implementation of the Revolutionary Council's expansive edict passed eight months earlier was suspended, and deep differences remained within the cabinet.

By May 1981, the issue reached a boiling point. More than a hundred parliamentarians appealed to Khomeini to reinstate the provisions of the April 1980 Land Reform Law requiring division of large property holdings. As with other economic policy issues, the debate over land reform hinged upon the question of institutional legitimacy and authority. Khomeini's ultimate decision reflected careful maneuver; he refrained from invoking the authority of his office but rather endorsed the power of parliament to enact emergency legislation, so long as it was temporary in duration and subject to review and accountability.[37] This proved to be the beginning of a process of accommodating the requirements of economic management to the constraints of Islamic law and the peculiarities of the postrevolutionary Constitution, which culminated in 1988 with the establishment of a suprainstitution empowered to overrule the canons of both *shari'a* and the Constitution.

In the short term, Khomeini's intercession tilted the precarious factional balance in favor of the Islamic Left. Still, despite his preeminence, the divisions persisted and deepened further, as economic policy making became more mired in ideology and partisanship. Over the ensuing months, land reform advocates pressed the issue to little avail, as the parliament and the government remained at odds. It was not until December 1982 that the parliament passed a new version of the law, one with a less far-reaching scope. This brief respite hardly settled the matter; land reform remained a recurrent bone of contention between left-wing Islamists and their more conservative opponents within the

---

[37] Khadija V. Frings-Hessami, "The Islamic Debate about Land Reform in the Iranian Parliament, 1981–86," *Middle Eastern Studies* 37:4 (October 2001), p. 140.

parliament. In 1986, they went another round and this time, too, the left wing once again prevailed, albeit in less ambitious form than originally envisaged.

The debates over land reform highlighted the uneasy equilibrium between the factions; on the one hand, there was broad-based support for a radically populist economic agenda, but it remained bounded by Khomeini's unwillingness to disregard the constraints of *shari'a* – or the opposition of powerful clerics.[38] The objections to land reform included its impact on clerical landholdings, typically incorporated in Islamic charitable endowments. Traditionalist clerics, including many in the Majlis, maintained that Islamic law empowered only *vaqf* administrators to determine asset disposition and rejected aggressive measures for state appropriation of badly needed urban properties. Similar objections were also raised when the government attempted to institute oversight of *vaqf* property sales.[39] Beyond the ideological disagreements, the early land reform efforts were undermined by the regime's misreading of rural preferences. "The illusion that villages were the repositories of traditional culture contradicted sharply the visceral desire of the rural population to gain access to the modern goods and services that were readily available in the cities."[40]

Ultimately, the tortuous struggle over land reform produced an outcome that favored neither the landlords nor rural villagers. Instead, the only real victor was the state.[41] The battle over land reform encouraged the expansion of institutions outside the realm of the formal government, including peremptory expropriations and revolutionary organs such as the Jehad-e Sazandegi and the Seveners' Commissions.[42] As land was redistributed, loans for new construction were financed by the Bank-e Maskan (Housing Bank) on the basis of referrals from various *bonyad*s and revolutionary organizations.[43]

The second hot-button dispute that splintered Iran's ruling Islamists was the state's role in foreign trade, an issue that served as a proxy for

---

[38] Shaul Bakhash, "The Politics of Land, Law, and Social Justice in Iran." *Middle East Journal* 43:2 (Spring 1989), pp. 199–200.

[39] See Asghar Schirazi, *The Constitution of Iran Politics and the State in the Islamic Republic* (London: I. B. Tauris, 1997), pp. 176–7, 181–3. The latter provisions were later modified by the Council of Guardians to preclude any supervision of *vaqf* properties by the Housing Ministry, retaining the preeminence of the *faqih*'s authority in this area.

[40] Ehsani (2006), p. 89.   [41] Baktiari (1996), p. 88.

[42] For background on these organizations and issues surrounding land reform, see Asghar Schirazi, *Islamic Development Policy The Agrarian Question in Iran* (Boulder, CO: Lynn Rienner, 1993).

[43] Valibeigi, p. 64.

broader questions of the public sector's size and scope and the issue of Iran's international orientation. The determined efforts to exert state authority over foreign trade reflected widely held suspicions toward the monarchy's international attachments. Trade was seen as the primary lever of imperialist influence over Iran, and so its regulation was essential to preserving the revolution and the country's independence. This issue first emerged during the Constitution drafting, when Islamic leftists succeeded in inserting a reference to state control of foreign trade in article 44, which defines the parameters of the postrevolutionary economy.

After the first parliament's inauguration, several representatives sought to further this agenda by putting forward a bill encouraging the government to implement this commitment. The Reja'i administration proved unenthusiastic but compliant, proposing legislation that established an extensive state role in foreign trade and domestic distribution networks. In the chaotic atmosphere of war, sanctions, and economic disruptions, this bill passed easily. However, it was quickly rejected by the Guardians' Council, which tended to favor conservative interpretations of Islamic law and aligned more closely with *bazaar* and private sector interests.

For the measure's supporters, the war compounded its urgency; the revolution and war had greatly disrupted normal trade relations and access to foreign exchange, and the state was best positioned to allocate them in a just and equitable manner. Shortages and escalating prices – presumed to be the by-product of wartime profiteering – further cemented public support. With populist rhetoric and attacks, including public floggings, against alleged profiteers, the regime itself exploited and escalated the public mood. Opposing this view were those who saw the measure as an unjustified violation of Islamic law and its protections for private commerce, and as an infringement on the historic role of the *bazaar*. In his capacity as committee chairman, Mohammad Musavi Khoeiniha objected to the bill on the grounds that it would transform the government into a "big employer, which violates the religious rights of those who are involved in trade and oar [*sic*] activities and, therefore it restrains their freedom."[44]

This dance was repeated three additional times during the subsequent two years, a tug-of-war between radical parliamentarians and a Guardians' Council determined to serve as a bulwark against creeping socialism

---

[44] Ibrahim Razzaghi, *Eghtesad-e Iran* [The Iranian Economy] (Tehran: Nashr-e Ney, 1367), p. 631, in Mehrdad Valibeigi, "The Private Sector in Iran's Post-Revolutionary Economy," *Journal of South Asian and Middle Eastern Studies* XVII: 3 (Spring 1994), p. 5.

in an Islamic guise. The debate raged for an epic six years, drawing Khomeini's typically inconsistent advocacy on behalf of both arguments and helping to force the establishment of a new governmental body to mediate the conflict. The outcome on trade proved mixed, as did so many contentious issues within postrevolutionary Iran. The revolutionary state saw little constraint in the legislative failure, since the highly bureaucratic system erected in the immediate aftermath of the revolution had already established vast government oversight over international trade.

The postrevolutionary nationalization spree had put most major firms involved with trade, transportation, and storage directly under government control. In addition, the government had already established a network of Procurement and Distribution Centers, each affiliated with a state ministry and charged with managing imports for a particular sector of the economy. The process was cumbersome, costly, and inefficient, and as such was deeply resented by the influential merchant class. By 1990, the private sector was responsible for only 37 percent of Iran's imports, with the public sector, state-owned enterprises, and other state-affiliated bodies handling the rest.[45] Still, the ultimate legislation represented a substantial retrenchment from the radicals' original goals, as Prime Minister Musavi himself acknowledged. "The original interpretation of our needs are now different. Five years of experience has taught us to depart from our original approach."[46] And the years of wrangling over the legislation deepened Iran's factional acrimony, contributing to the alienation of the leftists from institutions such as the Guardians' Council and their eventual reorientation around the primacy of elective institutions, as the reform movement.

The third issue of fierce contention among the wartime leadership was taxation. The war and the tremendous volatility in Iran's oil revenues reinforced the need for mitigating the state's reliance on external rents, but taxes represented an issue of tremendous sensitivity for the regime. Although Khomeini's prerevolutionary writings suggested that Islamic taxes, paid to the clergy by believers, provide both the justification for and the wherewithal of an Islamic state,[47] the revolutionary state effectively preserved the existing status quo. After the Iraqi invasion,

---

[45] Valibeigi, 1994: p. 5.
[46] Mehrzad Valibeigi, "Islamic Economics and Economic Policy Formation in Post-Revolutionary Iran: A Critique," *Journal of Economic Issues* 27:3 (September 1993), p. 803.
[47] Khomeini, *Hukumat-i Islami*, as translated in Algar, trans. (1981), pp. 45–6, 77, 79, 137.

Khomeini used the conflict to help justify the need for civil taxes, arguing that *sahm-e imam* would be insufficient to finance the war effort and that the state constituted a "primary Islamic ordinance" and thus was authorized to levy taxes. Other senior clerics, including traditionalist supporters of the Islamic Republic such as Ayatollah Azari-Qomi, disputed this interpretation, and the Guardians' Council upheld their position that civil taxes contradicted Islamic law.[48] Khomeini's intervention enabled the enactment of the 1988 Law on Direct Taxation, which had languished for several years in parliamentary gridlock.

The final economic issue of major contention throughout the 1980s was that of workers' rights and status, as crystallized in the debate over a new Labor Law. The first proposal, introduced in 1982 by Labor Minister Habibollah Asgharowladi, adhered to a conservative interpretation of Islamic jurisprudence, offering minimal state oversight and assurances to workers.[49] Submitted to a leftist-dominated parliament in a period of wartime hardship, the bill provoked such vehement resistance that Asgharowladi resigned and the bill was scrapped. Over the subsequent three years, the government struggled to produce legislation that incorporated robust protections to workers while conforming to *shari'a*. Given the Guardians' Council's leanings, the bills progressed slowly through the parliament in anticipation of ultimate rejection. The government appealed repeatedly to Khomeini for support, which he readily provided, culminating in a fatwa in December 1987 that endorsed the state's right to undertake the interventions in the labor market set out in the legislation. A flurry of statements and inquiries followed this extraordinary ruling, which was interpreted as sanctioning further inroads by the parliament's statist faction into what conservatives considered the doctrinally sacrosanct terrain of private property. Khomeini stood his ground, clarifying that "the government is empowered to unilaterally revoke any lawful agreements with people if the agreement *contravenes the interests of Islam and the country*"[50] (emphasis added). In this fashion, the factional and philosophical divide on the economy triggered the most consequential rationalization of temporal authority in the Islamic Republic's history, which would eventually be institutionalized in the establishment of the Expediency Council, as discussed later.

The divisions over these economic policy issues not only stymied development within Iran – they helped paralyze the state. During

---

[48] Schirazi (1998), pp. 67; 237–9.   [49] Schirazi (1998), pp. 207–15.
[50] *Ettela'at*, January 8, 1998, as quoted in Baktiari (1996), p. 142.

this period, the Guardians' Council rejected 48 percent of legislation approved by the parliament.[51] The parliament itself was deeply polarized by the differences over economic policy, and throughout this period, the two poles of Iran's domestic politics traded accusations of culpability for the country's worsening economic predicament. The radicals saw scarcity and inflation as further evidence of the *bazaari* greed and believed that the failure to institutionalize state dominance over the economy fully was an abandonment of the revolutionary commitment to Islamic justice. For their part, conservatives blamed the intrusive government policies enacted by Musavi and parliamentary leftists for inhibiting the market; they saw the substitution of thinly veiled socialism for Islamic canonical protections on private property as both heretical and inefficient. The doctrinal disputes were legitimately damaging, but neither side could acknowledge the more significant obstacle to growth in revolutionary Iran: the leadership's antagonisms with its neighbors and with the West, and its determination to pursue the war with Iraq until absolute victory.

REGIONAL AND INTERNATIONAL IMPLICATIONS

The war greatly heightened the hostilities that had erupted between revolutionary Iran and the rest of the Arab world, in particular its neighbors to the south. Iran's ruling clerics viewed the Gulf sheikhdoms and Saudi Arabia with barely concealed loathing. Khomeini's determined agitation and appeals for revolutionary upheaval across the Islamic world highlighted the fundamental contradictions between Tehran's universalist aspirations and the central Saudi narrative, which positions Riyadh as protector of Islam's most holy places and the declared leader of the Muslim world.

An array of other issues stoked the mutual enmity: Arab-Persian ethnic antipathies; the second-class status of the kingdom's Shi'a minority; doctrinal antagonisms stemming from the purist Wahhabist view of Shi'a practices; and the Islamic Republic's resentment of the institution of the monarchy and alliances with Washington. The force of all these frictions was magnified in the wake of the sectarian tremors that shook the Arabian Peninsula, starting with the November 1979 seizure of the Grand

---

[51] From Iran Times, June 27, 1989, p. 1, as quoted in Nader Entessar, "The Challenge of Political Reconstruction in Iran," in *Iran and the Arab World*, eds. Hooshang Amirahmadi and Nader Entessar (New York: St. Martin's Press, 1993), p. 229.

Mosque in Mecca and the violent demonstrations in the Shi'a majority city of Qatif that followed.

With this backdrop, Gulf support for Iraq was virtually assured, despite their wary relationship with Saddam's Baathist regime. Particularly after the Iraqi incursion began to founder, financial assistance from the Gulf began to flow to Baghdad. Throughout the conflict, just as U.S. intelligence and materiel boosted Iraq's defensive capabilities, Gulf economic assistance of $7–8 billion (supplemented by copious U.S. and European support)[52] enabled Baghdad to persist even as the war dragged on. "It's clear that it's finally hit the Iraqi population," an analyst from a British think tank said after a visit to Baghdad in 1986. "There are all kinds of economic shortages. If the American Government wasn't supplying flour, I doubt there would be bread."[53]

These intrinsic frictions escalated into a two-front proxy war through the 1980s, with the Saudis funding Saddam Hussein's war effort and Tehran cultivating Shi'a separatists in the kingdom's strategic Eastern Province and sponsoring violence in Kuwait and Bahrain. Riyadh attempted to mitigate its insecurities through a dramatic intensification of its diplomatic and military relationship with Washington. The U.S. sale of advanced air defenses helped the Saudis flex their muscles vis-à-vis Tehran, shooting down two Iranian fighter planes in 1984. However, even during this fractious period, the Saudis sought to manage the hostilities and occasionally indulged in overtures aimed at conciliating an uncompromising Iran, including the 1982 reparation offer; serious 1984–5 efforts to facilitate a cease-fire, including new reparations offers; facilitation of covert U.S. arms sales to Tehran; and Riyadh's decision to export refined products to Tehran even at the height of the tanker war in the Gulf.

By contrast, the Islamic Republic was less restrained during this period. With the exception of the occasional mollifying comment from Rafsanjani, the clerical regime frequently castigated its southern neighbors as American lackeys and "palace dwellers," openly scoffed at Riyadh's Islamic pretensions, and transformed the annual pilgrimage into a "vehicle for pan-Islamic agitation" and an occasion for harassing Riyadh over a variety of presumed transgressions, including and especially their

---

[52] John H. Sigler, "The Iran-Iraq Conflict: The Tragedy of Limited Conventional War," *International Journal* XLI (Spring 1986).

[53] John Kifner, "Arabs Fearful of a Breakout by Iran Army," *New York Times*, September 23, 1986, p. A9.

U.S. ties.[54] Tehran rejected King Fahd's 1984 invitation to Rafsanjani to perform the *hajj* and dismissed subsequent Saudi feelers that dangled war reparations as an incentive for terminating the conflict. Iran's view of the *hajj* as an inherently political event collided with the Saudi determination to safeguard (and control) the ritual and the hundreds of thousands of annual participants. The resulting clashes between demonstrating Iranian pilgrims and Saudi security forces peaked in 1987, with the death of more than four hundred pilgrims, most of them Iranian. In Tehran, mobs stormed the Saudi Embassy, Khomeini announced that the Saudi royal family "had forfeited the right ... to rule over the holy places," while Rafsanjani exhorted that "the Saudi rulers have chosen an evil path, and we will send them to hell."[55] The Saudis severed diplomatic relations in April 1988, and by the war's end, the Gulf's two heavyweights remained openly at odds. These bilateral scuffles took place in the shadow of an increasingly open U.S. military campaign against Iran in the Gulf.

Conversely, the war greatly advanced the incipient relationship between revolutionary Iran and Baathist Syria. Damascus emerged as a key ally and conduit for intelligence and weaponry funneled to Tehran from the Soviet Union, Libya, and Algeria; it also proved vital to the creation of an Iranian proxy force among Lebanese Shi'a. Beyond its utility to the embattled state's regional reach, the nascent alliance with Syria helped Tehran's efforts to stabilize its own economy and erode Iraq's reserves. During the war's initial phase, Hafez Al Assad sought to maintain a fig leaf of neutrality and promised to secure Iraq's export pipeline to Baniyas. His April 1982 reversal of that decision denied Iraq 400,000 bpd in exports, constraining Baghdad's revenues and leaving its remaining exports far more vulnerable to sabotage. This act cemented a closer alliance with Tehran and instigated a new phase of regional violence. It remained an awkward and asymmetrical relationship, however, and as the two states' interests and incentives diverged, the alliance experienced increasing pressure. In 1986, pressed for cash, Tehran sought to defer or curtail its subsidized oil supplies to Damascus, which had become increasingly unreliable about paying its bills. At the same time, the Syrians were unhappy with Iran's open meddling across the region.

---

[54] Henner Fürtig, *Iran's Rivalry with Saudi Arabia between the Gulf Wars* (Ithaca, NY: Cornell University Press, 2006), p. 43.

[55] Fürtig (2006), p. 48.

OIL WARS

Despite the open hostilities expressed between Tehran and its neighbors in the Gulf, the Iranian leadership acknowledged its ongoing reliance on oil income, and by extension its commitment to ensuring the regional flow of oil exports. As speaker of the parliament, Hashemi Rafsanjani insisted that Tehran "is not adventurous," adding that the government "realizes that the oil is essential for the world's economy today and it does not want the oil cut . . . in this region we are in greater need of security than the Gulf sheikhs. The security which we will maintain will stop others who want to violate it."[56]

After initial consideration of constraining production and seeking to drive oil prices upward through aggressive pricing, Tehran by necessity shifted tactics to expand its revenue base. This new approach included efforts to raise production far above its OPEC quota of 1.2 mbpd and offering price discounts to secure additional contracts. Having previously accused Kuwait and Saudi Arabia of boosting their own production to assist Baghdad, Tehran demonstrated little regard for its OPEC partners – the most important of which were already funding Saddam – or for the cohesion of an organization that they saw as a vehicle for U.S. influence. "The Saudis can't do anything before the end of the war, and after we win the war, you can be sure that they will do nothing," a senior Iranian oil ministry official said in 1982.[57] This bravado was expressed as Tehran sought to maintain market share amid Iraq's costly attacks by unilaterally lowering its export prices. Still, there was episodic cooperation – in 1983, Tehran agreed to an OPEC price cut despite official declarations to the contrary.

For much of the early war period, both sides sought to avoid taking the conflict to the Gulf. As the war dragged on, however, Iraq became more desperate and turned its focus toward economic targets with far greater efficiency.[58] In 1985, two dramatic developments altered the course of the war and slashed Iran's immediate revenue stream and long-term economic prospects. The first was the Iraqi decision to launch attacks in the Gulf, a shift facilitated by the provision of French Mirage fighter jets, which markedly enhanced the accuracy of Iraqi attacks on

---

[56] Bernard Gwertzman, "Iran Says It Will Not Be 'Adventurous' in Gulf," *New York Times*, May 29, 1982, pp. 1–2; Chubin and Tripp (1988), p. 164.

[57] "Iranians Challenge Oil Limits," *New York Times*, November 8, 1982.

[58] Kanovsky (1997), p. 9.

Iran's oil infrastructure. Then, in August and September 1985, Iraqi attacks on the massive Kharg Island facilities halved Tehran's export capabilities and quickly forced the revolutionary state to adjust its export logistics drastically.

Tehran responded by targeting Gulf oil exports and other shipments transiting the strategic waterway – first, through the unconventional resources of the Revolutionary Guard's nascent naval command, and by 1986 through the dispersal of indigenously produced mines. In addition, the revolutionary leadership embraced a mantra of shared consequences – that is, Tehran proclaimed that the safety of the Gulf was in essence a communal good, and any threat to its exports would be reciprocated by all the littoral states. Like so many of the patterns established and exacerbated by the war, this Iranian view of Gulf security persisted long beyond the conflict. Then, as now, Iran was equally if not more vulnerable than all of its neighbors to a protracted interruption of Persian Gulf shipping.

The tanker war phase underscores the importance of economic warfare to the broader strategies of both combatants. The war was, of course, first and foremost a military conflict – a brutal one at that, with a massive human toll. But the economic dimensions could not be avoided, particularly as the conflict became a protracted one. If a clear-cut victory could not be obtained on the battlefield, both Tehran and Baghdad calculated that the collapse of the enemy could be achieved by raising the costs. And through economic warfare, each side sought to erode the advantages of its adversary.

In addition to Iraqi tactics, the Islamic Republic had to contend with the market-generated fluctuations in oil prices. Worldwide oil markets remained caught in the throes of upheaval, most recently price spikes provoked by Iran's revolution. In addition, despite its prior successes, OPEC remained an inchoate force, its membership frequently at odds over political issues and its strategy for shaping supply still indeterminate. The war exacerbated these tendencies and elevated oil politics as the key arena for Iranian-Saudi tensions. This shift reflected the gradual decline in oil prices and revenues, as well as the success of Iraq's strategy of targeting Iranian oil installations, which began to reap benefits. Tehran and Riyadh began to feud openly in OPEC, and Riyadh's 1985 decision to enforce a more unified approach to OPEC quotas by flooding a weak market with production raised the temperature even further.

Iran's oil production and revenues declined precipitously – from $21.2 billion in 1983 to $13.7 billion in 1984 and $6.3 billion in 1986. Meanwhile, insurance rates on tankers increased, and Iraqi-inflicted damage to

Iran's refining capacity initiated a steadily increasing reliance on refined petroleum imports that eventually emerged as a gaping economic vulnerability and an almost intractable political dilemma. Iran's economy began to grind to a halt – the GDP crashed, and key sectors such as manufacturing and construction were disproportionately impacted.[59]

The Saudi move was widely seen by Iranians as a deliberate effort, with Washington's active collusion, to cripple Iran's economy and its military capability. The Saudis "sell oil which belongs to the Muslims and the oppressed, God-given wealth, at bargain prices. They pour it down the pockets of the superpowers at cheap prices in order to defeat revolutionary Iran," inveighed Ayatollah Montazeri in 1986.[60] This view has been echoed repeatedly, including by outside historians.[61] In reality, Washington harbored little expectation that an oil price war would modulate Iranian policy; as a senior U.S. official noted at the time, "You are not going to stop this kind of religious war by denying money to Iran."[62]

Nor does evidence support the theory that the price collapse was primarily motivated by Saudi fears of an Iranian victory in Iraq. In fact, the dramatic oil price fluctuations during the mid-1980s primarily resulted from ineffectual Saudi management of global oil markets. Having assumed OPEC's swing producer role in 1983, Riyadh was forced to adopt severe production cuts to maintain the official price. The recession, U.S. and European conservation efforts, and expanding non-OPEC supply meant that, as one American oil analyst commented in mid-1985, "all the pressure on prices is downward."[63] Saudi exports sank to 2.15 mpd in 1985, approximately half of its formal OPEC quota and a mere 25 percent of its 1980 exports.[64] Meanwhile, most OPEC members routinely disregarded their quotas and produced well beyond their allotted volumes. Riyadh's decision to ramp up production was less about Iran than about two profound concerns: its massive fiscal commitments,

---

[59] Kanovsky (1997), p. 10.   [60] Furtig (2002), p. 232.

[61] The conspiracy theories were echoed elsewhere, albeit with different complexions. Another popular theory held that the Reagan administration had persuaded Saudi Arabia to collapse oil prices in order to drive the Soviet Union into economic crisis. See Robert Lacey, *Inside the Kingdom: Kings, Clerics, Modernists, Terrorists, and the Struggle for Saudi Arabia* (New York: Penguin Books, 2009), p. 92; Steve Yetiv, *Crude Awakenings: Global Oil Security and American Foreign Policy* (Ithaca: Cornell University Press, 2004), p. 145.

[62] Clyde H. Farnsworth, "OPEC Deal: A Bid To Draw Iran Out?" *New York Times*, August 9, 1986, pp. 1, 32.

[63] "OPEC to Meet Earlier: Price Pressure Is Seen," *New York Times*, June 4, 1985, p. D1.

[64] Amuzegar (2001), p. 44.

primarily for domestic development projects but also its international initiatives, were jeopardized by the rapid declines in its annual oil income. In addition, the Saudis feared a long-term erosion in market share, and by extension its geostrategic role.

The Saudi move could not have been a surprise to Tehran; Saudi officials loudly signaled their dissatisfaction with the prevailing price slump, and senior Saudi officials explicitly warned that the kingdom was prepared to revert to exports at official quota levels. "For the kingdom of Saudi Arabia, it is the same case," Fahd declared in September 1985. "What others permit themselves, we do not forbid for ourselves. We are in need ourselves as they are."[65] Riyadh's unusual bluntness was motivated in part by an ultimately futile effort to persuade non-OPEC producers to align their production and export policies more closely with those of the oil cartel. Additionally, in advance of the June 1985 OPEC meeting, the Saudi foreign minister visited Tehran, the first such high-level visit since the revolution, and discussed the kingdom's growing frustration with its export predicament.

Riyadh's ramped-up production followed dramatic setbacks to the Iranian war effort. Baghdad had launched a series of successful strikes against Iran's export facilities and capabilities, and Iraqi oil officials were pressing for an increase in their own OPEC quota from 1.2 mbpd to 2 mbpd. Some analysts saw a Saudi hand in Iraq's new tactics, arguing that Baghdad's decision to push the war into the Gulf, and directly engage Iran's export facilities, was instigated by Riyadh to escalate oil prices.[66] Throughout 1985, the Saudis sent feelers to Tehran based on the expectation that the losses after the Kharg Island bombing might spur reconsideration of a cease-fire. As part of this strategy, Riyadh sought to break the Iranian alliance with Syria.

The oil strategy did not achieve all of Riyadh's intentions. While the kingdom managed to claw back market share, the crisis did not generate a newfound OPEC unity; nor did it produce near-term progress on subduing Tehran or cauterizing its regional influence. "Saudi Arabia thought that with its level of production it can enforce its wishes on our brothers in OPEC and the region," the Iranian oil minister fulminated.[67] Iranian leaders were determined to prove this presumption wrong. And the

---

[65] "Saudis' King Asserts Freedom to Cut Prices," *New York Times*, September 24, 1985, p. D24.

[66] William Safire, "Key to the Kingdom," *New York Times*, October 17, 1985, p. A27.

[67] *MEES*, January 31, 1983, p. D8.

strategy produced terrible blowback for the Saudi leadership, as its oil income similarly plummeted, to a mere \$18 billion in 1986 – approximately \$100 billion lower than its 1981 revenues.[68] "The national budget was in desperate need of the revenues. No one liked or wanted the low oil prices of the mid-late 1980s," remarked a Saudi government oil economist. "Everyone suffered, Saudi Arabia most of all. It was a very bad time."[69]

The price crash also hurt Riyadh's diplomatic sway, with regional clients as well as its American patron. Saddam Hussein voiced "friendly but also serious criticism" in mid-1985, noting that "we cannot possibly find convincing arguments in favour of this policy and its goals."[70] Washington was no less unhappy with the outcome than OPEC membership; then-Vice President George Bush was dispatched to Riyadh to plead the case that the Saudi gambit was eviscerating the American oil industry, whose costs were inordinately higher than those in any OPEC producer – a trip that only entrenched Iranian paranoia.

Tehran – with its oil infrastructure under attack and its prospects for expanding capacity almost nonexistent – was apoplectic at the Saudi move. At the March 1986 OPEC ministerial conference, Iran pushed back, bolstered by support from African producers, but made little headway against the "evident determination of Saudi Arabia and its Gulf region allies to depress prices by continued unrestrained production."[71] From his post as president, Ali Khamenei warned Riyadh that "the price war is no less important to us than the military war at the front."[72]

However, while the rhetoric remained at a high pitch and little progress appeared on the horizon, the precipitous decline in prices was forcing both sides toward the center. Gholamreza Aghazadeh, who assumed the Oil Ministry portfolio after the 1985 cabinet shake-up, visited Riyadh prior to the October 1986 OPEC meeting and eventually managed to wrest an accord from his Saudi counterparts. The deal entailed mutual compromises. The Saudis sensed that they had achieved their goal of establishing greater OPEC discipline and sought an exit strategy to stem the price erosion as well as the ongoing damage to their relations with

---

[68] Amuzegar (2001), p. 44.   [69] Lacey (2009), p. 92.

[70] Abbas Alnasrawi, "Economic Consequences of the Iran-Iraq War," *Third World Quarterly* 8:3 (July 1986), p. 889.

[71] John Tagliabue, "OPEC Ministers to Meet Amid Growing Dispute," *New York Times*, March 15, 1986, pp. 1, 33.

[72] John Tagliabue, "Stubborn Strategist: Sheik Ahmed Zaki Yamani; Squeezing OPEC – and the U.S.," *New York Times*, April 13, 1986, p. A6.

smaller producers, including the United States. Iran's yielding was more surprising, as it conceded a temporary boost to Iraq's production and by extension its adversary's bottom line.[73] Like earlier openings between the northern and southern Gulf powerhouses, however, any goodwill between Tehran and Riyadh that may have been generated in the hasty oil arrangements was soon shattered. Prospects for any durable improvement in relations were squandered by the Islamic Republic's opportunistic pageantry in the *hajj* and by the increasingly central role of the Gulf in the hostilities between the combatants and an ever-wider array of third countries, including the United States. The fragile accord on oil production between Tehran and Riyadh also proved short-lived, as continuing downward pressure on prices and Iran's war-imposed fiscal demands prompted renewed quarreling within OPEC by mid-1987.

PROBLEMS ON THE HOME FRONT

In the early weeks of war, Saddam Hussein was asked about his terms of settlement. "If Khomeini wants to continue the war, he can continue till eternity," Saddam responded. "But he has to know that war imposes its own demands which are greater than those that existed before the war."[74] This declaration would prove prescient for both embattled regimes. For Iran, the war generated demands on the regime both at home and around the region that were unanticipated or at least unappreciated at its outset. Despite the pressures of funding the war, social spending remained high. Approximately 20 percent of government spending was directed toward education between 1980 and 1986, and, relative to GDP, state support for education remained on par with that of the prerevolutionary era at approximately 3 percent of national income.[75] Still, the costs of the war far outweighed these investments and began to exceed the capacity of the government to absorb. Across the country, urban poverty more than

---

[73] John Tagliabue, "Iranian-Saudi Talks Created OPEC Pact," *New York Times*, August, 7, 1986, p. D3. Indeed, Iran's sudden flexibility on prices was surprising enough to provoke some observers to question whether it was connected to the arms-for-hostages dealings between U.S. and Iranian officials, although there has never been any serious evidence offered to substantiate such speculation. See Bill (1988), p. 312.

[74] Barbara Slavin and Milt Freudenheim, "War Is Costly, So Iraq Raises Its Price for Peace," *New York Times*, November 9, 1980, p. A6.

[75] Robert Looney, "War, Revolution, and the Maintenance of Human Capital: An Analysis of Iranian Budgetary Priorities," *Journal of South Asian and Middle East Studies* 25:1 (1991), p. 4.

doubled between 1983 and 1988, and income inequality widened significantly.[76] Not surprisingly, the war had a relatively larger economic
impact on the western and southwestern provinces, which were the scene
of the initial invasion and occupation. Poverty expanded at a relatively
higher rate during the war in these areas of the country.[77]

Beginning in 1983 and 1984, as the terror tactics associated with the
campaign against the Mojahedin began to wane and the burdens of the war
effort intensified, Iranians began to protest openly over the state of the
economy. Still, the problems continued. There were power cuts throughout
1985, and the subsequent year the government imposed a ration system for
gasoline. With mounting public frustration over the long, bloody conflict,
Khomeini tacked back to the left. "Count how many rich people have gone
to the fronts. How many of them have been martyred?... All our martyrs
come from the deprived masses and not from the *bazaar*."[78]

Domestic grievances were magnified by the inevitable revelations that
the revolutionary regime had begun to succumb to the temptations of
power. In 1984, news broke of a major corruption scandal in the Ministry
of Heavy Industry. This episode further eroded Musavi's standing
with his more conservative rivals and strengthened their case for a greater
role for the private sector.[79] Corruption allegations became the stock
and trade of factional warfare. There were criticisms leveled against the
Revolutionary Guard Corps (IRGC) for squandering resources and
helping to enrich a small circle of privileged merchants and industrialists.[80] In the debate over nominees for the 1988 cabinet, Said Rajai
Khorasani, an MP and former Iranian ambassador to the United Nations,
taunted Behzad Nabavi over his role in negotiating the agreement that
resolved the hostage crisis and dropped flagrant allusions to financial
improprieties.[81]

The ascendance of the parastatal *bonyad*s also emerged as a serious
irritant. Their ostensibly charitable mission made the foundations vulnerable to criticism and suspicion by the targets of government seizure.[82]
Within a year of the establishment of the Foundation for the Oppressed,
eight hundred complaints were submitted to a parliamentary

---

[76] Ahmad Assadzadeh and Satya Paul, "Poverty, Growth and Redistribution: A Study of
Iran," *Review of Development Economics* 8:4 (2004), p. 652.

[77] Ibid., p. 647.   [78] Baktiari, p. 121.   [79] Baktiari, pp. 119–20.

[80] Baktiari, p. 157.   [81] Baktiari, p. 156.

[82] Expropriation remains a routine tool of corporate consolidation for the foundations. See
Yeganeh Torbati, Steve Stecklow and Babak Dehghanpisheh, "To Expand Khamenei's
Grip on the Economy, Iran Stretched Its Laws," Reuters, November 13, 2013.

investigatory committee. That investigation was squelched, but changes were initiated after one of its first directors, Mohandes Khamoushi, was sacked over misuses of funds. Khomeini himself implied, in a play on his own rhetoric, that the institution had begun to serve the greedy rather than the needy (the *mostakbarin* rather than the *mostazafin*).[83]

In the 1984 campaign for parliamentary elections, the real issues of the day – the prospects for the war and the viability of the revolutionary state – remained off-limits for public debate. Instead, candidates competed for public favor on questions of economic policy. In part for this reason, the leftists managed to expand their bloc in the Majlis. Musavi described the election as having produced a parliament that "will be a true representative of all the toiling, self-sacrificing, and oppressed people."[84]

The four main actors in Iran's leadership drama – Khomeini, Khamenei, Rafsanjani, and Musavi – retained their roles after this election. But the tensions over economic issues had generated deep divisions among them, and between the executive branch and the parliament itself. A fault line between the prime minister and the president emerged over the immediate budget questions as well as the broader debates on trade and land reform. The schism reflected both the initial distance between them – Musavi was never Khamenei's first choice in the role of prime minister – and foreshadowed the even more consequential conflict a quarter-century later. The increasingly bitter differences among the warring camps exacerbated the already Herculean task of managing a war economy. Five members of Musavi's proposed cabinet failed to win parliamentary votes of confidence, and other nominees for key economic slots, including that leading the newly reconstituted Plan and Budget Organization, were rejected by the Guardians' Council. When he first took his cabinet to meet with Khomeini, the supreme leader castigated Musavi for the disastrous state of the economy, attributing the shortages and inflation to the prime minister's statist approach. After Khamenei's August 1985 reelection to the presidency, the frictions between Khamenei and Musavi increasingly centered on issues of economic policy as a proxy for their struggle to attain primacy in a contest for executive authority.

The costs of the war with Iraq were increasingly straining the resources of the revolutionary state; Rafsanjani would later assert that "some 60 to

---

[83] Moaddel (1993), pp. 249–50.   [84] Baktiari (1996), pp. 112–14.

70 percent of the country's income was spent on the war."[85] Managing this burden while engaging in an ambitious redistributional and development agenda and insulating the regime's preferred constituencies in the *bazaar* proved unsustainable. Nor could Tehran look to international capital markets for external sources of finance to sustain the war effort, unlike its adversary; both its ideological predilections and its ongoing antagonisms with Western governments inhibited any prospect of significant foreign borrowing.

These constraints provoked an agonizing debate about the theocracy's priorities, one that played out during the deliberations over the 1985/6 budget. Musavi sought to expand social spending, while the traditionalists opposed the implementation of additional tax authorities. "What should we do?" appealed Rafsanjani. "Stop the war, the universities, schools? Not paying taxes means disrupting all these."[86] This was the closest that the leadership came to acknowledging the increasingly painful trade-offs that sustaining the war had imposed on the once-ambitious agenda envisioned by Iran's revolutionaries. It proved an effective technique for cudgeling reluctant cooperation from the opposing factions around an economic agenda that reflected compromises on all sides. As the war approached its final years, the revolutionary élites mostly remained unwilling to challenge the ever-more-evident fiction that absolute victory over Saddam could be achieved without catastrophic cost to all the regime's other priorities.

The budget debate also signaled a shift in financing the war costs, which were increasingly exceeding the government's operating expenses. The oil price crash meant that new sources of revenues were required in order to support the growing burden of sustaining the offensive into Iraq. Much of this new income derived from taxes, which had grown from 19 percent of government income in 1974–8 to 54 percent by 1986.[87] During the revolution's first decade, Iran's economy became more inward focused, as exports declined from approximately 20 percent of GNP in the shah's final years to less than 4 percent in the penultimate year of the war.[88] Iran's leftists celebrated the reduction of the state's dependency on oil revenues and Western capitalism; as Musavi noted, "if we do not extract taxes, we will always be

[85] Hooshang Amirahmadi, *Revolution and Economic Transition The Iranian Experience* (Albany: State University of New York Press, 1990), p. 67.

[86] Baktiari (1996), p. 123.   [87] Amirahmadi (1990), p. 166.

[88] Steve Lohr, "The Big Dividends of a Gulf Peace," *New York Times*, August 13, 1988.

under the thumb of imperialism."[89] Conservatives conversely saw the shifts less positively, insisting that a rising tax burden hurt both the embattled, shrunken position of the private sector as well as the religious establishment itself. Ultimately, however, the evolving fiscal basis of the revolutionary state reinforced its populist pretensions. The theocracy's ambitious promises to advance social justice and a better life for ordinary Iranians were now being financed by the presumed beneficiaries – a factor that eventually would constrain the commitment to the war.

THE COST OF CONFLICT AND A TURN TOWARD OLD ADVERSARIES

Tehran's transactional approach to its difficult relationships with the superpowers was intensified by the oil price crash. The war's devolution into a frustrating, bloody stalemate created new pressures for the revolutionary regime. Khomeini and other senior leaders remained convinced that Saddam's absolute defeat remained not only possible but essential. However, materiel constraints on the war effort became increasingly problematic. A successful U.S. campaign, launched in 1983 and headlined Operation Staunch, had succeeded in closing off supplies of needed weaponry and spare parts to Tehran. Since Iran's military infrastructure was built entirely on U.S. arms, the operation intensified the impact of the estrangement with Washington; both legal and gray market avenues of military resupply became more difficult and costly to access.

Iran's resourceful maneuvers to acquire needed arms and other equipment pushed its leadership back into an unlikely association with its two most bitter adversaries, Israel and the United States. The war with Iraq and the increasingly violent Iranian footprint in Lebanon had heightened the antagonism among them, but also created new opportunities. Iranian military imperatives converged with U.S. interests in soliciting Tehran's help in freeing Americans who had been kidnapped in Lebanon. For some Reagan administration officials, longer-term strategic motivations came into play. Despite the de facto American tilt toward Baghdad, Washington still viewed Iran through a Cold War prism and sought to hedge against Soviet opportunism there. And there was the tantalizing hope of using a covert opening to Tehran as a means of facilitating regime change, or at least the ascendance of moderates who were opposed to

---

[89] *Ettela'at*, January 23, 1985, as quoted in Baktiari (1996), p. 122.

Ayatollah Khomeini's rule.[90] The White House was influenced in part by the involvement of questionable intermediaries, including Israelis and a motley array of sketchy arms dealers and discredited members of the Iranian diaspora. Having maintained a substantial arms pipeline to Iran throughout the early revolutionary period, Israeli officials remained convinced that the Islamic Republic was ephemeral and that cultivating moderate alternatives could revive the "true" Iran and its partnership with Israel.[91]

These American perceptions and aims contrast starkly with Tehran's goals in reviving contacts with the Great Satan. The revolution's pragmatists – most notably, Hashemi Rafsanjani – recognized the utility of overcoming the breach with Washington. Such a position hardly suggested opposition to the revolutionary state; Rafsanjani as well as the other Iranian officials involved with the clandestine U.S. dealings remained stalwart revolutionaries. Tehran's interests did not extend to repairing the U.S. relationship, and all the major players within Iran's increasingly fractured élite remained virulently anti-American. Khomeini's willingness to countenance the purchase of American arms spoke directly to his desperation and determination to prevail against Saddam.

For both sides, the Iran-contra affair remains a powerful cautionary tale. Beyond the legal and constitutional issues provoked by the diversion of the gambit's profits to Central American rebels, the Reagan administration was stung by the appearance that Washington had been manipulated by duplicitous Iranian clerics yet again. The United States delivered the missiles, spare parts, and intelligence that Iran so desperately needed but in return found its demands for the release of American hostages held in Lebanon stymied or delayed. The American view held that Washington

---

[90] Robert C. McFarlane with Zofia Smardz, *Special Trust* (New York: Cadell & Davies, 1994), p. 106.

[91] The January 17, 1986, U.S. Covert Action Finding by then-National Security Advisor John Poindexter argues that the Israelis saw arms sales as a means of acquiring "heretofore unobtainable penetration of the Iranian governing hierarchy. The Israelis are convinced that the Iranians are so desperate for military materiel, expertise, and intelligence that the provision of these resources will result in favorable long-term changes in personnel and attitudes within the Iranian government." As reproduced in Peter Kornbluh and Malcolm Byrne, eds., *The Iran-Contra Scandal: The Declassified History* (New York: New Press, 1993), p. 232. To Israel's enduring expectations of rapprochement, it is worthwhile to note then-Defense Minister Yitzhak Rabin's words at a 1987 press conference: "Iran is Israel's best friend and we do not intend to change our position in relation to Tehran, because Khomeini's regime will not last forever." Parsi (2007), p. 128.

fell prey to an Iranian bait and switch and that Tehran got the better of the deal. For Washington, the legacy of Iran-contra was an engrained aversion to quiet diplomatic outreach to Tehran, a distrust of self-proclaimed Iranian moderates, and an intense resentment of Iranian negotiating tactics, particularly the secrecy and exploitation of Western lives as leverage.

Within Iran, the arms deals reverberated throughout the polarized governing élite and ultimately entailed a tremendous political and human price. Only Khomeini's active intervention helped save Rafsanjani from the internal uproar once word of the dealings leaked, and the incident also helped hasten the downfall of Khomeini's designated successor, Ayatollah Montazeri, whose son-in-law was executed in connection with the revelations.

The arms relationship between Washington and Tehran did not facilitate a broader rapprochement, or even a more balanced American approach to the conduct of the war. Rather, the exposure of Iran-contra helped facilitate a more aggressive American effort to avert any Iranian advantage. As part of its war strategy, Iran was increasingly targeting neutral shipping, particularly the vessels of the Gulf sheikdoms that were generously subsidizing Iraq's war effort. For the Islamic Republic, complicity with the adversary made the Gulf commerce a legitimate target of retribution. The tone from Tehran grew once again more bellicose: "Any country which supports Iraq is subject to our retaliatory measures," proclaimed Iran's foreign minister, Ali Akbar Velayati. "In the past we have showed restraint but in future we will not." Washington initially balked at direct intervention, but when the Kuwaitis cleverly appealed to Moscow for assistance, the Reagan administration began to view the situation in a different light.

In mid-1987, the Reagan administration launched Operation Earnest Will to protect Kuwaiti oil shipments from Iranian attacks. Since American law prevented the U.S. Navy from escorting foreign ships, the Kuwaiti ships were reregistered under the American flag. Washington's direct engagement in the war sent Tehran's foremost adversary onto its doorstep: By August 1987, the U.S. had positioned forty ships, with twenty thousand personnel, in the Gulf.[92] The two sides exchanged a series of costly attacks; in August, a reflagged Kuwaiti tanker struck an Iranian-laid mine; in October, another was hit by an Iranian missile while

---

[92] Furtig (2006), p. 68.

in Kuwaiti waters, accompanied by a U.S. naval escort. Washington responded with force, attacking two drilling platforms at the Rashadat offshore oil field that had been utilized by the Revolutionary Guard for military purposes.

Beyond the immediate losses, the tanker wars had a longer-term impact on Iran's economy: Along with Tehran's rejection of cease-fire efforts, the outbreak of direct U.S.-Iranian skirmishing in the Gulf furnished the justification for the intensification of U.S. sanctions against Iran in 1987. "Everything changed after that attack," commented an American official – it created "a unified position of the American Government."[93] The new sanctions banned all Iranian imports to the United States and enacted export bans on a variety of dual-use goods, including motors, generators, and communications equipment. Even so, Secretary of State George Shultz tried to keep the door open to some form of dialogue, testifying in 1987 that Washington had an "obvious stake in better relations with Iran" and acknowledging the Iranian revolution as a "fact of history."[94]

SEEDS OF PRAGMATISM AND THE CEASE-FIRE

After the 1986 capture of the Fao Peninsula, many observers believed that victory was finally within the Islamic Republic's reach. Tehran proclaimed the "year of decision" and launched a series of massive new offensive campaigns intended finally to achieve an end to the sordid conflict. However, in part because of the remaining constraints on Iran's access to materiel and armaments, such a breakthrough continued to elude the revolutionary state. In this sense, Fao became a symbol of futility for the Iranian leadership: a sought-after milestone that failed to deliver the anticipated strategic prize, and eventually another humiliating setback in the final months of the war. Such developments underscored the limitations of Tehran's strategy of attrition; "it was a two-edged sword in that it could wear down Iran's will to fight as much as Iraq, with quite devastating consequences because of the importance of commitment in Iran's limited inventory of assets."[95]

As Tehran persisted in pressing a total war with Baghdad, the implications for the population – and for popular support for the revolutionary enterprise – came into sharp relief. During the crucial years of the war,

[93] Elaine Sciolino, "Reagan Bans All Iran Imports, and Curbs Exports," *New York Times*, October 27, 1987.
[94] As quoted in Hunter (1990), p. 67.   [95] Chubin (1989), p. 6.

flagging domestic support began to erode Tehran's singular advantage during the early phases of the war – manpower supremacy. Baghdad expanded and reorganized its infantry between 1986 and 1988 by approximately 150,000, whereas Iran's uniformed ranks fell by approximately 100,000.[96] Beginning in 1985, the government began experimenting with initiatives to expand military recruitment, focused on women, government employees, and other nontraditional draftees. By 1987, the service commitments of draftees were unilaterally extended to thirty months, an admission of the severe personnel shortage.

Khomeini's rivals appreciated the opportunity to adopt more strident public opposition to the war. Bazargan challenged his former ally directly, asserting in an open letter that "thanks to your misguided policies Iraq has fortified itself, its economy has not collapsed and it is we who are on the edge of bankruptcy. You say that you have a responsibility to those whose blood has been spilt. To this, I say, 'When will you stop the commerce with the blood of our martyrs?'"[97] The Freedom Movement was hardly the sole voice of doubt; commentaries from several influential senior clerics took aim at the decision to persist with the conflict. Meanwhile, the economy continued to worsen; as one merchant acknowledged shortly before Khomeini's decision to accept a cease-fire, "Basically, all trade now has been reduced to barter of oil, pistachio and other goods for what they want."[98]

These pressures manifested, slowly and fitfully, in the beginnings of the postrevolutionary rationalization of Iranian politics and policy. Together with – and indeed, facilitated by – the contemporaneous constitutional revisions and bureaucratic changes, Tehran began to advance a number of needed legal and regulatory measures to streamline revolutionary redundancies, clarify unresolved policy disputes, and enhance the state's efficacy. These included a new press law in 1986; legal reforms to the structure of the armed forces (passed in 1987 and amended in 1988); the 1987 dissolution of the Islamic Republican Party; 1988 legislation to impose value-added taxes on luxury goods.[99] Despite his continuing appeals to populist impulses, Musavi in fact began the process of seeking foreign loans as early as 1987; in hopes of blunting domestic opposition,

---

[96] Chubin (1989), p. 7.   [97] Moin (1999), p. 268.

[98] Youssef M. Ibrahim, "Economics of Revolution Bedevil Iran," *New York Times*, July 11, 1988.

[99] Hooshang Amirahmadi, "Economic Reconstruction of Iran: Costing the War Damage," *Third World Quarterly* 12:1 (January 1990), p. 37.

the government opted to pursue short-term instruments, a ploy that backfired as their terms ultimately imposed higher costs on Tehran.[100] In late 1987, Khomeini pushed for a tougher stance against hoarders and punitive measures for companies that sought to skirt taxes. This step eventually provoked a direct confrontation with the Guardians' Council and led Khomeini to issue an explicit, formal articulation of the primacy of national interests.

Perhaps the initiative with the greatest enduring impact on Iran's development was the embrace of an activist new agenda to address Iran's rapidly spiraling population growth. Khomeini had never explicitly endorsed a pronatalist agenda; however, the combination of a lag in the expected demographic transition and the implications of the social policies adopted by the Islamic regime helped to expand birth rates temporarily to an unprecedented high. The 1986 census suggested that Iran's population had grown to nearly 50 million, an expansion of almost 40 percent in less than a decade.[101] With the encouragement of the newly revitalized Plan and Budget Organization, the senior leadership adopted a two-prong plan that utilized public opinion surveys and an inventive family planning education program, implemented through the Ministry of Health's community health worker initiative. The sharp decline in fertility levels actually predated the political decision to embrace a new approach,[102] but the program and the senior leadership's public commitment accelerated and perpetuated the reduction.

The creeping moderation in Iran's domestic economic and social agenda corresponded to a shift in the leadership's discourse on the war. Throughout much of the long bloody conflict, Iran's senior leadership maintained an almost uniform commitment to their initial maximalist objectives: Saddam's defeat and the revolution's preservation. However, during 1987 and early 1988, the tone in official statements and Friday prayers modulated to reflect the nation's mood. When pressed by students on a call-in radio show in early 1989, then-President Khamenei acknowledged that the likelihood of victory had been "to a great extent weakened."[103]

---

[100] Pesaran (2011), p. 60.

[101] Homa Hoodfar and Samad Assadpour, "The Politics of Population Policy in the Islamic Republic of Iran," *Studies in Family Planning* 31:1 (March 2000), p. 22.

[102] Marie Ladier-Fouladi, "The Fertility Transition in Iran," *Population: An English Selection* 9 (1997), pp. 191–213.

[103] Elaine Sciolino, "Tehran Finds War Was Easier to Make than a Stable Peace," *New York Times*, January 2, 1989, p. 1.

This temperance of the public discourse belied a fierce behind-the-scenes debate over how to proceed, with the Revolutionary Guard pressing for redoubling the war effort while much of the political establishment sought to fashion an exit strategy. The Plan and Budget Organization, whose expertise had been derided by the revolutionaries and whose raison d'etre had been effectively superseded by the exigencies of the war, began to reemerge as an influential constituency. During the war's final years, the PBO undertook several initiatives to assess the resources that would be needed to continue the war and even studied the possibility of an intensified conflict involving the direct engagement of the United States.[104] However, the leadership had already begun to hedge its bets, as the exigency of maintaining popular support for the revolution had finally overcome the desire to punish Saddam.

Undoubtedly, a variety of factors fed into Iran's decision to take the war to an unsatisfying conclusion: the increasingly unfavorable battlefield prospects; Tehran's increasingly painful fiscal constraints; the civilian toll and the agitation on the streets; the lingering trepidation about Iraq's chemical warfare; the erosion of Iran's naval capabilities at the hands of stepped-up U.S. defensive measures in the Gulf; and finally, on July 3, 1988, the accidental downing of an Iranian civilian airliner in the Gulf by a U.S. Navy cruiser.[105] At the end, though, the move demonstrated Iran's pure pragmatism; Tehran's decision to end the war reflected a bitter cost-benefit analysis about the prospects and potential costs of any victory.

---

[104] Ahmadi Amoee (2003),pp. 254–6.

[105] The debate among the Iranian leadership over the decision to end the war continues in muted but increasingly direct fashion even today, more than two decades later. In recent years, Hashemi Rafsanjani has sought to burnish his own credentials as a moderate by releasing selective accounts of his advice to the supreme leader, as well as some documents penned by Khomeini himself. In 2006, Rafsanjani published a copy of the letter written by Khomeini explaining his decision to end the war, which cites budget constraints, battle fatigue among the population, Saddam's proclivity for chemical warfare, and the massive logistical and materiel requirements for any prospects of success. The former head of the Revolutionary Guards, Mohsen Rezaei, countered with a series of interviews, including one in which he insisted victory was both achievable, and within the financial capabilities of the Islamic Republic at the time. "I asked for approximately $4.5 billion be allocated for this purpose," Rezaei stated. "Considering our $10 billion in revenue for 1987, I was only asking for about 20 percent of our country's revenue over five years.... Of course, as I acknowledged, the damage would have been high. But the victory was achievable with the long-term plan." Interview with Mohsen Rezaei, published in Baztab, September 26, 2006, as translated and reprinted in James G. Blight, Janet M. Lang, Hussein Bani, Malcolum Byrne, and John Tirman, *Becoming Enemies: U.S.-Iran Relations and the Iran-Iraq War, 1979–1988* (Lanham, MD: Rowman & Littlefield, 2012), p. 343.

The Airbus downing reinforced Tehran's conviction that the war was an American conspiracy and the expectation that Washington was determined to prevent an Iranian victory. "This was in no way an accident, and in our view, it is a notification," a hard-line Iranian paper editorialized about the *Vincennes* attack.[106] After years of sporadic clashes with the United States in the Persian Gulf, the airliner incident was seen as the start of a new and more robust American military campaign directed at Iran. Compounding the perception that the war was now unwinnable was Baghdad's evident disregard for international law and human decency. Saddam's use of chemical weapons against Iranian troops as well as his own population helped persuade Iran's leadership that the world would turn a blind eye to indiscriminate attacks against Iran's cities.

This creeping resignation was not shared by the entire power structure. Powerful constituencies pressed for continuation and even intensification of the offensive, arguing that additional resources could win the day. When Rafsanjani cautioned restraint in response to the Airbus incident – arguing that "the Americans would like it if some amateurish action were taken in some corner of the world so that once again they can remove the wave of propaganda which is now heaped on America's head and divert it in another direction" – he was publicly ridiculed as defeatist by Ali Akbar Mohtashami, Iran's former ambassador to Syria and a leading radical in the Musavi cabinet.[107] In a letter to Khomeini released two decades later, the Revolutionary Guards commander Mohsen Rezaei appealed to Khomeini for a renewed mandate and additional materiel. Rezaei acknowledged that victory would likely require five additional years, and "350 infantry brigades, 2500 tanks, 300 fighter planes and 300 helicopters as well as an ability to make a substantial number of laser and atomic weapons."[108]

However, with supplies already running short at the front, Iran's civilian leadership countered that these requirements were beyond the country's capacity to provide, with Musavi insisting that the "government does not have the capacity for an appropriation of a single dollar."[109] Khomeini acceded to the cross-factional appeals to pragmatism, effectively recognizing that the domestic threats to the state's survival had

---

[106] *Jumhuri-i Islami*, July 19, 1988.
[107] Ed Blanche, "Destruction of Airliner Aids Radicals, but Others Urge Diplomacy," *AP*, July 6, 1988.
[108] Iranian Labor News Agency, September 29, 2006.
[109] Rajanews.com, March 10, 2008.

begun to exceed the dangers posed by its external adversaries. He announced that the decision to end the war "was more deadly than drinking hemlock.... Today's decision is based only on the interests of the Islamic Republic."[110]

Khomeini's decision reflected a range of factors, but ultimately it was the resource constraints that finally forced him to concede. The centrality of economic deficiencies in driving an end to the war reinforced the shift in state legitimacy from revolutionary ideology and charisma to state performance in the evolution of the Iranian political system. It is also notable that a consensus emerged on this question among the various factions of the regime that, until this point, had maintained profoundly divergent postures on economic policy. To draw together Musavi – the embattled prime minister, the advocate for social justice and the redistribution of the country's resources – and Khamenei – who had opposed Musavi at every turn – represented a convergence of tremendous significance. As the bitter battles of the reconstruction era would demonstrate, this convergence would not immediately heal the deep divisions within the regime over economic policy, but it set the stage for a widening consensus in favor of reform and rationalization of the state's approach to its domestic responsibilities. As Rafsanjani said in 1991:

We had serious difficulties in the economic aspects of the war.... We had a letter from the Minister of Economy and others who were responsible for the economy. We discussed it in the cabinet and took it to Imam [Khomeini].... The letter said that we had reached the red line in the use of our economic resources and budget. It said we had gone even below the red line, and people can't take it any more. We could not tell you that then, but I can say it now that the Governor of Bank Markazi wrote to us saying that although foreigners do not lend to us and we do not borrow from them, we have $12 billion in debts that we have to pay.[111]

After years of resisting any resolution to the conflict, Tehran now sought to expedite the cease-fire only to find its efforts resisted by both Baghdad and Washington. Sensing weakness, Iraq began to revert to its own maximalist aims of victory, while Washington apparently sought to exacerbate Tehran's vulnerabilities. The cease-fire was nearly undone by the resurgence of the Mojahedin-e Khalq (MeK), which saw an

---

[110] Kenneth Pollack, *The Persian Puzzle: The Conflict between Iran and America* (New York: Random House, 2004), p. 232.

[111] Sohrab Behdad, "The Post-Revolutionary Economic Crisis," Saeed Rahnema and Sohrab Behdad, *Iran after the Revolution: Crisis of an Islamic State* (London: I. B. Tauris, 1996), p. 112.

opportunity in Iran's epic concession from its Iraqi base of operations. Two days after the cease-fire was agreed upon, the MEK briefly seized several border towns.

The cease-fire culminated a process of convergence among the contending Iranian factions on the need to adopt policies that would preserve the revolutionary state. This process had its inceptions in the growing consensus surrounding the need for market-oriented reforms and economic restructuring, and it extended to other areas of Iranian policy, notably the revolutionary state's regional posture. Even before the war's end and the imam's passing, Rafsanjani signaled that Iran was on the cusp of a new era, offering a mea culpa in an interview on state television, coincidentally broadcast the day before the *Vincennes* downing, declaring that "one of the wrong things we did, in the revolutionary atmosphere, was constantly to make enemies. We pushed those who could have been neutral into hostility. It is part of the new plan that, in foreign policy, we should behave so as to avoid needlessly ceding ground to the enemy."[112]

Khomeini's views on this issue remained unchanged until his death – and well after. His final will advocates that "Muslims should curse tyrants, including the Saudi royal family, these traitors to God's great shrine, may God's curse and that of his prophets and angels be upon them."[113] Yet even as Iran's foreign minister was negotiating the cease-fire, Tehran began reaching out to the Gulf – and welcoming overtures from the same leaders it castigated for supporting Saddam – as early as August 1988. The Saudis appeared relieved at the prospect of the long war's end, and having helped pressure Saddam to accept the cease-fire, the Gulf States proved cautiously receptive to Iranian overtures. The same was true for Europe; after the cease-fire, Britain and France resumed full diplomatic relations, and trade revived quickly with a number of European states.

The reconstruction was primed in the cease-fire's immediate aftermath: Ministerial portfolios were shifted, and the PBO had already devised ambitious development plans for the postwar reconstruction, informed by technical expertise rather than ideology. The plan received overwhelming parliamentary approval before the year's end. In 1989, Mohammad Iravani, minister for economics and finance, came out in support of foreign debt as a source of investment capital, a position that directly

---

[112] Ed Blanche, "Destruction of Airliner Aids Radicals, but Others Urge Diplomacy," *AP*, July 6, 1988.

[113] Moin (1999), p. 305.

contravened the Musavi stance.[114] He was echoed by Morteza Alviri, who chaired the Majlis committee for planning and budget, who argued that "use of foreign sources can basically benefit us at the service of the development of the country, provided that it is not approached carelessly and negatively."[115] A new era had begun, one in which the old mandates would be reinterpreted by a state that had no choice but to reengage with the world.

A VOLATILE FACTIONAL BALANCE

Throughout this period, Iran's domestic politics continued to be riven by factional differences. Thanks to Khomeini's sympathetic invocations – he called on Iranians to support "candidates who have experienced poverty and who in word and deed defend the Islam of the bare-footed, the Islam of the oppressed" – as well as developments in the war, the 1988 parliamentary elections had produced a majority with leftist leanings.[116] Prominent radicals were elected, while several well-known traditional conservatives were defeated.

This ballot exacerbated long-simmering tensions between leftists and conservatives and precipitated a renewed skirmish between Musavi and Khamenei. The increased frictions within Iran's domestic politics contrasted sharply with the emergence of broad consensus around more pragmatic economic policies during the same period. Several factors explain the divergence: First, Tehran's perceptions of its own vulnerability were particularly acute as the conflict with Iraq dragged on and remained high even after it ended. For months and even years, war jitters in both capitals remained high, and the lack of a formal peace treaty between the two former combatants created trepidation across the region about the prospects for a relapse into hostilities.

In addition, public dissatisfaction over the war and over quality of life issues had been intensifying for several years. In such a context, Iranian leaders harbored intense fears that domestic adversaries would seize upon the cease-fire and exploit this costly, bitter failure to their own advantage. In Khomeini's letter dismissing Montazeri, he wrote at length about his former protégé's defection to the hypocrites, the regime's shorthand for the Mojahedin-e Khalq, betraying a persistent insecurity about the

---

[114] *Eqtesad*, July 1989, as quoted in Ehteshami (1995), p. 97.
[115] *Echo of Iran*, February 2, 1989, p. 18, as quoted in Ehteshami (1995), p. 98.
[116] Baktiari (1996), p. 147.

perceived collusion among the revolution's adversaries. The war had intensified the sense of siege among the leadership, the desperate paranoia surrounding the perception of a vast, determined conspiracy to unseat the revolution, and the belief that such searing experiences would ultimately strengthen the state and its capabilities.

In such an environment, it is hardly surprising that Khomeini sought to reinforce revolutionary fervor even before the government embarked upon reconstruction. This demonstrates that Tehran's embrace of pragmatic policies did not require wholesale abandonment of the provocative rhetoric or the support for violence; ending the war represented an exigency that did not extend to the modulation of its political domination or ideological commitments. The closing years of the war also saw escalating regime repression against internal dissent, culminating with the 1988 massacre of thousands of political prisoners in Evin Prison. Confronted about the executions on a call-in radio show, Khamenei defended the action, arguing that those who commit crimes against the state "should not be treated with sweets and candies."[117]

The most dramatic demonstration of the regime's determination to seize the upper hand occurred in 1989, when Khomeini issued a fatwa condemning the British-Indian novelist Salman Rushdie to death for his depiction of the Prophet Mohammad in his novel *The Satanic Verses*. Adding fuel to the fire, Khomeini deemed the mission to harm Rushdie one sufficient for martyrdom, and a parastatal government charity trumped that by pledging a $2.6 million bounty for any Iranian who might undertake the cause. The domestic passions and international recriminations served the purpose Khomeini sought – precluding the revolution from succumbing to its failures, reviving popular fervor for its ostensible ideological mission, and preserving Tehran's sequestration from the international community's dangerous embrace. The Rushdie affair succeeded in furthering these aims, and the ensuing costs to Iran's trade and diplomatic relations with the rest of the world were borne not by the imam but by the generations and leaders who succeeded him.

The episode also further attenuated Iran's ties with Europe. The British immediately protested to Tehran, conditioning any progress toward normalization on official Iranian renunciation of the threat; instead, a parastatal foundation in Iran pledged a multimillion-dollar bounty for Rushdie's death. Although most European states sought to move quickly

---

[117] Elaine Sciolino, "Tehran Finds War Was Easier to Make than a Stable Peace," *New York Times*, January 2, 1989, p. 1.

beyond the Rushdie controversy and returned their ambassadors to Tehran in April 1989, domestic politics on both sides as well as other irritants in the relationship delayed any parallel improvement for London. Diplomatic relations were formally resumed in September 1990, but divisions within the post-Khomeini order perpetuated the standoff for eight more years. Still, even as political frictions kept the two governments at odds, Iranian-British trade remained considerable – more than $1 billion by 1992, as the British benefited from both the arms trade during the early years of the war and the reconstruction opportunities thereafter.[118]

The war's conclusion also coincided with major changes in the international system, specifically the demise of the Soviet Union and the Eastern Bloc. These changes had benefits for Iran's nascent reopening to the international community, as Moscow and Tehran perceived a common interest surrounding expanded cooperation. For newly independent Russia, Tehran offered strategic inroads to the broader Middle East, and a prospective market for Russian armaments and technology – a better bet than Moscow's discredited former regional proxy, Saddam Hussein.

Khomeini died several months after issuing the Rushdie fatwa, in June 1989, having left his legacy and his state firmly yoked to professions of ideological fidelity even as the rationalization of the revolution was already well under way. The radicals' reascendance proved short-lived and illusory. During the subsequent year, as the post-Khomeini era began to manifest, the revolution's conservatives achieved the upper hand and sought to reorient Iranian politics toward a new center in which the interests of the system – rather than the advancement of the revolution – took precedence.

RESTRUCTURING OF THE SYSTEM AND SUCCESSION

The war compelled a considerable amount of decision making; however, throughout its duration, many important policies remained gridlocked by ideological differences and institutional competition. During this period, the Guardians' Council vetoed more than 100 pieces of legislation on the basis that they violated Islamic law and precepts governing the sanctity of private property.[119] The most bitter disputes concerned economic

---

[118] M. Milani (1994), p. 233.   [119] Abrahamian, *Khomeinism*, p. 55.

issues – taxation, land, labor, and trade – which struck at the core of the institutional ambiguities erected by the revolution.

This enduring conflict between the parliament and the Guardians' Council prompted an extraordinary ruling by Ayatollah Khomeini in January 1988, elevating the *velayet-e faqih* above "all ordinances that were derived or directly commanded by Allah."[120] A month later, he institutionalized this principle by establishing the Council for Assessing the Interests of the System (Majma-ye Tashkhis-e Maslahat-e Nezam), or the Expediency Council. The new organization was tasked with mediating between the parliament and the Guardians' Council on disputed legislation, as well as introducing independent legislation. It is also empowered to override both the Constitution and *shari'a* to shape outcomes deemed in the state's best interests. Among the first acts of the new institution was approval of the law on urban lands, one of the most contested elements of the postrevolutionary economic program.

As it became apparent that the end of the Khomeini era was near, the succession question began to loom larger. Khomeini personally selected Ayatollah Montazeri in 1982 as his heir apparent, describing his former student as "the fruit of my life" and "the hope of the people."[121] From the outset, however, Montazeri had limited support from within the Islamic Republic's senior ranks; many objected to the clandestine and nonrepresentative process of his selection, which contradicted Shi'a tradition – he was neither a *marja* nor a grand ayatollah – as well as the Constitutional procedures.[122] Montazeri shared Khomeini's worldview, but he became increasingly alienated from the institutions and individuals closest to the supreme leader. He had earned open opposition of figures such as Rafsanjani and Ayatollah Mohammad Reza Golpayegani,[123] and his vituperative disputes with others among the establishment were exacerbated by the serious rivalry that existed between his staff and that of Khomeini.[124]

[120] Schirazi (1997), p. 64.
[121] Shahrough Akhavi, "Elite Factionalism in the Islamic Republic of Iran," *Middle East Journal* 41:2 (Spring 1987), p. 194.
[122] After his promotion, the media referred to Montazeri as a grand ayatollah, but it was understood that this derived primarily from his political, rather than theological, qualifications.
[123] Marvin Zonis, "The Rule of the Clerics in the Islamic Republic of Iran." *Annals of the American Academy of Political and Social Sciences* No. 482 (November 1985), p. 94.
[124] Moin (1999), pp. 277–93.

In addition to his other perceived transgressions, Montazeri staked a more pragmatic position on economic policies. He was closely aligned with the *bazaar* and consistently defended the private sector's role. Montazeri's searing critique of the system's economic policies was voiced as public support for the war effort had waned. His manifesto cited "shortages, injustices, inflation, lack of sufficient income, extreme price discrepancies – the source of which is the Government itself – lack of expertise and compassion, a miserly attitude, rigidity of certain trade officials in the country's import-export sector, interference and usurpation by many organizations."[125] Montazeri also clashed repeatedly with the judiciary over the treatment of Iranian expatriates, whom he saw as a vital source of capital and expertise rather than a political threat.[126]

The final breach followed the cease-fire with Iraq, when Montazeri publicly denounced the regime's brutal repression of dissidents, including the mass executions at Evin. His broad-based attack on Khomeini's rule emphasized the Islamic Republic's material failings, writing,

I agree with the new generation of the revolution that there is a great distance between what we promised and what we have achieved ... mismanagement, a failure to give jobs to the right people, exaggeration, self-centeredness, monopolization, factionalism, the denial of people's rights, injustice and disregard for the revolution's true values have delivered the most severe blows against the revolution to date. Before any reconstruction [takes place], there must first be a reconstruction of the country's thinking about administration and its quality.[127]

In March 1989, Khomeini sent an angry, accusatory dismissal to Montazeri, stripping him of his position and the title of grand ayatollah. Recognizing the void and its urgency, Khomeini swiftly appointed a special body to revise the Constitution.[128] He also formally elevated the absolute mandate of the jurist to the highest order of divine commandment, to bolster the office of the supreme leader in his anticipated absence. He did not move quickly enough, however; approximately six weeks later – before the assembly could ratify new succession

---

[125] Elaine Sciolino, "Teheran Finds War Was Easier to Make than a Stable Peace," *New York Times*, January 2, 1989, p. 1.

[126] Shahrough Akhavi, "Institutionalizing the New Order in Iran," *Current History* (February 1987), p. 54.

[127] *Kayhan Hava'i*, February 8, 1989, as quoted in Moin (1999), p. 280.

[128] Critics note that the Islamic Republic's Constitution was originally drawn up by a popularly elected body. Schirazi (1997), pp. 110–11.

procedures – Ayatollah Khomeini died at age eighty-seven, leaving the Iranian polity in the unenviable position of having to replace the "irreplaceable."[129]

This grave event sparked grief among Iran's revolutionaries, jubilation among its opponents, and trepidation about the path ahead among many. The system moved quickly, with Rafsanjani and Ahmad Khomeini orchestrating the Assembly of Experts in selecting then-President Khamenei as supreme leader. At the time, Khamenei was considered a *hojjatoleslam*, literally "proof of Islam," which is a commonplace, middling clerical rank. His elevation as *faqih* implicitly earned him a notch up in the religious hierarchy, as the state media began referring to Khamenei as "Ayatollah."[130] Khamenei benefited from a strengthened office; on the basis of a letter penned by Khomeini shortly before his death,[131] the constitutional revisions downgraded the religious qualifications required of the leader, explicitly prioritized political standards over theological in the selection, and eliminated provisions for delegating the *velayet-e faqih* to a council of jurists in the event an appropriate individual could not be identified. Having previously subordinated religious law to state interest, the ostensibly theocratic Islamic Republic formally separated its political leadership from religious leadership.

As a result, even as its standing within the religious hierarchy waned, the office of the supreme leader absorbed greater authority over the state. The office's powers were expanded; in several areas where it had always claimed supervisory power – such as the *bonyad*s – the office of the supreme leader assumed sole jurisdiction. The new Constitution also eliminated the prime ministerial position, reducing the competition for authority at the highest level. The revision stipulated that the supreme leader commanded "absolute general trusteeship" over the three branches

---

[129] Mohsen M. Milani, *The Making of Iran's Islamic Revolution: From Monarchy to Islamic Republic* (Boulder, CO: Westview Press, 1994), p. 219.

[130] Wilfred Buchta, *Who Rules Iran?* (Washington, DC: Washington Institute for Near East Studies, 1999), p. 15. Saskia Gieling, "The *Marja'iya* in Iran and the Nomination of Khamanei in December 1994." *Middle Eastern Studies* 33, No. 4 (October 1997), p. 778.

[131] In the letter, Khomeini claimed, among other things, that he had never supported the requirement of *marja* status for the holder of the *velayet-e faqih*, and that it had been forced upon him by others. There is at least some plausibility to this claim, as Khomeini's own status as a *marja-ye taqlid* was not entirely certain at the time of the revolution. However, Schirazi comments that this "assertion contradicts the relevant passages in Khomeini's book on the Islamic state." Schirazi (1997), p. 107.

of government to the powers of this office.[132] The constitutional revisions were finalized in the months after Khomeini's death and, together with the election of Hashemi Rafsanjani as president, helped secure the new order.

The departure of its charismatic founder, whose tactical genius, impeccable religious standing, and magnetic persona had facilitated the functioning of a diverse and discordant system, represented the state's greatest challenge. Since Khomeini personified the revolution and the state, such an orderly transfer of power at a time of regional uncertainty testifies to the institutional resilience of the revolutionary state. Khamenei's elevation underscores the transformation in the criteria of authority and legitimacy since the inauguration of the Islamic Republic.

CONCLUSION

The war forged the revolutionary state, even as it bled the nation of opportunities and locked its leadership into a perennially paranoid and insecure state. In 1985, Rafsanjani acknowledged that the government had spent somewhere in the neighborhood of $43–$54 billion on the war effort to date, a sum that he acknowledged might have enabled Iran to become "one of the most powerful industrial countries in the world" had it been directed in a more constructive fashion.[133] Subsequent analyses have suggested that the final tally was significantly greater – $592 billion in damage to the Iranian economy and infrastructure by one analyst's estimate.[134] A comprehensive assessment of the economic toll would have to include a much wider array of expenses: the human toll, both in terms of deaths as well as ongoing physical and psychological impairment; damage to Iran's military capabilities; the productive activities invested in the war that might have been directed elsewhere; the value of the subsidies distributed domestically as well as the discounted oil provided to Syria; the environmental damage.

Beyond the literal balance sheet, the war institutionalized dysfunction within Iran's political economy in ways that persisted for decades. Rationing begat political pressure to maintain unaffordable subsidies, and the various damages to Iran's petroleum sector created a reliance on refined product imports. The conflict further enshrined the myth of self-sufficiency, and a confidence in Iran's capacity to thrive under

---

[132] Schirazi (1997), pp. 77–8.   [133] Chubin and Tripp (1988), p. 128.
[134] Amirahmadi (1990), p. 64.

pressure that romanticizes the survival of the fledging revolutionary state and obscures the actual erosion of any philosophical temptations toward autarky into a postwar embrace of trade and foreign investment. The continuing sensitivities surrounding the leadership's conduct of the war inhibit open debate around most of the unfortunate implications that resulted from it, including the central role of economic constraints in forcing Tehran to yield in accepting the cease-fire.

And while the war's end coincided with measures undertaken by the revolutionary state to rationalize its bureaucracy and overcome the ideological divisions that had stymied state institutions, it also fueled new factional divisions. Revolutionary Guard commanders saw the cease-fire as a betrayal of their sacrifice and of the ideals of the revolution and the imam. For others, the profound losses experienced during the war and the cynical appreciation of the realities of power drove a reconsideration of the revolution's course, and a reinterpretation of the ideals for which it had been fought. For the senior leadership, the war engrained a persistent sense of insecurity and a persecution complex, fed by the perception that Saddam could not have endured without the world's active assistance, and in particular that of Washington and its regional allies. These convictions fed policy decisions outside the economic sphere, including the revival of Iran's nuclear program, which ultimately had devastating impact on the country's economy.

The war period is often depicted as the precipitant of an inevitable Iranian revolutionary Thermidor – the incineration of Iran's revolutionary fervor and the triumph of a rational, cost-benefit approach to national decision making over one distorted by ideology, religious dogma, and revolutionary zeal. However, a closer examination of the creeping onset of pragmatism suggests that the adoption of economic pragmatism was decoupled from that of political moderation. Even as economic pressure forced the Islamic Republic to retrench, its leadership was not prepared to concede its primacy or its ideological domination.

Still, as Iran's mortal enemy foresaw, the war imposed its own demands. The war's end initiated a new phase in Iran's political and economic development, as the regime threw the resources, popular energy, and ideological invocation that had previously been reserved for the war effort into an expanded program of reconstruction and economic development. In many respects, the unsatisfying conclusion of the war made such an investment a necessity – "A peace dividend must be found for the supporters of the revolution if the virus of discontent is not to spread and affect the very legitimacy of the revolution."[135] The conflict's exigencies forced the government to invest heavily in infrastructure and the provision of material goods to a population that served as its arsenal and reoriented the priorities of an ideological and divided leadership. Most importantly, reinforcing the historical linkages between account-ability and legitimacy that stretched back at least as far as the Tobacco Revolt, the war created an ironclad expectation on the part of both the regime and its citizenry that the state's foremost role entailed its distribu-tion of resources and providing economic opportunities and benefits represented the foremost role of the revolutionary state. In this fashion, the Sacred Defense ultimately eroded the religious justification of the postrevolutionary regime and replaced it with one that was firmly grounded in the mundane.

[135] Chubin (1989), p. 16.

5

The Reconstruction Jihad, 1989–1997

With the war's end, a momentous new chapter in the Islamic Republic's history began. Its leadership confronted the task of recapitulating the system and adapting to the void opened by Khomeini's death, while also harmonizing its ideological verities with the calamitous realities wrought by the revolution and the war. The reconstruction program had a self-sustaining logic arguably as compelling as that of the war. The sheer exigencies of Iran's collapsing economy drew the political elite to an unusually swift consensus around both the leadership transition and the details of a plan to rehabilitate what was damaged by the war and revive Iran's stalled potential. The shock associated with the long conflict's sudden end, and Khomeini's death just a year later, helped facilitate the convergence, offering a clean break for his heirs to reinterpret his mandate.

The reconstruction era expedited trends already under way within Iran, prodding the Islamic Republic from revolutionary to routinized, from messianic to mundane. However, the process of normalizing the revolutionary state proved neither smooth nor wholly successful. Over time, the postwar agenda faltered, as a result of the factional contention and institutional dualism that have been the Islamic Republic's hallmarks. Major economic reforms were undertaken, but the fundamental reorientation stalled amid political opposition and financial pressures.

The reconstruction era played a major role in shaping Iran's subsequent evolution. The clashes between Rafsanjani, the reforms' architect and chief advocate, and the Islamic leftists, who remained wedded to state-centric policies and viewed capitalism as a betrayal of the revolution's ideals, precipitated a transformation in the Islamic Republic's ideological battleground. From these tensions emerged the first serious movement to reconsider the tenets of Iran's Islamic state. Having found themselves suddenly sidelined on the margins of the state they had helped create, Iran's "Islamic leftists" began to reassess their handiwork and plot their way back to power. Their ascendance would close the door on Rafsanjani's presidency and, at least temporarily, on the path he had adopted.

Rafsanjani's reconstruction program also deepened the alienation of another element of the revolutionary power structure – a younger generation of hard-liners who saw the new order as a distortion of the revolution and a vehicle for enriching regime insiders. Both these sociopolitical blocs emerged as major power centers as the revolution entered its second generation, and each defined its strategy in relation to its perceptions of the reconstruction era. And while their ideologies and policy prescriptions diverged considerably – even violently – the reformists and the neoconservatives inherited and internalized a substantially revised mandate from that of the revolutionary generation, one in which the state's primary responsibilities were rooted in satisfying public expectations for economic advancement. This remains the reconstruction era's foremost legacy. Although the program failed to fix Iran's underlying economic challenges, the intense national debate ultimately transformed the basis of the revolutionary state.

The reconstruction period also elevated Rafsanjani to a pivotal role in negotiating between the revolution's ideological imprimatur and its partisans' social and political demands. His embrace of reconstruction and economic development transformed the underlying social contract from one of revolutionary opposition and existential defense to one grounded in expectations of development and progress. Although the language of revolutionary Islam remained essential to the regime's legitimacy, his presidency confirmed that the most critical component of the regime's capacity to rule was its ability to satisfy popular demands for a better life. This postwar shift also began subtly to reshape the regime's foreign policy, as new Iranian priorities begat the conscious utilization of economic diplomacy as a means of mitigating the regime's challenges. Yet even as they sought to reintegrate the Islamic Republic into the global economy, Iranian leaders continued to nurture old antipathies, an inconsistency that ultimately contributed to the stumbling of their agenda.

THE POSTWAR ECONOMIC CHALLENGE

The Rafsanjani presidency is often conflated with the postwar reconstruction period – not without reason, since Rafsanjani championed that program throughout his two terms. However, they were not perfectly contemporaneous; the interceding year between the war's end and Iran's leadership change was "a year of tremendous change," as the scholar Mark Gasiorowski has commented.[1] The expense of mounting a total war had ended, but the economy remained in free fall. The penalties imposed on Iran after its attacks in the Gulf, including U.S. sanctions and a French oil embargo, remained in place. Oil prices had fallen again, nudged downward by Riyadh's revived production after the cease-fire. Iran's total exports collapsed by 25 percent during the first half of 1988 as compared with the previous year, prompting the government to slash prices near year's end. Tehran was also forced to rely on barter trade, since political risk made it difficult to secure import financing or investment; some of the reconstruction era's early megaprojects, such as the Mobarakeh Steel facility in Isfahan, were tied to long-term crude supply deals with foreign partners.

The war's fallout remained the leadership's most urgent challenge. Rafsanjani acknowledged prior to his 1989 election that Iran's manufacturing capabilities were operating at 40 percent capacity without any corresponding cost reduction.[2] The war had shrunk per capita income by 45 percent, inflation was approaching 29 percent, and war damages (direct and indirect) totaled somewhere in the neighborhood of $1 trillion.[3] During the same period, consumer prices rose by 600 percent, more than offsetting a 120 percent increase in wages and salaries.[4] Millions of Iranians remained displaced, and Iran's largest port facilities and oil export facilities were in ruins. Meanwhile, the postrevolutionary baby boom produced a population explosion, along with higher demands for infrastructure and jobs. As late as 1992, only half of Iran's sixty thousand villages had access to electricity.[5] In addition,

---

[1] Blight et al. (2012), pp. 246–7.   [2] Amirahmadi (1990), p. 85.

[3] Ehteshami (1995), p. 93; Jahangir Amuzegar, *Iran's Economy under the Islamic Republic* (London: I. B. Tauris, 1993): pp. 276, 304.

[4] *Iran Times*, October 16, 1992, as quoted in Kaveh Ehsani, "'Tilt but Don't Spill': Iran's Development and Reconstruction Dilemma," *Middle East Report* (November/December 1994), n. 13, p. 21.

[5] Vahe Petrossian, "Generating the Power for the Next Century," *MEED*, January 31, 1992, p. 14.

Iran continued to experience a massive refugee influx, primarily from Afghanistan but soon from Iraq as well.

The war's toll and chaotic economic policy had an enduring impact on Iran's relative position in the world economy. It upended the country's long-term growth patterns – by 1988, GDP per capita hovered around 54 percent of its 1976 high.[6] These declines were felt even more acutely by the population, which despite the isolating effects of a decade of revolution and war, remained engaged and informed about the world around them. By 1988, Iran's per capita income was 25 percent less than that of Turkey, which it had exceeded in the 1960s, and a mere 23 percent of per capita GDP in Western Europe, from 64 percent in 1976.[7] Similar differentials can be seen in comparison with made by other middle-income developing states, including Malaysia and South Korea.[8] The war had torpedoed an Iranian trajectory to secure high middle-income status, perhaps permanently.

The debate on the crisis became more frank as the Rafsanjani government sought to make the case for its agenda. In October 1992, the Central Bank governor Mohsen Nourbakhsh argued before the parliament that "we should not forget that this country was at war for eight years, and the previous administration had unrealistically increased expectation by involving the government in every economic activity from the service industry to banking and finance. Today, we want to increase private investments, and to do so we need to create the necessary ground work."[9] In 2001, Dr. Mousa Ghaninejad of the journal *Eqtesad-e Iran* (*The Economy of Iran*) acknowledged that "the economic infrastructure was deplorable. This means that the government faced a big danger; this was a sort of economic collapse. They had no option but to put up reforms."[10]

For Tehran, the postwar, post-Khomeini unease ran deeper than even these imposing physical and financial balance sheets. War fatigue and economic malaise had weakened popular support for the theocratic state. Proposed responses to this challenge diverged along Iran's established factional fault line. For some – particularly Islamic leftists, but also many conservatives – the revolution's fervor required periodic rekindling

---

[6] Esfahani and Pesaran (2008), p. 8.   [7] Esfahani and Pesaran (2008), pp. 7–8.

[8] Massoud Karshenas and Hassan Hakimian, "Oil, Economic Diversification and the Democratic Process in Iran," *Iranian Studies* 38:1 (March 2005): p. 16.

[9] *Resalat*, October 28, 1992; *Iran Times*, November 22, 1992, as quoted in Baktiari (1996), p. 225.

[10] "Effective Forces in Iran's Political Economy: Interview with Dr. Mousa Ghaninejad," *Hamshahri* (Monthly Economic Supplement), June 2001, pp. 12–15.

through mobilization, commemoration, and occasional provocation, such as the Rushdie *fatwa*. Others appreciated that passion plays could not sustain a system whose coffers were empty and whose citizens were impatient to experience the better life promised by the revolution and the peace.

Rafsanjani was the standard bearer of the latter group. As he prepared to take on the presidency, Rafsanjani was blunt about the country's predicament. "In the ten years after the revolution we were not able to attend to the everyday lives of people because of the war," Rafsanjani mused during the brief campaign, adding, "I have a series of hopes for the future of the country which may or may not square with the potentials at hand. I will try to realize what is practical."[11] However, even as Rafsanjani laid bare the economic imperatives, Ahmad Khomeini – the imam's sole surviving son and a central political player – vowed to prevent any deviation from the revolution's mandate. "I tell you that our officials will slap America on the mouth and drive it out of the Middle East," Khomeini warned. "Today the world is waiting to see how our officials move after the Imam. Will problems such as economic hardships make them go astray from the real path of the Imam and the revolution?"[12]

THE POLITICS OF THE NEW ORDER

Of course, that decision was now in the hands of a new leadership. Khomeini's passing gave way to what initially appeared to be a stable partnership. Khamenei always enjoyed "considerable prestige" among traditionalist clergy for his "passionate but methodical style of speech" and for his survival, despite grievous wounds, of a 1981 assassination attempt.[13] Having served as one of Tehran's Friday prayer leaders, a symbolically important role, Khamenei carefully utilized his authority to appoint *imam jomeh*s and personal representatives in government agencies to disseminate regime ideology and instill loyalty. He bolstered organized clerical groupings, such as the Society of Qom Seminary Instructors, and established networks in the country's important theological colleges.[14] And

[11] Kamran Fazel and Andrew Gowers, "Rafsanjani Faces Up to a Morass of Problems," *FT*, July 28, 1989.

[12] Mohammad Zargham, "Rafsanjani Assumes Presidency, Khomeini's Son Issues Warning," *Reuters*, August 17, 1989.

[13] Kianouche Dorranie, "Khamenei, Iran's Supreme Leader, at Center of Crucial Vote," *AFP*, October 21, 1998.

[14] Paul Taylor, "Tale of Two Ayatollahs Mirrors Iran Politics," *Reuters*, February 17, 1999.

he cultivated important power bases in the military and among the *bonyad*s, which helped fund his office's activities outside the public budget.[15]

Rafsanjani moved into the presidency with an ease that belied the factional divisions that had beset Iran for the previous decade. At the outset, his new position appeared an enviable one. Constitutional revisions had strengthened the office, curtailing the parliament's authority while empowering the executive branch. Khamenei unveiled the constitutional revisions publicly, noting that "all have accepted that many problems arise from non-centralised management.... It is impossible for two people to cut cloth with one pair of scissors: both fingers should belong to the same person."[16] The establishment of the Supreme National Security Council and the newly reinterpreted elections procedures enhanced the president's influence over foreign policy and the domestic power struggle. And Rafsanjani could boast a long experience at the epicenter of postrevolutionary politics as well as the implicit endorsement of the fallen leader, based upon his long-standing association with Khomeini, including responsibility for navigating an exit strategy from the war.

In the hastily organized election, Rafsanjani ran virtually uncontested; the Council of Guardians rejected all but one of the eighty others who applied. His opponent, Abbas Sheybani, a former agriculture minister and parliamentarian, was described as merely "a name to fill out the ballot sheet."[17] The sense that the election was purely procedural was confirmed when Sheybani declined to accept campaign funds, advising his supporters instead to donate to charity. The only individual whose influence rivaled Rafsanjani's was Khomeini's son Ahmad, but he opted to remain outside the bureaucracy, rebuffing appeals to run for parliament or accept another leadership post in favor of a slot on the newly-established Supreme National Security Council and overseeing his father's mausoleum on the outskirts of Tehran. Rafsanjani won easily, with respectable but not extravagant turnout that fell short of the historic popular mandate anticipated by some of his supporters.

---

[15] Ali Nourizadeh, "Editorial," *Al-Moujez an-Iran* 7, Number 6 (February 1998); Farhang Rajaee, "A Thermidor of 'Islamic Yuppies'? Conflict and Compromise in Iran's Politics," *The Middle East Journal* 53: 2 (Spring 1999), p. 228.

[16] Mohammad Zargham, "Iran to Change 'One Man; Two Scissors' Constitution," *Reuters*, July 12, 1989.

[17] Eric Hall, "Iran Names Two for Presidential Poll; Rafsanjani Favourite," *Reuters*, July 9, 1989.

It is a testament to the establishment's commitment to regime stability that the death of the revolution's founder and charismatic center was managed with so little turbulence, and that the transition displayed such ready consensus. The depth of Iran's economic predicament was directly responsible for the decision to conclude the war without achieving its intended aims, and so the cease-fire and succession generated a sense of a new consensus around the exigency of reconstruction. "In my country a big debate has gone on," Gholamreza Aghazadeh, Iran's then-oil minister, told a Western reporter in February 1989. "Now we have decided that the number one priority in this country is the reconstruction of the economy."[18]

And yet the debate was not truly settled, and the divisions within the system remained as fierce and as fresh as ever. The ideological battles over reconstruction represented as ferocious an internal debate as anything the revolutionary regime had yet experienced. The Islamic left saw the talk of reconstruction as the first step along a slippery slope of foreign debt and a return to Iran's formerly dependency. And they feared the population's sacrifices throughout a decade of upheaval and conflict would be squandered to little lasting benefit. "If the curbs on the private sector are lifted, we will have neither bread nor religion," a candidate for the fourth Majlis warned.[19] In early 1989, a broadside in a hard-line journal charged the revolution's leaders with betraying its ideals:

If the war has ended because of the Imam's *maslehat* [prudence], does it mean that the cruel offensive of world arrogance, from more narrow and undetectable angels has come to an end? Would they leave us alone? The wounded snakes of world arrogance led by America with its external and internal agents are plotting to undermine our revolution in its moral and cultural aspects. These plots are far more dangerous and destructive than their war fleets, missiles, air and land offensives and chemical bombs. If we do not pay attention and remain on our guard, God forbid, they will destroy us by our very own hand....

Because the supporters of revolution – the faithful, the Hezbollahis, the families of martyrs and the war veterans – are angry, disappointed and fed-up with this situation; the singers, dancers, musicians and their friends and cronies, on the other hand will never be happy with this system.... The more concessions you make to them, the more the "elephant feels homesick for India."... Stop it before it's too late.[20]

[18] Youssef Ibrahim, "Iran May Borrow at Banks Abroad to Revive Economy," *New York Times*, February 3, 1989.

[19] Bahman Baktiari, "Parliamentary Elections in Iran," *Iranian Studies* 26:3/4 (Summer–Autumn 1993), pp. 382–3.

[20] *Pasdar-e Islam* 86 (January/February 1989), pp. 41, 17, as quoted in Moin (1999), pp. 281–2.

The Islamic left's opposition to Rafsanjani's reconstruction program was not purely, or even primarily, an ideological issue. Rather, institutional politics came into play, as well as the impact of the new approach on the shifting tides of the factional power struggle. During the debate over revising the Constitution, leftists opposed the elimination of the prime ministry and the consolidation of greater authority under the presidency – hardly surprising given their strong majority in the 1988 parliamentary elections. Once the change had been approved, the Islamic left responded to what they perceived, correctly, as a power grab by leaders whose flexibility and commitment to revolutionary dogma were suspect. They sought to challenge Rafsanjani as a means of asserting their place in the postrevolutionary order.

The leftists moved almost immediately, first seeking to prevent Rafsanjani from assuming his new post until the expiration of Khamenei's term in October 1989. The gambit failed, and on August 17, 1989, Hashemi Rafsanjani took the oath of office and made his commitment to reconstruction and development explicit in his speech. "It isn't right to safeguard the nation with the hungry, poor people always marching forward and giving their life," Rafsanjani asserted. "It cannot go on that way.... This country has great potential for economic growth, but since we came to power, we have not done much (to achieve it)."[21] However, he sought to prevent the perception that his agenda contradicted Khomeini's principles, noting that "a new era, if it means turning against the main line drawn by our dear Imam, will never come in our revolution."[22]

Rafsanjani began his first term by taking on the leftists directly, nominating a cabinet that was heavily oriented toward a pragmatic ideological posture. He maintained an important element of continuity, as the scholar Anoushiravan Ehteshami notes, since all the key posts were filled by individuals who had held portfolios at some point during the Musavi years.[23] However, the slate consisted primarily of technocrats – men of executive experience and higher education (several in the United States), more engineers than clerics. He also replaced one of the scions of the Islamic left, Interior Minister Ali Akbar Mohtashami, with whom he had publicly squabbled over war termination and Western hostages in Lebanon. The postwar debates over foreign policy and the reconstruction program made clear that their worldviews continued to differ dramatically;

---

[21] "Rafsanjani Is Sworn in as President," *Los Angeles Times*, August 18, 1989.
[22] Baktiari (1996), p. 188.   [23] Ehteshami (1995), p. 102.

Mohtashami scorned the February 1989 visit of the French foreign minister, questioning the need for diplomatic relations with France. Rafsanjani also removed another vocal radical, Mohammad Musavi Khoeiniha, from the post of prosecutor general.

Despite parliamentary opposition, Rafsanjani managed to secure endorsements for his entire team, asserting his weight to set the agenda for the newly reconfigured system. The cabinet incorporated Mohsen Nurbakhsh, who held a Ph.D in economics from California State University, as finance minister; Mohammad Husayn Adeli, a Berkeley Ph.D in economics and business administration, as Central Bank governor; Mohammad Ali Najafi, who held an M.A. in mathematics from Massachusetts Institute of Technology, as education minister; and Mohammad Nejad-Husaynian, an M.A. in economics from George Washington University, as minister of heavy industries. Perhaps most notable was Rafsanjani's pick for culture minister, Hojjatoleslam Mohammad Khatami, who secured the widest margin of parliamentary support. Rafsanjani appealed to his former Majlis colleagues to consider nominees on their merits, rather than using the vote to debate the reconstruction program itself. "I picked the proposed members of the cabinet on the basis of their personal capabilities and not for their political leanings," Rafsanjani argued. "They are practical men and are from all factions."[24] And the new president dismissed objections to his nominees' Western education or concerns about the extent of their opposition activism prior to the revolution. "You know [prison experience] is a credit, but not essential," he said.[25]

The parliamentary leftists opted to yield; they remained unconvinced by Rafsanjani's agenda, but they also recognized the weakness of their negotiating position. Reconstruction commanded widespread appeal within the system, and the leftists' mistrust of both its advocates and its processes set them apart from Iran's other influential factions, particularly the traditional conservatives, who were eager to capitalize upon new economic opportunities. His victory in gaining approval of his cabinet would not be Rafsanjani's last skirmish with the Majlis. A number of developments, including the radical Mehdi Karrubi's election to replace him as speaker, and Mohtashami's win in a parliamentary by-election, perpetuated the system's political and

[24] Baktiari (1996), p. 190.
[25] Patrick E. Tyler, "Iranian Parliament Endorses Rafsanjani's Cabinet Choices," *WP* August 30, 1989, p. A31.

ideological rifts. Ultimately, these conflicts complicated Rafsanjani's hope of securing Majlis support for reconstruction.

The new president made several other administrative decisions: The Plan and Budget Organization was shifted to a direct subsidiary of the presidential office, after having been elevated to ministerial status during the war; the PBO chief would eventually take on vice presidential status. In addition, Rafsanjani resigned his position as acting commander in chief of the armed forces in September 1989 to prioritize the economic crisis confronting the revolutionary state. Rafsanjani eventually became synonymous with the corruption and opportunism – both political and financial – associated with the revolutionary system and resented by segments of the establishment as well as many ordinary Iranians. At the time that he assumed Iran's second highest office, however, Rafsanjani's rhetoric and policy positions represented a dramatic break from the past in an explicitly accommodating direction. Rafsanjani reflected a powerful embrace of internationalism by the revolutionary system, one that was at least as consequential as that of his successor eight years later.

FIRST DEVELOPMENT PLAN

With his cabinet in place, Rafsanjani appeared well positioned to advance reconstruction and related economic reforms aggressively. Iran's first postrevolutionary development plan was already in place, having been devised even before the war had ended. The draft proposal was completed only three months after the cease-fire by the Plan and Budget Organization, whose rehabilitation after a decade of revolutionary disregard signaled the rising power of the technocracy. Rafsanjani helped organize a parliamentary committee to work with the planners on the specifics, and as president, he sought to begin implementing elements of the plan even before the Majlis passed it. The plan was designed around goals of promoting growth, restraining government deficits, addressing Iran's trade imbalance, and revitalizing the stagnant oil and gas sector. In addition, improvements to Iran's defensive capabilities and infrastructure constituted an important part of the postwar agenda.

The draft Five-Year Plan focused primarily on promoting industrial growth, curtailing the role of government, improving the tax system, and reopening the economy to foreign investment and capital. The budget deficit was to be slashed from approximately 50 percent to 4.2 percent. It envisaged the construction of nearly 2.5 million new housing units, more than one-third of which were to be built in rural areas; as well as ninety-seven hundred kilometers of roads and about eleven hundred kilometers of railways. In addition, the plan set aside $10 billion to be invested in heavy industry; $3.5 billion for expanding oil and gas production. Increases in capital for exploration and production, as well as reconstruction of war-damaged oil fields and export facilities and the return of foreign investment, were intended to boost production to 4.5 mbpd.[26] The architects of the plan looked to Malaysia and China as models to emulate and sought to move the basis of economic policy "from privileging revolutionary commitment (*ta'ahod*) and the poor to championing expertise (*takhasos*) and the professional classes."[27]

The influential PBO head, Masoud Roghani Zanjani, argued that the make-or-break factor for the plan's success was continuing the state's nascent family planning initiative, which was formally launched in 1989. Khamenei himself endorsed the program during the final days of his presidency, appealing to Iranians in a Friday prayer sermon not to "use the Prophet as an excuse to have more children."[28] The high-level investment paid off – population growth rates fell from 3.3 percent in 1988 to 2.9 percent in 1993, and a low of 1.8 percent in 1994.[29] This decline was steeper and more rapid than even the PBO's ambitious plans. However, this success did not mitigate the immediate challenge: the disproportionately large youth cohort, which was beginning to come of age and enter labor markets. This young population entailed massive new investments in expanding basic infrastructure, for example, to accommodate a student cohort that had doubled from 5 million to 10 million between the revolution and the early 1990s.[30]

The population boom impacted Iran's domestic economy as well as its political evolution, fueling the postwar construction boom and the corresponding tensions within various arms of the government itself, and between state and local institutions and individuals and social groups, over real estate costs and availability. The youth bulge contributed to the

---

[26] "Iran's Economy in Dire Straits, Budget Chief Says," *MEED*, August 19, 1989; "Making the Most of Oil," *MEED*, October 18, 1991.
[27] Kaveh Ehsani, "Survival through Dispossession: Privatization of Public Goods in the Islamic Republic," *Middle East Report* 250, Spring 2009, http://www.merip.org/mer/mer250/ehsani.html
[28] Mohammad Zargham, "Don't Use the Prophet to Justify Big Families – Khamenei," *Reuters*, June 2, 1989.
[29] Amirahmadi (1996), p. 128.
[30] Djavad Salehi-Isfahani, "Human Resources in Iran: Potentials and Challenges," *Iranian Studies* 38:1 (March 2005), p. 124.

shift in Iran's center of gravity from predominantly rural to overwhelmingly urban and to the emergence of new urban centers throughout the country. This put intense pressure on the government to provide services, infrastructure, and of course jobs.

In parallel with Rafsanjani's inaugural warnings, the PBO chief, Roghani Zanjani, explicitly linked the reconstruction plan to the revolutionary state's legitimacy, warning Musavi in the final days of his prime ministry that the population could not withstand the same level of sacrifice in peacetime as throughout the long war. There was a broad consensus surrounding the need for substantial economic reform and intensive government investment and reconstruction. "We are preoccupied with a sick, dependent and bankrupt economy," lamented the committee head Morteza Alviri in August 1989. "Jobs seem to get scarcer by the day despite the fact that the nation has embarked on a broad reconstruction programme in which hundreds of towns and cities are to be rebuilt."[31]

Still, Iran's Islamic left faction harbored deep misgivings about the framework for reform. The plan did not reassure the skeptics that the new president intended to sustain the revolutionary emphasis on Islamic values and independence. The leftist critique focused on two main themes: first, the argument that the plan would facilitate individual enrichment and undermine the state's obligation to advance social justice and Islamic values. With no limits on concentration of wealth, the new orientation would encourage greed and exploitation. This was not purely ideological; once again, the Islamic left reflected a keen concern about further empowerment of the *bazaar* and the factions affiliated with the merchant class.[32]

In addition, the leftists focused to the point of obsession on their expectation that the ambitious reconstruction agenda would entail government overcommitments and ultimately require foreign borrowing – an eventuality that they likened to the subjugation of the revolution. Even new arrangements to repay foreign contractors with a proportion of production from their investments – a model that was applied to upstream oil investments as the "buyback" contract – provoked outrage in the parliament, including from MP Abulhassan Haerizadeh, who charged that the buybacks enabled "foreigners to make policies for our basic industries ... they will become the real investors while we will

[31] "Iran's Economy in Dire Straits, Budget Chief Says," *Reuters*, August 19, 1989.
[32] Moslem (2002), pp. 163–6.

be reduced to a broker between them and the Third World where the products will be sold."[33]

The leftists were hardly alone; there were many elements of the reconstruction agenda that unnerved more traditionalist elements of the revolutionary regime. MP Morteza Alviri, who chaired the Majlis Budget Commission, acknowledged to a *Reuters* reporter that "the extreme rightists consider birth control programmes, a scheme to use conscripts as rural teachers, government control on distribution of goods and regional crop policies violate their interpretation of individual freedoms in Islam."[34] Supporters of the plan actively contested the critiques. Ghassem Shoaleh-Sadi, a representative from Shiraz, argued that the Islamic left was "digging the wrong hole, at a time when we are light years away from affluence, they enter the arena with notions that poverty creates independence.... They are not aware that when poverty enters our house, faith departs."[35]

Still, the plan and its key elements survived four months of parliamentary inquisition, passing both the parliament and the Guardians' Council in January 1990[36] with the support of some prominent leftist deputies. This success reflected the relative isolation of the left's statist views after a decade of political dominance and poor economic performance, the ongoing implosion of the socialist economic model worldwide, and the brief coherence among the conservatives within the system, whose interests diverged on many issues but who generally supported the aims and framework of the plan. The cross-factional support for the program also revealed its proponents' success in linking efforts to address Iran's economic exigencies with compelling security concerns. In Rafsanjani's telling, Iran's planning process represented its new contest with the West. "With the implementation of the first five-year development plan, the arrogant powers have realized that they have lost the game," he added.[37]

---

[33] *Kayhan-e Havai*, 14 Day 1367, p. 24, as quoted in Amirahmadi (January 1990), p. 33, n23.

[34] Sharif Imam-Jomeh, "Iran's Five-Year Plan Unlikely to Face Major Changes," *Reuters*, January 30, 1990.

[35] Baktiari (1996), p. 197.

[36] Full text of the plan available in Persian from the Expediency Council Web site at http://www.maslehat.ir/Contents.aspx?p=17e0f3f3-5988-4069-a89b-73ad17f87e9d

[37] Jerome Socolovsky, "Rafsanjani Says U.S. Has 'Lost the Game' in Effort to Isolate Iran," *AP*, January 7, 1994.

The plan's implementation began immediately. In 1990–1, the government announced the beginning of privatization by selling off four hundred of its three thousand enterprises, a quantity bounded only by questions affecting the legality of the scheme. Many of the largest state firms remained off-limits because of constitutional mandates. In all, the first period of privatization – composed of offerings from 1990 to 1994 before the Majlis suspension – resulted in total sales of 1.7 trillion rials. The privatization effort would later resume between 1995 and 1997, when a reported 1.8 trillion rials in shares were distributed only to workers and war veterans.[38] Just more than 3.3 trillion rials in shares were distributed to the private sector through 1376 (1997/8), according to Iranian Privatization Organization (IPO) statistics.[39]

The privatization program, while consistent with conventional wisdom on development, was undertaken independently rather than in cooperation with international financial institutions such as the World Bank or International Monetary Fund. *The Economist* noted at the time, "Iran has voluntarily adopted the principle of IMF's restructuring rules, albeit without asking for IMF loans in return."[40] This distance was deliberate, as the architects of Iran's reconstruction understood that any perception that the program had been devised or dictated by the international community would exacerbate the suspicions of its internal critics. Indeed, even the minimal relationships established during this period with the IMF and other organizations provoked conservative media diatribes.

Rafsanjani also made the first significant attempts to reform Iran's foreign investment system, hoping to address postwar capital needs, but met with difficulties in tapping Western sources. Modest progress in formulating a clear and open legal framework for investment helped spur the process. In 1992, the Finance Ministry announced new provisions permitting full foreign ownership of Iranian firms and providing indemnification against nationalization and protection for capital repatriation.[41] In 1995, the Iranian Council of Ministers made a series of

---

[38] Jahangir Amuzegar, "Islamic Social Justice, Iranian Style," *Middle East Policy*, Fall 2007.

[39] The IPO table, which does not appear to adjust figures for inflation, includes a column to show that the period of 1370–6 accounted for less than 1 percent of the total value of shares distributed in the Islamic Republic through the end of Ahmadinejad's first term. Iranian Privatization Organization, "Statistics: Distribution from 1370 to 1387," http://www.ipo.ir/index.aspx?siteid=1&pageid=525

[40] Kamran M. Dadkhah, "Iran and the Global Finance Markets," in *Iran Encountering Globalization: Problems and Prospects*, 2003, ed. Ali Mohammadi.

[41] "Iran Allows Foreigners to Buy Its Companies," *New York Times*, June 29, 1992.

decisions to clarify ambiguity arising from Article 81 of the Constitution that foreign partners could indeed own majority stakes in joint ventures.[42]

In addition to the privatization program, the government moved quickly to liberalize the exchange rate. Through 1989–90, the tiered system included twelve different exchange rates. The highest rate was the free-market rate, which hovered around 1,200 to 1,400 rials/$, for imports not favored by the government.[43] For transactions not explicitly approved by the government, however, a significant parallel market emerged. With the stringent artificial restrictions put on the exchange rate, the market rate for dollars rose steadily throughout the years following the revolution, and by 1990, the parallel market premium topped 2000 percent over the official rate – among the highest discrepancies ever observed internationally.[44] The primary beneficiary of this system was the state, as well as individuals and institutions with privileged access to foreign currency, who earned massive profits in the parallel market. Sales of foreign currency were a major source of revenue for the state, which reportedly took in as much as 5 percent of GDP (1989–91) via foreign currency sales. The tiered rate also appears to have enabled the government to mitigate its spiraling budget deficits, which ballooned from 51 percent of total government spending in 1989 to a mere 6.7 percent four years later.[45]

To rationalize the system, Tehran narrowed the rates for imports to three in January 1991 – the basic official rate of 70 rials/$, the competitive rate of 600 rials/$, and the floating rate, maintained by Bank Markazi, which was comparable to the open-market rate and rose to as high as 1,460 rials/$ in March–April 1992. Sixteen essential consumer goods, in addition to defense and development goods, were eligible to be imported via the basic rate; these accounted for nearly two-thirds of all imports. An additional 290 items, mainly raw materials and intermediate goods, were eligible for the competitive rate, while all other goods (approximately

---

[42]	Iran Trade Point. "Foreign Investment – Guide to Iranian Market," http://www.irtp.com/howto/foreig/b13.asp. Accessed November 2008.

[43]	Amuzegar (1993), p. 165.

[44]	Adnan Mazarei, "The Parallel Market for Foreign Exchange in an Oil Exporting Economy: The Case of Iran, 1978–1990." IMF Working Paper 95/69, July 1995, pp. 2–3.

[45]	Abbas Valadkhani, "An Empirical Analysis of the Black Market Exchange Rate in Iran." Queensland University of Technology, School of Economics and Finance, Discussion Papers in Economics, Finance and International Competitiveness 144 (May 2003), pp. 2–3.

10–15 percent of imports) had to use the floating rate.[46] The parallel market was composed of a combination of active and closely linked markets, including an offshore market in Dubai, which was officially recognized and operated by domestic commercial banks, as well as the illegal street market.[47]

Consistent with the efforts to unravel the architecture of the war economy, there were plans to tackle the subsidies on fuel and consumer staples. Adeli, then-Central Bank governor, insisted in 1991 that the government was "trying to differentiate between items that need continued subsidies and those that do not. Instead of subsidies, we will gradually move toward making cash payments to the poorest so that they can choose what they want to buy."[48] There was also a recognition that such cash subsidies were necessary to cushion the impact of foreign exchange reform. In July 1991, ration coupons for chicken and eggs were replaced by direct cash subsidies. Planned price increases on products such as bread were deferred indefinitely. In an effort to restrain the inevitably inflationary impact, Adeli in July 1990 announced a 25 percent hike in profit (interest) rates.

Not all the economic reforms conformed to the plan, or to the preferences of the reconstruction-oriented executive branch. Although Rafsanjani was able to push through the major elements of his agenda at the outset of his first term, Iran remained greatly influenced by the interests and preferences of the leftists in parliament, who hoped to use the war's end to reinvigorate the state's efforts to advance social justice. Their continuing clout helped facilitate the passage and enactment of the 1990 Labor Law, which remains on the books and continues to be seen as a major obstacle to job creation and entrepreneurial activity.

The legal framework for labor had been debated inconclusively throughout the war, against the backdrop of recent historical experience with disruptive labor unrest and political change. The ability of the government to shape conditions of employment had served as an opportunity for Khomeini to advantage the leftists. The 1959 Labor Law had set a flat-rate minimum wage for the entire country, and employment

---

[46] Amuzegar (1993), p. 175.
[47] Oya Celasun, "Exchange Rate Regime Considerations in an Oil Economy: The Case of the Islamic Republic of Iran." IMF Working Paper 03/26, 2003.
[48] Judith Miller, "Iran Tries to Decentralize Economy, Causing Widespread Pain," *New York Times*, April 9, 1991.

had long proven inelastic; after the 1986 oil price collapse, output crashed by 32 percent but employment fell only 6 percent.[49]

The new law passed in 1990 recognized the rights to organize and to collective bargaining; outlawed child labor; required paid maternity leave and feeding/day care time; and mandated that large employers provide housing, training, and sports facilities to workers.[50] However, it also imposed stringent restrictions on firing workers. Overall, the law has proven problematic in a number of areas: First, the strict definition of workers' rights increases labor costs significantly and decreases incentive to hire.[51] In addition, the new labor law undermined privatization efforts; limits on abrogating labor contracts foisted bloated payrolls on private buyers of new firms.[52]

"The law is not ideal, we know," Iran's Central Bank governor conceded in 1991. "But it would have been far more radical if we had let the workers' unions draft it."[53] Iranian firms have frequently sought and found means of circumventing the terms of the law, utilizing a variety of work-arounds, including renewable short-term contracts (not covered by the law) and indirect employment through service companies and cooperatives, to circumvent its requirements. In this sense, the Labor Law's inflexibility has contributed to slower growth and hiring hesitancy rather than fulfilling its intended design to enhance job security.[54] Exploitation of these loopholes has generated vocal opposition from labor leaders and workers, sometimes in the form of antigovernment rallies.[55] Conversely, the government has used the law as a mechanism for constraining labor activism, since it insists that labor organizations operate "in a manner guaranteeing the protection of the interests of society as a whole."[56] In 1993, the government tried but failed to amend the law, and Rafsanjani's allies were left to comfort themselves with the

---

[49] Hamid Tabatabai and Djavad Salehi-Isfahani, "Population, Labor, and the Employment Problem in Iran," in *Labor and Human Capital in the Middle East*, ed. Salehi-Isfahani (Reading, UK: Ithaca Press, 2001), p. 80.

[50] Djavad Salehi-Isfahani, "Labor and the Challenge of Economic Restructuring in Iran." *Middle East Report* 210, Spring 1999, pp. 34–7.

[51] Ibid.   [52] Ibid.

[53] Judith Miller, "Iran Tries to Decentralize Economy, Causing Widespread Pain," *New York Times*, April 9, 1991.

[54] Ibid., pp. 34–7.

[55] "Iran: Workers Stage Rally outside Majles to Protest Temporary Contract Law," *IRNA* (English), November 20, 2005.

[56] Ibid.

recognition that they had at least blunted some of the more radical elements of the proposal.

Iran's economy performed reasonably well during this period, although the role of the Five-Year Plan itself was probably less relevant than the simple dynamics of postwar exuberance. In 1991, Iran's foreign minister declared to participants attending an international conference in Isfahan that a "new order" was emerging in which "economic considerations overshadow political priorities."[57] Most of the growth during this period can be attributed to government spending, much of it financed by foreign debt.[58] And while nonoil exports began to expand, the increases were largely attributable to traditional products such as carpets, rather than industry.[59] Opposition to the reconstruction program remained fierce from the parliamentary leftists. Mohstashami continued to denounce the government's efforts to secure external capital, arguing that "borrowing money abroad won't solve our economic problems but will enslave us."[60]

Throughout it all, Rafsanjani and his allies recognized that they were fighting an uphill battle in trying to reform and revitalize the economy. "There are so many obstacles to growth here at so many levels," the Central Bank governor Adeli remarked in 1991. "Islamic militants are doing everything they can to prevent this place from opening up. But Rafsanjani's people are different. They do think first of Iranian interests, not Islamic interests and that, at least, is a start."[61] On the streets, the initial reforms contributed to a sense that the revolutionary siege was lifting. "It's getting to be like it was under the Shah," a Jewish Iranian man told a *New York Times* reporter in 1991. "This long, dark period for us is ending."[62]

EARLY OPENINGS, DIPLOMATIC AND ECONOMIC

Parallel with his domestic economic reforms, Rafsanjani sought to build a more conducive international context for the reconstruction program.

---

[57] Elaine Sciolino, "Is Iran's Urge to Prosper Overtaking Its Islamic Zeal?" *New York Times,* June 2, 1991, p. A2.

[58] Khajehpour in Esposito and Ramazani, eds. (2001), p. 98.

[59] Amirahmadi (1996), p. 133.

[60] Claude Van England, "Gulf Crisis Helps Iranian Leader in Internal Struggle," *Christian Science Monitor,* December 19, 1990, p. 1.

[61] Judith Miller, "Iran Tries to Decentralize Economy, Causing Widespread Pain," *New York Times,* April 9, 1991.

[62] Judith Miller, "After the War: Islamic Radicals Lose Their Tight Grip on Iran," *New York Times,* April 8, 1991.

Central to the reconstruction strategy was a recognition that Tehran could no longer afford to foster its old enmities. Oil prices and politics no doubt played a part in these calculations; OPEC was in disarray, thanks to a self-defeating battle for market share among the major Gulf producers, and the outcome was a growing supply glut and weakened oil prices. Immediately after the Iran-Iraq cease-fire, the Saudis ramped up production considerably, far above its 4.5 mbpd OPEC quota. The other major Gulf producers, Kuwait and the United Arab Emirates, effectively sat out of the cartel's deliberations throughout the rest of the year.[63]

Iran's reopening to the world also reflected a crucial, if typically implicit, nod to public expectations and the regime's awareness of the system's need for continuing public support. Iranians viewed the Khamenei-Rafsanjani dual leadership as a signal that the long siege of isolation had ended. As an Iranian predicted to a Western reporter shortly before the 1989 presidential election, "Rafsanjani will make up with the West and they'll rebuild our industry and it'll be like before."[64] In the end, the process of rehabilitating Iran's reputation and repairing its ties to the world proved more difficult than anticipated, and the outcome would remain quite different from what it had been "before."

As with subsequent bouts of international outreach, Tehran began the process within its own neighborhood. The Gulf states remained suspicious but were receptive to a fresh start. Rafsanjani sought to disavow the use of terrorism and subversion, stressing that Tehran now "is not thinking of exporting our revolution through direct intervention or by force. The policy of force is not a successful policy."[65] By early 1989, Iran had resumed full diplomatic relations with Kuwait and Bahrain; engaged in quiet talks with Riyadh; welcomed the Omani foreign minister to Tehran; and undertaken high-level visits to Qatar, Bahrain, and the UAE. There were a series of intervening incidents, including Riyadh's decision to ramp up oil production dramatically in the wake of the cease-fire, that slowed progress toward a better relationship with Iran's neighbors. It would take Iraq's August 1990 invasion of Kuwait and Rafsanjani's consolidation of power to nudge the process of regional détente past the finish line; however, the stage had been firmly set with the early measures.

---

[63] "OPEC Seeks Kuwait and Emirate Oil Cut," *Reuters*, November 25, 1989.

[64] Kamran Fazel and Andrew Gowers, "Rafsanjani Faces up to a Morass of Problems: The Tasks Facing the Man Elected President in Tehran Today," *FT*, July 28, 1989, p. 4.

[65] Ed Blanche, "Iran Reaches Out to End Isolation despite Opposition," *AP*, October 1, 1988.

Tehran also spread its wings well beyond the region. "Our postwar foreign policy will be more open than our policy during the war," Rafsanjani declared in August 1988. "We must take this opportunity to explain our aims and talk with the people of the world."[66] Iran intensified its involvement in Afghanistan after the Soviet withdrawal in 1989, supporting groups that would eventually morph into the Northern Alliance. Rafsanjani traveled to Moscow within weeks of Khomeini's death in June 1989 and later, in 1993 and 1995, exchanged visits with the Indian prime minister. For the first time, Tehran appointed envoys to the Organization of the Islamic Conference and later to the Economic Cooperation Organization. Rafsanjani praised South Korea and Turkey as models of development and began courting Seoul as a possible replacement for the Japanese firm Mitsui in building the long-delayed Bandar Khomeini petrochemicals plant.

The early openings inevitably became intertwined with the internal competition for influence, as in the Romanian dictator Nicolae Ceausescu's December 1989 state visit. Tehran and Bucharest had long-standing and valuable economic ties, but the timing – amid intensifying unrest across Eastern Europe and the violent repression of Romanian protesters in Timisoara – could not have been worse. Only days after leaving Tehran, Ceausescu was deposed and executed, and left-wing Islamists in the Majlis, including the former revolutionary prosecutor Sadeq Khalkhali, used the episode to denounce the Foreign Ministry as incompetent and raise questions about the theocracy's odd embrace of a corrupt, violent autocrat. Iran's leadership briefly scrambled for moral righteousness, firing the country's envoy to Romania, before sternly drawing the episode to a close. Khamenei publicly defended Foreign Minister Velayati; conservative newspapers inveighed against "irresponsible statements" and attacks on the state's institutions "as a platform to settle sectarian scores." The Tehran *bazaar* closed in sympathy with the government, and similar petitions were circulated within the parliament. In the end, Khamenei's defiance won the day, and the radicals were put on the defensive.

Domestic politics also played into another vexing foreign policy question, the aftereffects of the 1989 Rushdie *fatwa*. The Rushdie affair gravely disrupted Iran's diplomatic relations with Europe, which historically served as Iran's main trading partner and which offered the most propitious source for the investment and technology that were critical to

---

[66] Ibid.

Rafsanjani's reconstruction agenda. The genius of Khomeini's grand-standing on Rushdie, however, was the issue's durability as a source of regime mobilization and a cause of frictions abroad. Even after the imam's death, it was virtually unthinkable for any Iranian political figure to disavow its most esteemed cleric. Commemorations of the verdict, as well as new threats and actual violence against individuals associated with the book, ensured that the image of a reradicalized Iran played on a perennial loop in the global news feed. Rafsanjani and his Foreign Ministry sought to distance Iran's elected institutions from the *fatwa*, but these efforts were undercut by Khamenei and hard-liners close to the regime, who repeatedly reaffirmed its validity and pledged its implementation.

Eventually, the issue receded from the agenda in Iran's relations with Europe. West Germany's foreign minister visited Tehran in November 1989 with a 112-member delegation in tow and inked preliminary agreements on industrial investments and training – all facilitated by a new stream of West German credits.[67] Senior European officials began adding Tehran to their travel schedule, and in 1991 the "troika" of European Community presidents met with Rafsanjani.

Tehran's post-Khomeini international outreach was explicitly intended to support the reconstruction effort with renewed investment and trade. "If people believe we can live behind a closed door, they are mistaken," Rafsanjani noted. "While we must be reasonably independent, we are in need of friends and allies around the world."[68] He ended Iran's self-imposed estrangement from foreign capital markets and international financial institutions. Tehran resumed consultations with the International Monetary Fund, and the World Bank concluded its first loan to Tehran since the revolution for earthquake relief after a devastating June 1990 temblor, which generated $10 to $15 billion in direct damage.[69] Notably, even Washington supported the bank's assistance to Tehran after that crisis. Tehran also launched dozens of technical cooperation programs with UNIDO.

The reconstruction program began to unshackle Iran's antipathy toward those investors and industries associated with the monarchy. Tehran sought short- and long-term export cover from South Korean, Japanese, and European banks.[70] The value of Iran's exports rose by

---

[67] Elaine Sciolino, "Tehran Finds War Was Easier to Make than a Stable Peace," *New York Times*, January 2, 1989, p. 1.

[68] *Ittila'at*, August 10, 1991.

[69] *Kayhan-e Hava'i*, 20 Tir 1369, p. 2, as quoted in Amirahmadi (1990), p. 67.

[70] Vahe Petrossian, "Rafsanjani Scores Economic Points," *MEED*, October 27, 1989, p. 9.

approximately 9 percent per year between 1987 and 2006 (although Iranian imports also expanded by a nearly commensurate pace).[71] Tehran managed to reconstitute its oil production, with an increase of a million barrels per day over a four-year period to reach 3.2 mbpd in 1990.[72] However, Rafsanjani and his team appreciated that Western technology and capital were required to sustain significantly higher production levels and revenues. As a result, he dispatched Oil Ministry teams to trumpet the reconstruction program in Tokyo and other capitals with valuable financial and technical capabilities. In 1991, Tehran signed preliminary agreements with Japanese and European companies for developing several oil and gas fields – the first foreign investments in the sensitive upstream sector since the revolution. His administration also welcomed the return of flagship American corporations such as Coca-Cola and Pepsi Cola, moves that appealed to the consumer market, and offered cheaper, domestically produced alternatives to imported sodas.[73]

Tehran also sought to rehabilitate the relationship between the Islamic Republic and the Iranian diaspora, in hopes of attracting repatriated investment. In April 1991, two senior officials met with four hundred Iranian expatriates in New York in an effort to generate interest in Iranian investment prospects. The campaign included assurances from the Iranian judiciary about legal protections accorded the diaspora.[74] In these efforts, Rafsanjani was countered by the same radicals who opposed his broader agenda, including Ahmad Khomeini. Early outcomes suggested only modest success; by 1993, twenty-six hundred Iranians had returned.[75]

Even as they ramped up trade and investment with their historic sources in Europe, Iran's leaders had begun looking toward the East in earnest. The primary vectors of Iran's foreign trade relationships were already in flux. The revolution itself had redirected Iran's oil exports away from the United States and to a lesser extent reduced the shares of Britain, Germany, and Japan. Meanwhile, even before the fall of the Soviet

---

[71] U.S. Government Accountability Office, Report to the Ranking Member, Subcommittee on National Security and Foreign Affairs, House Committee on Oversight and Government Reform, "Iran Sanctions: Impact in Further U.S. Objectives Is Unclear and Should Be Reviewed," December 2007, p. 27.

[72] Nomani and Behdad (2006), p. 48.

[73] "Islamic Republic of Iran: Industrial Revitalization," EIU-UNIDO Joint Publication (Vienna: UNIDO, 1995), p. xxiv.

[74] "Iranians Residing Abroad Welcome Home," *Kayhan Havai*, October 28, 1992, as quoted in Torbat (2002), p. 291.

[75] Torbat (2002), p. 293.

Union and the takeoff of the Asian economies, crude supplies to Eastern Europe, Turkey, and some Asian countries were already increasing.[76] The supply of weaponry and military materiel had also altered radically because of the transformation in Iran's political orientation. And the revolutionary disruptions had meant that Iran lost significant market share, probably permanently, for its traditionally important nonoil exports – caviar, carpets, and pistachios – as new, often cheaper competitors moved into the void.

Many of the new revolutionaries saw Tokyo as the standard bearer for an independent, interests-based foreign policy. "We have the oil, Japan the technology, China the labor and Central Asian countries the agriculture; therefore, an intermingling of these economies could bring prosperity to the continent."[77] Intellectuals, including the then-Culture Minister Khatami, who devoted a chapter of his book to the Russo-Japanese War, saw Japan's ascendance from feudalism and defeat as a model for Iran's rise. In addition to Tokyo, the revolutionary state began courting India. In 1992, the Indian Prime Minister N. K. Rao visited Tehran, and Rafsanjani returned the favor three years later.

Perhaps the most significant aspect of Iran's new international outreach was the initiative to expand relations with Beijing. This reflected official gratitude for China's wartime help in arms sales and missile development, as well as opportunism among an Iranian leadership more inclined toward economic liberalization than political moderation. The then-Foreign Minister Ali Akbar Velayati visited Beijing in late 1988, expressing Iran's desire to benefit from Chinese technology, labor, and industry, and met with qualified support from Premier Zhao Ziyang. Khamenei followed with a 1989 state visit. Rafsanjani praised Beijing as a "true friend of Iran"[78] and set out to encourage China's involvement in the reconstruction program. During this period, China also began to play an integral role in reviving Iran's nuclear program. Iran's outreach corresponded to China's economic transformation, the energy demands of a supersize economy growing at epic rates, and Beijing's desires to counterbalance U.S. political domination of the world.[79]

---

[76] Katouzian (1989), pp. 61–2.
[77] *Tehran Times*, February 22, 1993, in Menashri (2001), p. 203.
[78] Shireen T. Hunter, *Iran and the World: Continuity in a Revolutionary Decade* (Bloomington: Indiana University Press, 1990), p. 161.
[79] Garver (2006), pp. 106–7.

A series of high-level visits helped spur a gradual expansion in Chinese assistance; in 1993, China issued its first three formal loans for Iranian trade and development activities.[80] During this period, China's need for raw materials and energy grew substantially, and in addition to the expanding energy trade, Chinese companies began investing in the exploitation of Iran's mineral resources, a sector that featured prominently in Iran's first Five-Year Development Plan. Projects included a joint venture on a $350 million copper mine in East Azerbaijan in 1996 and a contract to build a $200 million aluminum smelter in Arak awarded to a Chinese state-affiliated firm in 2001.[81] Other Chinese investments in Iran included dam building, hydroelectricity, thermoelectricity, manufacturing, and agricultural development. Still, even in this early phase of postrevolutionary economic ties, China posed as much of a threat to Iran as an opportunity – as Beijing increasingly became a mass producer of "Persian" carpets that were considerably less costly than their authentic Iranian competitors.[82]

Bilateral trade doubled between 1996 and 1999, and over the subsequent five years, China's exports to Iran expanded by 360 percent, a larger expansion than any other Chinese market.[83] Much of this involved infrastructure projects, such as the construction of the Tehran metro, which at the time represented "one of the largest electrical and mechanical export contracts China has ever had overseas."[84] Beginning with $573 million in contracts signed with the Chinese firms CITIC, NORINCO, and the China National Technology Import and Export Corporation, Chinese firms were instrumental in the construction of the first two phases of the mass transit system, particularly after Iranian officials balked at the high bids submitted by European firms in the early 1990s.

WASHINGTON, TEHRAN, AND A STALLED OPENING

Iran's fitful international overtures reflected a broader modulation in the tone of its foreign policy after Rafsanjani's election. However, it was the relationship, or lack thereof, with Washington that had the capacity

---

[80] Garver (2006), pp. 244–5.   [81] Garver (2006), p. 254.

[82] Youssef M. Ibrahim, "The Magic Has Left the Persian Carpet," *New York Times*, February 12, 1995.

[83] Nicolo Nourafchan, "Constructive Partner or Menacing Threat? Analyzing China's Role in the Iranian Nuclear Program," *Asian Security* 6:1 (2010), p. 36.

[84] Nicolo Nourafchan, *Asian Security* 6:1 (2010), p. 37.

to make or break Iran's future. The George H. W. Bush administration took office just as the Islamic Republic was experiencing the complex transitions from war to reconstruction and from Khomeini's primacy to the leadership of his heirs. Washington's approach to Tehran was now less focused on the Gulf and more directed toward addressing the threat of Iranian-backed terrorism emanating from the Levant. The most immediate manifestation of the threat was the Lebanese civil war, and the seizure of Americans and Europeans as hostages by a variety of armed militants there.

Even before he assumed the presidency, Rafsanjani made no effort to disguise Iran's expectations of remuneration for any assistance provided in resolving the fate of the hostages; in 1987, he told a reporter of an American newspaper that "if you expect us to do something for you, you must do something to show you are not against us."[85] Despite the scandal associated with Washington's last effort to persuade Iran to cooperate on this issue, Bush again looked to open a channel to Tehran on the hostages, most notably in his inaugural address, when he urged Iranian leaders that "assistance can be shown here, and will be long remembered. Good will begets good will. Good faith can be a spiral that endlessly moves on." Bush buttressed his oft-quoted inaugural rhetoric a number of steps to demonstrate his seriousness, including the first authorized back-channel intermediary from the U.S. president to his newly installed Iranian counterpart, Hashemi Rafsanjani.

Predictably, Khamenei publicly denounced the overture. "Now the new U.S. President has stated that he is ready to resume relations with Iran, subject to this and that. He is setting conditions! We do not accept your conditions! You have nothing to say to us. We object, we do not agree to a relationship with you! We are not prepared to establish relations with powerful world devourers like you! The Iranian nation has no need of the United States, nor is the Iranian nation afraid of the United States."[86] For his part, Rafsanjani countered with his trademark pragmatism. In an August 1989 sermon that was one of his first as president, Rafsanjani diverged briefly from the standard revolutionary invective toward America to make an explicit appeal to the White House to work cooperatively toward a solution to the Lebanese civil war and hostage ordeal. A few days later, a senior Iranian official close to Rafsanjani was

---

[85] Susan J. Smith, "Bonn Sends Envoy to Tehran to Ask Help on Hostages," *AP*, January 29, 1987.
[86] Khamenei Friday prayer sermon, January 7, 1989, as quoted in Fuller (1991), pp. 255–6.

quoted as suggesting that Washington could expedite the hostages' freedom by releasing Tehran's remaining frozen assets.[87]

During the ensuing months, the Bush administration pointedly left the door open to improved ties through rhetoric and modest gestures on Iran's outstanding assets and its diplomatic presence in the United States. A November 1989 administration judgment by the U.S.-Iran Claims Tribunal at the Hague in the cases of several contentious outstanding debts to Iran contributed to the perception that Washington was preparing the ground for rapprochement.[88] Additionally, Bush reiterated an interest in rapprochement, declaring, "Look, we don't have to be hostile with Iran for the rest of our lives," adding that "there are many ways that countries who are estranged can get back together."[89] The mutual feelers and episodic appearance of flexibility persisted throughout the Bush years. In fact, in February 1990, Bush personally took the telephone for nearly half an hour to speak with an imposter posing as Rafsanjani. When the mishap was made public, the Iranian president seemed to delight in its absurdity, celebrating the incident as vindication of Tehran's leverage. "Can it be that such a global power, with all its means, can talk to a person it cannot identify?" Rafsanjani chortled in a Friday prayers sermon. "America is very much in need of talking to Iran and praise be to God, is deprived of this. Iran is so important that the biggest power in the world, the biggest bully on earth, tries to contact its officials by telephone."[90]

Still, neither American gestures, nor the subtle signaling, nor back-channel messages managed to launch a serious bilateral dialogue as Iran entered the post-Khomeini era. Both sides' feelers failed to reach far enough to bridge the existing gap or overcome domestic political disincentives. The legacy of the disastrous arms-for-hostages dealings continued to loom large and created divergent preferences on the modalities

---

[87] In August 1989, Rafsanjani said, "I wish to say – I address the White House – that Lebanon has a solution; the freedom of the hostages is solvable." Bernard Weinraub, "Iran's President Offers U.S. Help in Hostage Crisis," *New York Times*, August 5, 1989; Maureen Dowd, "Iran Is Reported Ready for a Deal to Recover Assets," *New York Times*, August 9, 1989. Also notable was a 1990 opinion piece in the newspaper *Ettela'at* by Rafsanjani ally Ata'ollah Mohajerani, who advocated a new opening to Washington on the basis of Iran's national interests. *Ettela'at*, April 26, 1990.

[88] Scheherazade Daneshkhu, "West Scrambles for Share of Iranian Market – Tehran Is Back in World Trade Fold," *FT*, December 4, 1991, p. 7.

[89] Maureen Dowd, "Bush Says 'Clear Signal' from Iran on Hostages Could Reopen Ties," *New York Times*, August 16, 1989.

[90] Youssef M. Ibrahim, "Iranian Leader Mocks Bush over Hoax," *New York Times*, March 10, 1990.

for any direct talks. Tehran needed secrecy more than ever, while no U.S. politician dared deal with the Islamic Republic except in public.[91] Tehran's paranoia toward Washington remained high – not without reason. In early 1989, Tehran unmasked a U.S. spy network in the Iranian military,[92] and American intelligence assistance to Saddam Hussein continued until a few months before his 1990 move into Kuwait.[93]

The stakes were especially complicated for Rafsanjani's efforts to press his interest in improving Iran's relationship with Washington. On one side of Tehran's precarious political equilibrium were Islamic leftists, who dominated the Majlis and were positioned to shape his reconstruction agenda. This was the faction that led the embassy takeover, agitated for export of the revolution, nurtured Hezbollah, and excoriated the pragmatists for purchasing arms from the Great Satan. However, he also had to contend with Khamenei and the revolution's conservative wing. Khamenei's posture on this issue was crystal clear. In May 1990, amid a whispering campaign about the possibilities for American investment or renewed ties, he categorically rejected any prospect of negotiations and insisted that any future shift in position would require his support.[94] Several years later, Khamenei stepped into this contested terrain once again; after reports that several high-level officials were urging a reconsideration of Iran's stance toward the United States, Khamenei announced that "relations with the United States at this stage are neither possible nor beneficial [for the country]. They [Americans] have yet to show a genuine change in their position towards Iran."[95]

Any explicit overtures toward Washington risked furnishing both poles of Iran's factional divide with common cause against Rafsanjani, and dooming his economic reform program. In a sense, Iran's pragmatic president was caught between a rock and a hard place. To advance Iran's postwar domestic agenda, he needed to fulfill multiple requirements simultaneously – transform Iran's international image in order to attract foreign investment, while neutralizing Iran's Islamic radicals and assuaging the regime's constituencies among the clergy and merchant community. Such a juggling act would prove difficult, if not impossible, to sustain.

---

[91] The State Department reportedly fielded multiple overtures for dialogue with Iran, but none were willing to pursue public discussions. Crist (2012), p. 383.
[92] Crist (2012), pp. 372–9.   [93] Crist (2012), p. 385.
[94] *Kayhan*, May 2, 1990, as quoted in Siavoshi (1992), p. 45.
[95] Moslem (2002), p. 226; *Ettela'at*, October 24, 1993.

As a result, Rafsanjani continued his low-key efforts to free the Western hostages in Lebanon, but in that complicated quagmire, progress was slow and subject to reversal, with atrocities such as the 1989 murder of Lt. Col. William Higgins and the seizure of new hostages even as some Westerners were freed. Moreover, the Iranian president failed to curb Iran's support for terrorism elsewhere. Throughout his eight-year presidency, attacks against Iranian dissidents in Europe continued, such as the August 1991 murder of the former Prime Minister Shahpour Bakhtiar in Paris.

Iranian assistance in Lebanon was not wholly unrewarded, as is sometimes suggested; Washington advanced several significant settlements from the financial claims still in arbitration from the revolutionary upheaval. In addition, Bush publicly offered to intercede with Israel to ascertain the status of Iranians missing in Lebanon as a goodwill gesture. And Tehran was thanked publicly by Washington for its contribution to the process that freed individual hostages, an acknowledgment of its sway intended to satisfy Iran's sense of importance. However, the Islamic Republic remained on the U.S. government's list of state sponsors of terrorism, and Washington soon intensified economic penalties against Tehran, including pressuring a number of U.S. allies to rescind trade deals for dual-use technology. The consequence of these feelers was a sense within both capitals that the back and forth had served their side poorly, and that their adversary had gotten the better of the transaction. Still, the testing did not end with the hostage diplomacy. Before the end of his presidency, Rafsanjani would attempt a dramatic economic opening to Washington, one that ended very differently than he might have hoped.

THE GULF WAR, AND BEYOND

Other developments conspired to complicate Iran's efforts to chart a new course in the world. First was Iraq's August 1990 invasion of Kuwait, which aligned Washington and Tehran against a common enemy but also sent hundreds of thousands of American troops to Iran's periphery. Unwilling to jeopardize its warming relations with the Gulf states, Tehran remained neutral and offered what President Bush described as "indirect assurances" that it would not assist Baghdad in subverting the international embargo.[96] Saddam's miscalculation posed some immediate

---

[96] Andrew Rosenthal, "Confrontation in the Gulf: Iraq Air Blockade Is Backed by Bush," *New York Times*, September 18, 1990.

benefits for the Iranian leadership – specifically, Baghdad's sudden willingness to sign off on Tehran's demands as part of the protracted war termination talks. However, it also created intense new threats, such as the U.S. presence and the complications of the failed postwar uprising among Iraqi Shi'a.

Shared interests in penalizing Saddam did not necessarily move Tehran closer to détente with Washington, in part because Iranian rhetoric and policies remained hostile. Khamenei condemned the American effort to evict Saddam from Kuwait and implicitly slammed the Saudis for their role. "It is necessary for us to inform the Muslim nations that we are strongly opposed to the American presence here.... Utter shame on those governments who allow aggressive America to come here in pursuit of its own interests."[97] These views were shared not just by Iran's conservatives, but also by the leftists, who were convinced that the effort to liberate Kuwait represented a toehold for America's imperial ambitions that would inevitably menace the Islamic Republic.

The war helped to ratchet up oil prices, at least temporarily, boosting Iran's oil revenues above $16 billion in the year ending in March 1991, approximately 50 percent higher than the previous year.[98] The temporary loss of Kuwaiti crude and Baghdad's postwar export challenges proved to be a multibillion-dollar bonanza for Tehran. Still, even this windfall was not without diplomatic complications and fiscal disappointments. Expecting that Saddam's latest misstep would spark a sustained rise in oil prices, Iran resented Riyadh's decision to ramp up production in order to compensate for lost Iraqi and Kuwaiti exports. Tehran had to settle for the short-term gains, only to see the price of oil remain low over the next few years.[99]

The brief buoyancy of the Iranian economy, sustained in part by the conflict among its neighbors, had important implications for Iran's political economy as well. The perception that the reconstruction was responsible for a new abundance in Iran bolstered the case for continuing liberalization, and Rafsanjani gained much-needed traction to push forward his broader program of privatization and economic reform and marginalize his left-wing adversaries. That sense of optimism and prosperity proved fleeting, and within a few years, the

---

[97] *Iran Times*, September 21, 1990, as quoted in Siavoshi (1992), p. 45.

[98] Pamela Ann Smith, "Looking for Prosperity in the 1990s – 17th Tehran International Trade Fair," *MEED*, September 27, 1991.

[99] Furtig (2002), pp. 233–5.

reconstruction program and its champion found themselves facing a bitter and multifaceted backlash.

Although the Gulf War led tangible economic and diplomatic opportunities to Tehran's doorstep, the attendant burdens imposed by the conflict should not be discounted. As one diplomat remarked at the time, "Last fall Iran looked like a big winner, but now I think it's better to say Tehran may be a short-term winner but likely long-term loser."[100] The conflict drew another 1.2 million refugees into an economy already overstretched by the demands of reabsorbing demobilized military personnel. In contrast to earlier refugee flows, in particular the Afghan exodus, Tehran sought to establish an effective system for managing the prospective Iraqi refugee crisis. From the outset, the regime established temporary camps, developed a resettlement strategy aimed at repatriating Iraqis, and actively appealed for international assistance. This stance had unexpected long-term consequences; the tight perimeter around Iraq's borders inadvertently facilitated the growth of autonomous Kurdistan, a situation that would eventually create new strategic opportunities and complications for Tehran after the fall of Saddam Hussein.[101]

Notably, similar efforts were applied to Iran's substantial Afghan refugee population, with the imposition of new limits on the duration of refugees' legal residence in Iran and the establishment of a new organization intended to facilitate mass repatriation. From the mid-1990s forward, most Afghan refugees who have entered Iran have not been accorded legal residency; their status subjects them to arbitrary deportation and generalized insecurity. Tehran took other measures to pare down its expenditures on refugees, including revoking health and educational subsidies.[102]

Tehran's constructive neutrality facilitated the restoration of some diplomatic ties with Riyadh in 1991. Still, nearly a decade passed before Iran's cold peace with the kingdom progressed to normalcy. In the interim, Tehran continued to agitate at the *hajj* and stoke regional radicalism as part of a wide-ranging rivalry with Riyadh. Frictions with the Gulf intensified once again in August 1992, when Tehran dispatched naval forces to occupy three small islands in the Gulf that are jointly claimed by the UAE. The Saudi embrace of the U.S. security umbrella – along with its pointed exclusion of Iran in the March 1991 "Damascus

[100] Jonathan C. Randal, "Iran's Failings Limit Bid to End Isolation; Tehran No Longer Seen Gaining from War," *WP*, April 27, 1991, A14.
[101] Rajaee (2000), p. 51.   [102] Rajaee (2000), p. 58.

Declaration" by the GCC, Egypt, and Syria – ran directly counter to Tehran's efforts to mobilize the Islamic world against Washington and the nascent Arab-Israeli peace process. Still, Rafsanjani continued to appeal to the Gulf for improved relations, emphasizing that "no country should be concerned about Iran's power." In a February 1993 interview, he stressed, "We do not have any unfriendly attitude towards any of our neighbours. We proved this during the Iran-Iraq war. Many Arab countries in the south acted badly toward us during the war. They gave money to Iraq, they provided her with assistance, but we overlooked all these issues. We have extended a hand of friendship towards them."[103]

And just as Iran was seeking to reintegrate itself into the international system, that system itself was in a state of epic change. The various factions saw the changes under way across Eastern and Central Europe through the prism of their own ideological parameters. The left remained virulently mistrustful of the West even as the Cold War ended. In 1991, the left-wing standard bearer and future Khatami cabinet member Behzad Nabavi published a pamphlet contending that the notion of a "new world order" represented a new American scheme for world domination.[104]

The combination of developments – Saddam Hussein's transformation from proxy to pariah and the demise of the Cold War – created mixed opportunities for ending Iran's isolation. After the war, some U.S. officials considered the possibility of a postwar role for Iran in American-led regional initiatives; Secretary of State James Baker outlined plans for a Gulf security framework that would exclude no regional state and explicitly envisaged Tehran "as a major power in the Gulf."[105] This coincided with similar thinking among Iranian pragmatists in the Foreign Ministry and elsewhere in the bureaucracy. Finance Minister Mohsen Nourbakhsh envisioned a "Gulf common market" and argued that economic cooperation offered a better pathway so that "true stability is ensured, rather than by trying to build up military strength."[106]

However, the perverse confluence between Iran's domestic political competition and the complicated dynamics of a region in flux conspired to undo some of the benefits of Iran's tentative détente in its neighborhood. In October 1991, the first peace talks between Arabs and Israelis in eighteen years prompted an Iranian counterreaction in the form of a

---

[103] Furtig (2006), p. 153.   [104] Moslem (2002), p. 124.

[105] http://query.nytimes.com/gst/fullpage.html?res=9D0CE0D91030F934A35751C0A9
67958260&sec=&spon=&pagewanted=2

[106] "The Opening of the Door," *MEED*, June 14, 1991.

dueling conference featuring Palestinian terrorist organizations and individual leaders. Rafsanjani contributed predictably provocative rhetoric – including a quickly backtracked pledge to send forces should the Palestinians choose to fight Israel for their state – but it was the parliamentary radicals, such as the former Iranian ambassador to Syria Mohtashami, who most exulted in the opportunity for grandstanding. Tehran remained profoundly out of step with the rest of the Middle East, and the continuing rejectionism cast doubt on Rafsanjani's rhetorical efforts to distance the state from support for terror.

In the end, despite relief that Iranian policy helped facilitate Saddam's retreat, Rafsanjani's efforts to use the Gulf War to end Iran's isolation did not fully succeed. In a speech to the Assembly of Experts in July 1990, Rafsanjani almost seemed to plead for greater openness, arguing that "the present age is the age of international organisations and of communication," and without these connections, "we will not be able to live." He also repeated one of his frequent themes, arguing that the Islamic Republic should "not make enemies without any cause."[107]

ELIMINATING THE LEFT: ELECTIONS AND OTHER POLITICS

Iran's international outreach was set within a context of fierce domestic infighting, focused primarily on Rafsanjani's economic reforms. Immediately after the war, the radicals had been outnumbered or successfully co-opted into signing on to the five-year plan, but their foreign policy adventurism and resistance to the post-Khomeini leadership were prompting shifts in their rivals' tactics. The first test was the 1990 ballot for the Assembly of Experts. With Khamenei's support, Rafsanjani persuaded the twelve-member Council of Guardians to revise the vetting process for approving candidates; for the assembly, this now entailed incorporating a test of religious learning to determine electoral eligibility. Karrubi, Mohtashami, and Khalkhali apparently failed the test; Khoeiniha, an MP who served as the spiritual leader of the hostage takers and the former prosecutor general, rejected the examination. In October 1990, fistfights erupted in the parliament over accusations that the balloting was being stage-managed to serve the interests of the leadership and of the reconstruction agenda, while marginalizing its rivals.

---

[107] "Rafsanjani and Radicals Exchange Harsh Words," *MEED*, August 3, 1990, p. 15.

In the end, the elections drew a mere 37 percent of the population to the ballot box – a historic low for the Islamic Republic, and particularly worrisome given the timing, just a year after the assembly's first utilization for its sole purpose, the leaders' appointment. However, the ballot served its purpose in humiliating the scions of the leftist movement and ensuring that the assembly remained a reliably pliant instrument of state control. The episode offered Khamenei and Rafsanjani a successful test case in utilizing institutions to outflank their rivals, a method they would use repeatedly but one that would also eventually work against them.

The battle lines thus drawn, the showdown between the radicals and the Rafsanjani initiative intensified during 1991, on both domestic and foreign policy. At home, the parliament sought to impeach several cabinet ministers and reached out to the only recently repudiated Ayatollah Montazeri. The tactics only bolstered Rafsanjani's determination to strengthen his hand and further undercut the radicals in the parliament, where they held the greatest sway and where they were positioned to delay – or at least politicize – the legislative framework for the reconstruction program. "The elections will be a turning point, I think," Adeli said. "The results will draw the line ... and hopefully pave the way for accelerated reforms."[108]

First, the president's allies in the parliament helped usher through an amendment to the elections law that required *absolute* fidelity to the supreme leader as a requirement for candidates seeking to run in elections. In addition, the Guardians' Council was once again deployed to intensify its scrutiny of candidates, and it performed precisely as intended – a whopping 1,060 aspirants, roughly 35 percent of the pool of 3,150 prospective candidates, were struck from the list. The shrewdness of this approach was to strike down many of the pillars of the Left while sparing their leaders, such as Karrubi and Mohtashami. As a result, forty incumbent MPs were blocked from running, including Khalkhali, the deputy speaker Assadollah Bayat, the student leader Ibrahim Asgharzadeh, and Hadi Ghaffari, a cleric who was reputed to have fired the shots that killed the monarchical prime minister, Amir Abbas Hoveyda. Finally, rumors were deliberately stoked to discredit the leftists as corrupt and linked to foreign interests.[109] Khamenei publicly inveighed against "those seditious people who have caused trouble for the government and told lies in their newspapers. People should not vote for their candidates."[110]

---

[108] "Bank Markazi Plans for Economic Recovery," *MEED*, November 15, 1991, p. 5.
[109] Baktiari (1993), p. 387.   [110] *Ettela'at*, March 28, 1992.

Unsurprisingly, the results of the ballot strongly favored the center-right factions, as even Karrubi and Mohtashami lost their seats.

The procedural manipulation of the ballot enraged the leftists. Asgharzadeh and Khoeiniha promised that "the results of this election aren't the end but the beginning," adding that "this is the start of a real political confrontation."[111] In retrospect, it remains unclear whether the election engineering surrounding the 1992 elections was necessary and, separately, whether it advanced Rafsanjani's cause in the long term. Iran's radical Islamists had already exhausted much of their natural constituency; the intellectuals were in disarray over the changing regional and international context, and more importantly Iran's citizenry had become more interested in results than in rhetoric. The Left's anti-American demonstrations during the Gulf War drew relatively slim turnout, and despite vehement criticism of the government over economic policy, the leftists had not managed to articulate a compelling counterproposal for dealing with the central problems that concerned most Iranians – jobs and the cost of living.

Moreover, the election results seemed to complicate Rafsanjani's predicament rather than alleviate it. In many cases, the new MPs were determined to assert their independence. Mohsen Mojtahed-Shabestari warned that "whenever the government will make a mistake, we will be the first to criticize, and no leniency will be given in this connection."[112] Only weeks after the new parliament was seated, rising criticism over perceived "cultural liberalism" forced the resignation of Rafsanjani's culture minister, Mohammad Khatami, who was uncharacteristically pugnacious in his departure. Khatami denounced "the rising retrograde and stagnant influence and the climate of insecurity that increasingly bedevils cultural activities."[113] The new parliament also refused to approve several of Rafsanjani's key ministers after his reelection, and its legislative agenda challenged the president's reconstruction efforts, including pressure to reconfigure the budget and other aspects of the economic plan when problems arose.

The long-term consequences of the 1992 electoral manipulations diverged dramatically from what Iran's two most senior power brokers might have intended. Forced from government, the leftists retreated to

---

[111] Peter Waldman, "Budding Economic Reforms in Iran Still Face Threat from Hard-Liners," *WSJ-Europe*, April 21, 1992, p. 2.
[112] Baktiari (1996), p. 222.
[113] "Culture Minister Explains His Resignation," *AFP*, July 18, 1992.

academia and think tanks, where their experience informed a rethinking of the institutionalization of the revolution. When they returned to the political fray, they posed the single greatest threat to the supreme leader's far-reaching authority and the revolutionary state's viability. Rafsanjani found the parliament's new ideological configuration no more compliant with his agenda than before, and when the reconstruction program began to founder, he came to appreciate that he had helped facilitate a process of centralizing power under the unelected auspices of the office of the supreme leader, a development that would increasingly cleave the system and its leadership. The bargain was a bad one; having ceded this advantage, Rafsanjani found that the maneuver produced little positive momentum on his economic agenda.

In the short term, both the president and the supreme leader sought to enhance their own legitimacy in varying fashion. Rafsanjani ran for a second term in 1993, campaigning on a record of what he described as "great tasks." He seemed to bristle when publicly queried about the track record, contending that "a president who carries out the policy of readjustment and carries out the process of reconstruction after the war and after the earthquake, as well as carrying out many infrastructural tasks at the cost of reducing the expenditure and, still, gains two-thirds of the people's votes in a free election, should be considered as very successful in my opinion.... None of these would have been possible without the economic readjustment policy."[114] He handily defeated his slate of opponents; however, his capture of 65 percent of the vote reflected a distinctly more competitive environment than the virtual coronation he received in 1989, when he won with 95 percent of the vote against a candidate who essentially declined to campaign. Perhaps most disquieting was the relatively strong showing of Ahmad Tavakkoli, a conservative who served in parliament as minister of labor and was a founder of the influential daily *Resalat*. Tavakkoli took a full 24 percent of the vote, a reminder that Rafsanjani's rivals from the Right were at least as potent as those from the left.

Khamenei also sought to consolidate his authority and assert the prerogatives of his position. After 1993 and 1994 deaths of several senior clerics, there was an effort to elevate Khamenei as *marja-ye taqlid*, a move that would have reestablished the convergence between religious and

---

[114] Vision of the Islamic Republic of Iran Network 1, June 7, 1994, from BBC Summary of World Broadcasts.

political authority that existed during Khomeini's tenure. Muhammad Yazdi, then-Iran's chief justice, and Majlis Speaker Ali Akbar Nateq Nuri mounted a campaign that was brazen by historical standards of clerical politicking and that emphasized the political and bureaucratic criteria for his ascension.[115] The controversy drew in the parliament, and in a telling demonstration of the limits of the leader's sway, only 155 of the 270 Majlis deputies signed the petition of support for Khamenei's bid, and 113 actually championed a competing effort to promote the dissident Montazeri to this role.

Khamenei was eventually forced to disavow the effort publicly and withdraw himself, noting wryly that "the people are the most uncompromising on the subject of the *marja'iyat*."[116] He did assert himself as the *marja-ye taqlid* for the Shi'a outside Iran, on the basis of a lack of senior religious models in Bahrain, Saudi Arabia, Kuwait, Iraq, and Lebanon, but even this presumption was widely rejected.[117] His bid to assume the highest post in the religious hierarchy withered without seriously damaging his mandate as the highest authority in Iran's political hierarchy. The initiative should be understood in its proper context; while many of the contemporaneous analyses of the post-Khomeini power structure depicted Khamenei as a weak or moderate leader, the historical record demonstrates otherwise. His collaboration with Rafsanjani to exert greater control over the electoral process, together with his efforts to formalize his transnational leadership, betray early evidence of the expansive ambitions that are evident in his later actions.

---

[115] Those organizations were the Qom Society of Seminary Teachers and the Society of Combatant Clerics of Tehran *(Jame-ye Ruhanyiat-e Mobarez* or JRM). Ayatollah Ahmad Jannati voiced the prevailing opinion among Khamenei's backers that the traditional requirements for the *marja'iyat* are insufficient, and that political awareness and the ability to defend Islam as taught by Khomeini should hold the highest priority for selection of a new *marja*. Yazdi argued similarly that the *marja* must have "political and social consciousness so as to manage the Islamic community and society" and that the Islamic community had a compelling interest in limiting the *marja'iyat* to a single individual. See Gieling (1997): pp. 779–80.

[116] Khamenei's speech as broadcast by the Voice of the Islamic Republic of Iran, December 14, 1994.

[117] Sheikh Mohammad Husayn Fadlallah, "arguably the most influential Shi'I cleric in Lebanon" as the spiritual leader of Hezbollah, has backed the candidacy of Grand Ayatollah Ali Mohammad Sistani, an Iranian cleric in Najaf. See Augustus Richard Norton, "Hizballah of Lebanon: Extremist Ideals vs. Mundane Politics" (New York: Council on Foreign Relations, 1999), pp. 21, 34.

SOCIAL UPHEAVAL

Ultimately, the efforts to shape the parliament's composition did not generate the compliance that Rafsanjani had envisioned. If anything, the perception that Rafsanjani no longer had political obstacles to his reconstruction program only raised public expectations higher. Inflation, unemployment, and the persistence of product shortages and other market disruptions originally attributed to the revolution or the war continued to erode public confidence. Moreover, the ripple effects of the reconstruction program were highly disruptive. As the government flexed its muscles across all areas of society, Iranians expressed a sense of profound frustration surrounding the failure of the state to sustain basic improvements in their day-to-day lives. In the "Hello *Salaam*" column of a pathbreaking newspaper, which documented reader comments and grievances, one Iranian demanded, "How come the government is capable of rounding up all the satellite dishes but is incapable of stopping inflation?"[118]

In May 1992, some of these tensions simmered over after municipal efforts to evict squatter camps in Arak and Mashhad. In Arak, violent protests erupted after a twelve-year-old boy was killed. In Mashhad just a few days later, thousands of demonstrators set buses, government buildings, banks, and stores ablaze. Central government authorities reacted harshly, and Ali Akbar Nateq Nuri, the newly elected speaker of the parliament, demanded that security forces and the judiciary "deal with the offenders decisively," adding, "There is no room for Islamic compassion for them."[119] Hundreds were arrested, four individuals were hanged, and others were sentenced to prison terms and lashings. In a harbinger of Iran's anguished future, the Revolutionary Guard established antiriot brigades in order to deal with any further unrest. Publicly, Rafsanjani took a less combative stance, declaring in a Friday prayers sermon a few days after the turmoil that "part of the population has problems but they are not bad and do not act illegally even if they have criticisms."[120]

---

[118] Elaine Sciolino, "Khomeini's Legacy – a Special Report: Fear, Inflation and Graft Feed Disillusion among Iranians," *New York Times*, May 30, 1995, p. A1.

[119] Sharif Imam-Jomeh, "Iran Demotes Riot Police Chief, Disciplines Others," *Reuters*, June 8, 1992

[120] "Revolutionary Guards Has Anti-Riot Brigades," APS Diplomat Arab Press Service Organization (36: 24), June 13, 1992.

In late 1993, an anonymous group claiming association with leading clerics in Qom circulated a petition criticizing Iran's social and economic deterioration since Khomeini's death; the appeal demanded that "either things will become right again or we demolish the badly built structure and start a new one with the hands of another builder."[121] At a February 1994 ceremony marking the fifteenth anniversary of the revolution, shots were fired in Ayatollah Khomeini's mausoleum while Rafsanjani was speaking. And in mid-1995, another spate of violence erupted, including mass demonstrations in Islamshahr and Qazvin over price escalations and water shortages.

A BOTCHED BID AT EXCHANGE RATE UNIFICATION

Perhaps the most important dimension of the postwar reconstruction agenda of economic reforms was the liberalization of Iran's exchange rate. In March 1993, Tehran attempted to impose a unified rate, set at 1,538 rials to the dollar, a substantial devaluation from the existing trade-weighted average rate of 786 rials/dollar.[122] The government proved unable to correct its balance of payments deficit, and concerns about its inability to meet its foreign debt obligations prompted a growing divergence between the free market exchange rate and the floating rate later that year. Rapid depreciation ensued, exacerbated by lax financial policies that increased liquidity and lower-than-expected oil prices. The government was forced to halt the float and institute a fixed rate of 1,750 rials/$ in December 1993, which in turn led to a high premium on the unofficial parallel rate.[123] Over two days of that month, the currency lost 10 percent of its value, prompting one of the government's most prominent critics, Ezzatollah Sahabi, to warn that "if the existing policies are not significantly altered, Iran will undergo social and political disintegration."[124]

This black market price spiraled upward, climbing as high as 6,800 rials/$ by May 1995. The government, facing a massive foreign exchange shortage, declared all foreign exchange transactions conducted outside its official network to be illegal and reinstituted a multiple rate system in May 1994, this time with just two rates. These were the official, ostensibly

[121] Youssef Azmeh, "All Is Not Well for Iran's Ruling Mullahs," *Reuters*, February 2, 1994.
[122] Hossein Farzin, "The Political Economy of Foreign Exchange Reform." In Saeed Rahnema and Sohrab Behdad (eds.), *Iran after the Revolution: Crisis of an Islamic State* (London: I. B. Tauris, 1995), p. 186.
[123] Celasun (2003), p. 4.
[124] "Iran's Currency Tumbles as Economy Falters," *New York Times*, December 18, 1993.

floating rate, still at 1,750 rials/$, which was applied to hydrocarbon export receipts, imports of essential goods, and imports for large national projects, and the "export" rate, first fixed at 2,345 rials/$ for nonoil exports and all nonessential imports. With high inflation from an expansionary monetary policy and the announcement of new U.S. sanctions against Iran, the parallel market rate peaked in May 1995. Tehran responded by devaluing the rial at the export rate to 3,000 rials/$. The renewed controls served to exacerbate the shortage of foreign currency, causing a sharp drop in imports throughout the mid- to late 1990s.[125] Inflation remained a debilitating issue, and the government was forced to reintroduce ration coupons.

The disarray contributed to the August 1995 resignation of the PBO chief, Roghani Zanjani. Rafsanjani appointed him to an advisory position and moved Hamid Mirzadeh from vice president for executive affairs to take over the PBO. Throughout 1996 and 1997, the fixed official rates further appreciated by approximately twenty-five percent. July 1997 saw the introduction of another exchange mechanism via the Tehran Stock Exchange (TSE), mainly used for imports. The unification of 1993 ended this source of revenue, but the government again began profiting from the reintroduction of a dual rate system.[126] Many have suggested that the government has also been a major player in foreign currency sales on the black market, which provided an important and unaccountable source of income for the leadership.[127]

The system ingrained inefficiency in the Iranian economy for several reasons – first, there was the obvious implicit subsidy for goods eligible for the official rate, which reached as high as 1985 percent at the highest level of the floating rate. The larger state-approved importers benefited most from the subsidized rates, and so the system effectively favored larger domestic industries, particularly those with high import content and a low share of value added in output. Further, there was evidence that

---

[125] V. Sundararajan, Michel Lazare, and Sherwyn Williams, "Exchange Rate Unification, the Equilibrium Real Exchange Rate, and Choice of Exchange Rate Regime: The Case of the Islamic Republic of Iran," IMF Middle Eastern Department, Working Paper 99/15, January 1999; M. Hashem Pesaran, "Economic Trends and Macroeconomic Policies in Post-Revolutionary Iran," in *The Economy of Iran: Dilemmas of an Islamic State*, ed. Parvin Alizadeh (London: I. B. Tauris, 2000), pp. 87–8.

[126] Hassan Hakimian and Massoud Karshenas, "Dilemmas and Prospects for Economic Reform and Reconstruction in Iran," in *The Economy of Iran: Dilemmas of an Islamic State*, ed. Parvin Alizadeh (London: I. B. Tauris, 2000), pp. 54–5.

[127] Coville (2002), p. 37.

manufacturing firms could frequently gain a higher percentage of their transactions at the competitive rate by arranging a deal to persuade their foreign supplier to buy back a certain percentage of their output, encouraging corrupt prearrangements. Finally, the preferential rates given to state-owned enterprises and *bonyad*s, many of which were in import-substituting industries, and the poor terms of exchange for nonoil exports essentially misallocated resources from export-oriented industries to protected public firms.[128]

The lifting of wartime restrictions and the devalued rial helped expand the value of nonoil exports in the 1990s, but the effects of devaluing the Iranian currency in nominal terms were undermined by other policies. Another effect of the early 1990s' devaluation – which was largely undertaken as part of an effort to streamline state activities and reduce the government command over the economy – was, ironically, precipitating greater government expenditure. This was due to the increase in the value of oil exports in rials (even as the dollar value of such exports decreased between 1992 and 1994), which more than compensated for the loss of government profits under the previous, multiple-rate system.[129] Expansionary fiscal policies pursued during the 1992–5 period in Iran triggered lower levels of exports and greater importation – and the real exchange rate actually continued to rise, with the rial remaining overvalued and Iranian nonoil exports continuing to be unattractive to the world market.[130]

FOREIGN INVESTMENT

The Rafsanjani era also saw the first significant attempts to reform Iran's foreign investment system, in response to the crushing lack of capital and foreign exchange after the war. Iran continued to find opening up a flow of investment from the West, particularly the United States, difficult and subject to factional opposition. Modest progress in formulating a clear legal framework for investment helped spur the process. In 1992, the Finance Ministry announced new provisions permitting full foreign ownership of Iranian firms and providing indemnification against

---

[128] Farzin (1995), p. 176.   [129] Hakimian and Karshenas, pp. 56–7.

[130] Ahmad R. Jalali-Naini, "Capital Accumulation, Financial Market Reform and Growth in Iran: Past Experience and Future Prospects," in *Iran in the 21st Century: Politics, Economics and Conflict*, eds. Homa Katouzian and Hossein Shahidi (London: Routledge, 2008).

nationalization and protection for capital repatriation.[131] In 1995, the cabinet clarified constitutional ambiguities to permit foreign partners to own majority stakes in joint ventures.[132]

Tehran also began a long-term experiment in cultivating duty-free zones as a beacon for foreign investment, as part of the first five-year plan. The ambitious effort offered investment guarantees, more lenient labor regulations, waiver of entry visa requirements, and a variety of other liberalized parameters of the prevailing foreign investment framework.[133] However, the free-trade zones (FTZs) have underperformed as compared to initial expectations and their potential. Broader obstacles to Iran's ability to attract foreign investment, such as political risk and legal constraints on capital repatriation, have inhibited outside interest in the FTZs. In addition, the zones failed to create dynamic hubs for export-driven investments; instead, the FTZs imported 10.5 times as much in total value as they exported.[134] This is at least in part related to provisions enabling Iranians to purchase limited quantities of imports via the FTZs; this loophole has helped generate a quasi-legal smuggling industry that uses the zones for domestic resale. This provision costs the Iranian government any applicable tariff revenue, while middlemen profit from the exploitation of the loophole.[135]

Rafsanjani's efforts to attract foreign investment were hampered by a variety of factors, political as well as economic. Within Iran, residual antipathy toward the international community was exploited, often by domestic competitors, who in part acted out of competitive interests as much as ideological motivations. After a 1993 franchising agreement between Coca-Cola and a local Iranian firm, the head of the Foundation for the Oppressed disparaged the agreement as an attempt by the West to

[131] "Iran Allows Foreigners to Buy Its Companies," *New York Times*, June 29, 1992.
[132] Iran Trade Point. "Foreign Investment – Guide to Iranian Market," http://www.irtp. com/howto/foreig/b13.asp. Accessed November 2008.
[133] World Bank Social and Economic Development Group, Middle East and North Africa Region, "Iran Trade and Foreign Exchange Policies: Reform Agenda, Economic Implications and Impact on the Poor," Report No. 22953-IRN, 1 November 2001, pp 33–4. See also Mehrzad Ebrahimi, Masoud Noonejad, and Mahdi Ebrahimi, 2008, "A Study of Iranian's Free Zones Throughput; Success or Failure in Achieving Proposed Goals?" *Journal of Applied Sciences* 8(8), pp. 1576–80.
[134] Mehrzad Ebrahimi, Masoud Noonejad, and Mahdi Ebrahimi, 2008, "A Study of Iranian's Free Zones Throughput; Success or Failure in Achieving Proposed Goals?" *Journal of Applied Sciences* 8(8), pp. 1576–80.
[135] World Bank, *op. cit.*, p. 34.

corrupt Iranian culture with this challenge: "God willing, we will soon drive all foreign Coca-Cola plants out of Iran." The outburst provoked parliamentary and newspaper debates, as well as reported labor unrest and supply disruptions. The episode illustrated to other potential investors that the *bonyad*s were a force to be reckoned with; for example, when Pepsi-Cola (which bore not simply identification with the United States, but a historical association with a well-known royalist and Bahai) returned to the Iranian market the following year, the company affiliated itself with a subsidiary of the Astan-e Qods foundation, based at the Mashhad shrine of Imam Reza.[136]

RECONSTRUCTION UNRAVELS

The initial outcomes of the postwar embrace of market reforms appeared quite encouraging. Even though Iran was facing imposing challenges, the war's termination generated a new sense of dynamism and opportunity. In the immediate aftermath of the cease-fire, the price of foreign currency on the Iranian black market fell steadily, and as the rial appreciated, consumer prices fell. The postwar recovery built upon the broad structural changes that had been under way in the Iranian economy and society since the revolution.

Other elements of the Rafsanjani era legal changes played a constructive role. The 1994 revision of the penal code, which raised fines markedly, apparently had a positive impact on curbing smuggling.[137] Rafsanjani also sought to reorganize the government in hopes of boosting efficiency and rationalizing some of the distortions associated with the first decade of revolutionary management. As part of this effort, the Ministries of Industry and Heavy Industries were merged in 1994, and he sought to restructure the military as well. As is described in greater detail in Chapter 8, the oil sector underwent significant shifts, with dramatic expansion of petrochemicals capability in the four years after the war's end and the establishment of the National Petrochemical Company in 1994. Iran's existing social safety net was expanded in 1994, with the parliamentary approval of a universal health care bill.[138]

---

[136] "Iran: 200 Demonstrators Oppose Return of Coca-Cola Company," *MEED*, May 23, 1994; "Iranian Official Vows to Close Coca Cola Plant," *Reuters*, January 18, 1994; *Resalat*, July 28, 1994, 13, 15, from FBIS-NES-94-168-S.

[137] Mohammad Reza Farzanegan, "Illegal Trade in the Iranian Economy: Evidence from a Structural Model," CESIFO Working Paper No. 2397 (September 2008), p. 22.

[138] Harris (2010), p. 735.

However, as the economy bounded back from revolution and war, the influx of resources fueled demand for consumer goods. Rural Iranians invested in durable goods, such as electronics, appliances, and cars. During this same period, prices stabilized and began a modest increase, but the revenues only fueled "an illusion of prosperity"[139] and further whetted Iran's appetite for imports, which rose from $11 billion in 1988 to $24 billion by 1991. In the same year, government spending was double the budgeted figure.[140] At the same time, the botched bid at exchange rate reform in 1993 entailed precipitous increases in costs for Iran's newly emerging private sector.

Much of this trade was absorbed by European suppliers – imports from Germany jumped by 95 percent between 1990 and 1991, while Italy and the United Kingdom experienced increases of approximately 50 percent.[141] Other beneficiaries of Iran's newfound openness (and the world's reembrace of the Islamic Republic) included the Soviet Union, which saw arms sales skyrocket after the Iraq war to approximately $1 billion per year, and Japan, which with $1 billion in exports to Iran remained the country's second largest trade partner (after Germany).[142] Much of this trade was financed by debt, and nearly two-thirds of Iran's newly assumed international obligations had relatively brief payback periods.[143] The debt crisis was compounded by softening oil prices; between 1993 and 1994, Iranian oil revenues fell by 30 percent.[144] The constraints on hard currency only further contorted Iran's domestic economy. A risky internal black market emerged for products, such as caviar, that were primarily reserved for export.

In 1989, the oil minister insisted that foreign borrowing would be limited to revenue generation schemes and would not exceed $3 billion over the subsequent five years.[145] And yet by early 1994, Tehran was confronting at least $20 billion in short-term debt, with approximately one-third already in arrears. As Figure 5.1 suggests, the dramatic expansion of imports, often financed by short-term debt, in the early post-war

[139] Hooshang Amirahmadi, "Iran's Development: Evaluation and Challenges," *Third World Quarterly* 17:1 (1996), p. 126.

[140] Pamela Ann Smith, "Looking for Prosperity in the 1990s – 17th Tehran International Trade Fair," *MEED*, September 27, 1991.

[141] Ibid.   [142] Ibid.   [143] Amirahmadi (1996), p. 133.

[144] Elaine Sciolino, "Iran's Difficulties Lead Some in U.S. to Doubt Threat," *New York Times*, July 5, 1994, p. A1.

[145] Youssef Ibrahim, "Iran May Borrow at Banks Abroad to Revive Economy," *New York Times*, February 3, 1989.

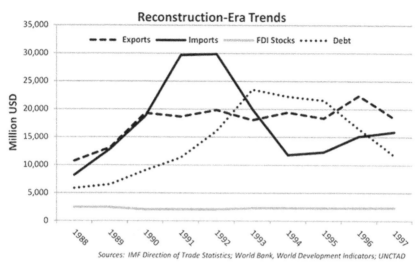

FIGURE 5.1. Reconstruction-Era Trade and Investment Trends

period significantly outpaced exports, quickly piling up a significant trade deficit and debt burden. Iranian officials appreciated all too keenly their predicament; political pressure within the country as well as from Washington made long-term borrowing difficult if not impossible. Tehran expressed bitterness about European eagerness to access the Iranian marketplace and corresponding unwillingness to negotiate improved repayment terms. "While Germany has exported tens of billions of Deutschmarks' worth of goods to Iran in recent years, it is refusing to reschedule between two and three billion marks of Iranian debt," an Iranian parliamentarian complained to a German official in 1994.[146] Ultimately, Washington played a disproportionate role in shaping the options available to Tehran for dealing with the crisis. As Adeli, the Central Bank governor, acknowledged, "The U.S. is going to put further pressure on European countries, as well as on Japan, in the Paris meeting on the so-called debts of Iran. In fact the U.S. wanted to see what concessions it could get from the Islamic Republic.... We do not owe the U.S. anything, but that country along with Britain will continue to initiate a negative stance against Iran."[147]

---

[146] Vahe Petrossian, "Bilateral Deals May Solve Debt Problem," *MEED*, January 24, 1994.
[147] Sharif Imam-Jomeh, "Iran Says Washington Tries to Turn G7 against It," *Reuters*, January 13, 1994.

With inflation mounting, government officials sought to defend the reconstruction program publicly, explaining that the country had few good alternatives for dealing with the legacy of the war. "Therefore we were placed in a cycle which, due to the population and consumption growth and the absorption of current capitals, we had only one possibility, which would have been to spend the existing capital on our daily needs and leave everything as it was. In that case the present generation could have lived in a relatively stable situation and basically forget about future requirements. That was the reason why, during the year [13]68 (March 1989) and in the first [development] plan, it was decided to break such a cycle, the cycle which would have, God forbid, forced us to a slow death."[148] The financial crisis took a direct toll on the effort to reorient the economy – with respect to both resources and political will.

The crisis hit just as the government was struggling to move toward the next phase of reconstruction. The launch of the privatization program and exchange rate liberalization measures were intended to be accompanied by measures to relax the system of price controls that had been precipitated by the war. In his 1993 reelection campaign, Rafsanjani made an impassioned plea for adjusting consumer and industrial prices to reflect their true market values, arguing that subsidies and price manipulation were "bearable at the time when there were shortages of commodities. But this cannot be tolerated now. We have, thus, planned to stop the practice of overcharging. We, however, believe that it is in the country's interest to reach real prices. A large portion of the resources used to subsidize some commodities unfairly in the past, is now transferred to reconstruction.... We have to bring up the prices to their real level if we wish to achieve a healthy economy. Subsidized prices will never allow an economy to take shape."[149] In 1993, prices on airfare, postage, medicine, and propane were permitted to rise to offset the higher cost of foreign exchange for the respective government institutions; however, in response to public protests, the state interceded to roll back price hikes on rail tickets and moderate higher telephone charges.

A similar dynamic unfolded a year later, when the government tried to impose greater order on the *bazaar* by requiring posted price tags on all goods. However, "even as municipal officials soldered shut the gates of

---

[148] "Review of the week," Vision of the Islamic Republic of Iran Network 1, February 1, 1994, from BBC Summary of World Broadcasts.

[149] Vision of the Islamic Republic of Iran Network 1, June 7, 1994, from BBC Summary of World Broadcasts.

merchants who did not comply, Interior Ministry officials went around the capital cutting them open again."[150] The parliament revolted against the executive branch's efforts to remove subsidies and passed legislation requiring Majlis approval of any proposed price increases. In their debates over the March 1994 budget, the deputies pushed back on plans to raise fuel prices, despite intense lobbying by all of the Rafsanjani cabinet as well as the Plan and Budget Organization. "We are presently paying an 11,000-billion-rial fuel subsidy and if this process continues and we fail to find a solution, we will have more problems in the next development plan," Oil Minister Aghazadeh argued, appealing to the parliament not to reject the price adjustments without identifying other solutions to the country's rising oil consumption.[151] "If you vote for the elimination of the provision on fuel price rises, perhaps you could assign me a new task in the Oil Ministry and tell me what to do."[152] For his part, Iran's energy minister, Bijan Namdar Zanganeh, retorted that "social justice does not demand payment of such subsidies or more subsidies for bigger consumers."[153]

The parliament peremptorily shaved 20 percent off what Hassan Rouhani described as an "unrealistic" government budget for the 1994/5 year, and adopted austerity measures that scaled back expenditures by 12 percent.[154] The revised budget included a 30 percent reduction in the funds available for importing wheat, cooking oil, sugar, and meat, and a slightly smaller reduction in the crude volumes available for financing imports of refined petroleum products. A debate over plans for surplus revenues ended in compromise to the chagrin of many MPs, who preferred a faster dispatch of the government's external debts. Underlying these fierce debates was an equally powerful turf battle. The parliament sought to wrest control of the shape and pace of Iran's economic policy away from Rafsanjani and his technocratic advisers. As one MP sought to remind the president in 1994, he might be "the guardian of policy, culture, society and religion, economics is another matter."[155]

[150] Elaine Sciolino, "Iran's Difficulties Lead Some in U.S. to Doubt Threat," *New York Times*, July 5, 1994, p. A1.
[151] Voice of the Islamic Republic of Iran Network 1, January 30, 1994, from BBC World Service, Summary of World Broadcasts.
[152] "Iranian Majlis Blocks Oil Ministry Plan – Bid to Link Tax to Construction Nixed," *Platt's Oilgram News* (72: 22), February 1, 1994, p. 4.
[153] Voice of the Islamic Republic of Iran Network 1, January 30, 1994, from BBC World Service, Summary of World Broadcasts.
[154] "Iran Adopts Austerity Budget," *AFP*, February 1, 1994.
[155] Elaine Sciolino, "Iran's Difficulties Lead Some in U.S. to Doubt Threat," *New York Times*, July 5, 1994.

The debt crisis prompted European and Japanese firms and financial institutions to reconsider their interest in Iran investments. In January 1992, Germany, Belgium, and France suspended export guarantees to Iran, and a development deal for the first phase of the massive South Pars gas field – the first upstream tender since the revolution – also collapsed as a result of new reluctance from the intended Italian financing agency. At the same time, the debt crisis also dampened Tehran's eagerness for foreign capital. Stung by the difficulty of obtaining financing abroad, and under pressure from domestic constituencies that were deeply suspicious of foreign firms, the president shifted gears and began to reemphasize domestic capabilities. "Designing and implementing such projects in Iran seemed far-fetched only a few years ago.... But now we can build them with internal resources at a much lower cost than offered by foreign contractors," Rafsanjani declared in 1994.[156] In the process, he also sought to revamp and expedite the privatization process, but nationalist sentiments in the parliament again created roadblocks, and in 1994 the Majlis stopped all privatization until a process could be found to offer the shares first to veterans and families of martyrs from the revolution and the war.[157]

Opposition also mounted over issues such as inflation and exchange rate reform. Although Rafsanjani had focused on defusing leftist opposition, frustration over internal conditions now spanned the factional divide. And many within the regime pinpointed Rafsanjani as the culprit. "Instead of promising heaven, the government should also be thinking about solving this deadly inflation," Ayatollah Meshkini fulminated in early 1994. "But I know that this problem of high prices will not be solved until those who have luxurious lifestyles ... and who do not feel social problems and who use their expertise to manage their own affairs are no longer in power. And there are many of them."[158] Angry over the effects of free-market reforms, the Majlis rejected Mohsen Nourbakhsh for a second term as finance minister in 1993, apparently seeking a scapegoat for inflationary trends.[159] Rafsanjani quickly named him to a vice presidential position and considered the PBO chief, Roghani Zanjani, for the ministerial slot before

[156] "Dam Project Goes to Revolutionary Guards," *MEED*, October 3, 1994.
[157] Sohrab Behdad. "From Populism to Economic Liberalism: The Iranian Predicament," in *The Economy of Iran*, ed. Alizadeh (London: I. B. Tauris, 2000), pp. 125–9.
[158] Scheherazade Daneshkhu, "Stop Promising Heaven, Rafsanjani told," *FT*, January 26, 1994.
[159] "Reform-Minded Finance Minister Is Rejected by Iranian Parliament," *New York Times*, August 17, 1993.

deciding that he was "too valuable in his present post."[160] Meanwhile, the halting of privatization prompted the influential PBO official Mohammad Tabibian to resign.[161] Ever the savvy politico, Khamenei began hedging his support for the reconstruction agenda in his own public rhetoric.

CORRUPTION

Another aspect of the reconstruction program that emerged as a thorny problem for Rafsanjani was the question of corruption. Over time, this issue would become the president's trademark – an association that remained firmly planted in the realm of popular caricature for many years and one that would eventually haunt and hamper Rafsanjani's future political aspirations. Allegations of corruption and abuses of power strike at the core of the state's Islamic legitimacy and thus threaten to sully the system itself; the claims to moral authority and the centrality of social justice in the revolutionary ideal leave its leadership more vulnerable to such charges than that of a secular autocracy might be.

However, corruption took on a variety of forms in the boom-time economy that characterized the reconstruction era. One dimension was individual enrichment, the stench of which would remain personally identified with Rafsanjani. This was the era of the *aghazadeh* – men of means and influence – who began as revolutionary functionaries, but utilized their positions within the hierarchy, access to insider information, and preferential standing to accumulate wealth and status. Most notorious, given Iran's history and antipathy toward monarchical institutions, was the hereditary dimension of the *aghazadeh* phenomenon – the wealthy and powerful routinely engaged in familial nepotism that resulted in the replication of influence across the generations. This is exemplified by the political and business empire associated with Rafsanjani himself: His brother Mohammad Hashemi served as his vice president for executive affairs during his second term in office and previously as head of the state television broadcasters; his eldest son, Mohsen, headed the multibillion-dollar development of the Tehran metro system; his son Mehdi Hashemi assumed prominent positions in the Oil Ministry and subsidiary firms; his two daughters, Faezeh and Fatemeh, have served in parliament and run a major charity; and his nephew Ali Hashemi helped

---

[160] "Former Minister Tipped for Top Economic Post," *MEED*, September 6, 1993.
[161] Laura Secor, "The Rationalist," *New Yorker*, February 2, 2009, p. 31.

facilitate the arms sales that became public as part of the Iran-contra scandal and later served in parliament on the energy commission.[162]

The most notable of the *aghazadeh* were the inner circle of the regime – not simply Rafsanjani, but his intended successor Ali Akbar Nateq Nuri, Ayatollah Abbas Vaez Tabasi (administrator of the foundation attached to the Imam Reza shrine in Mashhad),[163] and many others – and the phenomenon of enrichment by proximity extended well beyond the highest echelons of the state. A reformist journalist later accused Rafsanjani of seeking "to appease its top level managers by giving them material rewards. The salaries and bonuses given to senior managers at the time of Mr. Rafsanjani had such a substantial growth that had no precedence in the history of both Iran and the world."[164] Unfortunately, similar critiques would attach themselves to his successors.

Beyond cultivation of a new economic elite, the reconstruction era saw a flurry of cases involving outright theft and embezzlement. A number of senior Oil Ministry officials were accused of taking bribes to facilitate a $300 million contract. Perhaps the most notable case of embezzlement involved Bank-e Saderat, a scandal involving the embezzlement of $450 million, which came to be known as Iran's "trial of the century" – the first of several that would elicit that moniker. Among those prosecuted was Morteza Rafiqdust, brother of Mohsen Rafiqdust, the former Revolutionary Guards' minister and sitting head of the Foundation for the Oppressed. The scandal captured popular imagination, reigniting the rhetoric of the radicals and threatening to taint the Rafsanjani era economic liberalization with the stigma of personal enrichment and oppression – themes markedly reminiscent of the opposition movement under the monarchy.[165] And it unleashed an unprecedented level of criticism

---

[162] As referenced in Chapter 7, the family would be caught up in the postelection turmoil that was unleashed after the 2009 presidential ballot; Mehdi and Faezeh were imprisoned and Ali Hashemi was implicated as well.

[163] Vaez Tabbasi's sons, Mostafa and especially Naser, drew pointed criticism for their style of dress and trappings of wealth, as well as for their contacts with the West. Reports in April 2002 suggested that Naser Vaez Tabbasi had fled the country to avoid imminent corruption charges. Naser Tabbasi came under particular fire for his wife's decision to travel to the United States to give birth to their child, thus assuring the child U.S. citizenship. See Adelkhah (2012), p. 26.

[164] Reza Alijani, "Mr. Hashemi Rafsanjani's Economic Adjustment Pattern," *Iran-e Farda* 67 (February 2000), pp. 2–3.

[165] Ahmad Ghoreishi and Dariush Zahedi, "Prospects for Regime Change in Iran," *Middle East Policy* V: 1, (January 1997), pp. 87–8; notable is the castigation of both the embezzlement *and* the handling of the case by the government from Ayatollah Ali Akbar Meshkini, then-head of the Assembly of Experts (which selects the Faqih). Meshkini

against the foundation and its leadership, which (perhaps by implication or perhaps by unconfirmed involvement) was closely associated with the cover-up.[166] The Saderat corruption case was hardly the first instance of financial malfeasance under the Islamic Republic; nor was it the sole evidence of the growing enrichment of those with preferential access to political leaders and state assets. But it was the first instance of an intense public scrutiny of the problem of corruption, and the first time the revolutionary state sought to appease public demands for elite accountability through the implementation of rule of law, albeit as a scapegoat.

Coverage of the Saderat scandal prompted the arrest of journalists who soon became closely identified with the reform movement. Ultimately, the Saderat case did little to stimulate strengthening of public institutions or ethics, and each of Rafsanjani's successors would be confronted with similar scandals involving the banking and oil sectors. Perhaps not coincidentally, in each of these cases, the president's ideological opponents sought to use the scandals to impugn his administrations and policies. Thanks to the overwhelming preference of Iran's senior leadership to contain any scandal spillover, neither Saderat nor its successors provoked any public upheaval. The scandals' eruption and resolution primarily served as vehicles for factional warfare.

While the Saderat inquiry dominated Iranian headlines, in fact the problem of corruption had become far more extensive and engrained. Beyond Saderat, the issue of spin-off companies and parasitic privatization presented a major problem for the reconstruction effort. Since these earliest anticorruption crackdowns, rent-seeking behavior among government enterprises merely became more resourceful. The proliferation of private companies attached to government ministries – which utilize government

voiced frustration that has been echoed in the popular press with the impression of favoritism in the prosecution of the case, saying in a sermon, "When people of low rank commit a crime or an offence, they are immediately pursued, imprisoned, locked up and ruined. ... However, when we find some big shot, they merely move him from one town to another and give him another post, maybe even higher than his previous post." *Reuters World Service*, July 23, 1995.

[166] Con Coughlin, "Banking Fraud Overstretches Mullahs's Credit," *Sunday Telegraph*, August 6, 1995; "Brother of Powerful Iranian in Fraud Case," *Reuters*, June 29, 1995; "Iran: Bank Fraudster Hanged," *MEED*, December 1, 1995, 14; *Kayhan*, May 23, 1996), 2, from FBIS-NES-96-143; "Khatami Cabinet Voices Utmost Disappointment over Karbaschi Arrest," *Tehran Times*, April 7, 1998, 1, 3, 15, from FBIS-NES-98-109. The noted journalist Abbas Abdi makes the allegation explicitly in a series of *Salaam* columns published in his book *Qudrat, Qanun, Farhang: Yaddashtha-ye Siasi-i Ruznameh-i Salaam* (Tehran: Tarah-e No, 1998), 84–9.

resources, but serve to benefit private groups or individuals – has been exacerbated by the inadequate regulatory control.[167] An Iranian academic has described the mechanics of this recycling of assets: "The procurement department of a given ministry would function as a company, selling supplies acquired with the ministry's funds to the ministry, for profit. The profits were then distributed among shareholders, who were mostly the same ministry's personnel. This was a way to augment the faltering purchasing power of the state employees, but these companies also had a parasitic nature, milking the state budget and giving the private sector a bad name."[168]

One example involves the investigation into a string of government-owned, profit making dummy corporations set up to perform subcontracting services for the Construction Jihad ministry. Since government ministries were prohibited from creating such companies, the scheme was facilitated by the "gift" of three corporations from the Foundation for the Oppressed in 1987. These three holding companies encompassed fifty-three productive units, employing twenty-three thousand workers and making an estimated 200 billion rials in annual profits – and, after a somewhat acrimonious debate, were eventually accorded status as non-governmental public institutions themselves. The Majlis has in fact encouraged such development, creating mechanisms for seemingly non-commercial government divisions such as the Education Ministry to establish corporate subsidiaries and seek private financing.[169] Rafsanjani himself played a role, explicitly encouraging government organizations to engage in business beginning in 1992–3.

One economist estimated that more than 120 of these organizations are responsible for 35 to 40 percent of Iran's national income. While such figures are impossible to confirm and unlikely to be accurate, given the centrality of petroleum revenues in national income calculations, they hint at the profound lack of transparency that characterizes Iran's economy.[170] Through such quasi-legal maneuvers, government resources were effectively transferred outside the purview of the state, enriching well-placed individuals along the way and contributing to the escalation of

---

[167] Rahim Moqaddam, "Interview with Mohammad Reza Bahonar, Majles Deputy from Tehran," *Keyhan*, July 2, 1997, 7, in FBIS-NES-97-258, September 15, 1997.

[168] Karbassian (2000), p. 637.

[169] "Extensive Report on Two Majles Sessions," *Resalat*, November 27, 1999, p. 5, in FBIS-NESE-2000-0102.

[170] See interview with Ali Rashidi in *Sobh-e Emruz*, as reported in the "Farsi Press Watch" of *Iran Daily* (Internet version), May 16, 1999, p. 2.

prices through noncompetitive bidding.[171] The proliferation of state-affiliated enterprises – sometimes referred to as "first-generation" companies or spin-off firms, to indicate their degree of distance from actual government ownership/control – represents one of the most serious problems for the Iranian economy.

Another dimension of the corruption issue during the Rafsanjani era derived from the dualistic dimension of Iran's economic structure. Thanks to their origins in the mass expropriations and their preferential access to credit and foreign exchange, the *bonyad*s were perceived by many Iranians as a kind of institutionalized corruption – an entire network of organizations and firms that operated outside the accountability of the executive branch or parliament. The distortion of the foundations was magnified by the decision shortly before Khomeini's death to subsume their supervision with a general headquarters known as Setad Ejrai-ye Farman-e Hazrat-e Imam.[172] Protests erupted in Shiraz in 1992 over *bonyad* mismanagement,[173] and subsequently in Mashhad.

The Foundation for the Oppressed withstood a parliamentary investigation in 1995–6, which reportedly concluded that the foundation had engaged in influence peddling.[174] The investigation was headed by the noted conservative deputy Ali Movahedi Savoji, and while newspaper reports suggested that the report demonstrated serious failings in the foundation's charitable activities on behalf of veterans, as well as illegal sales and transfers of property, the specifics of the investigation or its findings were never released publicly, and in Movahedi-Savoji's only comment, he stressed the "positive points" in the report and the cooperation of the foundation's staff.[175] Parallels can be drawn between the rising resentment of the *bonyad*s and the critique of the Pahlavi Foundation prior to the revolution.[176]

---

[171] "Iranian Deputy on Wealth Accumulation," reprinted in *Resalat*, August 27, 1997, pp. 1, 13, from an interview in *Sobh*, in FBIS-NES-97-261, September 18, 1997.

[172] Steve Stecklow, Babak Dehghanpisheh, and Yeganeh Torbati, "Khamenei Controls Massive Financial Empire Built on Property Seizures," *Reuters*, November 11, 2013.

[173] David Menashri, *Revolution at a Crossroads: Iran's Domestic Politics and Regional Ambitions* (Washington, DC: Washington Institute for Near East Policy, 1997), p. 55.

[174] "Iranian Foundation Head Denies Accusations of Corruption," *New York Times*, January 8, 1995, p. 8; "Iran: Committees in Fourth Majlis Strongly Criticise Bank Markazi and *Bonyad* Mostazafin & Janbazan," *MEED*, June 3, 1996; "Iran Probe Blasts Central Bank for Mismanagement," *Reuters Financial Service*, May 26, 1996.

[175] "Majles to Receive Report on Investigation," *Resalat*, April 13, 1995, p. 11, in FBIS-NES-95-106.

[176] Annabelle Sreberny-Mohammadi, and Ali Mohammadi, *Small Media, Big Revolution: Communication, Culture, and the Iranian Revolution* (Minneapolis: University of Minnesota Press, 1994), 125–6.

It was not just the parastatal organizations that experienced public criticism during the reconstruction period. Rafsanjani sought to utilize the resources and authority of the military to advance the reconstruction, as a means of both engaging the millions of demobilized soldiers and quickly ameliorating the war damage and underdeveloped infrastructure across the country. During this period, the Revolutionary Guard established an institution that eventually became Khatam al-Anbia (also known by the acronym GHORB) and, under its auspices, established companies active in agriculture, industry, mining, road building, transportation, export, and education. In fact, there was considerable prerevolutionary precedent for employing the military in this fashion, and it had been explicitly foreseen in article 147 of the Islamic Republic's Constitution.[177]

From the perspective of military commanders, the burgeoning role in the economy offered an important new mission, still vital to the survival of the revolutionary enterprise, at a time of transition and uncertainty about its future; according to Ali Saidi, Khamenei's representative in the IRGC:

This defence [sic] has a different form and shape in every period. After the war, the damages and ruins had to be reconstructed so that the revolution wouldn't be faced with threats. Given its engineering facilities and the experiences of its experts, it could help the then government and could provide a positive response following the request of the then president, Mr. Hashemi-Rafsanjani, and also the agreement of the Supreme Leader in this relation. Of course, this assistance was conditional, the condition of which was for the IRGC not to distance themselves from their core duty.[178]

The IRGC extended its influence into the economic activities of the Islamic Republic via its ties to other revolutionary organizations, and even during this early phase of IRGC activities outside the military sphere, criticism began to emerge over the perception that the Revolutionary Guard was squandering resources and helping to enrich a small circle of privileged merchants and industrialists.[179] The role of the IRGC economic organizations, like that of the *bonyad*s and satellite firms, would eventually expand to complicate Iran's economy, and even to threaten the

[177] Constitution of the Islamic Republic of Iran. Available at http://www.servat.unibe.ch/icl/ iro0000_.html
[178] Hoseyn Sokhanyar. "We Went to Extremes in Democracy." *E'temad*, December 22, 2008.
[179] Baktiari, p. 157.

autonomy of the civil authorities of government and squeeze out the small private sector.

ANOTHER RUN AT WASHINGTON

Although domestic opposition remained intense, and the challenges of low oil prices and a heavy debt burden continued to hamper his political fortunes as well as the implementation of the reconstruction agenda, Rafsanjani began his second term as president with an emboldened sense of initiative. He courted international media, quite a shift from revolutionary leaders' traditional antagonism toward the Western press, and flaunted his embrace of "modernity" in the form of satellite television access to CNN – something that remains prohibited under Iranian law.

Rafsanjani also sought to undercut the possibility that his hard-fought reconstruction would be reversed or even ruined by yet another conflict – this time with an even more dangerous adversary than Saddam Hussein. Tensions with Washington were running high, thanks to both sides' deep-seated mistrust of the other's intentions. The Clinton administration had taken office in 1993, determined to isolate both Iran and Iraq under the rubric of "dual containment." Several senior U.S. officials, including Secretary of State Warren Christopher, who had helped negotiate the Algiers Accords, carried scars from historical experience dealing with Iran. Washington sought formally to brand the Islamic Republic as a "rogue" state and draw the international community into unprecedented cooperation around isolating Tehran. The bilateral tensions manifested themselves from Israel to the Gulf, and U.S. and Israeli officials were predicting that Tehran might have a nuclear weapon "within five years."[180]

Still struggling to maintain consensus around economic reforms, Rafsanjani sought to push back against U.S. pressure. He accused Washington of leading "an orchestrated propaganda campaign ... to discourage Iranian people by exaggerating our economic difficulties." But, he added, "their weapon of oil is no longer effective against us and the recent price shocks have only hurt their friends." He insisted Iran had achieved self-sufficiency in food production and could survive "even if it was forced to stop exporting oil."[181]

---

[180] Chris Hedges, "Iran May Be Able to Build an Atomic Bomb in Five Years, U.S. and Israeli Officials Say," *New York Times*, January 5, 1995.

[181] "Iran Can Withstand US Pressure: Rafsanjani," AFP, January 7, 1994.

In addition to rhetorical bluster, Tehran sought to co-opt U.S. companies through investment opportunities. In March 1995, the Oil Ministry announced that Conoco had won the contract for Iran's first major upstream development deal awarded to an IOC since the revolution – a decision that seemed to catch both capitals by surprise. Tehran clearly sought to mitigate domestic opposition, with Iranian media coverage describing the winning bidder as a Dutch firm, in reference to the Netherlands-based subsidiary that served as Conoco's formal signatory on the contract. U.S. policy makers initially struggled to balance strenuous opposition to the development with an acknowledgment of the deal's lawfulness. The latter quickly gave way to the former, and within a week the contract had been repudiated by Conoco and formally blocked by President Clinton. As detailed in Chapter 9, the episode sparked the enactment of two executive orders that extended the existing U.S. trade embargo on Iran to nearly all bilateral business dealings, and subsequent legislation attempting to penalize foreign companies over future Iran energy investments.

Like so many episodes in the tortuous history of U.S.-Iranian relations since the revolution, the foiled Conoco contract has been woven into the narrative of both sides' grievances. The countervailing depictions speak to the depth of mutual suspicions. U.S. officials interpreted the offer as a crafty tactic designed to divide Europe from Washington and undercut the intensifying pressure within and from Washington.[182] One senior official described it as "an attempt to thwart our pressure on European oil companies by highlighting our hypocrisy."[183] Such motivations surely were in play, but so too was the exigency of the financial and technological challenges facing Tehran – challenges that an American company would have been uniquely valuable in overcoming.

Conversely, several Iranians and external analysts have argued retrospectively that the Conoco deal was intended to promote a full diplomatic reengagement between the two countries, an overture that was foolishly rebuffed by an American establishment bent on hostility toward Tehran. These latter interpretations reflect the long-nurtured grievances among Iranians that have animated advocates of engagement for decades; however, they clearly overstate the case. It strains credulity that Rafsanjani, still struggling with intense factional opposition at home and crippling

---

[182] Martin Indyk, *Innocent Abroad: An Intimate Account of American Peace Diplomacy in the Middle East* (New York: Simon & Schuster, 2009), p. 168; Pollack (2004), p. 271.
[183] Indyk (2009), p. 168.

economic problems, sought to defy one of the animating convictions of the Islamic Revolution.

Rather, what Rafsanjani was seeking was what another Iranian pragmatist, Mohammad Javad Larijani, described in 1992 as a "marriage of convenience"[184] – an expanded U.S.-Iranian trade relationship existing independently of, and irrespective of, the bilateral diplomatic estrangement. The decision to offer the deal to Conoco, rather than the presumptive French favorite Total, reflected Rafsanjani's newfound sense of empowerment, thanks to the elimination of the political threat from the leftists, as well as his keen awareness of the obstacles confronting Iran's initial efforts to restore foreign investment to the petroleum sector. A $1.7 billion contract for the initial phases of South Pars first issued in 1993 to a consortium of Italian, Japanese, and Russian firms imploded after concerns about Tehran's debt levels scuttled the anticipated financing. With economic conditions inside the country worsening and Washington targeting Iran's access to financing, Iran's president understood another misfire might imperil his efforts entirely. With the Conoco offer, Tehran sought to leapfrog the anticipated risks – specifically, American opposition – to another European-financed deal by approaching the source directly.

Rafsanjani's retrospective analysis of the episode was measured but rueful. "We invited an American firm and entered into a deal for $1 billion.... This was a message to the United States, which was not correctly understood. We had a lot of difficulty in this country by inviting an American company to come here with such a project because of public opinion."[185] This was, no doubt, an understatement – beyond his left-wing critics, who had been largely eliminated from the parliament but were only temporarily neutralized, Rafsanjani had to contend with the supreme leader, who never wavered from his position that the United States was "the most hated country before the Iranian nation and the conscious people of the world" and made clear that "the definite policy of the Islamic Republic of Iran is not to have relations or hold negotiations with America."[186] And Khamenei differed pointedly from his president on the utility of an economic relationship, arguing that "countries facing

---

[184] Elaine Sciolino, "Distrust of U.S. Hinders Iran Chief," *New York Times*, April 10, 1992, p. 3.
[185] Elaine Sciolino, "Iranian Leader Says U.S. Move on Oil Deal Wrecked Chance to Improve Ties," *New York Times*, May 16, 1995.
[186] "Iran's Khamenei Rules out Ties with U.S.," *Reuters*, August 26, 1993.

America should know that it is possible to live, have calm and progress without America."[187]

Of course, just as Washington's suspicions about the deal misread Iranian intentions, Rafsanjani's supposition that a billion-dollar deal could cement a new economic relationship with its old adversary even as the two countries continued to clash across the region proved similarly misguided. Rafsanjani's innate opportunism was not simply inconsistent with the Clinton administration's vision of the Middle East – it was out of step with the realities of a competitive global economy. Rather than the cunning tactic imagined by U.S. officials, the Conoco deal instead was a manifestation of Iran's naiveté about Washington's outlook and its influence in world markets.

By July 1995, Rafsanjani's public posturing on the deal had noticeably soured. In an interview with Christiane Mansour, he denounced "Zionist propaganda" for having "poisoned" Washington against Iran but sought to emphasize that Tehran did not "have any problem with the American people ... it would be better if there were some type of economic and cultural relationship, because both nations of Iran and the US will have to cooperate with each other at some point in the future." The Clinton embargo "will only increase hatred between the two nations and it will have negative effects. We should not further this type of tension between us."[188]

It was too late, however – the tensions were already multiplying. The 1995 sanctions prompted an immediate, serious slide in the value of the rial, compounding Tehran's economic problems and intensifying the popular dissatisfaction that was increasingly evident on the Iranian streets. The following year, Washington would up the ante, with the first serious effort to extend U.S. restrictions to third countries by threatening penalties against foreign companies that invested more than $20 million in the Iranian energy sector. Over time, the tightening of U.S. sanctions fed Tehran's increasingly assertive campaign against American influence and allies in the region. During Rafsanjani's second term, Iran intensified its involvement with anti-American activities and organizations in the Gulf: increased surveillance of U.S. government facilities and installations in the region, a 1996 failed bid to oust Bahrain's emir, harassment of U.S. naval vessels, and the June 1996 catastrophic bombing of Riyadh's Khobar Towers, a housing complex for U.S. forces based in Saudi Arabia.

---

[187] Ibid.   [188] "Rafsanjani Tells Us 'Door Is Open,'" *MEED*, July 10, 1995.

These actions should not be read as a direct response to U.S. economic pressure; however, the sanctions played an important role in shaping Iranian perceptions of American policies and may have helped persuade the regime to adopt a more aggressive posture toward its old nemesis.

THE EMERGENCE OF KARGOZARAN

Rafsanjani's response to the political frustrations facing his agenda was multifaceted. One key element was his cultivation of a new political organization, which became known as Kargozaran-e Sazandegi, or Servants of Construction. Kargozaran's formal launch coincided with the opening of the 1996 parliamentary election campaign, in which the two main clerical-backed political groupings had essentially frozen out Rafsanjani's allies. At its creation, Kargozaran's mission advocated "the use of experts and creation of a domestic environment where ideas flowed."[189] Mohammad Husayn Adeli, who had led the Central Bank and later served in senior Foreign Ministry positions, was emblematic of Kargozaran's technocratic identity and agenda. Adeli dismissed the role of ideology in shaping Iranian policy making, arguing that "economic laws have no connection with ideology ... [since the end of our war with Iraq we have realized] that economic problems should only be dealt with from an economic perspective."[190] The group itself remained highly personalistic, centered around the sixteen signatories and a few fellow travelers rather than evolving into a mass-based political party. And yet it became an important player in Iran's subsequent electoral dramas.

One of Kargozaran's defining political personalities was Gholamhusayn Karbaschi, who was appointed mayor of Tehran during Rafsanjani's first year in office and helped transform the overcrowded capital through a dynamic approach to governance. Karbaschi had pioneered aggressive urban renewal programs as mayor of Isfahan, and under his management, Tehran literally blossomed. Six hundred new public parks were constructed, and the periphery of the megacity was recultivated with woodlands. Hundreds of cultural and sports centers were established, and thirteen thousand empty lots were transformed into recreation areas.[191] Equally important were the social implications of his innovations; as one analyst noted, "These new mixed social spaces became havens of

---

[189] Hamshahri, February 27, 1996.
[190] *Salaam*, December 23, 1992, as quoted in Siavoshi (1992), p. 33.
[191] A. Bayat (2007), p. 56.

relative freedom and accelerated the emergence of new social actors."[192] Karbaschi, assumed publication of the newspaper *Hamshahri* and transformed it into an advertisement-heavy, full-color broadsheet intended to appeal to the broad segment of popular opinion.

Karbaschi's genius was not simply the reimagination of the physical landscape of the capital, but the exploitation of ambiguous authority and a creative approach to assembling resources. His initial success in Isfahan drew national attention precisely because he had managed to counter the financial pressures that beset other urban areas during this period. Karbaschi, represented the empowerment of a new class of technocrats and political entrepreneurs and their subsequent repression. In addition to his civic beautification and cultural development projects, Karbaschi, can be credited with the incorporation of informal elements of Iran's urban economy in a way that served as an important model for development around the country. Instead of battling with street vendors, Karbaschi established traditional flea markets, which facilitated better regulation of their activities and enhanced opportunities for worker mobilization.

Karbaschi, was emblematic of the Rafsanjani way of politics: The process was subsidiary to the outcome; legal niceties were an unnecessary extravagance; and pay-to-play represented a perfectly reasonable approach to governance. Well before he became a target of political reprisals, Karbaschi had earned the enmity of many Tehranis, developers and disenfranchised alike, who fell afoul of his plans or who believed the mayor was reaping financial as well as political profits at their expense.[193] This perception of elite opportunism ultimately hurt the men and their cause. As Chapter 7 details, Karbaschi became an early political victim of the heightened factional conflict that characterized the reform era.

RECONSTRUCTION BEGETS REFORM

Rafsanjani's economic reforms unwittingly helped generate a broader impetus for political and social change within Iran. Demographic factors played an important role in this process, including the maturation of the revolutionary generation as well as the emergence of a vast, energetic postrevolutionary baby boom. The opening to the world, at a time of epic

---

[192] A. Bayat (2007), p. 57.

[193] Anecdotes about high permit costs and quasi-legal shakedowns under the Karbaschi municipal reign are commonplace. See, for example, Vahe Petrossian, "Put to the Test – President Rafsanjani Faces Tough Decisions," *MEED* (June 25, 1992), p. 6.

change within the region and the international system, contributed indirectly too. With the lifting of the constraints of the war, the attempt to destigmatize economic liberalism inadvertently provoked a broader reconceptualization of the ideological verities of the revolution.

In tandem with the intensification of elite factionalism, private entrepreneurism, and societal pluralism sparked by the successive system shocks of the war's end and Khomeini's death, the press rebounded with vigor, as newspapers tripled in number over the ensuing three-year period.[194] These included the progenitors of the reform movement, such as the provocative paper *Salaam*, which implanted themselves firmly in Iran's slowly expanding political space and deftly skewered the establishment and official policies. The postwar media activity benefited from Rafsanjani's appointment of a relatively moderate culture minister, Mohammad Khatami, whose 1992 resignation demonstrated the limits of official tolerance for this new pluralism.

Salaam, launched in 1991, provided one of several important vehicles for disseminating the tenets of the reform movement on a broader basis, and it pioneered the intellectually challenging, investigative analysis that would become the hallmark of the reformist press. One retrospective eulogy described the paper as "a torch to shed light on the movement ... a political current to safeguard the fruits ... an academy to give its staff a chance to grow, evolve, and enlighten themselves."[195] Along with the journals *Kiyan, Zanan (Women), Jamaeh-ye Salem (Healthy Society)*, and *Iran-e Farda (Tomorrow's Iran)*, *Salaam* adopted a more directly political slant, reflective of its ambitious publisher, Mousavi Khoeiniha, who had been forced out of the 1990 Assembly of Experts elections. The paper's column dubbed "Hello *Salaam*" reprinted reader grievances along with responses that ranged from informative efforts to facilitate more effective bureaucratic responses to acerbic commentaries on the politics of the day.

The contentious 1996 parliamentary elections also fueled the media revitalization. As the factional divide grew more acute, loose confederations of like-minded politicians converged in protean political parties looking for vehicles to advance their agendas. Newsprint was their only asset. Rafsanjani's government sought to restrain the burgeoning

---

[194] Statistics from *Ettela'at* (February 26, 1991) and *Salam* (November 24, 1992), as quoted in Schirazi (1997): p. 137.

[195] Karim Arghandehpur, "On the Eve of the First Anniversary of the Banning of the Newspaper *Salam*: They Don't Want to Respond to *Salam*s (Greetings)," *Goonagoon* 1 (No. 3), 3, (accessed via Internet, August 15, 2000).

publishing industry as part of its broader effort to purge Iran's politics of internal dissent, deploying a variety of instruments to silence the media, including publication closures, journalists' arrests, and denial of subsidized newsprint to offending periodicals.

In a host of other ways, often inadvertent, the reconstruction program continued to advance the possibilities of reform. For example, Rafsanjani invested heavily in upgrading Iran's communications technologies and linkages, unwittingly putting Iran at the forefront of the information revolution and tapping into rising popular expectations for information. "As a government, it is now not enough to just provide food, electricity, and water," Iran's telecommunications minister remarked in 1997. "We must provide an information infrastructure, too."[196] At the time, Western information and entertainment were presumed to be threats to Iran's moral fiber and were seen as a Western conspiracy to contaminate the nation culturally. In 1989, the parliament contemplated lifting its ban on videos but was overruled by the Guardians' Council. However, by 1992, Ali Larijani assumed the Culture Ministry portfolio and began to legalize videos. In a failed bid to maintain government control over new technology and a rapidly changing social environment, he eventually announced the creation of government-sponsored "video clubs."

In other ways, economic liberalization accelerated other social trends already in progress, including the expansion in women's role and opportunities. This began in part as a response to economic necessity, particularly as the postwar reconstruction boom gave way to a debt crisis and recession.[197] Some of the state's most important social policies, including the literacy campaign and the belated embrace of family planning, succeeded as a result of the mobilization of women through traditional charitable organizations as well as state-led NGOs. Once organized to advance state-sanctioned projects, women typically extended these same skills to pressing the government for better services.[198]

The cultural opening went only so far, and state repression of writers and dissidents remained the norm. And even the entrepreneurs of the reconstruction era remained convinced that a wholesale embrace of freedom would imperil Iran. Gharazi, the telecommunications minister, rejected arguments for unfettered competition and open access to information at a June 1997 industry conference in Singapore. Gharazi argued that "the right of society is more important than the right of the

---

[196] "Developing Situations," *TELE* 2:3 (tele.com), March 1, 1997.
[197] Bahramitash, *Critique*, Spring 2004, p. 41.   [198] Ibid. pp. 41–4.

individual," adding that "we respect very much giving people all the information. But we must not be giving them bad information. Social problems will arise, against the [benefit] of society."[199]

Still, the state's focus on economic reform also reinforced a shift under way among the Islamic leftist faction. Iran's economic challenges had created obvious incentives to relinquish the state's grip on the economy, and the ongoing collapse of the Soviet system and the embrace of market reforms in formerly socialist states across the Eastern Bloc and Asia prompted Iran's left-leaning faction to reassess its principles. The transformation began to manifest precisely on one of their prime areas of advocacy, the economy. A 1992 interview with Musavi Khoeiniha published in *Salaam* is indicative of the process of change under way:

Production should be open to the private sector and necessary encouragement given to it.... We are not averse to the argument that growth in productive capacity [policy of reconstruction] of the country is the most important economic solution for the present situation ... and that state monopoly in economic management will not lead to growth in production ... [but] giving total freedom to the private sector and eliminating the government [in the economy] is not the solution.[200]

FINAL PRAGMATISM

During Rafsanjani's final months in office, he sought to consolidate his influence at home and secure his changes in Iran's relationship with the world. After briefly floating the notion of constitutional revisions to enable him to run for a third term, Rafsanjani was forced to prepare himself for a postpresidential role. The Expediency Council was expanded and empowered in 1997, in preparation for Rafsanjani's assumption of the reins.[201] It was apparent that the council was intended to serve as a vehicle for his personal political ambitions, as well as the further distancing of the Iranian state from theological bases. While the Expediency Council remains a crucial body for charting ultimate legislative outcomes, subsequent developments have reinforced the primacy of the executive and legislative branches in establishing day-to-day policies.

Iran's outreach to the world continued apace during Rafsanjani's final days in the presidency. Rapprochement with Britain received a major

---

[199] Laurinda Keys, "Iranian Minister Discuss Open Telecom Market," *AP*, June 13, 1997.
[200] *Salaam*, April 23, 1992, as quoted in Sussan Siavoshi, "Factionalism and Iranian politics: The Post-Khomeini Experience," *Iranian Studies* 25:3/4 (1992), pp. 32–3.
[201] Olivier Roy, "Tensions in Iran: The Future of the Islamic Revolution," *Middle East Report* (Summer 1998), p. 40.

boost from traditional conservatives in the Iranian government aligned with Khamenei in February 1997, when MP Mohammad Javad Larijani met with the Foreign Office's Middle East chief in London. Larijani also headed the campaign of Iran's presumptive next president, and in his London discussions, he promised to settle the Rushdie issue and open new trade links.[202] Leaked transcripts of the meeting drew recriminations against Larijani, but after the presidential elections later that year, British ties with Tehran continued to expand.

The executive branch saw the hard-fought debt rescheduling, together with the new signs of European investment and export credits, as evidence that its perseverance in the face of internal and external obstacles paid off. "Despite all the pressures from U.S. sanctions, we have succeeded in reopening credit lines," the Central Bank governor Mohsen Nourbakhsh proclaimed. "There was some hesitation at first, but no more.... Finally we are on the right track. With all the unemployment here in Europe, they need to do business with Iran, and we are ready to do business."[203]

The final press for pragmatism was very nearly derailed, however, by external events. In April 1997, a German court ruled that the Iranian leadership was complicit in directing attacks against Iranian dissidents in Europe. In response, European diplomats were recalled; in Tehran, thugs surrounded the German Embassy and domestic opponents of Iran's tentative opening pushed back against Europe, which remained Iran's largest trade partner. "We don't give a damn about your ending the critical dialogue," Khamenei fulminated. "We never sought such a dialogue, and we have more criticism against you than you do against us."[204] However, as the ensuing years would show, Iranian leaders recognized all too well the need for continuing and even expanding international trade and investment.

CONCLUSION

The reconstruction program initiated during Rafsanjani's tenure has had prolonged impact on the structure of the Iranian economy, including facilitating the greatest growth over the course of the past three and a

---

[202] Ali M. Ansari, *Iran, Islam and Democracy: The Politics of Managing Change* (London: Chatham House, 2006), p. 106.

[203] Alan Friedman, "Iran's Central Bank Chief Hails Cooperation from 'Partners,' Citing Failure of U.S. Sanctions," *New York Times*, February 3, 1997.

[204] Tom Buerkle, "Standoff over Terror Ruling Is Worsening : EU and an Angry Iran Turn up War of Words," *New York Times*, May 2, 1997.

half decades. It helped to generate a tremendous amount of dynamism in its early phases. However, "as soon as the economic engine started running, it overheated dangerously."[205] The scholar Kaveh Ehsani cites media accounts from this period highlighting the disconnection between the initiative and energy demonstrated by Iranians and the eventual outcomes: thirty-five thousand agreements signed for new industrial enterprises, which produced a mere four thousand projects, and only ninety thousand new jobs.[206] The failure was not a single decision or mistake. It was the combination of factors – a recovery that was not well managed, the pent-up public appetite for imports and consumer products, the poorly timed exchange rate reforms, among others. And, perhaps most importantly, the undoing of Rafsanjani's reconstruction program stems from the persistence of the tensions with the world's sole remaining superpower, in large part due to Tehran's continuing constraints on domestic politics and its refusal to relinquish the ideological imperatives that continued to guide its regional diplomacy.

Rafsanjani played a vital role in the transformation of the Iranian economy and, by extension, the evolution of its political debates. His unapologetic embrace of internationalism and pragmatism – "Yes I am a pragmatist," the president said in 1993. "I am interested in facts and practicality"[207] – helped legitimize an interests-based approach to governance and decision making. Moreover, Rafsanjani's policies succeeded, in the sense that they contributed to the first real postrevolutionary economic growth, at least up until the debt crisis. However, unlike the oil boom of the subsequent decade, the population did not experience – or perceive itself to experience – the anticipated benefits of the Rafsanjani era economic turnaround. Inflation remained high throughout the reconstruction era, averaging nearly 19 percent during the first plan, more than 25 percent during the second plan, and reaching as high as 49 percent at times.[208] Unemployment also remained a stubborn problem throughout Rafsanjani's two terms.

Among the lessons of the Rafsanjani presidency are the fundamental contradictions posed by Tehran's attempt to reintegrate into the international economy without overcoming its antipathies toward and

---

[205] Ehsani (1994), p. 19.   [206] Ehsani (1994), p. 20.
[207] "Iran's Rafsanjani – the Pragmatic Revolutionary," *Reuters*, June 12, 1993.
[208] Vahid Mahmoudi, "Poverty Changes during the Three Recent Development Plans in Iran (1995–2007)," *African and Asian Studies* 10 (2011), p. 159; Karshenas (2005), p. 69.

disagreements with the largest player in that economy, the United States. Rafsanjani was explicit in promoting his agenda as intended to preclude compromising either the values of the revolution or the increasingly vocal expectations of the population for improved economic opportunities, acknowledging that "Iran will stick to revolutionary principles of Islam and at the same time try to get as much as it can from the West."[209]

The continuing frictions with Washington and the imposition of new American economic pressure persuaded some within the Iranian system that Tehran would need to find alternative markets and investors. The parliamentarian Hassan Rouhani argued in a 1996 speech, "Our relationships with important developing countries need to be expanded, in order to be able to resist the United States. We need to develop better relations with Russia, China, and Japan as they are big industrial powers."[210] However, as even Rafsanjani's adversaries came to appreciate, an international opening that sidesteps the United States is unlikely to generate the intended benefits. The unique American role in the Middle Eastern strategic landscape and the global economy could not be disregarded. "If we are supposed to go out of isolation by a policy of detente," Mohammed Musavi Khoieniha wrote in 1992, "as long as we have not brought about a detente with the U.S., detente with its satellites will solve no problems."[211]

This dilemma transcended the question of Iran's posture toward Washington, and it helps explain the disappointing outcomes of Rafsanjani's reconstruction program. Any number of factors contributed to constraining the positive impacts and undercutting the long-term viability of the postwar economic reforms; navigating the contradictions among ideological, political, and economic imperatives is a precarious course, particularly within a system as fractured and competitive as the Islamic Republic. The immediate demands of containing the factional fallout over his intended economic reforms took priority over defending his agenda and implementing the most effective policies. The same is true for Rafsanjani's approach to institutions and governance, in which he failed to appreciate what an early parliamentary critic described as

[209] "Iran's Rafsanjani – the Pragmatic Revolutionary," *Reuters*, June 12, 1993.
[210] Hassan Rouhani, *Islamic Revolution: Roots and Challenges* (Tehran: Afsat Company, Islamic Consultative Assembly of Iran, 1997).
[211] Jonathan C. Randal, "Iran's Failings Limit Bid to End Isolation; Tehran No Longer Seen Gaining from War," *WP*, April 27, 1991, p. A14.

the "symbiotic relation between economic liberalism and political freedom."[212] Pragmatism was both his genius and his curse.

Since leaving office, Rafsanjani has staunchly defended his record. Even as the former president has seen his ethics and his policies pilloried by reformists, and later by younger conservatives, he has continued to assert the wisdom and efficacy of his strategy. In a recent interview, he commented that "through the implementation of two five-year plans, the Construction Government gained huge achievements for the country. I was keen to implement the country's comprehensive movement towards overall progress.... We had a 51 per cent budget deficit. Five provinces involved in the eight-year war were destroyed. Most of the country's infrastructure was damaged.... All of Iran was turned into a landscape for building the country during the Construction Period, and everybody multiplied his efforts to cooperate. Of course, this cooperation was gradually weakened in the second term of my presidency and problems slowly appeared."[213]

---

[212] "Pre-Agenda Speeches by the Deputies in the Third Majles," *Resalat*, August 26, 1991, as quoted in Baktiari (1993).

[213] Rafsanjani interview, *Etemad*, April 3, 2012.

6

Ayatollah Gorbachev: Reform within the Red Lines, 1997–2005

The May 23, 1997, election of Muhammad Khatami unexpectedly closed the door on the Rafsanjani era and vaulted a new social movement into the highest echelons of the revolutionary state. Khatami was not the progenitor of the reform movement; nor was he its operational leader. Nonetheless, after his unexpected ascendance to the presidency, Khatami came to represent the reform movement as its standard bearer to both a domestic and an international audience. His policies and political choices defined the pathway for reform as explicitly incremental. The president's agenda was centered on a campaign that advanced the concepts of moderation, tolerance, accountability, and the supremacy of man-made law. These were revolutionary ideas in theocratic Iran; however, Khatami and his partisans scrupulously avoided revolutionary action.

These challenges, and the reformists' struggles to surmount them, earned the Iranian president unwelcome comparisons with another erstwhile reformer, Mikhail Gorbachev, whose program of liberalization and minor political reforms inadvertently generated the collapse of the Soviet system and the shrinking of its imperial borders. The moniker that became attached to him – Ayatollah Gorbachev – first by his adversaries and later by his allies offers a pithy summary of both the promise and the problems associated with reforming the Islamic Republic. Khatami's detractors, beginning with his opponent in the 1997 elections, relished linking the president with the final Soviet premier.[1] This analogy became the frequent theme of conservative journals and politicians, and it was

---

[1] "Farsi Media Focus," *Iran Daily*, October 8, 1998, p. 4.

deployed as a potent implicit warning about the consequences of unchecked reform and the hidden hand of American domination.[2]

The comparison is subtly powerful – in implicating Khatami personally, it also evoked the more profound perils of an inevitably eroding system. For this reason, the supreme leader, among others, rejected the analogy and its implications.[3] By the same token, Khatami's more ambitious allies increasingly brandished the resemblance to suggest the inevitability of public impatience and the imperative for the president to push harder for change.[4] They warned that the Soviet Union's collapse demonstrated the unsustainability of repressing popular movements. "Accepting the people's demands and gradually reforming all the pillars of the state is the only remaining way," opined one influential newspaper. "Let us learn from history."[5] Among Western observers, the epithet of "Ayatollah Gorbachev" initially bore a flattering veneer, implying as it often did that the new Iranian president might be capable of reconciling Islamic dogma with liberal economic and political philosophies, and thereby ushering in a similarly profound transformation in its policies.[6] However, the allusion grew more pointed, a subtle reminder that the path of moderation in immoderate political environments rarely achieves longevity.

The sobriquet "Ayatollah Gorbachev" highlights the dilemmas inherent within the reform movement's explicitly *evolutionary*, rather than revolutionary, approach to Iran's challenges. Khatami held inherently contradictory positions: He headed the government while serving as the symbol of its opposition, and he revitalized Iran's liberal tendencies and representative institutions while also leading the state that repressed them.

---

[2] *Resalat*, the newspaper of the traditionalist conservative establishment, was particularly vocal on this theme, in columns authored by "Khatami and Values," *Iran*, June 27, 2001, p. 3.

[3] Khamenei pronounced that the "collapse of communism in the Soviet Union with plausible slogans for reforms and reformations, would never work for Iran" and attributed the perestroika phenomenon that overtook the USSR to Western conspiracies. See "Khamenei Rejects Western-Style Reforms, Lashes out against US, Britain," *AFP*, July 10, 2000.

[4] "Two Tactics," *Asr-e Ma*, December 22, 1999, p. 3.

[5] "The Tragedy of Monopoly," *Hayat-e No*, August 30, 2000.

[6] The *New York Times* columnist Thomas Friedman became particularly enamored of the analogy, referring to the prospect of an "Ayatollah Gorbachev" in columns published both before and after Khatami's election. See "Waiting for Ayatollah Gorbachev," *New York Times*, September 8, 1996; "Broken China" *New York Times*, January 26, 1999; "Ayatollah Deng," *New York Times*, July 20, 1999.

These paradoxes defined, and ultimately undermined, his mandate and his two terms in office.

THE STRATEGY OF REFORM

For its tacticians, reform in Iran represented the art of the possible. The politicians who spearheaded the movement began as loyal adherents to the Islamic system – eager participants in the revolution frustrated as the state assumed more autocratic features. Many – including the future president – found themselves sidelined by Rafsanjani's efforts to push forward his reconstruction program. In fact, Khatami was recruited to run in 1997 as a token opposition candidate, in hopes that a decent showing would jolt the leftists' ranks and restore their political viability.[7] The reform movement's leadership neither rejected the Islamic system's fundamental premise nor sought its wholesale removal. Rather, they wanted to rehabilitate the Islamic Republic by implementing its limited guarantees of representative government, equality, and freedom.

For Khatami and his cohorts, advocating reform through rule of law represented more than mere rhetoric; it guided their agenda for change. "The law must be the law," Khatami argued. "It should be the criterion for assessing our behavior. Not that we should do whatever we like and then justify it legally. That is no different than lawlessness."[8] Their liberal reading of Iran's constitution facilitated the quadrupling of the country's press outlets in Khatami's first two years, which helped repoliticize a new generation of Iranians and challenge Iran's prevailing orthodoxies and oligarchies. Insistence on rule of law empowered an investigation into the shadowy intelligence war against dissidents and some pushback against the indiscriminate violence perpetrated by the country's security bureaucracy. By implementing long-disregarded constitutional provisions for local elections, Khatami expanded national support for democratic institutions and dispersed some authority from the center to Iran's provinces. Couched on the safe terrain of standing law, reformists pushed for a wide range of political, social, and economic changes in the months and years

[7] Massoud Sadroldin, "The Heroes Address the Excited Ones," *Hayat-e No,* October 28, 2000, p. 11.
[8] "Khatami Addresses Red Crescent Society, Stresses Political Development," speech broadcast on the Vision of the Islamic Republic of Iran Network 1, May 8, 2002, as transcribed and translated in World News Connection IAP20020509000114.

following the 1997 elections and appeared poised to erode the conservative stranglehold on ultimate authority from within.

This cautious agenda represented the authentic impulses of politicians whose careers were forged within the Islamic system. Improbable as it may seem given the tremendous obstacles they faced, some reformers – including, most of all, Khatami himself – remained convinced that the Islamic Republic actually could accommodate freedom and democracy. Equally importantly, the focus on rule of law represented a key component of their overall strategy for effecting change, which emphasized the very permissibility of their activities. Khatami and his allies were not naïve; rather, having battled back from political oblivion, many were profoundly cynical about the system as well as about Iran's political culture, which has condoned successive suppressions of representative rule. They learned to utilize the system's suppleness to their own advantage, to deploy the cult of Khomeinism and the hard-liners' dogma against them. Iran's reform movement explicitly set out to avoid any overt challenge to the boundaries of permissible political discourse and to capitalize on the room for maneuver accorded to the regime's mainstream political elite.

Once in office, the tactical deliberation behind the reform movement initially served Khatami and his allies well. They adopted a binary strategy – under the catchphrase "Pressure from below, negotiation at the top" – that acknowledged burgeoning public demands for accountability while exploiting their return to positions of influence. With a compromise cabinet and a short window of opportunity, the new president had to pick his battles carefully. To turn up the heat "from below," hundreds of new publications were licensed, censorship guidelines were loosened, and permits for student gatherings were issued. Meanwhile, within the government itself, the reformers refrained from defying the supreme leader overtly. Instead, they focused on expanding their institutional power bases, taking full advantage of constitutional provisions for limited democracy to move the political competition into the public arena.

However, reform within the "red lines" failed to anticipate the intensity of the reaction from both the conservatives, who recognized it as an unambiguous threat and responded in kind, and the populace at large, which inevitably inflated the reformers' mandate with buoyant expectations. The reformers' prudence may have preserved their place in Iranian politics, but it did not protect them or their agenda. The hard-liners appreciated that the reformists' slogans and subtle policy steps aimed at nothing less than the reconfiguration of the Islamic Republic.

The articulation of this challenge by "insiders" within the system only intensified conservative umbrage. "These people are delivering the biggest blows at Islam in an Islamic garb,"[9] raged the hard-liners' ideological stalwart, Ayatollah Mohammad Taqi Mesbah Yazdi. Their vociferous opposition blocked Khatami from implementing his broader vision and reversed many of the reform movement's achievements. The conservative campaign made a mockery of the Constitution's legal protections and the reformers' strategic self-restraint.

While pragmatism helped preserve the reform movement, it also eventually eroded much of the public and international confidence in the movement. Iranians became disenchanted with the glacial pace of change and the president's reluctance to confront his adversaries in the face of repeated provocation. The president was also pressed by his allies, as several leading voices of reform agitated publicly for a more aggressive strategy. In the short term, the strategic differences within the reform camp produced mainly internecine squabbling and squandered some credibility on ill-conceived gambits, but generally failed to mobilize a meaningful replacement to moderation. The reform movement's popular mandate represented its most potent implicit asset, but one that was too risky to wield casually, or perhaps at all. Khatami, for one, never demonstrated the stomach for this level of gamesmanship, particularly after the shattering violence that erupted across the country when security forces aided by hard-line thugs crushed student protests in July 1999.

The reformists' incrementalist approach had other consequences, particularly in the international arena. Their embattled status further complicated efforts to resolve outstanding international disputes. The reformists sought détente – in fact, it was a key element of their agenda – but their rhetoric and actions tended to focus on domestic issues, where progress was more viable. Highly sensitive matters of foreign policy – such as the Arab-Israeli peace process – remained either too hot to handle, outside their scope of action, and/or consistent with their own ideology. The failure to ameliorate these areas of significant tensions with Washington and its allies played into existing suspicions among Western policy makers that the reformists were either irrelevant or insincere.

---

[9] As quoted in "Injustice That Is Done in the Name of Islam," *Asr-e Ma*, January 27, 2001, pp. 1, 8.

THE REFORMIST APPROACH TO THE ECONOMY

Khatami was elected on the basis of an agenda that focused almost entirely on sociocultural liberalization; however, once in office, he found himself confronted with immediate challenges on the economy. And none of these issues confronting Iran – neither the demand for political participation nor the need for new investment and employment nor the exigency of reintegrating Iran into a rapidly changing global marketplace – could be addressed in isolation.

Still, the reform movement was primarily focused on social, cultural, and political issues, as evidenced by its initial standard bearer Khatami, who had been forced out of Rafsanjani's first cabinet because he was perceived as too liberal. Khatami's campaign platform focused almost exclusively on sociocultural liberalization. Moreover, he had limited command of economic issues, and his advisers remained wedded to statist economic policies consistent with their leftist orientation.[10] In his campaign, Khatami insisted that "we definitely do not want capitalism. But we respect the value of capital."[11]

Once in office, however, he was confronted with the urgency of the country's economic stagnation and international isolation. The reformists' response was to approach the problem sequentially. Khatami and his allies saw gradual political change as the first step to resolving Iran's multiple challenges, arguing that:

> our society faces serious problems and solving those problems requires cooperation and peace and calm.... In order to establish minimum stability and development, we have no option but to set the country's economic development at six percent and the growth of investment at just above seven percent in the country. This requires an atmosphere of agreement and cooperation, without tension. We need private investment. We need the private sector's investment. We need foreign facilities. Naturally, with moderation and calm, we can better move on this path.[12]

The prioritization of political over economic reforms derived directly from the reformists' historical experience. They believed, as Ayatollah

---

[10] Of the many excellent books that address the reform movement and the Khatami presidency, one of the best is Ali Ansari's absorbing narrative of its rise and fall, *Iran, Islam and Democracy: The Politics of Managing Change* (London: Royal Institute of International Affairs, 2006).

[11] IRIB Television Second Program Network, May 21, 1997

[12] "President Khatami Addresses Students on Reform, Extremism," *IRNA*, December 23, 2001.

Montazeri once said, that "before any reconstruction [takes place], there must first be a reconstruction of the country's thinking about administration and its quality."[13] For the reformists, this process of reorienting the relationship between state and society was essential to the state's legitimacy and survival, and by extension to the success or failure of a market economy in Iran. They also were reacting to their understanding of the monarchy's development agenda; as a reformist journal opined, the shah "was in a great hurry to implement a number of reforms in order to achieve economic development and mainly government investment, without the political participation and supervision of the people. He was hoping to isolate all his opponents and critics and his possible rivals by creating a great economic power and a great civilization, but we saw what happened."[14] Even Khatami's lieutenants charged with jump-starting the economy, such as Oil Minister Bijan Zanganeh, celebrated the reform agenda's focus on "software and in rearranging and reorganizing ideas and thoughts" as "creating the grounds and necessary conditions for facilitating economic activities."[15]

Beyond their philosophical leanings, this sequential approach to reform also reflected deep frustration with the Rafsanjani years. Rafsanjani occupied an outsized position in the reformist intellectual discourse as well as their fumbling for factional advantage. The journalist Akbar Ganji's epic dissection of the brutality committed during the Rafsanjani era and endorsed, at least tacitly, by the president himself electrified the political elite. Attitudes toward Rafsanjani figured prominently in the debates that led up to the 2000 parliamentary elections, the apex of the reformist electoral successes. For his part, the former president largely avoided the fray at the time but has since sought to defend his legacy robustly.

The reformists argued that Rafsanjani had failed precisely because he was more interested in economics than in the country's political institutions. Reformists saw Rafsanjani as having condoned political repression while distributing little to none of the dividends of reconstruction through growth or enhanced competitiveness.

"The experience of the reconstruction period has shown that we have given priority to economic matters and spent our energies in this sector,

---

[13] *Kayhan Hava'i*, February 8, 1989, as quoted in Moin (1999), p. 280.
[14] "Obedience or participation?" *Iran-e Farda*, Mordad 1377 (July/August 1998), pp. 2–4.
[15] "Oil Minister Supports Buy-Back Agreements; Lauds Government's Economic Performance," *Hamshahri*, September 5, 2000, pp. 4, 15.

in the hope of resolving the country's problems," the prominent reformist activist Mohsen Armin explained.

The experience showed itself to be the wrong solution and that attention to the economic structure without corresponding attention to the political structure and the distribution of power would not resolve anything. If we are negligent of political transparency and the creation of political control mechanisms, then economic efforts will only lead to powerful economic poles and the formation of a new economic aristocracy. Problems will thus remain and we will not be able to prevent the widespread abuse of economic privileges. So before all else, we must think of the transparency of power and of placing authority next to responsibility.[16]

Although Rafsanjani protégés and allies composed an important segment of the reformist leadership, Khatami's administration explicitly rejected his approach. Instead, the reformists argued for strengthening civil society and rule of law, anticipating that this progress would create spillover effects on the economy; as an influential reformist journal opined, "It is through this feeling of participation and social cohesion that the economic wheels will start to turn."[17]

The decision to sequence political reform in advance of economic restructuring also reflected the enormous obstacles facing the state. A serious program to promote economic growth and competitiveness would entail dismantling the manifold inefficiencies of the prevailing system—its subsidies, state monopolies, labor safeguards, and overall structural distortions. All these measures would generate long-term gains but also short-term public pain. The reformists saw public support as their most potent asset, and so the political costs of undertaking meaningful economic liberalization would have severely threatened their political viability.

At the outset, the reformists' strategy of anchoring their mandate to the promotion of fundamental principles rather than individual pocketbooks resonated reasonably well with a populace that felt too disenfranchised and disconnected from any benefits that might derive from economic reform. Ultimately, however, the reformists' incrementalist strategy reflected a misreading of the popular mood as well as the force of regime opposition. The reformists' gradualism could not meet public expectations; nor could it neutralize the state's inherent contradictions. The conservative response shuttered reformist newspapers, obstructing

---

[16] "Reforms Need Changes in the Political and Legal Structure," interview with Mohsen Armin, *Kar va Kargar*, September 20, 2000, p. 10.
[17] "Obedience or participation?" *Iran-e Farda* 45 (Mordad 1377/July-August 1998), p. 3.

their legislative program, and filled Iran's prisons with a new generation of dissidents. Khatami's presidency became mired in political paralysis and a bitter power struggle. With their monopoly on authority and a readiness to use extralegal instruments, hard-liners rescinded the reformists' tenuous hold on Iran's electoral institutions and undercut their popular mandate as well.

The conservatives were aided by the reformists' own missteps, in particular their inability to transcend their elite origins. The reformists remained a cliquish group of political insiders with an inherent distrust for mass politics, who failed to create political parties capable of mobilizing their potentially broad social base. In addition, the reformists' inability to make a persuasive case for addressing Iran's economic dilemmas contributed to the perception that their leaders were out of touch, eroding the movement's popular support. And despite enacting modest economic reforms, the reformists' failure to leave the economy in fundamentally better shape than they inherited it left them vulnerable to the redistributionist rhetoric of their successor, Ahmadinejad, who campaigned around the need to put Iran's oil revenues on its citizens' dinner tables.

EARLY CULTURAL AND POLITICAL BATTLEGROUNDS

Khatami was initially compelled to accept a compromise cabinet, composed of ministers from the center and the Right of Iranian politics. He managed to place influential leftists in two critical portfolios, the Ministry of Culture and Islamic Guidance and the Interior Ministry; both individuals, Ataollah Mohajerani and Abdollah Nuri, quickly became lightning rods for the conservative backlash and both were forced from office (and in Nuri's case, into prison). Khatami also insisted on selecting particular deputy ministers to form a sort of shadow cabinet of reformers.[18] In addition, he broke new ground, albeit in a typically wary manner, by naming two women as senior advisers, managing portfolios on the environment and on women's issues. These appointments reinforced Khatami's progressive reputation and underscored the importance of the female vote in catapulting him into the presidency.

On the economy, Khatami assembled a disparate – some might say, divergent – team. His finance minister, Husayn Namazi, had held the

---

[18] Massoud Sadroldin, "The Heroes Address the Excited Ones," *Hayat-e No* (accessed via internet), October 28, 2000, p. 11.

same post in the Musavi government and remained an ardent advocate of statist economic policies. Zanganeh, who had served as energy minister under Rafsanjani, moved over to take on the Oil Ministry and emerged as a significant figure in shaping the most consequential element of the Khatami era economic agenda, the return of international oil companies and cultivation of foreign investment in the petroleum sector. Nourbakhsh stayed on at the Central Bank, and the well-respected Mohammad Ali Najafi took on the PBO.

Emboldened by their electoral success, reformists hoped to build greater popular momentum and extend their institutional strongholds by mounting a coordinated campaign in October 1998 elections for the Assembly of Experts (Majlis-e Khobregan). The institution itself was quite marginal to the practice of politics in the Islamic Republic; its function was limited to succession decision making, although by law the council's responsibility for replacing the leader might be construed as its oversight of his performance.[19] Despite the assembly's low profile, reformist strategists anticipated that another populist victory at the ballot boxes would intensify the momentum for change and reinforce public support for the Khatami agenda. This proved an early miscalculation. As an institution with no day-to-day relevance to government decision making, the Khobregan commanded very limited popular interest. Moreover, the Guardians' Council was fully prepared to deploy its vetting authority against what the hard-liners perceived as an impudent transgression by the Islamic Left on their turf. In the end, voter turnout was a respectable 46 percent – a full 10 percent higher than the previous Khobregan ballot – but the most influential reformists were blocked from running.

In addition to enhancing the role of electoral politics, the focus on the Khobregan elections highlighted another objective of the reformist strategy – the gradual erosion of the autonomy and authority of Iran's theocratic institutions. This set the reformists on a collision course with the supreme leader's defenders, who used their vetting authority to block any prospect of another reformist electoral claim. Still, the 1998 elections heightened the profile of the Khobregan, spawning criticism of the

---

[19] Schirazi concludes that the responsibility for selection and, if necessary, replacement of the *faqih* places the Assembly of Experts "above the leader because it can dismiss him and choose another in his place. By exploiting this power the majority in the council can, at any given moment, put pressure on the leader to bow to their will." Schirazi (1997), p. 297.

assembly as inadequate and inappropriate to carry out the duties with which it was charged.[20] Iranian reformers began pressing the organization for active supervision of the institutions under the leader's purview and his performance in the office.[21] This presaged similar efforts to increase pressure on another key conservative-controlled institution, the Guardians' Council, later in the Khatami presidency. And it was consistent with the reformist focus on transparency and accountability, principles that they sought to extend throughout the bureaucracy including the economy. In fact, the supreme leader endorsed this notion. "No one, not even the leader's establishment, is above supervision," Khamenei confirmed in February 2001. "Everyone must be overseen, all those who have power and wealth in their hands."[22]

Even as they sought to rein in the state's unelected institutions, the reformists also tried to bolster the representative aspects of the Iranian system. After the frustrating Khobregan experience, Khatami and his allies pivoted, announcing the first-ever round of city and municipal council elections across the country, held in early 1999. This simultaneously fulfilled a previously disregarded constitutional provision and facilitated some decentralization of authority, while reviving the reformists' momentum and popular mandate in the lead-up to parliamentary elections the subsequent year. That ballot proved to be the apex of what was sometimes referred to as the Khatami spring, a brief halcyon moment when the reformist coalition won more than four times as many seats as their conservative rivals and managed to oust several long-standing stalwarts, including their bête noir, Rafsanjani. The exuberant show of force prompted a sustained backlash, from which the movement never recovered.

During this same period, the fragile roots of free expression that the president helped sow while culture minister were revived. Khatami approached the press as an integral component of a viable democracy and the resolution of the country's problems. He argued that "critique is the source of the country's progress, the cause of the improvement of the affairs and the achievement of better methods, the clarification

---

[20] Two members of the Assembly of Experts coincidentally passed away in September 1999, only days before a meeting of the group. This prompted the need for midterm elections, held along with the parliamentary elections in February 2000, as well as some sniping in the press about the age and lassitude of the assembly as a whole.

[21] "The Assembly of Experts' Performance," *Khordad* (accessed via Internet), September 8, 1999.

[22] "Iran Supreme Leader Defends Reformist Press Curbs," *Reuters*, February 28, 2001.

of ambiguities and the removing of shortages."[23] After his inauguration, new publications proliferated thanks to the intragovernmental commission on the press. Newspapers served as proxies for political activism, since other avenues remained proscribed under the Islamic Republic's strictures. "The press was never intended to be the spearhead for Khatami's political reforms," Ahmad Borqani, who served as deputy minister of culture and Islamic guidance, later acknowledged, "but it was soon apparent that it offered the fastest path to political liberalization."[24] One of the most determined reformist editors, Hamid Reza Jalaiepour, similarly explained that the rejection of his application for a licensed political party prompted him to turn to newspapers. "Instead, I saw that press licenses were easier to get, so I opened a newspaper."[25]

Despite the flourishing of the reformist press, comparatively less effort was devoted to the establishment of mass political parties. After the 1987 demise of the Islamic Republican Party, influential coalitions emerged to fill two of the typical functions of a political party – the differentiation and advancement of policy positions and individual ambitions. They failed, however, to provide meaningful mechanisms for collective action or linkages between the population and the state. The reformists would eventually make a halfhearted bid at establishing a real party, the Islamic Iran Participation Front. However, even at its height, it remained a relatively small-scale organization and quickly receded into paralysis after the reformists lost the parliament.

KHATAMI ON CNN

Khatami's strategy throughout his two terms in office prioritized steadiness, gradualism, and moderation. And yet one of his first important moves as president reflected a surprising gamble. The new president's January 1988 decision to sit for an extended interview with CNN was unusual. Khatami's predecessors in leadership positions within Iran had engaged sporadically with media outlets based outside Iran, but certainly in nothing that might be described as an international charm offensive. The timing – at the outset of his term – as well as the language and

[23] "Iran: President Khatami Addresses Majlis on Government Performance," Vision of the Islamic Republic of Iran Network 1, BBC Monitoring 1820 GMT, March 11, 2001.
[24] Kaveh Ehsani, "'The Conservatives Have Misjudged': A Conversation with Ahmad Bourghani," *Middle East Report* 212 (Fall 1999), p. 37.
[25] Afshin Molavi, "Extra! Extra! Extra! Iran's Newspapers at War," *Washington Post*, August 30, 1999, p. A13.

demeanor represented a stark departure from any prior interaction between Americans and Iranians since the revolution.

Invoking the legacy of the Puritans and the experience of de Tocqueville, Khatami jump-started a public debate – both at home and within the Washington policy circles – over the state of the bilateral relationship. When asked about the revolutionary mantra "Death to America," Khatami explained its symbolism and noted that "not only we do not harbor any ill wishes for the American people, but in fact we consider them to be great nation." He appealed for "a crack in this wall of mistrust to prepare for a change and create an opportunity to study a new situation" and insisted that "nothing should prevent dialogue and understanding between two nations." He proposed the establishment of people-to-people exchanges involving academics, writers, scholars, artists, journalists, and tourists and tackled a range of more sensitive issues – the Arab-Israeli peace process and the nuclear question – with reason and diplomacy, if not objective arguments.[26]

The interview provoked a flurry of commentaries within Washington about its purpose and the prospects for meaningful changes in the tenor or substance of the U.S.-Iranian relationship. Within Tehran, the speech sparked a vociferous debate in the media, as both the Islamic Left and the traditional conservatives sought to reframe Khatami's apparent overture. Nine days later, in a Friday prayers sermon, Khamenei defended his new president, noting, "I listened to it carefully. All the things that should be said were said. ... Everything was very good." However, just as he had in previous years, the supreme leader sought to reinforce the revolution's ideological bona fides and discourage any conciliatory impressions. "They ask, 'Why do you call us the Great Satan?'" Khamenei said. "What does Satan mean? If you don't do satanic acts, then we will stop calling you that." He also insisted that "negotiations and dialogue with America are harmful for us."[27]

Khatami scrambled to clarify his stance and his presidency. In a speech ten days later at Khomeini's tomb, the new president offered a rendition of American history more familiar to his audience, the assembled political élite of the Islamic Republic. Asserting Iran's independence, Khatami denounced past and present U.S. policies toward Tehran as dictatorial.

---

[26] Transcript of interview, *CNN* (Internet edition), http://www.cnn.com/WORLD/9801/07/iran/interview.html

[27] Elaine Sciolino, "Chief Iranian Cleric Assails Washington but Backs Overture," *New York Times*, January 17, 1998, p. A1.

"Both before and after the revolution, American politicians acted toward the world as if they were the masters," he said. "They want to impose their own domestic law on the world. The world will not tolerate a master any more.... The embargo has led America into isolation. America's politicians are betraying the American people."[28]

For the remainder of Khatami's two terms in office, meaningful debate or substantive overtures on the issue of rapprochement with Washington continued to be constrained by Khamenei's insistent antagonism and ensnared by the power struggle as the symbolic centerpiece of patriotism and political strife. Washington sought to reach out to Tehran through a variety means – quietly communicating through the Swiss channel, using exhortatory rhetoric by senior officials, easing visa restrictions, and encouraging people-to-people dialogue. The president himself spoke out on Iran repeatedly,[29] and his secretary of state, Madeleine Albright, made several high-profile speeches in which she appealed to Tehran for mutual confidence building. The administration also made tangible overtures, such as designating the regime's most reviled expatriate opponent, the Mojahideen-e Khalq, as a foreign terrorist organization and relaxing sanctions on several key Iranian exports. In 1999, instead of launching retaliatory action against Tehran over evidence of its involvement in the 1996 Khobar Towers bombing, the administration endeavored to "set up a separate, discreet channel to Khatami."[30]

The prospects were complicated – probably, quite deliberately – by domestic developments within Iran, including the June 1999 arrest of Jewish Iranians on charges of spying for Israel. The trial prompted intense international criticism and intensified suspicions while deterring the already hesitant overtures from both sides. Khatami and his allies fell back on the traditional Iranian formulation of demanding deeds rather than words as a mechanism for establishing a formal dialogue. For his part, Khamenei publicly disparaged the need for resuming relations, arguing that "Iran will undoubtedly undergo

---

[28] Elaine Sciolino, "At Khomaini's Tomb, Iran's President Switches Tune on U.S," *New York Times*, January 20, 1998.

[29] In President Clinton's videotaped January 1998 Eid Al-Fitr message, he announced that "the United States regrets the estrangement of our two nations. ... We have real differences with some Iranian policies, but I believe these are not insurmountable. ... I hope that the day will soon come when we can enjoy once again good relations with Iran." See Indyk (2009), p. 222.

[30] Indyk (2009), p. 227.

improved economic conditions without having to give in to the bullying typical of the Americans."[31]

This assessment was not strictly accurate, and the advent of reform facilitated a much more open discussion surrounding the relative costs and benefits of the estrangement with the United States. "What has been our attitude toward America?" Ali Rashidi, a renowned economist and political activist, posited. "Now, let us assume that American had wrongly supported the shah, and she has paid the penalty for that. However, continuing this present situation will result in nothing but harm for Iran; because in every part of the world America has blocked our potential involvement. For instance, she does not allow us to take a loan from the International Monetary Fund, or prevents Japan from investing in Iran. At least on 30 occasions America has blocked our international activity."[32] Like so much of the reform movement's advancements, the early forays at staking new ground on U.S. relations were necessary but insufficient.

ACKNOWLEDGING THE ECONOMIC CHALLENGES

No sooner had the president assumed office than he was confronted with a bitter economic crisis. The price of oil fell below $10/barrel in late 1998, the lowest level in a quarter-century, precipitating a parallel slide in government oil revenues from $19 billion in 1986 to $10 billion in 1998. Khatami's first budget was based on a $17.50 oil price. "If the government is not capable of solving the economic problems, the economic problems could ultimately overwhelm the government," one economist commented.[33] Moreover the specter of the 1993 debt crisis haunted the new administration, as the government struggled to service the same $5.9 billion package of European debt that Rafsanjani was forced to reschedule in 1993.[34]

His speech followed on the heels of an intensive, and somewhat contentious, process of deliberation within the neophyte administration about economic policy and the ways to respond to the predicament facing the state. That debate reflected an intellectual confrontation between

[31] "Leader: US Position on Iran Essentially Unchanged," *Iran Daily*, November 4, 1998.
[32] Mohsen Shemshiri, Interview with Dr. Ali Rashidi, *Mobin* 316 (May 16, 1998), pp. 1, 4.
[33] Douglas Jehl, "Iran Discontent Rises as Oil-Based Economy Falls," *New York Times*, December 13, 1998.
[34] Ibid.

advocates of market reforms and the defenders of Iran's unique brand of Islamic socialism. In the end, the unavoidable realities of massive employment demands and constrained revenues made the direction of Khatami's economic policy uncontestable: He would have to seek additional foreign investment and privatization if he was to have any hopes of meeting the expectations of a newly reinvigorated Iranian citizenry. Khatami described the Iranian economy as "chronically ill," adding that "this will continue to be so unless there's fundamental restructuring."[35]

Among his proposed remedies were promises of bureaucratic reform, efforts to create jobs and boost productivity, improvements to the regulatory and security framework for foreign investment, and efforts at tax reform and promotion of nonoil exports. He appealed for patience and cooperation, noting that he was not advising "don't criticize, but criticism is different from sabotage," and he promised that "the future will be better." He hedged, however, by refusing to disavow the revolutionary emphasis on social justice, calling it "the focal point of our policies" and adding that "we are even ready to slow down economic growth for the sake of social justice."[36]

All told, it was a strong speech, although short on details or innovations. It launched Khatami's "Economic Recovery Plan," a vague but encouraging document that laid out the president's aspirational economic agenda; it prioritized social justice but included an embrace of foreign investment. The speech also heralded the formulations of a more permanent exercise in state-guided development in the form of the third five-year plan, which entailed an intensive effort over several years by one thousand experts.[37] Khatami remained more persuasive as a political philosopher than a manager of government operations. And yet it was encouraging to many Iranians that the new president seemed to appreciate the need to achieve objectives in both arenas.

REGIONAL DÉTENTE AND DIALOGUE AMONG CIVILIZATIONS

As with domestic policy, the reformists' foreign policy agenda reflected the art of the possible. At the outset, the reform movement appeared

[35] Kianouche Dorranie, "Khatami Unveils Policies to Heal Iran's Economy," *AFP*, August 2, 1998.

[36] Jonathan Lyons, "Iran's Khatami Outlines Economic Recovery Plans," *Reuters*, August 2, 1998.

[37] Jahangir Amuzegar, "Iran's Third Development Plan: An Appraisal," *Middle East Policy* 12 (3) (Fall 2005).

prepared to exploit the international goodwill that Khatami's surprise election and the genesis of new popular support for the regime offered. After a bravura performance hosting the Organization of the Islamic Conference in late 1997, the president helped cement the burgeoning reconciliation with Iran's Gulf neighbors and undertook the unenviable task of repairing Iran's reputation on the world stage. The reformers initially believed that the linkages between domestic political reform and international détente could be harnessed to the advantage of their cause. Reducing frictions with the world could generate much-needed tranquility at home, and that in turn would augment the system's security.

The reformers contented themselves with pursuing a generalized program of détente that was carefully orchestrated to ensure the broadest possible support from the country's fragmented political élites. During Khatami's two terms, Tehran pursued a number of diplomatic initiatives that commanded broad consensus across the fractured factional landscape, including developing more constructive relations with the GCC states, advancing peace negotiations in the Azeri/Armenian conflict and the Tajik civil war, and withdrawing the small coterie of Revolutionary Guards still positioned in southern Lebanon. The moderation extended well beyond the region, as the Iranian government undertook major initiatives to woo investors and government envoys alike from across Europe and Asia.

The 1997 summit of the Organization of the Islamic Conference marked a high point for Khatami. Although bookended by Khamenei's orthodoxy, Khatami's call for the revitalization of "Islamic civil society" clearly signified a new tone was welcomed by the array of senior Arab officials in attendance, including the then–Saudi Crown Prince Abdullah. The summit success was followed by a series of historic visits to and from the kingdom: former president Rafsanjani's visit in 1998, President Khatami's in 1999, and routine ministerial exchanges. The two states even signed a series of agreements on trade, culture, science, and technology, including a 2001 security pact, and launched a number of joint projects. In a surprising goodwill gesture, Riyadh even appointed a Shi'a ambassador in Tehran.

The Saudis had to manage their smaller neighbors', particularly Bahraini, concerns about Iran's role in ongoing sectarian tensions, and the UAE's objections to Iran's occupation of three Persian Gulf islands claimed by both states. In particular, reducing tensions with the UAE required continued intervention of Riyadh and other Arab interlocutors (particularly Qatar and Oman) on Iran's behalf. In June 1999, a GCC exhibited a rare bout of public dissension, when its ministerial session ended without agreement on a closing statement addressing the GCC's position toward Iran. After several weeks of mutual sniping in the press, the Qatari emir, Sheikh Hamad bin Khalifa Al Thani, eventually brokered an agreement in crisis talks with his Saudi and UAE counterparts. In March 2000, the Emirates forced the Arab League to rescind an invitation to Iran's foreign minister to attend its annual summit, which was expected to focus on the Middle East peace process and the future of Lebanon.

Iran's relations with Kuwait, another state that harbored justifiable grievances against Tehran for its subversive policies in the 1980s, fared better. Rapprochement appeared to be spearheaded by the next generation of the ruling family: Sheikh Mohammad Al Salem Al Sabah, the country's former Washington envoy and then-minister of state for foreign affairs, traveled to Tehran in 2001, the highest ranking member of his government to do so since the revolution. And Kuwait's government appointed a prominent member of the ruling family's younger generation, Sheikh Nasser Al Ahmad Al Sabah, to lead efforts to foster greater cooperation with Iran. The ideological edge in Iranian-Gulf relations appeared to have dulled, and remaining disputes focused on territorial claims. In addition to the islands issue with the UAE, Iran's claim to the Dorra gas field raised tensions with Kuwait in 2000. However, by spring 2002, Kuwait and Saudi Arabia were moving to begin exploiting its resources, and the Kuwaiti government was discussing compensation to Iran for relinquishing its claim.

The opening to the Gulf facilitated direct cooperation between Tehran and Riyadh on oil policy. The steady drop in oil prices had pushed both states to the brink of a renewed financial crisis, and with memories of the fallout from the 1985–6 price crash still fresh in the minds of decision makers, there was a newfound readiness to work together within OPEC to fashion a mutually beneficial solution. In reaching out to Tehran, the Saudis reflected a consistency with their own preferences for hedging their more powerful neighbors and preventing price wars within OPEC.[38]

However, in pursuing this policy, the kingdom was explicitly diverging from the preferences of Washington, whose policy remained focused on isolating Tehran. In contrast to the 1985–6 price collapse, when concerns

---

[38] As discussed in Chapter 4, Riyadh made several overtures to Tehran in an effort to advance a cease-fire, most notably in 1985 as concerns about Saudi price and export declines were at their height.

about domestic American producers coincidentally aligned the Reagan administration's oil price preferences with those of Tehran, Washington now explicitly opposed the new trans-Gulf effort to boost prices. Also complicating the effort was the fact that the Saudis had to assume the larger proportion (25 percent) of the burden for export cuts agreed upon at the March 1999 OPEC meeting.[39] The newfound comity between the old adversaries did not eliminate their differences, and only a few months after the Vienna deal, the two countries clashed over an Iranian bid to push its own candidate to lead OPEC.

DOMESTIC POLITICAL BACKLASH

Even as Iran began to make inroads internationally, the domestic environment was degenerating. Once the hard-liners recovered from the shock of their electoral defeat – so unexpected that the conservative parliament commissioned a study to explain it – they regrouped and began to take revenge. Inveighing against the reformist press quickly emerged as a standard refrain in Friday prayer sermons, conservative publications, and official statements released by conservative institutions. Paralleling the "West-toxification" discourse under the monarchy, conservatives adopted similar imagery to impugn the reformists. "Poisonous thought and articles serve as a microbe in the society," Ayatollah Mohammad-Taqi Mesbah Yazdi, an Assembly of Experts member well known for his bombastic sermons, opined. "Government should prevent the publication of harmful articles just as it checks the distribution of adulterated or contaminated foodstuff and medicine."[40]

The threat to the public welfare was not a diffuse one; for conservatives, articles criticizing the government and contravening the official narrative risked eroding morality and authority, presaging the recurrence of external domination. Thus, hard-liners traversed a logically facile path from press freedom to American imperialism. The early contours of the conservative offensive against the reform movement crystallized in mid-1998, when Tehran Mayor Karbaschi, – a key Khatami campaigner – was prosecuted on dubious fraud charges, and the notoriously liberal interior minister was first impeached and then, along with the culture minister,

---

[39] Nawaf Obeid, *The Oil Kingdom at 100: Petroleum Policymaking in Saudi Arabia* (Washington, DC: Washington Institute for Near East Policy, 2000), p. 82.

[40] "Mesbah-Yazdi Asks Gov't to Stop Publication of Harmful Articles," *IRNA*, March 24, 2001.

physically harassed by thugs outside the Friday prayer ceremony. From these early efforts, the basic components of the conservative strategy can be discerned – the targeting of individual reformist leaders, the selective use of violence to intimidate and create diversions, and the central role of the judiciary, along with other conservative-dominated state institutions, in blocking genuine reform.

Although he was typically portrayed as mediating between the two opposing camps, much as Khomeini had, Khamenei in fact aligned himself firmly with the hard-liners. He repeatedly argued that democracy represented a nefarious Western-orchestrated plot against the developing world, advocating instead a divinely guided government focused on advancing justice. In a 2001 speech before the Assembly of Experts, Khamenei declaimed that "democracy is not everything. Justice, which is the basis of correct government, does not exist there [in the West]."[41]

Khamenei's rhetoric underscored the conservative interpretation of the reform movement as a Trojan horse of external subversion. Well before the emergence of Iran's second-generation hard-liners such as Ahmadinejad, the hard-liners accused reformers of facilitating external pressure. All politics was not in fact local, despite the conventional wisdom; Khamenei perceived that the West was determined to reassert its former dominance over Iran and sought to use the reformists as its instrument of influence. "Today, the greedy expectations that they, particularly the Americans, had from our country are no longer feasible. This is not a small loss for the centers of international political power and domination. What can they do to return to the past situation? In the early days of the revolution, they ineptly opted for a face-to-face war. However, when their noses were rubbed in dirt, they realized that this method could not serve their interests. They therefore resorted to a cultural war."[42]

In tandem with insinuations that reformist activism constituted treason, the conservatives increasingly deployed allegations of apostasy. The use of the charge of *mohair* – waging war against God – only exacerbated reformist alienation. As one new agency commentary posited, "Does Islamic justice necessitate that one who takes up a weapon and terrorizes people is not proven *mohareb* and that one who takes up a pen and informs and enlightens, is treated as an agent of the enemy? Is the

---

[41] Khamenei speech to the Assembly of Experts, February 15, 2001. From the Voice of the Islamic Republic of Iran Radio 1.

[42] Khamenei address at Amir Kabir Science and Technology University, Tehran, February 27, 2001, from the BBC Summary of World Broadcasts.

national security of the Islamic Republic so vulnerable that it is threatened by one speech or one article, so secure that it is not injured by the cancerous tumors of the Information [Intelligence] authority and political terrorists?"[43]

The most comprehensive backlash was directed at the press, particularly after an April 2000 speech in which Khamenei accused the reform newspapers of serving as "bases of the enemies." The supreme leader took pains to portray himself as open-minded and suggested that he had been "forced" to address an increasingly serious problem within Iran, involving "some segments of the press concentrate their efforts on inciting the public, sowing discord and making the people pessimist about the system.... Ten to fifteen papers are seemingly guided by one center. ... Those segments of the press dash hopes of the youth, weaken the confidence of people in the country's officials, and insult the very basic foundations of the country."[44]

The *jihad* against the journalists continued during the rest of Khatami's tenure and negated even the meager constitutional protections awarded to the press. In its first year, at least fifty periodicals were shuttered and more than one thousand journalists lost their jobs.[45] At the outset of the clampdown, a number of reformist editors shrewdly parried the closure of each paper with the inauguration of a successor, in some cases retaining the entire staff and the style of the predecessor explicitly to flaunt the linkage. Thus, in the best known case of what came to be disparaged by conservatives as the "serial newspapers," *Jameah* morphed into *Tous*, albeit briefly, which begat *Neshat*, and then *Asr-e Azadegan*.[46] The conservatives adapted to this ploy, however, by targeting individual reporters, editors, and publishers under the harsh new press law, revised in 1999, and by deflecting bids to resurrect banned publications under new names. The crackdown reached such proportions that Iran's social security organization proposed classifying journalism as a hazardous

---

[43] "Statement of the Tehran Council of the Unity Consolidation Movement Regarding the New Cycle of the Judicial System's Conflict with the Reformers and the Students," *Iranian Students' News Agency*, February 28, 2001.

[44] "Leader: Press Should Respect Constitution, Islamic Values," *IRNA*, April 20, 2000.

[45] "Press Freedom Association Issues Watershed Communiqué," *IRNA*, April 28, 2001; government officials claimed that the closures reduced circulation from 3 million to 2 million. "Deputy Culture Minister Reports Drop in Circulation since Press Closures," *IRNA*, August 17, 2001. "Unemployment Haunts Journalists after Press Crackdown," *AFP*, April 27, 2000.

[46] Jalaeipur unveiled *Nosazi* in May 2000, but it was banned after only five issues.

profession, to enable higher pay rates, shorter hours, and other prerogatives for Iranian reporters commensurate with those in other high-risk
endeavors, such as mining and oil-rig work.[47]

The crackdown also reinforced the conservatives' certainty about the
media's existential threat to the future of the Islamic Republic. Khamenei
never wavered in exhorting more coercion, dismissing journalists'
protests as further evidence of their seditious intentions.[48] "From now
on, government officials have no right ... to be soft on those who abuse
freedom and act against the interests of the people and Iran's destiny,"
Khamenei told a Tehran student gathering in February 2001. "No
government would stand by and allow others to axe at its roots. For
reasons we have tolerated that for some time. No longer. We cannot wait
until a catastrophe takes place."[49] For his part, Khatami's public response
was tepid at best – "I don't agree with the methods used," he demurred
after the August 2000 closure of nearly thirty papers.[50] This stance only
intensified dissatisfaction among reformists and within even apolitical
segments of society.

The press crackdown continued throughout Khatami's second term,
partially blunted by the advent of new communications technology.
During earlier periods of unrest in Iran, *shabnameh* ("night letters,"
political pamphlets distributed anonymously over night), mimeographs,
cassette tapes, and a host of "small media" managed to perpetuate a
strong channel of opposition communication regardless of the government's media monopoly. More recently, the technological challenge to the
system's propaganda gradually became nearly universal: cellular tele-
phones, bootleg videos, satellite television reception – with "programs
from 2,494 TV channels as well as 1,099 radios," one newspaper noted
pointedly[51] – and the Internet. As a result, the press closures by no means
managed to choke off all communication from outside Iran or foreclose
dialogue among Iranians themselves. "Until yesterday, the closure of each

---

[47] "Iran Labels Journalism 'Hazardous' Profession," *Reuters*, September 4, 2000.
[48] For example, in June 2000, Khamenei rejected the reformers' remonstrations over the first
wave of newspaper closures. "Some political factions are seeking, through creating
ballyhoo, to undermine the authority and dignity of the judiciary and intimidate its
officials in order to force them to give into their demands." Ali Akbar Dareini, "Iran's
Top Leader Urges Judiciary to Ignore Pressure for Press Freedom," *AP*, June 27, 2000.
[49] "Iran Supreme Leader Defends Reformist Press Curbs," *Reuters*, February 28, 2001.
[50] "Khatami Slams Press Closures," *AFP*, August 21.
[51] "Rumors Abound When News Is Not Available: Daily," *IRNA*, August 21, 2000,
quoting editorial from *Iran News*, August 21, 2000.

newspaper only increased the people's inclination toward foreign radios," one newspaper columnist warned. "But today, this inclination is flowing toward Internet sites too. And tomorrow, technology will open another way of acquiring news."[52]

The backlash against reformist journalists extended to the political strata. Thugs also were frequently deployed, either informally or organized via the Basij mobilization corps or local *komitehs*. In November 2000, the renowned dissident Ezzatollah Sahabi found himself blocked from presenting a scheduled speech by an unruly group of thugs, who flipped over a car and threatened to burn down the house where the writer was to stay.[53] In addition to the Tehran mayor and the former interior minister, parliamentarians were prosecuted, including several on the basis of speeches given on the floor of the Majlis. In late 2001, Husayn Loqmanian, who represented Hamedan after losing a leg in one of the Iraq war's notoriously bloody battles, was jailed for criticizing the judiciary, and only pardoned by Khamenei after a rare show of defiance by the reformist parliament. Convictions of other MPs, including Bushehr's Mohammad Dadfar, were upheld, along with prison terms and fines. The crackdown netted a variety of reformist figures, including activists, clerics, and officials, such as the provincial governor of Kurdestan, who was accused of breaching the "red lines" of permissible discourse in comments reported in the press. And the conservatives did not fully spare those whose personal connections might have assured them a zone of protection; Hadi Khamenei – the supreme leader's proreform brother – was summoned to the Special Court for Clerics in September 2000.[54]

In addition to the individual prosecutions and harassments, Iran during this period experienced a series of gripping dramas – what Khatami would describe as a crisis every nine days – that consumed the political class, undermined institutional effectiveness, and threatened the eruption of factional warfare. The chain murders, the student protests, the tape makers' case, the Berlin conference trial, the former interior minister Abdollah Nouri's trial, the shooting of the political strategist Saeed Hajjarian: These episodes fed into one another in what appeared a relentless loop of persecution and violence, particularly as the regime

[52] Shahram Sharif, "Closing Press and Welcoming Alternatives," *Hambastegi*, April 10, 2001, p. 10.

[53] "Opposition Dissident Ezzatollah Sahabi Is Threatened by Hardliners," *IRNA*, November 5, 2000.

[54] Ali Akbar Dareini, "Iran Leaders' Kin Summoned to Court," *AP*, September 11, 2000.

began targeting defense lawyers in human rights cases. For the most part, the public discussions of these episodes, while unprecedented, typically only featured the tip of the iceberg of the Islamic Republic's abuses against its own people.

TARGETING KARBASCHI

During Khatami's tenure, the persistent use of allegations of financial impropriety to target political rivals intensified. The inequities of the reconstruction era boom and bust continued to draw public ire, and conservatives fulminated against consumerism and the encroachment of Western goods. One *Kayhan* editorialist equated economic reform with greed and despotism, calling capitalists "this wealthy and prosperous class, which has no interest in preserving the ideals of the revolution and only wants revolution to continue for the sake preserving its capital, has become a filthy sore in society's economic and social body, and the elimination of its dangers and the harm it has caused will be more difficult than many of the development programs."[55]

Tehran Mayor Gholamhusayn Karbaschi offered a tempting mark for chastening the new entrepreneurial class and cowing their political ambitions as well. His ambitious urban development programs earned him broad support from Tehranis who benefited from improvements in city services and facilities. However, these same programs – and the tactics, such as new taxes and preemptive fines, that enabled Karbaschi to undertake them – also affronted the traditional commercial sector, as did his strident campaigning on behalf of Khatami. In the politicized postelection atmosphere, Karbaschi's 1998 arrest and trial quickly became a battle of good versus evil, televised nightly to a rapt national audience. And though his conviction was interpreted by observers of the Iranian political scene as a setback for political liberalization, the consequences were perhaps more ambiguous.

The Karbaschi verdict evidenced a shift in the political discourse over the nature of the Islamic Republic's economy, consistent with the reform-era obsession with rule of law. The arguments from both sides over the propriety of Karbaschi's business dealings largely focused on efficiency and equality before the law, avoiding for the most part the issues of Islamic doctrine that so divided the clerics, or even the standard populist

[55] *Keyhan*, July 1, 1997, p. 2, in FBIS-NES-97-238.

homage to concerns of social justice. In addition, the debate among the general public centered not on these issues or on the strict legality of his actions – many Tehranis openly conceded that the mayor may well have violated laws on land development and appropriations – but on the greater national good. In the Karbaschi episode, popular sentiment sided with the proponents of political reform, but ironically, against the interests of financial transparency. However, in Iran's fluid factional contention, declining material well-being eventually galvanized outrage over corruption and the disregard of the revolution's redistributive mandate.

What was most remarkable about the Karbaschi conviction was how limited the ripples within society proved to be in response to his plight. The mayor whose reimagination of the massive capital city had improved the lives of millions commanded only the most limited sympathy within the hearts of his constituents. And the arrest of a popular, transformative figure was greeted by the population not as an outrage against what was right, but as yet another indication of the broader corruption of the system itself. The deal struck on Karbaschi's behalf, limiting his prison term and presumably incorporating some imposed period of political inactivity, was equally telling with respect to the arbitrary nature of the law and authority in reformist Iran.

The rise and fall of the Tehran mayor highlights the limited mass appeal of Iran's erstwhile pragmatists, but also their institutional embeddedness. Karbaschi, like the Kargozaran Party that he helped to establish, never managed to capture and sustain public loyalty – a seeming irony, given the grassroots nature of his mayoral agenda. He was targeted for his ambitions but insulated by the fact that he remained *khodi*, or an insider. Ultimately, during their earliest years, the pragmatists were not much interested in mass political mobilization; their project was one of élite reformation, and as such subject to easy reversal by a contending elite. Their successors – particularly Hassan Rouhani, who would capture the presidency fifteen years later – appear to have appreciated the need for broadening their base.

Karbaschi was not the only case of a rising reformist politician scapegoated on corruption charges. After Khatami's successful reelection, the reformist politician Behzad Nabavi became the focal point for repeated investigations and accusations of corruption. In addition to his parliamentary seat, Nabavi headed Petropars, established in the 1990s as the lead partner for foreign investors in Iran's massive South Pars gas field. The Guardians' Council secretary Ayatollah Ahmad Jannati announced that ministry officials had "plundered millions and millions in the oil empire and transferred the money to their foreign accounts."[56] At the time, Oil Minister Bijan Zanganeh – himself a target of murmured accusations – called the charges "politically motivated." Khatami himself personally intervened, publishing a letter to Nabavi in July 2001 that questioned why the Guardians' Council was "disturbing public opinion and not handing over his information to competent authorities."[57] The campaigns had a serious cost. For the oil industry, "the main reason for the delay in concluding oil agreements is the court summons received by several Oil Ministry managers," according to the head of the Majlis Energy Committee, Hussein Afarideh.[58]

Not all of the corruption cases that captured the public imagination during the reform period involved senior officials or political figures. A range of lower-level officials were targeted for exploiting their positions, including several of Karbaschi's deputies as well as then–Minister of Culture and Islamic Guidance Mohajerani. Perhaps the most notable corruption case during the Khatami tenure was a massive bank embezzlement scandal. Editorials in *Kayhan* and remarks by prominent conservatives attempted to link the reform movement to the young businessman Shahram Jazayeri's crimes, including the allegation that he had funneled his proceeds to more than sixty members of the Majlis.[59] In his trial, Jazayeri implicated several political figures, both reformist and conservative, including the Majlis speaker Mehdi Karrubi; Hadi Khamenei, brother of the supreme leader and the editor of one of the most prominent reformist dailies at the time; as well as bureaucrats in the exports administration and children of senior clerics.[60] Jazayeri emphasized that the transfers were intended for charitable activities rather than as bribes. Reformists saw the trial and accusation as an attempt by their hard-line opponents "to score points" in service of their "ultimate objective ... the total neutralization of the Majlis as an effective political entity."[61] The case grew to encompass at least fifty defendants, and while Jazayeri

[56] *IRNA*, July 17, 2001.

[57] Ali Akbar Dareini, "Khatami Backs Oil Ministry over Fraud Allegations," *AP*, July 9, 2001.

[58] "Moves against Oil Ministry Officials Criticized," *Iran Daily* (internet edition), May 16, 2002, p. 3

[59] "60 MPs, One Deputy Minister and 11 Offsprings of the Elite," *Kayhan*, January 2, 2002.

[60] "Brother of Iran's Supreme Leader Cited in Corruption Trial," *AFP*, January 21, 2002; "More Names Mentioned in Corruption Trial," *AFP*, January 23, 2002.

[61] *Iran News*, January 13, 2002.

was eventually convicted and sentenced to twenty-seven years in prison, as well as fifty lashes, all the parliamentarians referenced were exonerated, and several of those with powerful connections (e.g., the son of the former intelligence minister) were given very light sentences. In offering a glimpse into the scope of illicit payoffs, shakedowns, and profiteering among the revolutionary élite of all political stripes, the trial seemed to confirm the ethical bankruptcy of the Islamic Republic. In what was perhaps a sign of pervasive public cynicism, the fracas generated little public reaction, but at least one reformist daily acknowledged the damage done by the trial:

People are dissatisfied with a lot of our actions and performances. They see that a lot of authorities and officials behind the tinted windows of their brand new cars are going from this high-rise to another one. The accumulation of wealth in the hands of some off-shoots has really made the people angry. The huge barefoot population is still barefoot, and they have hurt and bruised their feet by long walks.[62]

The legacy of the Jazayeri case remained fresh long after his conviction and imprisonment; in 2007, it was reported that he had "escaped" from prison during a transfer and was subsequently found in Oman. The escapade prompted another round of accusations against political figures, bureaucrats, and journalists for collusion. And again in 2009, Ahmadinejad used the Jazayeri case to undermine the criticisms of Mehdi Karrubi, then contesting Ahmadinejad's reelection.[63]

The intense public debate on corruption, even where the charges appeared politically motivated, as in Karbaschi's case, proved self-sustaining, particularly in an environment of considerable press activity. Journalists and activists used the Karbaschi case to raise questions about other individuals and organizations, such as the various parastatal *bonyad*s. "Equally, people ask why the judiciary has not investigated the reports of the Research Committee of the Islamic Consultative Majlis concerning the Foundation of the Oppressed or the Voice and Vision [radio and television]," a newspaper column queried in 1998. "These double standards have strengthened the public suspicion regarding the political nature of the trial of the mayor of Tehran."[64] Another reformist

---

[62] *Aftab-e Yazd*, January 24, 2002.
[63] Hiedeh Farmani, "Ahmadinejad, Karroubi Clash over Economics, Ethics," *AFP*, June 6, 2009.
[64] Commentary by an unidentified Iranian attorney, "Three Important Distinctions of the Trial of the Mayor," *Mobin*, July 18, 1998, pp. 2, 4.

journal audaciously questioned the subsidies to the prosperous Bonyad-e Astan-e Qods-e Razavi – one of the oldest religious endowments, which supports Iran's holiest Shi'a shrine – suggesting that transfers should in fact occur in reverse. In a thinly veiled jab at Bonyad-e Mostazafan and the other large parastatal foundations, the magazine continued: "Nongovernmental foundations which receive limitless and unaccountable government funds, and which are not answerable to the government or the nation, are among the most difficult economic, political, cultural, and even foreign policy problems of the country."[65]

IRAN'S SHORT FUSE

Throughout the reform period, the sense of political entitlement generated by the elections and the fierce contention among the regime's power brokers helped to encourage a much more forceful expression of public opinion on political issues. Street protests became a regularity, not a rarity. The most serious episode unfolded in July 1999, when students gathered for days in central Tehran to demonstrate against the closure of *Salaam*, the pathbreaking reformist newspaper, for publishing Intelligence Ministry documents related to its violent campaign against dissidents. The closure occurred only days after the parliament's ratification of a regressive new press law. Student groups organized protests on university campuses in Tehran and several other Iranian cities. Security forces eventually moved into a dormitory to break up the Tehran demonstrations, and the ensuing violence devastated the reform movement's popular base, especially the student leadership. Fifteen hundred students were arrested, and the minister of higher education offered his resignation amid sharp criticism of the repression.

The official response offered a microcosm of the divergent impulses of Iranian leaders. In classic Khatami fashion, the president endeavored in vain to steer a middle course through a precarious situation. He used an institutional mantle (that of the Supreme National Security Committee, which as president he chaired) to decry the upheaval, express sympathy with the students, appeal for restraint by the protesters, and offer modest concessions in the form of an inquiry commission and the resignation of a senior police commander. The communiqué satisfied no one, and the failure of the president to champion his most dedicated constituency

---

[65] *Iran-e Farda*, No. 37, September 23–October 22, 1997, pp. 25–8, in FBIS-NES-98-049, February 18, 1998.

personally bred resentment and a verdict that Khatami's personal weakness was the primary failing of the movement. For his part, Khamenei briefly struck a slightly softer tone, calling the police assault on the dormitory "this bitter incident [that] has broken my heart," but also inveighed against the CIA and what he described as "hidden hands behind the scenes directing this," an allusion to the U.S. role in unseating Mosaddeq.[66] Also notable during this episode was the role of the Revolutionary Guard and senior military commanders, who issued an unprecedented warning to Khatami that evoked harbingers of a military coup:

> We can see the footprints of the enemy in the aforementioned incidents and we can hear its drunken cackle. You should understand this today because tomorrow will be too late. If you regret this tomorrow, it will be impossible to retrieve the situation. O noble Seyyed: Look at the speeches made by your so-called friends and insiders at the gathering of students. Is what they said not tantamount to encouraging chaos and lawlessness? ... Mr Khatami: Look at foreign media and radios. Can you not hear their joyful music? Mr President: If you do not make a revolutionary decision and if you do not fulfil your Islamic and national mission today, tomorrow will be far too late. It is unimaginable how irretrievable the situation will become. In the end, we would like to express our utmost respect for your excellency and to declare that our patience has run out. We cannot tolerate this situation any longer if it is not dealt with.[67]

The warning was sent privately to Khatami, but quickly leaked and initiated a debate among the political élite nearly as intense as that provoked by the protests themselves. The threatened intervention of the military proved a harbinger of things to come, as the Revolutionary Guard emerged during Khatami's second term as a political and economic force to be reckoned with.

The episode marked a turning point, but one that was not immediately obvious. Khatami sought to use the episode to remind his supporters that aggressive tactics would backfire. Neither the economic reform initiative nor the associated efforts to promote a better relationship with the world were manifestly impacted by the events. The stock exchange merely hiccoughed in response to the upheaval, and the largest British trade delegation since the revolution arrived in Iran just a few weeks later. Some conservatives sought to link Khatami's handling of the crisis with his economic policies, such as the hard-line newspaper *Shoma's* use of the

[66] Elaine Sciolino, "Police Move to Crush Protests in Iran," *New York Times*, July 13, 1999; Jonathan Lyons, "Supreme Leader Says U.S. Sought New Coup in Iran," *Reuters*, July 30, 1999

[67] *Jomhuri-ye Eslami*, July 19, 1999.

episode to indict the Khatami administration as "impotent in its entirety," contending that "an interior minister who is unable to protect his ministry's gate against rioters ... and a central bank governor unable to stabilise the currency, what more do they have to say to the people?"[68] Ultimately, the denouement of the July 1999 upheaval confirmed for many of Iran's highly politicized youth the fundamental inadequacy of the reform movement itself and the sheer impossibility of advancing gradualist moderation of an absolutist system. This sense of despair left a lasting rift among the reformist activists themselves, as well as between the population and the movement's leadership – one that was reinforced in even more serious protests a decade later. Among the hard-liners who opposed Khatami, the events of July 1999 confirmed that his strategic and temperamental inclination toward moderation was his Achilles' heel, a realization that informed the increasing forcefulness of their campaign against the reform movement.

After July 1999, Iran remained on edge. The popular aspirations that had animated the reform movement – and were heightened by its initial victories – continued to roil Iran. However, the turmoil appeared to deflect any impetus to use street demonstrations as a means of advancing political positions. Instead, as during the revolution's early years, small-scale collective actions over various mundane concerns took place on an increasingly regular basis – students dissatisfied with university conditions, workers angry about lack of pay, farmers enraged by drought conditions, citizens irritated over administrative decisions that impacted local budgets and opportunities. Teachers repeatedly struck over complaints about low pay in 2001, 2002, 2004, and thereafter; administrative issues produced surprising backlash – Sabzevar in 2001, Quchan in 2002 over the division of Khorasan, Oqlid in 2007 over the division of Fars, and Semiran in 2003 over the division of Isfahan. There were notable exceptions, such as the August 2000 violence in Khorramabad over security forces' efforts to block speeches by two prominent religious intellectuals.

Generally, however, the public's apparent unwillingness to go to the street in large numbers over a sustained period over political grievances can be interpreted in varying fashion, either as vindicating the reformists' disinclination to mobilize their mandate or reflecting the dearth of an assertive leadership or strategy. This trend reinforces the extent to which the metric by which the Iranian population gauges its own government is

---

[68] Mehrdad Balali, "Unrest May Set Back Khatami Economic Reforms," *Reuters*, July 19, 1999.

that of performance and competence, rather than ideology. "The people should not be made disappointed because their disappointment is like the calm before the storm," Hajjarian warned in mid-2002.[69] This view was shared across the political spectrum: "The survival of the regime depends on the actions of those at various levels of power," Ayatollah Ibrahim Amini, a conservative prayer leader in Qom and vice chairman of the Assembly of Experts, warned in May 2002. "The people are very discontented and they are right to be so, and I swear to you that society is on the brink of explosion."[70]

THIRD FIVE-YEAR PLAN

The impetus for economic reform remained centered on the need to forestall just such an explosion. Awareness of the risks facing the system did not necessarily make the task easier, however, since sensitivity to popular sentiment offered as tempting platform for populism as for market-based reforms. Khatami had to navigate these countervailing sensibilities within his own cabinet and among his own advisers, many of whom remained skeptical toward, if not wholly opposed to, market-based reforms. And yet the government's draft of Iran's Third Five-Year Development Plan represented the most ambitious effort in the postrevolutionary period in terms of structural reforms to the economy.

In addition to the Asian economic crisis and its negative impact on oil prices, the driving motivation for the plan was underscored by another challenge that emerged during Khatami's second year in office. Beyond the precipitous drop in oil revenues, Khatami confronted another significant challenge to the nation's economy from forces beyond his control – a historic drought. Iran charted a 45 percent drop in average annual rainfall in 1999–2000, a weather cycle that had cataclysmic effects on the agricultural sector and ultimately on the government's budget and trade balance more broadly. The drought severely impacted more than half of Iran's provinces, with at least $1.7 billion in direct economic losses and health effects caused by disruptions to the drinking water supply that affected approximately half the population.[71]

---

[69] "Khatami's Threats Serious," *Iran Daily* (internet edition), May 18, 2002, p. 1.

[70] "Religious Leader Warns, Iran on Edge of Social Explosion," *AFP*, May 16, 2002.

[71] Habibollah Salami, Naser Shahnooshi, Kenneth J. Thompson, "The Economic Impacts of Drought on the Economy of Iran: An Integration of Linear Programming and Macroeconometric Modeling Approaches," *Ecological Economics* 68 (2009): pp. 1032–9.

The conservative-dominated sixth parliament approved the plan with relatively minimal debate; however, they did opt to strip out several important proposed policy changes, including an initiative to subject the *bonyad*s and other revolutionary organizations to taxation and a third measure that would have freed state-owned enterprises from price controls.[72] The Majlis also blocked another component of the plan that would have reduced subsidies, insisting on price ceilings for key goods and demanding more social welfare spending. Khatami's oil minister, Bijan Zanganeh, lobbied for the reforms, just as his predecessor had six years earlier, arguing that doing so was "the only way to reduce domestic consumption and decrease imports."[73] Domestic oil consumption continued to rise, reaching the equivalent of a record 17.5 barrels of crude oil per person in the year ending in March 2002. The average growth in energy consumption was increasing more quickly than the rate of population increase.[74] Without a fix in the works, the government paid 1,050 rials per kilogram of flour but could only sell the same volume to bakeries at a mere 60 rials.[75]

However, consideration of the draft plan happened to coincide with a parliamentary election year, and eliminating subsidies risked not just social tranquility, but also MPs' claim to populist credentials.

---

[72] The fifth parliament did in fact take a number of steps to try to exert supervision and authority over the *bonyad*s. In November 1998, the Majlis floated a proposal to separate the charitable activities of the Bonyad-e Mostazafan from its economic sectors. *Hamshahri* (Internet version), November 25, 1998; *IRNA*, November 24, 1998. Such a reorganization would entail a strict partition between the economic and charitable sectors in order to divorce the operating budget and lines of authority of the productive enterprises from those of the philanthropic division. In November 1998, the Majlis held a closed session to discuss concerns about the Bonyad-e Mostazafan's treatment of veterans; when the deputies emerged, a member of the parliamentary executive council called for the foundation to increase its activities on behalf of veterans. *Jomhuri-ye Islami* (internet version), November 25, 1998. The parliament took direct aim at the tax exemption, including provisions in the 1378 budget bill for lifting the tax exemption that had heretofore been granted to the foundations. In the final version of the budget, however, the Council of Guardians added an explicit note of caution about the foundations' status. The edict that established Mostazafan and the other foundations clearly referenced their lines of authority to the office of the leader, and thus even senior Khatami officials acknowledged that this implied the Majlis had no authority to rescind their tax exemption or to change their status in any way. "With Approval of Majles, Taxation Exemption of Foundations and Private Institutions Tied to Government Repealed," *Kar va Kargar*, January 16, 1999, pp. 1–2.

[73] Douglas Jehl, "Iran Discontent Rises as Oil-Based Economy Falls," *New York Times*, December 13, 1998.

[74] "Energy Consumption up," *Iran Daily* (Internet edition), May 16, 2002, p. 3.

[75] Ehsani (2006), p. 92.

"I doubt it is correct to move towards a market economy when our welfare system is not in order and people are financially pressed," the independent parliamentarian Hassan Sobhani complained. "To impose this could lessen popular support for the system. Policy makers must keep in mind the people's income."[76] Other conservatives opposed any measures to reduce the subsidies for fear of sparking another inflationary bubble.

PRIVATIZATION

Over the course of its two terms, the Khatami presidency managed to tackle several broad and complex economic issues – privatization, significant enhancements to the trade and investment framework, exchange rate unification, and the establishment of a sovereign wealth fund to hedge against oil revenue volatility. The government moved slowly in the direction of a meaningful retreat from its economic dominance, including privatization plans that extended to the energy, water, and power sectors. In 2001, the National Privatization Organization was established. The Twenty-Year Perspective document, issued in late 2003 by Ayatollah Khamenei, explicitly advocated privatization but cautioned that any sell-off must be in accordance with the Constitution as well as consistent with national security and "the preeminence of Islamic and revolutionary values."[77]

In 2004, a revision to article 44 of the Constitution that was passed clarified the roles of the public and private sector in Iran's economy. While leaving a few critical industries – notably, upstream oil and gas – as the domain of the state, the new interpretation of article 44 mandated the disengagement of the government from sectors deemed to be in the private sector by the end of the fourth five-year development plan (March 2010). These included – with several exceptions for particular firms – the sectors of heavy industry, mining, downstream oil and gas, international trade, banking and insurance, power generation, dams, irrigation, aviation, shipping, roads, railways, and telecommunications.[78]

---

[76] Mehrdad Balali, "Iran Officials Doubt Quick Economic Recovery," *Reuters*, November 30, 1999.

[77] Full text of the plan can be found in Persian in various places; see, for example, http://www.dolat.ir/PDF/20years.pdf

[78] Atieh Associates Legal Newsletter 4 (2), October 2004. http://www.atiehassociates.com/law/newsletters/Newsletter200410.pdf

During this period, Tehran also began experimenting in privatizing the financial sector. In 2000, the parliament approved legislation authorizing the establishment of private banks, a move that in theory began to roll back one of the key areas of postrevolutionary nationalization. Over the subsequent five years, four new institutions received licenses – Bank-e Parisian, Bank-e Saman, Bank-e Karafarin, and Bank-e Eqtesaed-e Novin – and carved out a small but growing segment of the marketplace. The opening of the banking sector also extended to foreign banks, with Standard Chartered receiving the first license for an offshore branch in July 2004.

OIL STABILIZATION FUND

The past experiences of revenue plunges in the oil busts of 1986 and 1997–8, coupled with the examples of oil revenue funds that had been set up by such nations as Kuwait, Oman, and Norway, inspired the OSF's creation.[79] Iran's Oil Stabilization Fund (OSF) was established as a foreign currency account at Bank Markazi in 2000, intended to insulate Iran's budget from oil price volatility. Management of the fund was assigned to an executive committee composed of various senior officials.[80]

According to the fund's original guidelines, transfers for budget expenditures above the reference oil price – the effective expected price of oil based on budget plans – required Majlis approval. If actual oil export revenues fell below budget allocations by the end of the eleventh month of the fiscal year, then Bank Markazi would draw the shortfall from the OSF and transfer it to the treasury for government expenditure.[81] No more than half of OSF assets could be lent out domestically to the private sector via domestic banks. Firms were permitted to borrow from the OSF over periods of up to eight years, with repayment requirements in later years and collateral including land, machinery, equipment, or corporate bonds.[82] The Fourth Development Plan amended the guidelines to direct minimal proportions (10 percent) of all future OSF allocations to the agricultural sector, as early private sector lending was dominated by industrial firms.[83]

---

[79] Jahangir Amuzegar. "Iran's Oil Stabilization Fund: A Misnomer," *Middle East Economic Survey* 48 (47), November 21, 2005, p. 28.

[80] Abdelali Jbili, Vitali Kramarenko, and José Bailén. *Islamic Republic of Iran: Managing the Transition to a Market Economy* (Washington, DC: International Monetary Fund, 2007), p. 77.

[81] Ibid.   [82] Ibid.   [83] Amuzegar (November 21, 2005), p. 30.

The initial OSF framework ostensibly precluded the use of funds from the OSF to offset fiscal deficits.[84] Unfortunately, these restrictions were frequently disregarded, and the financing amounted to substantially less than the original guidelines demanded. Instead, the fund has been raided for withdrawals against the guidelines of article 60 of the Third Development Plan, and the budget allocation was repeatedly changed to enable more oil revenue to be spent as it came in, also against the fund's rules. Within a year of its inception, there were already allegations of improper withdrawals from the OSF. In 2001, left-leaning members of Khatami's cabinet reportedly pressured the then–Central Bank Governor Mohsen Nourbakhsh to access OSF reserves for public sector spending. Reports, denied by the bank, suggested that several billion dollars were spent in the first year on such areas as government bonuses and pensions, foreign debt repayment, and unfinished infrastructural projects.[85] The raids were facilitated (and to some extent encouraged) by unexpected increases in oil prices during Khatami's second term; projected oil revenues remained relatively low, but the OSF accrued far less than the differential between anticipated and actual oil revenues – a mere $29 billion rather than the estimated $74 billion.[86] The Majlis frequently bypassed the OSF board for withdrawals totaling nearly $17 billion from 2000 to 2005 – for reasons not approved in the original law, such as drought relief and police equipment, as well as budget overruns and losses associated with the exchange rate unification. Between 2000 and 2005, nearly $17 billion of the fund's total assets was used in public sector spending, while only $3.7 billion was loaned to the private sector. In 2005, at the end of the Third Plan, the OSF's total assets consisted of only $9.4 billion in cash and $3.5 billion in outstanding loans.[87] According to one analysis, the treasury itself owed a debt to the OSF of at least $6.5 billion by March 2005.[88]

---

[84] Amendment to Article 60 of the Third Socio-Economic and Cultural Development Plan of the Islamic Republic of Iran, 2000–2004. Available at http://www.irtp.com/laws/3socio-economic/ap2.htm. Accessed October 22, 2008.

[85] BBC Monitoring Middle East. "Iranian Paper on 'Surplus Oil Revenues.'" February 1, 2001.

[86] World Bank, Office of the Chief Economist of the Middle East and North Africa Region. *Middle East and North Africa: Economic Developments and Prospects 2006: Financial Markets in a New Age of Oil*, 2006, p. 21. Available at http://siteresources.worldbank.org/INTMENA/Resources/MainReport.pdf. Cites Amuzegar (November 21, 2005); Amuzegar (November 21, 2005), p. 29

[87] Amuzegar (November 21, 2005), pp. 29–30.

[88] Amuzegar (November 21, 2005), p. 30.

REFORM AND THE WEST

Khatami assumed office only two years after the Clinton administration began erecting the most rigorous unilateral sanctions regime since the hostage crisis. His election and the advent of a moderate political trend in Iran prompted frenzied U.S. efforts to parlay these changes into a bilateral détente. After a flurry of signals from both sides, including then–Secretary of State Madeleine Albright's proposal for a "road map" to rapprochement, the same American administration that had significantly intensified sanctions whiplashed in the opposing direction.

Tehran's internal infighting had forestalled any real movement on this issue for Khatami's first several years. Still, as the president's "dialogue among civilizations" initiative began to win plaudits and lure investors, Iran's Islamic leftists began to see foreign policy – and more specifically, rapprochement with Iran's old adversaries – as a "useful and constructive ballast for his domestic policy ... a valid sphere of political operations which, if well harnessed, could have a positive bearing on internal developments."[89] Moreover, as the reform movement evolved, new thinking on relations with Washington began to percolate in Iran. Several prominent reformists – including those who had been the standard bearers of anti-Americanism during the 1980s – began forcefully advocating détente. "We believe the taboo over negotiations with America should be broken," MP Mohammad Naimipur said. He was echoed by Ali Mazroui. "Iran and America cannot ignore each other. We can make best use of our position without giving up our interests."[90]

In fact, the intellectual experimentation with revising the revolutionary formulation toward Washington extended well beyond the Iranian reformists. The conservative editor Taha Hashemi argued that incentives and confidence-building gestures could persuade even Khamenei, who had been reflexively hard-line on the issue, to endorse rapprochement. "If the scenario is planned and prepared wisely and he becomes confident that this relationship won't hurt our national pride and won't make the Islamic Republic passive, I believe he would not be far from accepting."[91] Publicly, however, Iran's primary power brokers appeared unmoved. "We will not bow down before the Americans," Rafsanjani said after the February 2000 reformist parliamentary victory. "They have wronged

---

[89] Ansari (2006), pp. 130–1.
[90] "Reformists Urge Iran-US Contact," *Oil Daily*, April 19, 2002 (52:75).
[91] "'Islamic New Thinker' Sees Formula for Iran-U.S. Ties," *Reuters*, May 29, 2001.

us in the past and they should rectify their past mistakes."[92] Khamenei maintained his uncompromising public opposition to negotiations with the United States. "These people who talk about negotiations with the US are unfamiliar with the ABC of politics and the ABC of honor."[93]

As Iranian perspectives appeared to be in flux, the Clinton administration undertook the most dramatic series of overtures toward Tehran since 1979, including measures to ease existing sanctions on caviar, carpets, and pistachios; these steps are discussed in greater detail in Chapter 9. The most important aspect was their failure to generate any reciprocal gesture or broader improvements to the estrangement. U.S. officials continued to seek mechanisms for signaling receptivity to dialogue with Tehran; for example, in September 2000, Albright disregarded standing policy and attended Khatami's UN General Assembly speech, because as a U.S. official declared, "we wanted to send a signal to the Iranians that we're willing to listen to what they have to say."[94] However, neither the overtures nor sanctions themselves that succeeded them seemed to have significant impact in inducing positive changes to Iran's most problematic policies.

At the same time as Washington was fumbling with vague road maps, Europe had launched a full-fledged love affair with reformist Iran. Khatami's kinder, gentler persona appealed to European leaders, and his "dialogue of civilizations" initiative offered a useful balm for a continent still wrestling with its own demographic demons. The furor over the Mykonos verdict was supplanted after six months by efforts to reach out to Iran's new president in hopes of reaping diplomatic and mercantile rewards. The EU's "critical dialogue" policy quickly gave way to "constructive engagement," with a flurry of senior policy maker visits to Tehran and an explicit European goal of sustaining and advancing reform. That such partisan language did not noticeably lessen Tehran's readiness to improve the relationship speaks to the urgency of Iran's economic predicament, and the significance of European capital, at this time.

Tehran's rare forbearance quickly reaped tangible benefits – the 1997 return of European ambassadors to Tehran, the 1998 resumption

---

[92] "Rafsanjani Says No Change in Iran's Stance," *Reuters*, February 25, 2000.

[93] Guy Dinmore, "Khamenei Rails against Backers of US Dialogue," *FT* (internet edition), May 23, 2002.

[94] "President of Iran Praises His Country's Civilization," *New York Times*, September 6, 2000.

of full diplomatic relations with Britain, and a series of diplomatic "firsts" and new trade opportunities. In 1999, Khatami visited Italy and France in what was the first Iranian state visit to Europe since the revolution. It was not a coincidence that the visits followed quickly on the heels of a massive new Iranian deal with ENI and Elf Aquitaine, or that announcements of sizable flows of new export credits were made at each stop along his route. A similar visit to Germany in June 2000 proceeded in very similar fashion.

THE ECONOMY AS A POLITICAL VULNERABILITY IN KHATAMI'S REELECTION CAMPAIGN

Throughout his presidency, Khatami drew barbs from conservatives over his alleged inattention to economic issues. In July 1999, after the student protests, a prominent conservative business advocate, Ali Shams Ardakani, who had previously headed Iran's Chamber of Commerce, accused the government of "paying more attention to the tug of war to settle political problems. It cannot afford to let go of economic problems, especially with respect to the great army of unemployed youth." "Those grappling with political issues have no concern about feeding people and creating employment. They don't take responsibility for the negative consequences."[95] For the most part, however, this critique was muted by the consistency between the reformist economic approach and Rafsanjani's business-friendly reconstruction agenda. For this reason, most of the first-term disapproval levied against Khatami focused on issues of greater disagreement, such as cultural policies and efforts to strengthen representative institutions.

After the 2000 Majlis elections, the conservative critique shifted from one focused on "values" and ideological conformity with the revolution's tenets to a fierce critique of Khatami's approach to the country's faltering economy. It was a utilitarian transformation, one that implicitly acknowledged the centrality of popular legitimacy to the political fortunes of the contentious factions, and it had the virtue of consistency with the conservatives' broader sense of superiority. "All these pieces of evidence, and other similar ones, reveal the fact that the government and the 'Majlis of reforms' have no idea and plan for solving the economic problems of the people, and by means of political games, support for criminals, and futile

---

[95] Mehrdad Balali, "Unrest May Set Back Khatami Economic Reforms," *Reuters*, July 19, 1999.

controversies, they try to attribute these problems to critics who at present have no role or responsibility in the decisions of the government and the Majlis."[96]

The 2001 presidential campaign naturally directed the criticism against Khatami personally, and his attempts to give greater emphasis to the nation's economic problems appeared only to sharpen the attacks. A ecommuniqué issued by a *bazaar* group prior to the 2001 elections rebuked Khatami explicitly:

> Our respected president recently said, "The administration's most important task is to deal with the unemployment problem." He also called on certain apparatuses to find ways to solve this problem. We thank President Khatami for his attention to the issue, but we wish he could have occupied himself with it earlier on in his presidency, not during the last weeks of his term in office. If the administration had put "dealing with the unemployment problem" at the top of its agenda when it first came into office, tens of thousands of job-seekers, particularly young people, would have had their demands answered by now.[97]

Although he had a credible record on the economy, Khatami continued to ground his appeal to voters in the argument that political engagement would generate prosperity. "Society needs its daily bread. What do you need politics or freedom for? You should all go and seek your daily bread," Khatami acknowledged, but added,

> if there is no freedom, if there is no enthusiasm, if there is no public presence and participation, if there is no sense of affiliation to a government or society, if there is no bond between government and society, if the people do not consider the government their own.... If that does not exist you can be sure that we would not progress in the economic arena. It is wrong for us to say that we should put aside politics for the time being and have nothing to do with it, and that I, the President, and the government do whatever we want and, God willing, your daily bread will be provided, and young men and young ladies will be able to find homes very soon and get married, and all the problems will be solved.[98]

---

[96] Abbas Darvish-Tavangar, "After Four Years!" *Resalat*, February 19, 2001, pp. 1–2, in FBIS-NES-2001-0315.

[97] Society of Islamic Trade and Market Associations, "Nation's Self-Esteem Depends on Parliament's Ability to Cope Intelligently with People's Problems," *Resalat*, February 25, 2001, p. 2, in FBIS-NES-2001-0315.

[98] "Khatami Addresses Red Crescent Society, Stresses Political Development," speech broadcast on the Vision of the Islamic Republic of Iran Network 1, May 8, 2002, in IAP20020509000114.

He was firmly countered by Karrubi, who reminded the president that "this country belongs to 60 million people and we should not think that only we have dropped down from heaven and we are concerned about Islam."[99]

Ultimately, part of the reluctance of the reformists to prioritize economic progress stemmed from their apparent apprehensions about the capacity to rally the Iranian people around such issues.

How can it be acceptable that with more than $400 billion in oil revenues at the prices of 1975 [1996/1997] in the past 20 years, the Iranian economy has been one of the lowest-return economies of the world, and in terms of per-capita income comparable with the economies of African countries? How can one convince the Iranian people despite the huge investments in the past and the numerous economic resources, the national economy must be necessarily in recession and the Iranian people remain sleeping and suppressed in economic lethargy, similar to Africa?

demanded the parliamentarian Shahrbanu Amani-Angeneh.[100]

According to domestic research surveys, Iranians ranked economic issues highest among their priorities for the government in 2000, with 75 percent of those surveyed describing the economy as their primary concern, versus a mere 0.5 percent who described lack of freedom as their principal interest.[101] The parliamentarian Hoseyn Ali Qasemzadeh argued that "shouting slogans of reforms is very easy," adding that

the just expectation of the people is that practical steps will be taken.... In the area of the economy, today we are facing a sick economy and its very negative consequences.... Indeed, who should improve this chaotic economic situation, begin reforms in the area of the economy, and make serious and rapid decisions about the people's sustenance and daily bread? Is it not the government? If it is, and of course it is, why does it not take practical steps? Who is responsible today for saving the millions of Iranians who live below the poverty line, and who should reform this tragic situation? Is it enough for us to every day only shout the slogan of the government of reforms? Should this slogan not be put into practice and plans made for it?... Why are the reformers, instead of engaging in solving the problems of the people's daily lives, only satisfied with the slogan of political reforms? Is the main problem of our society today actually not having newspapers?[102]

As the economist Fariborz Raisdana pointed out, "the fact that the number of unemployed rose from 1.5 million to three million in the past

---

[99] *Jomhuri Islami*, October 29, 2000.   [100] *Ettela'at*, November 9, 2000, p. 8.
[101] Abbas Darvish Ravangar, "Once More on the Main Problem of the People," *Resalat*, June 22, 2000, p. 10.
[102] *Ettela'at*, November 9, 2000, p. 8.

five years indicates that the Khatami administration followed in the footsteps of previous government without attempting to remove the weaknesses."[103] Job creation during the implementation of the Third Five-Year Plan (2000–4) missed its target by almost one-quarter, with only 580,000 of an intended 765,000 jobs created each year.[104] Programs intended to expand employment opportunities, such as a much-vaunted effort to provide subsidized loans to enterprises that created jobs, appear to have foundered as a result of insufficient oversight.[105]

The parliamentarian Hoseyn Ali Qasemzadeh criticized the reformist economic track record, arguing that

shouting slogans of reforms is very easy. But the just expectation of the people is that practical steps will be taken.... In the area of the economy, today we are facing a sick economy and its very negative consequences.... Indeed, who should improve this chaotic economic situation, begin reforms in the area of the economy, and make serious and rapid decisions about the people's sustenance and daily bread? Is it not the government? If it is, and of course it is, why does it not take practical steps? Who is responsible today for saving the millions of Iranians who live below the poverty line, and who should reform this tragic situation? Is it enough for us to every day only shout the slogan of the government of reforms? Should this slogan not be put into practice and plans made for it?... Why are the reformers, instead of engaging in solving the problems of the people's daily lives, only satisfied with the slogan of political reforms? Is the main problem of our society today actually not having newspapers?[106]

In an odd paradox, given the vehemence of the economic critique and Khatami's vulnerability to it, the president's reelection campaign actually benefited from a modest improvement in economic conditions during early 2001. Inflation dipped down to 11.3 percent from a high of 50 percent in 1995, thanks in part to the government's success in opening up trade and reforming the foreign exchange market.[107] Of the nine opposing candidates, none managed to generate ardent support from the conservative élite or a significant popular base, and Khatami outdid his 1997 mandate, at least in terms of sheer votes, capturing 21,659,053, or 77 percent of the turnout.

---

[103] "Economic Practices Undemocratic" *Iran Daily* (internet edition), May 22, 2002, p. 3.
[104] Zahra Kazimi, "Financing Job Guarantee Schemes by Oil Revenue: The Case of Iran," Levy Economics Institute of Bard College Working Paper No. 527 (January 2008), p. 6.
[105] Ibid., p. 9.   [106] *Ettela'at*, November 9, 2000, p. 8.
[107] Oya Celasun and Mangal Goswami, "An Analysis of Money Demand and Inflation in the Islamic Republic of Iran," IMF Working Paper WP/02/205, (December 2002), p. 6.

POWER OF THE PRESIDENCY

Throughout most of his two terms in office, Khatami struggled with the constraints on his authority, imposed by the Constitution as well as the aggressive interpretation of the supreme leader prerogatives since its revision. His proposed remedy conformed to his philosophical and strategic tendencies, reflecting his focus on institutions. In November 2000, Khatami issued an extraordinary statement to a parliamentary commission established to monitor constitutional issues, acknowledging his frustration with the limitations on his authority. The office of the president, Khatami argued, "is responsible for the implementation of the constitution. This is an exclusive duty of the president. In addition to this, in the oath of office that he has taken, provided the president is committed to religion, the president has a religious duty, a divine and national duty, which also includes upholding the constitution. ... After three and a half years, I should declare that the president does not possess sufficient authority in order to perform this duty." [108]

This speech, like many of Khatami's tactics, produced controversy; it drew vociferous public objections from conservatives, who dismissed the appeal as a gambit to reconfigure the system through constitutional revision, precisely what they suspected the reformists ofe seeking all along.; meanwhile others read the acknowledgment as confirmation of Khatami's utter impotence and, therefore, his irrelevance. After his reelection, he sought to redress his frustration by sponsoring two pieces of legislation aimed at bolstering the presidency; the proposal became known as the "twin bills." The first, introduced by Khatami in September 2002, aimed at limiting the Guardians' Council's "approbatory supervision," or aggressive vetting of prospective candidates. The Majlis passed versions of this bill twice, but both were rejected by the Guardians' Council and eventually foundered.

Even Khatami's closest advisers acknowledged that "there is no clear horizon ahead for the democratic transfer of power in Iran." [109] As his second term ground to an even more frustrating stalemate than the first, Khatami again began to issue vaguely worded warnings that he would prefer resignation to blatant irrelevance. Still, the president explicitly

---

[108] "Iranian President Addresses Constitution Conference in Tehran," Vision of the Islamic Republic of Iran Network 2, BBC Monitoring, 1818 GMT, November 26, 2000.

[109] "Hussein Valeh: Answering the People's Political Demands in the 84 (2005) Elections Will Be Very Difficult," *Nowruz*, May 18, 2002, pp. 3–5.

rejected a referendum on the country's future, arguing that hard-liners would disregard the outcome of such a ballot as easily as they did the 1997 vote. "Today they are talking about the referendum," he exhorted skeptical students in December 2001. "How many times do you think the people must take part in referendums? Didn't the people say what they wanted through their participation in the presidential elections, the parliamentary elections, the city-village council elections, and even the recent Golestan province by-elections...? If there are people who do not want to comply with the wishes of the people and all these referendums, they would not give in to the would-be referendum either."[110]

But few beyond Khatami seemed convinced that patience was the most effective way to combat conservative intransigence, and his arguments about the futility of further elections appeared likely only to play into the hands of those who had advocated a complete break from the system. The disempowerment of the president also served the conservatives' interests. "They want to keep the president in office, and use his popularity at home and abroad, while he has no power," the writer Ahmad Zeidabadi told a Tehran University rally in April 2000.[111]

SECOND-TERM ECONOMIC INITIATIVES: TRADE AND INVESTMENT REFORMS

After Khatami's reelection victory in 2001, the reformists intensified their focus on economic issues, a belated recognition of their centrality to their popular mandate and ultimately to their political fortunes. The centerpiece of this newfound economic initiative was a proposed revision of the country's framework for foreign investment. President Khatami and his reformist allies eventually achieved their goal of improving the legal platform. On May 25, 2002, the Expediency Council ratified Iran's new foreign investment law, the Foreign Investment Promotion and Protection Act (FIPPA), which had been approved by the Majlis on March 10 of that year. Prior to reforms, foreign investment in Iran was governed by the strict regulations of the Law of Attraction and Protection of Foreign Investment (LAPFI), which had been in effect since 1955. "This is only one of the levers that can attract investment," MP (and Rafsanjani nephew) Ali Hashemi said in July 2000. "But we need political and

---

[110] *Islamic Republic News Agency*, December 23, 2001.
[111] Guy Dinmore, "Tehran Students Protest at Closure of Reformist Media," *Financial Times*, April 26, 2000.

economic stability too because a foreign investor to invest needs to take into account the investment risk, the cheap energy supply and the manpower and such."[112]

As in any period of postrevolutionary political history, the victory mattered, at least insofar as the factional balance was concerned. The reformists sorely needed a big win, and the state itself needed to demonstrate that Iran had moved beyond the administrative dysfunction of the war period, when debates on urgent economic issues remained unresolved for years. In addition to FIPPA, nontariff barriers were replaced with tariffs, most export restrictions were eliminated, import licensing was streamlined, and the tariff structure was rationalized. The parliament approved an international arbitration convention in May 2001, and Tehran joined the World Bank's Multilateral Investment Guarantee Agency.

As with its predecessor, the Khatami administration continued to seek and receive support from international financial institutions for a variety of minor projects, including two World Bank loans for sewage management and primary health care. This engagement prompted bitter opposition from Washington as well as from Israeli officials, one of whom noted that "above all, what Iran wants is international legitimacy. It's not so much a question of money. Iran wants to show everybody it has support from an international organization. It's very much a political issue. It doesn't need loans for these projects. It has enough money."[113] During Khatami's November 2000 visit to Japan, Iran scored an agreement for an officially backed $3 billion credit facility tied to crude oil exports to Iran.[114]

Some reformists also sought to promote an Iranian application to the World Trade Organization (WTO), with little success, arguing that "participation in the World Trade Organization is a bitter drug that has to be poured into the mouth of the country's sick and faint economy, so that the existing parasites and infectious lumps will come out and show their ugly face."[115] This issue, like other economic policy options, demonstrated the counterintuitive fracturing that had begun to take place

---

[112] "Foreign Investment Protection Law Will Boost Employment: Hashemi," *IRNA*, July 16, 2000.

[113] Janine Zacharia, "World Bank Set to Consider Iran Loans," *Jerusalem Post*, May 10, 2001.

[114] "Nico Gives NIOC Greater Access to Outside Finance," PIW, December 11, 2000.

[115] Hassan Samini, "World Trade Organization: A Bitter but Curative Drug," *Hayat-e No*, November 16, 2000, p. 10.

within Iran's established factional alignments as a result of political shifts and economic opportunities. The chief of the Chamber of Commerce, Industries, and Mines as well as the new head of the Foundation for the Oppressed and War-Wounded emerged as a public advocate for WTO membership, while some reformists – including Khatami's own minister of labor – publicly cast doubt on the benefits of WTO membership. Husayn Kamali argued that "in our present conditions, WTO membership will mean nothing other than an end to domestic manufacturing and an ensuing crisis, unemployment, and so on ... we must appoint a team of experts to carefully consider the country's conditions, and come up with a program within a fixed period to create the right social, political, and economic conditions for Iran's membership in the WTO."[116]

These Khatami policy initiatives can be credited with some significant steps forward. In 2002, Iran okayed the first foreign takeover of a domestic company under FIPPA, when the German chemical company Henkel snagged a 60 percent share in Pakvash, an Iranian detergent outfit. Other sectors boomed as a result of the new political and legal context. Iran's car industry skyrocketed between 1997 and 2006 – expanding from 80,000 units to 817,000 cars produced and assembled, a growth rate that was among the industry's highest around the world.[117] The Japanese and Europeans reopened the spigot of export credit instruments, in many cases for the first time since the revolution, and the EU was preparing to negotiate a Trade and Cooperation Agreement with Iran. In July 2002, Iran's first bond issue in two decades was oversubscribed.

Chinese trade and investment continued to expand, including an $836 million deal awarded to NORINCO in May 2004 for a nineteen kilometer expansion of the Tehran metro.[118] A November 2003 trade delegation to Beijing led by Iran's transportation minister netted preliminary agreements on $3–$4 billion in investment in similar projects over the following three years.[119] All of the major European and Asian energy companies had returned to Iran, along with a wide array of foreign industrial conglomerates and financial institutions hoping to get in on the ground floor of the next great wave of opportunity generated by the opening of a formerly closed economic system.

---

[116] "Minister of Labor: WTO Will Finish Off Iran's Industry," *Hayat-e No*, March 15, 2001, p. 15.
[117] Javad Abedini and Nicolas Peridy, "The Emergence of Iran in the World Car Industry: An Estimation of Its Export Potential," *World Economy* (2009), pp. 792–3.
[118] Garver (2006), pp. 261–4.   [119] Garver (2006), p. 259.

The Free Trade Zone (FTZ) experiment was also expanded, despite its mixed track record. Several new FTZs were established in 2003 at Aras, Anzali, and Arvand. By 2002, Kish drew up to 1 million tourists each year, and $100 million in spending.[120] Cultural restrictions were less stringently enforced than on the mainland, although the parameters remained contested. Kish's new development bore a strikingly resemblance to its prerevolutionary heyday, but the ventures persuaded at least some conservatives that entrepreneurial opportunities justified adapting cultural standards. "There is nothing un-Islamic here," said one conservative Friday prayer leader, Hojjatoleslam Mohammad Ali Talib, as he attended the opening of a dolphin show at one of the hotels on the island. "Kish was barren and deserted before Mr. Sabet (the hotel developer) started this place. Our religion favors pleasure and entertainment as long as it is not provocative. Plus, he has created jobs, and tourists are bringing money to the island. There is nothing un-Islamic about that."[121]

Still, Iran struggled to translate this domestic progress to a meaningful export market – the thriving automotive industry remained largely inward-focused, as remaining barriers to foreign competition at home generated robust demand for Iranian vehicles at home and made them less competitive abroad. Much the same could be said for the FTZs, where domestic investment continued to outpace foreign capital by far. Between 1996 and 2004, the three original FTZs (Kish, Qeshm, and Chabahar) drew only $2.099 billion in foreign investment, compared to $30.576 billion from domestic sources, and Kish's overseas exports in 1998 and 1999 only averaged $1 million, or 1 percent of the volume of its exports to mainland Iran.[122]

EXCHANGE RATE UNIFICATION AND OTHER ECONOMIC REFORMS

In addition to the efforts to facilitate foreign investment, Khatami's second term saw broader forward momentum on the economy, for which the reformists reaped little popular gratitude. Perhaps most importantly, Tehran intensified the gradual exchange rate reform that had begun in 1998, when a foreign exchange bourse was added to the Tehran Stock Exchange (TSE); the price was permitted to float and became known as

---

[120] Nazila Fathi, "A Little Leg, a Little Booze, but Hardly Gomorrah," *New York Times*, April 15, 2002, p. 4.
[121] Ibid. [122] World Bank, *op. cit.*

the TSE rate. In May 1999, the Central Bank moved to depreciate the TSE rate significantly and established an open deposit facility to absorb excess reserves from commercial banks. The export rate was phased out and eliminated altogether by the end of March 2000, and the TSE rate became the main market rate applied to all official transactions except imports of subsidized basic commodities and debt service payments (which remained at the official rate of 1,750 rials/$).[123]

The plan then turned to the full unification of exchange rates. March 2002 saw all previously TSE-based transactions shifted to a newly established interbank market, and the elimination of the basic official rate. The exchange rate was unified at the prevailing TSE market rate before the unification.[124] This was facilitated by the authorities' more explicitly subsidizing the difference between the previous rates on certain imports and the new unified rate, particularly for "necessities" such as pharmaceutical products, medical equipment, fertilizers, defense items, scholarships, and capital goods for state-owned enterprises. Some delays resulted from existing contracts for imports at the eliminated official rate with SOEs; surplus oil revenues and Central Bank assistance offset these costs.[125] In May 2002, Tehran adopted an "ersatz float," in which the market set currency rates, but only within undefined parameters maintained by the Central Bank. The new exchange rate system represented a critical step to reducing corruption, and to rationalizing Iran's industrial spending, but it faced bitter opposition among many merchants in the *bazaar*.

Even as the reform movement's political agenda appeared stymied, the Khatami era approach to economic reform was beginning to pay off. By 2002, Iran had paid down its short-term debts to approximately $6.2 billion, with another approximately $14 billion outstanding in longer-term debts. The reformist-led sixth Majlis succeeded in amending the Labour Law in 2003 to exempt small firms – those with five or fewer workers – from some of its restrictions. The Tehran Stock Exchange had attracted 3 million shareholders, and Khatami's personal appeal helped facilitate intensified efforts initiated by Rafsanjani to attract expatriate investment. Thousands of Iranians who fled during the brutal early years of the revolutionary regime overcame their antipathy and

---

[123] Celasun, pp. 4–5.
[124] According to data from OANDA, this rate appears to have been 7,900 rials/$, which went into effect on March 2, 2002.
[125] Celasun, p. 5.

mistrust of the government to return to Iran, at least for short periods – a flow of individuals and capital that has mushroomed since the 1997 election. In addition, the cumulative effects of the reconstruction program, combined with the Khatami administration's efforts on poverty, were continuing to raise overall living standards; for example, statistics on malnourishment and underweight children fell from 10.9 percent in 1998 to 5 percent in 2004.[126]

This period also marked the further rationalization of the bifurcated revolutionary bureaucracy with the merger of the Agriculture Ministry with the Jihad-e Sazandegi, forming the Ministry of Agricultural Jihad. The Construction Jihad had emerged after the revolution as a parastatal organization, tasked with rural development and extending the regime's authority into the countryside as it built infrastructure. Over time, the Construction Jihad collaborated with the IRGC on land seizures and progressively assumed the role of the Guards' de facto "corps of engineers" for its military operations during the Iran-Iraq War, eventually making it a subordinate organization.[127] This merger remained intact, but a separate mobilization corps, the Construction Basij, was also established and would expand rapidly during the Ahmadinejad presidency.

And then there were the smaller-scale initiatives, which often had a disproportionately dramatic impact on the daily lives of ordinary Iranians. The international financial institutions resumed lending to Iran, despite American objections. Improvements to the banking system also facilitated the country's evolution beyond a purely cash-based economy. In 2001, Tehran began instituting an electronic banking network (Shetab), which was intended to provide a uniform payment network across the banking system and generated a rapid expansion in consumer access to electronic banking. Between 2001/2 and 2003/4, the number of transactions conducted via automatic teller machines in Iran jumped more than 100-fold, from 360,341 to 38,333, 093.[128] By the time Khatami left office, Iran had more than 3,887 ATMs and an additional 47,000 point-of-sale ATM terminals, distributed around the country.[129]

---

[126] Mahmoudi (2011), p. 160

[127] Kenneth Katzman. *The Warriors of Islam: Iran's Revolutionary Guard* (Boulder, CO: Westview Press, 1993), p. 41.

[128] Data made available on the Web site of the Central Bank of the Islamic Republic of Iran, http://www.cbi.ir/page/2806.aspx

[129] Data made available on the Web site of the Central Bank of the Islamic Republic of Iran, http://www.cbi.ir/page/2807.aspx

Most of these achievements represented wholly insufficient remedies to Iran's overall economic problems – they do not produce sufficient employment, or mitigate escalatory pressures on prices, or address the myriad distortions that exist within the Iranian system. And yet they also reflected a more holistic approach than that of Rafsanjani, which was designed to grow the economy beyond its inefficiencies as quickly as possible. "Experience has shown that an important boost to the Iranian economy comes not from an increase in the government's foreign exchange income but from a drastic and fundamental change in the economic policies and legislation of the land," wrote the economist Saeed Leylaz in his column in a reformist newspaper. "The main problem of Iran's economy is not in financial resources but in economic approaches, policy-making and, most importantly, the overall climate of security for investments and investors."[130]

The Khatami period also helped solidify the shift in the political culture that had begun during the reconstruction period more firmly in favor of capitalism. As an industrialist told a Norwegian researcher in 2003, "The situation is getting better. Some days ago, I was in a meeting with the governor of Mazandaran. He told me straight out that 'after the revolution, we made a mistake. We have regarded the capitalist as a deceiver. Today, however, we understand the government, the country and the regime depend on an active economy. And for the economy to function, we need to protect and encourage the capitalist.'"[131]

However, many other initiatives contemplated or attempted by the Khatami economic team foundered as a result of continuing factional differences and an unwillingness to undertake risky changes to the country's economic framework. For example, the reformists attempted to address the perennial issue of consumer price subsidies but were once again stymied in the parliament. Reform of the 1990 Labor Law suffered a similar fate; the law was widely perceived to impose costly inefficiencies on the market and constrain the expansion of job creation. Khatami's strong association with the Left, with its emphasis on job protection rather than policies likely to spur job creation, affected his presidency greatly, especially in his early years in office. He was unable to break with these labor elements to provide substantially greater economic freedom to

---

[130] Saeed Leylaz, "80 Budget: Continuation of the Strategy of Liberalization," *Nowruz* (internet edition), December 23, 2001, p. 4.
[131] Selvik (2005), p. 12.

accompany his idea of a civil society in Iran.[132] A number of other reforms languished in the parliament, including capital market regulation, a proposed VAT risk-based banking supervision, and anti–money laundering policies. "We do not have a clear economic direction," the former PBO head Masoud Roghani Zanjani lamented. "Our regulations reflect a confused system of thought. If we are moving towards market economy, our laws must conform to our practice. We cannot have two different logics."[133]

AMERICA, OPPORTUNITY AND THREAT

Even as the Khatami team was navigating an increasingly difficult domestic dynamic, the embattled reform movement found itself once again confronted with a crisis – only this time, it was along Iran's borders rather than among its power brokers. The terrorist attacks that struck New York and Washington on September 11, 2001, quickly transformed the regional context, sending the full force of the U.S. military back to Iran's doorstep once again to assist an Iranian-backed coalition of Afghans in removing one of Tehran's fiercest and most troublesome regional adversaries. Given the long-standing parallels in their official positions toward the Taliban, many anticipated that the U.S. military campaign in Afghanistan might create new opportunities for formal cooperation and diplomatic overtures between Washington and the Islamic Republic. Indeed, for the first few months this appeared to be the case, with some new high-level contacts initiated and several small but significant gestures from the Iranian side. However, as the Taliban position crumbled, the Bush administration shifted its concern from the need for local allies, where Iran by virtue of its influence in Afghanistan and prior support for the Northern Alliance was considered valuable, to the need to forestall warlordism and to buttress the central government, where Tehran's continuing involvement was seen as part of the problem. As a result, the very same factors that generated a new dialogue between the United States and Iran contributed to an increasingly ominous view among U.S. policy makers of Tehran's role and intentions.

---

[132] Djavad Salehi-Isfahani, "Population, Human Capital, and Economic Growth in Iran," in *Human Capital: Population Economics in the Middle East*, ed. Ismail Sirageldin (Cairo: American University in Cairo Press, 2002), p. 157.

[133] Mehrdad Balali, "Iran Officials Doubt Quick Economic Recovery," *Reuters*, November 30, 1999.

Tehran traversed the complicated new terrain carefully. Tehranis mourned the attacks with a candlelight vigil and the traditional chants of *"Marg bar Amrika"* ("Death to America") were briefly absent from the mass Friday prayers session held in Tehran and other major cities. A reformist parliamentarian signed a book of condolences proffered by the U.S. Interests Section at the Swiss Embassy. However, while Iranian leaders – including Khamenei – condemned the attacks and expressed sympathy for their victims, they also warned against U.S. military action. And neither sympathy nor pragmatism deterred Iranian leaders, including Rafsanjani, from repeatedly invoking some of the basest hoaxes about the episode.[134] Similar sentiments were encouraged in the state-sanctioned media, which compared the events of September 11 to seminal events in the American Revolution.[135]

Tehran insisted that it would remain neutral in the event of any U.S. military action in Afghanistan. "How can America, which has tampered with Iran's interests, demand help from Iran to attack the suffering, oppressed and Muslim nation of Afghanistan?" Khamenei demanded, adding that "it is wrong to say that those who are not with us are with the terrorists. No, we are not with you, and we are not terrorists."[136] In fact, however, the Islamic Republic provided quiet assistance to the campaign, in terms of logistics and coordination with the Northern Alliance. Indeed, Iranian officials later boasted that it was the Revolutionary Guards who built the bridges that U.S. forces used in their initial incursion into Afghanistan. And Tehran played an integral role in the success of the Bonn Conference, which established the post-Taliban government in Afghanistan, and made a number of subsequent overtures toward Washington intended to build upon cooperation in Afghanistan.[137] And for eighteen months, the two old adversaries engaged in direct bilateral talks on Afghanistan – the first such sustained official dialogue since the end of the hostage crisis.

---

[134] "Rafsanjani Condemns Israeli Attacks against Palestinian Refugee Camps," Voice of the Islamic Republic of Iran, March 8, 2002, from BBC SWB.

[135] "Daily Draws a Parallel between Sept 11 Events and 1773 Boston Tea Party," *IRNA* (Internet edition), March 12, 2003.

[136] Nazila Fathi, "Iran Won't Join U.S. Campaign, Leader Says," *New York Times*, September 27, 2001.

[137] James Dobbins, "Negotiating with Iran," statement before the Committee on Oversight and Government Reform, Subcommittee on National Security and Foreign Affairs, U.S. House of Representatives, November 7, 2007.

However, the prospect of rapprochement remained firmly beyond reach. A series of incidents added new frictions to the relationship, ranging from the Israeli seizure of a ship packed with clandestine Iranian arms reported to be en route to the Palestine Authority to President Bush's inclusion of Iran in his self-defined "Axis of Evil," to the conviction of an Iranian-American dancer on morals charges. New disclosures about Iran's past terrorist activities, including the 1994 bombing of a Jewish community, stoked the distrust of senior Bush officials of an Iran that remained trapped within a precarious process of transformation. The August 2002 revelation of Iran's covert development of an indigenous uranium enrichment capability was seen in Washington as confirmation of the threat posed by Tehran – a supercharged state sponsor of terror engaged in a secret race for the bomb. Finally, Iranian involvement in post-Saddam Iraq returned the two adversaries to the dangerous conditions of undeclared warfare that had existed for the latter years of Tehran's war with Iraq.

Throughout this period, Iran periodically lit up with rumors related to some possible rapprochement: Had Khatami established a high-level committee to study the possibilities for engagement? Were secret negotiations already under way? Would the reformist parliamentarians pursue suggestions from U.S. congressmen, including then-Senator Joseph Biden, for a legislative exchange? Similar speculation periodically transfixed Washington, such as the revelation of a bold proposal for a bilateral "grand bargain" to resolve the estrangement that was offered to the Bush administration by the Swiss ambassador to Tehran, purportedly with the endorsement of senior Iranian diplomats.

None of these gambits managed to progress, and despite the confluence of interest and the relative political tractability of the Iranian regime during this period, the estrangement with Washington remained as well entrenched as ever. "As long as they are threatening, insulting and humiliating us, neither myself nor the nation is ready to accept any relations," Khatami said in May 2002. "My policy is a policy of détente. From the beginning we said we wanted to implement this policy to include the United States. We have never said we never want relations with the United States."[138] For their part, the conservatives remained unconvinced that rapprochement represented the Holy Grail for Iran that the reformists seemed to presume. "Foreign exchange cannot work miracles nor is it

---

[138] Parisa Hafezi, "Khatami on US Ties," *Reuters*, May 14, 2002.

a solution to every problem. We should not think that as soon as the ice in relations with the United States thaws, capital would begin to pour into the country all of a sudden. We should not forget our imprudent planning. We should not attribute every shortcoming to lack of relations with the United States or lack of foreign investments in order to justify inefficiency."[139]

Initially, the post-9/11 environment appeared to open up new economic opportunities for Tehran; Washington's removal of its most formidable regional adversaries, the Taliban and Saddam Hussein, expanded two markets where Iran could claim the benefits of proximity, familiarity, and familial and ethnoreligious ties. The removal of Saddam Hussein in Iraq did not merely eliminate Iran's most fearsome regional adversary; it opened a valuable new market for Iranian goods and services, and an increasingly vital channel for hard currency and other necessities that were impacted by sanctions. Tehran moved quickly to muscle in on opportunities in Iraq. Establishing free trade zones in Iran's border provinces helped facilitate increasing transit of goods through neighboring states such as Iraq and Afghanistan.[140] The regional turmoil added ballast to an Iranian economy that was already rising on steroids as a result of the oil price hike. During this period, Iran's bilateral trade with Russia also expanded by a whopping 43 percent between 2003 and 2004, and the two governments initiated discussions about the merger of their power grids.[141] Khatami maintained his avid international travel schedule, which paralleled Iran's expanding trade horizons, including a visit to New Delhi in January 2002.

CONSERVATIVE REVIVAL AND THE RISE OF THE REVOLUTIONARY GUARD

Long before the end of the Khatami presidency, the signs of a conservative revival were clear. Having absorbed the lessons of the reformist ascendance, an array of hard-line activists and political aspirants began to flex their muscle, first through electoral institutions, dominating the 2003 city council elections and then the 2004 parliamentary ballot. In each of

---

[139] Kaveh Eshtehardi, "Rafsanjani Administration Purchased $23 Billion More than Oil Incomes," *Jam-e Jam*, 3:608–9 (June 22–3, 2002).

[140] http://www.ostan-kd.ir/Default.aspx?TabId=50&nid=22005

[141] Talal Nizameddin, "Squaring the Middle East Triangle in Lebanon: Russia and the Iran-Syria-Hezbollah Nexus," *Slavonic and East European Review* 86:3 (July 2008), p. 489.

these contests, the active intervention of the conservative power structure facilitated their advancement, but ultimately they managed to draw support at the ballot box too. New conservative political organizations – which are most easily identified by their shorthand names *Isargaran* ("Devotees"), *Abadgaran* ("Developers"), and *Usulgaran* ("Principalists") – emerged during this period and began to reshape the landscape of factional politics. The rise of the "new Right" paralleled a slow-motion reformist collapse, thanks to a failure to define a viable agenda or make a compelling public case that they could achieve their agenda. The 2004 parliamentary elections began to close the door on the reform era, as the disqualification of thousands of candidates including eighty sitting Majlis representatives mostly drew public apathy. For many Iranians, a brief sit-in by the representatives only confirmed their cynical suspicions of the movement's self-interest.

The mobilization of a younger generation of conservatives around the ballot box and Iran's representative institutions began to make its influence felt in other arenas of the system, especially the economy. The new Right was built through personal as well as institutional linkages with the Revolutionary Guard, and many observers interpreted the shift in Iran's factional balance as confirmation of the militarization of its politics. Indeed, during this period, the explicitly political and economic role of the Revolutionary Guards expanded rapidly, and by 2004 the Guards and the political figures associated with them were brashly assertive in their pretensions to predominance. The Guards' role had been long in the making, but its full expression seemed to require a conducive political context that was lacking until the reformists' waning days.

The most dramatic example of the IRGC's new sway occurred on May 8, 2004, when the Guards' closed the newly constructed Imam Khomeini Airport outside Tehran in apparent anger over the failure to win the valuable deal to build and operate the facility. Khatami's then–transportation minister, Ahmad Khorram, accused the Guard Corps explicitly. Khorram was quoted as saying, "One reason that the Imam airport was closed down was that the armed forces had failed to sign a lucrative contract. Iranian companies usually make bids for such contracts and there were companies which were under the management of the armed forces.... However, the price they were asking was too high and, consequently, they were not chosen." Further suggesting that the closure was designed to circumvent free competition, he added, "We are not against the Revolutionary Guards winning contracts. Some of their companies already have contracts with us, but first they have to win the tender."[142] Khorram would be removed in impeachment proceedings later that year, and Tehran was eventually forced to compensate the Turkish company Tepe-Akfen Vie (TAV), which had been awarded an 11-year contract for the new airport terminal

The Turkish telecom firm Turkcell also met with similar obstacles as it pursued projects in Iran. In September 2004, Turkcell signed a $3 billion contract to develop Iran's first private cellular phone network, purchasing a 70 percent stake in Irancell. On February 15, 2005, the Majlis reduced the firm's stake in Irancell to 49 percent, in contravention of FIPPA guarantees. This move prompted the deal's eventual collapse and a Turkcell lawsuit seeking $10 billion in damages. Tehran prevailed in an Iranian court, whereupon Turkcell turned to international arbitration.[143] In response, a leading reformist lamented that the "international repercussions will stay with us. I believe that it has damaged the basis of trust, which is the cornerstone of bilateral relations between nations."[144]

The Revolutionary Guards' new bid for economic primacy represented a conservative counterreaction to one of the reformists' seminal achievements, the ratification of a new foreign investment framework. The conservative-dominated seventh parliament sought to reverse some of the provisions of FIPPA, requiring parliamentary approval for all foreign contracts, and extended this authority retroactively to already-signed deals. The legislation explicitly targeted the Turkcell and TAV deals. Proponents of the legislation based their support on both economic and security concerns about ceding control over such sensitive infrastructure to foreign firms; in this sense, the move reflected a twenty-first-century version of resource nationalism.

CONCLUSION

If Khatami entered the presidency like a lion – jolting Iran and the world with an astonishing shift in the tone of Iranian diplomacy and domestic politics – he left like a lamb. His allies and advocates had been driven from office, his policies of openness and tolerance were under siege by institutional repression as well as public indifference, and his

---

[142] "Iran's Transport Minister Accuses Hardliners over Airport Closure," *Agence France Presse*, August 30, 2004.

[143] Economist Intelligence Unit. "Iran: Investment Regulations," *EIU ViewsWire Select*, March 19, 2008.

[144] *Tehran Sharq*. "Head of Islamic Iran Participation Front Criticizes Majles over Impeachment," October 6, 2004.

much-vaunted dialogue of civilizations – the cornerstone of his tenure, and the one element that appeared to attract cross-factional backing – was collapsing under the weight of the intensifying nuclear standoff with the West. There is a certain irony in his undoing, in that the critique with the greatest popular resonance concerned the frustration with the reformists' disregard of economic issues. In fact, the Khatami track record on the economy compares favorably to any other period of postrevolutionary history in Iran. This is scant praise, given the persistent inability or unwillingness of the Islamic Republic to address the major structural deficiencies in the Iranian economy. Still, for all the understandable frustration over the persistence of unemployment and inflation, the reformist era had in fact enacted significant enhancements to the country's economic framework.

Where Khatami failed, however, was in instilling an appreciation of the benefits of these reforms for the broader population and, equally importantly, in creating confidence in the government's capacity to advance an agenda that could manifestly improve citizens' lives. What the reformist rise and demise demonstrated was that twenty-five years after the revolution, ideological legitimacy was no longer sufficient to sustain a popular mandate, irrespective of the appeal of the principles articulated. The country wanted a government that worked – where institutions were not perpetually at war with one another, where the senior elected official could implement his own directives, where the massive resources of the state and nation raised standards of living and created new opportunities. In fact, Khatami's menu of reforms aimed at achieving these objectives, but the unrelenting setbacks eroded his credibility and his base of support, along with those of his allies in government. For that reason, even before the electoral shenanigans that helped catapult Mahmoud Ahmadinejad into the presidency and maintain him there, the reformists were already being beaten at their own game by an array of clever hard-liners.

Just as he always insisted, Khatami was no Gorbachev, if only because resource rents and nationalism helped entrench the Iranian system more durably than the Soviets' dying days. The better analogy for the Khatami era is that of another temperate revolutionary, Mehdi Bazargan. As head of the Provisional Government, Bazargan had the unenviable task of trying to hold the center as competition within the revolutionary coalition pushed rivals to vie for the extremes. Bazargan's efforts to reestablish central authority entailed by definition deliberation, collaboration, and moderation – which happened to be his personal and political hallmarks. Such attributes were foiled at every turn by his rivals' readiness to utilize informal channels of influence and absolutist tactics. Like Khatami, Bazargan found himself outmaneuvered and disempowered, operating by his own description as "a knife without a blade."[145] Both men left office to assume a principled place on the fringes of the system, and in their wake another revolution followed.

[145] This is an oft-repeated line from Bazargan's memoirs, *Shura-ye Enqelab Va Dowlat-e Movaqat* [The Council of the Revolution and the Provisional Government] (Daftar-e Nehzad-e Azadi, 1983). As quoted in Mohsen Milani, "The Ascendance of Shi'i Fundamentalism in Revolutionary Iran," *Journal of South Asian and Middle Eastern Studies* 13, Nos. 1 & 2 (Fall/Winter 1989), p. 10.

7

Populism, Version 2.0: The Ahmadinejad Era, 2005–2013

Had Iranians set out to find the absolute antithesis of Khatami to succeed him as president, they could not have achieved a more perfect paradox than Mahmoud Ahmadinejad. The 2005 presidential election instigated a dramatic transformation in the character of the presidency. Khatami, a genteel and literary cleric who valued dignity, respect, and rule of law, found himself replaced by a provocateur from the security forces who reveled in political strife. On domestic policy, where Khatami favored incrementalism, Ahmadinejad opted for shock therapy. Across the world, the reformist mantras of détente and dialogue among civilizations were jettisoned in favor of confrontation and creeping isolation.

Nowhere were the distinctions between the Khatami presidency and the Ahmadinejad era more evident than in the economy, where government policy, political debates, and actual conditions experienced striking shifts, mainly negative ones. Each of the perennial problems afflicting the economy – inflation, unemployment, corruption, and mismanagement – worsened during Ahmadinejad's eight years in office, despite a period of record oil revenues. These outcomes, and Ahmadinejad's legacy, are inextricably tied to the nuclear standoff and the 2009 elections upheaval, which together facilitated an unprecedented sanctions regime and severe disruptions to Iran's place in the global economy.

The Ahmadinejad era is best understood as the product of Iran's unique metamorphosis over the past three decades and is particularly rooted in the basic forces of Iran's postrevolutionary political economy. His populist rhetoric and program – particularly the ostentatious efforts to dispense the state's largesse after taking office – revived themes that were central to the early postrevolutionary period.[1] The roller-coaster ride that was the eight-year presidency of Mahmoud Ahmadinejad may have been the most unexpected dimension of a political narrative that has been persistently unpredictable since its inception in 1979. As the scholar Ali Ansari commented, "(E)ven for those Iranians who were bored of politics, Ahmadinejad was making life dangerously interesting."[2]

Precisely for that reason, however, gleaning the implications of the Ahmadinejad era has been a frustrating exercise. The president's propensity for incitement, both at home and abroad, has made it all too easy for analysis to devolve into moralizing. His presidency was frequently depicted as a spasmodic anachronism – a throwback to the heady early revolutionary period, when radical anti-Westernism was in vogue and confrontation was the budding theocracy's modus operandi. Alternatively, Ahmadinejad was simply written off as a rube or a fool – an unsophisticated charlatan who was out of his depth in the Islamic Republic's second highest office. There are elements of truth in each of these explanations, but neither is wholly accurate. Ahmadinejad was thoroughly contemporary in both his outlook and appeal, and he proved surprisingly skillful as a politician. His catastrophic management of the economy and bombastic approach to the world represented the perfect culmination of the contradictions of the revolution's mandates. His campaign slogan, which promised to put the country's oil income on the *sofreh* (tablecloth) of each Iranian, reflected and reinforced the extent to which the legitimacy of the theocracy is now determined by the delivery of improved living standards.

AHMADINEJAD'S ASCENT

Ahmadinejad owed his unlikely ascent from administrative obscurity to the pinnacle of power to his successful exploitation of Iranians' frustration with their living standards and economic opportunities. His dark horse victory benefited from the well-organized political machines associated with his various constituencies – which originally consisted of a young conservative political grouping, some elements of the Revolutionary Guard and Basij corps, and voters in Tehran and Ardabil, where he

---

[1] Abrahamian; Manoucher Dorraj, *From Zarathustra to Khomeini: Populism and Dissent in Iran* (Boulder, CO: Lynne Rienner, 1990); Dorraj, "Populism and Coporatism in Post-Revolutionary Political Culture," in *Political Culture in the Islamic Republic*, eds. Samih K. Farsoun and Mehrdad Mashayekhi (London: Routledge, 1992).

[2] Ali M. Ansari, "Iran under Ahmadinejad: The Politics of Confrontation," Adelphi Paper 393 (London: Routledge, 2007), p. 51.

had previously served as governor general. In addition, several of his rivals as well as other influential Iranians have suggested that the supreme leader's office helped seal his election through a variety of tactics.

Still, it is nonetheless notable that Ahmadinejad managed to do what no preelection analysis predicted – persuade a sizable proportion of Iran's electorate to endorse a defender of the theocracy. He accomplished this feat by focusing on issues of everyday economic hardships and inequities. In his campaign, Ahmadinejad spoke bitterly about the indignities of Iran's grinding poverty and pointedly contrasted his humble lifestyle with that of his chief rival, the profiteering former President Rafsanjani. Ultimately, Ahmadinejad's victory represented an endorsement of the system, but a rejection of the status quo and a mutiny by an electorate more concerned with jobs and the cost of living than with slick campaigns or implausible pledges of political change.

His ability to leverage economic grievances should not be interpreted as evidence that those grievances had in fact intensified. As the scholar Djavad Salehi-Isfahani has demonstrated, "While the populist movement that toppled the Shah in 1979 might have drawn strength from rising inequality in the 1970s, the one that defeated the reformists in 2005 was most likely not" a direct result of worsening inequality.[3] In fact, the 2005 election took place nearly midway through the largest bonanza Iran had ever experienced with respect to oil revenues. Ahmadinejad's campaign successfully exploited Iranians' misgivings about their own future prospects, even as climbing oil prices were supplying unprecedented largesse to the state.

The election outcome surprised many, as most prevote analyses presumed that Ahmadinejad stood no chance of prevailing over the presumptive front-runner Rafsanjani. The former president seemed a shoo-in, either through vote tampering or simply as a result of his name recognition and Iranians' underlying eagerness for a powerful chief executive. Ultimately – like so many political shifts in the postrevolutionary narrative – the 2005 ballot upended the conventional wisdom on Iran. In the Khatami administration's waning days, many presumed the reform movement's stalemate would benefit Iran's pragmatists. One researcher posited that the private sector's "newfound legitimacy" would elevate its political influence and popular appeal.[4] Ahmadinejad's ascension reinforces the dominance of ideology in interpreting Iranian

---

[3] Salehi-Isfahani (2009), p. 18.   [4] Selvik (2005), p. 17.

political trends, and the corresponding failure to appreciate the importance of economic forces in shaping both public expectations and leadership decisions. The combination of state largesse and popular economic grievances offered an opening not for the pragmatists – who have tended to step to the fore precisely when the theocracy's challenges are most urgent, such as the war's end – but rather for populists and agitators.

Until the campaign's final days, Ahmadinejad drew little attention, and jockeying among the conservatives, focused on preventing a Rafsanjani victory, kept the race fluid even by Iran's hectic electoral standards. Early in the presidential posturing, many presumed that Ali Larijani had the supreme leader's endorsement; he was an intense and loyal establishment man who offered the symmetry of having replaced Khatami in 1992 after he was forced from Rafsanjani's cabinet. Larijani's candidacy failed to gain steam, however. Next surged Mohammad Baqr Qalibaf, a former Revolutionary Guards commander and former chief of the national police, who ran a sophisticated, well-oiled campaign. However, as the election date approached, rumors circulated of Qalibaf's fall from grace over his flashy style and grandiose ambitions, epitomized by his self-characterization as a "Hizbollahi Reza Shah," presumably intended to emphasize his decisiveness and developmental credentials. Qalibaf had other baggage, including his signature on the infamous warning from military commanders to Khatami over the July 1999 student protests and, conversely, his criticism of the Guardians' Council culling of reformist candidates in the 2004 parliamentary elections.

By contrast, Ahmadinejad ran an unobtrusive campaign. And in a field that included such revolutionary stalwarts as the two-time parliamentary speaker Mehdi Karrubi, secretary of the Expediency Council Mohsen Rezaei, and Mostafa Moin – the only Khatami official to resign in protest over the July 1999 crackdown – Ahmadinejad seemed destined to be an also-ran. However, Ahmadinejad's profile corresponded perfectly with Khamenei's articulated priorities: the mayor's apparent personal simplicity, his dogged emphasis on revolutionary values, and his mettle in delivering effective jabs to his rivals. Ahmadinejad's occasional habit of helping Tehran's street cleaners, while donning their neon uniforms and extolling their vocation, underscored the humble pretensions of a politician who described himself first and foremost as "a child of the Islamic Revolution and a servant of the people, and so I am ready to stand against any enemy who threatens our nation and revolution."[5] With literally no personal wealth – his campaign declaration listed a thirty-year-old car and near-empty bank accounts – the mayor ran a peripatetic, shoestring campaign, "a textbook definition of the populist leader."[6]

Still, even in this protean phase, there could be no mistaking the future president's brash style. Throughout the campaign, he resisted pressure from other hard-liners, including the influential *Kayhan* editor Husayn Shariatmadari, to withdraw to prevent splitting of the conservative vote. And even before the official campaign was under way, he demonstrated a flair for insubordination in relation to the perks of the established political élite, as in his upbraiding of the then–sitting president over Khatami's critique of Tehran traffic after a late arrival at a ceremonial event.[7]

In response Ahmadinejad advised Khatami to "take a bus," saying that had Khatami remained in his downtown office instead of moving to a complex in the fashionable and wealthy northern part of the city, he would be more in touch with the people's everyday problems. He pronounced himself "delighted to see that the President got stuck in Tehran traffic at least once, in order to experience up close what it feels like."[8]

Ahmadinejad also benefited from the enthusiastic support of an emergent political movement on the Right, the Abadgaran (Developers), which had won a parliamentary majority in 2004. After eight years of the reformists' public agonizing, the allure of a fresh and decisive candidate riding an energetic new political movement appealed to many Iranians, including Khamenei. A generation earlier, his predecessor regretted the appointment of the moderate Bazargan to lead the Provisional Government; Ayatollah Khomeini lamented that "we made a mistake, we did not act in a revolutionary way.... We should have appointed a young and resolute candidate, and not an impotent one."[9] In 2005, Khamenei opted for the young and resolute candidate, although he would ultimately harbor regrets at least as profound as those Khomeini expressed.

[5] *Mehr News Agency*, May 14, 2005.

[6] Kasra Naji, *Ahmadinejad: The Secret History of Iran's Radical Leader* (London: I. B. Tauris, 2008), pp. 220, 222.

[7] "Repercussion of Ahmadinezhad's Remarks in Response to Khatami Complaint: People Will Vote for Those Whose Social and Political Manners Befit a President's," *Aftab-e Yazd*, April 30, 2005.

[8] *Iran Daily*, May 1, 2005, as quoted in Anoushiravan Ehteshami and Mahjoob Zweiri, *Iran and the Rise of Its Neoconservatives: The Politics of Tehran's Silent Revolution* (London: I. B. Tauris, 2007), p. 61.

[9] *Sahifeh-ye Nur* 12, (Tehran 1361/1982), p. 253, as quoted in Moin (1999), p. 222.

ECONOMIC POLICIES – POPULISM REDUX

Like those of the reformists, the economic policy positions of Ahmadinejad and his fellow travelers were shaped by Hashemi Rafsanjani's postwar reconstruction program. Their antipathies to the former president's pragmatism led them down a very different path from that of the Left's push for greater transparency, more robust legal protections, and an expansion of popular participation. To the contrary, the new Right perceived the reconstruction agenda as a betrayal of the revolution's promises of justice.

The construction government's economic team justified its policy by reasoning that the economy cake (national production) must expand and then be divided fairly. A larger cake would mean a larger cut for every group; it is not too important if those cuts are unequal.... Despite the economic progress and postwar reconstruction effort, the people retain some very bitter memories from the construction period. The construction government's economic policies gave rise to the privileged offspring and discriminatory wages. Some became wealthy overnight and people felt the discrimination. The younger generation aspired to the same life, but the path was blocked for them. Bank loans were exclusive to a very few people, while a measly marriage loan took so much effort that people would give up halfway. The US dollar went from 65 tumans to 900 tumans, crushing the people under the wheels of the economic adjustment policy. Meanwhile, the Executives of Construction promised a better tomorrow, but, with the seventh Majlis in office replacing the price-raising policy with the price-fixing policy, the results of the economic adjustment policy became clear. There were widening gaps between the wealthy and poor in every province. Some found vast amounts of wealth, while others were deprived of the basics.[10]

It was fitting, then, that Rafsanjani was the race's de facto front-runner and Ahmadinejad's sole opponent in the runoff round. The "shark," as the former president is popularly known, provided a convenient foil for the mayor's populist projections. The 2005 runoff provided those who inveighed against Iran's post-Khomeini moderation with a fresh opportunity to redress what they saw as Rafsanjani's ruinous shift in the revolution's course, miscalculations that were further exacerbated by the reformists' liberalizing influence. Personality politics and other issues almost surely play a role in sustaining the new Right's loathing of Rafsanjani.[11]

---

[10] Qasem Ravanbakhsh, "Weekly Note: True Principle-Ists," *Partow-e Sokhan*, July 31, 2006.

[11] Fouad Sadeqi, "What Is Ahmadinejhad's Problem with Hashemi?" *Mardom-Salari*, January 14, 2008.

The focus on inequity, and the advocacy of redistributional remedies, was not unique to the hard-liners. During the campaign, the candidate Mehdi Karrubi pledged to distribute 50,000 tomans (approximately $55 at the prevailing exchange rate) to each Iranian adult. The funds were to be offset by spending cuts and increases to gasoline prices, and Karrubi billed the proposal as a means of distributing Iran's rising oil revenues in a more evenhanded fashion. This move was alternatively depicted as a bald attempt to buy voter support or Karrubi's inability to relinquish the statist economic policies of the 1980s.[12] The cross-factional convergence around social justice reflected the legacy of revolutionary rhetoric and the 1980s economic policy disputes. However, the dramatic expansion of Iran's revenues also contributed, thanks to the rebounding global economy. Rapidly increasing demand from India and China fueled a tight oil market and unprecedented price escalation – from $17.50 per barrel in 2002 to more than $60.00 per barrel by the time of Ahmadinejad's August 2005 inauguration. This unexpected influx raised the stakes among the élites and intensified public expectations during Ahmadinejad's two terms in office.

Although there were some similarities between Karrubi's left-leaning populism and the Abadgaran approach to the economy, there were also significant differences. Karrubi's policy positions had evolved over the course of his long career, and by 2005, he articulated a relatively forward-learning internationalism. He emerged from the ballot as the most forceful and innovative defender of democratic institutions within the theocratic establishment. By contrast, the new Right fused a commitment to social justice with a profound antipathy toward the West and a mistrust of foreign investment that bordered on aversion, a posture that was not dissimilar to the stance of the Islamic leftists, including Karrubi, during the early revolutionary period.

The Abadgaran caucus entered the Majlis in the 2004 elections and subsequently led an effort to assert greater parliamentary authority over foreign contracts. They also objected to provisions in the fourth Five-Year Plan that advanced privatization. Ahmadinejad's economic agenda on the campaign trail paralleled the Abadgaran critique. He advocated radically reorganizing the bureaucracy, criticized Iran's post-war economic policies as unnecessarily increasing income inequality,

---

[12] Larijani chastised Karrubi that "we shouldn't portray the entire country as a relief committee by making such promises." See "Until the Election of the Sixth President: The Candidates' View of the Next Administration," *Keyhan*, June 6, 2005.

and emphasized his desire to disperse investment and resources beyond Tehran.[13] He deftly exploited revolutionary themes of social justice, inveighing against élite enrichment and appealing for redistribution of the nation's wealth to benefit the "dispossessed." For Iran's traditionalists and especially among its hard-line clerics, these sentiments resonated deeply. "We must move toward Iranian and Islamic theories," Ahmadinejad explained in 2008. "Economic theories must be based on justice, on eliminating deprivation, on helping to encourage our people's talents to blossom and on securing the comprehensive progress of our dear Iran."[14] One of his key allies described his appeal as "a sincere return to the revolution's slogans. People saw the sincerity in his slogans and stance such as justice, being of service to God's beings, affection, prosperity and promotion of the country. People demanded a new generation of managers be in charge of executive positions in the country and advance the affairs."[15]

In addition to the emphasis on social justice, there are several other aspects of the new Right's approach to the economy that became apparent during Ahmadinejad's administration. First, consistent with their own intense partisanship, many standard bearers for the new Right advocated the primacy of ideology in orienting Iranian diplomacy and trade relations. In this sense, Ahmadinejad devoted considerable effort and capital to sustaining special relationships between Iran and an array of states that similarly reject Western dominance, including Cuba, Syria, and Byelorussia. Kazem Jalali, then rapporteur of the Majlis National Security Committee, questioned in 2008 the rationale for maintaining trade with Britain, arguing that "we should seriously revise our economic ties with the countries with which we have political disagreements." Jalali added, "The economy is one of the most important elements of diplomacy."[16] As part of this synergistic approach to ideology, foreign policy, and trade, the new Right has embraced and advocated an eastward shift in Iranian diplomacy to correspond to the increasing importance of Asia to the global economy.

---

[13] Didgah ("Outlook") program, Voice and Vision of the Islamic Republic First Network, June 3, 2005, from *BBC Monitoring Middle East*.

[14] Speech by Iranian President Mahmud Ahmadinejad, May 27, 2008, as broadcast on Islamic Republic of Iran News Network Television and translated by World News Connection.

[15] Najmeh Bozorgmehr, "Interview: Mojtaba Samareh-Hashemi," *FT*, May 30, 2008.

[16] "Iran Should Revise Economic Ties with Hostile Countries: MP," *Mehr News Agency*, November 26, 2011, http://www.mehrnews.com/en/newsdetail.aspx?NewsID=1470162

At the outset, Ahmadinejad's outsider status and his proclivity for tough talk unnerved some in the business community. Hamidreza Jalaeipour, a political analyst and reformist newspaper publisher, opined that Iran's conservative power brokers were intent on "implementing a North Korean model.... They are closing economic, social and political liberties."[17] Other analysts and business people pointed to the new president's comments on corruption and the stock exchange – which he implied was un-Islamic – and saw a more ominous picture for the economy under the new Right's stewardship. Indeed, the stock market crashed in the wake of his electoral victory. It was a fitting omen.

THE NUCLEAR CRUCIBLE

Ahmadinejad assumed the presidency at a particularly sensitive time in the unfolding drama over Iran's nuclear ambitions. The August 2002 disclosure of Iran's nuclear activities shocked Western capitals, as the full scope of a sophisticated, self-sufficient, and diversified Iranian nuclear program became apparent. During the reform era, Tehran engaged reluctantly and truculently with the French, Germans, and British in an attempt to head off international reprisals over the nuclear issue. In 2003, as Washington launched its ill-fated invasion of Iraq, laborious negotiations produced a compact between Iran and the Europeans. The agreement included Iranian commitments for confidence-building measures, including suspension of its enrichment activities and ratification of the Additional Protocol of the Nuclear Non-Proliferation Treaty.

Even as the deal was struck, however, Iran's politics were in the process of taking a turn toward the right, and the ascension of hard-liners in the parliament and subsequently in the presidency. Their withering critiques of the reformist bargaining stance and the benefits – or lack thereof – that accrued to Iran for its concessions contributed to the overall hardening of the Iranian position. When the parliament refused to ratify the Additional Protocol, the government voluntarily adhered to its provisions in order to assuage international concerns. The supreme leader later asserted:

At that stage, because of the cooperation with westerners and the retreats that were made, the enemies advanced so much that I had to step in personally. At that time, westerners became so insolent that even when our government officials became satisfied with only three centrifuges, the westerners expressed their

---

[17] Nazila Fathi, "Conservatives in Iran Battle the Spread of Foreign Investment," *New York Times*, October 10, 2004.

opposition even to that, but today we have eleven thousand centrifuges that are active in the country. If those retreats had continued, today there would be no nuclear advances and no scientific dynamism and innovation in the country.[18]

Khamenei's intercession resulted in Iran's abrogation of the commitments made under the 2003 Paris Accord – a decision often associated with Ahmadinejad but actually taken prior to his election. In April 2005, the supreme leader ordered the government to resume nuclear fuel activities, and on August 8, after a frantic back and forth with the Europeans, Tehran reopened the Isfahan uranium conversion facility. The move was deliberately cast with cross-factional support, "independent from the change of governments," with Khatami, Ahmadinejad, and Rafsanjani present for the pronouncement. The fourth official participant was the former prime minister Mir Husayn Musavi, who would later play a dramatic role in the denouement of the Ahmadinejad presidency.[19]

Of course, even as the eminences of the Islamic Republic sought to portray a unified stance on the nuclear issue, Ahmadinejad's new role had the opposite effect. Even before his election, Ahmadinejad sought to use the nuclear issue as a central plank in his agenda. Through speeches, ceremonies, and an assiduous cultivation of the popular attachment to the program, the president gradually fused his presidency to the program's fate. He dismissed concerns about international reaction to the program as a conspiracy by Iran's adversaries to

create a false mood. They want to portray the situation as critical, while there is no crisis here.... The problem can be solved with prudence and wisdom, by utilizing opportunity and relying on the endless power of the Iranian nation, through our self-confidence. ... One cannot impede scientific progress. You can see scientific progress everywhere in the world. One cannot obstruct this movement.[20]

ON THE WORLD STAGE

Ahmadinejad's tenure began with a maiden voyage to New York to participate in the United Nations General Assembly (UNGA) annual meeting. The new president's quick embrace of this international forum took some observers by surprise, since his previous travels were relatively limited and it was so early in his tenure to court the international

---

[18] "Supreme Leader Meets Government Officials," *Fars News*, July 24, 2012.
[19] "Resumption of Nuclear Activity Is a Collective Decision by Iranian Top Officials," *Xinhua News Agency*, August 2, 2005.
[20] *IRNA*, excerpts from Ahmadinejad interview with the IRIB, Wednesday, June 8, 2005.

spotlight. Khatami had used UNGA as part of his charm offensive, and while Ahmadinejad seemed determined to turn the page on that era, the limelight's lure proved too much to resist. This first U.S. visit provoked intense debate even before it began; the Bush administration seriously contemplated denying the Iranian president a visa, an extraordinary breach of diplomatic protocol, over allegations of his complicity in the U.S. Embassy seizure and mistreatment of the Americans held hostage during that period.[21] And the meetings began only weeks after Tehran had revived its nuclear fuel work, the first breach of the Paris Accord that deepened international concerns about the nuclear program.

Washington reluctantly green-lighted Ahmadinejad's visa, only to reap an unexpected public relations victory in his rambling and defiant discourse. The new leader catapulted himself into that rare pantheon of world leaders who are simultaneously reviled and ridiculed. The speech helped expedite the Bush administration's efforts to mobilize international pressure over the nuclear issue and prompted new derision among the president's domestic rivals. Ahmadinejad's post–New York remarks relating his perception of divine intervention during his UNGA speech instigated much mockery among Iranians and intensified international skepticism. Weeks later, the International Atomic Energy Agency voted to refer concerns about Iran's nuclear activities to the Security Council. As a result, Ahmadinejad was welcomed back to New York each subsequent September with perverse anticipation of his proclivity for galvanizing opposition to Iran's most objectionable activities.

Shortly after his UN debut, Ahmadinejad once again made headlines, this time with his invocation of one of the aphorisms associated with Ayatollah Khomeini, loosely translated as "Israel should be removed from the page of history." Although this sort of rhetoric was hardly unique to Ahmadinejad and was deployed repeatedly throughout Iran's postrevolutionary history, its revival underscored the ideological shift in the Iranian presidency and generated swift and fierce reprisals. In subsequent months, the new president upped the ante with a discursive diatribe on the "myth" of the Holocaust and the suggestion that Israelis be resettled in Europe, Canada, or Alaska. Ahmadinejad chose the December 2005 meeting of the Organization of the Islamic Conference in Mecca as one of the occasions for such musings, embarrassing his Saudi hosts and further jeopardizing the precarious relationship between

---

[21] Nazila Fathi and Joel Brinkley, "U.S. Pursuing Reports That Link Iranian to Embassy Seizure in '79," *New York Times*, July 1, 2005.

the two countries. Compounding the offense, Ahmadinejad next tasked the Foreign Ministry's think tank, which had previously served as a conduit for Western contacts, to host a conference on the issue, inviting an absurd showcase of hate-filled Holocaust deniers. If there was a silver lining to this repugnant phase of Iranian public diplomacy, it was the firestorm of debate within Iran that was incited by the provocations, which included fierce denunciations of the president's rabble-rousing from Iranians across the political spectrum.

Although bilateral tensions mounted during this period, both Tehran and Riyadh appeared committed to avoiding a full-fledged resumption of the 1980s cold war. Ahmadinejad was openly reviled by many Gulf leaders, who mocked his lower-class origins and deeply resented his millenarian sympathies and penchant for stoking radicalism. His posture on Israel, Lebanon, and even Bahrain, particularly after a conservative newspaper published revanchist views, stirred fears about the possible resumption of Iranian efforts to destabilize its southern neighbors. The real source of Gulf anxiety was Iraq, and by extension Iran's deepening sway in Lebanon and among the Palestinians. "To us, it seems out of this world that you do this," Saudi Foreign Minister Prince Saud Al Faisal told an American audience in September 2005. "We fought a war together to keep Iran from occupying Iraq after Iraq was driven out of Kuwait. Now we are handing the whole country over to Iran without reason."[22]

Still, both sides sought to preserve some modicum of official amity and prevent the deterioration of the relationship even as regional tensions ratcheted upward. Tehran repeatedly dispatched envoys to Riyadh to assuage concerns, including the former foreign minister Ali Akbar Velayati, the supreme leader's personal adviser on foreign affairs, who first embarked on a damage control mission after Ahmadinejad's outrageous performance at the December 2005 Organization of the Islamic Conference summit. As Ali Larijani acknowledged, "We do have our disagreements in certain areas, but overall the relations between Iran and Saudi are very dignified with excellent underpinning."[23]

---

[22] Prince Saud Al Faisal, remarks at the Council on Foreign Relations discussion on "The Fight against Extremism and the Search for Peace," New York, September 20, 2005. Transcript by Federal News Service, text accessed at http://www.cfr.org/publication/8908/fight_against_extremism_and_the_search_for_peace_rush_transcript_federal_news_service_inc.html

[23] Open Source Center, "Larijani: Discusses Nuclear Issue; Improvements in Iraq Due to 'Iran's Assistance," Islamic Republic of Iran News Network Television, September 13, 2007.

Despite their profound trepidation about Iran, the Saudis signaled sporadic overtures toward Tehran. Riyadh actually hosted Ahmadinejad several times, including for the December 2007 *hajj* pilgrimage – a first for a sitting Iranian president and remarkable given the Saudis' traditional consternation over Iranian troublemaking at the pilgrimage. Riyadh also undoubtedly sanctioned another unprecedented act of regional comity, Ahmadinejad's participation in the annual summit of the leaders of the Gulf Cooperation Council in December 2007, where he proposed a regional security pact and new economic cooperation between Iran and its historic adversaries. At the same time, however, the Saudis agreed to massive new arms sales from Washington and played a central role in the implementation of international economic pressure against Iran during Ahmadinejad's second term.

THE POPULIST PRESIDENT IN ACTION

Just as his early international foreign policy ventures appeared bent on reversing the postwar openings, Ahmadinejad's attempts to reframe the country's domestic policies got off to an even more tumultuous start, although not necessarily by design. Despite the confluence in their ideological views, the new president and the parliament soon were in conflict over the cabinet composition. Ahmadinejad's nominations left almost no sitting ministers intact, in contrast to past precedent, and his attempt to install little-known bureaucrats in sensitive posts provoked parliamentary outrage. Like his predecessors, the president sought to surround himself with political allies, including a number of activists who had long-standing personal relationships with him, such as his adviser Mojtaba Samareh-Hashemi, whose association dates back to their university days, and Esfandiar Rahim Mashaei, who was related by marriage to the president and was initially given a tourism post.

The approach provoked an early power struggle with the parliament. Four separate nominations, and four full months, were required before the approval of a permanent oil minister, and even then Ahmadinejad was forced to settle for the official who had assumed caretaker responsibilities during the process. Each prior bid was rebuffed by a parliament dominated by conservatives, who resented his apparent disregard for such a critical industry. His ultimate choice, Kazem Vaziri-Hamaneh, served for a tumultuous two years until Ahmadinejad managed to force him out. The Oil Ministry ranked high on the president's priority list – after all, the central themes in the campaign involved the mass distribution of oil revenues and the eradication of what Ahmadinejad described as the "oil mafia." In 2011, Ahmadinejad sought to install himself as caretaker oil minister, a move that prompted protests and a demand for an inquiry by members of parliament.

It might be tempting to ascribe these difficulties to Ahmadinejad's inexperience at the upper echelons of decision making in the Islamic Republic. However, the ministerial selection drama would recur on several subsequent occasions, suggesting at least the possibility that these were calculated gambits to assert his authority vis-à-vis the Majlis, and vice versa. If that is the case, the outcomes were likely unsatisfactory to both sides – Ahmadinejad was repeatedly forced to accept the mandate of the Majlis, and the parliament experienced pushback as well. As with the early debate on the pick for oil minister, the issue of credentials proved to be a recurrent point of contention between the parliament and the president. Several of his ministerial nods, including one of his key allies, Vice President Mohammadreza Rahimi, were revealed to have faked their educational pedigrees, and an education minister was accused of plagiarism. The scandal underscores the extent to which ideological competition has only further the rationalization of the revolution; an advanced degree is now a prerequisite for any senior position in Iran, to the extent that degree mills and forged credentials have become an almost predictable scandal for Iranian presidents.[24]

"THE THIRD REVOLUTION"

Shortly before his inauguration, Ahmadinejad declared his victory to be the "third revolution" – the first two corresponding to the eviction of the shah and the seizure of the U.S. Embassy. A prominent dimension of this "revolution" were the president's efforts to associate himself directly with the distribution of state resources, whether through his peripatetic predilection for all-cabinet road trips or his solicitation of personal appeals for state largesse, which began even before his inauguration.[25] Consistent with his populist campaign, Ahmadinejad ordered the publication of his office telephone number and e-mail address to expedite

[24] The political analyst Sadeq Zibakalam describes this as "one of the main reasons for our underdevelopment" and chronicles a litany of analogous incidents. "Kordan – Convicted or Unjustly Accused?" *Kargozaran*, October 18, 2008.

[25] Michael Slackman, "The Guy up the Alley? Just a Neighbor. Chats, Gives Parties. Will Be Running Iran," *New York Times*, July 2, 2005.

direct receipt of individual petitions. (Like so many Ahmadinejad gambits, this backfired, snarling the phone lines for months.) His assiduous regional politicking was unprecedented in Iran, where national politics typically focus on the capital and, to a lesser extent, the religious leadership in Qom. It was patrimonial politics, and by the end of his second term, the president had visited many of Iran's thirty-one provinces as many as four times each to assemble a network of support outside Tehran – not an unwise strategy, given the obstacles he faced among the political establishment.

The provincial trips represented the tip of the iceberg of Ahmadinejad's freewheeling spending. Because he had assumed the presidency near the peak of the global oil price spike, his administration had no experience with austerity. And, as with the provincial trips, the president favored personally branded initiatives that conveyed direct individual benefits. Among his trademark initiatives were the Imam Reza Love Fund and the Mehr Housing Project. Both were widely caricatured as vanity projects; yet each addressed a high-priority social issue, the viability of youth transitions to adulthood and the unavailability of sufficient affordable urban housing. The Mehr Housing initiative consisted of a $10 billion loan fund to facilitate the construction of affordable residential units for first-time buyers on unutilized land. However, irrespective of their merits, the implementation of these initiatives elicited powerful criticism on the grounds that they did not serve their target populations effectively.[26] Others have suggested that these large infusions into the economy exacerbated inflation by contributing to the rapid expansion of liquidity, which by 2013 was at least seven times higher than at the start of Ahmadinejad's first term.

The issue of government spending is one that looms large in any review of the economic debates of the Ahmadinejad era. More than $700 billion in oil revenues accrued to Tehran during the president's first term alone. Initially, his expansive approach to the national purse appeared to command broad political support, even in the parliament, whose conservative majority was predominantly skeptical of the neophyte president. Instead, the primacy locus of opposition, somewhat surprisingly, was Ahmadinejad's cabinet. His first appointee as governor of the Central Bank, Ibrahim Sheybani, resigned in protest after the president insisted on cutting interest rates well below the rate of inflation. In Danesh Jafari's

---

[26] Kamal Ettehari, "Promises of Controlling the Housing Market," *Etemad*, April 6, 2013.

April 2008 resignation speech, the minister broke down in tears while lambasting Ahmadinejad's handling of the economy – particularly policies that stoked inflation to near 20 percent. "During my time, there was no positive attitude towards previous experiences or experienced people and there was no plan for the future," Danesh Jafari blasted.[27]

The resignations over Ahmadinejad's fiscal policies were representative of a broader cycle of bureaucratic instability and unprecedented turnover at the highest levels of the government. Sheybani's replacement, Tahmasseb Mazaheri, lasted only a year in the post before Ahmadinejad fired him, once again in a dispute over interest rates, spending, and Central Bank autonomy. During his two terms in office, at least four individuals cycled through the post of deputy governor for foreign exchange matters. His first foreign minister, the career diplomat Manouchehr Mottaki, was dismissed while on an official trip to Senegal in 2010. Of all the principal officials who entered office with Ahmadinejad's 2005 election, none – save the president himself – remained by the end of his second term. One of the implications of this institutional competition for authority was a fiercer, faster, more dynamic power struggle among the political elites. Many of the individuals who were elevated to ministerial slots and later thrust aside by Ahmadinejad emerged as vocal critics of his policies: Mazaheri, former foreign minister Mottaki, former economy minister Danesh Jafari, and nuclear negotiator-cum-parliamentary speaker Ali Larijani.

Ahmadinejad's economic policies and rhetoric generated a steady stream of opposition from across the political spectrum within Iran, including, as already noted, from within his own cabinet. On four occasions, he was the recipient of open letters from Iranian economists, who wrote in excruciating detail about the irrationality and counterproductive dimensions of Ahmadinejad's policies.[28] The economists' letters were the tip of the iceberg; In January 2007, 150 members of parliament published a similarly devastating critique. This was consistent with the undercurrent of hostility toward Ahmadinejad that was evident within the parliament from the outset and deepened as a result of acrimonious tussles over almost every aspect of his economic policy. Gholamali Mesbahi Moqqadam, then-chairman of the Majlis Economics Commission and a former spokesperson for the conservative clerical association,

[27] "Ahmadinejad under Fire on Economy," *BBC*, April 23, 2008.
[28] Letters were published in 2006, 2007, 2008, and most recently 2013. See http://www.ilna.ir/news/news.cfm?id=50213

stated that "however infuriated I became and however much I shouted when I looked at the budget bill for 1385 [2007], they did not listen and they said we have no inflation. Now also the government says whatever has happened is because of imports using foreign currency. I swear to God this is not right." Mesbahi Moqqadam added for dramatic flourish that his rage was so intense that he was afraid he would die on the floor of the parliament: "I recited my articles of faith because I am a Muslim and I believe in the Islamic Republic and also in the government of Ahmadinejad. I want to help this government so that it does not create inflation."[29]

In addition to the substantive critiques, Ahmadinejad became the subject of derision among ordinary Iranians even as he retained the confidence of the system and the supreme leader. In 2008, a journalist at a reformist newspaper offered this anecdote about shopping in a nearby supermarket:

When I asked the shopkeeper to give me tissues, he asked whether I want the Iranian brand or imported ones. I asked: "Do we import tissues too?" He said as a matter of fact at the moment they didn't have the Iranian brand, but only the exported one. I looked at it carefully and saw that it was made in Germany. So that's where the oil revenues go! I bought a box and went home. After the dinner when I was wiping the table with the tissue I actually saw the oil income on my table! The oil revenue is spent on importation.[30]

In typically Iranian fashion, humor was used to deflect the profound popular frustration and sense of disempowerment.

LABOR LAW REFORM

Even as his policies were primarily populist in nature, Ahmadinejad also sought to address some of the long-standing distortions in the Iranian economy, including the question of subsidies and the problems with the 1990 Labor Law. In 2006, Ahmadinejad attempted to amend the Labor Law, which was widely recognized since its inception as overly rigid. Then–Labor Minister Mohammad Jahromi argued that the amendment would enhance productivity, allowing employers to dismiss permanent workers without penalty by paying sizable

---

[29] "Majlis Approves the Government Withdrawal of 45 Thousand Billion Rials from Foreign Exchange Reserve Fund," *Aftab-e Yazd*, June 30, 2008.

[30] Alireza Behdad, "Government Should Prevent Lavish Costs," *E'temad* web site on December 21, 2008.

severance fees.[31] Jahromi and his allies contended that the reforms would increase job security by encouraging job creation.[32]

However, the labor movement recoiled at the law's relaxation of constraints on firing workers. Further, the amendment permitted the payment of apprentice workers (during a period of up to three years) at only 70 percent of the minimum wage. MP Ali Reza Mahjub of Labor House also alleged that the proposal would enable employers at hundreds of firms that were in arrears in salary payments to fire any workers who complained about back pay.[33] He later argued that Labor Law reform would cost Iranian workers their most basic rights and allow employers to define minimum labor standards.[34] The government's own Social Security Organization (SSO) also opposed the move on the grounds that it would cause more than 4 million permanent workers to be laid off and create an unsustainable burden for the SSO itself.[35]

Labor unions, both sanctioned and illegal, mobilized opposition to the amendment via letters, statements, and demonstrations. An open letter penned by an assembly of unions accused Ahmadinejad of betraying revolutionary principles.

Is the government, the government of Islam, not the government of the deprived and the needy? Are the workers not under the shadow of pure Mohammedan Islam? Is this year not called the year of the great Prophet? Why do you let all these values be sacrificed for the sake of incorrect policies and the stubbornness of Labor Minister Dr. Jahromi? Was Mr. Jahromi appointed by and given the vote of confidence in the Majlis to suppress and annihilate the workers, or to serve the labor community, administer justice and equality, and establish job security and peace of mind for this noble layer of society?[36]

---

[31] "Social Security Organization: 4 Million Workers to Be Laid Off as Result of Implementation of Labor Law Amendment," *Kayhan*, September 13, 2006.

[32] "Labor Minister: Labor Law Reform Will Increase Job Security," *Fars News*, September 13, 2006, http://www.farsnews.net/newstext.php?nn=8506220305; "Chairman of the House of Industry: Labor Law Must Give Executives Management Security," *Fars News*, August 13, 2006. http://www.farsnews.net/newstext.php?nn=8505210606

[33] "Workers House General Secretary: Wages of 200,000 Workers Three to 50 Months Overdue," *Farhang-e Ashti*, November 1, 2006.

[34] "Ali Reza Mahjub Referring to Those Complaining about the Labor Law: They Want to Deprive the Workers of Their Minimum Rights," *Mardom-Salari*, October 1, 2007.

[35] "Social Security Organization: 4 Million Workers to Be Laid Off as Result of Implementation of Labor Law Amendment," *Kayhan*, September 13, 2006.

[36] "Letter of Islamic Labor Associations of Saveh to Ahmadinezhad: 'Labor Minister Has Endangered Workers' Job Security,'" *Mardom-Salari*, October 13, 2006.

Although Labor Law reform had been on previous presidents' agenda, Iranian moderates and reformists largely opted to side with their ideological allies in the labor movement.[37] Their stance was bolstered by the government's heavy-handed response to labor actions during this period. In December 2005, the independent workers' syndicate of Tehran's Vahed Bus Company launched labor stoppages to push for higher pay and protest the use of short-term contracts to dodge legally mandated worker protections.[38] The government responded with a crackdown that included hundreds of preemptive arrests and repeated arrests and charges of "acting against national security" for the union's leader, Mansour Ossanlu.[39]

Job creation remained sluggish as well, with less 800,000 jobs created annually, and youth unemployment that routinely ranked at twice the national average. These figures spoke to the persistence of unemployment, and the failure of successive governments to identify and implement successful job creation programs. The unemployment quandary also highlighted one of the fundamental underlying distortions of Iran's rentier economy, the conspicuous lack of connection between jobs and revenues because so much of Iran's revenue stream derived from its (low-labor) petroleum sector. As an Iranian economist noted, "Unemployment rates in 2006 (during [the] oil boom) were close to those in 1986 (at the height of the Iran-Iraq War and the lowest oil prices.)"[40]

DIVESTMENT THROUGH "JUSTICE"

One of the central planks in Ahmadinejad's economic policy was a renewed push for privatization. This initially was at the behest of the supreme leader, who in July 2006 mandated a plan to sell off 80 percent of all state-owned enterprises. The goal was the full privatization of all industries permissible under the Constitution by the end of the fourth Five-Year Plan – an anticipated total value of 1 quadrillion rials worth of

---

[37] "Why Strike?" *Kargozaran*, May 7, 2007; "The Right to Strike for the Workers," *Kargozaran*, May 7, 2007; Iranian Organization of Graduates. "Hammer on Trade Unions and Councils," *Etemad*, May 14, 2007.

[38] "Deputy Head of Tehran Bus Driver's Association Comments on Strike," *Iranian Labor News Agency (ILNA)*, December 25, 2005.

[39] "'You Can Detain Anyone for Anything': Iran's Broadening Clampdown on Independent Activists," *Human Rights Watch* 20:1 (January 2008), pp. 30–1.

[40] Zahra Kazimi, "Financing Job Guarantee Schemes by Oil Revenue: The Case of Iran," Levy Economics Institute of Bard College Working Paper No. 527 (January 2008), p. 6.

state firms.[41] Khamenei continued to play a direct role in prodding the process over subsequent years.

The privatization program was threatened by other reforms championed by Ahmadinejad. In 2007 and 2008, the president launched an initiative to create a system of interest-free banks, merging several state-owned banks, including Banks Tejarat, Saderat, and Mellat, with charitable loan funds (*qarz ol-hasaneh*). The government's plan was officially to merge, culminating in the establishment of the Mehr Iran interest-free bank, while other state-owned banks, such as Bank Sepah, would be turned into other interest-free banks. This led to discussion of shelving the privatization plans for the banks in question. Esma'il Gholami of the Iranian Privatization Organization explained, "With the banks becoming interest-free institutions, their privatization and inclusion in the list of bourse companies will no longer be possible, given that in such a case, no one will be prepared to buy the shares of interest-free banks."[42] According to Mehr Iran's Web site, the bank was eventually established by using capital from state banks, but the government opted to allow the banks themselves to remain intact.[43]

However, evidence suggests that much of the selling of state assets actually constituted a recycling through the network of public and semi-public institutions within Iran. Significant shares in six petrochemical and power plants were floated by the government directly to SATA (the Armed Forces Social Welfare Organization, a Revolutionary Guard–affiliated pension fund), prompting private sector criticism. Backlash halted a direct offering of another state entity, the International Conferences Organization, to the pension fund in 2010.[44] One of the most controversial cases took place in September 2009, when a majority share in the Telecommunications Company of Iran was sold – also through the IPO on the Tehran Stock Exchange – directly to Etemad-e Mobin, an IRGC-controlled consortium, with no competition. The value

---

[41] *Fars News Agency* (Persian), "Mohsen Rezai in Press Conference: 100 Thousand Billion Tomans of State Property Will Be Privatized and Distributed to the Public [Mohsen Rezai dar Jam'-e Khabarnegaran: 100 Hezar Milliard Toman az Malekiat-e Dolati beh Mardom va Bakhsh-Khosusi Vagozar Mishavad]," July 5, 2006 (14 Tir 1385), http://www.farsnews.net/newstext.php?nn=8504140273

[42] *Etemad*, "A Plan for a Revolution in the Banking System: Draft Plan for Transforming Eight Major State Banks to Interest-Free Banks," May 26, 2008, BBC Monitoring translation

[43] http://www.qmb.ir/AboutBank/History.aspx

[44] *Mehr News Agency* (English), April 9, 2010.

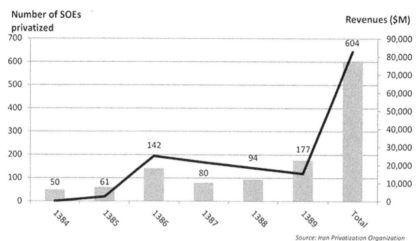

FIGURE 7.1. Privatization Activity during the Ahmadinejad Administration

of the sale was reported as high as nearly $8 billion (though elsewhere reported as $5 billion).[45] a record for a sale on the bourse. The noncompetitive nature of the sale revived public opposition, but the deal was finalized in November 2010 nonetheless.[46] One of the major beneficiaries was reportedly the Social Security Investment Company, which manages the assets of the Social Security Organization.

As the Figure 7.1 suggests, Ahmadinejad sought to advance his populist agenda through a revived and reconfigured effort at privatization. A new dimension of the privatization program during the Ahmadinejad era was the introduction of the "justice shares" program, which was intended to carry through on the president's electoral pledges of redistributing the benefits of Iran's oil rents. Low-income families and those with privileged status as a result of war service and other revolutionary credentials received shares in state-owned enterprises (SOEs), which ostensibly paid dividends from any SOE profits. By mid-2010, Ahmadinejad's minister of economics claimed that 49 million Iranians had registered, and 39 million had received shares.[47] Iranian officials defended the program as having achieved its redistributional aims, noting that

---

[45] Julian Borger and Robert Tait, "Financial Power: 'A Business Conglomerate with Guns' – How Militia Took Control of Economy," *Guardian*, February 16, 2010.

[46] *Country Commerce Select*, "Political/Commercial Background: State Role in the Economy," April 1, 2010.

[47] "Minster of Economics Came to Parliament: Report to Majles on Privatization," *Donya-ye Eqtesad*, August 22, 2010.

16 million of a total of 22 million rural Iranians received shares, and that a significant proportion of lower-income workers including taxi drivers and construction workers had participated as well.[48] The effect of the privatization program on poverty alleviation efforts is questionable – the scholar Kaveh Ehsani writes that the average value of shares received by the recipients was only approximately $220.[49]

Rafsanjani emerged early on as one of the most vocal critics of Ahmadinejad's handling of privatization, questioning his commitment to the program, the pace of progress, the heavy involvement of quasi-governmental firms in the bidding process for SOEs, and insufficient transparency and competition. In December 2008, Rafsanjani blasted the government's slow progress on privatization as the cause of Iran's lagging behind other nations in attracting foreign investment as well as a reason for capital flight out of Iran, asking, "Why can't Iran make use of the people's participation to build and administer the country, and why should Iran's capital assets be transferred to Dubai? Why can't Iran attract billions of Iranian nationals' capital?"[50]

After Khamenei's July 2006 decree, a *Siyasat-e Ruz* editorial prognosticated that the privatization scheme would not be successful for several domestic reasons: "In the current situation, the domestic private sector is not sufficiently talented to handle a huge part of Iran's economy through privatization. It is worrisome that certain figures with secret relations might make the best use of privatization. The government should pave the way for foreign investment and seriously think about investment by Iranians living abroad."[51] Other newspapers, including *Quds*, echoed the concern that well-connected individuals would corrupt privatization for their own goals.[52] Ali Akbar Nateq Nouri previously assailed Ahmadinejad's economic record for the same reason, saying, "We see that assets are transferred from an open to a shadow government."[53]

[48] "Minster of Economics Came to Parliament: Report to Majles on Privatization," *Donya-ye Eqtesad*, August 22, 2010.

[49] Kaveh Ehsani, "Survival through Dispossession: Privatization of Public Goods in the Islamic Republic," *Middle East Report* 250, Spring 2009, http://www.merip.org/mer/mer250/ehsani.html

[50] *Fars News Agency* (English), "Rafsanjani Criticizes Government Bodies for Not Implementing Article 44," December 11, 2008.

[51] *Siyasat-e Ruz*, July 11, 2006. Mideast Mirror translation accessed via Nexis.

[52] *Quds*, May 4, 2010.

[53] Ali Akbar Dareini, "Iranian Conservative Attacks President on Economy," *AP*, August 31, 2008.

In December 2007, Ahmadinejad blamed the lack of "necessary infrastructure" for the failure to implement the 3.5 trillion rials in budget-mandated privatization, implying that the stock exchange was not equipped for such a task. However, he expressed optimism that in the following year, three thousand companies would be privatized and argued for efforts to broaden the program's reach, saying, "By private we mean anyone who has the capability can come and set up a factory for example. We should not offer the factory to five people and then say the business has been privatized. This is not privatization."[54]

OFFICIAL OPACITY

The concerns about spending and skepticism about the real scope of the privatization program were linked to a broader systemic issue in evaluating Iran's economic conditions. Ahmadinejad's presidency compounded the long-standing opacity in Iran's economic decision making. In his defense, the debate over the timely release and reliability of government data did not originate with Ahmadinejad. The sociologist Charles Kurzman noted that "Iran has long suffered an overabundance of statistics," citing skeptical accounts of British and American diplomats toward Iranian official number crunching that stretched back as far as 1848.[55] The challenges to acquiring credible data on Iran's economic predicament have been exacerbated by questionable approaches to the task itself. In 1998, the prominent economist Ali Rashidi complained that distortion of statistics had undercut Rafsanjani's capacity to address Iran's real problems during the reconstruction era and called on Khatami's government to adopt a more realistic and honest approach to the release of information.[56] The intensification of the internal factional struggle only further degraded the clarity of Iranian economic data by intensifying the inevitable temptation to manipulate data for partisan advantage. In 2005, the surveys for assessing employment data were revised ostensibly to adhere to International Labor Organization standards; since that time, employment figures have broadened to include a mere hour per week of

---

[54] *BBC Monitoring Middle East*, "Banking Sector Main Cause of Liquidity not Government – Iran President," December 18, 2007.

[55] Kurzman (2004), p. 96.

[56] Mohsen Shemshiri, Interview with Dr. Ali Rashidi, *Mobin* 316 (May 16, 1998), pp. 1, 4. Rashidi continued his criticism of Iranian policies and politics and was imprisoned during Ahmadinejad's second term, after the release of a petition by the revived National Front, which bore his signature among others.

work, as well as those individuals engaged in unpaid domestic labor and full-time study.[57]

And yet even by Iran's own historical standards, the aversion toward both the investigation and the dissemination of economic statistics during this period was striking, precisely because of the president's association with this very issue. The increasing secrecy surrounding economic data became a source of considerable consternation about the system itself, with routine denunciations in even the progovernment press of the constraints placed upon the Central Bank and other state institutions for data release. Ahmadinejad and his backers insisted that any irregularities were the responsibility of other institutions, notably those with which the president had had strained relations.

The unwillingness to disseminate accurate data on the state of the economy paralleled a broader evisceration of the Islamic Republic's capacity for economic planning and projections. As part of his first cabinet, Ahmadinejad named Farhad Rahbar to head the Management and Planning Organization (MPO), but little more than a year into his first term the president ordered the seconding of MPO provincial offices to the local governors, who in turn reported to the Interior Ministry. The move prompted numerous resignations, which coincided with the departure of longtime oil sector technocrats (including the former UN ambassador Mohammad Hadi Nejad-Husaynian), as well as many others across the state bureaucracy. During this same period, Ahmadinejad dissolved the Money and Credit Council, the government body charged with devising monetary policy, as part of a broader clash with government bankers over interest rates, lending policy, and inflation.

The disdain for bureaucratic hierarchy and the disinterest in transparency compounded Tehran's difficulties in managing the relatively short-lived economic hiccoughs that the country experienced during Ahmadinejad's first term in 2008 when the U.S. credit crunch rocked the world economy, and oil prices collapsed almost overnight. At the outset, many Iranian officials saw the global recession as evidence of divine retribution against its adversaries. In October 2008, Mahmoud Dehghani, a Majlis representative, publicly described the economic crisis facing America and the Western world as divine punishment against the oppressive behavior of the West toward the Islamic Republic as well as Palestine, Afghanistan, Lebanon, and Iraq. "The West wanted to

---

[57] "A Selection of Labor Force Survey Results, the Year 1390," Statistical Centre of Iran, p. 3, http://www.amar.org.ir/Portals/1/Files/labor-force-1390.pdf

create a crisis for the revolution and the nation of the Islamic Republic of Iran, but as it is a divine promise that the oppression of the oppressor returns to himself, today a type of crisis, specifically the economic type, has latched onto the West," he said.[58] Others including Ahmadinejad saw the slowdown in more opportunistic fashion, suggesting that Iran's minimal integration in the global economy was a distinct advantage that could attract potential investors.[59] As the oil prices dropped from a high of $147 per barrel to below $40, regime stalwarts such as Hassan Rouhani warned that "this is just like us rejoicing when the house of our neighbor is on fire because he is our enemy, ignoring the fact that the flame of that fire will spread to the house of others, as well as to our own house." Rouhani's prediction proved accurate, and Iran was forced to scramble as its revenues fell dramatically in mid-2008.

The 2008 chaos prompted new debate over the lack of clarity in the national budget and the lack of discipline in respecting institutional checks and balances, in particular those surrounding the Oil Stabilization Fund (OSF). After its establishment by the Khatami administration to facilitate long-term savings and insulate Iran from revenue volatility, the fund was repeatedly raided by the government as well as by the parliament. The off-books use of the fund only intensified during the Ahmadinejad years, despite the historic oil revenues throughout most of this period.[60] Much of the unsanctioned spending appears to have been directed toward infrastructure projects and other pet projects of particular interest to Ahmadinejad and other influential elements of the regime. Among many other reported uses of the funds were $500 million in 2006/7 to renovate Iran's public rail and air transport fleet,[61] $1 billion in 2006 for projects in the western border provinces aimed at "the reconstruction of Iraq,"[62] $4.7 billion withdrawn in mid-2007,

---

[58] *Javan Daily*, "Bohran Eqtesadi-ye Qarb Mosdaq-e Tahaqqoq-e Vedehha-ye Alhi Ast [The Western Economic Crisis Is Evidence of the Realization of Divine Promises]," 28 Mehr 1387, October 19, 2008, http://www.javannewspaper.com/1387/870728/dakheli.htm#s430677

[59] "India, Iran Broaden Prospects for Trade," *IRNA*, October 17, 2008.

[60] IMF. "Islamic Republic of Iran: Selected Issues," August 2008, IMF Country Report No. 08/285, http://www.imf.org/external/pubs/ft/scr/2008/cr08285.pdf, table III.2.

[61] Central Bank of the Islamic Republic of Iran [Bank Markazi Jomhouri Islami Iran]. Annual Review: 1385 (2006/07), English Available at http://www.cbi.ir/page/4848.aspx, p. 14

[62] *BBC Monitoring Middle East*. "Iran Allocates 1bn Dollars to Western Provinces to Help Reconstruct Iraq," November 19, 2006.

mainly for government construction projects,[63] approximately $1 billion for an infrastructural project to deliver gas to villages.[64] In 2009, the fund reportedly disbursed $1 billion to Iran's Revolutionary Guard Corps (IRGC) to help fund projects that the IRGC's construction wing had been awarded in the development of the South Pars gas reservoir. Revenue Watch, an international organization that promotes transparency, estimated that at least $150 billion was withdrawn between 2006 and 2011 "without clear economic justification" and that an estimated $36 billion in additional revenues should have been deposited in the OSF but did not appear in government reporting.[65]

In May 2008, the fund was reconfigured, its governing board dissolved, and the Government Economic Committee put in charge of oversight of the new fund, which in early 2009 was renamed the National Development Fund.[66] This was a move first proposed during the Khatami presidency; its advocates then were technocrats in the oil sector who were seeking more reliable streams of revenue for massive infrastructure projects. Under Iran's fifth Five-Year Plan, which runs from 2011 to 2016, 23 percent of all oil and gas revenues were to be directed toward the fund, with that proportion increasing to 32 percent by the plan's conclusion. The new fund was not intended for budget support; however, the crisis atmosphere introduced by sanctions' intensification and Tehran's enduring unfamiliarity with budget discipline raise doubts about the durability of any newfound insulation for the state's windfall revenues.

The habitual raiding of the reserve fund has generated considerable debate over the years. In 2008, Musa Ali-Reza Servati, then-member of the Majlis Budget and Planning Commission, publicly deplored the paltry balance of $7 billion, just as the oil boom hit its peak. He was rebutted by the commission's deputy chair, Asghar Geranmayeh-Pour, who insisted that the fund's balance was $25 million.[67] Prior to his 2013 election to the presidency, Hassan Rouhani excoriated Ahmadinejad's government for its reliance on high oil prices, noting $45 billion in withdrawals during

---

[63] *BBC Monitoring Middle East.* "Iran Spends 4.7b Dollars from Oil Savings Fund," September 19, 2007.

[64] *Fars News Agency* (Persian). "A Justification for the Withdrawal of 950 Billion Tomans from the Oil Stabilization Fund Has Been Offered," 26 Mehr 1387, October 17, 2008, http://www.farsnews.net/newstext.php?nn=8707260008

[65] Heuty (February 2012), p. 1.

[66] IMF. "Islamic Republic of Iran: Selected Issues," August 2008, IMF Country Report No. 08/285, http://www.imf.org/external/pubs/ft/scr/2008/cr08285.pdf, p. 39.

[67] *MEES*, March 11, 2008; *MEES*, June 10, 2009.

Ahmadinejad's first three years in office, much of it to cover budget deficits, in violation of the guidelines of the law.[68] The former president Rafsanjani has also bemoaned the weak controls, arguing that a more robust reserve fund would help Iran weather the "economic tsunami" facing the world.[69] However, as Iranian institutions have themselves noted, the responsibility lies not simply with the president and the executive branch, but more broadly with the parliament as well. A 2008 audit critiquing the government's misuse of the fund also implicated the parliament for effectively granting approval to the executive branch for such liberal use of the reserve fund.[70] There were conflicting reports about the size of the fund at the end of the Ahmadinejad presidency; in late 2013, the former finance minister Seyyed Shamseddin Husayni and the former Central Bank governor Mahmoud Bahman rejected assertions that Ahmadinejad had left the government treasury empty, insisting that $32 billion remained in the fund.

THE RISE OF THE REVOLUTIONARY GUARDS

One of the most notable features of Ahmadinejad's tenure was the ascendance of the Revolutionary Guard. In many respects, this should be considered neither surprising nor new. Iran's armed forces have represented a high priority for all contemporary Iranian leaders, and in the prerevolutionary expansion of the state and defense spending, the military assumed a prominent role in the industrial sector through massive investments in defense-related industries. Even during the monarchy, the military's role in the economy extended to the financial sector, through the establishment of Bank Sepah and cooperative organizations for servicemen, as well as development activities, with the creation of the Literacy and Health Corps under the auspices of the Pahlavi military.[71]

For Iran's hard-liners, the more recent expansion of the Guards' economic activities represented a new chapter in the defense of Iran and the revolution against enemy plots, with sanctions replacing Saddam

---

[68] "Rouhani: Taking from the Foreign Exchange Reserves Has Always Been Tempting," *Tabnak*, October 20, 2008, http://tabnak.ir/pages/?cid=22312

[69] *BBC Monitoring Middle East.* "Iran's Rafsanjani Expresses Concern over 'Drastic Slump' in Oil Prices," October 24, 2008.

[70] "Head of State Inspectorate Calls Government Forex Reserve Withdrawals Lawful," *Javan*, November 17, 2008.

[71] Robert E. Looney, "The Role of Military Expenditures in Pre-Revolutionary Iran's Economic Decline," *Iranian Studies* 21(3–4): 1988, p. 54.

Hussein as the American instrument.[72] As described in Chapter 5, the economic role of the IRGC began in earnest during the postwar period, and has since expanded to incorporate hundreds of subsidiary firms. The largest affiliate engaged with the economy is its engineering arm, Gharargah Sazandegi Khatam al Anbia, often referenced by the shorthand "Khatam al-Anbia" or alternatively by its acronym, GHORB. According to its own Web site, Khatam al-Anbia has been awarded more than 750 construction contracts and 150 technical consulting projects over its entire life span; the firm claims to employ approximately twenty-five thousand engineers and staff.[73] According to a Fars News report in early 2008, the company had carried out more than fifteen hundred projects nationwide,[74] and some estimates put the firm's employment at forty thousand.[75]

Khatam al-Anbia's director, Abdolreza Abed, insisted that the firm's construction activities are kept "completely separate" from the IRGC's military activities; he added that 90 percent of Khatam's workers were non-IRGC subcontractors.[76] However, some profits of Khatam al-Anbia are used to support defense projects of the IRGC.[77] Khatam al-Anbia is still heavily infused with revolutionary rhetoric. It has representation from the office of the supreme leader, which ensures a prominent ideological bent to the public face of the organization.

Contracts awarded to Khatam al-Anbia and its subsidiaries during Ahmadinejad's presidency included construction of a line of the Tehran Metro, construction of several lines of the Tabriz metro, part of the Tehran-Tabriz railway, infrastructure and shipping capabilities for the South Pars gas field, numerous dams, expansion of the Shahid Beheshti port at Chabahar, and a no-bid $1.3 billion nine hundred kilometer gas pipeline from the South Pars shore base at Assaluyeh to Iranshahr in the province of Sistan and Baluchestan.[78] Khatam al-Anbia became very active in energy exploitation as well, having been awarded

---

[72] Abbas Haji-Najjari, "The IRGC in the Balance of the System's Authority," *Javan*, June 25, 2012.

[73] Wehrey et al., *op. cit.*, p. 60.

[74] *BBC Monitoring Middle East – Political.* "Iranian News Agency Reports New Appointment in Islamic Revolution Guards Corps," January 14, 2008.

[75] Abbas William Samii, "The Guards Run the Show in Iran," *Christian Science Monitor*, October 5, 2007.

[76] Wehrey et al., *op. cit.*, p. 63; Reza Zandi, "Corps' Engagement in Economic Contracts," *Sharq*, June 26, 2006.

[77] Reza Zandi, "Corps' Engagement in Economic Contracts," *Sharq*, June 26, 2006.

[78] Wehrey et al., *op. cit.*, p. 61.

projects by the government such as a no-bid \$2.1 billion contract for the development of Phases 15 and 16 of South Pars. Khatam al-Anbia was selected among six firms to participate in a thirteen-month-long project to find "appropriate locations" for the construction of new nuclear power plants.[79]

At least some proportion of the Guards' economic activities is clandestine. During his time as Majlis speaker under Khatami, Mehdi Karrubi indirectly accused the force of operating sixty illegal jetties unsupervised by the government.[80] The Guard operates Payam Airport, located northwest of the capital, where multiple flights per day ferry smuggled goods as well as Iranian travelers.[81]

The IRGC's increasing activity in the economy prompted fierce debate within Iran, as well as intense scrutiny from other governments. Within Iran, critics asserted that Khatam al Anbia and other affiliates benefited from unfair advantages over the private sector; that their expanding role undermined privatization efforts and violated the Constitution; and that Ahmadinejad's administration spawned deeply problematic patterns that empowered military contractors while subverting civilian authority and debilitating the true private sector. Hassan Rouhani blasted the government for using privatization as a pretext for transferring government resources from other sectors into the military.[82]

Reformist newspapers including *Farhang-e Ashti, Etemad-e Melli*, and *Sharq* openly postulated that Ahmadinejad's factional preferences catalyzed the acceleration of the IRGC's extension into the economy.[83] Other critics charged that contracts were intended to buy the Guards' support for Ahmadinejad in the 2009 presidential election.[84] The former Tehran mayor Gholamhusayn Karbaschi lamented the Guards' seeming predominance, asserting that "some of the wealth that was formerly in governmental hands is now in the hands of those affiliated with the

---

[79] Aresu Eqbali. "Iran Picks Firms to Hunt for New Nuclear Plant Sites," *Agence France Presse*, August 19, 2008.

[80] Wehrey et al., p. 64.

[81] Mohammad Reza Farzanegan, "Illegal Trade in the Iranian Economy: Evidence from a Structural Model," CESIFO Working Paper No. 2397 (September 2008), p. 10.

[82] Nasser Etemadi "Qodrat-e Eqtesadi-ye Sepah-e Pasdaran. (The Revolutionary Guards' Economic Power.)" Radio France Internationale (Farsi), November 19, 2008. http://www.rfi.fr/actufa/articles/107/article_4366.asp

[83] BBC Monitoring International Reports. "IRAN PRESS Iranian Ministry Awards Economic Projects to Guards Corps," July 6, 2006.

[84] Alireza N. Haghighi and Victoria Tahmasebi. "The 'Velvet Revolution' of Iranian Puritan Hardliners," *International Journal* 61(4) (Autumn 2006), p. 959.

military. This means that economic power has bolstered the armed power of military affiliates." He described Ahmadinejad's economic policies as "militarization instead of privatization."[85] Reformist parliamentarians protested the no-bid contracts given to Khatam al-Anbia, particularly the South Pars deal and the offer of $2 billion in financing from the Oil Stabilization Fund, which was designed by law to facilitate loans solely to the private sector.[86]

Elsewhere, however, the Guards' economic role commanded influential support, based on claims of constitutionality, ideology, national security, and economic efficiency. The then-Oil Minister Kazem Vaziri-Hamaneh justified awarding the lucrative Assaluyeh-Iranshahr pipeline project to Khatam al-Anbia without a competitive bidding process, arguing that "holding a bid requires at least one year, and we had to work fast to implement this project and transport gas to deprived areas. Meanwhile, pipeline projects usually have a defined structure, and this is why, with the knowledge we have of the resources and equipment available to the Khatam ol-Anbiya Development Headquarters, we preferred to hand the job to them without holding a bid and by dispensing with formal procedures."[87] He was echoed by Mohsen Rezaei, a former Revolutionary Guard commander and an Ahmadinejad rival, who maintained that the Constitution stipulated the use of the military for development projects during peacetime, according to Rezaei, adding that "a large amount of the country's budget would be wasted if these institutions did not take part in the reconstruction of Iran."[88]

Guard commanders asserted that its subsidiaries' success was based solely on their ability to make the lowest bids on appropriate projects. Khatam al-Anbia's director Abed insisted that the organization's no-bid contract for the Assaluyeh-Iranshahr pipeline was awarded "because they have seen our work. We must have done something for them to be willing

[85] Roshanak Taghavi, "Iran Reformist Eyes Privatization Drive as Vote Looms," *Dow Jones Newswires*, June 11, 2009.

[86] Open Source Center. "Iran: Majles Minority Wing Questions No-Bid Deal for IRGC Developing South Pars," June 30, 2006. Translation of "The Minority Deputies Demand an Explanation from the President Regarding the Recent Economic Contracts Awarded by the Petroleum Ministry to the Revolution Guards – Objection to $7-Billion No-Bid Deal," *Sharq*, date unknown.

[87] "Oil Minister: The Latest Situation with Regard to Oil and Petrol Bourse Contracts," *Etemad-e Melli*, June 8, 2006.

[88] *BBC Monitoring Middle East – Political*. "Iran Guards Corps Economic Activities Questionable – Agency," July 6, 2006. Translation of report from *ILNA*, July 5, 2006.

to award us the contract without bidding."[89] Abed added that the IRGC's military activities and Khatam al-Anbia's construction projects were completely separate, and that the firm's patronage did not imply preferential bidding status. Of critics who accused Khatam al-Anbia of abusing its military power to secure contracts, he said, "They eventually learn that they were mistaken. We are contractors and we must observe our terms of contract. If we do not, we cannot last." He also dismissed the assertion that Ahmadinejad's election expanded the military's economic opportunities. Asked whether the corps had demanded its "share of the cake," he responded, "No, not at all. There is need. The government needs to do work. And it will employ anyone that can work. Not only the base [Khatam al-Anbia], but private contractors as well."[90]

Another military organization that expanded during the Ahmadinejad presidency was the Construction Basij, which was founded in 2000 as a summer youth employment program by the Construction Jihad (then a parastatal organization, since merged with the Agriculture Ministry) and the paramilitary Basij mobilization corps.[91] The then-President Khatami publicly extolled its establishment, calling the Construction Basij an example of "a greater cooperation among various government organizations and the Basijis" that "would benefit the system"[92] The Construction Basij frequently cooperated with Khatam al-Anbia on larger projects,[93] and as with the Guard affiliates, its mission was often intertwined with security objectives and preservation of the revolution.[94]

A law passed in January 2008 and ratified the following month called for the Construction Basij to be "the implementer for ... public and governmental plans that are approved by the Majlis" in line with article

[89] Zandi, *op. cit.*   [90] Zandi, *op. cit.*
[91] BBC Summary of World Broadcasts. "Ayatollah Khamene'i Calls for Unity in New Year Day Speech," March 24, 2001. Transcript of speech aired by Voice of the Islamic Republic of Iran on March 21, 2001.
[92] BBC Monitoring Middle East – Political. "Iran: President Khatami Addresses Commanders of Basij Resistance Force," November 29, 2000. Transcript of speech aired by Voice of the Islamic Republic of Iran Network 2 on November 27, 2000.
[93] Open Source Center. "Iran: Revolution Guards, Paramilitaries Carry Out Large Projects in Southeast," November 27, 2007. Transcript of broadcast on Vision of the Islamic Republic of Iran Sistan-Baluchestan Provincial TV on November 27, 2007.
[94] For example, a General Qorbannezhad, speaking on provincial TV in West Azerbaijan about the Construction Basij's work building 300 homes for the poor in the province, took the opportunity not only to highlight the group's infrastructure projects but also to stress "the need for border residents to be aware of criminals and counterrevolutionaries." "Iranian Paramilitary Units Build Homes for Poor in Northwestern Province." September 27, 2008.

147 of the Constitution. Government organizations were thus permitted to delegate projects for "quick-responding and low-cost" implementation to the Construction Basij, which was authorized to receive a set annual budget from the administration. The law also stipulated that, in order to have "necessary forces," the Construction Basij could each year take "a number" of conscripts performing their mandatory military service to supplement their volunteers and "Basij youngsters."[95]

Although the law passed by a large margin, it precipitated harsh criticism. Private sector groups, such as the Iranian Society of Consulting Engineers, argued that the law would damage their livelihood by taking projects away from them.[96] A reformist paper described the move as a government expansion and reversal of privatization efforts.[97] The parliamentarian Bijan Shahbazkhani argued that the law would give the Basij an unfair advantage against private firms, as it would be able to use its "cheap human and logistic resources" and lack of required Majlis oversight to submit low bids for government tenders.[98] The influential conservative parliamentarian Elias Naderan suggested the law would turn the Basij into an arm of the government and further the state's control of the economy.[99] Others, including the then–Majlis Speaker Gholam-Ali Haddad-Adel, rejected the criticism and dismissed concerns about the bill, saying, "This bill is so the Basij may compete for government contracts and have its own legal character . . . not that the government absorb it and assign all contracts to it."[100] Brigadier General Khorasani of the Construction Basij told reporters that the act would allow the group to undertake "limited" government projects and that it would be no threat to private contractors. Rather, he claimed that 70 percent of the organization's assignments entailed "helping young people to build and develop Islamic Iran, and its policy is to guide young talents in the private sector to develop Islamic Iran." He also rejected any assertions that the law infringed upon the Article 44 privatization efforts or that it granted unfair

---

[95] "President Sends New Construction Basij Law to Defense Ministry," *IRNA*, March 3, 2008. Translated by Open Source Center.

[96] "Iranian Society of Consulting Engineers: Entrusting Development Plans to Construction Basij Is Harmful," *Etemad-e Melli*, March 2, 2008.

[97] "Contradictions in the Popular Economy," *Etemad-e Melli*, January 26, 2008.

[98] "Iran MPs Pass New Basij Construction Law," *Tehran-e Emrooz*, January 22, 2008.

[99] "Naderan: Basij Hamchenan Basij Bemanad va Dolati Nashavad [Naderan: Let the Basij Remain the Basij as Is and Not Become Governmental]," *Islamic Consultative Majlis News Agency (Khaneh-ye Mellat)*, January 21, 2008. http://mellat.parliran.ir/News/Parliament/2008/1/14598/Default.aspx

[100] *Islamic Consultative Majlis News Agency*, op. cit.

advantages to the Basij, saying the militia group would have to go through the same tender process as private firms and that it was proffered no tax or insurance breaks by the government.[101] The then–IRGC commander Yahya Rahim-Safavi made similar assertions prior to the law's ratification, arguing that "some individuals and political groups may have a wrong and incorrect understanding of both Article 44 of the constitution and the Basij Construction. These two issues are completely separate from each other."[102] Still, the law appears to have facilitated a dramatic expansion in the role of the Construction Basij in undertaking government projects, which tripled in the first year after its passage.[103]

It is important to avoid oversimplifying the role of the military in the economy; the security services' economic activities derived from complex political motivations, and often their activities were exploited for factional advantage or diplomatic leverage. Some argued that public attention had tended to overstate the scope of the Guards' activities, suggesting that approximately two-thirds of the IRGC's engineering capabilities were deployed in activities directly related to the core defense mission of the Guard.[104] And after the 2013 presidential election, senior Iranian officials acknowledged that at least some of the high-profile contracts awarded to Khatam al-Anbia were just for show – an effort to bolster confidence in the economy as foreign investors retreated as a result of sanctions.

THE 2009 PRESIDENTIAL ELECTION AND ITS AFTERMATH

During his first four years in office, Ahmadinejad managed to polarize Iranians and much of the world as well by deftly deploying outrageous rhetoric on Israel and stoking nationalist opinion on the nuclear issue. His disdain for technocrats and reckless spending habits fueled record inflation and squandered the epic bounty of recent high oil prices, and his confrontational international approach undermined Iran's historic trade relationships and helped generate wider support for sanctions. As a result, the opportunity to block his second term attracted intense interest. After

[101] "Brig-Gen Khorasani: Construction Basij Authorities Revision Act No Cause for Private Sector's Concern," *Javan*, March 10, 2008.
[102] *BBC Monitoring Middle East – Political.* "Iranian Commander Says Guards Strategy Change Was Necessary," August 17, 2007.
[103] Esfandiar Sefari. "Three Thousand More Government Projects for the Basij," *Rooz*, July 1, 2008, http://www.roozonline.com/archives/2008/07/post_8098.php
[104] Zandi, *op. cit.*

much negotiation among the reformists, the former prime minister Mir Husayn Musavi emerged as his chief opponent, along with the former parliamentary speaker Mehdi Karrubi. Mohsen Rezaei filled out the field of officially approved candidates.

The campaign proved fierce and fascinating, particularly a series of live debates featuring dramatic accusations and an intense argument about the economy. Despite a relatively unassuming personality, Musavi assumed an outsized role in this drama. After a self-imposed withdrawal from political life, he seemed to relish his new opportunity, and his candidacy drew the vigorous backing of former president Khatami. Although he was relatively unknown among Iranian youth, Musavi's vibrant campaign appeared to energize cynical and disengaged voters. In the days before the ballot, his supporters formed a human chain that stretched for miles along Tehran's main avenue. They dubbed themselves the "Green Wave," surely stoking the existing paranoia among Iranian security forces, whose commanders were convinced that the reformists represented coconspirators in a Western plot to oust the revolution.

The other reform-oriented candidate, Mehdi Karrubi, was a septuagenarian cleric who had occupied some of the state's highest positions since the revolution but whose fourth-place finish in the 2005 presidential election had left him embittered. His debate exchanges with Ahmadinejad left the former parliamentary speaker, in the words of one journalist, "almost quivering with outrage" over the president's shameless misrepresentation of his economic track record. "Do you think I came from the desert, and that I don't know anything about figures?" Karrubi demanded.[105]

After such a buildup, the election outcome came surprisingly quickly and gave the embattled Ahmadinejad a landslide victory for a second term. The tally reinforced the conviction among his rivals, and among many others, that Ahmadinejad's win was achieved through heavy-handed rigging. The president retained a considerable constituency, thanks to his copious distribution of Iran's oil revenues as well as his strident nationalism and indignant denunciation of corruption. But the margin and other factors defied credulity. Musavi and Karrubi rejected the official vote tally, and its certification by Khamenei, and called their supporters into the streets. Days of mass protests in Tehran and other major Iranian cities were suppressed only by a massive show of official

---

[105] Robert F. Worth, "As Iran Gets Ready to Vote, Economy Dominates," *New York Times*, June 10, 2009, p. A6.

force, and for at least the six months subsequent to the ballot, Iran remained rocked by periodic protests, turmoil, and an acceleration of the decades-old brain drain.

The upheaval compounded the ongoing challenges confronting Iran's economy and further polarized long-standing divisions over economic policy. The scenes of street protests and the regime's violent response catalyzed world opinion and dramatically transformed Europe's posture toward Tehran. The events reinforced foreign investors' concerns about political and reputational risk, consistently with the drumbeat of U.S. government efforts to persuade international firms to exit the Iranian market voluntarily. The alienation of regime stalwarts including Hashemi Rafsanjani, whose influential offspring were first forced into exile and later imprisoned, raised questions about the Islamic Republic's long-term viability and strengthened the resolve of states, including those in the Gulf, that had historically hedged on Iran. And even though the system proved more than capable of riding out the storm, the unrest and the violent response stripped Ahmadinejad of his revolutionary appeal. The elections may have given him the veneer of a popular mandate, but the aftermath left him more vulnerable to elite rivalries and left Iran more isolated in the world.

In this respect, the deterioration of Iran's domestic political dynamics paralleled and exacerbated a simultaneous erosion of its international standing. The election outrage was compounded by the unease over Iran's role in Iraq, the intensifying nuclear dispute, and Iran's evident indifference to international norms, as evidenced by episodes such as the seizures of British sailors in 2007 and 2009 and the November 2011 attack on the British Embassy in Tehran.

As Iran's internal politics deteriorated, its nuclear diplomacy became increasingly erratic. In October 2009, Iranian negotiators agreed to a fuel swap for its medical research reactor, which would have resulted in the export of most of its low-enriched uranium stockpile. The bargain was proffered by Washington in hopes of jump-starting a sustained process of negotiations to resolve the crisis. However, after the agreement became public in Iran, criticism of its terms erupted, and Iranian officials began repudiating the bargain. The demise of the deal, and its timing on the heels of the violent repression of street protests and elite challengers, consolidated support in Washington and elsewhere for ratcheting up economic pressure on Tehran in hopes of incentivizing negotiations. That strategy proved extraordinarily successful in sustaining an international coalition to disrupt Iran's economy.

SUBSIDY REFORM PROGRAM

Iran's leadership recognized the looming threat of intensified sanctions and their foresight precipitated a bold step to address one of the system's most profound vulnerabilities, its reliance on imported gasoline and other refined petroleum products. Remarkably, given the fresh memories of widespread internal unrest, Ahmadinejad opened his second term in 2009 by launching a massive new effort to address a costly distortion that his predecessors had failed to tame. The cost of underwriting absurdly low prices for energy and other staple goods – with direct costs estimated at about $100 billion per year – was long seen as seriously inefficient. The misleading price signals had helped Iran's domestic energy consumption grow faster than that of almost any country on the planet, with massive associated waste – approximately 30 percent of subsidized bread was either thrown away or smuggled out of the country.

The objective of rationalizing subsidies on wheat, bread, gasoline, and other consumer goods had been incorporated in the 2004 fourth Five-Year Plan, but resistance to price increases remained quite powerful, particularly in the parliament. In 2007, Tehran began rationing gasoline by limiting drivers to 120 liters per month, and this process served as a precursor for the broader subsidy reform program three years later. The basis of the plan was income-tested individual payments as a mechanism for offsetting the impact of the staged rationalization of prices.

In 2008, Ahmadinejad launched a public campaign around the plan, which immediately sparked resistance from conservative power brokers, including the Majlis economics commission chairman, Gholamreza Mesbahi-Moqaddam, and Ahmad Tavakkoli, chief of the Majlis Research Center.[106] "I do not know on what basis the president has promised to pay the money," Mesbahi Moqqadam remarked in October 2008. "Does the president have some money the Majlis is unaware of? Why doesn't he pay his debt to the staff of the Education Ministry? Why doesn't he pay his debt to the banks? Why doesn't he pay his debts to the Central Bank?" Fierce parliamentary opposition remained a constant feature of the political landscape for the planning, implementation, and revision of the subsidy reform program, overcome only by the

---

[106] "Where Will the $32 Billion Come From?" Mohammad Sadeq Jenansaft, *Donya-e Eqtesad*, Persian, October 9, 08, http://www.donya-e-eqtesad.com/Default_view.asp?@=125649; "Ahmadinejad: Direct Subsidy Plan Set to Begin," *Fars News*, English, October 9, 2008, http://english.farsnews.com/newstext.php?nn=8707180671

supreme leader's explicit support for the initiative. The dichotomy in the conservatives' political imperatives complicated and intensified the debate and exacerbated hostilities between the president and the Majlis.

From the outset, the divisions centered on several elements of the proposed reform plan: the size of the preliminary phase, the locus of authority for funds dispersal (the Majlis or the executive branch); and the mechanics of assessing income eligibility for payments intended to offset price increases. Ultimately, these disputes reflected the traditionalists' deep-seated mistrust of Ahmadinejad, and their preference for shrinking presidential authority in favor of the parliament's prerogatives. In a 2009 speech intended to promote his reelection prospects, Ahmadinejad highlighted subsidy reform as a key aspect of his agenda:

God almighty has provided us with huge resources for man's survival, for his evolution and for the comfort of society. Huge natural resources, mines, seas, fuel and fossil energy are among the blessings and sources that the God Almighty has given us. These resources belong to all citizens; they belong to successive generations. They belong to future generations. The right and appropriate usage of these resources is the duty of the Islamic state and of every individual. Nobody has the right to invade these resources or use them in a way that is against justice and against the national interest. No one has the right to waste or destroy these resources. Nobody has the right to allocate these resources to inappropriate consumption. . . . My dear friends, it is an absolute obligation for the government and the individuals to make sure that national resources are protected and properly used.[107]

In 2010, a compromise was struck, restricting the program cost to $20 billion but according the president decision-making authority over spending and implementation.[108] The program was also expanded and simplified to provide modest cash payments to every Iranian household. A test of the distribution system for cash payouts began in late May in Ilam, North Khorasan, and Gilan. After a prolonged, acrimonious battle in the Iranian parliament, the targeted subsidies plan was formally launched in December 2010. Early steps included quadrupling the price of gasoline as well as a range of other goods. As part of a massive public education campaign, the government had distributed payments worth at the time approximately seventy-seven dollars to each Iranian household several months earlier, deposited in bank accounts that were locked until

[107] Speech in Isfahan, Islamic Republic of Iran Network Television, from World News Connection, April 8, 2009.
[108] "End of the Economist Sheikh's Day of Silence," *Khabar Online*, May 17, 2010, http://www.khabaronline.ir/news-62308.aspx

the price increases were implemented. Whether cowed by threats or convinced by the prolonged public debate, the program launch initially proceeded more smoothly than expected. There were a variety of small-scale problems, particularly as cash payments were based on voluntary household surveys. However, during the early months, data suggested substantial declines in consumption of electricity and gasoline. And there were inadvertent benefits: Use of Tehran's anemic public transportation system boomed. The banking sector rushed to attract new clients. And anecdotal reports suggested that initial payouts helped stimulate investment in small-scale entrepreneurship.

Although the reforms were plagued with inefficiencies and contradictions from the outset, the lack of violence during the initial phase refuted the worst fears of many Iranian politicians and observers alike. The program won plaudits from the International Monetary Fund and others, even as conservatives and reformists in the parliament maintained a barrage of criticism. Universalizing the program proved an effective strategy for selling the reform program, but one that raised the cost and intensified the enmity toward Ahmadinejad. "Paying allowance to individuals and families will not resolve the country's economic problems and the problems we have in production. After a while, this [practice] might even turn into huge economic problems such as spread of unemployment and laziness."[109] Still, the program's launch occurred as economic and political grievances prompted intensified turmoil and popular activism across the region, and the payments briefly may have helped insulate Iran from the unrest that beset other Middle Eastern states.

And yet as sanctions pressure mounted, the regime launched an informal campaign to persuade middle- and higher-income Iranians to forgo their monthly payouts. The same factors persuaded the government to delay the second phase of the subsidy reforms. The program was blamed by a number of officials for exacerbating Iran's rampant inflation levels, which rose to rates among the highest in the world. Moreover, the collapse of the currency as a result of the 2012 U.S. and European banking restrictions dramatically shrank the effective value of the payout – from forty-five dollars per person per month at the 2010 outset to an estimated fifteen dollars by mid-2013. Ahmadinejad launched a voluble campaign to raise the monthly payments to 250,000 rials, but his opponents in the Majlis accused him of electoral manipulation.

---

[109] *Fars News Agency*, May 2, 2012.

The parliament remained a source of severe criticism, and the main grievance seemed to focus on the program's failure to resolve the underlying distortions in the Iranian market. The former economics minister Danesh Jafari noted that even as the reform program began to reshape consumer behavior, the government had not made sufficient efforts to boost industrial production. "In economic theory, when the price of essential for production goes up, the overall prices go up and consequently production levels come down. With the implementation of the subsidy reforms, we face lower production, which means recession, unemployment, and higher overall prices. But this was not the goal of this project. How do we get out of this situation?... we have to have a plan to increase production."[110] The government fought back against accusations that the reform stoked disastrous inflation. Economics Minister Shamseddin Husayni retorted, "Over these years that we've been giving excessive subsidies to energy and other sectors, has inflation been under control? Definitively, the answer is no."[111]

ARAB SPRING AND NUCLEAR WINTER

Even as the revolutionary state was struggling to manage epic internal political and economic challenges, Tehran found itself suddenly confronted with massive and unexpected regional flux. A popular movement instigated by the actions of a single frustrated young Tunisian managed to ignite the long-frozen politics of the region, quickly dethroning the seemingly unshakable autocrats who ruled Tunisia and Egypt and inflaming brittle tribal states in Yemen, Libya, and Syria. Elsewhere across the Arab world, popular agitation and a profound sense of uncertainty about the future became the order of the day. After a flutter of activism in Tehran that was quickly dispersed by the most modest show of the regime's repressive capabilities, Iran's leaders settled into a satisfied role of opportunistic onlooker for several years. Perhaps unexpectedly to Western observers, who hoped that the loss of old Arab allies might be compensated by Iranian instability, the Arab spring did not infect the Islamic Republic, despite the fact that it was only two years after its own legitimacy appeared fatally compromised.

---

[110] "Finding a Solution for Better Production," *Donya-ye Eqtesad*, January 3, 2012.
[111] BBC Persian, "Beginning of Subsidy Targeting Trial in Three Provinces," May 15, 2010, http://www.bbc.co.uk/persian/iran/2010/05/100515_l13_iran_subsidies_vid.shtml

For Iran's revolutionaries, the Arab uprisings were welcome; the initial Tunisian and Egyptian dynamics struck a chord with their own revolutionary experience in upending a seemingly stable American ally. And the brief ascendance of Islamist politics seemed to confirm Tehran's long-held theory that the Islamic Revolution would be replicated across the region. Moreover, Tehran's strategic interests initially were enhanced by the crisis, which put Washington freshly on the defensive and shattered the regional balance of power aligned against Iran. The implosion of a regional order that Iran implacably opposed was an unexpected windfall, without a single rial or any political capital expended. Just when Iran faced the prospect of full-fledged isolation, Arab unrest – and the undercurrent of mistrust for Washington – offered Tehran vital new inroads. The zero-sum logic of Iran's strategic competition with Washington meant that the weakening of U.S. capabilities and partnerships in the Middle East could only be a boon.

Of course, there was one nagging contradiction – Syria, which for decades had been the Persian theocracy's sole Arab ally, whose steady descent into a ferocious civil war threatened Tehran with the loss of its most reliable regional partner and its vital channel of access to Lebanon and the Levant. And it imposed real economic costs, in terms of significantly expanded military and economic support to the Syrian leader Bashar Al Assad. Iran maintained a contingent of Revolutionary Guards in Syria, and its security cooperation was always oriented toward mutual defense as well as deployment of force against civilian populations and joint support of terrorist groups such as Hezbollah and Hamas. Amid increasing attention surrounding the role of Al Qaeda–linked groups among the armed opponents of Damascus and Washington's unmistakable reluctance to intervene, Iranian leaders appeared confident that that they could maintain the upper hand in Syria vis-à-vis the West.

Regional insecurity precipitated by the Arab spring helped ratchet oil prices back up to $125 per barrel in 2013, and the persistence of tensions in the neighborhood mitigated against a repetition of the 2008 crash in oil prices. The prospect of a sustained $100 per barrel price band seemed to promise a substantial cushion against the creeping costs of Iran's estrangement from its traditional trade partners and the impact of unprecedented international economic sanctions adopted by the United Nations, the European Union, and other states in 2010.

This regional boost and corresponding revenue rebound helped strengthen Tehran's nerve in its dealings with the international community on the nuclear issue. Ahmadinejad's second term offered little evidence of diplomatic progress, despite the imposition of tough new sanctions. United Nations Security Council Resolution 1929, enacted in June 2010, opened the flood gates for a series of unilateral measures by the United States, the European Union, and a host of other countries restricting arms sales to Iran, further constraining Tehran's relationship with the international financial system, curtailing European energy investment in Iran, and blocking sales of refined petroleum products to Tehran. After the collapse of the October 2009 preliminary agreement that would have traded fuel for Tehran's research reactor for the export of most of Iran's low-enriched uranium, Washington and its allies turned their focus to intensifying the economic pressure on Tehran. Six months later, Washington dismissed an attempt by Iran, Turkey, and Brazil to resurrect the fuel swap arrangement in considerably watered-down form as a ploy to avert new Security Council penalties.[112]

CURRENCY CRISIS

In the absence of diplomatic movement, Washington and Europe sought to ratchet up sanctions in hopes that pressure would convince Tehran to accept curbs on its nuclear activities. A series of measures – detailed in Chapter 9 – began to create havoc for the Iranian economy, with dramatic impacts on Iran's oil exports and revenues, as well as a corresponding crisis for the value of the national currency.

Just as during previous periods, economic pressure prompted renewed factional conflict but also forced the reconsolidation of the regime's warring factions around a path forward. Khamenei declared 2011/12 to be the year of economic jihad and later described Iran's response to the sanctions as the elevation of "the economy of resistance." "Economy of resistance does not mean putting a fence around ourselves and taking defensive measures. Economy of resistance means providing a nation with the possibility to continue to grow and flourish even under pressure. ... Economy of resistance means an economy that can guarantee the growth and development of the country under pressure, sanctions and severe hostilities."[113] Mohammad Nahavandian, chair of the Chamber of

---

[112] For specific criticisms of the proposed Turkish-Brazilian-Iranian deal by Obama administration officials, see Michael Slackman and David E. Sanger, "U.S. Is Skeptical on Iranian Deal for Nuclear Fuel," *New York Times*, May 17, 2010.

[113] Translation of Khamenei's August 6, 2012, speech before a university student gathering in Tehran, broadcast on IRIB Channel One on August 7, 2012, and translated and transcribed by BBC Monitoring, August 10, 2012.

Commerce, inked an agreement with the Central Bank to establish an experts' committee for managing foreign exchange policies. Nahavandian also lobbied against aggressive antiprofiteering and antismuggling campaigns, arguing that they tended to be ineffective.[114] And institutions such as the national oil company sought to use the crisis to advance their own agendas – initiatives that might have been exacerbated by the severity of the sanctions' impact, but that existed independently of the sanctions themselves.

The "chicken crisis" referenced at the outset of this volume emerged as a kind of shorthand for the broader economic distortions generated by the latest intensification of the international restrictions, and an unusually robust debate emerged in the media and among government officials about the causes and prospective remedies. A number of prominent conservatives used the chicken shortage to highlight the shortsighted economic policies of the Ahmadinejad administration; it was a slow-moving calamity – one that could have been averted or at least mitigated had the government heeded the concerns raised early in the year by poultry farmers unable to import needed feedstocks. Others pointedly alluded to the contrasts to the war period, when rationing and hardships were willingly accepted by a nation under siege.[115]

Even as the situation deteriorated, however, Iranian officials across the political spectrum maintained a persistent confidence that the sanctions would ultimately unravel, in part because of Western economic vulnerabilities and insecurities. As MP Ali Moruri, the vice chair of the Majlis's Energy Commission, declared several weeks after the U.S. and European sanctions had been fully implemented, "The possibility of the elimination of Iran's oil does not exist because the world needs Iran's oil and Iran's oil cannot be ignored under any circumstances such as reduction of consumption or the increased production of other countries."[116] The head of the Iranian-Chinese Chamber of Commerce declared that trade with five countries – Russia, China, India, Turkey, and Malaysia – could sustain Iran even if the rest of the world fully embraced sanctions.[117]

The domestic debate on sanctions during this period focused on Ahmadinejad himself, who was openly blamed for the state of the

---

[114] "Head of Chamber of Commerce Announces Foreign Currency Agreement with Government Officials," *Donya-ye Eqtesad*, February 27, 2012.

[115] "In an Interview with Hamshahri Online, Fuladgar Discussed: Expressing Concerns Over Multi-Rate and Double-Rate System," *Hamshahri*, July 21, 2012.

[116] Ali Moruri, "We Have Become Immune," *Tehran-e Emruz*, July 22, 2012.

[117] *Fars News*, February 11, 2013.

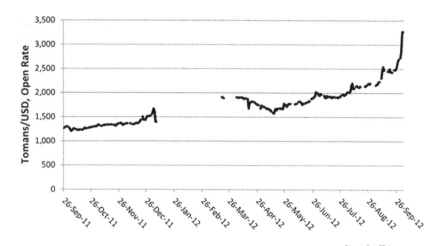

Source: SarafiTehran.com

FIGURE 7.2. Central Bank Sanctions and the Value of the Rial

economy – including but hardly limited to the external pressure. Rafsan-jani repeatedly blasted Ahmadinejad's management, noting that "impru-dence and unnecessary measures to create enemies have taken this high potential and capability from us and we are witnessing an ever-growing decrease of the number of regional and global friends and an ever-growing number of enemies." The former president added, "At present, sanctions have strengthened and have a new format. If we do not take balanced and thoughtful steps they could have negative impacts. We should not make enemies without any reason."[118] Other political figures lamented the president's spending spree and the opportunities lost as a result of his actions. "The policies that we have implemented in the gas and oil sectors were such as though we had decided to implement Amer-ica's policy of sanctions," asserted Ali Shams-Ardakani, then-chairman of the Chamber of Commerce Energy Committee. "America has banned investment in oil and gas sectors, and we have also wasted our own capital, and this has enabled the Americans to achieve their goal.... In my view, due to the fact that we did not invest in oil and gas sectors and have spent our oil revenue on importing oranges and grapes, we have done exactly what America wanted us to do."[119]

Beyond the rhetoric and the factional jousting, Iranian officials engaged in a frantic effort to mitigate the impact of the 2012 sanctions

---

[118] Rafsanjani interview, *Etemad*, April 3, 2012.
[119] "Iran Lacks Energy Diplomacy," *Etemad* (supplement), February 1, 2010.

and to address their ripple effects throughout the economy. The most urgent arena for action concerned the currency. Even before the Central Bank measures were fully implemented, the news of their approval had a cataclysmic impact on trading of the rial.

"We have stockpiled our gold for 15 years to be able to answer their challenges," the Central Bank governor asserted in August 2011. "We do not have a problem with reserves."[120] In September 2012, Tehran established an official Foreign Exchange (forex) Center, intended to stabilize the currency by providing foreign exchange at a slightly discounted rate as compared to the black market. The opening of the forex center also signaled the demise of Iran's hard-fought effort to unify its foreign exchange rates, which was only completed during the reformist period. The approach adopted in 2012 provided cheap dollars (12,260 rials/$) for government use as well as for high-priority items such as meat and grains; a slightly discounted "non-reference rate" for other goods (which stood at approximately 24,000 rials/$); and, of course, the open market rate, which fluctuated considerably on the basis of domestic and diplomatic developments but typically hovered at least 50 percent lower than the nonreference rate (36,000 rials/$). Later that year, the government announced a list of seventy-seven "luxury" products whose import was banned, in order to conserve foreign exchange. In mid-April 2013, the government once again revised the system, scaling back the list of items for which preferential foreign exchange rates were available to a mere handful of agricultural imports.

The sanctions rippled across the Iranian economy. As parts became difficult or more costly to import and long-standing relationships with foreign firms were ruptured, much of Iran's indigenous industrial capacity was devastated. In the Iranian year beginning March 2012, domestic car production fell significantly, after the government doubled the prices of new cars.[121] The government put a six-month moratorium on pistachio export in early 2013 in hopes of stabilizing prices through the Noruz holiday. Reports of escalating costs of basic foodstuffs abounded – meat prices reportedly increased by 60 percent; cooking oil by 35 percent – although in some cases the time frame and base reference rate seem vaguely defined. "People can't eat meat, they can't eat beans, should they

---

[120] "$6 Billion of False Demand," *Donya-ye Eqtesad*, August 2, 2011.
[121] Youssef Naseri, "Auto Industry at the Bottleneck of Price," *Tehran-e Emruz*, March 15, 2013.

also not eat broth which requires a spoon of oil?" the conservative parliamentarian Ahmad Tavakkoli demanded in April 2013.[122]

As Iranian analysts themselves pointed out, the spiraling prices had their roots in a range of policy distortions – injecting too much liquidity into the monetary system, the maintenance of a distorted fixed exchange rate, the declining productivity of Iranian industry.[123] The same inflationary pressures also constrained Iran's nonoil exports and domestic industries.

Iranian mitigation efforts staunched some of the damage; import expenditures declined and nonoil export revenues apparently increased, although the specifics were subject to some dispute given the paucity of official data. The Iran-China Chamber of Commerce head Asadollah Asgharowladi rejected government claims of $45 billion in nonoil exports, noting that perhaps as much as one-fourth of the revenues was unpaid, and that the real foreign exchange rate was not used in the calculations.[124]

Still, even as Iran sought to muddle through, the long-term implications were painful. The growth rate fell into negative numbers, and inflation rates of 30 percent defied government efforts to manage. Reliance on barter trade expanded the deluge of cheap Chinese goods into the Iranian market, further decimating Iran's domestic manufacturing capabilities and textile industry. The domestic flower industry protested the import of cheap artificial flowers from China. In July 2012, a columnist in the hard-line *Qods* newspaper inveighed against government officials at a conference intended to promote domestic industry, many of whom were sporting Chinese-made suits.[125] Analysts have suggested that the dramatic increase in East Asian imports may have also exacerbated the sense of insecurity and frustration over lack of employment opportunities.[126]

The history of the Islamic Republic's turbulent economy looms large for any comparative measures, and certainly many Iranian officials continued to argue – perhaps correctly – that the sanctions had not yet reached the level of disruption that the regime had experienced in previous crises, such as the war, the 1985 oil price crash, the 1993 debt crisis, or subsequent global recessions in the late 1990s and 2008. Still, by the

---

[122] Yeganeh Torbati, "Iran Withdraws Cheap Dollars for Most Imports, Price Rises Feared," *Reuters*, April 24, 2013.

[123] Ahareh Oryani," Six Reasons for Inflation in Iran's Economy," July 22, 2012.

[124] "The Need to Reform the Statistics of Non-Oil Exports," *Jaam-e Jam*, December 1, 2012.

[125] Khosrow Motazed, "Apartments Have Become Dreams, Suits Are Hard to Find!" *Qods*, July 1, 2012.

[126] Salehi-Isfahani (2009), p. 25.

start of the Iranian new year in March 2013, Iran was facing a crisis that even domestic experts viewed as more complicated and more precarious than any of these precedent episodes; the respected economist Saeed Leylaz argued that the combination of radically reduced oil revenue, spiraling inflation, high unemployment, flat or negative overall growth, and expansionary spending commitments ranked the nuclear crisis as the "most dangerous" in the country's postrevolutionary history.[127]

FROM RISING TO REVILED: AHMADINEJAD

Ahmadinejad's antics and influence throughout his first six years in office were facilitated by a unique condition – the supreme leader's assiduous protection. It was Khamenei's explicit endorsement of Ahmadinejad and his repeated defense of the president that enabled Ahmadinejad to assert his influence well beyond the bounds of the office's relatively limited authority and to play an outsized role in the international arena. Predictably, however, Ahmadinejad eventually overstepped, and as with each of his predecessors his personal ambitions proved no match for a system constructed to ensure its own preservation and the supreme leader's unchallenged authority.

Ahmadinejad's success always derived from his willingness to assert himself without any legal authority or obvious political support. Time and again, the president positioned himself in such a way as to force his own relevance, whether it was on the economy, the nuclear issue, or matters of lesser significance. His proclivity for transgressing protocol and institutional boundaries exacerbated the Iranian establishment's disapproval from the outset; irrespective of ideological orientation, much of Tehran's political elite viewed Ahmadinejad as an uncouth, incompetent interloper who was only tolerated because of the supreme leader's public backing. During his two terms in office, Ahmadinejad jousted, sometimes subtly but often quite openly, with nearly every political actor within the Islamic system: a "who's who" of parliamentary power brokers, high-ranking clerics, and revolutionary patriarchs.

The long-standing struggle for influence morphed into a transparent grab for institutional advantage and control. In 2010, Ahmadinejad sought to assert control over Azad University, established under Rafsanjani as a means of absorbing skyrocketing public demand for higher education. It was Iran's first and only private university system,

---

[127] Saeed Leylaz, "Next Year and the Year That Has Passed," *Mardom-e Salari*, March 24, 2013.

with more than 350 campuses, with a reputation for high tuition, academic mediocrity, and a cozy relationship with the ruling system. Rafsanjani denounced the uproar as an assault on his legacy, contending that "this great and wonderful success, that can be unique in many ways, is now infected with political and factional contests. They seek to either seize it or weaken it for the purpose of confronting me."[128] Ultimately, Khamenei interceded, and his guidance quieted the uproar while settling neither side. Two years later, an Ahmadinejad ally was appointed chancellor of the Azad system, belatedly advantaging the president over his repeated rival. It was, like so many of Ahmadinejad's partial victories, a temporary one, as the leadership changes were effectively undone after his August 2013 departure from office.

However, episodes like the Azad University tussle only whetted Ahmadinejad's appetite for greater authority. In April 2011, he moved to dismiss the intelligence minister – only to see his order revoked by the supreme leader and the intelligence minister reinstated. In fact, cabinet turmoil was a hallmark of Ahmadinejad's tenure, but the intelligence portfolio has traditionally remained the leader's prerogative. Ahmadinejad responded with a public tantrum, refusing to attend cabinet meetings for eleven days despite apparent efforts on the part of much of the establishment either to persuade or to threaten him back to his office.[129] This was a bold challenge to Khamenei's precedence that seemed to challenge the previously unshakable support of the supreme leader. Ahmadinejad's cabinet boycott, intended to force Khamenei's hand, backfired spectacularly. Khamenei publicly rebuked the president with language that unleashed the torrent of antipathy that the political establishment had harbored since his initial elevation. Ahmadinejad eventually was forced to submit to a humiliating interpolation before the parliament, which threatened to impeach him. Even to the end, he seemed unmoved by his own marginalization, and in his parliamentary defense of his track record, Ahmadinejad seemed to relish the opportunity to grandstand:

Do you think that being pure, round-the-clock efforts, service, defending the people's rights, fighting against greed people and encroachers upon collective property, fighting against corruption, insisting on the people's rights, monotheism and justice, implementation of big projects, making Iran nuclear and space

---

[128] Rafsanjani interview, *Etemad*, April 3, 2012.
[129] Hojjat ol-Eslam Mojtaba Zonnur, the deputy representative of the leader to the Revolutionary Guards, claimed in an interview that 200 officials sought to persuade Ahmadinejad to return to work. See *Mehr News*, June 21, 2011.

country, accelerated scientific and technological progress, implementation of the targeted subsidies plan, Mehr Housing, Justice Shares, multiplying construction activities, increasing the volume of non-oil export for over 6.5 times, fulfilling the entire slogans of all the previous governments, interaction, tolerance and respect for the freedom and rights of the people, love for the people, encouraging kindness, justice and thousands of other services can be called deviation? If it is so then almost the entire Iranian nation is moving along this path. Whether you admit it or not, most of the attendees of this session are moving along this path.[130]

The unprecedented questioning only cemented the hostility between the president and the parliament. As a result, for the final two years of his second term, Ahmadinejad was effectively sidelined, reduced to playing a convenient foil for intraélite skirmishing while Khamenei publicly mused about simply eliminating the presidency altogether and reverting to a prime ministerial structure. Ahmadinejad's fall from grace was ironic, but probably not surprising, given Iran's proclivity for dramatic factional fluctuations. And like the reformists before them, the suddenly sidelined hard-liners who were aligned with the mercurial president discovered the utility of institutional constraints on absolute power.

Ahmadinejad seemed determined to reject any quiet submission to his political fate. During his final months in office, he revived his provincial visits and organized a mass rally that was widely interpreted as an electoral nod to his protégé Esfandiar Rahim Mashaei. In April 2013, he told an audience in Khuzestan, "some people tell me 'if you get too cocky, we will sort you out,' but I will remain at the service of justice, the revolution, belief in Shi'i imams and the *velayat* (guardianship) until the end of my life. Thousands of Ahmadinejads will sacrifice their lives for an iota of justice and a strand of the hair of the people of Iran."[131]

"CLEANSING" THE REVOLUTION

A vigorous anticorruption agenda featured prominently in Ahmadinejad's initial campaign for the presidency, and it remained at the forefront of the political turmoil within the regime during his eight-year tenure, although perhaps not quite in the same way that the president envisioned. Despite promising to clean up what he described as a system filled with fraud and malfeasance, Ahmadinejad found himself and his circle of allies under attack for influence peddling and worse. The low point was the revelation

---

[130] "Iran President Rejects All Grievances of Majlis Members – Full Text," *BBC Monitoring Caucasus*, March 14, 2012.
[131] *ILNA*, April 23, 2013.

of the embezzlement of nearly $3 billion in a scandal that transfixed the country, brought down the heads of two major Iranian banks, and implicated several of the president's closest allies. The main conspirator in the Bank Arya case managed to obtain fraudulent letters of credit, which were used to secure loans to purchase privatized companies and obtain additional loans.

As with the two prior blockbuster corruption cases in the Islamic Republic – Morteza Rafiqdust in 1997 and Shahram Jazayeri in 2001 – the 2011 revelations about banking fraud were timed perfectly to distract an increasingly restive public and further corrode the influence of a second-term president who had sought to exceed the constraints of his limited authority. Rafsanjani, no stranger to accusations of corruption himself, rejected any comparisons between the embezzlement and a similar scandal that transpired during his own presidency, both by virtue of its magnitude as well as that "the efforts of bodies for deflecting responsibility and accusing others created a base so that the real issue would not be learned by the people."

"People who have given 200,000 martyrs for this establishment do not expect to witness from it such a violation of its banking system," declared the parliamentarian Aziz Akbarian, noting that the scandal had "aroused a public distrust of the system."[132] The president was personally vulnerable on this issue – not simply because he had brandished it against his political adversaries, but because he had revived the revolutionary themes of purity and austerity. Moreover, even in the midst of evidence of widespread abuses – which arguably represented an endemic aspect of the postrevolutionary economy – Ahmadinejad continued to defend the Islamic Republic as "the purest and most healthy system in the world," adding that "since it is pure, even little spots are not bearable in it. One violation, a single personal interest seeking, one misuse, one misuse of the Public Treasury, one misuse of connections, are all bad. It is an honor for the Iranian nation to raise their voice against these.[133]

What made the scandal especially salient for Iran's factional arena were allegations that Ahmadinejad's closest adviser and hand-picked protégé, Esfandiar Rahim Mashaie, had ties to the scandal. From the start, concerns radiated from the established Ahmadinejad's "brother-in-law-cracy" – shorthand for the president's proclivity to reward his original

---

[132] "Iran Bank Chiefs Lose Jobs over Fraud Scandal," *RFE/RL*, September 27, 2011.
[133] Speech by Iranian President Mahmud Ahmadinejad, May 27, 2008, as broadcast on Islamic Republic of Iran News Network Television and translated by World News Connection.

inner circle.[134] This was hardly a new phenomenon in the Islamic Republic, to witness not simply the proliferation of Hashemi Rafsanjani family members in senior bureaucratic positions, but also those of other prominent politicians in the postrevolutionary era. Neither the Khameneis nor the Khatamis can offer a credible retort. This may be seen as a testament to the modernization of political expectations and debates, that the appearance of official nepotism has become seen as a disqualifying factor. Alternatively, it may be an indication of the hostility with which the president and his closest cronies were viewed by Tehran's political establishment.

The Arya Bank scandal was hardly the only example of corruption during the Ahmadinejad era. The sanctions, and the government reintervention in the foreign exchange market, expanded the space for speculators and profiteers, with a corresponding increase in publicity surrounding prosecutions. And then there was the strange issue of the Palizdar case. In 2008, Abbas Palizdar, an Ahmadinejad functionary ostensibly working on the staff of the Judicial Inquiry and Review Committee, gave several speeches in which he made blockbuster allegations about official corruption, citing an array of senior officials and prominent clerics. Palizdar was immediately disowned by all elements of the Iranian political establishment, including Ahmadinejad, and arrested for "propagating lies" and "spreading misinformation," as well as charges involving a defaulted loan.

The issue of corruption became a major, if incredibly opaque, obsession as Ahmadinejad's relationship with the supreme leader and the rest of the conservative establishment deteriorated. His remaining close allies, including Mashaie and the first vice president, Mohammadreza Rahimi, drew intense scrutiny, particularly as Ahmadinejad's opponents saw his every move during his final months in office as intended to bolster his flagging legacy and secure one of his protégés as his successor.[135]

Unlike his predecessors, however, Ahmadinejad had absorbed the lessons of three decades of partisan deployment of corruption allegations, and he proved that he could give as good as he got. The president managed to shock the normally unflinching Iranian political establishment on multiple occasions by deploying what he claimed were intelligence files on his rivals, most notably in February 2013, when he played excerpts from a taped bribery solicitation by the brother of Ali Larijani,

---

[134] Abbas Pazouki, "70 Family Appointments: Ninth Government Has Stepped Back from Truce of Meritocracy," *Mardom Salari*, April 24, 2006.

[135] "Are the 'Main Figures' around Ahmadinezhad or in Ahmadinezhad's Pocket?" *Fars News*, June 13, 2012.

the speaker of the parliament, in an address given on the floor of the parliament. He was rebuked by no less than Chief of the General Staff of the Armed Forces of Iran General Seyyed Hassan Firouzabadi for "unacceptable" allegations against the system. As his second term drew near a conclusion, the president traded jabs with a variety of his adversaries in the parliament and other official institutions, clearly itching for an opportunity to release publicly a list of 312 individuals for whom he claimed to have evidence of official malfeasance.

For the president's critics, all of these scandals were part of a seamless pattern of misdeeds by Ahmadinejad. The former aide to the president Ali Samari argued that the network of Ahmadinejad cronies taking advantage of the system had

> become like a cancerous tumor attacking the health of the public treasury.... The only justification for this fraud is that the top echelons were involved in it. The deviated group has turned the banking system into its own backyard, and all their economic efforts are in line with this attempt. The problems of the Oil Ministry leading to the dismissal of the minister, the problems of the Intelligence Ministry and the president boycotting his office for 11 days, the issues of Kish Island and incomplete projects, Qeshm tenders, airline programs, the tourism organization's financial problems, and the wandering funds of the Council of Iranians Abroad are all proof of this claim.[136]

For his part, Ahmadinejad continued to insist on the purity of his presidency, arguing in fact that it was his very diligence in pursuing corruption cases that had produced such an onslaught of criticism, including allegations of financial misdeeds, against his administration. "I am stressing again that I am the only president who has announced that if anyone sees an offence committed by me or those related or affiliated to me should report it to the Judiciary to be dealt with according to the law," Ahmadinejad declared in a June 2011 news conference, adding "maybe the reason that we are receiving so much pressure is because we are insisting on our position."[137]

IRONIES OF THE AHMADINEJAD ERA

Ahmadinejad's divisive disposition, his repressive predisposition, and the contentious history that led him to and kept him in power have fixed him

---

[136] "Embezzlement and Economic Corruption in Free Zones Go Back to People Close to the President," *Qods*, September 21, 2011.

[137] News conference by Iranian President Mahmud Ahmadinezhad with foreign and domestic correspondents in Tehran; broadcast in progress by Islamic Republic of Iran News Network Television (IRINN), June 9, 2011, from World News Connection.

firmly in the role of a buffoonish nemesis to the democratic aspirations and institutions that remain just under the surface of the Islamic Republic. And yet at least some of the Ahmadinejad experience would ring frustratingly familiar to a partisan of Khatami or the reform movement more broadly. Despite his own authoritarian instincts, Ahmadinejad found himself perennially outmanned in the turf battles that define the day-to-day politics of revolutionary Iran. "An institution which is outside the authority of the president and the ministers should not get a budget from Majlis," the president argued in a speech to the Majlis. "These institutions should implement the government's and Majlis decisions. I don't want to mention everything, but there are right now, some institutions or organisations which receive a budget but go exactly the opposite directions of what the government had decided, while the president or a minister is responsible for their actions."[138]

Ahmadinejad's criticisms of the reliance on central planning and the obscurities of the budget process that have facilitated parliamentary horse trading are not necessarily inappropriate critiques, even if they are partisan in genesis. Instead, he argued, "the budget bill should be understandable for anyone knowing to read and write" and lamented that "the [state] treasury has become a source from which everyone with a hose can have an item number and pump out the budget."[139] The budget battles between Ahmadinejad and the parliament provided a proxy for a large struggle over institutional authority in the Islamic Republic. In this respect, Ahmadinejad's efforts were not dissimilar to those of Khatami, who repeatedly sought to expand the powers of the presidency to no avail.

CONCLUSION

The turning of the tides of Iran's turbulent politics did not appear to demoralize Ahmadinejad. All the characteristics of his early ascendance and his brutal reelection victory – the pugnacious self-confidence, the mastery of minutiae, the proclivity for surprise attacks on political adversaries, and, most of all, his absolute conviction in his own righteousness – remained fully intact in his public persona. The sanctions provided a useful scapegoat for any perception of error or disappointment in his agenda and appeared to have only stiffened the embattled president's spine, at least insofar as his economic policies were concerned. Asked in

---

[138] Saba Azarpeyk, "The Simple Budget in Parliament," *Etemad*, January 12, 2008.
[139] *Ibid.*

February 2013 how – with the wisdom of hindsight – he might have approached the targeted subsidy plan differently, the president only offered a critique of the parliament's decision to defer the second phase of the program. He met reporters who interrupted what was intended as a solo interview with a burst of critical queries on the failure to fulfill projected increases in nonoil exports, agricultural production, and other economic targets with similar defenses of his approach and sunny projections that future growth would offset any recent difficulties.

Sounding eerily like the shah – who reveled in predictions that Iran would overtake European economies – Ahmadinejad explained that the sanctions crisis was merely a bump along the unswerving road of the Islamic Republic's ascendance. "We need to pass this juncture, in order to do so we should turn into the first or second most powerful country in the world in terms of economy within four or five years," the president explained. "Because this is a very heavy battle, of course an economic battle. But the Americans have utilized all of their economic power. The most powerful economy in the world is at war with the 10th most powerful country in the world." He compared Washington to a "mega weight athlete [who] is fighting against a light-weight one," adding, "well, this imposes pressures, but it makes us much stronger. They might have thought that with the first shock, Iran's economy will be destroyed. Well, they have inserted a few shocks to our economy but it has survived."[140]

In a fitting finale, the live broadcast of the interview on Iranian state television was suddenly disrupted when one of the reporters apparently veered too close to sensitive territory – the $3 billion corruption scandal – and Ahmadinejad's responses on corruption and popular dissatisfaction with the subsidy reforms were redacted from the initial press coverage of the episode. However, Iran's factional politics has a tendency to facilitate a selective transparency, and the full text of the president's remarks quickly emerged in the official media. They underscore Ahmadinejad's combative – and arguably delusional – confidence. "We believe that the government has put oil money on the people's table, why not?" he challenged, later adding, "I believe that the country's economic situation is very good."[141]

---

[140] Morteza Heydari interview with Ahmadinejad, broadcast on Vision of the Islamic Republic of Iran Network 1, February 26, 2013, from World News Connection.
[141] *Mehr News*, February 23, 2013.

8

Energy and the Islamic Republic

In March 1979, when Iran's nascent Islamic Republic resumed crude oil exports after sixty-nine days of revolutionary disruptions, it seemed to herald a new era. Iranian oil workers had played a central role in driving the shah from the throne, and issues related to Iran's oil sector had mobilized Iranian oppositionists for nearly half a century. A government established through popular action now had not simply authority over the formidable instruments of state power, but also – for the first time in Iran's history – unqualified authority over the country's foremost asset, its petroleum endowments.

From its outset, the Islamic Republic realized the objective that had eluded the determined efforts of Reza Shah, Mosaddeq, and Mohammad Reza himself. At the ceremony that marked the resumption of exports, Hassan Nazih, a human rights lawyer who initially led the postrevolutionary national oil company, became emotional at the revolution's early achievement. "This is the greatest moment of my life.... I hope it is an omen of a bright future for our country and our people."[1] Unfortunately, Nazih's optimism proved premature. He was quickly purged for ideological differences, and the new state's sway over the country's incredible resources has not translated into the propitious future that he envisioned. Instead, Iran's oil production has never returned to its prerevolutionary heights, and the sector has been battered by government policy, sanctions, war, and political risk.

---

[1] "Oil Flow from Iran Resumes; First Two Tankers Get Loads Priced at $20 a Barrel," *New York Times*, March 6, 1979.

The energy sector is ground zero for all of the revolutionary state's dilemmas. It represents the wellspring of modern nationalism and continues to generate the bulk of Iran's foreign exchange, as well as its access to and prominence within the global economy. The Islamic Republic's founders sought to reconfigure the role of energy in the postrevolutionary economy, so that the country's new authorities maintained a decisive upper hand over the international oil companies, as proxies for Western power, and the sector's revenues were used to advance Islamic values and sustainable growth, rather than exploitation, immorality, and the monarchy's apish ambitions.

The outcome has proven far more murky. The energy sector offered both the vehicle and the vulnerability for the persistent struggle between Iran and its neighbors for regional domination. After the war, Tehran's efforts to use oil as a pathway to diplomatic redemption and economic rehabilitation became mired with political debates over shielding its patrimony from foreign rapacity and eventually with fallout from the nuclear standoff. And while Iran's oil revenues have surely funded infrastructure development, they have sustained the same rentier patterns and mundane impulses that undermined the shah. Corruption and cronyism thrive as the Islamic Republic's feuding factions vie for their share of the bounty – even as the same politicians continue to rely on populist rhetoric to bolster public support for the regime.

As a result, Iran's energy development, like so much else in the country's contemporary experience, is profoundly paradoxical. Ultimately, Iran's ties to the energy industry have gradually facilitated the partial rationalization of its postrevolutionary political economy. Since 1979, Iranian energy policy has been driven less by ideological imperatives than by the inescapable need of the postrevolutionary state for revenues to meet popular expectations to have the oil money on their tablecloths, as Ahmadinejad so memorably argued in his 2005 presidential campaign. However, the legacy of Iran's contentious history with international oil companies and Western governments remains firmly entrenched. Perhaps uniquely in the modern era, the Islamic Republic has attempted to balance a central place in the global economy with fierce ideological hostility to the most important factor in those markets. And nowhere has that contradiction played out more dramatically than in the energy sector.

PREREVOLUTIONARY PETROLEUM SECTOR

For Mohammad Reza Shah, control over Iran's oil resources – and the corresponding revenues – was the sine qua non of regime power, internal stability, and international clout. If he did not absorb that lesson from his father's bitter failure to renegotiate the Anglo-Persian concession, it was surely thrust upon him during the nationalization campaign and the rapid denouement of Mosaddeq's domestic power base during the British embargo. With the memory of these skirmishes looming large and the prospective upside from any improvement in the government's terms seemingly boundless, energy was naturally a central preoccupation.

The shah devoted considerable energy to mastering the workings of the oil markets and the requirements of Iran's resource base. "I know everything there is to know about oil, everything," the shah boasted to a reporter in the midst of the dramatic 1973 oil price spike.[2] He was buttressed by talented technocrats within the executive branch and NIOC. However, their hard-won education into the industry's financial and technical aspects could not dissuade the shah of the belief that the international oil companies and Western governments had ill used Iran. He was determined to redress the imbalance in influence and economic returns, and in contrast to his ambivalence toward nationalization a generation earlier, he was fully prepared to play hardball to achieve this.

The shah invested enormous energies in wresting control of production and price decisions from the consortium and in carving out production deals outside the consortium territory. And despite some initial skepticism toward OPEC, the shah also came to appreciate the additional clout that the nascent producers' cartel afforded. The monarchical obsession with energy served both the shah's domestic motivations and foreign policy ambitions. Oil revenues fueled development programs that the shah saw as essential to his own legitimacy and to the required betterment of the nation. And for the first time, the gas that had long been flared would be utilized to jump-start the country's industrial development. But energy was also integral to his view of Iran's place in the world – no longer a supplicant to world powers or subjugated by their machinations, but the architect of its own future. "No one can dictate to us," the shah declared in 1974. "No one can wave a finger at us, because we will wave a finger back."[3] This vision of oil as a vehicle to move the country from exploited to empowered persisted long after the monarchy expired.

---

[2] William D. Smith, "Oil Watchers Focus on Shah of Iran," *New York Times*, March 7, 1974, p. 55.
[3] "Shah Rejects Bid by Ford for Cut in Prices of Oil," *New York Times*, September 27, 1974.

The shah himself played a dominant role – the "pivot in the price hike," as one memoir describes him – in the epic reconfiguration of the international energy business.[4] He personally engineered OPEC's successful push for higher prices and greater host government control over operations and exports. This initially provoked a muted competition with the Saudis, who sought a less provocative approach. The rivalry between the two Gulf heavyweights, with very different fiscal exigencies and popular mandates, persisted and mutated over the next four decades in ways that would prove deeply problematic for successive Iranian governments.[5]

In the early 1970s, the Pahlavi dynasty appeared to hold the advantage. The shah's success in seizing control of the concession's operations and simultaneously escalating global prices reaped fantastic benefits for Iran and ratcheted production to historic levels. Over the dozen years prior to the revolution, Iran's output increased an average of 8.7 percent per year, expanding from slightly more than 1.9 mbpd in 1965 to 5.3 mbpd in 1978, with a high of more than 6 mbpd in 1974.[6] Iran would never again attain those epic production rates.

Much as his successors used oil exports and investments to cement their influence, the monarchy used nascent command of energy to extend its diplomatic reach. After successfully brokering the 1971 concession renegotiation, the shah described his achievement as "the oil problem solved, rain for our crops and Iran's leadership of the whole Middle East acknowledged throughout the world."[7] Washington always figured front and center, and his Midas touch meant access to the most advanced technology and defense capabilities. He used Iran's newfound wealth and weaponry to assert himself across the region – in Iraq, Oman, and a scattering of Gulf islands – and to embark on a less clientelistic relationship with the United States.

Iran's oil connections under the shah extended to its robust relationship with Israel, which relied on Iran for as much as 75 percent of its

---

[4] Afkhami (2009), p. 278.

[5] See Andrew Scott Cooper, *The Oil Kings: How the U.S., Iran, and Saudi Arabia Changed the Balance of Power in the Middle East* (New York: Simon & Schuster, 2011) for a dramatic interpretation of the 1970s interplay among the shah, the Saudis, and the U.S. government over oil prices and military sales.

[6] Data from *BP Statistical Review*, 2011.

[7] James Buchan, *Days of God: The Revolution in Iran and Its Consequences* (London: John Murray, 2013), p. 169.

domestic supply in 1970.[8] The relationship entailed secret partnerships between NIOC and the Israeli government for the development of the Eilant-Ashkelon pipeline, enabling Tehran to gain experience marketing its production, reap premium prices for its crude, and access Israeli military technology.[9] The legacy of this quiet cooperation fed the Israeli conviction that the revolution need not abrogate this pragmatic partnership, a misapprehension that facilitated a sporadic flow of medicine, weapons, and other vital goods to the postrevolutionary regime until the Iran-contra affair.

The shah adopted a similar approach to the Soviet Union. In 1965, countering domestic opposition over the intensifying U.S.-Iranian relationship, Tehran sought to bolster its nascent opening to the Soviet Union with a landmark gas deal. In return for supplying gas, Iran would receive military equipment as well as steel and machine tool factories – capabilities that commanded outsized importance for Iran's rapid industrialization strategy. Over time, the success of the Soviet gas arrangement also opened the possibility of Iranian oil sales to the Eastern bloc.[10] It was a bold strategy – one that required the shah to assuage Soviet concerns about Iran's industrial application of gas and American anxieties over strategic trade with its adversary. Among Iranian technocrats, the export deals provoked a debate that continues today about the relative advantages of exports versus domestic utilization, particularly for reinjection in Iran's oil fields. On balance, however, the shah's approach to gas proved an unmitigated success, achieving additional leverage vis-à-vis Washington and readying Iran's gas sector for massive expansion, which occurred only after the revolution.

The Iran Gas Trunkline I (IGATI) from Bid-Boland in the south to Astara along the western coast of the Caspian Sea was inaugurated in 1970 and represented the first major attempt to monetize Iran's gas resources, previously wasted through flaring. It served as the backbone of a massive domestic gas utilization system, freeing additional volumes of crude oil for export and eventually offering a mechanism for mitigating the limitations of international sanctions. Although IGAT-1 was built to supply the Soviet contract, its construction also prompted the

---

[8] Parsi (2007), p. 76.

[9] Uri Bialer, "Fuel Bridge across the Middle East-Israel, Iran, and the Eilat-Ashkelon Oil Pipeline," *Israel Studies* 12:3 (Fall 2007), pp. 29–67.

[10] David A. Andelman, "Iran Emerging as Major Alternative in Eastern Europe's Search for Oil," *New York Times*, November 21, 1977.

development of local spur lines for gas-fired industrial development including a cement plant in Shiraz. Additional gas export projects were in the works at the time of the revolution, including a second trunkline intended to deliver gas to Europe via swaps with Moscow. At the same time, Tehran was pressing liquefied natural gas (LNG) export plans with Japanese, European, and American companies. In 1978, two U.S. firms sought U.S. Department of Energy approval of 300 million cubic feet (mcf)/day in LNG imports from Iran.[11]

The shah's energy strategy entailed considerable risk and contradiction. His crusade against the companies unnerved his advisers, who remembered the consequences of prior battles with the companies and the world powers who relied upon their stable supply of energy. He walked a fine line with his neighbors and fellow OPEC heavyweights by opting out of the Arab oil boycott but utilizing the episode to expand Iran's market share and cement its alliance with Washington without significant cost. After his successes in leveraging greater control and revenues from the Western companies in the early 1970s, the shah struggled and ultimately failed to achieve rising prices and revenues in the second half of the decade. This period marked the apex of Saudi dominance of oil markets and OPEC and exacerbated Iran's overheated economy at a critical turning point.

POSTREVOLUTIONARY PETROLEUM SECTOR: INSTITUTIONAL AND LEGAL FRAMEWORK

The revolution, and the accompanying chaos, changed everything, or so it seemed. Oil worker strikes through late 1978 devastated the monarchy, and the disarray was prolonged by the departure of thousands of technocrats, the ongoing divisions among the revolutionaries, the perpetuation of worker activism and ethnic unrest, and the Iraqi invasion, which massively impacted energy-related facilities and transportation. Compounding these oil disruptions were the new regime's political imperatives. Initially, the revolutionary leadership was split over management of Iran's oil resources and sector. The legacy of 1953 meant resource nationalism was an integral dimension of revolutionary ideology, and the conviction that Iran's patrimony had been squandered by the shah and exploited by the West was shared across the political spectrum. However,

[11] "Two Utilities Seek Iranian Gas," *New York Times*, June 28, 1978, p. D11.

there was also a profound realism, as then–Prime Minister Rejai once acknowledged, that "oil is the lifeblood of the revolution."[12] As with other economic issues, Khomeini bridged the divide, disparaging the nationalization movement but insisting that Iran could overcome its oil dependency.[13]

The postrevolutionary regime cancelled the consortium agreement and other concessions, consolidating upstream joint ventures under NIOC control. Initially, production was deliberately limited, and with full authority over crude marketing, Tehran favored independents and the spot market in its export contracts. Even its oil and gas fields were renamed; "imperial connotations" were exchanged for names that evoked Iran's Islamic heritage.[14] Massive gas export projects were abandoned, with a devastating impact on Iran's role in the international gas trade. Downstream joint ventures in South Africa and South Korea were also abrogated. Among other energy projects abandoned at this time were billions of dollars in contracts for constructing nuclear reactors.

Perhaps the most important aspect of the revolutionary transformation of the hydrocarbons sector was the Constitution's explicit provisions imposing expansive but nebulous limitations on foreign involvement in the energy sector. Article 81 prohibits concessions to foreign firms or individuals, while Article 153 forbids "any form of agreement resulting in foreign control over the natural resources, economy, army, or culture of the country." The former provision elicited considerable debate among the body tasked with devising the postrevolutionary Constitution, and, eventually, repeated attempts at interpretive guidance from the Guardians' Council.

After the war, the government sought to circumvent these restrictions, by developing a contract that nominally adhered to the proscription against foreign ownership while facilitating the international oil companies' return. The "buyback" contract borrowed from the various countertrade schemes Tehran had undertaken in other sectors during the war and the reconstruction program. Under the buyback, foreign firms

---

[12] Ettelat-e Eqtesadi va Siasi, October 13, 1985, as quoted in Morady (1996), p. 13.

[13] "Khomeyni reportedly said of Mosaddeq: 'They say he nationalized [Iranian] oil. So what? We did not want oil, we did not want independence, we wanted Islam.'" Homa Katouzian, *The Political Economy of Modern Iran, 1926–1979* (London and Basingstoke: Macmillan, 1981), p. 362, as quoted in Yann Richard, "The Relevance of 'Nationalism' in Contemporary Iran."

[14] Mahnaz Zahirinejad, "The Role of Political Structure in Iran's Energy Decision Making Policy," *Journal of Third World Studies* 29:1 (Spring 2012), p. 234.

assumed investment risks in exchange for a predetermined rate of return that typically hovered below 10 percent. The contract also set the project's duration. Foreign firms have argued that the buyback offers insufficient incentives, relative to other opportunities; conversely, many Iranian technocrats contend that the buyback encourages companies to cut corners and discourages lasting commitments to the optimal development of Iran's resources. "The contract must create an incentive for performance," a BP executive commented in June 2002. "This does not yet exist in Iran."[15] The debate over the buyback framework and terms continues, sharpened by sanctions and the departure of nearly all Western firms. This contention speaks to a broader issue: persistent and mutual dissatisfaction between the government and foreign companies over the development of Iran's oil and gas resources.

Still, excepting the obstacles to foreign investment, ideological preferences occupied a secondary place in postrevolutionary energy management. Despite the new regime's mistrust of foreign oil companies and states, no serious thought was given to downsizing Iran's energy sector, if only because of its labor force's political sway. The revolutionary rhetoric on independence and the critique of the shah's policies did not prompt significant changes in the basic structure of the Iranian petroleum industry, or its relationship to the state.

Today, energy remains the lifeblood of the Iranian state and its economy, and Iran's energy sector remains dominated by the state and semi-governmental entities. The 1980 establishment of the Ministry of Petroleum for the first time endowed an institution – rather than a single ruler – with responsibility for policy and supervision of the operating companies. The ministry oversees the flagship National Iranian Oil Company (NIOC) and its counterpart businesses for gas, petrochemicals, and refining and distribution. (NIORDC was originally a subsidiary of NIOC but was elevated in 1991 as a parallel business line.)

NIOC remains the epicenter of Iran's energy sector, and while the postrevolutionary system has created an array of subsidiaries, spin-off companies, and other structural changes, it remains the fourth largest state oil company in the world, with 180,000 employees as of 2007 – an increase of more than 300 percent since the revolution.[16] The ministry's

[15] Hugh Pope, "Internal Hurdles Restrict Business in Iran," *Wall Street Journal*, June 14, 2002.

[16] Mahnaz Zahirinejad, "The Role of Political Structure in Iran's Energy Decision Making Policy," *Journal of Third World Studies* 29:1 (Spring 2012), p. 237.

creation nudges the Iranian oil sector toward greater rationalization; however, it has succeeded only marginally in shifting policy making away from the company and toward the political establishment. Episodic attempts to reform the sector in order to establish greater accountability have run aground.

This deficiency left a vacuum that the parliament was eager to fill. Parliamentary activism dates back to nationalization and its role in shaping the national budget and international agreements. As a result, the parliament has often proved interventionist. However, under the Islamic Republic, the relationship between the Majlis and the Oil Ministry as well as with NIOC and its affiliates served as a proxy for Iran's broader factional competition within the political establishment. At times, the parliament has vigorously asserted itself on energy policy issues in an effort to champion its institutional dominance vis-à-vis the executive branch, and in hopes of weakening individual technocrats – such as Bijan Namdar Zanganeh – perceived as exceeding their deliberately constrained authority. During other periods, however, the ministry has managed to co-opt the parliament, as in the 2012 election to a seat of the former oil minister Masoud Mirkazemi, whose tenure as chair of the Majlis Energy Commission proved notably lenient toward his successor – perhaps in part because of opportunistic placement of former commission members in NIOC subsidiaries.[17]

The ideological opposition to foreign companies and constitutional restrictions on ownership, combined with an adverse environment for foreign investment, count among the sector's major challenges. However, the Islamic Republic has confronted an array of more prosaic obstacles in its energy development. One of these has been the failure to establish organizational coherence and clear lines of authority. Although oil production has never reached prerevolutionary heights, employment within the industry itself ballooned. This expansion initially compensated for the departure of foreign oil experts and workers. Exploration and development remain under NIOC auspices, with subsidiary Pars Oil and Gas charged with the largest gas fields including the epic South Pars gas field, and other geographically delimited subsidiaries that oversee development of the various other fields. In parallel with opening the hydrocarbons sector to foreign investment, an array of spin-off companies were established to manage specific projects.

---

[17] Yong and Hajihosseini (January 2013).

Oil production never regained pre-revolutionary heights

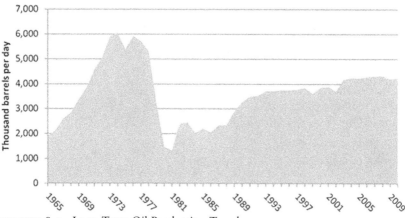

FIGURE 8.1. Long-Term Oil Production Trends

The other persistent issue facing the petroleum sector is financing. Because Iranian law directs crude revenues into the hands of the central state, NIOC's capital budget for exploration and production activities is chronically underfinanced and vulnerable to political diversion. Product sales remain within the company's purview, but given price controls they do not provide a firm basis for investment and stable planning. Guidelines for the National Development Fund direct 14.5 percent of total profits from oil and gas revenues to NIOC for investment purposes. However, because the budget allocation is based upon a presumptive oil price, the actual distribution of revenues has been subject to manipulation. Ahmadinejad's maneuverings proved particularly difficult to track, even within Iran, as his administration stopped releasing accurate data and the subsidy reform program began to require massive outlays of cash from the central government. The volatility and limitations of the revenue stream have proven frustrating and problematic for ensuring predictable capital investment. The ministry and NIOC – with the recent cooperation of the Majlis Energy Commission – have sought to utilize sanctions as a rationale for revising the calculation of the sector's budget allocation.

The Islamic Republic has managed its revenue constraints by focusing on volume. Restoring production to prerevolutionary levels has been a major priority for NIOC, one that has proven to be persistently beyond reach, as Figure 8.1 demonstrates. In 1992, Iran's oil minister predicted that Iran's production capacity would reach 5 mbpd by the March 1993

Source of Iran's gas resources

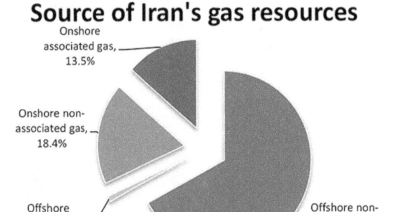

Onshore associated gas, 13.5%

Onshore non-associated gas, 18.4%

Offshore associated gas, 1%

Offshore non-associated gas, 67.1%

Source: FACTS Global Energy, U.S. Energy Information Administration

FIGURE 8.2. Source of Iran's Gas Resource

new year.[18] In 2000, his successor made the same promise,[19] and similar boasts continued throughout the subsequent decade. Yet the failures to meet these unrealistic expectations of the industry's proponents should not mask NIOC's underlying achievements. Despite heavy political constraints and severe restrictions in its access to foreign technology, expertise, and capital, Iran has managed steadily to increase its oil production capabilities, reaching a postrevolutionary high in 2008 of 4.184 mbpd.[20]

Notably, despite other energy struggles, the Islamic Republic can claim something of an energy success story in the explosion of gas production and consumption. Although overall energy production has declined since the revolution, the past three decades have witnessed a dramatic upsurge in annual gas production of more than 670 percent, from approximately 1.6 bcf/day in 1979 – and this was a reversal of the previous four years of declining production – to 13.4 bcf/day in 2010.[21] As Figure 8.2 indicates, more than two-thirds of Iran's proven gas reserves lie in offshore,

---

[18] Youssef M. Ibrahim, "Pumping Oil: Iran's New Muscle; Rebounding Iranians Are Striving for Regional Leadership in Gulf," *New York Times*, November 7, 1992.

[19] "Oil Production in Iran to Reach 5 mn bpd in Five Years to Come," *AZER Press*, July 18, 2000.

[20] *MEES*, November 2, 2008.

[21] These are estimates; figures from *BP Statistical Review 2011*

nonassociated fields, and their development has necessitated massive new investments in infrastructure and technical capabilities.

OIL AND THE NEW ORDER

The postrevolutionary government focused on diversifying the economy and attenuating its integration in the international energy business, which its leaders saw as draining Iran's patrimony and subjugating the country to Western capitalist interests. For the first several years after the revolution, the Oil Ministry held that "oil should be used as a political and economic weapon."[22] There was a broad consensus that a more diversified economy, oriented to the interests of the Iranian people rather than Western consumers, would place less emphasis on petroleum and the quick accumulation of wealth. Still, from the start, Khomeini appreciated the leverage offered by Iran's oil production; during the height of the Kurdish rebellion, for example, he announced that he had ordered NIOC to put a single day's oil receipts for development projects in Iran's Kurdish provinces as a means of acknowledging and, at least nominally, assuaging local grievances.

Husayn Nazih, the human rights lawyer initially tapped to head NIOC, quickly found himself in an impossible situation – trying to revive production, deal with sabotage and terrorism, assuage political sensitivities as well as labor grievances, mitigate the loss of some six hundred foreign experts, and manage a sector that he knew only superficially, all in the midst of profound political infighting. He was quickly overcome by revolutionary turmoil, and after a brief but abortive bid for the Assembly of Experts, Nazih fled to France over feared backlash from revelations that emerged as a result of the embassy seizure of his meetings with U.S. diplomats.

Nazih was replaced by Ali Akbar Moinfar, another left-leaning technocrat, who still had the Islamists' confidence. The new leadership announced its readiness to revive production and maintain export relationships with the former consortium companies. To some surprise, Tehran was able to command a premium for its initial postrevolutionary spot sales. Other than demands to preclude reexport of Iranian crude to Israel and South Africa, the new regime's early crude deals hewed closely to the country's prior trade patterns: Most of Iran's crude remained destined for Europe and Japan. Tehran did abandon several prerevolutionary joint ventures, including refining deals with South Africa and South Korea.

---

[22] "Iran to Use Oil Meeting to Seek Aide's Release," *Reuters*, December 13, 1979.

The structure of oil contracts and the psychological impact of the revolution had precipitated another sudden and severe price spiral.[23] During the hostage crisis, Tehran appealed – futilely – to fellow OPEC members to limit their own production in sympathy with its "antiimperialist struggle."[24] Iran also sought to shift away from requiring dollars in its export transactions and embargoed oil sales to U.S. companies. These measures did not significantly disrupt oil markets, which were already in turmoil from prerevolutionary panic and price escalation. However, they "amplified the overall nervousness and anxiety in the market" and ultimately enabled Tehran to ratchet prices and revenues upward.[25]

However, by mid-1980, the price hikes associated with revolutionary upheaval were already beginning to abate. In April 1980, Japan rejected Iranian price demands, instead expanding their imports from Saudi Arabia and the UAE. Other IOCs, including BP and Shell, also began to balk at Iranian demands. The pricing dispute coincided with new Japanese and European sanctions on Iran over the hostage crisis. Tehran brushed off the dispute, with Moinfar questioning, "What would be the use in trying to produce more when we have no use for the money? We are not interested in piling up dollars in foreign banks and then having no use for them."[26] Already, though, the lure of oil rents split the new leadership, with Prime Minister Rejai arguing to expand production during debates over the 1981 budget. The breach with Tokyo lasted ten months until a new agreement allowed Japanese imports to resume at 170,000–180,000 bpd.

THE WAR AND IRAN'S ENERGY SECTOR

With the September 1980 Iraqi invasion, revenue requirements began to force the rapid reconstitution of an industry that had been battered by pre- and postrevolutionary turbulence. The war threatened the permanent loss of production from Khuzestan to Iraq's voracious appetites. Taha Ramadan, Iraqi vice president, declared that Iran's oil production or, as he put it, "Arabistan's oil will be Iraqi as long as Tehran will not negotiate."[27]

---

[23] Yergin (1991), pp. 684–8.
[24] "Iran Asks Other OPEC Members to Limit Oil Output Next Year," *Wall Street Journal*, December 3, 1979.
[25] Yergin (1991), p. 702.
[26] "Iran Reports Big Oil-Income Loss," *New York Times*, June 13, 1980.
[27] "Iraqi Aide Says Aim Is to Seize Iran's Oil and Then Negotiate," *New York Times*, October 22, 1980, p. A1.

One of the initial Iraqi offensives near Abadan captured the acting oil minister; the next permanent minister, Mohammed Gharazi, gave to the post an industry background as well as impeccable revolutionary credentials that included stints in the shah's prisons as well as Najaf and French exiles. Gharazi helped to found the Revolutionary Guard Corps and served as deputy governor of Khuzestan, where he won plaudits for uncovering and viciously repressing an alleged plot against local military forces. He maintained his office in central Ahwaz even after the Iraqi incursion, declaring that "if Iraqi MiGs attack the city and hit this building, I will be the first to die."[28] Gharazi was influential enough within the early postrevolutionary power structure that in 1981, Khamenei pressed for him as prime minister after the president's first choice – Ali Akbar Velayati, who went on to serve instead as foreign minister – was rejected by the parliament on the basis of insufficient revolutionary credentials. Gharazi's nomination was also quashed, a move that paved the way for a government led by Mir Husayn Musavi.

The war devastated Iran's petroleum sector, in both direct and indirect fashion. The conflict destroyed vital facilities, including the Abadan refinery, and Iran's main oil export terminal was also targeted repeatedly. During the revolution's first decade, Tehran struggled to revive production and maintain exports as its facilities and transportation corridors were bombed and its economy was subsumed by both sanctions and war mobilization. Overall trends were intensely negative – from an average production level of 3.17 mpbd in 1979, despite massive unrest and labor actions in the oil sector, average production fell to 1.5 mpbd as a result of the Iraqi invasion the subsequent year.[29]

The same problems that plagued Iran's military resupply – sanctions, foreign exchange shortages, and a profound lack of either credit or credibility – hurt Tehran's ability to revive oil production. The war also exacerbated Iran's weak position within OPEC. After the revolution, Tehran lost its opportunity for an OPEC leadership role, and Saudi Arabia responded to the Iraqi invasion by ramping up production and filling the supply breach for a dozen countries. Tehran repeatedly pressed for a higher OPEC quota, based on the exigencies of war: "We have a series of expenses the others do not have," argued Gharazi.[30]

---

[28] Richard Johns and Terry Povey, "Opec's Most Political Animal," *FT*, January 29, 1983, p. 34.
[29] Salehi-Isfahani in Rahnema and Behdad (1995), p. 153.
[30] James Crawford, "Yamani Sees Hope of Oil-Sharing Pact," *Globe and Mail*, December 20, 1982.

Still, over the first half of 1982, in part out of a desperate need for hard currency revenues, Tehran made major strides in reviving production and putting damaged facilities back on line. Iranian exports expanded from 400,000 bpd in early 1982 to 2 million bpd six months later. At the same time, Tehran sought to improve its position within OPEC, in hopes of shifting its competitors' production policies in its own favor. Iranian representatives advocated quotas based on each state's population and financial requirements. The Iranian oil minister Mohammad Gharazi invoked a Persian proverb in making the case that "those who have more roof gather more snow."[31] When that gambit failed, Tehran sought to grab market share and expand its revenue base by instituting price cuts that defied the cartel's agreed price band, risking an open breach with OPEC. At a 1983 ministerial meeting, Gharazi declared that "every reduction in Saudi production that is added to ours means a victory."[32]

Despite struggles in maintaining production and achieving needed revenues, the Iranian leadership sought to use oil trade as a political weapon. In 1983, after a French sale of advanced strike jets equipped with Exocet missiles to Baghdad, Tehran threatened to blockade all Gulf exports by threatening safe passage through the Straits of Hormuz. Rafsanjani predicted that if the sale went through, the West "would face a very cold winter."[33] However, when the inevitable occurred – an Iraqi attack on tankers at Iran's main export terminal, Kharg Island – Tehran hunkered down. The relative imbalance in the two combatants' dependency on oil revenues limited Tehran's options, since it had almost no recourse to compensate for lost export opportunities while Baghdad had an array of deep-pocketed supporters.

As discussed in Chapter 4, the Saudis engineered the mid-1980s collapse of oil prices, which fortuitously undermined the Iranian economy and by extension Iran's war prospects. Later, when the "tanker war" phase of the conflict escalated to direct skirmishes between Iranian and American naval forces, Tehran faced prolonged risks in its traditional Gulf export routes, and in 1987 Iran's oil minister launched talks with

---

[31] Milton Freudenheim and Henry Giniger, "Knocks, Pings at OPEC Session," *New York Times*, December 26, 1982.

[32] William Drozdiak, "OPEC Output Pact Collapses; Yamani Hints at Price Cut," *Washington Post*, January 24, 1983, p. A1.

[33] Thomas Lueck, "Iran-Iraq Oil Threat Minimized," *New York Times*, October 17, 1983.

Moscow to pursue the possibility of utilizing the IGAT-1 gas trunkline for oil exports.[34]

By the mid-1980s, Iran was reportedly producing at levels well above its 2.3 mbpd OPEC quota and relying on spot market barter deals to offload its excess – which over time constituted as much as 25 percent of its exports. As the terms became increasingly less advantageous, Tehran sought to shift its pricing model away from barter deals, primarily at the behest of industry technocrats, who saw barter as eroding Iran's control over prices and destinations as well as contributing to soft market conditions.[35] On the other side stood the Foreign Ministry, which valued barter trade as a mechanism for extending Iranian influence.

During this same period, the Iranian leadership began to recalibrate its approach to oil politics. In November 1985, Gholamreza Aghazadeh was appointed oil minister. Although Aghazadeh was not a trained oilman, he was better equipped than his predecessors to work collaboratively with his Saudi counterparts, initially crafting a common response to the 1985 price collapse after nearly a year of feuding with Riyadh over production policy. The comity did not last long, however. Frictions with Riyadh continued to manifest throughout the war. In 1987, Iran's OPEC representative Husayn Kazempour-Ardebili stormed uninvited into a cartel committee meeting, demanding aggressive Saudi action to curtail rampant overproduction and accusing Riyadh of risking "a price war."[36]

Beyond the strategic competition with the Gulf for market share, Tehran during the war period undertook a dramatic expansion in gas production, shifting focus from its associated gas, gas that is produced as part of oilfield development which accounts for approximately 15 percent of Iran's total gas resources, to its massive nonassociated fields, particularly South Pars. In 1983, NIGC began production at Gavarzin, on Qeshm Island in the Persian Gulf, which supplied the Bandar Abbas power station among other uses; Gavarzin was followed by Khangiran in 1984; Sarkhun, Masduran (Sarakhs) in 1990; Aghar-Dalan (1995).[37] Gas production increases were sustained even while oil production remained relatively stagnant.[38] Flaring was reduced threefold, and gas reinjection in Iran's aging oil fields as a means of maintaining pressure

---

[34] Elaine Sciolino, "U.S. Escorts Quietly Take 2 More Ships into Gulf," *New York Times*, August 9, 1987.

[35] Kathy Evans, "Exports Maintained Despite Difficulties," *FT*, April 1, 1985.

[36] Steven Greenhouse, "Iranian Assails Saudis over OPEC Production," *New York Times*, September 11, 1987, p. D1.

[37] *APS Review Gas Market Trends* 38:19, May 18, 1992.   [38] Ibid.

expanded from 11 bcm in 1985 to 18 bcm in 1989.[39] Still, flaring continued in significant volumes; in 2008, the World Bank ranked Iran the third leading source of flared gas, at an estimated 10 bcm per year.[40]

Despite rising production, gas exports did not factor high on the postrevolutionary energy agenda. In the months before the revolution, labor unrest disrupted gas exports to the Soviet Union, and the successor regime ultimately cancelled all other gas export projects as part of its broad repeal of monarchical-era energy contracts. Although Tehran grudgingly relaxed its opposition to foreign investment in oil and gas, particularly after the war's end, the consequences of its gas export cancellations should not be underestimated. The rescission of Iran's burgeoning gas exports had long-term consequences for the country's place in the global economy; had IGAT II moved forward as initially intended, it would have been "the biggest gas corridor in the world after the Soviet Union's."[41] Instead, gas exports to the Soviet Union tapered off after the Iraqi invasion, with Tehran diverting supplies for domestic consumption while demanding higher prices from Moscow. Meanwhile, other competitors – particularly Qatar, whose massive gas field is part of the same geological structure as South Pars – found an open field as the international gas trade began to boom.

Even in the Islamic Republic's early years, the revolutionaries did not close the door entirely to foreign presence in the energy sector. At this same time, Iran began exploring possibilities for a return by international oil companies, despite the constitutional prohibitions on foreign ownership. In late 1981, Iran contracted for technical assistance with Romania to rebuild facilities damaged by the war.[42] In 1982, Tehran began working with Agip to extend pipelines from the Kangan gas field.[43] That same year, Tehran signed a memorandum of understanding with Ankara for a feasibility study to examine the prospects for constructing a pipeline via Turkey to transport Iranian gas to Europe.

One of the casualties of the war was a long-delayed petrochemical plant at Bandar Khomeini (Shahpour prior to the revolution); after repeated setbacks and price escalations, the complex was nearing completion at the time of the revolution. Despite revolutionary disruptions,

---

[39] Ibid.

[40] "Natural Gas Liquids Supply Outlook 2008–2015," International Energy Agency, 2008, p. 23, http://www.iea.org/textbase/nppdf/free/2010/NGL2010.pdf

[41] Afkhami (2009), p. 341.

[42] "Iran Embargo Just Partial Success," *Reuters*, November 16, 1981.

[43] "Iranians Challenge Oil Limits," *New York Times*, November 8, 1982.

the project was sustained by the 50 percent stake of the Japanese company Mitsui and Tokyo's reliance on Iran for nearly 10 percent of its oil consumption. Mitsui sought to walk away from the project repeatedly but recommitted itself in 1983 after Iran agreed to sell Japan oil at below-market prices.[44] Ultimately, however, repeated Iraqi bombings devastated the complex, and in 1988 Mitsui finally withdrew. Its demise represented the largest loss in the Mitsui Company's post–World War II history.[45]

FUELING RECONSTRUCTION

After the war's end, the Iranian leadership understood that rebuilding the energy sector and reviving production and exports would be vital. In this respect, the Iraqi invasion of Kuwait offered a well-timed windfall, albeit a brief one. Tehran reaped the benefits of higher oil prices as a result of the Iraqi invasion of Kuwait and subsequent disruptions to both countries' exports. However, the conflict also underscored the ongoing and seemingly irresolvable opposition of Saudi Arabia and Iran, particularly on the issue of oil production and pricing policies. For Tehran, the crisis in the Gulf offered a well-timed opportunity to staunch the slide in prices and the overproduction and quota busting that plagued OPEC's interactions and effectiveness. The Saudis saw the conflict in very different terms – existential ones, naturally – and sought to ramp up production in order to bolster Western commitment to the kingdom's security and Saddam Hussein's expulsion.

Riyadh's approach was consistent; after all, problems of oversupply and quota cheating contributed to Saddam's decision to seize Kuwait in August 1990. The continuing divergence between Saudi and Iranian oil policies checked the cautious reengagement under way between the two countries. It also contributed to the stumbling of Rafsanjani and his reconstruction program. In the next several years, as the Saudis continued to expand production, the price remained low. Iran's oil revenues declined precisely at the same moment its postwar reconstruction economy began to overheat and its debt burden grew too quickly. Tehran's income for the Iranian year ending March 1994 had fallen by 25 percent over the previous year, and 20 percent lower than budgeted.[46]

[44] Steve Lohr, "Japanese to Resume Big Project in Iran," *New York Times*, May 19, 1983.
[45] Henry Scott Stokes, "Iran's Japanese Hostage," *New York Times*, November 30, 1980.
[46] Furtig (2002), p. 235.

Still, the revived Saudi-Iranian frictions over oil policy helped persuade both sides of the utility of greater cooperation on energy. Persistent tensions – including Iranian military efforts to stake a claim to several small Gulf islands, which provoked intense hostility – meant that the rapprochement process required an additional five years beyond the Gulf War. In the interim, Tehran feuded again with the Saudis within OPEC in 1992, as Riyadh pushed the cartel to endorse its expanded market share formally. The outcome reflected a compromise, with the Saudis winning a short-term extension of their higher production quotas.[47] In addition to these domestic and regional political challenges, Tehran's postwar attempt to revive its oil exports faced oil markets that had changed dramatically in the years since the revolution. The boom and bust of the previous decade had tempered the producing countries' clout. As Djavad Salehi-Isfahani notes, "This introduce[d] a strategic element into Iran's export policy which did not exist before the revolution."[48]

Iran's postwar reconstruction agenda was grounded in a realistic appreciation of the need for a substantial increase in oil production and a full-fledged reengagement with the international economy. Efforts to reopen the energy sector to foreign investment were hard fought internally. The resulting framework, as codified in the 1987 Petroleum Law and much later in the 2002 Foreign Investment Promotion and Protection Act, was carefully constructed to prevent or at least mitigate anticipated domestic opposition. This resulted in a cumbersome and unattractive contract model, known as the buyback. Launched in 1990 and revised repeatedly since that time, the buyback contract has proven a major impediment to attracting and maintaining foreign investment in the energy sector. The relatively limited time frame and the cap on the rate of return soured relationships between the IOCs and their Iranian counterparts and deterred others from investing. The drawbacks to the buyback are exacerbated by the time-consuming and often quixotic decision-making process within the energy sector.

In conjunction with the launch of the buyback contract model in 1990, the second Five-Year Plan approved by the Iranian parliament also included specific authorization for the government to seek up to $3.2 billion in foreign investment for the development of South Pars. In the

---

[47] Fareed Mohammedi, "OPEC since the Gulf War," *Middle East Report* 176 (May–June 1992), pp. 39–40, 42.

[48] Djavad Salehi-Isfahani, "The Oil Sector after the Revolution," in Rahnema and Behdad (1995), p. 151.

next several years, NIOC undertook talks with a range of prospective partners over an array of oil and gas projects, including Total, Chevron, Agip SpA, Japan National Oil Company, British Petroleum, and the Soviet Machinoexport.

At the time, the focus on South Pars was something of "a surprise" to external analysts given Iran's fiscal vulnerabilities and the sufficiency of its existing gas developments. In the late 1980s, Iran had initially explored the possibility of jointly developing the resource with Qatar. Qatar's September 1991 launch of North Field developments drew international headlines and capital, and until the scope of the Iranian structure was better understood, there was a presumption among many in the industry that Tehran was simply seeking to shake down its Gulf neighbor.[49]

Despite its mammoth reserves, South Pars development has proven prone to complications since its outset. In 1993, Tehran revoked a $1.7 billion contract issued to Italian, Japanese, and Russian firms the previous year, after the government's external debt load imperiled prospects for European financing. At the same time, the collapse of the Soviet Union and changes under way across Eastern Europe unexpectedly eliminated Iran's sole gas export relationship, which had only just been painstakingly reconstructed after a decade of inactivity. The situation soured some Iranians on the hard-fought opening to foreign investors; in the words of one official at the time, "if foreign companies want to be active in the oil sector, they'd better change their terms and make them less demanding."[50]

After the rescission of the Italian/Japanese/Russian deal, an NIOC spin-off firm, Petroleum Development and Engineering Company (Pedec), took over in 1994. Pedec's difficulties in attracting financing meant that little progress was made until the project was shifted once again to the newly established Petropars in 1998. During the same period, in a flurry of negotiations with a wide array of European and Japanese firms, Tehran pushed forward the development of subsequent South Pars phases. In 1997, a consortium that comprised Total (France), Gazprom (Russia), and Petronas (Malaysia) agreed to develop Phases 2 and 3, with Hyundai (South Korea) serving as the primary subcontractor for onshore construction.

[49] "Saipem and TPL Near Accord on South Pars Field," *MEED*, July 26, 1991.
[50] Randall Palmer, "Iran Snubs Foreign Firms in Oil/Gas Contracts," *Reuters*, August 31, 1994.

Three years later, Phases 4 and 5 went to the Italian firm ENI and Petropars, and in 2002 Tehran announced that Statoil had been selected as the operator for Phases 6, 7, and 8. LG won Phases 9 and 10 the same year. Financing for the projects had a variety of domestic sources, including NICO, as well as foreign banks and entities such as Mitsui & Co. These deals defied a new American push to extend its own prohibitions on energy investment to third countries, via the Iran Libya Sanctions Act. Iran's success in attracting IOCs called into question the viability of U.S. pressure on Iran and seemed to herald the internationalization of Iran's energy sector. The port city of Assaluyeh took off with the construction of processing facilities and managerial activities for South Pars; it was "a contractor's dream," and tens of thousands of new jobs were created.[51] In 1998, the Pars Special Economic Energy Zone was established in order to facilitate foreign investment in and around the South Pars projects.

At the time, many within the Iranian establishment viewed foreign investors and the return of Western capital, technology, and expertise as essential to the country's future. This reflected a decade of hard-fought postwar efforts to reconstruct the economy and to achieve a domestic consensus around a central role for international oil companies in the future of the country's petroleum sector. And there was little confidence in the domestic industry's capabilities; the two main Iranian contractors – Petropars and Pedec – struggled to meet their project deadlines and obtain needed capital. The deals were also perceived as a valediction of the newfound reform movement, which was posited on the notion of Iran's reintegration into the world economy.

However, the sector and the role of foreign investors evolved much differently than early optimism might have suggested. The early optimism eroded under the weight of delays and differences between Tehran and the foreign contractors about the pace of the projects and viable rate of return. There were inherent conflicts between Iranian interests and those of their prospective foreign investors. Ultimately, Iranian sought precedence for utilizing the gas to satisfy the country's domestic demand – an NIOC official described Iran's EOR requirements as "unlimited" – whereas foreign investors would have preferred projects that capitalized on international gas demand.[52] The companies considered doing business in Iran's contentious political environment frustrating, and several found

---

[51] Nassir Shirkhani, "South Pars Boom Town," *Upstream*, November 24, 2000.
[52] "Iran – Homeward Bound," *Energy Compass*, July 21, 2000.

themselves enmeshed in costly corruption scandals that damaged both their profile within Iran as well as their international reputation.[53] Increasingly, as international sanctions intensified, new project tenders were subject to repeated delays and revisions, and new opportunities began to present themselves, as in Iraq and Libya, the enthusiasm of the international oil companies for Iran began to wane.

In 1989, Tehran and Moscow agreed to revive the IGAT I export swaps and negotiated similar deals with Bulgaria, Romania, and Yugoslavia, as well as talks with Czechoslovakia, Poland, and Greece. Those deals collapsed with the demise of the Soviet Union and the Eastern bloc, raising questions about the markets for South Pars production. "Just as it seemed the long-planned but seemingly fated plan to export to Europe via Turkey was entering the home straight, someone shifted the entire track."[54] The loss of the Soviet market for major infrastructure projects – Moscow had helped finance several major dams as lower costs than other bidders – helped drive Iran's decision to open the energy sector, and the broader economy, to investment from Western Europe, Japan, and even America.

Alongside the initiative to develop South Pars, Iran has sought to revive other gas export possibilities, including pipeline and LNG deals that echoed the prerevolutionary plans. In 1993, Tehran signed a preliminary agreement with Gaz de France for feasibility studies into various pipeline and LNG export options. At the time, the Petroleum Ministry envisioned exports of approximately 50 bcf/year by 2000, half of which was intended for European and Pakistani markets.[55] In 2001, Oil Ministry officials projected that gas export revenues would gradually rise to levels commensurate with historic patterns, predicting $6 billion from South Pars alone.[56]

These projections proved overly optimistic. Tehran's export capabilities have been constrained by a variety of forces: domestic mismanagement and volatility in the petroleum sector, sanctions-imposed limitations on access to technology and capital, and fierce rivalries over establishing dominant export corridors from competitors including Qatar, Russia,

---

[53] Both Total and Statoil were alleged to have paid bribes as a means of securing and maintaining their stakes in South Pars. "Total Takes $390 Mil Settlement Provision over US Probes of Iranian Gas Deals," *Platts*, July 27, 2012.

[54] "Events Buffet Iran's Export Plans," International Gas Report, *FT*, January 10, 1992.

[55] "Making the Most of Oil," *MEED*, October 18, 1991.

[56] "Special Report Oil & Gas – Pars Oil & Gas," *MEED Weekly Special Report*, March 23, 2001.

and the Central Asian states, the latter the recipients of substantial U.S. government backing. Still, Iran managed to achieve modest export levels to Armenia and Turkey via pipeline and arranged two separate swap arrangements with Azerbaijan, one of which provides Iranian gas to the Azeri enclave of Nakhchivan.

Turkey remains the longest-standing of Iran's export relationships, and its chaotic history speaks to Iran's challenges in positioning itself as a reliable gas source. Talks between Tehran and Ankara began shortly after the revolution and culminated in 1982 in a gas export deal.[57] However, a supply agreement was not signed until 1996, and sanctions and financial issues further delayed the launch. The pipeline linking Tabriz to Ankara was completed in 2001 with a capacity of 28 Mcm/day.

Shortly after its initial foray into IOC investment went awry in South Pars, Tehran extended the buyback model to upstream oil, only to face similar obstacles. In 1994, an Iranian spin-off company, IOEC, sought foreign partners in developing the Abuzar oil field, but an American, French, and Japanese consortium failed to raise sufficient funds.[58] Once again, financing problems and the aftereffects of the debt crisis thwarted a politically sensitive international deal. Still, despite these stumbles, Iranian officials perceived themselves in the driver's seat as they sought foreign investment in the upstream. "If foreign companies want to be active in the oil sector, they'd better change their terms and make them less demanding."[59]

This backdrop helps to explain why Conoco won Iran's first postrevolutionary upstream oil contract awarded to a foreign firm. Prior to 1995, ideological preferences and factional infighting deterred Tehran from serious pursuit of American firms for exploration and development openings. However, the difficulties in securing financing for South Pars Phase 1 and Abuzar commended consideration of a more influential partner – one that might overcome official U.S. opposition and financing restrictions. In March 1995, Tehran announced Conoco's selection to lead development of the Sirri A and E offshore oil fields – a deal estimated to be worth $1 billion and one in which the French firm Total was perceived as the favorite.

[57] "Iran Agrees to Supply Natural Gas to Turkey," *New York Times*, September 11, 1982.
[58] "Local Firms Given Lead in Oil and Gas Schemes," *MEED*, September 5, 1994.
[59] Randall Palmer, "Iran Snubs Foreign Firms in Oil/Gas Contracts," *Reuters*, August 31, 1994.

The decision generated a fierce backlash. Although Conoco officials had invested heavily in their bid, the public outcry in the United States quickly persuaded the company to back away even before Washington issued its formal ban on oil investments a few weeks later. The project reverted to Tehran, where initial frustration and concerns quickly gave way to renewed interest from multiple European firms. Still, the unsettled political environment had shifted the commercial context, and ultimately Shell dropped out of the bidding. Total went on to develop the Sirri fields in Conoco's place and shortly thereafter assumed a major role in the first round of South Pars exploration and production contracts that went to foreign firms.

Iranian officials scrambled to shift gears, depicting the episode as an important triumph in their efforts to parry American efforts to isolate the country. After the Total deal, Tehran was almost giddy with expectation; Iran's deputy oil minister announced that twelve projects, worth a total of $6.5 billion, would be tendered to international companies.[60] "We have an excellent response from the industry, it's outstanding.... I don't anticipate any problem at all," Bonakdar Hashemi, NIOC's deputy general manager for overseas participation and international agreements, declared in 1995.[61]

During this period, Tehran also sought to leverage its strategic location to serve as a hub for Central Asian oil and gas exports, offering land-locked Caspian states a route for getting their production to market and enabling Iran itself to optimize its domestic energy balance. Consistent with efforts to isolate the Islamic Republic, Washington countered, devoting considerable resources and effort over the course the 1990s and beyond to the promotion of alternative pipeline routes. To the extent that the U.S. strategy succeeded, it was aided by market forces. With the establishment of new pipeline systems with its neighbors largely precluded by U.S. sanctions, Tehran was forced to rely on oil swaps, which offered only marginal revenues and cut into the country's OPEC quota. An Iranian MP revealed that Iran's total revenues over nine years of swaps totaled a mere $146 million, and when swaps were abandoned in 2010, then–Oil Minister Massoud Mir-Kazemi described them as "completely disadvantageous for us."[62]

---

[60] "Iran to Offer 12 Oil Projects to Foreign Firms," *Reuters*, July 27, 1995.

[61] "Iran's NIOC Upbeat over Energy Projects Tender," *Reuters*, September 7, 1995.

[62] Ebrahim Gilani, "Iran's Decision to End Loss Making Oil Swaps Could Reduce Its Influence in the Caspian Region," Institute for War and Peace Reporting, October 7, 2010.

To service swaps that oil officials predicted could reach levels of 500,000 bpd, Tehran invested $400 million in a 240-mile pipeline from the Caspian port of Neka to Tehran and sought to expand refinery capacity in the north of the country to support the trade. By summer 2003, Turkmenistan was exporting 50,000 bpd via Neka-Tehran, with smaller volumes from Russia and Kazakhstan (25,000 bpd and 20,000 bpd, respectively beginning in 2002).

Iran has sought for decades to construct a viable petrochemicals industry, although the effort was significantly set back by the revolution and the war, which deferred new industrial investment and destroyed or damaged many existing facilities. After the war, a major joint venture that had been undertaken with Japan just before the revolution was reconstituted as the Bandar Khomeini Petrochemical Complex, as well as rehabilitation of existing plants and major investments in new facilities in Arak, Tabriz, and Isfahan.

The reconstruction era also saw the first of what would prove many unsuccessful debates around how to stem the explosion of domestic consumption of petroleum and its by-products. Despite its massive hydrocarbon resources, Iran historically relied on imported supplies of refined products to meet domestic demand. During the earliest development of Iran's oil sector, Iran imported significant quantities of gasoline and kerosene, mostly from Russia, thanks to the underdeveloped transportation and distribution networks at the time.[63]

The postrevolutionary leadership envisioned constraining domestic consumption as part of a broader reconfiguration of the economy to reduce reliance on energy revenues. In 1979, then-Deputy Prime Minister Husayn Bani Assadi urged Iranians "to stop this wave of car-buying and the feverish consumption of electricity and gas by the rich."[64] Still by 1993, Iran was consuming one-third as much energy as the country produced, in contrast to a mere 4 percent two decades earlier.[65] In 1995, then–Energy Minister Zaganeh appealed for reduced consumption, which was growing at 5.5 percent per year, arguing that a 40 percent reduction in domestic demand would save Iran at least $5.6 billion each year by making more oil available for export.[66]

---

[63] Fesharaki (1976), pp. 32–6.
[64] Youssef M. Ibrahim, "Inside Iran's Cultural Revolution," *New York Times Magazine*, October 14, 1979.
[65] Salehi-Isfahani in Rahnema and Behdad, p. 151.
[66] "Iran Should Curb Energy Use – Energy Minister," *Reuters*, January 25, 1995.

The driving element of explosive demand growth has been the artificially low domestic price of gasoline and other fuels. This was a deliberate strategy of appealing to the sense of national resource ownership that was part of the new state's legitimacy – an early articulation of what Ahmadinejad would later describe as the oil revenues on every citizen's tablecloth. Second, some Iranian leaders saw the country's resource base as providing a distinct comparative advantage – low energy costs – that could facilitate Iran's rapid industrialization.

However, as a wide range of analysts and political figures, including those in Iran, have long critiqued, "Neither of these theories was realistic. Ownership should not have been the reason to give Iranians the right to squander their God-given national assets. As for subsidizing industrial energy, this was calling for its wasteful use in all domestic factories."[67] The consequences of depressing real energy costs were uniformly negative – depriving NIOC of much-needed revenues, since domestic product sales represented a major component of the resources available to the sector for new investment.

For this reason, the postwar reconstruction program envisaged mechanisms to curtail refined petroleum imports and rationalize demand in accord with real prices. In 1994, the parliament attempted to cap gasoline imports at 190,000 bpd; however, the Oil Ministry balked at the restriction, arguing that it would be impossible to avoid either shortages or price escalations unless imports were permitted to rise to meet demand.[68] Similar efforts were undertaken on multiple occasions after this misfire, with nearly identical results. Iran's factional infighting inevitably situated the executive branch and the parliament in opposition on implementation of these reforms. Thirteen years passed before the first serious initiative was launched, after the intensification of international economic sanctions provided additional impetus to address such a gaping economic vulnerability. By that time, Tehran was importing 200,000 bpd of gasoline, and energy subsidies consumed at least 12 percent of GDP, according to a 2005 IMF study. Significant proportions of Iran's cheap gasoline were smuggled outside the country or consumed by Iranians with sufficient means to pay competitive prices.

---

[67] A. M. Samsam Bakhtiari and F. Shahbudaghlou, "Energy Consumption in the Islamic Republic of Iran," *OPEC Review* 24:3 (September 2000), p. 224.

[68] Sharif Imam-Jomeh, "Iran Deputies Vote for Food, Fuel Import Cuts," *Reuters*, March 8, 1994.

THE SPIN-OFF COMPANIES

The opening of Iran's petroleum sector to foreign companies prompted the establishment of new entities to handle specific projects and/or tasks, often with little or no real supervision by the state. Many of these were created as semiprivate entities. In addition, there are a range of additional direct and indirect (semiprivate) subsidiaries performing as subcontracted developers of the fields, in cooperation with international and foreign national oil companies in some cases. The proliferation of these companies began during the Rafsanjani presidency but reached its peak during Khatami's tenure. At least one hundred "affiliated and subsidiary companies" have staked a claim in one or more of Iran's current and future upstream projects.[69]

The NIOC spin-off companies have their roots in the distribution of the spoils. They operate with a larger degree of autonomy than NIOC and its immediate subsidiaries, but they are and always have been directly controlled by the government and fully publicly capitalized. Not surprisingly, authority over South Pars has been the subject of persistent turf battles; the multiplicity of cutouts ultimately reflects countervailing impulses toward distribution of the spoils and periodic efforts at rationalization and promotion of competition.

One of the largest of these is Petropars, which is engaged in South Pars Phases 1, 4 and 5, 6 through 8, 12, and 19. Petropars was established in 1997 as an offshore company, registered in the Virgin Islands, to manage South Pars projects. Its original shareholders were the NIOC Pension Fund (60 percent) and the Industrial Development and Renovation Organization Pension Fund (40 percent). As with other aspects of Iran's economy, its origins reflect a short-term fix to long-term problems; its leadership argued that "the services we need are not available in our banking system, or our insurance system. It's not quick enough to be competitive. So we prefer to work as an offshore company."[70] However, criticism of Petropars's structure, role, and leadership quickly mounted, motivated in equal parts by hard-liner suspicions toward reformists and resentment of an industry newcomer with a foreign registration and preferential access.

---

[69] Mahnaz Zahirinejad, "The Role of Political Structure in Iran's Energy Decision Making Policy," *Journal of Third World Studies* 29:1 (Spring 2012), p. 237.

[70] Then-Petropars Chief Akbar Torkan in Hugh Pope, "Internal Rules Limit Businesses in Iran," *Wall Street Journal*, June 29, 2002, p. B11.

Investigations by the parliament and the State Inspectorate Organization prompted the 2002 reconstitution of Petropars as an Iranian firm. It was then quietly transferred to Naftiran Intertrade Company, the Swiss-registered overseas arm of NIOC. Throughout its history, Petropars has been implicated in a series of scandals and allegations of corruption, but aside from the eviction of several high-profile reformists from its management, the scrutiny has generated little meaningful restructuring, other than further delays to South Pars development. Sanctions have thrust Petropars into an even more central role in South Pars's future development, and its role has evolved from facilitator of foreign investment to a favored vehicle for Iranian involvement in overseas upstream projects, including in Venezuela and Angola.[71]

In addition to Petropars, an array of well-connected spin-off firms has emerged with significant stakes in key upstream projects:

- Pedec was established in 1994 to serve as the main domestic partner for buyback projects. In 1997, Mehdi Hashemi, son of then-President Ali Akbar Hashemi Rafsanjani, managed to assume control of Pedec in what was perceived as a battle for turf, influence, and rewards. He was later replaced by Mehdi Husayni, a deputy oil minister and later the head of Kala in London.[72] During the Khatami period, Husayni was known as "Mr. Buyback," for his role in devising the contract model and negotiating many of the early deals. By 2000, Husayni was moved to Kala Naft in London, and Mehdi Mirmoezzi, deputy minister for exploration and production, took over Pedec. The firm's mandate was limited to three fields: Salman, Sirri C&D, and Farzam.[73] In 2000, responsibility for the buybacks was shifted to Pedec, led at the time by Ali Akbar Al-e Agha.

- IOEC was created in 1994 as a general contractor for the petroleum sector. Mehdi Hashemi headed IOEC in the 1990s, but the firm failed to win major deals, instead evolving into an engineering subcontractor and holding firm for other small technical firms. IOEC did manage to take a claim as a partner to Pedec. The company remains active in the

---

[71] Petropars has performed reservoir studies for several Venezuelan prospects and assumed a 26 percent stake in developing the Dobokubi oil field in Venezuela, in conjunction with the Venezuelan state oil company PDVSA. F. Milad, "Tehran, Caracas to Sign $2 Billion Oil Deal," *McClatchy-Tribune Business News*, May 29, 2012.

[72] "Iran – Who's Who," *Energy Compass*, October 6, 2000.

[73] "Iran – Homeward Bound," *Energy Compass*, July 21, 2000.

energy sector, constructing platforms and other facilities for several phases of South Pars.

- Petro-Iran Development Company, or Pedco, was also established in 1998 and incorporated in Jersey. Headed by Mostafa Khoee, the former chief of NIOC's offshore subsidiary (Iran Offshore Oil Company), Pedco emerged as a major player quickly when it won buyback contracts for the Salman field (with IOEC).[74]
- OIEC is another of the older subsidiaries, with a history that traces back to 1993. OIEC is a jointly owned subsidiary of NIOC (40 percent), NIOC Pension Funds (20 percent), and NIOC management (40 percent). OIEC took on minority stakes in Shah Denis (10 percent) and Lenkoran Denis (10 percent), another Caspian project under the auspices of TotalFinaElf.[75] In 2000, OIEC partnered with British Gas on a bid for South Pars Phases 9 and 10 and 11 and 12. During the Khatami period, OIEC was initially chaired by Ali Hashemi, who later chaired the parliament's Energy Commission. In 1999, the former construction minister Gholamreza Forouzesh took the helm and later acquired a 10 percent interest in the Soroush/Nowruz field development.[76]
- Naftiran Intertrade Co. (Nico) has emerged as one of the most important instruments of NIOC's arsenal, and an essential dimension of Iran's international commercial activities. It was created in 1992 in order to undertake barter deals in East Africa. In 1999, Iran's former ambassador to Italy, Majid Hedayatzadeh, took over Nico and brought to bear his prior diplomatic experience as well as his background as international relations chief for NIOC. Nico technically falls under the auspices of NIOC International but tends to overshadow its ostensible oversight body. Over time, Nico became an integral link in Iran's burgeoning financial relationships with the international banking system – the $3 billion credit facility negotiated during the Khatami era, for example, utilized Nico as the conduit.[77]
- A similar phenomenon has occurred in the petrochemicals sector, where privatization during the Ahmadinejad presidency has facilitated the establishment of numerous nonstate actors in this sector. In the process, "the petrochemical industry was cut into pieces and awarded to a group of individuals who only sought higher profits in

---

[74] Paul Sampson, "Who's Who in Iran," *Energy Compass*, May 25, 2001.
[75] "Iran – Who's Who," *Energy Compass*, October 6, 2000.
[76] Paul Sampson, "Who's Who in Iran," *Energy Compass*, May 25, 2001.   [77] Ibid.

the short-term," according to the head of the state petrochemical company in April 2014.[78]

THE ZANGANEH ERA

After Khatami's 1997 election, Bijan Namdar Zanganeh was named oil minister. Zanganeh was more technocrat than reformist – he had helped found the Reconstruction Crusade and led that organization during the war. During his two-term tenure as Rafsanjani's energy minister, he was widely credited for rehabilitating the sector. The experience also gave him a keen appreciation of the importance of Iran's gas sector for its domestic economy, as well as the distortions caused by price subsidies for domestic energy use. In taking over the Oil Ministry – by definition, a vital post – Zanganeh pursued an ambitious agenda of increasing production, securing foreign investment, and reforming the sector itself. He argued that "Iran's oil industry has two choices; either it wants to be an updated mainstream industry and be present globally or else this is absolutely not important for it," adding, "we opted for the first choice."[79]

Zanganeh unleashed a barrage of new tenders for upstream activity, although the pace of decisions proved more difficult to accelerate. Foreign firms vying for a share of the spoils during the reform period included Agip/ENI, BHP, British Petroleum, British Gas, Elf/Total/TotalFinaElf, Enterprise, Gaz de France, Gazprom Lasmo, Maersk, Royal Dutch/Shell, and Petronas. At least $15 billion in upstream deals were signed during Khatami's first term, and in several cases the arrangements included enhancements to the existing buyback terms that offered the foreign firm a larger role in production decisions and other key aspects of the deal. In 2005, in the last round of international tender activity on South Pars, Phases 15 and 16 drew bids from four separate partnerships of foreign and domestic firms, including Hyundai/Foster Wheeler/Isoico, Technip/OIEC/Saff, Petropars/Daelim/Chiyoda, and Sabra/AK Kvaerner/Khatam al Anbia. During this period, even U.S. firms sought to position themselves for a future role in South Pars, buying technical data packages and leading Iranian officials to predict they might receive U.S. bids for Phases 9–12 in 2000.[80]

---

[78] "Wrong Privatization Paralyzed Petchem Sector: NPC Chief," *IRNA*, April 19, 2014.
[79] "Candid Chat with the Oil Minister about the Nation's Oil Performance and Strategy," *Noruz*, July 21, 2001, p. 15.
[80] "US Companies Seen Submitting Bids for Iran Gas Field – Official," *Dow Jones Energy Service*, November 5, 2000.

Demonstrating a savvy appreciation of the political opportunities as well as the shifts within the sector, Tehran also reached out beyond the traditional IOC heavyweights to the national oil companies that were beginning to emerge as major industry players. Petronas and Gazprom joined TotalFinaElf in a successful bid for Phases 2 and 3 of South Pars in 1997. In 1998, BG submitted a joint bid for construction of the Neka-Tehran pipeline but found themselves outbid by a joint effort by Mapna and a Chinese-led consortium.[81] In August 1998, Bonyad-e Mostazafan partnered with CNPC for gas exploration in southern Iran.[82] The courting extended beyond well beyond Asia, however, particularly as sanctions and political risk began to erode the competitive position of Western companies. Brazil's Petrobras won a license to explore in the Gulf in 2003 and a year later was granted drilling rights in the Caspian. In 2000, after signing a series of European firms to major gas and oil deals, Iran's oil minister described U.S. sanctions as "a joke," adding that "the only thing it has succeed [ed] in doing is preventing American companies from investing in Iran."[83]

However, the track record of projects spearheaded by domestic Iranian firms has been marked by financial and logistical headaches. In 1998, Tehran was forced to shift from a domestic-led effort to boost production at the Nowruz field to an international tender when OIEC was unable to secure financing.[84] IOEC's buyback contract for developing the Soroush experienced similar issues, which cleared the way for Shell and Enterprise Oil to claim the contract. One of the difficulties was the parliament, which rejected efforts to insert flexibility in the fulfillment of buyback deals.'[85]

In October 1999, Tehran announced the biggest oil find since the revolution, the Azadegan field in southwestern Iran near the Iraqi border. At the time, Azadegan was believed to hold somewhere between 26 and 70 billion barrels of oil, with a potential production profile of 300,000–400,000 barrels per day for decades. The discovery seemed ideally timed for Tehran, since the advent of a reformist presidency had restored confidence among prospective investors in Iran's energy sector and political stability. Initially, a consortium of Japanese firms won the

---

[81] "Iran – Who's Who," *Energy Compass*, October 6, 2000.   [82] Ibid.
[83] "Iran Makes More Headway on Gas Developments," *Energy Compass*, August 4, 2000.
[84] "Local Iranian Firms Struggle to Fulfill Own Contracts," *Petroleum Intelligence Weekly*, June 15, 1998.
[85] Ibid.

right to develop Azadegan, in a transaction that offered Tehran a $3 billion loan.

The lure of investing in Iran was not limited to European and Asian firms. Throughout the 1990s, American oil companies actively sought to position themselves for the future in Iran, lobbying against American sanctions, buying technical data on tendered projects, sending represen-tatives to industry events in Iran, and mapping out prospective cooper-ation with foreign firms that did not face legal constraints and had already entered the Iranian market.[86] For his part, Zanganeh openly agitated for American firms' return to the Iranian oil sector. "I don't think [sanctions are] good for open and free trade. It's a decision that goes against both sides. It deprives U.S. companies from participating in our projects. We have money to develop our fields, but we would prefer to have the participation of first-class foreign companies."[87] This public advocacy of resumed U.S. investment contributed to Zanganeh's unpopularity among Iran's hard-liners.

Having experienced the most direct loss as a result of the intensification of American sanctions on Iran, Conoco lobbied publicly and strenuously against the restrictions and actively sought to maintain its position in Iran despite the sanctions. When Iran's parliamentary speaker, Mehdi Karrubi, and other MPs visited New York for the September 2000 UNGA, they attended a reception with U.S. oil executives – as well as members of Congress. Conoco even acknowledged in 2001 that its UK subsidiary had analyzed the data package for the Azadegan field.[88] For most other U.S. companies, however, Iran represented a potential danger zone rather than an imminent opportunity, and American firms typically opted to follow Iranian developments from afar and sought to avoid reputational or legal jeopardy in dealing directly with Iran.

Despite his apparent success and his centrist political stance, Zanga-neh's tenure at the Oil Ministry was profoundly controversial. He emerged as a lightning rod for criticism and corruption allegations, primarily emanating from traditionalists who opposed the opening. In 2001, Ayatollah Ahmad Jannati, head of the Council of Guardians, inveighed against what he described as an Oil Ministry conspiracy to

[86] "US Companies Seen Submitting Bids for Iran Gas Field – Official," *Dow Jones Energy Service*, November 5, 2000.
[87] Neela Bannerjee, "Five Questions for Bijan Namdar Zanganeh; Toward Oil Price Stabil-ity, Step by Step," *New York Times*, June 25, 2000.
[88] Paul Sampson, "Politics in Limbo," *Energy Compass*, March 30, 2001.

embezzle funds, promising to name names. The parliament began agitating for more transparency, especially on terms of agreements concluded with IOCs. Because of its inherent limitations, the buyback model attracted criticisms even from supporters of foreign investment in the oil sector. NIOC Vice President Ghanimifard damned the contract model with faint praise as "the least damaging" mechanism for attracting foreign investment in the sector.[89] Technocrats within the sector and even the critics in the parliament appreciated that the risk-reward tradeoff was not sufficiently attractive to IOCs and argued that Iran bore the consequences of projects that were not optimally developed as a result of the lack of a long-term time horizon on the part of the foreign investors.

However, the debate on opening the sector to IOCs became caught up in partisan efforts to subvert Khatami as well as an ideologically motivated reluctance to embrace foreign development of Iran's petroleum resources. Much of the postrevolutionary élite remained convinced that foreign oil companies served as stalking horses of external influence and advocated using Iran's newfound surplus oil revenues for enhanced investment. Still others argued for deliberate restrictions on Iranian output to reduce dependence on petrodollars and/or preclude any weakening of worldwide prices as a result of expanded supply. And there was an overwhelming push for maintaining a dominant role for Iranian firms. Mostafa Taheri Najafabadi, chairman of the reformist parliament's Energy Committee, grumbled that the buybacks were "costly and not in our country's interests," adding that local firms "can do the projects on our own and step by step, making direct use of foreign loans and expertise."[90]

Senior officials doggedly refuted these arguments, engaging in an informal public education campaign that was not dissimilar to efforts undertaken to shift the official stance on birth rates and, later, on subsidy distribution. Iranian technocrats attempted to correct widespread misperceptions, particularly the notion that any dealings with the IOCs were inherently zero-sum in terms of their benefits. However, the official vindication campaign for buybacks was undertaken belatedly and was hampered by the industry's discomfort with transparency of its contractual arrangements. Ultimately, the barrage of domestic reproaches was sufficient to prompt the Expediency Council to intercede in February

---

[89] "Buy-Back Deals in the Dock," *MEED*, August 4, 2000.   [90] Ibid.

2001, overruling a Guardians' Council attempt to strike down the buy-back as a viable contract form.

One of the difficulties facing the advocates of further opening of the oil and gas sector was the fact that some of the critiques raised valid issues, particularly regarding the lack of transparency and the facilitation of corruption. Ministry officials sought to avoid public disclosure or discussions surrounding the modifications of the contract terms that were made to persuade companies to invest. In addition, subsequent revelations of bribes involving firms such as Total and Statoil and Iranian coconspirators such as Mehdi Hashemi, Rafsanjani's son, hint at the extent to which the IOC reentry to Iran was facilitated by financial self-interest on the part of individual Iranian authorities.[91] The perception and the reality that the return of the IOCs had empowered an "oil mafia" became woven into the popular imagination and eventually emerged as a powerful dimension of the political discourse with the rise of Iran's second-generation conservatives, particularly Ahmadinejad.

Zanganeh adopted an activist agenda with regard to the structure of the petroleum sector and promoted a skilled group of technocrats within his own inner circle. The downturn in oil prices during the mid- to late 1990s forced a broad retrenchment of government spending that extended to the petroleum sector. During this period, Zanganeh launched a closely watched reorganization of the ministry and NIOC, building a tightly woven network of supercharged technocrats, with Seyyed Mehdi Mirmoezzi as his upstream chief, Mohammad Aghaie as his downstream chief, Mohammad Reza Nematzadeh spearheading petrochemicals, and Hamdollarh Mohammad Nejad overseeing gas; Husayn Kazempour Ardebili as deputy minister for international affairs; Fereidun Saghafian, deputy minister for planning and board member of OIEC.

Zanganeh sought to place Mohammad Forouzandeh, a former defense minister, in a newly created position of managing director in 1997; he was rebuffed, and Forouzandeh instead moved to the Bonyad-e Mostazafan, which then began to make inroads into the petroleum sector for the first time.[92] In 1999, Mirmoezzi was appointed deputy managing director of NIOC, replacing Ali Hashemi – a move intended to expedite the sluggish bidding process. Hashemi's removal from these posts, along with the 1998 establishment of Petropars, was intended to promote a more

---

[91] Jacques Follorou, "Inquiry into Total's Activities in Iran Shifts toward Dubai," *Le Monde*, September 6, 2007.
[92] Paul Sampson, "Who's Who in Iran," *Energy Compass*, May 25, 2001.

rational, competitive approach to the petroleum sector.[93] In 1999, Zanganeh created and empowered NIOC International, under the leadership of Ahmed Rahgozar, who had formerly headed the London-based Naftiran Services; NIOC International was given authority over all oil exports as well as all gas and LNG projects.[94] Also within NIOC International were Majid Rouhani, a former senior NIOC official in London, who headed international business development in NIOC-International, and Hojatollah Ghanimifard, a vestige of the Aghazadeh era, who oversaw oil marketing as acting VP for international affairs.

The adoption of the Third Development Plan established the Council for Energy Planning, composed of cabinet members with economic portfolios and a handful of senior technocrats. Reforms to the structure of the industry that were considered during Khatami's second term were aimed at enhancing the competitiveness of the sector and clarifying the relationship between the government, in the form of the ministry, and the corporate decision-making structure. The sector was targeted as part of the broader Khatami era privatization effort, but labor unrest and accusations that the move was a vehicle for private enrichment derailed the plans.[95] Plans launched to privatize the National Iranian Drilling Company and the National Iranian Tanker Company proved in effect to be Ponzi schemes – the putative buyers included the NIOC pension fund and other government affiliates.[96] Protests by oil workers and accusations of corruption forced Khatami to shelve the plans, but they were revived by Ahmadinejad.[97]

On the downstream side of the industry, the Khatami period witnessed the beginnings of an expansion in capacity after two decades of neglect. The Khuzestan Refinery, a $4 billion project of the National Iranian Oil Refining and Distribution Company, was launched by the Khatami administration at the Arvand Free Trade Zone and began operations in 2011.[98] In addition, in parallel with the efforts to expand production, the Khatami government like its predecessor sought to rein in consumption.

One of the key dimensions of the reformist stewardship of Iran's hydrocarbons sector was the dramatic shift in Iran's posture within OPEC, which was part of a broader regional rapprochement and

[93] "NIOC Revamp Lends Confusion to Investment Tender," *PIW*, July 20, 1998.
[94] Paul Sampson, "Iran – Chipping Away," *Energy Compass*, November 24, 2000.
[95] Paul Sampson, "Double Your Money," *Energy Compass*, November 3, 2000.
[96] "Iran – Chipping Away," *Energy Compass*, November 24, 2000.
[97] Paul Sampson, "Double Your Money," *Energy Compass*, November 3, 2000.
[98] "Refinery Tracker," *World Refining and Fuels Today*, January 20, 2009.

outreach to Saudi Arabia. Like his predecessor, Zanganeh established good rapport with his Saudi counterparts and successfully navigated a precarious period for both the industry and the region. Curiously, the fragile cooperation between Saudi Arabia and Iran within OPEC appeared to sustain itself during this period, even as frictions between Tehran and Riyadh over developments in Iraq were on the rise. The newfound cooperation was driven by a fundamental shared interest of the two governments in avoiding any disruption to the steady escalation in oil prices, while sustaining global economic growth. And it was framed by relatively fresh memories of the 1985–6 price crash.

In 2005, OPEC even held its annual summit in Isfahan – the first since the revolution and a testament to the "rare unity among Gulf oil producers" and the organization's revived "cohesiveness and discipline."[99] Iran's representative to OPEC, Kazempour Ardebili, explained that "the situation has changed in the region.... Ideology has no place in our negotiations within OPEC. All players are competitors on the market, but before that they are partners within OPEC."[100] The newfound rapport was surely facilitated by the high prices, which helped satisfy the revenue ambitions of historic price hawks such as Iran, as well as a greater sense of unity in the face of rising production from non-OPEC sources such as Russia and Norway. The durability of the cooperation seemed to suggest that OPEC might have overcome some of the internal dysfunction that characterized its policies during the 1980s.

Through his tenure as Khatami's energy envoy the oil minister proved a tempting target, and the parliament continued to pursue allegations that he was unfairly privileging foreign investors over domestic firms for petrochemicals projects, along with a range of other concerns. Zanganeh defended his efforts to lure foreign investment to Iran's oil sector from criticisms that he had unfairly passed over equally well-qualified domestic competitors. "If you become sick and don't have the medicine, would you wait to make it yourself and risk your life or would you go to someone who already has it?"[101] However, the mood had already begun to shift, and the populist sentiments that have persistently manifested in Iran's economic policies began to revive. Iranian disillusionment with their

[99] Jad Mouawad, "With Rare Unity, OPEC Ministers Gather in Iran," *New York Times*, March 15, 2005.

[100] Mouawad (March 15, 2005).

[101] Amir Paivar, "Iran's New Guard Rethinks Investment Strategy," *Euromoney*, September 2005.

experience negotiating and working with IOCs was already growing. When the South Pars Phase 1 gas refinery was inaugurated, in 2004, then-President Khatami hailed the project as "a great honor in the country's economic and industrial arena," adding that "the bigger honor is that its construction work was carried out by Iranian engineers, designers and managers."[102]

AHMADINEJAD AND OIL ON THE TABLECLOTH

President Ahmadinejad took office pledging to eradicate what he described as an "oil mafia" that had plundered Iran's resources, a thinly veiled reference to the former president Rafsanjani and other officials who had enriched themselves and their families through their government connections. Ahmadinejad succeeded in engineering a broad turnover in the energy sector's senior leadership, although there is little evidence that he achieved anything other than a shift in the vector of patronage to his own circle of crony capitalists. Many technocrats with long experience in the industry and in dealing with international energy companies were sidelined, and in their place Ahmadinejad in 2006 authorized the establishment of a Petroleum Council within the ministry, intended to oversee the awarding of contracts.

Ahmadinejad's efforts to dominate the oil sector met with substantial opposition. He feuded repeatedly with the parliament over selecting successive oil ministers. The president's first three nominees – several of whom were his close cronies – either were rejected by the parliament on the grounds of insufficient experience in the oil sector or chose to withdraw in the face of likely rejection. Ahmadinejad finally conceded and put forward the caretaker minister, Kazem Vaziri Hamaneh, and at one point in 2011 attempted to install himself as acting minister. The Majlis also thwarted the president's effort to merge the petroleum and energy portfolios in his cabinet. After several years of turbulence at the top, Rostam Qasemi was confirmed in August 2011, and his background as a senior officer in the Islamic Revolutionary Guard Corps construction and engineering wings signaled the fusion of the military with the most prized and lucrative arena of economic activity and revenues.

Under Ahmadinejad, the traditional sinecures of the petroleum sector found themselves under siege. In 2007, the Petroleum Ministry

---

[102] "Khatami Unveils Iran's South Pars 1 Gas Plant," *IRNA*, November 20, 2004.

announced that twenty-one of the various subsidiary companies to its four primary operating consortia would be privatized but made little real progress in implementation.[103] There was also talk of shifting the country's vital enterprises outside Tehran and dozens of Ministry of Petroleum subsidiaries were included on the list of more than 160 government firms directed to move their operations away from the capital.[104]

Meanwhile, the aftereffects of sanctions shattered the long-standing NIOC monopoly of participation in oil and gas development. Historically, the state-owned oil company jealously guarded its turf and precluded all but a few favored state enterprises, such as IDRO, from gaining inroads into the sector. But Ahmadinejad's mercurial managerial style in relation to the withdrawal of foreign investors shifted that paradigm. These plans involved both the entry of new players into both the upstream development of fields and downstream marketing of crude sales, as well as the shift to seeking domestic financing through the sale of "participation bonds" in specific phases/projects of South Pars. Companies affiliated with the Revolutionary Guard, including but not limited to the Khatam al Anbia construction firm, reportedly secured as much as $25 billion in projects in the oil and gas sector in recent years, as did other domestic semigovernmental firms, including those associated with several large parastatal foundations that had previously been excluded from such activities.

The opening of the Iranian energy sector to private development also extended to the downstream. In 2008, Tehran launched an "oil stock exchange" on Kish Island as a means of facilitating direct sales in crude, petrochemicals, and refined products, including fuel oil and gasoline. In 2009, the oil ministry granted authority to the Bonyad-e Mostazafan, then headed by a former military officer who had once been intended to take over NIOC itself as managing director, for oil sales. In April 2012, Hassan Khosrowjerdi, who then headed the Association of Oil, Gas and Petrochemicals Products Exporters, suggested that private companies had been responsible for $18 billion worth of exports in refined petroleum products over the previous year, and he as well as other industrial officials indicated that the government may also facilitate upstream

---

[103] "Iran Oil Ministry Names Twenty-One Firms Set to Be Privatized," *Mehr News Agency*, July 14, 2007; F. Milad, "Iran Plans to Privatize 95% of Oil Ministry's Subsidiaries," *McClatchy –Tribune Business News*, January 25, 2012.

[104] "One Hundred and Sixty Three Government Firms to Leave Tehran," *Hemayat*, May 20, 2010.

involvement.[105] Notably, most of these companies appeared to be linked to holding firms associated with the Revolutionary Guard Corps, calling into question whether they were actually independent of government ownership or control. At least three private sector consortia were established with the specific intention of trying to "bypass" sanctions.[106]

In addition to reconfiguring the sector to cope with sanctions, among the other hallmarks of the Qasemi management of the oil sector were revived concerns about the exploitation of shared fields and the prospects for conflict with Iran's neighbors over the faster pace of development in Iraq and the Gulf. There were mounting critiques of Qatar's rapid exploitation of its North Field, which is part of the same geological structure as Iran's South Pars, as well as Kuwaiti and Saudi efforts to develop the Arash (Dorra) gas field in the Gulf. Tehran sought to assert what the leadership considered to be its sovereign rights to fields adjacent to disputed boundaries in the Caspian Sea and along the border with Iraq, and it is hardly inconceivable that as tensions mount over sanctions and Iranian regional influence, direct conflict could erupt in one of these areas as Tehran seeks to flex its muscles and intimidate its neighbors. In July 2012, Mahmoud Zirakchianzadeh, managing director of the Iranian Offshore Oil Company, announced that Tehran was seeking to develop Arash (Dorra) jointly with Kuwait, but added that "if Iran's positive diplomacy is turned down, we will be carrying on our efforts at Arash field unilaterally."[107] Add to these suspicions the simple reality that through their expanded production and other measures to blunt Iran's oil might, the Gulf states played a significant role in enabling the sanctions on Iran to succeed. Such a context tempts some within Iran's security establishment to periodically issue vague warnings of possible reprisals against the ability of neighboring states to export their own oil and gas.

China Rising

Although Iranian leaders initially directed their efforts to luring foreign investment from traditional European trade partners, the energy relationship with China quickly took on increasing significance. Iranian leaders

---

[105] http://shana.ir/184656-en.html; http://shana.ir/188364-en.html

[106] Narges Rasuli, "Three Consortia Have Been Formed to Bypass Sanctions," *Etemad*, July 12, 2012.

[107] "Gas Field Development – Iran to Cooperate with Kuwait," *Pakistan and Gulf Economist*, July 29, 2012.

explicitly sought to utilize China as a bulwark against Western pressure, deliberating privileging Chinese companies with major deals in the expectation that this would both reinforce Chinese disdain for sanctions as well as splinter the increasing coherence of the international effort to isolate Tehran. Beijing appeared willing to expand its economic ties with Iran irrespective of – or perhaps as a subtle but tangible rebuff to – increasing Western agitation over Iranian foreign policy.

In 2004, in the midst of a major American push to escalate pressure on Iran, Sino-Iranian economic ties began to expand dramatically through a series of blockbuster energy deals. These included a $20 billion agreement inked in March 2004 with a Chinese state oil company, Zhuhai Zhenrong, for 2.5 million metric tons of LNG per year for twenty-five years, billed in typically inflated terms as the world's largest natural gas purchase to that date.[108] Later that year, Sinopec signed a $100 billion deal for a 51 percent stake in the Yadavaran field. Iranian politicians trumpeted these investments as evidence that sanctions cost the West more dearly than they did Iran.[109] Washington openly criticized the deals, suggesting that they would "undermine" international efforts on the nuclear file; however, Chinese officials shrugged off the rebuke, arguing that commercial arrangements should have no bearing on security issues, and vice versa.[110] China eventually supported international pressure on Iran over the nuclear issue, but the energy deals signaled its growing stake in the region's upstream assets.

After three years of delays, the first Yadavaran development contract was signed with Sinopec in December 2007, with the National Iranian Oil Company awarding a $2 billion deal to the Chinese firm for the first stage of the field's development. Shortly after the deal was signed, it was reported that Sinopec was increasing its imports of Iranian crude from 60,000 b/d in 2007 to 160,000 b/d in 2008, singlehandedly increasing China's Iranian oil imports by one-third. A NIOC source reported that this increase was tied to the Yadavaran deal.[111] Analysts suggested that more attractive terms to the buyback contract used in the Yadavaran deal reflected Tehran's desire to induce Chinese participation and blunt

---

[108] John W. Garver, *China and Iran: Ancient Partners in a Post-Imperial World* (Seattle: University of Washington Press, 2006), p. 271.

[109] "Baztab-e Gostardeh-ye Emza-ye Qarardad-e Nafti-ye Iran va Chin [Widespread Reaction to the Signing of the Iran-China Oil Contract]." 19 Azar 1386, December 10, 2006. http://www.shana.ir/121108-fa.html

[110] "China Stands by Iran Deal," *Oil Daily*, December 13, 2007.

[111] "China to Buy More Iranian Crude," *Oil Daily*, December 17, 2007.

Beijing's cooperation with American efforts to strengthen international sanctions on Iran.[112]

The United States openly criticized the Yadavaran deal. However, China vociferously defended the contract as "commercial cooperation in the energy sphere undertaken by a Chinese company with Iran following the principle of equality and mutual benefit."[113] Just one day before the UN Security Council passed Resolution 1696 in 2006, threatening Iran with sanctions if it did not suspend enrichment within a month, Sinopec signed a $2.7 billion deal to upgrade and expand the Arak refinery.[114]

However, from that high point, Chinese investments in Iran's energy sector began to stumble as Beijing assumed a more direct role in the nuclear negotiations with Tehran. Following a December 2006 memorandum of understanding, a deal between China National Offshore Oil Corporation (CNOOC) and Iran for the development of the North Pars gas field was significantly delayed – reportedly because of U.S. opposition.[115] It was not until March 2009 that Oil Minister Gholam-Husayn Nozari announced that CNOOC had signed the deal to develop the field for LNG export. The upstream phase of the project was projected to cost $5 billion and the downstream phase $11 billion; it was projected to be completed by 2012, when CNOOC was expected to purchase half of the output, or 10 million mt/yr, for twenty-five years.[116] However, sanctions kept any actual investment on ice, and after Iran's 2013 presidential election returned many technocrats to the oil sector, Tehran reportedly nullified the Chinese contract.

Beijing did seek to take some advantage of departures of other prospective foreign investors. In January 2009, China National Petroleum Corp. (CNPC) signed a $2 billion deal to develop the North Azadegan onshore oil field, to be carried out under a "revised version" of Iran's frequently used buyback scheme.[117] Even as Total renewed its hesitancy to follow through with its plans to develop South Pars, in March a senior

[112] Paula Dittrick. "Yadavaran Buyback Contract Signals Better Iranian Terms," *Oil & Gas Journal,* January 14, 2008.

[113] "China Stands by Iran Deal," *Oil Daily,* December 13, 2007.

[114] Clara Tan, "China's Sinopec Signs Iran Refinery Deal, Despite Crisis," *International Oil Daily,* August 2, 2006.

[115] "China's CNOOC, Iran LNG Deal Delayed on US Concerns, Talks Still On – Source," *Xinhua Financial News,* April 8, 2008.

[116] "China's CNOOC, Iran Sign North Pars Deal," *Platts Oilgram News,* March 17, 2009.

[117] Paul Sampson. "CNPC Deal with Iran Poses Foreign Policy Test for Obama Administration," *Oil Daily,* January 15, 2009.

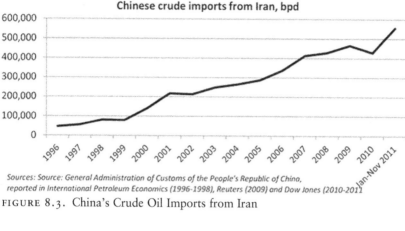

FIGURE 8.3. China's Crude Oil Imports from Iran

government official in Iran reported that an unnamed Chinese consortium had signed a $3.2 billion three-year deal for the field, with cooperation planned with an unnamed European nation. This occurred just two days after a renewal of U.S. sanctions by the Obama administration.[118]

Since 2010, the disparity between the universally applicable sanctions imposed under various United Nations resolutions, which carefully avoided any specific measures directed at the petroleum sector, and those more narrow measures adopted by Washington and its allies created a gaping need for Tehran and a fortuitous opportunity for Beijing to expand their cooperation on energy. The combined impact of long-standing U.S. sanctions and more recent measures adopted by the EU, Norway, Japan, South Korea, and several other states prohibited virtually all major Western oil companies from new investments in the Iranian energy sector and eventually from selling refined petroleum products to Tehran as well.

In such a context, China was left as the most significant international actor in Iran's energy sector. As Figure 8.3 demonstrates, Beijing represented an increasingly important destination for Iranian crude exports. Chinese companies, faced no direct legal constraints – they were the only major players left standing in the Iranian energy sector after the 2010 intensification of pressure on Tehran. Sinopec moved forward on its development of Yadavaran field, and other Chinese companies sought stakes in developing major oil and gas fields, including Azadegan (North

[118] Borzou Daragahi, "Iran, China Sign Gas Deal; The $3.2-Billion Pact to Develop An Offshore Field Stymies Sanctions," *Los Angeles Times*, March 15, 2009.

FIGURE 8.4. China Represents a Growing Proportion of Iran's Crude Exports

and South), South Pars (Phase 11), and North Pars. In addition to its upstream stakes, the financial and political premiums ensured that Beijing was content discreetly to flout the threat of U.S. sanctions against its companies that continued to sell gasoline and other fuels to Tehran.

Chinese companies also engaged in preliminary discussions with Tehran surrounding plans to boost refinery capacity and performance. In this fashion, China became the indispensable foreign partner for Iran's energy sector. In 2011, China imported an average of 540,000 bpd from Iran, nearly 20 percent of Iran's total exports – making Beijing Tehran's most consequential customer in terms of both volume as well as strategic value. At 8.4 percent of China's total crude import basket in 2011, Iran's share was still significantly lower than Chinese imports of Saudi crude and oil products (14.5 percent.) In other words, as Figure 8.4 under-scores, China became more important to Iran's bottom line, even as Iran became comparatively less significant within Beijing's supply alternatives.

Chinese companies moved carefully not to absorb major new upstream projects after 2010, when in the wake of the new sanctions, U.S. officials warned that any Chinese "backfilling," or replacement of departing European firms, in energy projects would provoke tensions with Washington. Sinopec and CNPC clearly slow-rolled their investments in Iran with a careful eye on the $20 million ceiling for the applicability of U.S. sanctions under the 2010 Comprehensive Iran Sanctions and Divestment Act (CISADA, which succeeded and expanded upon the Iran-Libya

Sanctions Act and its heirs). The slow pace of China's activities earned the ire of senior Iranian officials, including public recriminations from Oil Minister Rostam Qasemi and blunt discussion of replacing the Chinese firms. Still, Tehran's alternative options were drastically limited by the U.S., European, and other investment bans, and domestic critics of the leadership scoffed at the regime's attempt to browbeat Beijing into a more forthcoming posture.[119] In recent years, China's monthly imports from Iran varied considerably, from a high of more than 730,000 bpd in May 2009 to a low of less than 189,000 bpd a year later. These fluctuations continued after the imposition of the Central Bank sanctions, albeit at lower overall volumes, reflecting seasonal shifts in demand and pricing disputes.

Iran's Great Gas Game

Iran's gas industry remains heavily focused on development of the massive South Pars field, appropriately so since the field contained 47 percent of the country's total recoverable gas reserves. The first ten phases of an anticipated twenty-four-plus-stage development plan are already online, and while this is zealously celebrated by regime officials, Iran's technocrats quietly grumble about the extent to which development has lagged and the costs this has imposed on Iran.[120] Production from South Pars accounts for approximately one-third of Iran's gas production, and the investments in the field helped fuel exponential increases in Iran's gas consumption over the course of the past two decades. Production from South Pars Phase 1 totals 28.2 bcf per day (800 mcm/d) and rose to more than 35 bcf per day (1 bcm/d) by the end of the Iranian year in March 2013.[121]

During the Khatami presidency, these expansions prompted concerns within the international energy sector that Tehran would "end[s] up with more gas than it can handle."[122] However, development of South Pars, the crown jewel of Iran's gas reserves, moved considerably more slowly

---

[119] *Donya-ye Eqtesad* (online), "The Oil Minister: 'Chinese! Do Not Delay,'" September 19, 2011.

[120] Zoreh Kamizi, "Iran Lacks Energy Diplomacy," *Etemad* (supplement), February 1, 2010.

[121] "Gas Production Capacity of South Pars Phase 1 to hit 1b sqm," *IRNA*, July 23, 2012, http://irna.ir/News/Economic/Gas-production-capacity-of-South-Pars-phase-1-to-hit-1b-sqm/80243151

[122] Vahe Petrossian, "Iranian Gas at the Crossroads," *Upstream*, July 13, 2001.

than originally planned, and additional gas remained urgently needed to fulfill domestic requirements, including reinjection to maintain production levels in the country's aging oil fields. The phased but interconnected approach to South Pars development meant that delays on early phases – for example, Petropars's difficulty in bringing Phase 1 on line – cascaded into delays for subsequent projects, such as Phases 2 and 3, which were intended to be fueled by production from Phase 1.

More recently, virtually all Western investors in the energy sector exited Iran as a result of international pressure and frustrations with the Iranian investment climate. One of the last remaining Western firms in the upstream, Edison International, withdrew from an agreement to explore the Dayyer offshore gas field as part of a settlement with Washington over its prior commercial activities in Iran. In their absence, Chinese and Indian firms assumed symbolic stakes but slow-rolled capital commitments and project development. However, even here frustration was mounting; Iranian leaders expressed resentment about the pace of development by Chinese companies. In 2012, Iranian reports suggested that CNPC had withdrawn from its lead role in Phase 11, following months of warnings by Tehran that the contract the contract was jeopardized by lack of progress. A year later, Iran shifted the project to a domestic firm, Petropars.

The bluster that characterize the political leadership with respect to the state of Iran's petroleum sector was not wholly shared by technocrats, or even by the informed politicians who had long engagement in this arena. Hamidreza Katouzian, a longtime member of parliament who served as head of the Majlis Energy Commission, acknowledged in 2010 that Iranian petroleum development had fallen behind, and the disparity between Iran and its competitors was only growing. "Twenty years after discovering this gas field, we are behind Qatar in projects, investments, and exploitation," Katouzian lamented. "While Qatar has completed the building of refineries and drilling, Iran has not even reached halfway through its development projects. We are losing because whoever exploits more will gain more."[123] The relative difference in pace with tiny Qatar is highlighted in Figure 8.5.

Senior officials cited insufficient gas volumes as an explanation for the precipitous declines in oil production (2012 production was down by an

---

[123] "Chairman of Majles Energy Committee Criticizes Performance of Oil Ministry," *Mardom-e Salari*, November 19, 2010.

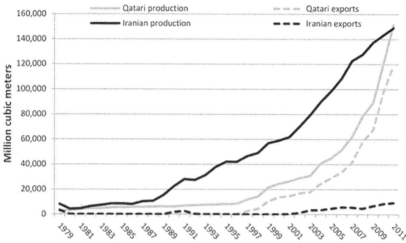

FIGURE 8.5. Comparing Qatar and Iran: Gas Production and Exports

average of 300,000 bpd over 2011), although surely the intensifying sanctions and their negative impact on the availability of capital and technology played a significant role here. Estimates suggested that Tehran may need to boost its reinjection rates – which ranked at the top of the region – to somewhere in the range of 10 bcf/d by the middle of the decade. This represented production equivalent to Qatar's entire LNG exports.[124] The country's difficulties in arresting the declines prompted serious concerns among Iranian political figures as well as industry technocrats. The subject arose repeatedly at a 2011 conference on the future of the oil industry. Hamidreza Katouzian, then-chair of the parliamentary Energy Committee, commented in 2011 that the reinjection program was "not proceeding well at the moment."[125]

Most of the gas available for reinjection derives from South Pars Phases 6 through 8, with additional volumes anticipated from Phase 12 (and potentially others), which had originally been intended for the Iran LNG project. Already, Tehran had launched what was considered to be the world's largest gas reinjection project, with somewhere in the range of

[124] Fereidun Fesharaki and Siamak Adibi, "Iran's Oil and Gas Industry: Short- and Long-Term Drivers Impacting the Future of Petroleum Production and Export Revenues," September 18–19, 2009, presentation accessed at http://dornsife.usc.edu/conferences/iran/documents/USCIranOilandGasIndustry-FereidunFesharaki-8-24.pdf

[125] "Analyzed at the 'Oil Outlook' Conference: Nation's Negative Oil and Gas Trade Balance," *Donya-ye Eqtesad*, April 25, 2011.

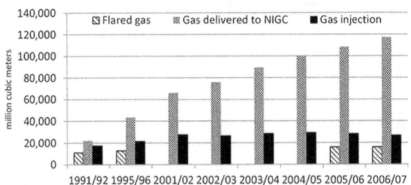

FIGURE 8.6. Iran's Increasing Gas Production and Usage

3 bcf destined to boost production at the Aghajari field from 140,000 bpd to 200,000 bpd, utilizing gas produced in Phases 6, 7, and 8 of South Pars.

Beyond domestic demand, power generation, and reinjection, Tehran sought to capitalize on its gas to buttress a petrochemicals industry that until recently had been growing at rapid pace. Sanctions and related difficulties in obtaining sufficient capital contributed to delays in completing two major new gas processing plants, Bid Boland-2 and Parsian.[126]

Iran's gas trade with Turkey was interrupted on a regular basis by political, security, and market issues, including Turkish terrorism and problems from both the demand and supply sides of the equation. Turkish demand repeatedly came up short, and under the terms of agreement Turkey was obligated to pay $600 million in 2009. Iran's gas exports to Turkey rebounded in 2010 by nearly 50 percent, but Ankara continued to press Tehran for price reductions. In 2011, Tehran demanded compensation for yet another interruption but was rebuffed by Ankara. The greater disappointment was that the Turkish deal never fulfilled the larger ambitions of Iranian policy makers – that is, to serve as a gateway to European exports and situate Iran as the hub of a robust supply network.

As part of its fifth Five Year Plan, launched in March 2010, Tehran set out an agenda of massive investments in the gas sector that included the construction of the ninth in the IGAT pipelines. Iran continued to pursue

---

[126] "Iran Gas Plants Face Delays," *MEES*, January 31, 2011.

piped gas export projects that showed little sign of immediate viability from either a political or a commercial perspective, including a pipeline to Pakistan (and in some guises, India) as well as a joint project with Iraq, Syria, and Lebanon that would extend to serve European demand as well. In each of these cases, Tehran sought to create facts on the ground by developing domestic pipeline capacity to service anticipated export routes and signed a variety of preliminary agreements with Islamabad and Damascus in order to facilitate discussions on pricing and infrastructure. Khatam al-Anbia was tapped to build a portion of the next IGAT, intended to serve future gas exports to Europe.[127]

It is not coincidental that Tehran sought to depict each of these projects in ideological terms – the official Iranian media and industry sources dubbed the South Asian pipeline as the "peace pipeline" and the Syrian route the "Islamic pipeline." Beneath the posturing lay a sense of Iran's evolving strategy for navigating the constraints of its ongoing frictions with the world – identifying prospective trade and investment partners with shared antipathies and limited options. This was hardly a recipe for prosperity or sensible development of the gas sector – neither the South Asian pipeline nor the Arab route had a viable business model in the near or medium term.

The "peace pipeline" to South Asia was in the works since at least 1994 but was repeatedly stalled by political frictions, security concerns, and difficulties in agreeing upon a pricing formula. In May 2009, Tehran signed a Gas Sale and Purchase agreement with Pakistan and subsequently inked a gas transportation agreement with additional guarantees intended to facilitate the countries' respective construction of the pipeline in 2010. Tehran claims that it has completed the domestic portion of the pipeline, and in 2015 Pakistan was in talks with a CNPC subsidiary to complete its segment of the pipeline.

By virtue of necessity, Iran's approach to gas exports was characterized by opportunism. When talks with Pakistan on piped gas foundered, Tehran revived the dormant Iran LNG project that had been associated with South Pars Phase 12 as a prospect for gas exports to India. The Arab pipeline network also shifted form to adapt to changing geopolitical circumstances and/or opportunities. With sanctions impinging on its finances and energy partnerships, Tehran turned its attention to utilizing the gas domestically and serving as a regional electricity hub, including

---

[127] "IRGC Company Wins Two Pipeline Contracts," *MEES*, March 4, 2011.

major projects for electricity supply to Iraq, Afghanistan, Pakistan, and other neighboring states including Armenia, Azerbaijan, Turkey, Turkmenistan, and Russia.

Iran also pursued the possibility of gas exports and/or joint development projects with neighboring states, but these projects have not yet generated exports, and the regional political climate effectively deterred any possibility that they would come to fruition until sanctions were lifted. Even before the escalation of frictions between Iran and the Gulf States, a combination of political and pricing obstacles had scuttled prior efforts to establish meaningful gas trade within the region. Iran's protracted negotiations to supply 500 mcf per day of gas to the UAE produced only acrimony on both sides; a deal with Dana Gas, based in Sharjah, collapsed over pricing disputes. Tehran engaged in period negotiations with Kuwait, Oman, and Bahrain and signed preliminary agreements with Kuwait in 2003 and 2010. Often these talks appeared designed to serve as public relations gambits. After Rouhani's election, Tehran pursued gas export deals with Oman and Iraq with apparent new seriousness.

Iran sought to develop LNG production from the initial development of South Pars. Three major projects – Iran LNG, Persian LNG, and Pars LNG – were originally devised, with plans for initial exports to begin in 2011. Pars LNG and Persian LNG were intended to utilize South Pars production Phases 11 and 13 and 14, respectively, and had attracted strong interest from foreign investors including TotalFinaElf and Petronas in Pars LNG and Shell/Repsol in Persian LNG. However, both projects were formally suspended in 2010, in an implicit acknowledgment of the impact of sanctions as well as the shifting realities of the global gas trade.[128]

The pair of 5.4 mt/year trains envisioned as part of Iran LNG were reassigned from Phase 12 of South Pars to Phase 11, to enable the volumes produced from the already-underway Phase 12 to feed into the IGAT trunkline system and supplement volumes available for domestic consumption. The political environment and sanctions regime deterred investors and prospective purchasers alike – generating a self-perpetuating cycle of failure that Tehran could do little to mitigate, as early discussions and preliminary deals with companies such as Sinopec and OMV withered on the vine.

Without the technology and without firm contracts for purchase, there was little that Tehran could do to advance these projects. A number of the

---

[128] Benoit Faucon and Spencer Swarz, "Iran Curbs LNG-Export Ambitions," *Wall Street Journal*, August 12, 2010.

foreign firms involved with the projects had already withdrawn or signaled their disinterest in moving forward and wrote off tens of millions in costs associated with the aborted projects. Some facilities associated with the Iran LNG project, including storage tanks constructed by the Iranian firm Panahsaz Iran Engineering Company, were left effectively idle. "We do not dare buy given the political issues. What would happen if we sign a deal?" an Asian buyer queried a reporter in 2011, adding that beyond the sanctions, "Iran's sluggish progress on construction of the liquefaction plant and its lack of any prior track record in LNG makes prospective customers very skittish."[129]

Tehran continued to promote a vision of the country as a major supplier to its neighbors as well as to demand centers in Europe, with the intention of expanding Iran's share of the international gas market from 1 percent to 10 percent.[130] In 2013, Javad Owji, then head of Iran's gas company, predicted that gas exports would triple to 100 mcm by 2014, as pipeline sales to Iraq and Pakistan expanded upon the modest levels of Turkish exports. Owji forecast that gradually these projects would shift the basis of Iran's resource rents from oil to gas.[131] However, the vision of Iran as a major gas exporter appeared to be largely divorced from reality; beyond the sanctions , Iranian officials seemed to disregard the historic shifts in the gas market that had ensued with the emergence of unconventional supplies, including shale. Iranian officials reportedly were rebuffed in efforts to launch gas export talks with a range of European and Russian firms.[132] Meanwhile, Iran's only remaining European export prospect – a preliminary agreement signed in 2008 with a Swiss company for 20–25 mcm in gas exports – remained in limbo as routes and supply options were considered. Still, Tehran claimed to be banking on a future as a diversified exporter, with a projected 6.35 bcf/day (180 mcm/d) intended for Turkey, Europe, and South Asia.[133]

Beyond its modest pipeline exports and continually deferred dreams of LNG, Tehran managed to establish a growing revenue stream from South Pars condensates production. Exports of condensates brought in more

[129] "Iran LNG Advances, Buyers Still Balk," *World Gas Intelligence*, April 27, 2011.
[130] Ali Khajavi, "Strategies for Iran's Effective Interaction in the Global Gas Market," *MEES*, January 21, 2011.
[131] Ladane Nasseri, "Iran to Boost Gas Exports in Efforts to Cut Oil Sales Reliance," *Bloomberg News*, April 7, 2013.
[132] "EU Advisor: Aipg, Repsol, LukOil Reject Iran's Gas Proposal," *Iran Economy Review*, July 31, 2012.
[133] "Iran Plans to Export 180 mcm of Gas per Day," *Shana News Service*, June 9, 2012.

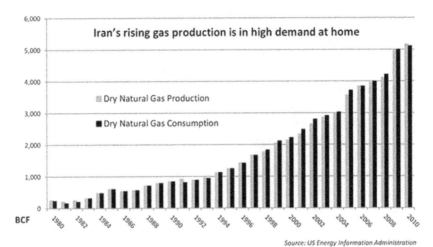

FIGURE 8.7. Nearly All of Iran's Gas Production Is Consumed Domestically

than $9 billion in the Iranian year that concluded in March 2012, and Tehran planned to build two additional gas refineries aimed at expanding production threefold.[134] There is an inherent tension between seeking to monetize condensates production via exports and utilizing the production to offset the need for imports of refined petroleum products. However, the U.S. sanctions on Iran's Central Bank, which imposed limitations on oil export volumes, inadvertently encouraged the expansion of condensates exports, which were not subject to the restrictions.

Because of the distance between supply and major centers of domestic demand, Tehran also established import relationships with several Central Asian neighbors and imported small but steady volumes from Turkmenistan via the Korpezhe-Kurt Kui pipeline from 1996 to enhance gas supplies available to northern Iran. A second pipeline was launched in December 2009 and expanded in November 2010 to facilitate as much as 45 mcm/day eventually, taking advantage of the Dowlatabad field. With another northern neighbor, Azerbaijan, Tehran established a swap arrangement that exchanged Iranian supply to the Azeri enclave of Nakhchevan in Armenia and in 2011 agreed to another deal for up to 5 bcm/year by 2015.

[134] Al Kroner, "Condensate Trade Will Reshape Oil, Gas Markets East of Suez," *Oil & Gas Journal*, February 6, 2012.

Finally, NIGC began testing its first gas storage facility at Serajeh, near Qom, with plans to inject as much as 1.5 bcm by the end of the Iranian calendar year in March 2013. Serajeh was part of a broader initiative to build underground gas storage to 14 bcm by 2015, according to the fifth Five Year Plan.[135]

Although much domestic and international attention focused on refined oil products consumption, the most dramatic shift in Iran's post-revolutionary energy policy was the explosion of domestic gas consumption. Thanks to massively undervalued resource prices, the Islamic Republic had one of the least energy-efficient economies in the world, and the cost in terms of both dependence on gasoline imports and reduction in available fuel exports forced the government to adopt the controversial subsidy reform plan since 2010. This compounded a trend that reflected the government's long-term strategy of "gas replacement" – increasing crude volumes for export by utilizing gas for domestic requirements.[136] As a result, it is hardly surprising that most of Iran's gas production today is directed toward internal consumption for residential, commercial, and small industries usage.

In part as a consequence of the pressure of rapidly expanding domestic energy demand, Tehran relied heavily on gas for domestic power generation, and increasingly for transportation as well. Slightly more than half of all consumption derived from the residential sector, with power generation at 30 percent and major industries (including petrochemicals) at 16 percent.[137] From a gas network that served 51,000 households at the time of the revolution, Iran expanded access to nearly 19 million households by 2011/12, with similar but lower trends for industrial usage. In 2012 there were 921 cities connected to the domestic gas transmission network, as compared with 9 at the time of the revolution three decades previously.[138] The domestic pipeline network supplies more than three-quarters of the country with gas, reaching virtually all urban centers and approximately 57 percent of

[135] "Iran Testing Middle-East's 1st Underground Gas Storage Facility," *Fars News Agency*, June 12, 2012.

[136] Ali Arrecchi, "Iran's Gas Vision: Priorities and Potentials," in *Shia Power: Next Target Iran?*, eds. John Laughland and Michel Korinman (London: Valentine Mitchell, March 2007), p. 228.

[137] Ali Khajavi, "Strategies for Iran's Effective Interaction in the Global Gas Market," *MEES*, January 21, 2011.

[138] Ahmadinejad address, broadcast on state television, July 26, 2012, from BBC Monitoring Middle East, July 28, 2012.

the rural areas.[139] Industrial usage also skyrocketed – from approximately 280 plants in 1980 to 1,100 by 1993. Demand was estimated to increase at approximately 3.8 percent per year through 2030.[140]

Iran has thirty-one gas-fed power plants, and during periods of peak usage – most notably, during winter freezes – residential demand escalates sharply, and on repeated occasions the government was forced to cut supply internally, constraining petrochemical plants, oilfield reinjection and other industrial usage, as well as to export customers such as Turkey in order to fulfill household demand. Iran's transmission capacity of 750 mcm per day has outpaced production capacity (650 mcm/day), but Tehran is preparing for additional phases of South Pars feeding into the system, seeking to add some 9,000 km of pipelines and sixty-five pressure boost stations by 2015.

Sanctions have helped foster domestic utilization, in limiting Iran's export options and in providing additional impetus for the 2010 implementation of subsidy reforms. The program targeted multiple aspects of the vast government support for basic commodities, whose direct tab had totaled $66 billion by 2009. Approximately 15 percent of that total related to gas, and to date the initiative has had conflicting impacts on gas consumption and future demand.[141] One of the primary goals was to reduce a major vulnerability for the Iranian economy – the reliance of a country with among the largest energy reserves in the world on imports of gasoline and diesel for as much as 40 percent of domestic usage.

In order to mitigate the consumer shock of raising gasoline prices and to dampen the persistently rising domestic demand for gasoline that had left the country dependent on product imports for much of its daily usage, Tehran undertook a major effort to shift the country's transportation fleet to compressed natural gas (CNG). This initiative included the adoption of smart cards for all vehicles and fuel pumps that ration lower-cost gasoline on the basis of consumption and subsidized conversion for individual vehicles to CNG. The outcome of this effort was a massive increase in CNG capacity. By mid-2012, Iran claimed to have established more than nineteen hundred of an anticipated twenty-five hundred CNG stations, with 2.8 million vehicles on the roads fueled by CNG.[142]

---

[139] Qasemi address to parliament, *Shana News Service*, June 25, 2012.
[140] Brumberg/Jaffee paper, p. 26.
[141] Ali Khajavi, "Strategies for Iran's Effective Interaction in the Global Gas Market," *MEES*, January 21, 2011.
[142] *Shana News Service*, June 20, 2012.

The subsidy reform initially had a positive impact on fuel consumption overall and, in particular, smuggling. Estimates suggest that prior to the increase in gasoline prices, approximately 5–10 million liters of gasoline and other fuels were exported illegally to Afghanistan, Pakistan, Iraq, and Turkey. The subsidy program was also intended to reduce residential consumption of gas by 20 percent over a five-year period, combined with other measures such as reduced flaring, enhancing the efficiency of the power grid and related equipment such as outdated air conditioners, ostensibly in order to generate additional gas volumes for exports. Gas prices for industrial projects were raised to approximately two dollars per million British thermal units (MMBtu) from a previous rate of forty to fifty cents per MMbtu, and further increases were initially envisaged for future stages of the reform program.[143] Initial reports suggested that consumption declined by as much as 15 percent for households in the capital.[144] However, the price hikes proved unsustainable for residential customers, and as many as 30 percent of households simply failed to pay their gas bills. By late 2014, consumption was continuing to increase and the National Iranian Gas Company was forced to declare bankruptcy due to more than $3 billion in unpaid debts.

At the same time, Tehran sought to balance rising domestic demand for gas and concerns about the viability of expanding exports by focusing more on conservation and preventing waste and leakages. According to Javad Owji, then-managing director of NIGC, more vigorous conservation measures could save as much as 100 mcm per year – as much as four phases of South Pars production.[145] As long the nuclear issue remained unresolved, the perennial tension about the most efficient utilization of any new gas volumes was mooted by the logistical and financial constraints of sanctions on export options, as well as by the increasing reinjection supply that will be required to maintain pressure in Iran's aging oil fields.

The increasing gasification of the domestic economy has been intensified by the distortions imposed by sanctions, subsidy reform, and Iran's limited access to foreign capital and technology. The overwhelming majority of Iran's gas production is dedicated to internal consumption

[143] R. Smith, S. Adibi, and S. Khimasia, "2012 Petrochemical outlook: Middle East," *Hydrocarbon Processing*, May 1, 2012.
[144] "Gas Consumption Drops after Withdrawal of Iran's Subsidies," *MEES*, January 17, 2011.
[145] "Energy Official: Iranians' Waste 100 mcm of Natural Gas," *Iran Economy Review*, July 16, 2012.

needs, with considerably smaller volumes utilized for reinjection as part of enhanced oil recovery efforts to contend with declining pressure in some of Iran's older oil fields. This imbalance is likely to be exacerbated by the continuing efforts to mitigate lack of foreign capital and technology in the energy sector overall.

THE SANCTIONS ERA AND THE FUTURE OF IRANIAN ENERGY

In the absence of foreign investors and external sources of finance, Tehran has been forced to pony up enormous capital investments to compensate for the loss of anticipated foreign investment (funded through the National Development Fund, a revamped version of Iran's Oil Stabilization Fund, where the Oil Ministry's investment allocation under the official budget fell short). For South Pars Phases 15 and 16, Tehran claimed to have drawn on $2 billion from a combination of NDF support, Oil Ministry funds, and domestic banks.[146]

With no viable mechanisms for accessing foreign credit facilities, Tehran resorted to issuing bonds to domestic investors as an additional source of finance for major energy projects like South Pars to supplement traditional sources, such as the state capital budget and National Development Fund. More than $1.6 billion in bonds were sold in 2012 to finance South Pars, and as of early 2015, plans were in the works for another substantial bond issue ($80 million) for an array of upstream projects. And sanctions only exacerbated the demand constraints; Iran's subsidy reform program, undertaken at least in part to reduce Iran's dependence on imported gasoline, diverted additional volumes toward satisfying domestic transportation and power generation requirements. As a result, instead of a surfeit of gas, Iran continued to import gas in order to satisfy domestic demand, as discussed in the subsequent section.

Still, even as external pressures on Iran were intensifying, the government sought to accelerate the timetable for South Pars, for both face-saving and practical reasons. Full development of South Pars was initially slated to be completed in 2023, a schedule that would have proven ambitious given the difficulties faced in getting the early phases off the ground.[147] Iranian oil ministers have repeatedly pledged to accelerate the pace of development. Then-minister Qasemi pledged to the parliament to

---

[146] "Iran Claims South Pars 15–16 Progress," *MEES*, March 4, 2011.
[147] "Special Report Oil & Gas – Pars Oil & Gas," *MEED Weekly Special Report*, March 23, 2001.

achieve full development of the field by March 2013. A task force composed of senior regime officials with responsibility for economic issues was appointed, and crews were reportedly working around the clock in order to meet these self-imposed deadlines. "Completing the work will require great investment, which will entail serious help by honorable Majlis representatives because with the completion of the South Pars phases our production will equal Qatar's," Qasemi emphasized.[148] In July 2012, Tehran allocated $5 billion from the NDF for South Pars investments, out of a total $14 billion in new NDF support for the petroleum sector. Still, after Qasemi left office as a result the 2013 presidential elections, his replacement was his predecessor Zanganeh, who acknowledged that "we are lagging far behind the schedule" and made similar pledges of rapid progress and intense focus to accelerate South Pars development.

In addition to slowing its upstream development, Iran's petrochemicals trade was also hit by U.S. sanctions, as both U.S. (Executive Order 13590, November 2011) and EU measures specifically targeted this growing segment of Iran's energy revenues. As a result, countries such as Taiwan and South Korea scaled back or curtailed imports entirely after the Central Bank sanctions were implemented. Tehran was forced to absorb the shipping costs, which increased commensurately from $45–$55/mt to $100/mt.[149]

Iran's leadership also persistently sought to use its oil clout to blunt American efforts to isolate the Islamic Republic, striking deals with and offering preferential terms to potential investors that might block international measures against Iran, shifting its crude sales to nondollar currencies as Washington began to target its financial institutions individually with sanctions, and periodically invoking threats against the Strait of Hormuz. The Iranian leadership was explicit in acknowledging its deployment of its oil clout as a disincentive for further sanctions, although from its rhetoric it appeared that Tehran might overestimate its leverage in this arena, particularly as technology and market fundamentals facilitated the development of resources that were previously uneconomic.

---

[148] "South Pars Projects Will Be Completed by March 2015," *Mehr News Agency*, June 24, 2012.

[149] "Iran Issues vs Economic Woes Drive China Methanol Price Volatility," *Platts*, May 23, 2012.

Even before the implementation of U.S. sanctions targeting Iran's imports of refined petroleum products, the government was already racing to expand refinery capacity and gasoline production. Abadan, the country's oldest and largest facility, which was nearly wholly destroyed during the Iran-Iraq War, was the focus of ongoing expansion work. According to Ahmadinejad, refinery capacity rose by 29,000 megawatts (mw) of capacity from an original basis of 35,500 mw.[150] Tehran repeatedly announced plans for significant Chinese investment, and in 2009 a memorandum of understanding was signed by Sinopec and NIORDC. However, there was little evidence of progress on that deal. In 2008, the first privately financed refinery opened in the Aras FTZ in northwestern Iran, and as of 2012, there were plans in the works for two additional refineries (Anahita and Persian Gulf Star) to be constructed with full or majority private capital.[151] By June 2012, Iran had achieved a gasoline surplus, with exports totaling 132,000 tons during the previous calendar year, netting $134 million in revenue. Approximately 40 percent of those exports ($51.6 million) went to Afghanistan.[152]

During this period, Tehran continued to seek to diversify its export options and expand its energy cooperation with its neighbors. The Azali FTZ incorporated a $400 million new port, intended to increase Iran's ability to handle oil and container-based trade with the other Caspian Sea nations significantly.[153] The port had the potential to serve as a duty-free conduit for Turkmen or Kazakh hydrocarbons to the world market via an exchange arrangement for the former Soviet states to bypass Russia, export to Iran via the Caspian, and receive equivalent amounts of oil or gas from a Persian Gulf or Gulf of Oman port.[154]

Finance and sanctions remain the most important and most urgent issues facing Iran's energy sector today. However, they are hardly the only forces that will shape its future. As suggested previously, Iranian resource nationalism has frequently translated into efforts to assert sovereignty

[150] Ahmadinejad address, broadcast on state television, July 26, 2012, from BBC Monitoring Middle East, July 28, 2012.

[151] "Market Overview – Iran: Oil and Gas Infrastructure – Q2 2012," *Business Monitor International Industry Insights*, May 5, 2012.

[152] "Iran's Tondgouyan Refinery to Produce 2.8 Million Liters of Gasoline per Day," *Trend News Agency* (Azerbaijan), July 6, 2012.

[153] Sohrab Mehrabian. "New Caspian Port to Increase Iran's Import Capacity," *American Metal Market*, November 12, 2008.

[154] John C. K. Daly. "Analysis: Iran Develops Bandar-e-Anzali," *UPI Energy*, May 21, 2008.

over contested territories. The issue of Iran's twenty-eight fields whose geological structures are shared with neighboring states has been raised with greater frequency in recent years. Then-Oil-Minister Rostam Qasemi has repeatedly raised the question of extraction rates from twenty-eight fields that straddle Iran's borders with its neighbors, including Iraq, Kuwait, Saudi Arabia, and, most sensitively, Qatar. In August 2012, Qasemi declared, "it is the right of the people of Iran to have not an equal share but a bigger share of these resources." Another senior Oil Ministry official declared that Iran had "a national duty for us to protect this capital."[155]

In July 2001, Tehran dispatched naval gunships to warn off an Azeri oil exploration vessel operating in Caspian Sea waters that Iran claims as its own in its ongoing dispute with the other five Caspian littoral states over the post-Soviet division of the waters. The incident ended peacefully, and successfully from Tehran's perspective, with the research vessel, leased to BP, retreating and representatives of both the company and the British government assuring Iranian officials that no further actions would be taken so long as the territorial claims remained unresolved.

The relative status of South Pars's exploitation is the subject of increasing anxiety for Tehran; the geological structure is shared with Qatar's North Field, and the disparity between development and depletion rates on the Qatari side has sparked concerns that the delays and obstacles experienced by Tehran will eventually forfeit the field's potential. One expert estimates that Doha has gained $55 billion and is set to earn another $100 billion in part because of the lack of serious competition from Iran.[156] This assessment of a production imbalance favoring the Qataris is not universally shared; in fact, some analysts contend that Tehran may bear some share of culpability in depleting the reservoir at a sharper decline rate than its relative share of the asset would imply.[157] At the same time, with financial pressures mounting along with frictions

---

[155] "The Widespread Extraction from Joint Oil by Arabs," *Donya-ye Eqtesad*, August 21, 2011.

[156] Kamizi, *Etemad* (supplement), February 1, 2010.

[157] Witfield (2011) argues that "the classic problem of drainage only exists if one party in a non-unitized field produces more than his share of the reserves. Since the North Field reserves are roughly twice those in South Pars, balanced production would have Qatar producing twice as much as Iran. It is important to note that Iran is currently producing more than its share would justify. If Iran is ultimately successful in developing its 22 South Pars blocks, its planned production would substantially drain reserves from Qatar's much more modest development plans." Alex Witfield, "Understanding Middle East Gas Exporting Behavior," *Energy Journal* 32:2 (2011), p. 215.

with Iran's neighbors, the Iranian tone on South Pars and other shared fields, including the Arash gas field, which is shared with Kuwait, tended to sharpen.

In addition, Iran is confronting a huge challenge in adapting to a changing international gas market. Tehran played an early, enthusiastic role in the establishment of an organization of gas exporting nations intended to evolve into a gas analogue to OPEC. To date there is little evidence that a suppliers' cartel can achieve even the minimal level of cohesion and efficacy that characterizes OPEC's experience, which itself benefited from a broad initial shared interest among the host governments in wresting greater control of price and production decisions from the concessionary companies. The Gas Exporting Countries Forum, or GECF, can claim no such collective sense of mission; its primary advocates, which include Russia and Qatar as well as Iran, developed their industries quite differently and are direct competitors for export markets. Even as the organization has sought to establish itself, changes in energy markets – specifically, the advent of hydraulic fracturing technology – have dramatically expanded supply, depressing gas prices and introducing new prospective heavyweight producers into the marketplace, including the United States, further dissipating GEFC's early prospects.

Although Iran has little rationale or capacity to move beyond its conventional resources, the Petroleum Ministry has sought to position the country for the new era of gas, announcing several studies including those to ascertain shale prospects as well as gas hydrates. However, the NIOC exploration director, Mahmoud Mohaddes, has already acknowledged that shale is "not economical" given Iran's conventional reserves.[158]

Finally, Iranian decision-makers will have to engage more serious in the debate over how to attract and maintain foreign investment in the energy industry. Many within the energy technocracy appreciate that the buyback contract is a problematic model for the country's development simply because its terms are not terribly beneficial to international companies and tend to discourage the sort of long-term sense of shared investment that is most conducive to optimizing Iran's resources. However, the opposition to foreign ownership runs deep within the existing system, and Iran's historical experience has inculcated a long-standing and widely shared sense that the country's national wealth was stolen for decades by its original foreign oil partner. Even as technocrats resumed

---

[158] "NIOC Conducting Study on Shale Oil," *Shana News Service*, July 15, 2012, http://shana.ir/192440-en.html

influential positions throughout the oil sector and state economy, deep mistrust of foreign companies and governments will remain intense as it relates to Iranian petroleum resources. For that reason, the legal rejection of foreign ownership of petroleum resources (and the corresponding implications for the ability of international companies to "book" reserves) is likely to remain intact irrespective of any future shifts in the ideological complexion of the Iranian regime.

9

Sanctions and the Sacred State

The 1979 revolution was never simply about Iran: Its ambitions were explicitly transnational, and its demons – the forces that animated the movement and the state that it generated – always transcended Iran's borders. The revolutionaries harbored profound bitterness toward Washington and other major powers, as well as toward the international system that empowered them and sustained the monarchy; such sentiments have only been exacerbated by three and a half decades of international pressure. At the same time, as this book details, the Islamic Republic has remained intricately engaged with the global economy through its reliance on energy production and exports.

Revolutionary Iran's engagement with the international economy has been molded by a variety of factors: its historical legacy; the politics of protectionism; heavy-handed exchange rate management, which has facilitated imports and depressed nonoil exports; and of course Iran's prickly relations with the West. The country's trade patterns shifted considerably over time thanks to the Islamic Republic's policies, as well as in response to regional and global changes – the demise of the Soviet Union; conflicts in Lebanon, Iraq, and Afghanistan; the rise of Asian economies.

However, the revolution added a new factor – international economic restrictions – that has persisted and loomed ever larger in dictating new patterns of engagement with the world, and eventually reconfiguring the Iranian economy. From the initial measures undertaken after the 1979 embassy seizure to the mushrooming labyrinth of restrictions imposed after Iran's 2006 referral to the United Nations Security Council, understanding the sanctions regime – and Iran's responses to it – is critical to appreciating the political economy of the Islamic Republic.

SANCTIONS AND THE HOSTAGE CRISIS

The November 1979 embassy seizure achieved what the revolution itself had not[1] – an immediate and abrupt transformation of the economic relationship between Tehran and Washington. The U.S. policy framework was established in the earliest hours after the embassy staff was taken hostage. As a former senior State Department official recalled, "almost as soon as policy discussions began on [the day after the embassy was overrun], the members of the crisis team in both the White House and the State Department focused on a two-track strategy." The objective then was to "open the door to negotiation" while also "increas[ing] the cost to Iran of holding the hostages." Since then, the U.S. formula for influencing Iran via a combination of pressure and incentives has remained fundamentally intact.

The embrace of a dualistic approach reflected divisions within the Carter administration, between those such as Secretary of State Cyrus Vance, who favored negotiations, and others, including National Security Advisor Zbigniew Brzezinski, pressing for coercive options. However, the military options available in November 1979 – including a rescue mission and retaliatory strikes or raids – did not offer compelling prospects for successfully extracting the captive diplomats. With their safe release as the paramount U.S. policy objective, Washington sought to exhaust nonmilitary measures before resorting to force. Even economic pressure was not universally endorsed, particularly in the Congress, where skepticism toward sanctions as a foreign policy tool ran high, as did concerns about collateral damage to a stagnant American economy.

Still, U.S. efforts to persuade Tehran to release the hostages ultimately relied heavily on economic pressure: prohibitions on U.S. imports of Iranian oil, a freeze of all Iranian state assets held by U.S. institutions, and eventually a travel ban and a comprehensive embargo on nearly all forms of trade. Even here, the Carter administration opted for incrementalism, anxious to avoid endangering the hostages or further entrenching Iran's revolutionary paranoia. For this reason, the sole measures undertaken in the immediate aftermath of the embassy seizure were the ban on importing Iranian oil and the assets freeze. The uncertainties surrounding Tehran's prospective reactions to U.S. measures

---

[1] Iran's non-oil exports to the U.S. actually increased in the months immediately following the revolution. Mehrdad Valibeigi, "U.S. Iranian Trade Relations after the Revolution," p. 212

weighed heavily on the minds of American decision makers, in particular whether Iran might seek to cripple the world economy by withdrawing all its exports or shifting its oil sales to nondollar currencies in response to the U.S. import ban. Indeed, Iran's oil minister made just these sorts of threats. Washington also had to consider the impact of its measures against Iran on the world economy – the assets freeze represented a new frontier in economic warfare, and its extraterritorial scope had the potential to provoke deep discord even among U.S. allies. In a telling reminder of the inherent codependencies of energy producers and consumers, U.S. officials took pains to emphasize that American measures against Iran were not intended to reduce Iranian oil production or worldwide supply.[2]

Of all the measures undertaken during the course of the fifteen month crisis, the assets freeze proved uniquely powerful; in one fell swoop – precipitated at least in part by concerns that Iran planned to withdraw its U.S. deposits – Washington "effectively immobilized $12 billion in Iran's assets, including most of its available foreign exchange reserves."[3] The decision to freeze the assets was prompted at least in part by concerns that Tehran was planning to withdraw its dollar deposits from U.S. banks, an action that could have destabilized the financial system. Iranian officials subsequently suggested that despite pronouncements of this nature by senior officials, this was not their aim. "Iran did not have sufficient money in American banks whose withdrawal would hurt US banking system," Rafsanjani told an interviewer.[4]

As the crisis persisted, frustration among both the American public and the policy community in Washington over the lack of progress in effecting the hostages' release grew more intense. President Carter publicly mused about the possibility of a naval blockade, an idea that Brzezinski had proposed early on. Tehran responded with a promise to close the Strait of Hormuz – the first of many such threats. Notably, the intensification of economic penalties against the revolutionary regime throughout the 1979–81 episode reflected a deep-seated unease with the viability of using military force to free the American captives in Iran – one that extended well beyond the Carter administration.

---

[2] Steven Rattner, "Thrust and Parry: The Economic Warfare Was Also Psychological," *New York Times*, November 18, 1979, p. E1.

[3] Robert Carswell and Richard J. Davis, "Crafting the Financial Settlement," in Christopher et al. (1985), p. 252.

[4] *Iqtisad-i Siysasi-i jumhuriya Islami*, pp. 58–9.

The failure of the April 1980 rescue mission reinforced that trepidation; in its aftermath, Congress made its first use of the War Powers Act to ward off any further attempts by President Carter. Instead, the same U.S. officials who urged caution on launching a war with Iran appealed for tougher economic penalties – Senator Barry Goldwater endorsed that the military undertake aerial bombing of Iran's oil facilities "and let them sit there and starve to death."[5] The farm lobby even announced that it would support measures prohibiting grain sales to Iran, a unique exception to its long-standing opposition to agricultural sanctions.[6] The lack of credible military options against Iran that could command broad-based support and the common moral outrage against Tehran's actions created an escalating spiral of economic pressure, a dynamic that would repeat itself more recently over the nuclear crisis.

It is difficult to quantify how much damage the U.S. measures inflicted to Iran's economy, which was in a state of revolutionary chaos and, eventually, wartime siege. Beyond the assets freeze, the most consequential dimension of the sanctions was its impact on Iran's military readiness and resupply capabilities. Here, too, the ideological impulses of the post-revolutionary regime were already driving a breach in bilateral military sales. After the Iraqi invasion, the U.S. embargo on weapons and spare parts had a catastrophic impact on Tehran's campaign against Iraq, with considerable unforeseen implications for its domestic dynamics and foreign policy.

However, a Congressional Research Service analysis early in the crisis suggested that Tehran had effectively insulated itself – to a degree – from Washington's influence because the revolutionary government had already begun to reorient its trade away from the United States.[7] America imported relatively little oil from Iran prior to 1979, and agricultural imports such as wheat, rice, and feed grains, which had been the mainstay of America's nonmilitary exports to Tehran, had already declined substantially as a result of a combination of both chaos and the ideological preferences of the new regime.

The financial constraints imposed by the assets freeze may not have fully crippled the Iranian economy, which was already reeling as a result of revolutionary chaos, but they magnified the negative consequences of Iran's inept and ideological management and, eventually, the pressures of the war. Notably, the freeze did not include assets of private individuals

---

[5] Bowden (2006), p. 210.   [6] Rattner (November 18, 1979), p. E1.
[7] Steven Rattner, "Iran Shifting Trade from U.S.," *New York Times*, December 18, 1979.

or corporations, in contrast to other similar cases, a measure that protected the sizable and relatively well-off Iranian-American community. However, Washington's decision to apply the measure to Iranian assets held in other countries proved powerful and foreshadowed persistent American efforts to extend U.S. sanctions' writ to third countries. Tehran responded in kind to the economic measures unveiled in the early weeks after the hostage seizure, largely through efforts to boycott the dollar and other measures intended to undermine the stability of U.S. currency.

The deployment of economic pressure against Tehran was facilitated by the fact that some bureaucratic groundwork had already been accomplished. The shah's initial ouster had already prompted U.S. government contingency planning, and the private sector undertook similar efforts to hedge its exposure vis-à-vis Iran. Some analyses have suggested that American policy toward Tehran during this period was unduly influenced by U.S. banking interests, but these allegations have not been borne out by impartial investigation, and it is apparent that the Iranians themselves did not put much stock in such purported intrigue, which Rafsanjani described after the fact as "not correct." Predictably, Tehran instead favored a broader conspiracy, as Rafsanjani confirms: "Our view was that they admitted the Shah to America to use him as a plot against us."[8]

The array of stakeholders and the complexity of the legal, financial, and political issues at stake complicated Washington's options. Some American firms had already taken legal action against Iran over business disputes, and there was some ambiguity about whether Carter's decision to freeze all Iranian assets took precedence over judgments already awarded or in process.[9] However, the multiplicity of interests and parties in this opening installment of the U.S.-Iranian estrangement contributed to a resolution of the hostage crisis. For example, representatives of several American banks remained in regular contact with designated mediators for Iran's Central Bank governor and finance minister throughout much of the standoff. This dialogue was separate from the various channels that eventually led to the final resolution, although the U.S. government was fully informed of its details.[10] The bankers' and lawyers'

---

[8] *Iqtisad-i Siysasi-i jumhuriya Islami*, pp. 58–9.

[9] Kate Gillespie, "US Corporations and Iran at The Hague," *Middle East Journal* 44:1 (1990), p. 21.

[10] John E. Hoffman, Jr., who was the lead counsel for Citibank at the time, writes that "I was never told what other lines of negotiation were open, and it was not until the government negotiations through the Algerians had commenced and were reported upon

exhaustive discussions over the assets freeze and other outstanding bilateral financial claims helped facilitate the eventual agreement once a political commitment to a resolution had been achieved on both sides. As one of the negotiators of that agreement has argued, the vast and complex financial claims between the two countries, many involving private disputes stemming from the revolution, would have effectively obligated both sides to engage in negotiations even if no political imperative for doing so had existed.

As suggested in Chapter 3, this crisis offers a striking example of sanctions' efficacy in producing demonstrable Iranian concessions, as well as in establishing an ongoing constructive vehicle for conflict mediation (the U.S.-Iran Claims Tribunal). However, the episode also underscores the limitations of economic pressures as a tool of influencing Iranian policy and highlights the difficulty in achieving multilateral support for penalizing Iran. Despite broad sympathy with Washington and outrage over the affront to international law and diplomatic protocol, even America's closest international partners proved reluctant to jeopardize their economic interests with Iran or undertake measures that might alienate opinion elsewhere in the Muslim world. The Carter administration galvanized support for United Nations Security Council Resolutions 457 and 461, which exhorted Iranian cooperation. However, the resolutions did not require sanctions and specifically excluded purchases of Iranian oil from proposed measures. And Soviet opposition, aided by Iranian negotiating ploys, torpedoed a successor resolution mandating sanctions.

The diplomatic discord enabled Iran's trade partners – countries that also happened to be close U.S. allies – to sustain business as usual for many months. Initially, the Carter administration made relatively minimal demands for allied action, instead seeking support in accessing the hostages and mitigating fallout from the assets freeze. However, even these requests caused frictions, and they intensified as Washington embraced the need for a comprehensive embargo on Iran. In initial consultations, Europe and Japan promised "virtually universal support," but in practice these governments took no steps except to delay some military sales.[11] In fact, their actions contradicted their pledges of

publicly that I was much aware of activities beyond those in which I was personally involved," Hoffman, "The Bankers' Channel," in Christopher et al. (1985), pp. 251–2.

[11] Paul Lewis, "U.S. Urges Iran Sanctions, But Whom Will They Hurt?" *New York Times*, December 16, 1979, p. E2.

solidarity. Japan moved – "with unseemly haste," according to a U.S. official – to fill the void left by Washington's oil import ban by purchasing the cargoes that had been destined for the U.S. prior to the crisis and drew official recriminations from Washington for replacing American pharmaceutical imports to Iran.[12] Japanese banks also reportedly advised Tehran on mitigating the impact of Washington's assets freeze, to the chagrin of U.S. officials.[13]

Anecdotal reports document some informal cooperation, but Japan and the European Community did not adopt minimal trade sanctions until midway through the fifteen month crisis. And even those measures were loose enough to enable trade to continue to rebound from postrevolutionary disruptions.[14] Personal appeals by the hostages' families to European leaders produced little progress. Early in the crisis, when Washington sent a special envoy to Tokyo to appeal for greater cooperation, a senior Japanese official acknowledged, "We will treat him nicely and see him off at the airport, but basically we want nothing to do with really tough sanctions that we don't believe will work or can work, and are not in the interests of Japan."[15] The one tactic that was marginally effective in altering European cost-benefit analysis was the allies' concerns over a military escalation of the standoff. "We're not sure, frankly, what Carter intends to do," a European diplomat commented in the days before the botched American rescue mission in Iran. "He's given us a series of ambiguous and conflicting signals – perhaps purposely, perhaps not. In our situation, we feel we must do everything possible to buy time for reason to take hold."[16]

Absent such a threat, the allies' convictions as well as their interests diverged from those of Washington. "All were apt to speak of the Iran problem as an 'American' crisis, despite Europe's far-greater interest in the stability of the Persian Gulf area."[17] The Europeans had little respect for President Carter's foreign policy, and Washington's divisions over the hostage crisis exacerbated their mistrust. The botched rescue mission

[12] Richard Burt, "Administration Says Japanese Undercut U.S. Efforts on Iran," *New York Times*, December 11, 1979, p. A1.

[13] Richard Burt, "U.S. Is Moving Toward a Decision on Economic Boycott against Iran," *New York Times*, December 12, 1979, p. A1.

[14] "Europe Takes Steps to Lift Its Embargo," *New York Times*, January 22, 1981, p. A11.

[15] Henry Scott Stokes, "Japan Indicates It Would Not Join in Trade Sanctions on Iran and Soviet," *New York Times*, January 17, 1980, p. A1.

[16] R. W. Apple, Jr., "Allies' Unspoken Fear," *New York Times*, April 24, 1980, p. A1.

[17] Peter Jay, "America's Friends," *New York Times*, December 19, 1979.

prompted grumbling about American incompetence and the German chancellor, Helmut Schmidt, warned of the alliance's being inadvertently dragged into another world war.[18] Moreover, sanctions had been discredited by their apparent ineffectiveness elsewhere, and ongoing American efforts to halt grain and high-technology exports to the Soviet Union after its invasion of Afghanistan deepened multilateral reluctance to use trade to penalize other states. As a British newspaper commented, economic penalties "have no chance of reaching the sick old man (Khomeini)."[19] Such logic posited that sanctions were not simply ineffective; they were counterproductive. Moreover, many around the world remained convinced, as the then-Australian Foreign Minister Andrew Peacock explained, that "there is some benefit to the West in continuing a presence in Iran."[20]

And, of course, there were interests closer to home to protect. European governments pushed back hard against measures that they believed infringed upon their sovereignty, a prelude to future multilateral differences over Washington's extraterritorial reach. Iran supplied approximately 20 percent of Japan's crude imports, and European dependence ranged between 11 and 15 percent. American imports of Iranian crude traditionally were much lower, approximately 4 percent of total consumption, although they had risen to 10 percent in the year before the revolution.[21] Domestic upheaval had already halved Iranian oil exports, and escalating crude prices deepened the reluctance to act against Tehran. In the wake of several massively disruptive oil crises, another surge in energy costs risked severe and prolonged consequences for the global economy.

Iran's major European trade partners were also anxious to preserve their place in the country and hoped to avoid compounding the revolution's economic fallout. Britain was already experiencing new tensions in its bilateral relationship with Tehran, thanks to the long-standing perception of British malfeasance among Iran's revolutionaries, as well as many

---

[18] Flora Lewis, "Allies' Decision to Follow U.S. Lead: Necessity Mixed with Grave Misgivings," *New York Times*, April 23, 1980, p. A12.

[19] William Borders, "U.S. Allies, Asked to Back Iran Sanctions, Are Sympathetic But Cautious," *New York Times*, April 9, 1980.

[20] Borders (*New York Times*, April 9, 1980).

[21] From January to November 1978, approximately 10 percent of U.S. oil imports, and 5 percent of American oil consumption, originated in Iran. Historically, the proportion had been considerably lower, as little as 4 percent for most of the 1970s. Anthony Parisi, "Iran's Turmoil Cuts Oil Surplus," *New York Times*, November 6, 1978, p. 77.

other Iranians. The British Embassy in Tehran was briefly attacked, and Iran's revolutionary leadership renamed the street in front of the British Embassy in Tehran after the Irish hunger striker Bobby Sands. Other European states experienced similar disruptions. France had already seen its largest export contract, a multibillion-dollar deal to construct up to fifteen nuclear plants, abrogated by the new Iranian regime, as was another major infrastructure project to construct the Tehran metro system.

The European reluctance to sanction Tehran over the hostage seizure preserved its traditionally preferential place in the Iranian market, and trade remained steady during the early war years, nearly doubling in 1983 with more than $6 billion in European exports to Iran.[22] During this same period, Iran's trade with the Eastern bloc also expanded, with imports from the Soviet Union and Eastern Europe rising to approximately 15 percent of Iran's total import bill in 1981, three times the prerevolutionary level.[23] The rise of Eastern Europe among Iran's trade partners was facilitated by the preference of both sides for barter transactions.

Moscow also used the episode to its advantage, vetoing UN sanctions in January 1980 and dangling ambiguous offers of economic assistance to Tehran. Given that Moscow was subject to American-led economic penalties over its Afghan invasion, the Kremlin's opposition to multilateral measures against Iran hardly came as a surprise. The persistence of trade ties even during Iran's most ideological period speaks to the fundamental opportunism of both leaderships, and Soviet obstructionism carried a high cost to Washington. It doomed prospects for multilateral sanctions, as European governments insisted on a United Nations Security Council (UNSC) mandate. And continuing Soviet work on unfinished infrastructure projects such as the electrification of rail routes between the two countries helped ensure Tehran had alternative export routes to deter a U.S. naval blockade.[24] Trade with Moscow also helped Tehran blunt incipient European support by leveraging Cold War fears of Soviet encroachment on a former Western ally.

Like the Soviets, the Chinese maintained their modest economic ties to Tehran. Beijing's willingness to purchase increased volumes of Iranian

---

[22] "European Report: EC Export Surge to Iran May Ease," *Wall Street Journal*, May 8, 1984.

[23] Terry Povey, "Iran's Trade Shows Shift to Soviet Bloc," *FT*, March 10, 1982.

[24] Theodore Shabad, "Soviets Moving to Bolster Alternate Routes to Iran," *New York Times*, April 22, 1980, p. A12.

crude helped Tehran to manage the disruption with Washington and balance production with demand. This too offered a political payoff, by enabling Iran's revolutionary leadership to trumpet the failure of U.S. efforts to isolate the new government.[25] All told, these tactics helped entrench Iranian skepticism toward sanctions.

The deliberations over sanctions during the hostage crisis reflected a persistent overconfidence among U.S. officials about American capacity to impact Iran's ferocious power struggle in a positive fashion. Then as now, U.S. officials sought to craft a balance of inducements and penalties that would empower the theocracy's persistently embattled moderates. It is difficult to discern any meaningfully constructive influence that carrot-and-stick diplomacy had on the balance of power within the Islamic Republic.

As discussed in Chapters 3 and 4, Iranian officials repeatedly spurned the notion that their decisions on the handling of the hostages would be influenced by the American sanctions. American officials understandably saw the situation very differently; while the lead negotiator Warren Christopher acknowledged that Tehran might have achieved some "psychic satisfaction that outweighed the tangible disadvantages, at least for a time and at least in the minds of the most radical elements," he expressed confidence that no "nation would find such a psychic ride to be enough compensation for the massive losses Iran suffered."[26] This would not be the last time that Washington and Tehran would use very different standards of accounting to assess the relative utility of U.S. actions in altering Iranian policies. These tactics served their purpose and helped entrench Iranian skepticism toward sanctions.

The U.S.-Iran Claims Tribunal – and the intragovernmental agreement that established it – withstood early tests of its viability and credibility, including a somewhat predictable Iranian bid to revise the tribunal's mandate in Tehran's favor.[27] It saw a slow start (only 387 claims were settled by 1987), punctuated by periodic outbursts, including a 1984 assault by the Iranian judges against an independent arbiter.[28] However, over the course of the subsequent years, the tribunal managed

---

[25] *AFP*, "Iranians report China oil deal,"

[26] Warren Christopher, "Introduction," in Christopher et al. (1985), p. 14.

[27] Iran sought to introduce lawsuits by the government against U.S. firms, which was explicitly excluded under the terms of the Algiers Accords. When its bid was rejected, Tehran had to withdraw 1,400 claims from the purview of the Tribunal. See Gillespie (1990), pp. 22–3.

[28] Gillespie (1990), p. 26.

to settle thousands of outstanding claims among a panoply of American petitioners as well as U.S. and Iranian government claims, worth upwards of $2.5 billion.[29] Many other existing claims were settled privately; in fact, the value of those settlements dwarfed that of the tribunal's early awards, and often these arrangements incorporated some ongoing business dealings.[30] Nearly three-quarters of the filings involved sums less than $250,000, but the tribunal also managed to contend with a range of much more provocative diplomatic and legal issues.[31] However, after a productive early period, the tribunal's activities largely ground to a halt by the late 1990s. The private sector claims were by then fully settled, and the infinitely more complicated question of intragovernmental claims, and in particular the remnants of the prerevolutionary foreign military sales credits, remains largely unresolved.[32]

REAGAN, THE WAR, AND A CONVOLUTED RELATIONSHIP WITH THE WORLD

The Reagan administration entered office in tandem with the hostages' release and the end of the agonizing national ordeal. Although bilateral tensions remained high, the Algiers Accords included provisions that lifted trade sanctions, removing all legal impediments to Iranian-American economic interactions. Reagan's own approach was decidedly eclectic; on the one hand, he deployed a wide range of epithets against the Islamic Republic during his campaign, describing Tehran alternately as "barbarians," "criminals," and "kidnappers." Still, with the hostages' release, Reagan offered a public endorsement of renewed relations when "people of some sense and moderation would take over." He added, "I think there was a legitimate reason for us being allied with Iran to begin with and that reason still exists. I think the great threat to all of us is from the left. The Tudeh Party over there is waiting for this chaos to reach a point where it might be able to move in."[33]

---

[29] Allen S. Weiner, "The Iran-United States Claims Tribunal: What Lies Ahead?" *The Law and Practice of International Courts and Tribunals* 6 (2007), p. 96.

[30] Gillespie (1990), p. 29–30.

[31] Warren Christopher and Richard M. Mosk, "The Iranian Hostage Crisis and the Iran-U.S. Claims Tribunal: Implications for International Dispute Resolution and Diplomacy," *Pepperdine Dispute Resolution Law Journal* 7:2 (2007), p. 173.

[32] Weiner (2007), pp. 86–7.

[33] Lawrence Martin, "Reagan Plans Links with Iran Following Release of Hostages," *The Globe and Mail*, January 19, 1981, p. 11.

After the hostages' release, the sanctions were lifted quickly, and trade between the two adversaries quickly rebounded, although at greatly diminished levels. Twenty-five thousand tons of U.S. wheat flowed to Tehran within two months of the hostages' release, and by June 1981, Iranian wheat imports from the United States were returning to their prerevolutionary levels of 125,000 tons per month.[34] By 1982, total trade had risen to $300 million, after grinding to a halt only two years earlier. This even included purchases of Iranian crude by the U.S. Defense Department procurement agency, whose first cargo in April 1982 was interpreted by the U.S. private sector as a green light for revived oil sales and by others as a possible signal of new American interest in engaging with Tehran.

Similarly, the linkages between Iran and its traditional European trade partners also revived, reflecting Iranian desire to access better quality products than the domestic market could provide. For its part, Germany regained its leading role in the Iranian marketplace.[35] British trade remained robust even as the diplomatic relations between the two countries deteriorated; trade delegations were openly welcomed and the two countries did $600 million in business in 1982, including a new venture between Iran Khodro and the British car maker Talbot. Thanks to its shrewd decision to host Khomeini during his final months in exile, France initially found itself spared of the most direct revolutionary wrath – and even the focus of some preferential contracting opportunities. In 1981, Tehran awarded an exclusive contract for export of Iranian caviar to a French businessman, who predicted that sanctions would have little impact on American access to the luxury food. "There will be Iranian caviar in America like there are American arms in Iran."[36]

However, the French position shifted quickly after Paris granted asylum to former Iranian officials, including Shahpour Bakhtiar, the shah's final prime minister, and the former Islamic Republic president Abolhassan Bani Sadr. Further fueling Iranian fury was France's special relationship with Saddam Hussein, including a lucrative arms trade and a reliance on Baghdad for as much as 25 percent of its oil imports. When the French government confirmed delivery of Mirage fighter jets to

---

[34] "U.S. Wheat on Way to Iran," *New York Times*, March 6, 1981; UPI, "Iran Importing U.S. Wheat," *New York Times*, June 10, 1981.

[35] Kathleen Evans, "Western Salesmen Return to Tehran," *FT*, April 28, 1983, p. 20.

[36] Susan Heller Anderson, "Frenchman Signs Iranian Caviar Pact," *New York Times*, September 19, 1981.

Saddam in 1981, the Iranian Embassy in Paris declared that "the Iranian people will never forget this act" and French exports to Iran declined by 40 percent in 1982.[37] Similar dramas played on several subsequent occasions, as Paris opted to provide its Iraqi ally with advanced technology and weaponry and Tehran responded with threats to shut down Gulf oil exports. In 1983, Tehran severed commercial and banking ties with France and cut off oil supplies, which had risen to 6 percent of French imports in the previous year. In late 1986, Paris and Tehran settled a $1 billion dispute over loans made by the shah to the European enriched uranium facility Eurodif, and within days several Western hostages including two French citizens were released.

For the most part, Iran's new authorities tended to favor countries that did not have a deep relationship with the shah or strong ties with the West – primarily Eastern and Central European states, Turkey, and Asia. Courting regional powers and outcasts without close affiliation with Washington and underpinning these diplomatic relationships with tangible economic benefits helped Tehran to mitigate the restrictions it faced, including some self-imposed. This strategy proved attractive to a number of states. Turkish exports to the Islamic Republic increased sixfold between 1980 and 1982, and in 1982 Ankara and Tehran signed a trade agreement that helped boost trade further.

That same year, Tehran sent a trade delegation to Brazil in hopes of reviving the prerevolutionary trade relationship. Part of Iran's sales pitch involved promising Brasilia a major role in the eventual postwar reconstruction. The pitch succeeded; Brazilian officials opted to shift their oil purchases away from Baghdad, as an official explained, because "Iran has 40 million people, it has oil and it is going to win the war."[38] This presumption helped persuade even Iran's adversaries to get in on the action. Besides the Iran-contra episode, dealt with in depth in Chapter 4, Israel bought $36 million in Iranian oil in 1989 in hopes of encouraging Tehran to facilitate the release of three Israeli soldiers held captive in Lebanon.[39] And Australia and New Zealand took advantage of the American departure by expanding their food and agricultural exports to Iran.

---

[37] Milt Freudenheim and Barbara Slavin, "A Bombing Run down Memory Lane," *New York Times*, February 8, 1981; David Housego, "Tehran Retaliates for Jet Sale to Iraq," *FT*, November 11, 1983.
[38] Andrew Whitley, "Brazil Drops Iraq in Favor of Iran," *FT*, May 17, 1982.
[39] "Israel-Iran Oil Deal Disclosed and Tied to Captives," *New York Times*, December 20, 1989, p. A3.

An examination of long-term trends in Iran's international economic relations suggests that the Islamic Republic's turn toward the East intensified during the war with Iraq. Tehran's efforts to replace American products and services were sourced to states in Southeast Asia, such as Thailand and Indonesia. And Iran resumed imports of Toyota vehicles in mid-1981, after initially rescinding contracts in an effort to boost domestic auto production. Finally, China emerged as a vital source of armaments and materiel – particularly missiles and missile technology. Sino-Iranian trade beyond weapons or energy also began to reemerge in the 1980s, with projects including dam construction and fishery development, as well as the establishment of a Joint Committee for Trade, Science, and Technology Cooperation in 1985 to identify investment projects and participating firms.[40]

Still, trading with a revolutionary state engaged in a total war was hardly an easy proposition. The initial postrevolutionary trade regime was skewed and highly state-controlled. Iran's revolutionaries cancelled a wide range of contracts and major foreign investment projects. In theory, at least, luxury goods were to be eschewed and imports were to be discouraged as Iranian leaders extolled the virtues of national self-sufficiency. An elaborate procurement system was established, under the auspices of the Ministry of Commerce, requiring prospective importers to work through one of eleven different sectorally organized centers. Moreover, even those European states that managed to maintain trade ties with the Islamic Republic found that they were forced to contend with episodic crises and wild oscillations in the tenor of relations. Britain was plagued by a series of "diplomatic contretemps,"[41] which included a 1986 clash over the British refusal to accredit an Iranian diplomat because of his involvement in the U.S. Embassy seizure and the 1987 arrest of an Iranian consular officer in Manchester on shoplifting charges, which sparked the armed seizure and beating of a British diplomat in Tehran and a series of expulsions and reprisals that practically emptied the embassies on both sides. A thorny rapprochement with France was quickly scuttled over French suspicions of Iranian involvement in terrorist bombings the year earlier. Even Germany, which was at the time one of Iran's leading trade partners, found itself the subject of official Iranian recriminations and retribution in 1987,

[40] Garver (2006), p. 242.
[41] Cameron R. Hume, *United Nations, Iran and Iraq: How Peacemaking Changed* (Bloomington: Indiana University Press, 1994), p. 66.

after a televised comedy sketch involving an image of Ayatollah Khomeini and women's undergarments.[42]

As a result of all these factors, the Islamic Republic's early track record on trade was mostly dismal. Imports rebounded quickly – $7.9 billion in the first seven months of 1981 alone – and remained stubbornly high, even as oil exports remained at historic lows and hard currency revenues dropped precipitously.[43] Food and agricultural products revived most quickly, with Tehran spending $3.5 billion on commodities and other imported food in 1981, including 1 million tons of American wheat.[44] The rapid depletion of its reserves forced the government to retrench quickly, banning luxury imports and seeking short-term foreign financing for vital goods. The cash crunch also helped shift some Iranian trade to the Soviet bloc, where barter was the only viable transaction in any case. The share of industrial goods in Iran's nonoil exports plummeted, from 28 percent in 1976 to 2.2 percent in 1985.[45] Similarly, foreign investment also fell. From 1982 through 1990, UN statistics show a net decrease in FDI for every year with the exception of 1988. The total FDI stock dropped by more than $900 million over this period, from $2.99 billion at the end of 1981 to $2.039 billion at the end of 1990.[46]

Iran's posthostage crisis "cold peace" with Washington deteriorated dramatically during the Iraq war, creating new complications for its trade activities and economic management at precisely the same moment that oil prices had fallen and Tehran's revenues had hit a historic low. Washington began shifting from its previous neutrality in the long, bloody Iran-Iraq War to a distinct U.S. tilt toward Iraq, in part to avert the regional upheaval that would have ensued if Iran had succeeded in its aims to take Baghdad. American material, intelligence, and strategic support helped sustain the Iraqi war effort. At the same time, Iran stepped up its campaign of subversion against its neighbors and began cultivating terrorist proxies in the Levant.

---

[42] The TV station announced an apology, and the comedian himself issued a statement explaining that "if my gag about Ayatollah Khomeini has created anger in Iran, I regret it very much and wish to be pardoned by the Iranian people." James M. Markham, "Iran Chokes on German Joke," *New York Times*, February 19, 1987.

[43] "The Government of Iran May Soon Face a Cash-Flow Crisis," *FT*, September 9, 1981.

[44] "Hostages Released, Then Iran Resumed Buying U.S. Food," *Reuters*, January 8, 1982.

[45] Amirahmadi (1990), p. 226.

[46] UNCTAD. FDIStat Database, Major FDI Indicators, http://stats.unctad.org/FDI/TableViewer/tableView.aspx?ReportId=1254.

These developments persuaded the Reagan administration to ratchet up pressure on Tehran, through both military as well as economic coercion. Early measures included an aggressive campaign to prevent Tehran from securing desperately needed military equipment and the 1984 designation of Iran as a state sponsor of terrorism for its support of Hezbollah in Lebanon and its involvement with the 1983 bombing of a U.S. barracks in Beirut that killed 241 Marines. The terrorism list penalties included additional restrictions on dual-use exports and opposition to multilateral lending. These restrictions were relatively limited measures, at least compared to the hostage era sanctions, and whatever sense of urgency they may have conveyed to Tehran was surely undercut by the nearly simultaneous covert sales of U.S. arms to the revolutionary regime as part of the Iran-contra episode. Within a few years, the sanctions associated with the terrorism list expanded to include a broader arms embargo and prohibition on all U.S. economic assistance.

Still, Iran continued to export to the United States, $468.2 million in oil in 1986, plus an additional $51.7 million in carpets and $14.1 million in pistachios.[47] This expansion became politically embarrassing as the two countries were engaged in direct hostilities in the Gulf. This marked the sole period of direct armed conflict between Iranian and American forces, after Washington agreed to escort Kuwaiti oil tankers that had been under Iranian attack through the Gulf. Although senior U.S. officials continued to hold the door open to engaging Iran's leadership, the hostility between the two sides was at a historically high pitch.

Washington's wartime diplomacy increasingly became intertwined with the use of sanctions. The Reagan administration repeatedly sought to invoke penalties against Iran if it failed to end the war. Much as with the nuclear issue two decades later, Washington pressed for UNSC action in hopes of demonstrating to Tehran "that in our view at least there's a diplomatic way out of the mess."[48] For Iran's leadership, however, the Reagan formula of an end to the war "without victor or vanquished" was inconsistent with its national dignity and fundamental security interests. Surprisingly, the American push for multilateral sanctions achieved meaningful traction among the relevant players on the UN Security Council. In contrast to its posture in 1979, the Soviet Union joined the

---

[47] Mark Hosenball, "Trade with Iran: Importing Trouble?" *Wall Street Journal*, September 2, 1987, p. 1.
[48] Elaine Sciolino, "U.S. Asserts Iran Rebuffed Offers of Direct Talks," *New York Times*, November 2, 1987.

consensus, presumably galvanized by shared concerns about destabilization of the Gulf as well as a desire to insulate its Iraqi ally.

Even as Washington sought to use sanctions to force Tehran to end its campaign in Iraq, the Reagan administration began to embrace new unilateral measures against Iran that were unrelated to the status of the conflict itself. In 1987, Tehran was named a major narcotics producing state, a declaration that merely duplicated the penalties associated with the terrorism list. The same year also saw the reimposition of an American embargo on Iran. The administration was initially split on this step. Traditionally, Washington preferred to maintain low trade levels with Iran, because trade offered a potential source of information on and influence within the Iranian private sector and because, as one State Department official acknowledged in 1987, "it's so minimal right now that there is no effective purpose in reducing it."[49]

As direct military engagements in the Gulf escalated, Congress and the Pentagon pushed hard for a comprehensive trade and investment ban. Initially, opposition from the Commerce and State Departments scuttled any movement, but the underlying impetus for increasing pressure on Tehran remained strong. Reagan's hesitation reflected a hard-won realism about the limited impact of any U.S. oil embargo on Tehran, and about the impact of new U.S. sanctions on Washington's push for a multilateral arms embargo against Tehran and the residual activities of the bilateral claims tribunal.[50] In addition, his use of sanctions against the Soviet Union, Nicaragua, and Libya had generated little more than diplomatic headaches and had imposed higher costs on U.S. companies than on their ostensible targets. Still, the political imperatives were undeniable; the tempo of Iranian attacks on Gulf shipping simply made any kind of normal trade, particularly in a strategic commodity such as energy, indefensible. John Herrington, Reagan's energy secretary, welcomed the congressional action, arguing that "the American people would rather walk than buy Iranian oil," and "we do not want to support the Iranian war effort."[51]

Reports of increasing Iranian imports to the United States sparked renewed congressional activism in Congress. U.S. imports from Iran were surging, largely as a result of increased oil purchases to hedge against

---

[49] Elaine Sciolino, "U.S. Officials Called Bitterly Split Over Continuing Trade with Iran," *New York Times,* June 22, 1987, p. A1.
[50] Elaine Sciolino, "Iran Embargo: The Main Import Is Political," *New York Times,* October 11, 1987.
[51] "Herrington Supports Boycott," *New York Times,* October 7, 1987.

possible war-related disruptions of Gulf transit. Imports from Iran had increased from $600 million in 1987, with oil constituting approximately 75 percent of that total, to more than $1 billion in the first nine months of 1988.[52] Congress overwhelmingly passed sanctions bills, and ultimately, a series of encounters between U.S. and Iranian naval forces in the Gulf pushed the new measures over the top. Still, there was a keen awareness that the measures' impact would likely be symbolic. The then-House Speaker, Jim Wright, described the sanctions as a way to demonstrate that "we can assuage our anger," adding, however, "I don't believe it's the solution to our problems."[53]

Despite the severity of the new measures, the 1987 sanctions were perceived by Washington as part of a diplomatic continuum with Tehran that included ongoing efforts to engage in direct dialogue with the regime. The administration took pains to communicate its actions and intentions to the Iranian leadership through established channels and reached out on multiple occasions in hopes of luring Tehran to the negotiating table. In principle, Iran was not unwilling, but Iranian interlocutors made clear that the price of their participation was the delivery of arms purchased under the shah and impounded by President Carter after the hostage seizure.[54] That kind of haggling was anathema to post–Iran-contra Washington and any underlying willingness that remained in both capitals for some kind of relationship simply withered. Meanwhile, Tehran viewed the embargo as the Reagan administration's effort to redeem its hawkish credentials on Iran at home.[55]

Given past experience, Washington made only cursory efforts to persuade other states to join the embargo. The transatlantic differences over the U.S. approach to the Soviet Union – American sanctions against Moscow were deeply resented by many Europeans – cast a long shadow over the options on Iran. In fact, few joined it, citing among other rationales the desire to play a constructive role in mediating an end to the Iran-Iraq War. The British merely closed an Iranian military

---

[52] Neil A. Lewis, "U.S. Considers Boycott on Iranian Oil," *New York Times*, August 21, 1987.

[53] Jonathan Fuerbringer, "House and Senate Vote for a Total Ban on Iran Imports," *New York Times*, October 7, 1987.

[54] Sciolino (November 2, 1987).

[55] During a September 1987 visit to New York for the United Nations General Assembly meeting, Iran's then-president Ali Khamenei charged that because of domestic politics, Reagan was "dragging the Persian Gulf to war" in order "to project himself as a powerful and decisive person." Youssef M. Ibrahim, "Iranian Says Arms Affair Guides U.S. Actions," *New York Times*, September 24, 1987.

procurement office in London after a British tanker in the Gulf was attacked by Iranian forces. One of the exceptions was France, which embargoed Iranian oil for approximately sixteen months over suspicions of Iranian involvement in terrorist bombings in Paris in 1987. However, Japan and most other U.S. allies offered carefully parsed commitments to avoid profiting from the American withdrawal, a stance that earned them little sympathy in either Washington or Tehran.

Perhaps the most significant dimension of the 1987 measures was the application of the new restrictions to imports of Iranian carpets to the United States; the carpet industry had long ranked as one of Iran's leading nonoil exports, and at the time the United States exports constituted 30 percent of Iran's carpet trade.[56] The sanctions also eliminated Iran's niche position in the U.S. market for caviar. Still, the impact of the 1987 embargo was limited by its loopholes, particularly provisions that permitted U.S. companies to continue to purchase Iranian oil that had been refined elsewhere or to purchase crude for non-American markets. These ambiguities would eventually prove unsustainable for Washington as subsequent administrations sought to expand the reach of economic pressure on Iran and found their efforts undermined by the inherent inconsistencies in the U.S. stance.

POSTWAR OPPORTUNITIES: GOODWILL RUNS AGROUND

As discussed in Chapter 5, President George H. W. Bush's approach to sanctions was exemplified by his inaugural outreach to Tehran, as well as by his administration's sustained receptivity toward an improved relationship with revolutionary Iran. Bush's renowned "goodwill" offer was effectively an attempt at transactional diplomacy with Tehran – Washington's effort to make clear that cooperation would be rewarded. The U.S. stance during this period stands out for its persistent efforts to proffer or provide material incentives to Tehran in exchange for specific Iranian actions. This appears to be the single time in the postrevolutionary period when Washington and Tehran successfully extracted mutual trade-offs in return for reciprocal concessions. Yet on balance, the deals – conducted publicly but with a certain degree of plausible deniability – did not alter the bilateral estrangement or reopen bilateral trade channels.

After his inaugural rhetoric, Bush authorized multiple channels to reiterate his appeal for cooperation and specifically for assistance

---

[56] Keshavarzian (2007), p. 196.

on the hostage issue.[57] In addition, Washington put forward tangible unilateral concessions– none of them explicit or lavish, but in total representing a substantial investment by Washington in demonstrating the possible benefits of cooperation. Iran was in the midst of an unprecedented process of succession, and the administration watched Tehran's contradictory signals carefully.[58] Still, despite the uncertainty about Iran's power struggle, Bush was willing to test the waters. In November 1989, Washington agreed to return $567 million to Tehran to settle outstanding claims against U.S. banks. This was hardly the first judgment of its nature or size; a similar payment was made one year earlier. However, the president himself endorsed the move, saying, "I'd like to get this underbrush cleared out now," and a senior U.S. official reinforced the political gesture by declaring that "if Rafsanjani is serious, this should be a big milestone."[59] Washington also stepped up efforts to compensate the families of victims in the 1988 shooting down of an Iranian passenger plane by the USS *Vincennes*. Subsequent agreements were reached to resolve an array of outstanding bilateral financial claims in May 1990 and November 1991, timing that roughly corresponded to the release of American hostages in Lebanon.

A State Department lawyer described the confluence as "pure coincidence," noting that the agreements were long in the making and had been nearly finalized well before the public announcements.[60] However he also acknowledged that "there was no doubt whatsoever that what we were doing was helping to aid Iran in the release of the hostages."[61] Throughout this period, both governments essentially acknowledged that the hostage cooperation was predicated on the concept, advanced

---

[57] Crist (2012), p. 383; Blight et al. (2012), pp. 247–8.

[58] "I had a meeting with various agency experts on Iran, and I think the jury is still out as to what has happened internally there in Iran," President Bush mused at a press conference shortly before Rafsanjani's inauguration, adding "I think all our experts feel that there are some hopeful signs, and I would cite some of the comments by Mr. Rafsanjani. Then you've seen some countersigns, one as recently as yesterday, by Mr. Khamenei...So, I think we don't know yet." President George H. W. Bush news conference, August 15, 1989, as transcribed and published in the U.S. Department of State Dispatch, October 1, 1989.

[59] Elaine Sciolino, "Bush Hopes to Settle Iranian Assets Issue," *New York Times*, November 8, 1989.

[60] Ibid.

[61] Martin Fletcher, "Tehran's Millions Freed Western Hostages," *The Times*, January 20, 1992.

by President Bush and other senior U.S. officials, of an anticipated quid pro quo in the form of economic relief in exchange for Iranian assistance in securing the release of Western hostages in Lebanon. The undertaking entailed some cost to Iran; Tehran claimed to have provided $2 million to its Lebanese proxies for each freed hostage. In May 1990, Iran's ambassador to the United Nations, Kamal Kharrazi, publicly anticipated American reciprocity, declaring that "what is important is that the Government is determined to do its best on this issue and we have proved it.... This effort will continue, provided the United States encourages Israel to facilitate the process of releasing all hostages."[62]

During this same period, Tehran also appeared prepared to settle some of its old grievances with Washington – for a price, of course. Iran pursued claims against the United States for the destruction of two Iranian oil platforms by U.S. naval vessels during the "tanker war" phase of the war with Iraq. Its legal action cited the 1955 Treaty of Amity, Economic Relations, and Consular Rights signed by Washington and Tehran and specifically cited article I, which establishes "firm and enduring peace and sincere friendship between the two countries."[63] The reference to article I was rejected by the Court, and the case proceeded on the basis of an Iranian claim that the U.S. attacks had violated its "freedom of commerce" under article X of the same treaty – and based its arguments on the persistence of Iranian oil sales to the United States.

Amid profound domestic and international flux, the Bush administration's modest deployment of economic incentives toward Tehran generated little positive traction from Iran and left both governments dissatisfied with the experience. Washington was frustrated by what U.S. officials saw as insufficient Iranian efforts to live up to what was perceived as their end of the bargain – the release of the hostages. And while Iran may have been making a fitful, contested transition to greater pragmatism in its economic policies, one that included efforts to assuage tensions with its neighbors and other old adversaries, Rafsanjani's first years at the helm could hardly be described as a kinder, gentler Islamic Republic. The Rushdie verdict continued to echo, members of a U.S. espionage network were publicly hanged, Tehran was linked to the 1992 bombing of the Israeli Embassy in Buenos Aires (and a subsequent attack on a Jewish community center there), while the

---

[62] Robert Pear, "U.S. and Iran Move on Smaller Claims," *New York Times*, May 8, 1990.
[63] James A. Green, "The Oil Platforms Case: An Error in Judgment?" *Journal of Conflict and Security Law* 9:3 (December 1, 2004), pp. 359, 365.

Iranian leadership reveled in hate-filled invective as a counterpoint to the newly launched Arab-Israeli peace process. Iranian leaders remained steeped in resentment toward Washington for its support of Saddam Hussein during their long war, and too consumed with steering the reconstruction program through domestic turbulence to staunch the steady march of economic pressure by undertaking a diplomatic opening to their old adversary.

The first Bush administration's relatively limited agenda on Iran belies a hardening of Washington's attitude toward the theocratic state. One notable aspect was the creeping association between Iran and Iraq, - as part of a broader reconceptualization of a post-Soviet strategic land-scape dominated by threats from rogue states. Second, the administration's direct and fruitful immersion in the precarious terrain of Middle East peacemaking created a new imperative for antagonism between the two old adversaries. New sanctions enacted during this period were codified in the 1992 Iran-Iraq Nonproliferation Act, which prohibited any transfer of any goods or technologies that facilitate the development of chemical, biological, or nuclear weapons as well as desta-bilizing conventional weapons. This legislation represents another salvo of Washington's increasing reliance on threats of penalties against third countries to deter them from doing business with Iran. The administration also sought to strengthen multilateral restrictions on dual-use goods, albeit to little effect.

CLINTON, REFORM, AND SANCTIONS' NEW LIFE

The hardening intensified during the Clinton administration. Secretary of State Warren Christopher's experience leading the contentious negoti-ations that freed the hostages left a legacy of distrust toward Tehran and a revulsion for the Islamic regime's policies. He and other officials took office determined to avoid Iranian duplicity and to isolate Tehran, as well as Baghdad, in hopes of facilitating a "new Middle East" anchored by Arab-Israeli peace. The new U.S. policy became known as "dual containment," a deliberate shift away from the traditional American policy of counterbalancing one of the Gulf powerhouses by indulging the other. To achieve these aims, Washington sought to sharpen its penalties and deepen the isolation of both countries.

Washington focused on generating greater cooperation from its reluc-tant European allies to apply pressure on Tehran, a posture that was undermined by the persistence of considerable volumes of U.S. trade with

Iran. The inconsistencies in the 1987 embargo meant that U.S. oil companies continued to purchase large quantities of Iranian crude without violating any legal restrictions so long as they refined the crude and sold the products elsewhere. American firms were purchasing as much as 25 percent of Iran's exports by 1994 – more than any other state. For their part, the Iranians reveled in highlighting this discrepancy, presumably intended to undercut American pressure on Europe. Iran's Central Bank governor went on record asserting that American companies had exported $1 billion Iranian goods and suggested that U.S. efforts to persuade Europe to join the embargo were a competitive move aimed at eliminating rivals for the Iranian marketplace.[64] The disparity between Washington's advocacy and the behavior of American companies emerged as a political embarrassment and a tactical problem. In a joint press conference with President Clinton at the White House in February 1995, German Chancellor Helmut Kohl pointedly referenced reports on the large stakes of U.S. oil companies in Iran's export revenues.[65]

Washington began to focus on strengthening restrictions on U.S. companies as a means of persuading American allies to take its concerns about Iran more seriously. However, even within the U.S. government, there was no unanimity of views. In 1994, various U.S. agencies disagreed over a proposed sale of Boeing 747s to Tehran, with Commerce, Treasury, and even some Pentagon officials advocating its approval. State Department opposition killed the deal, in part by persuading the Saudis to condition a $6 billion aircraft purchase on the willingness of American aerospace firms to forgo the Iranian opportunity. The availability of alternative supplies – in this case, Airbus – meant that the move achieved little in imposing real costs on Tehran.

Torpedoing the Boeing sale was the first in what became an activist U.S. government agenda of sanctioning Iran and seeking to degrade its access to

---

[64] "Iran's Central Bank Says U.S. Imported $1B in Iran Goods," *Dow Jones News Service*, January 12, 1994.

[65] Kohl commented: "As far as Iran specifically is concerned, we are in agreement. We are not willing to support any policy in Iran which might entail the danger of fundamentalism, which to me is one of the greatest dangers we are facing today. We are not willing to add any support to fundamentalism. We have cut back economic relations with Iran considerably. Those were longstanding relations which we have cut back considerably. And if I'm not mistaken, Time Magazine being a respectable news magazine, has said quite a number of things this week about American oil companies, not German oil companies, mind you. And if you take a look, you'll have to conclude that these oil companies export into other countries, not our country." Transcript of Clinton-Kohl Press Conference (part 1 of 3), *U.S. Newswire*, February 9, 1995.

international trade and finance. In what would become institutionalized features of American foreign policy, Washington adopted a multipronged approach to economic pressure and weighed in with all its allies and partners to use moral suasion as a means of eroding international interest in economic opportunities in, and diplomatic dialogue with, Tehran. The Clinton administration track record in this regard is extensive, even outside the energy sector: Washington undermined Iranian efforts to reschedule debts, blocked loans by the World Bank and International Monetary Fund, reversed Japanese plans for a several hundred million dollar aid project in southern Iran, swayed Moscow to restrict its arms sales to defensive weaponry, and otherwise increased the costs and inconvenience to the Iranian economy at a time when Iran was still struggling to recover from the war and the aftereffects of revolutionary turmoil and mismanagement. American opposition helped constrain flows of capital into an Iran in flux. Even with the more outward-looking policies championed by Rafsanjani and, later, Khatami, the return of foreign direct investment (FDI) to Iran was slow throughout the 1990s. By the end of 2001, the stock of FDI had only rebounded to $2.492 billion.[66] Through this period, Iran's FDI compared to that of neighboring nations was abysmal – in 2001, Iran accounted for only 0.34 percent of all FDI inflows into the broader Middle East and North Africa region.[67]

As part of its efforts to cordon off Iran from the rest of the region, the Clinton administration also adopted a vigorous agenda on Central Asian energy. Officially, U.S. policy sought to promote multiple pipelines; unofficially, Washington sought to preclude Iran (and Russia) from participation in the newly developing energy linkages of the post-Soviet space. The capstone of this policy was official American advocacy for the $4 billion Baku-Tblisi-Ceyhan pipeline, which was formally committed in 1999 and officially launched in 2005. Unlike the thwarted Boeing deal, these policies did more than simply advantage a competitor – in this case, Turkey; they deprived Iran of a central role as the transit route for Central Asian and Caucasian energy supplies.

Still, pressure built within Washington for more aggressive action against Iran's slowly reviving trade and investment ties with the world,

---

[66] UNCTAD. FDIStat Database, Major FDI Indicators, http://stats.unctad.org/FDI/Table-Viewer/tableView.aspx?ReportId=1254.

[67] Massoud Karshenas and Hassan Hakimian. "Managing Oil Resources and Economic Diversification in Iran." In Katouzian and Shahidi (eds.), *Iran in the 21st Century: Politics, Economics, and Conflict* (London: Routledge, 2008), p. 197.

particularly among Republican leaders in the Congress. Led by Speaker of the House Newt Gingrich (R-GA) and Senator Alphonse d'Amato (R-NY), proposals for a wholesale embargo circulated Congress. The executive branch restrained these initiatives, arguing instead for targeted multilateral measures focused on arms transfers, dual-use technology, and the extension of official government credits and other financial support to Tehran. However, in March 1995, events conspired to put the administration on the hot seat. Tehran's award of its first upstream oil deal since the revolution to an American company sparked a firestorm and left the administration scrambling to denounce the deal while grudgingly acknowledging its permissibility under existing U.S. law. The deal immediately elicited passionate denunciations from every corner of Washington, including from Secretary of State Warren Christopher, who proclaimed, "wherever you look, you find the evil hand of Iran in this region," shortly before he recused himself because of a conflict of interest involving his previous law firm.[68]

Within a week, board members of Conoco's parent company, E. I. du Pont de Nemours & Company, had declared their objections, and Clinton announced that he would issue an executive order banning U.S. companies from financing, management, or development activities in Iran's energy sector. A second executive order two months later extended the embargo to all trade, financial, and commercial transactions involving U.S. firms and their overseas subsidiaries.[69] Clinton scorned the proposition that trade could positively influence Tehran's policies, noting that

many people have argued passionately that the best route to changing Iranian behavior is by engaging the country. Unfortunately, there is no evidence to support that argument. Indeed, the evidence of the last two years suggests exactly the reverse. Iran's appetite for acquiring and developing nuclear weapons and the missiles to deliver them has only grown larger. Even as prospects for the peace in the Middle East have grown, Iran has broadened its role as an inspiration and paymaster to terrorists. There is nothing to suggest that further engagement will alter that course.[70]

---

[68] "Christopher Attacks Conoco Oil Deal with Iran," *Reuters*, March 9, 1995.

[69] Executive Order 12957, signed on March 15, 1995, prohibits U.S. companies from investing in Iran's energy sector, http://www.treasury.gov/resource-center/sanctions/Documents/12957.pdf. E.O. 12959, which extends U.S. sanctions to a wide-ranging ban on all exports of goods and services to Iran as well as investment, was signed on May 6, 1995, http://nodis3.gsfc.nasa.gov/displayEO.cfm?id=EO_12959_.

[70] Todd S. Purdham, "Clinton to Order a Trade Embargo against Iran," *New York Times*, May 1, 1995.

Tehran castigated the new American restrictions and disdained the prospect that the move would hurt Iran's energy sector. "We do not need you," Iran's oil minister responded:

We, in the world, do not need them at all. It was they who came and pleaded to be allowed to participate in this tender. Why should we need them? What happened was a fully stage-managed show. They created a climate of adverse propaganda inside the USA. This is purely because this gentleman's [President Clinton's] position in the coming elections is a bit shaky. He is seeking to find a subject to exploit for propaganda purposes. But he is still behaving in a clumsy manner here. That is, no doubt this move will work against him too. In my opinion this was a very crude propaganda move. A panic reaction undertaken by the clumsy US government.[71]

Despite the bravado, however, the move did take a toll; Shell subsequently dropped out of a revived bid process, and the black market rate for the Iranian currency crashed from 2,500 to the dollar in January 1995 to 4,300 to the dollar by April and 6,500 to the dollar in May 1995.[72] The currency would never again recover its value, as future rounds of sanctions depressed its value even more dramatically.

The muscular new trade embargo did not end the Clinton administration's debates over Iran. Key congressional Republicans remained eager to press American allies further on Iran; even before new measures had been approved, Senator d'Amato approached international oil companies including Total to warn them that proposed new U.S. restrictions would target their business dealings with Tehran. And Washington's frustration with Iranian policies intensified with the 1996 escalation of terrorist violence in Israel. U.S. officials interpreted the attacks by Hezbollah and Palestine Islamic Jihad as a deliberate effort to exploit Yitzhak Rabin's assassination and obstruct efforts by his successor, Shimon Peres, to negotiate a Syrian peace deal.

As a result, after painstaking negotiations to incorporate waiver authority and a sunset provision, President Clinton signed the Iran-Libya Sanctions Act (ILSA) in August 1996; the law threatened penalties on third countries that invested more than $20 million in Iran's energy sector.[73] Not surprisingly, the measure generated backlash among

---

[71] Excerpts from discussion with Oil Minister Gholamreza Aghazadeh, on "In Line with People, in Step with Officials," March 16, 1995, Voice of the Islamic Republic of Iran Network 1, from BBC Summary of World Broadcasts.

[72] Menashri (2001), p. 200.

[73] The Iran-Libya Sanctions Act was signed in August 1996, http://thomas.loc.gov/cgi-bin/query/z?c104:H.R.3107.ENR:

Iran's Political Economy since the Revolution

Washington's allies, with formal protests from Europe and Asia and a
French decision to reinstate export credits to Tehran, among other rebuffs.
"Nobody accepts that the United States can pass a law on a global scale,"
the French prime minister Lionel Jospin fulminated. "American laws apply
in the United States. They do not apply in France," he said, adding that he
would "rejoice in" the news of the Total deal for Sirri.[74]

The European rejection of ILSA scuttled nascent convergence between
European and American policies toward Tehran. After initially welcoming trade opportunities created by Iran's postwar reconstruction,
Europe had ruptured ties with Tehran dramatically in 1997, only one
year after ILSA's enactment, as a result of the Mykonos verdict officially
linking Iran's leadership to the assassination of dissidents in Europe. The
frictions had begun at least a year earlier, when the Germans issued an
arrest warrant for Iran's intelligence minister, Ali Fallahian, for the
murders of Kurdish dissidents. The 1997 ruling by a German court
confirmed the complicity of the Iranian leadership in the attacks,
prompting Germany to recall its ambassador and expel several Iranian
diplomats, and not long thereafter Tehran arrested a German
businessman.

U.S. officials used the news as an opportunity to chastise Europe's
commercial ties to Tehran and appeal for Europe to join Washington in
penalizing Tehran. However, European leaders remained convinced that
dialogue remained the most effective tool for influencing Iranian policies
and were loath to jeopardize the steadily improving commercial ties
between the countries. Khatami's election shortly after the Mykonos crisis
erupted only solidified the European commitment to staying the course;
the changes in Iran's official leadership roster underscored the conviction,
declared by British Foreign Secretary Robin Cook, that "a policy of
isolation would be counterproductive."[75] These divergent views on
tactics precluded any closer coordination between Washington and its
allies on pressuring Tehran even during periods of Iranian provocation.

Eventually, Washington fashioned a compromise on ILSA, and once
the Clinton administration issued a formal waiver of the threat of penalties on Total and its partners for their involvement in South Pars Phases
2 and 3, U.S. measures proved less of a deterrent than the broader

[74] Roger Cohen, "France Scoffs at U.S. Protest Over Iran Deal," *New York Times*, September 30, 1997.
[75] Christophe de Roquefeuil, "New Cloud Hangs Over Iran-EU Relations As Tehran Seeks
New Basis for Ties," *AFP*, January 31, 1998.

frustrations of doing business in the Islamic Republic. For the next several years, ILSA presented a minor additional risk factor for Iran's prospective foreign investors, but there is no evidence to suggest that it succeeded in dissuading them. Even before the waiver, Total's CEO publicly dismissed ILSA and American pressure, describing the effort as "absurd" and arguing that his company saw "no obligation to apply an American law produced by a domestic lobby for narrow interests."[76] At the same time, Washington engaged frequently and contentiously with both Beijing and Moscow over the aspects of their own economic relationships with Tehran. Beijing opted to scale back its weapons exports and nuclear assistance to Tehran to assuage the tense relationship with Washington, although China continued to assist Iran in developing an indigenous arms industry.[77]

Despite the severity of the new measures, the Clinton administration had relatively limited objectives for sanctions and a realistic appreciation of the challenge of generating additional international support. The president advocated *against* secondary sanctions in a 1995 speech to the World Jewish Congress, on the basis that they "would cause unnecessary strains with our allies at a time when we need our friends' co-operation." That same year, Undersecretary of State Peter Tarnoff testified that the administration's "Iran policy is designed to make it even tougher for the Iranian government to obtain hard currency, and thereby constrict its ability to fund those policies that threaten our interests." Washington merely sought to take "a bite out of Iran's wallet" and deny resources to Tehran; expectations that financial pressure would quickly alter Iran's approach to the world were restrained.[78] The debate within Congress featured diverse views and pragmatic discussion of the prospective costs and benefits.

However, as the price of terrorism began to hit home, the Clinton administration also created new opportunities for individual action against Tehran for its involvement with terrorism. Prior efforts to seek compensation from the Iranian government for various offenses – including the embassy seizure and damages to tanker traffic during the Iran-Iraq

---

[76] Bhushan Bahree and Thomas Kamm, "Total Seeks More Pacts with Iran, Despite Threat of U.S. Sanctions," *Wall Street Journal*, March 17, 1998.

[77] Scott Harold and Alireza Nader, "China and Iran: Economic, Political, and Military Relations" (Washington, DC: RAND Corporation, 2012), pp. 4, 7.

[78] "The Pressure for Change: The U.S. Embargo against Iran," Peter Tarnoff, Under Secretary of State for Political Affairs, Hearing before the Senate Banking, Housing and Urban Affairs, October 11, 1995, http://www.iranwatch.org/government/US/Congress/Hearings/senbanking-101195/us-senbanking-tarnoff-101195.htm

War – were consistently rejected by the courts on the basis that governments cannot be sued. Prompted by the 1993 World Trade Center bombing, Congress in 1996 passed the Antiterrorism and Effective Death Penalty Act, revoking sovereign immunity for designated state sponsors of terrorism. The law facilitated a tidal wave of successful lawsuits against Iran, beginning in 1998 with a $247 million judgment against Tehran.

The proliferation of these lawsuits created awkward contradictions for the U.S. executive branch. Successful plaintiffs sought to collect on large judgments by attaching Iran's remaining diplomatic properties in the United States, and Congress repeatedly sought to facilitate lawsuits by the former hostages, in contravention of the provisions of the 1981 Algiers Accords. Administrations from both political parties have blocked such efforts on grounds of international law and diplomatic conventions. In October 2000, President Clinton signed a legislative compromise, which authorized $213 million in compensatory payment to successful plaintiffs against Iran and shifted responsibility for securing payments for these judgments to the U.S. government, while preserving the inviolability of diplomatic property.

As discussed in Chapter 6, the Clinton administration's assiduous efforts to fortify economic pressure on Iran were succeeded, and nearly matched in their intensity, by a serious, sustained initiative to engage Tehran in diplomatic dialogue undertaken in response to the ascendance of the reform movement during Clinton's second term. After Khatami's election, Washington used multiple channels to signal high-level interest in direct talks. The then-Assistant Secretary of State Martin Indyk explained that "as Iran's leaders have shown an interest in constructive engagement with the international community, we have sought to respond by highlighting our interest in encouraging changes in Iranian behavior and establishing through dialogue a road map for building a more cooperative relationship."[79]

These efforts included tangible abatements to the U.S. embargo. In 1997, only months after Khatami's election, the State Department formally designated the Mojahideen-e Khalq as a foreign terrorist organization, a move that blocked the group from fund-raising openly in the United States. A year later, Clinton removed Iran from the list of major drug-producing states. Because of the redundancy inherent in the multiple

---

[79] Martin S. Indyk, "U.S. Policy Toward the Middle East (testimony before the House International Relations Committee)," *U.S. Department of State Dispatch* (10:6), July 1, 1999.

layers of U.S. sanctions, this move did not open any new trade or investment opportunities to Tehran. And U.S. officials stressed that the decisions were based upon the evidence, rather than a politically inspired overture.[80] In all, Clinton adopted the most dramatic series of U.S. overtures toward Tehran since 1979, including authorization of the sale of spare airline parts and lifting of restrictions on sales of food and pharmaceuticals. The moves concluded with a wide-ranging March 2000 speech by the then-Secretary of State Madeleine Albright articulating U.S. regret for previous U.S. policies and lifting sanctions on caviar, carpets, and pistachio imports.

The March 2000 Albright statement reflected an unusual gamble for Washington; without any prior coordination, Washington lobbed a historic opening to an old adversary in hopes of a constructive reception. A U.S. official predicted that the Iranian reaction would be "cautious, mild, at the beginning. But they won't be dismissive."[81] However, even these modest expectations proved overly optimistic as the initiative generated no tangible response from Tehran. Some reports suggested that the Iranian government was caught off guard by the extent of Albright's mea culpa. Others blamed Albright's criticisms – deliberately narrowed so as not to construe wholesale American antipathy toward Iran – for exacerbating Iranian paranoia and prompting a backlash by the targeted Iranian institutions. "She specifically named the Islamic Revolution Guard Corps and the judiciary, which along with the previous stance of the Americans against the Guardian Council completed the chain of enmity with the heart – the leader – of the system."[82] Ultimately, the obstacle was not the specific phraseology or the logistics of Iranian preparation, but a more fundamental impediment: the intense factional divisions within the Iranian system and the fundamental unwillingness of Iran's supreme leader to countenance normalization with the "Great Satan."

Of course even as the executive branch was reaching out to Iran, Congress continued to expand the sanctions regime. In 1998, Congress passed legislation requiring the State Department to review issues of religious freedom, creating another checklist of international offenders

---

[80] Thomas W. Lippman, "U.S. Removes Iran from Its Drug List," *WP*, December 8, 1998, Page A23.

[81] Phillip Shenon, "Major Overture toward Iran Expected in Speech by Albright," *New York Times*, March 17, 2000.

[82] Mohammad Imani, "An Anarchical Understanding of Reform," *Kayhan*, April 3, 2000, p. 14.

that included the Islamic Republic. In March 2000, the Iran Nonproliferation Act of 2000 was signed into law, although only after a protracted dispute between the administration and Congress over executive waiver authority. In addition, even after the launch of overtures toward Khatami, existing sanctions required the administration to oppose World Bank loans and other international financial institutions' activities in Iran.

The Clinton era tightening meant that U.S.-Iran trade ties remained significantly lower than in any historical period other than the hostage crisis. However, the two instances of sanctions relaxation – the April 1999 rescission of all restrictions on exports of American agricultural and medical products and the March 2000 exemption of caviar, carpet, and pistachio imports – revived some trade between the two countries. Carpet sales surged, but U.S. tariffs established to protect American pistachio growers forestalled much expansion, while caviar exports were subject to newfound competition and recurrent disruptions over environmental concerns.

BUSH'S CARROT AND STICK

President George W. Bush took office amid expectations that the utilization of sanctions as a policy tool might wane. Such presumptions had less relation to Iran's internal conditions, which had influenced Clinton's policies, than to the president's background in the oil industry and the growing skepticism around sanctions in general because of the deteriorating situation in Iraq. However, the new administration's early months were marked by ambivalence toward Tehran, as Iran's domestic politics continued to regress and the Justice Department released new allegations of Iranian complicity in the 1996 Khobar Towers bombing. As a result, the administration's halfhearted effort to scale back ILSA when it came up for renewal in August 2001 made little headway. In July 2001, Washington chose not to prevent an Iranian bid to begin accession talks with the World Trade Organization, a modest opening at best, since Washington continued to oppose the talks.

Along with so many other aspects of U.S. foreign policy, the September 11 attacks changed everything with respect to U.S.-Iran relations, albeit not immediately or obviously. The crisis created a dramatic new impetus for robust U.S. policy instruments for dealing with the threat of terrorism. While Al Qaeda was the primary focus for the conceptualization or the initial implementation of those tools, their authorities were gradually deployed to deal with the threat from other terrorist organizations as well. And their utilization helped inform a more aggressive approach to pursuing the financial dimensions of international terrorism. The campaign to constrain and penalize Al Qaeda served as a model, one that arguably proved even more effective when applied to a state actor such as Iran with manifold interconnections to the international financial system.

The primary weapon in this new initiative was Executive Order 13224, a measure signed by President Bush a mere two weeks after the 9/11 attacks. E.O. 13224 freezes all assets of individuals and organizations designated as terrorists,[83] and in concert with other early measures, such as the October 2001 USA Patriot Act, proved "a powerful and flexible tool" by extending the reach of the U.S. Treasury Department's existing investigatory and punitive mechanisms.[84] Interestingly, although a number of Iranian-affiliated groups such as Hezbollah and Palestine Islamic Jihad were included on the initial list of sanctioned entities, the first Iranian group to be incorporated in the Treasury Department's E.O. 13224 designations was the Mojahideen-e Khalq. This designation was consistent with its inclusion on the State Department's list of foreign terrorist organizations, but it also may have served as a reward for the initial bout of cooperation between Tehran and Washington in the Afghan dimensions of the American war against terrorism.

It took four additional years, and the intensification of the standoff between Washington and Tehran over the nuclear program, before the new authorities were applied squarely to Iran. In the meantime, the bilateral relationship remained characterized by striking contradictions. Between 2001 and 2003, the Bush administration engaged in the most substantive direct dialogue with Iranian officials since the conclusion of the Algiers Accords, a process that facilitated unprecedented cooperation between the two adversaries in and on Afghanistan. However, even as these talks were under way, U.S. policy toward Tehran was hardening significantly; in January 2002, President Bush described Iran as part of an "axis of evil," and later that year revelations about Iran's covert nuclear activities put the two countries on a collision course in which economic pressure would increasingly assume a central place in Washington's strategy. Still, for most of Bush's first term, U.S. policy in the region remained

---

[83] The text of E.O. 13224, signed in September 200, is available at http://www.treasury.gov/resource-center/sanctions/Programs/Documents/terror.pdf

[84] Testimony bfore the Senate Committee on Banking, Housing and Urban Affairs, by Adam J. Szubin, Director of the Office of Foreign Assets Control, U.S. Department of the Treasury, September 12, 2006.

focused on Iraq, rather than Iran, with the expectation that Saddam Hussein's successful ouster would ultimately create the conditions for positive change within Iran.

Although Washington began to articulate a more absolutist approach to Iran than it had at any time since the hostage crisis, the administration sought to influence Iran through means other than sanctions. For most of the first Bush term, there were no serious efforts to intensify economic pressure, in part as a result of competing priorities as the war on terror and the Iraq campaign consumed senior policy maker attention. Moreover, within the administration and between Washington and its closest allies, Iran policy was subject to ambiguity. Hawks pushed for more aggressive penalties against Tehran and more explicit regime change efforts, tactics that concerned America's European allies, while administration moderates advocated expanded engagement with the clerical regime.

As a result, U.S. Iran policy during the early Bush administration was characterized by rhetorical excess and programmatic neglect. The administration presumed that the ouster of Saddam and the establishment of a pro-Western, democratic Iraq would undercut the legitimacy of Iran's Islamic Republic. On this basis, Washington abandoned nascent dialogue with Tehran on Afghanistan, and unofficial Iranian overtures, including an expansive proposal for a "grand bargain" proffered by the Swiss ambassador to Tehran with the input of several Iranian diplomats, were disregarded. For similar reasons, the Bush administration initially resisted European diplomacy on the nuclear issue. As the dispute became entrenched and Iraq erupted into civil war, U.S. officials accepted that a direct American role in that dialogue would offer greater leverage in dealing with the issue. In an attempt to provide incentives for Iranian cooperation on the nuclear talks, in May 2005, Washington dropped its objections to Iran's application to begin accession talks with the World Trade Organization and announced that it would consider licensing sales of spare parts for aircraft on a case-by-case basis.

Over time, as circumstances produced little evidence of positive change within Iran and the situation in Iraq created new bilateral tensions, Washington sought to alter the calculus of the Iranian leadership through the application of additional pressure. The first step occurred after Tehran's decision to abandon its commitment to suspend uranium enrichment and reprocessing. The August 2005 removal of the seals at the Natanz enrichment facility intensified Washington's attempts to expand the existing counterproliferation measures, with the application of a model crafted around the antiterrorism authorities. Such designations freeze any U.S.-based assets and preclude any American individual or institution from engaging in any transactions with them. This prohibition extended to the exceptionally tangential contacts that characterize the movement of capital in the modern international financial system, including what are referred to as "U-turn" transactions, which entail only indirect interaction involving a third-party bank or financial institution. The scope and reach of the U.S. financial system mean that such measures effectively blacklist the designated institutions from any contact with any individual or institution with U.S. business interests, and as such have a powerful extraterritorial dimension. President Bush signed Executive Order 13382 in June 2005 and designated Iran's Atomic Energy Organization, Aerospace Industries Organization, the Shahid Hemmat Industrial Group, and Shahid Bakeri Industrial Group under its authority.[85]

The real innovation, however, was in September 2006, when the U.S. Treasury Department for the first time designated an Iranian financial institution – Bank-e Saderat – as well as Iran's Qods Force under EO 13224 on the basis of their funds transfers to Hezbollah. The move prompted banks around the world to curtail transactions with Saderat, and the ripple effect encouraged Washington to strike again. One by one, Iranian banks were designated under the antiterrorism and counterproliferation authorities: Bank-e Sepah in January 2007, Bank-e Melli and Bank-e Mellat in October 2007, and eventually nearly all Iranian financial institutions. Along with the banks, the Bush administration sought to target Iran's security organizations, to hamper further their resources but also to underscore – as had the Clinton administration – that Washington's real differences lay with Iran's hard-liners rather than with its population. In addition, a series of official and semigovernmental institutions were listed alongside the banks and the military, including the Martyrs' Foundation, Al Qarz Al Hassan, and Khatam Al-Anbia and other IRGC-controlled companies.

Washington also unleashed a powerful public relations campaign aimed squarely at the compliance departments of financial institutions in Europe, Asia, and the Gulf, intended to highlight both the increasing legal roadblocks as well as the reputational risks of investing in Iran. Treasury Department officials described such moral suasion as a "force multiplier," noting that "financial institutions may do so because

---

[85] The text of E.O. 13382, signed in June 2005, is available at http://www.treasury.gov/resource-center/sanctions/Programs/Documents/wmd.pdf

they don't want to be hosting the business of terrorist organizations, even if it is legally permissible. They may cooperate because of reputational risk. Or, perhaps they do so because of fears of litigation or U.S. action.... As a result, our 'unilateral' actions are anything but."[86] Their efforts reaped some payoffs, particularly where U.S. pressures were compounded by problematic experiences in the Iranian marketplace. Total's 2008 withdrawal from its South Pars Gas field development project came in the immediate aftermath of Western condemnation of a new round of Iranian missile tests. The Total spokeswoman Lisa Wiler justified the decision by saying, "The conditions are not present for investing in Iran today. We hope that the political relations will improve so that we can invest."[87]

The outcome was dramatic; after more than two decades of trying to bring the rest of the world on board with American efforts to isolate and pressure Iran, Washington helped launch a wave of divestment from Iran simply by capitalizing on the unique role of the U.S. financial system to magnify the impact of U.S. restrictions. The U.S. federal measures were complemented by the proliferation of state-level measures, the cumulative effect of which was to reinforce the disincentives for any firm with American interests to deal with Iranian counterparts. Over time, the Bush measures began to achieve precisely what previous authors of sanctions legislation had sought but largely failed to do: to present firms from all over the world with a choice of trading with Iran or with the United States.[88]

While extraterritorial sanctions had provoked European opposition in the past, these bank designations received little overt pushback from either the diplomatic or the financial community. The surprising degree of adherence and support reflects a combination of effective U.S. diplomacy with allies, a more skeptical international mood toward Tehran, and the obliqueness of the measures, which ostensibly targeted merely the Iranian institutions but indirectly imposed constraints on any of their foreign business partners. Notably, and particularly as the restrictions began to take a more direct toll on Iran's ability to export oil, the international support was facilitated by changes in worldwide energy

---

[86] Testimony before the Senate Committee on Banking, Housing and Urban Affairs, by Adam J. Szubin, Director of the Office of Foreign Assets Control, U.S. Department of the Treasury, September 12, 2006.

[87] See, for example, Greg Keller, "French Energy Giant Total Says It's Too Risky to Invest in Iran, in Blow to Gas Deal," *Associated Press Worldstream*, July 10, 2008.

[88] AIPAC published just such an appeal in 1995. See Neal Sher, "Comprehensive US Sanctions against Iran: A Plan for Actions," (Washington, DC: AIPAC, 1995).

markets; the availability of additional oil and gas supplies due to technological breakthroughs and the advent of shale production helped mitigate the impact of the threat to and even the loss of some Iranian exports on the global price of energy.

During this period, the Bush administration succeeded in its long, arduous drive to refer the Iranian nuclear file to the United Nations Security Council. A trio of successive UNSC sanctions resolutions began amassing international consensus around penalizing Iran and specific institutions.[89] The UNSC measures deliberately targeted individuals and institutions associated with the nuclear program to prevent undue harm to the broader Iranian population or economy. The first measure, approved in March 2006, was largely hortatory and was succeeded by a consensus overture directed from the permanent five UNSC members – Russia, China, Britain, France, and the United States, plus Germany – that offered incentives to Tehran. When neither symbolic UNSC action nor the promise of enhanced nuclear cooperation appeared to sway Tehran, the subsequent two UN measures incorporated more specific sanctions.

In addition to unilateral American measures and Security Council action, the Bush administration began to reap the rewards of a new coordination with Europe on Iran, in the form of incipient European and multilateral actions to penalize Tehran. In October 2007, the Financial Action Task Force warned that "Iran's lack of a comprehensive anti-money laundering/combating the financing of terrorism regime represents a significant vulnerability within the international financial system" and called on members to exercise "'enhanced due diligence.'" This paved the way for an effort that would broaden until the entire Iranian financial system had been blacklisted by both Washington and the European Union.

The Bush administration also sought to enforce U.S. sanctions on Iran more rigorously, although it retained the same basic indifference to ILSA. Penalties were levied on Chinese firms – at least sixty-two separate instances of sanctions enforcement against Chinese companies during the Bush tenure alone – as well as European financial institutions. Aggressive enforcement was seen as a vital dimension in intensifying the impact of U.S. measures and persuading firms to forgo even legal trade or investment opportunities. In addition, the Bush administration encouraged the expansion in local and state-level measures to restrict trade and

---

[89] The text of the four sanctions-oriented UNSCRs and related resolutions can be found at http://www.un.org/sc/committees/1737/resolutions.shtml

investment in Iran, even in cases where such trade was indirect. From 2004 onward, more than a dozen states approved legislation requiring that state pension funds divest from companies doing business in Iran.

Still, even as Washington was sharpening sanctions and even as European companies began to reconsider reentering the Iranian market, Iran's trade and investment with other countries were on the rise. This is particularly true of Chinese companies, which outside the financial sector appeared largely unmoved by the Bush era unilateral sanctions on doing business with Iran. Major infrastructure projects were announced involving several prominent Chinese conglomerates, and Chinese imports to Iran rose at a faster pace than Iran's crude exports to China – 33 percent alone in 2011, for a total value of $14.8 billion.[90] A robust trade in consumer goods and arms helped elevate China to one of Iran's leading trade partners, second only to the traditional reexport hub in Dubai (through which a large volume of Chinese goods pass in addition to those attributed via direct trade).

OBAMA'S COERCIVE DIPLOMACY

In contrast to his predecessors as well as his rivals, candidate Barack Obama publicly campaigned on the exigency of a new approach to Iran; during the Democratic primary race, then-Senator Obama embraced the need for direct negotiations without preconditions. After taking office, the new president personally invested himself in reaching out to Iran, via a March 2009 video message commemorating the Iranian New Year (Nowruz), a greeting that was crafted to appeal to regime elites as well as regular citizens. In subsequent months, Washington reportedly initiated other gestures toward Tehran of a more private nature, including unprecedented correspondence from President Obama to the Iranian supreme leader.

However, Obama indicated from the outset that engagement would be given an early deadline to prevent Tehran from utilizing the process to dodge, and by the end of his first year, U.S. policy toward Iran had reverted to the familiar terrain of economic sanctions. And notably, even before his election, Obama supported economic pressure as a tool for altering Iranian policy. In 2007, then-Senator Obama introduced a bill that would eventually be reconfigured into the Comprehensive Iran Sanctions and Divestment Act, which he signed as president in 2010;

---

[90] "Sanctions Show Importance of China for Iran's Economy," *EIU*, July 24, 2012

his original support was predicated upon the belief that "there are signs that some Iranians understand the impact their regime's behavior is having on Iran's national interests.... We should send a message that, if Iran wishes to benefit from the international system, it must play by international rules. If it chooses to flout those rules, then the world will turn its back on Iran."[91]

Obama's approach to Iran retained the basic framework of the Bush approach; however, he succeeded in enhancing the persuasive power of U.S. policy – initiating early overtures toward Tehran as a means of demonstrating to Europe the seriousness of American readiness, making key compromises on issues at stake with Russia to draw Moscow into a more cooperative relationship on Iran, and investing in a protracted negotiation of the fourth UN resolution on Iran, Security Council Resolution 1929, so that it would serve as a platform for additional measures by individual states as well as the European Union.

The advantages of this synergy cannot be underestimated, and in many ways those subsequent unilateral sanctions are far more significant than the UN measure itself. Washington took other steps to encourage cooperation among "like-minded states" in Europe and in Asia, notably by utilizing sanctions policy to highlight human rights abuses in Iran and to restrict the government's access to technology used to control the free flow of information. These include the following:

- 2010 American[92] and European sanctions[93] that targeted Iran's imports of refined petroleum products and new energy investments, respectively
- 2011 U.S. measures targeting investment in or support to Iran's petrochemicals industry,[94] a step taken in tandem with a British move to sever all financial relations with Iran, including with the Central Bank.[95]

---

[91] THOMAS.loc.gov.;
  H.R. 2347, 110th Congress: The Iran Sanctions Enabling Act of 2007
  Congressional Record, Senate, May 17, 2009, p. S6309
  AIPAC, "Bill Summary: Iran Sanctions Enabling Act of 2007 – H.R. 2347." July 31, 2007, available at http://www.aipac.org/Publications/AIPACAnalysesBillSummaries/Bill_Summary_HR_2347.pdf
[92] Text available at http://www.treasury.gov/resource-center/sanctions/Documents/hr2194.pdf
[93] Text available at http://eur-lex.europa.eu/LexUriServ/LexUriServ.do?uri=OJ:L:2010:281:0001:0077:EN:PDF
[94] Text of E.O. 13590 is available at http://www.treasury.gov/resource-center/sanctions/Documents/13590.pdf
[95] Text of UK decision available at http://www.fco.gov.uk/en/news/latest-news/?view=News&id=695250182

- 2011 and 2013 measures imposed by the United States and the European Union targeting Iran's Central Bank,[96] its crude exports to Europe, and its access to European-based insurance services,[97] as well as other vital links to the international financial system.

In addition, European leaders joined, with varying degrees of enthusiasm, in the American-led effort to use moral suasion to reduce foreign investment in Iran. As a senior German official warned, "The company leaders should consider whether new deals with Iran are truly appropriate." On this basis, companies including Deutsche Bank and E.on-Ruhrgas were persuaded to forgo prospective opportunities in Iran, and worldwide more than eighty banks cut off interactions with their Iranian counterparts. However, some businesses recoiled at the notion that company/shareholder interests in seeking investment returns should be constrained without legal justification. "We cannot restrict business simply because a politician promises it," a businessman responded. "On what legal grounds should that then happen?"[98]

During Obama's presidency, American sanctions went through several stepwise changes in intensity. The first occurred in June and July 2010, with UN Security Council Resolution 1929 and the Comprehensive Iran Sanctions and Divestment Act (CISADA). The UN resolution represented a major victory for the administration, one that was hard-fought and required months of painstaking diplomacy with Europe, Moscow, and eventually Beijing.

CISADA represented a revamped and superpowered version of the former Iran-Libya Sanctions Act. The final law included a rescission of the prior exemption of caviar, carpets, and pistachios from U.S. sanctions, as well as a new array of extraterritorial measures including restrictions on sales of refined petroleum products to Tehran. In part because CISADA was enacted so quickly on the heels of the UN resolution, there was some grumbling, particularly from the Russians, that Washington

---

[96] The Central Bank measures were imposed via the National Defense Authorization Act, signed by President Obama on December 31, 2011 and text available at http://www.gpo.gov/fdsys/pkg/PLAW-112publ81/pdf/PLAW-112publ81.pdf, and a follow-up executive order (E.O. 13599) signed in February 2012 that freezes all assets of the Central Bank in the United States, http://www.gpo.gov/fdsys/pkg/FR-2012-02-08/pdf/2012-3097.pdf

[97] Text available at http://eur-lex.europa.eu/LexUriServ/LexUriServ.do?uri=OJ:L:2012:019:0022:0030:EN:PDF

[98] Beat Balzli, Konstantin von Hammerstein, Christian Reiermann and Wolfgang Reuter, "New Confusion: Tougher Iran Sanctions Could Backfire on Germany If Teheran Halts Debt Repayment," *Der Spiegel*, Sunday, November 18, 2007.

had exceeded its mandate. Still, the unilateral American actions did not provoke intraalliance tensions or defections from the overall cooperation with the campaign of pressuring Tehran from the international powers, but just the opposite – the sense of momentum that derived from broad multilateral support for the truly robust measures in UNSCR 1929 helped persuade many countries that had long hedged their relationships with Tehran to adopt much more rigorous standards for sanctions and their implementation.

The next major intensification of international economic pressure on Iran was in early 2012, thanks to a combination of strenuous new American and European measures, including the British prohibition of all financial transactions with any Iranian institution, including the Central Bank, in November 2011; new U.S. measures targeting Iran's petrochemical sector in November 2011; the U.S. decision to extend sanctions to the Central Bank on December 31, 2011; and the European Union's ban on all import, purchase, and transportation of Iranian crude oil, as well as a ban on insuring Iranian oil shipments and an assets freeze. The aggregated impact of these measures, as discussed in Chapter 7, dealt a body blow to the Iranian economy, feeding into an already-overheated economy and creating a persistent sense of crisis. Additional measures have compounded the damage: Later in 2012, the EU prohibited all but licensed financial transactions with Iran and proscribed any trade in natural gas, construction of oil tankers, or reflagging of Iranian ships. Meanwhile, in early 2013, the United States adopted new measures to restrict the ability of Iran's remaining crude customers to provide any direct form of payment, effectively forcing all trade to a barter system.

These measures dramatically reduced Iran's oil exports, effectively curtailed the government's ability to access revenues paid for the exports it has maintained, and deprived Tehran of the European market, which until recently had been its most substantial importer. Each of Iran's major crude customers – Japan, India, South Korea, Turkey, as well as China – scrambled to balance the need to avoid exposure to U.S. penalties while preventing any supply disruptions or escalatory spiral in the price paid by consumers at the gasoline pump. Moreover, days after President Obama signed the new measures, the State Department announced new designations of Chinese entities – in particular the prominent state-run trading firm Zhuhai Zhenrong – for their continued sale of refined petroleum products to Tehran. By early 2013, all of Iran's major crude customers had met Washington's criteria for 180-day waivers of the prohibition on Central Bank transactions, by making "significant reductions" in their petroleum purchases from Tehran. This ranged from a decrease in Iranian crude imports by approximately 50 percent, in the case of Japan, to 18 percent for China.

These reductions denote a broader trend of meaningful adherence to unilateral American restrictions by third-country governments and firms, a dramatic transformation that transpired so gradually from 2006 onward that it was underappreciated by the imposers of sanctions as well as by Tehran. This shift has been particularly evident in the response of a number of key trade partners for Iran, such as the United Arab Emirates. On the heels of the UN action, authorities in Abu Dhabi began stepping up enforcement almost immediately – freezing bank accounts, seizing a cargo of dual-use goods, and in July 2010 blocking permits for new Iranian companies to establish operations in the Ras al-Khaimah Free Trade Zone. The UAE also closed ports to transit by ships carrying gasoline cargoes to Iran later the same summer and began discouraging companies from providing insurance coverage to shipments bound for Iran.[99] Still, it is clear, as suggested previously, that trade links between Tehran and its Gulf neighbors remain significant. A particular source of consternation was the continuing purchase of Iranian condensate by the Dubai-based Emirates National Oil Company, which is required by law to provide subsidized gasoline to the domestic UAE market and has become reliant on cheap Iranian feedstock.[100]

Conversely, China found itself confronted with the dilemma of escalating sanctions even as its trade relationship with Iran continued to expand. This reflected the practical consequences of the increasing difficulties of nonbarter transactions, but also speaks to a convergence in the two countries' worldviews. Iranian leaders openly admire China's flourishing growth rates as well as its successful balancing act in fostering rapid economic development under conditions of authoritarian rule. The Islamic Republic applauds the disinclination of its Eastern trade partners to meddle in its internal affairs. Beijing has approached Iran as a fellow heir to a great civilization and as the inevitable heavyweight power in the Middle East.[101] China also values Tehran's pragmatic disinterest in agitating its restive Muslim population in Xinjiang.

[99] Nikolay A. Kozhanov, "U.S. Economic Sanctions against Iran: Undermined by External Factors," *Middle East Policy* 18:3 (Fall 2011), p. 153.

[100] Amena Bakr and Raissa Kasolowsky, "Dubai Fueled by Cheap Iran Oil As U.S. Steps Up Pressure," *Reuters*, October 18, 2012.

[101] Underscoring the realist streak in Beijing's approach to Tehran, Chinese official statements noting that Iran and China were both glorious nations humiliated by the ravages

Still, as Beijing calibrated its trade with Tehran in order to prevent frictions with Washington – "a strategy of opportunistic pragmatism in that they have sought to placate both US and Iranian concerns to maximize gains from both parties"[102] – Iranians began to perceive that they had once again become pawns in a great power rivalry. Analysts from both sides of the political spectrum cautioned that Beijing's economic interests in Iran will not trump its strategic relationship with Washington, or even its energy relationships with the Saudis or other competitors.

In response to American efforts to craft a consensus around new multilateral pressures on Iran, Beijing typically engaged in passive efforts to slow the process or blunt the impact of the measures themselves. However, China has taken care to ensure that its posture within Iran does not expand at a time when the rest of the world is departing. In late 2007, Iranian businesses complained about Chinese refusal to extend letters of credit needed to maintain trade ties,[103] and Tehran has cancelled several of the contracts awarded to Chinese companies in the oil and gas sector because of lack of progress.

These measures, and the general frustration with the degeneration of the business climate in Iran, presented a dire set of circumstances for Iran's energy business just at the moment at which its gas development had begun to take off. Major IOCs including Shell and Repsol walked away from signed deals for South Pars projects. Most other Western companies, including firms that were early entrants to Tehran's reopened energy sector such as Total, Statoil, and ENI, foreswore new opportunities in Iran, closing their offices in Iran and curtailing future prospects there. The major construction firms that had fabricated facilities and transportation networks associated with Iran's petroleum sector scaled back, or withdrew completely, and the European and Asian banks that provided much of the capital for several early phases of South Pars as well as a number of other upstream projects left. Ultimately, Tehran announced that all future development of South Pars would remain in the hands of Iranian firms, a face-saving attempt and tacit recognition of the country's return to isolation.

---

of imperialism – but ultimately emerging victorious over the western powers – were nearly identical at many high-level meetings both before and after the Islamic Revolution in spite of the drastic regime change that it brought. Garver (2006), p. 10.

[102] Nicolo Nourafchan, "Constructive Partner or Menacing Threat? Analyzing China's Role in the Iranian Nuclear Program," *Asian Security* 6:1 (2010).

[103] Nazila Fathi, "Iran hails U.S. report that it halted bid for nuclear arms," *New York Times*, December 5, 2007.

The Central Bank measure was carefully crafted to attempt to mitigate the likelihood of negative repercussions for crude oil prices and, by extension, the global economy. The statute provided the U.S. president with versatile waiver authority to ensure that the primary impact remains focused on Iran's crude oil revenue stream, rather than on crude supply or prices at the pump. Even so, the initial announcement of the new measure provoked some anxiety in the markets as well as more broadly, with concerns focused on the possibility of shortages, spiraling prices, and potential retaliatory action by Tehran. However, these concerns proved to be overblown, as a variety of factors coincided to check any price escalations. These factors included expanded output by other producers, principally Saudi Arabia; the slowdown in the global economy, particularly related to European financial and political woes; and increasing domestic North American oil production. To be sure, Washington made relatively liberal use of its waiver authority, granting six-month exemptions to twenty countries, including most of Tehran's major crude customers, from prospective U.S. penalties in recognition of reductions in Iranian crude imports deemed "significant" by Washington.

However, while global energy markets have been relatively unshaken by the sanctions to date, the impact on Iran was dramatic and unmistakable. The shift in the world's approach to sanctioning the Islamic Republic has culminated in what even Iranian officials acknowledge is unprecedented economic pressure on the Iran regime. Even before the full implementation of these sanctions, Iranians felt the impact, as the mere announcement of the new U.S. measures helped drive down the value of the rial by nearly half its value in just a matter of weeks. Once the initial grace periods incorporated into the latest U.S. and EU measures expired, Tehran was bleeding as much as $133 million per day in revenues, as oil exports fell from 2.3 mbpd in 2011 to an estimated 1.2 mbpd in 2012, and as a low as less than 1 mbpd in 2013.[104]

Some Iranian leaders began to appreciate the role that the revived sectarian frictions with Riyadh played in facilitating the sanctions strategy. "More important is the issue of oil," Rafsanjani said in a 2012 interview. "Would the West impose sanctions on us, if Saudi Arabia had good ties with us? Only Saudi Arabia could take Iran's place. Saudi Arabia does not need to do anything. If it produces oil according to OPEC limits, no one could harass us. As the world economy could

---

[104] Anthony DiPaola and Isaac Arnsdorf, "Iran Loses $133 Million a Day on Embargo, Buoying Obama," Bloomberg, August 2, 2012.

not carry on without our oil, I believe that it is still possible to establish good relations. However, there are people here who, as you see, do not want that."[105]

As discussed in Chapter 7, the Obama era sanctions had a dramatic impact on Iran's economy. The rial lost almost half its value over the course of 2012, in a precipitous decline sparked by the news of Washington's Central Bank measures. The disruption to its established contracts created management challenges for Tehran. Iran was forced to expand its floating storage from 28.0 million to 32.5 million barrels between November 2011 and January 2012.[106] Iran was forced to rely heavily on barter, smuggling, and other unconventional mechanisms for compensation, creating new complications for orderly management of its economy and petroleum sector.

For ordinary Iranians, the 2012 sanctions meant a reversion to the exigencies of the wartime economy. Over the course of subsequent months, inflation mounted, and while official reports put the rate at 22 percent, anecdotal evidence suggested this might have been an underestimation. Factories shut down for lack of imported raw materials, and much of the trade that continued was forced to rely on barter, circumstances likely to increase the flood of inexpensive Asian-produced textiles and intermediate goods and further decimate Iran's own manufacturing sector. The latest degradation was the nationwide chicken shortage referenced at the outset of this volume. This was itself the by-product of the months of feedstock scarcity, which generated lengthy lines and rationing around the country and a fierce national discussion about the "chicken crisis."

From a technical perspective, then, the sanctions functioned working precisely as intended – eroding Iran's economic power and, by extension, the capability and authority of its government, without impairing the global economic recovery or adversely impacting oil consuming countries. From a strategic perspective, however, deep uncertainties persisted on the nuclear issue or the host of other areas of vehement Western objections to Iranian policy, such as Syria. Sanctions have multiple objectives, and the constraints imposed by the restrictions had some utility in limiting the resources available to Tehran for the development of its nuclear program. However, achieving their stated purpose – achieving verifiable curbs on Iran's nuclear ambitions, as well as its other objectionable

---

[105] Fars News Agency, April 3, 2012.
[106] Javier Blas, "Oil groups begin to cut ties with Iran," *FT*, January 12, 2012.

policies – continued to elude, even the most severe and comprehensive sanctions regime in Iran's history.

Notably, the pressure has intensified the debate over the government's handling of the economy and intensified the existing divisions among Iran's contentious factions. Both ends of the tolerated political spectrum in Iran – regime hard-liners and reformist politicians – have utilized the sanctions to criticize Ahmadinejad in particular, who once dismissed the sanctions as not worth the paper they were written upon. "Complex events have happened in our foreign policy," the hard-line former MP Mehdi Tabatabai remarked shortly after the U.S. measures against the Central Bank were announced. "Unfortunately, some consider the enemy's resolutions to be useless sheets of paper. But in fact they have aroused troubles. There are problems regarding foreign currency and gold coins, and saboteurs have taken root in the government. The main cause of the problems is the government, and the government should apologize to the people."[107]

A strikingly similar refrain was also voiced by Mostafa Tajzadeh, an influential former deputy interior minister during the Khatami presidency whose arrest, imprisonment, and public recantations after 2009 had jettisoned his political career. Tajzadeh wrote an open letter to then-Foreign Minister Ali Akbar Salehi, widely presumed to be a judicious technocrat, skewering the official narrative on sanctions and arguing that "instead of ignoring such contradictions, winking at foreign powers, and holding a fire sale of Iran's interests and resources with the baseless hope of convincing the foreign powers to end their pressure, threats, and sanctions, it is better for you to devote part of your efforts to presenting the international realities to the [Supreme] Leader and convincing him to reconsider his rule."[108]

Until Iran's 2013 presidential campaign, the voices of reason were relegated firmly to the sidelines. Khamenei publicly maintained that sanctions would not succeed in altering Iran's nuclear posture, and that their economic impacts would remain tolerable, arguing that "continuing these sanctions for a long time is not in the interest of western countries" and that much of the world has "either been forced to go along with sanctions

---

[107] Iranian Labor News Agency, January 24, 2012.

[108] Muhammad Sahimi, "Tajzadeh to Foreign Sec'y Salehi: Tell Ayatollah Khamenei the Reality," PBS Frontline/Tehran Bureau, August 11, 2012, http://www.pbs.org/wgbh/pages/frontline/tehranbureau/2012/08/news-tajzadeh-to-foreign-secy-salehi-tell-ayatollah-khamenei-the-reality.html#ixzz23d7G1Gru

or they are just doing it as a ceremonial gesture. And these conditions will not continue."[109] The supreme leader extolled Iran's "economy of resistance" – one that "prepares the ground for the progress and flourishing of a nation even in times of pressure and sanctions."[110] This approach may not be wholly delusional; Iran has endured even more onerous economic circumstances in the past – during the war with Iraq, for example, when the fiercest fighting coincided with a worldwide collapse in crude prices that drove Iran's annual oil revenues to less than one-tenth of their levels as of late 2014.

IRANIAN RESPONSE TO SANCTIONS

The long history of sanctioning Iran has produced a number of readily identifiable patterns in Tehran's response. First and foremost is *denial*. Historically, Iranian leaders have tended to reject the significance of sanctions, at least rhetorically, and they have celebrated the country's capacity to withstand external economic pressure, particularly the measures imposed on Iran by Washington. Immediately after the revolution, this ethos was philosophically consistent with the revolutionary leadership's quest for independence and its ambivalence about capitalism and international entanglements. Over time, sanctions have been integrated within the regime's ideological narrative. Like the war with Iraq in the 1980s, economic pressure represents a component of the international conspiracy to undermine the Islamic Revolution, a plot that has been foiled by Iran's wise and righteous leaders, who have used sanctions to the country's benefit by strengthening its indigenous capabilities and sovereignty.

"They threaten to impose sanctions and economic embargoes on us," Khamenei proclaimed in a sermon in 2008. "Well, who has been harmed by the various economic embargoes you have been imposing on the Iranian nation for the past thirty years? Was the Iranian nation the loser? Not at all! We used the sanctions to the advantage of our progress. There was a day when we needed military equipment but they didn't even sell us the simplest military equipment. They used to say sanctions. We were able to use these sanctions. Today the Iranian nation has achieved some capabilities which have caused those who imposed sanctions on us to become agitated and worried about the Iranian nation becoming the number

---

[109] "Supreme Leader Meets Government Officials," Fars News Agency, July 24, 2012, http://english.farsnews.com/newstext.php?nn=9104251302
[110] "West economic woes stem from Capitocracy: Leader," *Press TV*, August 7, 2012. Text is available at http://www.presstv.ir/detail/2012/08/07/254909/west-econ-woes-stem-from-capitocracy/

one military power in the region. Well, this was the result of your sanctions. These sanctions didn't work to our detriment. We were able to create an opportunity out of this threat. It's the same today. We are not afraid of Western sanctions. With the blessing of God, the Iranian nation, in the face of any sanction or economic embargo, will demonstrate an effort which will double or increase its progress by many folds."[111]

In this respect, the hard-liners perceive merely surviving new sanctions – even at a significant price – as victory and will portray it as such to their base. Endurance has been elevated as a priority for Tehran even as the objectives of sanctions have expanded.

Self-Sufficiency: Iranian leaders have frequently sought to depict economic pressure as constructive, because it has provided the impetus for investing in domestic capabilities and weaning the country off its reliance on the West as well as on resource revenues. In February 2011, Khamenei implicitly acknowledged the constraints that the latest round of UNSC sanctions, including an arms embargo, posed for Iran's military in an address to the air force on the anniversary of the revolution.

Our industrial sectors were affected by sanctions. The countries that imposed sanctions on us had thought that those sectors would stop working. However, this backfired. The sanctions made our youth think and produce whatever the enemy did not like us to possess. They produced such things on their own and in some cases they produced even better versions. They produced less-costly, lighter, and more useful version of such things.

Similar justifications have been offered by Iranian political figures from across the factional spectrum, and while there is clearly a self-serving dimension of this rhetoric, it is also clear that the persistence of external economic pressure has fed into existing ideological preferences for self-sufficiency and economic independence. As sanctions have slashed Iran's oil exports and revenues, the leadership has publicly reveled in the opportunity to fulfill the revolutionary ideal of reducing state dependence on oil revenues.

Mitigation: The constraints imposed by sanctions have persuaded Tehran to take a number of steps over the years to mitigate its vulnerability to external pressure at critical junctures. Austerity has been a standard part of the repertoire, beginning with the budget retrenchments during the war with Iraq and recurring with each new shock to the economy. In response to the nuclear-related measures, the government has sought to

---

[111] Speech by Iran's Supreme Leader Ayatollah Seyyed Ali Khamene'i in Shiraz to the people of Fars Province on April 30, 2008, Vision of the Islamic Republic of Iran Network 1, from World News Connection, May 1, 2008.

slash spending, with cutbacks of as much as 20 percent beginning in June 2012. In addition, Iran's mercantilist diplomacy has deliberately sought to expand its network of trade partners and reorient its trade and investment patterns to privilege countries with international influence and minimalist interest in political interventions. Iranian leaders are experienced at replacing prohibited suppliers, finding alternative financiers, and absorbing additional costs in order to mitigate the impact of sanctions.

Tehran has also reoriented its trade to facilitate barter and other creative financing arrangements with a number of key partners after the dollar and the Euro do not provide viable vehicles for its isolated financial system. As antediluvian and inconvenient as it may appear, barter trade is not wholly unfamiliar to Iranian officials. Iran has a long history with barter trade; under the monarchy, barter was utilized to gain access to otherwise closed Soviet and Eastern bloc markets. It was also a central dimension of the Mosaddeq-era strategy for navigating external economic pressures, when Tehran concluded barter deals with Germany and France. After the Central Bank sanctions were imposed, Tehran has restored barter to manage its trade with a variety of countries including China; with others, such as Turkey, payments in local currency are utilized by Tehran to purchase gold to bolster its reserves (although this mechanism too was subsequently outlawed by Washington).

Perhaps the most dramatic example has been the adoption of the first serious effort to contend with Iran's most inefficient economic policy, the government's price support of key items, including fuel, bread, and other consumer goods. Curtailing expenditures on subsidies has ranked high on the agenda of each government since the reconstruction era – and yet never before were meaningful steps undertaken to reduce the country's reliance on imported petroleum products. While it is clear that the impetus for subsidy reform predates and transcends sanctions, the linkage is implicit in the timing and the justification for the colossal disruptions associated with the program.

In a 2007 sermon in 2007, Khamenei declared:

We pay billions to import gasoline or import other things in order that a certain section of us – or a segment of our society – can spend and be extravagant. Is this right, I ask you? We, as a nation, have to look at this as a national problem. ... They [the West] have launched sanctions against us time and again precisely because they pin their hope on this particularly negative characteristic of our nation. If we continue to be a wasteful and profligate nation, we will be vulnerable to difficulties. But a nation which refrains from such extravagance and takes care with its expenditures and revenues will not be vulnerable to these difficulties. In this case they can sanction the nation all they like. Such nation will not suffer if it faced sanctions.[112]

In its responses, Tehran has proven willing and able to make adjustments midcourse to cope with the impact of sanctions. As the 2012 measures targeting the Central Bank and other financial mechanisms began to shrink Iran's revenue stream, the parliament sought to defer and even roll back some elements of the subsidy reform program, which had morphed into a major financial commitment for the government. In November 2012, the second phase of the program, intended to rationalize industrial and utility spending, was put on hold, and further increases in individual payments were blocked. Ahmadinejad continued to press to see the plan fully executed, arguing that sanctions had elevated its urgency. "Naturally the sanctions create a series of problems, including a slowdown in the country's growth, pressure on wide swathes of people who have a fixed income, disruption in foreign trade, and certainly a gap between classes," he contended before the parliament in January 2013. "If this plan is fully implemented, wealth will be fairly distributed, national capital will be preserved, production efficiency will go up, the government's dependency on oil income will be reduced and poverty will be eradicated."[113]

While the subsidy reform program was the most prominent recent aspect of Iran's countersanctions economic planning, it was hardly the only one. Indeed, the Islamic Republic's economic agenda has been influenced from the outset by the need to compensate for the loss of trade, technology, and investment that was associated with its estrangement with Washington and frictions with a host of other states. Restrictions on access to external sources of weaponry and military materiel helped generate domestic manufacturing capability and indigenous technology development. Over time, these compensatory industrial investments have expanded well beyond the armaments industry; today, Iran has domestic capabilities for producing high-level inputs for much of its power generation sector as well.[114] In this arena, Tehran responded to the threat, and eventual implementation, of restrictions on gasoline imports by shifting the domestic public transportation fleet to CNG and embarking on a

---

[112] Khamenei sermon, October 13, 2007, from World News Connection.
[113] "Iran's Ahmadinejad pushes subsidy reform as antidote to economic woes," *Reuters*, January 16, 2013.
[114] Mehdi Majidpour, "Heavy duty gas turbines in Iran, India and China," *Energy Policy* 41 (2012), pp. 723–32.

major push for refinery construction and expansion. The national oil company has used sanctions as the justification for its effort to expand the sector's budget allocation, and some have even gone so far as to suggest the need to institute new revisions to the buyback model in order to lure back the foreign investment lost as a result of the nuclear standoff.[115]

In addition to shifting its patterns of trade and economizing at home, Iran's mitigation strategy in response to sanction has always incorporated the search for new revenues. During the long siege of the nationalization embargo, Mosaddeq's efforts to boost nonoil exports sustained the Iranian economy for nearly two and a half years. Since the nuclear crisis began, the Islamic Republic has sought mechanisms for expanding tax revenues to compensate for falling oil revenues in the short term and shrinking dependency on oil revenues in the long term.[116] While tax revenues have risen as a proportion of the annual budget, there is widespread consensus within the Islamic Republic that the current system is deeply flawed, and that tax reform would significantly enhance government income and insulate the Iranian economy against the volatility of reliance on resource rents. Recent efforts to institute specific new tax measures have generated social resistance and instill some uncertainty about the capabilities of the government to enact a serious program of tax reform. Still, during a similar period of budget exigency and catastrophic foreign policy – 1985/86 – Tehran managed to push through some tax hikes. And the precedent of the subsidy reform program suggests that the government remains fully capable of implementing disruptive economic policy shifts without significant corresponding social upheaval.

Blowback: Tehran has also sought to emphasize that the states imposing sanctions face higher costs from any new measures against Iran than Tehran itself does. Historically, Iranian officials highlighted the costs to U.S. companies, in terms of both profits and competitive advantage within their industries. The then-acting NIOC Vice President Hojjatollah Ghanimi-Fard remarked in 2001 that "the U.S. sanctions helped Iran get better acquainted with other world oil companies. And the disadvantage was for the U.S. oil companies is that they were deprived of the country's

---

[115] Yong and Hajihosseini (January 2013).
[116] "Oil income and tax evasion: two problems for the national budget," *Mardom-e Salari*, December, 17, 2012.

oil and gas reservoirs and projects that could have been of short- and long-term benefit to them."[117]

Iranian officials continue to reference the competitive disadvantages that sanctions impose on their architects. "Therefore, imposing sanctions on the Iranian market is also detrimental to the countries imposing sanctions because they will lose Iran's oil projects," asserted Mehdi Ghazanfari, Iran's minister of industry, mining, and trade in December 2011. He added, "At any rate, these sanctions make things more difficult, but not impossible, and the country imposing sanctions also loses. For us, these sanctions create opportunities of developing our domestic industries."[118]

More recently, this refrain has evolved, and Iranian officials have sought to remind U.S. allies and countries that have acceded to U.S. extraterritorial obligations that these actions, too, will have consequences. "Iran has imported gas from Turkmenistan and exported it to Turkey. If the banking system fails to operate, we will not import gas from Turkmenistan and, therefore, will not export gas to Turkey," warned Masoud Mirkazemi, the chairman of the Majlis Energy Commission and former oil minister, in late 2012. "If imports of gold from Turkey to Iran are banned, it will be Turkey which will face problems and will go to great expenses to make up its gas deficit. It will be impossible for Turkey to import gas from other countries easily. Thus, they should use liquid fuel and the process of changing their systems from consuming gas to systems consuming liquid fuel will be difficult. Therefore, this issue will not create many problems for Iran, and those countries which have close ties with Europe will be able to resolve their problems with them."[119]

Iran's most recent sanctions response strategy relies on expectations, cultivated by a decade in which oil prices had skyrocketed, of stable high prices for its crude. Despite the reminder over the course of 2008 and 2009 that such trends are not infinite, Tehran appeared caught off guard by the slackness in world crude markets when the 2012 measures took effect. It exacerbated existing tensions with

---

[117] "Foreign investment law inapplicable to buybacks," *Iran Daily*, July 23, 2001, p. 5.
[118] Mina Yousefi, "The Ministry of Industry, Mining and Trade Stressed the importance of setting the rate of foreign currency under the exports-oriented production approach," *Donya-ye Eqtesad*, December 3, 2011.
[119] Iranian Students News Agency (ISNA), December 8, 2012.

Riyadh, whose historically high levels of production were contributing to the price erosion.

An array of Iranian political figures – including and especially those in the "pragmatic" camp associated with the former president Rafsanjani – appeared convinced that concerns about prospective blowback to the world economic recovery would preclude full implementation of the new measures. According to Rafsanjani, the West "cannot impose such embargoes on Iran because the measure would leave a drastic effect on oil prices and pose a major threat to the already shivering world economy."[120]

Retaliation: The direct economic impact of sanctions is not the only risk facing the Iranian leadership today. The economic pressure that Iran experienced as a result of the nuclear standoff has predictably exacerbated the regime's innate animosities and paranoia and intensified the conviction, born of Iran's postrevolutionary isolation and the war with Iraq, that the world is aligned implacably against its survival. The revival and reinforcement of this approach to the world occurred at a particularly dangerous moment – one characterized by multiple sources of instability and potential conflict, any of which would have devastating consequences for Iran's energy prospects as well as the broader security of the Gulf.

Sanctions fueled a set of dynamics that are already deeply troubling and that threaten to instigate regional violence and destabilization. The departure of foreign investors has helped empower and enrich the Revolutionary Guards, whose ascendance is now depicted by hardliners as a new chapter in the institution's defense of the country and the revolution against the plots of the enemy, with sanctions as the American instrument.[121] Iranian leaders tend to believe that the best defense is a good offense and under strain are prone to lash out rather than to moderate their policies or yield to external demands. For Khamenei, and even more so for the younger generation hardliners who surrounded Ahmadinejad, there was no middle ground in dealing with Washington or the West. In their view, any act of compromise would merely initiate a perilous process of intensifying pressure intended to eliminate the Islamic Republic. "If you supplicate and

---

[120] "Rafsajani: West seeking to block investment in Iran's oil sector," *Fars News*, January 5, 2010.
[121] Abbas Haji-Najjari, "The IRGC in the balance of the system's authority," *Javan*, June 25, 2012.

show flexibility," Khamenei has warned, "arrogant powers will make their threat more serious."[122]

The regional climate could easily escalate from what is now a low-intensity proxy war between Iran and its Sunni Arab neighbors to a direct interstate conflict involving a number of key energy producers. The Arab spring has generated any number of opportunities to spark such a crisis – for example, Yemen and Bahrain are each rife with sectarian violence, external intervention, and the prospect for inadvertent escalation. However, the most likely arena for an Arab-Iranian conflagration is in Syria, where Iran's sole longtime ally in the Arab world is in the midst of a brutal and protracted implosion, one that has been cheered as well as facilitated by Saudi Arabia and the other Gulf States.

Moral Counterarguments: Tehran has also sought to use the humanitarian impact of sanctions as a mechanism to erode international support for implementation of nuclear-related measures and/or adoption of any more stringent restrictions. Over the course of late 2013, reports from Iran of drug shortages began to surface. The issue of drug shortages is particularly complicated, because it entails questions of Iran's overall health care system and its subsidy reform program. Complaints about drug shortages have been aired in the country's media for many years,[123] and in 2012 and 2013, senior officials alleged that the government had failed to allocate sufficient hard currency for imports.

There is a certain irony to focusing on pharmaceutical imports; in 1980, after the decision by the European Common Market to impose modest trade sanctions on Iran in response to its prolonged detention of U.S. diplomats, Tehran summarily nationalized the Iranian-based subsidiaries of a number of European pharmaceutical companies.[124] It is also worth recalling that sales of U.S. pharmaceutical products to Tehran featured prominently in the Iran-contra affair, when American medicines ranked alongside weaponry as the most valuable currency for Washington's efforts to reshape Iran's domestic balance of power.[125]

---

[122] Karim Sadjadpour, "Reading Khamenei: The World View of Iran's Most Powerful Leader," Carnegie Endowment Report (March 2008): 16.

[123] See "Medicament crisis is expected for the second half of the year," *Abrar*, August 21, 2008, p. 14.

[124] John Tagliabue, "European drug concerns are taken over by Tehran," *New York Times*, July 10, 1980, p. D11.

[125] Indeed, even as word of the U.S.-Iranian dealings leaked, a shipment of U.S. medical items was waiting to leave Israel for Iran. See Walter Pincus and Dan Morgan, "Arms delivery resumption was planned," *WP*, July 30, 1987, p. A1.

Statistics on Iranian imports of U.S. pharmaceutical products show a decline by approximately half over the same period; however, exports of other U.S. products, including vital goods – such as diagnostic equipment and medical instruments – remained stable or expanded after the initial intensification of nuclear-related sanctions. And though lower than the previous year, Iran's drug imports from the United States in 2012 remained considerably higher than they were a decade earlier. More pointedly, the question of the price and availability of medicine has been a long-running issue in Iran, with considerable criticism levied against the government, including by its own officials. In 2013, an official with the Ministry of Health's General Office of Drug and Narcotics Oversight predicted that prices would rise even further, by 20 to 30 percent for domestically manufactured medicines and as much as 100 percent for imported drugs, and attributed these price increases to the government's decision to withdraw discounted ("government rate") foreign exchange that was previously available for drug purchases.[126]

The medicine shortages have drawn widespread headlines outside Iran, and the Iraq precedent demonstrates the potential weight and utility of moral counterarguments in eroding support for sanctions and their implementation. A small but vocal movement began to emerge in the United States and elsewhere questioning the logic of sanctions and highlighting the increasingly dramatic impact the measures are having on the lives of ordinary Iranians.[127]

Breakout (of Isolation): Tehran sought to erode adherence to sanctions by the demonstration effect of its continuing engagement with the world. Coupled with the expectation of sanctions fatigue over time, Iranian leaders attempted to wait out and wear down both enforcement efforts and the international consensus to maintain pressure. Historically, Iran's leadership has proven deft at evading American efforts to isolate it. Even as international economic sanctions slashed Iran's oil exports and drove the country's businesses from the international financial system, Iran managed to persuade an array of world leaders, including the UN secretary general and – for the first time since the revolution – an Egyptian president, to attend the 2012 summit of the Non-Aligned Movement.

---

[126] Habib Qaani, "Medicine is still without a curing prescription; two- to three-fold increase in the price of medicine; 2.2bn tuman fund not just for medicine," *Qods*, April 14, 2013.

[127] See "A Growing Crisis: The Impact of Sanctions and Regime Policies on Iranians' Economic and Social Rights," International Campaign for Human Rights in Iran, 2013, http://www.iranhumanrights.org/2013/04/growing_crisis/

In a similar vein, Tehran has also utilized the far-flung diaspora community to access products and markets that have been put off limits by U.S. restrictions. Throughout the 1990s, a number of Iranian expatriates based in Canada were accused of assisting the Islamic Republic's weapons procurement efforts and smuggling other sanctioned items into Iran, an effort facilitated by licensing exemptions for U.S. military sales to Canada.[128]

Diplomacy: Finally, despite the poor track record of sanctions generally and in the Iranian case specifically, it would be inaccurate to suggest that sanctions have produced no diplomatic movement whatsoever. Iran has in fact resorted to diplomacy repeatedly in response to sanctions, or the threat of new measures. Ayatollah Khamenei's first and only visit to the United States occurred in 1987 as part of an effort to blunt progress toward UNSC action that would have threatened sanctions against Tehran unless the leadership agreed to a cease-fire. More than a decade later, the reform movement sought to rebuild ties to the region and to key European capitals as a means of counteracting American efforts to isolate Iran. This was not, of course, the sole purpose or even the primary genesis of the reformist interest in promoting détente and the "dialogue of civilizations," but a broad recognition of the exigency of maintaining trade relations with Europe was a key element of the cross-factional support for the Khatami foreign policy agenda. Reengaging with the world represented the most effective ammunition for rendering sanctions ineffective. The short-lived Paris Accord, in which Iran agreed to suspend its nuclear activities, represents another moment when Tehran embraced diplomacy – and nuclear concessions – as a means of averting international economic pressure.

Unfortunately, this view seemed to lose credence within the Iranian political establishment for a variety of reasons – the hardening of the domestic political debate, the appearance of American intractability, and the growing conviction within Iran that the locus of the global economy was shifting eastward, where sanctions held little appeal and political litmus tests were less relevant to the viability of trade and investment. Still, even in this more complex international environment, Iranian officials have sought to undermine international consensus on sanctions by wielding diplomatic opportunities in the recent past – most notably, the October 2009 preliminary deal on a fuel swap and the 2010

---

[128] Anthony dePalma with Lowell Bergman, "Sneaking U.S. jets to Iran: the Canadian route," *New York Times*, May 15, 1998.

Turkish-Brazilian proposal. The willingness of Iranian officials to proffer small concessions in each of these cases reflects an awareness of the potential price of continuing defiance. And the breakthrough diplomacy of 2013–14 that produced an interim nuclear accord suggests that the system is both willing and capable of negotiating and compromising on core security concerns as a means of averting the damage wrought by international economic pressure.

COLLATERAL DAMAGE

Sanctions tend to be a blunt instrument, and their impact can never be isolated with precision. However, it is clear that the measures enacted over the course of the past few years have expanded the fallout to a broader range of the Iranian population. While the present political circumstances make it difficult if not impossible to treat the results of any public opinion polling conducted in Iran as credible, a February 2013 survey conducted by Gallup nonetheless cannot be wholly disregarded. The poll suggested that 47 percent of Iranians blamed Washington for the fallout from sanctions, while only 10 percent attributed responsibility to the Iranian regime.[129]

Much has already been made of these problematic unintended consequences, including self-serving arguments by elements of the Islamic Republic political establishment and external analysts who are sympathetic to Iran's arguments. In the absence of sufficient opportunities for academics and journalists to conduct nonpartisan research in Iran, it is impossible to measure or even approximate the perceptions and sensibilities of any proportion of the Iranian population. Still, both common sense and episodic evidence from the Iranian press and social media provide credible reason to presume that the hardships imposed by sanctions are already transforming Iranian public opinion on domestic political and economic issues, as well as on their view of the world.

The sense that Iran has reverted to a war footing appears to be widely shared. Even worse, as one academic described in a March 2013 interview, today there is little confidence that the end of the crisis itself can generate the kind of hopeful investment in Iran that was seen in 1989 and beyond. "When the war ended we had all the problems in terms of raw materials but we endured because we were growing," Dr. Amir Hoseyn

---

[129] Mohamed Younis, "Iranians feel bite of sanctions, blame U.S., not own leaders," *Gallup World*, February 7, 2013.

Kakai commented. "At that time we believed there had been a war. After the war we also believed we should do reconstruction. These beliefs took public behavior in a positive direction, but it is the opposite now."[130]

As sanctions intensified, the concerns about the impact on U.S. and other business articulated by either government officials or business representatives correspondingly diminished. Whereas U.S. officials during the 1990s repeatedly invoked the need to prevent undue harm to prospective American economic interests in Iran as well as more broadly in discussing the need and utility of sanctions, this issue gradually became irrelevant as a political issue or a decision-making factor. And yet the costs of these measures to the imposing countries, as well as the target, are important to assessing utility and impact of sanctions. These cumulative array of multilateral, national, and sub-national level measures are rarely tallied, and their costs remain difficult to estimate. For example, in 2008, CalPERS estimated that if it had instituted its divestment rules on Iran and Sudan five years prior, it would have cost as much as $725 million.[131] Other studies have claimed that sanctions impose "staggering" losses of $175 billion to the U.S. economy, although such estimates derive from problematic methodology. [132]

Another of the counterproductive consequences of the robust sanctions regime and aggressive enforcement climate is their chilling effect on the desirable dimensions of U.S.-Iranian interaction. The sanctions mania has also prompted unfortunate compromises by organizations implementing the broader array of U.S. government promoted and/or supported activities vis-à-vis Iran. The Broadcasting Board of Governors, which oversees Voice of America and other official U.S. media enterprises, has opted to conduct audience surveys from outside Iran in order to avoid applying for a Treasury Department license that would be necessary for work conducted inside Iran, even though the external nature of the queries likely compromises the quality of results.[133] The Nobel Prize in peace winner Shirin Ebadi initially faced difficulties in publishing her memoir in the United States, and Iranian expatriates complain of harassment and complications in trying to maintain or access funds held outside the country.

---

[130] Youssef Naseri, "Auto industry at the bottleneck of price," *Tehran-e Emruz*, March 15, 2013.

[131] Clancy Nolan, "Buy Good, Sell Evil," *Portfolio* 2(9), September 2008, p. 36.

[132] Glenn Kessler, "The Claim That Sanctions on Iran Have Cost the U.S. $175 Billion in Lost Trade," *The Washington Post*, July 18, 2014.

[133] OIG Report No. ISP-IB-09-27, Inspection of Voice of America's Persian News Network, March 2009, pp. 22–3.

Sanctions have complicated the access of Iranians, particularly those who oppose the regime's policies, to the Internet and other forms of communications technology. An array of Internet companies sought to prevent the use of their products in Iran because of concerns about sanctions liability, and while Washington has sought to mitigate some of the obstacles since the 2009 elections upheaval, this effort has not been fully successful.[134]

Sanctions have also prompted the Iranian leadership to revert to informal mechanisms for moving funds around the world and hone their utilization of the black market and smuggling. Already adept at smuggling funds and procurement of illicit materials, Tehran now has no choice but to conduct all of its business via primitive and clandestine methods. These are hardly the sorts of capacities one would hope to enhance in a country whose ties to terrorist organizations are a subject of urgent concern. Cases of questionable money movements already abound. For example, the former Central Bank governor and economics minister Tahmasseb Mazheri was held in Germany in February 2013 after a check valued at $70 million in Venezuelan currency was found in his hand luggage, ostensibly for covering the costs of an Iranian firm operating in Caracas.[135] Even more dramatic is the massive drain of state resources by Ahmadinejad crony Babak Zanjani, who is alleged to have spirited as much as $2 billion out of the country with the encouragement of the president as a means of evading sanctions.

SANCTIONS: LESSONS LEARNED AND IMPLICATIONS FOR THE FUTURE

The Obama experience has refuted several long-held assumptions about sanctioning Iran, surprising many observers as well as Tehran itself. First, the success in generating real, robust multilateral support for U.S. measures, as well as implementation of separate measures by a "coalition of the willing," defy all prior precedent in dealing with Iran. This success reflects a number of factors: Improved U.S.-Russian bilateral relations helped coax Beijing to acquiescence. Public and private diplomacy emphasizing the potential political and commercial repercussions of

---

[134] For example, as of May 2013, Iranians will no longer have access to Samsung mobile applications as a result of sanctions liability concerns. "Samsung to close down access to app store in Iran over 'legal barriers'," AP, April 26, 2013.

[135] William Neuman, "Firm denies deception in big check linked to Iran," *New York Times*, February 5, 2013.

business links to Tehran persuaded a number of major international corporations to reduce their business ties with Iran voluntarily and helped prepare the ground for more formal measures. Additionally, the domestic developments within Iran have caused a variety of influential international constituencies to support measures against the regime. The 2009 elections turmoil swayed European publics toward a tougher line on Iran, while the investment in a decade of diplomacy has put pressure on their governments to support sanctions. At the same time, the shift in the Iranian balance of power in favor of the hard-line Revolutionary Guard unsettled states that are less concerned with democratic pretenses, such as Russia and China. Finally, Tehran's deliberately provocative rhetoric on the nuclear program, and the sheer frustrations of the decade-plus negotiating process, combined with the intensifying concerns of the International Atomic Energy Agency, have created a shared multilateral appreciation of the urgency of the need to address Iran's nuclear quest.

In addition, as international support for sanctioning Iran expanded, other previously fixed assumptions were abandoned as well. For most of the 1980s and 1990s, Washington's efforts to pressure Iran were constrained by a well-founded appreciation of the international community's unwillingness to undertake measures that might negatively impact the global oil markets, with respect to either supply or prices. Insofar as U.S. sanctions targeted Iran's energy sector, they were largely symbolic unilateral measures – such as the 1987 embargo on imports of Iranian oil – or exhortatory extraterritorial measures intended to have a modest, long-term impact on the availability of foreign investment and technology needed by Iran to maintain its production and exports. Increasingly, however, the ambitions of sanctions have expanded, and with ithem the readiness to risk destabilization of oil supplies and prices. While this emphasis can be interpreted as an indication of the determination of U.S. and other policy makers to prompt meaningful changes in Iran's nuclear policy, it may also highlight the transformation in global energy markets as a result of technological advancements and other factors. Saudi Arabia has fulfilled its traditional role as swing producer in ramping up production to offset the loss of 1–1.5 mbpd of Iranian exports; however, it is also clear that the additional 1.6 mbpd from new North American production has helped to assuage market forecasts and prevent price spikes.

Next, historically, sanctions represented one of several instruments of U.S. policy toward Tehran and their objectives were correspondingly restrained. Economic pressure was intended to achieve peripheral objectives – to deny or deter access to inputs for Iran's military, to elevate the price of specific aspects of Iranian foreign policy, or even simply to send a signal of American reprobation. And their application was preceded by at least some measure of debate over their prospective advantages and disadvantages, including the competitive cost to the U.S. economy, within the executive branch as well as between the administration and the Congress. Today, sanctions are assigned vastly more ambitious goals explicitly designed wholly to cripple Iran's energy sector and by extension its economy. And the scope and impact of sanctions vastly outweigh any other mechanism in use or currently available to Washington and its partners. The expansive objectives of international economic measures contain an inherently escalatory logic to a policy that is overly reliant on sanctions. Each time economic pressure has failed to achieve the desired objective, the instinctive response has simply been to intensify the pressure by expanding or enhancing the sanctions.

Fourth, the sanctions are now a semi-permanent fixture of American policy and of the Islamic Republic's interaction with the world. Although restrictions are, in principle at least, an instrument that can be fine-tuned, there are relatively few instances in which Washington has sought to relax American measures targeting Iran's economy: the 1981 Algiers Accords, which removed the hostage era sanctions; 1998 legislation exempting U.S. agricultural and pharmaceutical exports from all sanctions; and a number of gestures by the Clinton administration, including the authorization of the sale of spare airline parts, removal of Iran's designation as for narcotics production and transit, and the 2000 lifting of restrictions on caviar, carpet, and pistachio imports. Today, the redundant and interlocking array of measures and the reverberation upon ostensibly licit trade make any calibration or relaxation of restrictions infinitely more complicated, as evidenced by the negotiations surrounding the November 2013 interim nuclear accord and subsequent efforts to hammer out a more permanent resolution to the crisis. Even the modest sanctions relief provided in the interim deal provided Tehran little new trade or investment, thanks to the durability of the sanctions' legal and reputational barricades.

This highlights that the difficulty of deploying sanctions in advancing solutions to the Iranian nuclear issue is their relationship to the negotiating process. Unlike in previous cases, where Washington and the international community imposed sanctions as part of a long-term strategy of eroding regime legitimacy and state capacity, many of the economic penalties adopted by the international community toward Tehran are explicitly intended to be used as bargaining chips in extracting specific Iranian concessions.

There is a tendency to misperceive the appeal of specific prospective incentives to a sanctioned state. Much as in the case of North Korea, the utility of more general overtures – such as participation in the World Trade Organization – appears to be quite limited. These measures imply only limited and conditional benefits for the sanctioned state and may entail complicated domestic negotiations. Just as Pyongyang has preferred specific "targeted transfers" of food and funds from the West, Tehran may favor concrete benefits with short-term payout.[136] Overtures such as the 2005 decision not to oppose Iran's application to begin accession talks with the World Trade Organization proved highly unpersuasive to Tehran, simply because it conveyed no tangible assistance to the state's immediate challenges, and in fact entailed a rigorous and internally contested process of negotiating further economic reforms with an international body. The outcome proved unsatisfactory to both sides, and that failure exacerbates each government's sense of grievance and conviction that its adversary is fundamentally unreasonable.

In addition, even where incentives carry meaningful material benefits for the target state, in the Iranian case the attempt to use sanctions as incentives has been impeded by a persistent tendency to underrate their value. For example, the measures enacted unilaterally by the Clinton administration in March 2000 that removed restrictions on imports of Iranian carpets, pistachios, and caviar have been persistently derided by Iranians as well as advocates of engagement as trivial gestures. However, these products represented Iran's largest nonoil exports, and their production employed hundreds of thousands of Iranians. The sanctions relaxation, together with legislation exempting agricultural and medical products from all sanctions that had been passed by Congress two years earlier, led to a dramatic expansion of U.S. trade with Iran, and of Iran's exports of the newly unrestricted products. Just as efforts to intensify pressure have failed to generate conciliation from the Iranian leadership, these episodic attempts to provide tangible incentives to Tehran have produced no evidence of traction or reciprocal concessions.

Moreover, the attempt to utilize economic restrictions to persuade Tehran to change its policies inherently requires the Iranian government to reverse its posture and/or undertake concessions with a considerable

---

[136] Stephan Haggard and Marcus Noland, "Sanctioning North Korea: The Political Economy of Denuclearization and Proliferation," *Asian Survey* 50:3, p. 541.

degree of risk about the prospective payoff. This is not new to the nuclear sanctions; indeed, the two major precedents for the success of economic pressure as applied to Tehran – the 1981 hostage release and the 1988 cease-fire with Iraq – offer a stark reminder that in each case, the Iranian leadership effectively accepted a very uncertain gamble.

In the first case, it seems clear that the utility of the hostages as a tool for securing specific objectives had waned considerably. The shah's death mooted their symbolic value, and the Iraqi invasion unavoidably altered Iran's priorities. Still, since the embassy seizure was a crucial turning point for the fledging revolution and state, one that had helped consolidate its authority, releasing the hostages meant turning the page on that momentary sense of advantage and ceding a presumptive asset that offered both bargaining power and domestic legitimacy. As the intensity and chaotic nature of the final weeks of talks suggest, committing themselves to a resolution was neither effortless nor uncomplicated for the Iranian leadership.

What may have facilitated the decision to risk an end to the hostage ordeal were the framework for the settlement and the direct involvement of the banking channel, which provided a third-party guarantor to overcome the mistrust and ensure that the exchange was in fact a reciprocal one. Even so, Iran finally yielded even though considerable internal concerns remained about the capacity of the state to fend off the Iraqi onslaught. Even after the hostage release, Tehran continued to struggle to maintain solvency and secure international financing, and business analysts warned that there "isn't a company in its right mind that would deal with Iran right now."[137] A similar narrative of uncertainty and risk can be seen in the 1988 decision to accept the cease-fire with Iraq.[138]

At a basic level, a strategy for thwarting Iran's nuclear ambitions that relies on sanctions may fall prey to the incongruities that characterize the worldview of senior decision makers in the Islamic Republic today. Sanctions initially strengthened the position of hard-liners, in contradiction to the basic intent of sanctions policy – which was to promote moderation in Iranian foreign and domestic policies. Instead, sanctions play into a larger historical narrative of persecution at the hands of the

---

[137] Clyde Farnsworth, "Washington Watch: Reagan to drop an export curb," *New York Times*, February 16, 1981, p. D2.

[138] A recently released oral history offers a fascinating look at the way that the negotiations transpired, and in particular how Washington sought to slow or block the final outcome at the last moment. Blight et al. (2012).

West. And the current leadership assesses the risks and rewards associated with its various policy options through the lens of a unique and deeply conspiratorial worldview, a product of both ideology and historical experience. Throughout the decade of fitful nuclear diplomacy, Iranian leaders have made clear that they expect to be compensated in response for any concessions, and intensifying sanctions only escalates the price expectations of Iranian negotiators. As a result, the nuclear standoff seemed to be self-sustaining; even as sanctions succeeded in generating a more constructive negotiating process, the path to a durable resolution of the crisis appeared as uncertain as ever.

10

Conclusion

"Close your eyes. This is Tehran," an Iranian newspaper aligned with the reform movement inveighed its readers in April 2013. "This is Tehran in 92 [the Iranian year that began in March 2013], and second and third class fruits and vegetables and, of course, waste have become popular."[1] What was then a wearied, cautious debate on the economy and the toll of sanctions erupted just a few weeks later, when the campaign to replace Ahmadinejad began in earnest. After the 2009 upheaval, many observers anticipated the 2013 election to showcase an anodyne campaign as a display of mindless deference to the regime's ideological strictures – a Potemkin pageant to confirm a new unquestioning acolyte to Khamenei in the post of the presidency. Instead, something within Iran's mercurial system gave way, and the Islamic Republic's carefully stage-managed electoral process mutated into a serious dialogue on the crisis facing the country and a newfound popular relegitimization of a system that only four years earlier had made a mockery of its own democratic pretensions.

The campaign included a number of surprising twists, including the early rejection of Hashemi Rafsanjani's bid to contest the presidency once again. However, the most striking aspect of the entire process was the instigation of an unprecedented public questioning of the regime's nuclear diplomacy, focused on the costs of the impasse to Iran's economy. The issue was highlighted during a lengthy televised debate on foreign policy that took place only a week before the election, with approximately two-thirds of the country watching. The rival candidates assailed the presumptive

---

[1] "Close Your Eyes, This Is Tehran," *Bahar*, April 9, 2013.

front-runner, the nuclear negotiator Saeed Jalili, for failing to resolve the issue or deter the intensification of sanctions. Former nuclear negotiator Hassan Rouhani defended his own negotiating track record, previously much criticized by hard-liners, and deployed a well-practiced riposte that questioned the utility of spinning centrifuges when factories are idled.

The debate was far more significant than simply another sharp-elbowed display by an elite known for its fractiousness. The suddenly candid discourse on such a sensitive subject betrayed the Iranian establishment's awareness of the regime's increasing vulnerability. It was an intervention, initiated by some of the regime's most stalwart supporters, intended to rescue the system by conceding its precariousness and appealing for pragmatism to rescue it. And it was an acknowledgment that the sanctions-induced miseries of the Iranian public could no longer be assuaged with the nuclear pageantry of the Ahmadinejad era, or even the formerly reliable appeals to the system's unique blend of religion and nationalism. Although Iranian leaders continue to laud their ability to withstand and evade sanctions, the cost of defiance had reached a tipping point where the system was prepared to test its alternatives.

The most compelling interpretation of the unusual events of Iran's 2013 presidential election and its aftermath is simply that the divisions among the theocracy's political elite and the catastrophic costs of Ahmadinejad's final years in office forced a course correction. Just as in 1988, when Rafsanjani was given a mandate to end the devastating Iraq war and reconstruct Iran's economy and its relationship with the world, Iran's revolutionaries sought once again salvation in moderation. This time around, another member of the self-described "reasonable faction" regained the trust of the orthodox revolutionaries, including Khamenei, and won the votes of the citizens.

Rouhani branded his administration "the government of prudence and hope," and it has proven a fitting signature for his particular approach to the rowdy, unpredictable sport that is Iranian politics. In his first year in office, Rouhani lived up to his billing, thanks in part to the surprising room for maneuver he was accorded. The new president was allowed to install the most forward-leaning, Western-oriented cabinet in postrevolutionary history. In speeches and press conferences, he openly staked his presidency on resolving the nuclear impasse, promising more active diplomacy and efforts to build trust and transparency. He managed to secure an interim accord within a record one hundred days in office – a deal that entailed more in the way of unwelcome obligations than it afforded in the way of rewards. None of this would have been possible without Khamenei's explicit support.

Ultimately, Rouhani's success hinges on reviving the economy, and this objective drives his diplomatic ambitions. In April 2013, as the campaign to succeed Ahmadinejad was just beginning to take shape, Rouhani remarked on the change in Iran's fortunes under his stewardship. In 2005, he noted, "we had a quiet country with good foreign relations. We had a good economy with a relatively acceptable rate of unemployment and inflation. But whoever inherits this government will inherit the worst conditions of unemployment, inflation, value of national currency, social disputes, and unclear foreign policy."

Since taking office, Rouhani has insisted that the situation was even worse than he previously understood. On his hundredth day in office, he gave an address to the nation in which he described food shortages, epic inflation rates of 46 percent, and massive state debts of at least 2 trillion rials. He conceded that "the government that had the most revenues during its two terms" – Ahmadinejad presided over eight years in which Tehran earned more in petroleum exports than in the previous century of production – "left the most debts as well." Working with an experienced group of technocrats and economic planners, most of whom had been forced out of government by Ahmadinejad, Rouhani chose a "precarious balancing act" to rehabilitate the economy without adopting austerity budgeting.[2] His initial program was intended to impose enough fiscal and monetary discipline to control and reduce inflation, without triggering a deeper recession. The International Monetary Fund issued an assessment that Iran's "near-term outlook remains highly uncertain, with the distribution of risks becoming more balanced but still tilted to the downside." The fund expects that GDP contracted by 1.75 percent for 2013/14, with projected modest growth of 1–2 percent in 2014/15.[3]

Rouhani and his supporters emphasized Ahmadinejad's culpability for the country's economic state – a position that has some political currency given the former president's vilification among the Iranian elite. The critiques focus on his erratic and invasive management style, wildly indulgent spending, and massive corruption, as well as his failure to foresee the impact of international sanctions. The former Tehran mayor, Gholamhusayn Karbaschi, has charged that "Ahmadinejad's government

[2] Kevan Harris, "Rouhani's Next Test: Empty Coffers," *Iran Primer*, December 2, 2013, http://iranprimer.usip.org/blog/2013/dec/02/rouhani%E2%80%99s-next-test-empty-coffers

[3] IMF, "Islamic Republic of Iran: 2014 Article IV Consultation-Staff Report," April 4, 2014, p. 11. www.imf.org/external/pubs/cat/longres.aspx?sk=41463.0

tried to run the country on the basis of a series of very propagandist and noisy moves and slogans. They imagined that they could resolve all the issues with a great deal of noise and ballyhoo, but today we see the consequences of their actions that have afflicted the people and all political spectrums." For Karbaschi, as for others in Iran, a return to Iran's pre-Ahmadinejad state would represent a resounding success for Rouhani. "Of course, we hope that he will be even more successful than that and with the help of his friends he will be able to move the country forward," Karbaschi added.[4]

Apportioning blame to Ahmadinejad is fair, but within Iran's Islamic system it inevitably raises awkward questions. Specifically, why was Ahmadinejad's government permitted to run the economy in such dangerous and dishonest fashion? As Iran's supreme leader, Khamenei wields ultimate authority over all policies and institutions of the state; therefore, he and the massive parallel bureaucracy that he commands bear final responsibility for the "astronomical" graft, colossal losses, and wasted opportunities of the Ahmadinejad era. As Karbaschi lamented, "There is nobody to grab these people by their collars and ask them why they brought the country to a point that we had to import wheat from Brazil, America and the Soviet Union." Of course, there was somebody, but Khamenei and his lieutenants either did not know or did not care.

Several of Ahmadinejad's signature economic initiatives have been abandoned, wound down, or — in the case of the much-needed but badly implemented subsidy reform program — modified significantly to reduce costs, improve efficiencies, and avoid imposing new disruptions on the economy. However, not all of the aftereffects of the Ahmadinejad economy can be quickly or easily discarded. Rouhani's economic team was forced to contend with extensive nontransparency in the government's accounts as well as an array of makeshift mechanisms for coping with sanctions that impose ongoing or even increasing costs. Some of these were Potemkin arrangements with state-affiliated (and often Revolutionary Guard–affiliated) firms to mask the dramatic exodus of foreign investors; others were simply rash efforts fueled by panic and resource availability. Other sunk costs from the Ahmadinejad era come in the form of lost opportunities, such as Iran's slow pace in developing

[4] Saba Azarpeyk, "We Will Not Be Played; We Will Not Abandon Rouhani," *Etemad*, April 8, 2014, www.etemaad.ir/Released/93-01-19/204.htm

its offshore gas resources, which may have cost billions in unrecoverable revenues as a result of disproportionately higher Qatari production from its North Field.

Even seemingly sensible measures – such as the expansion of refinery capacity to mitigate Iran's reliance on imported fuel, a key vulnerability that Washington and Europe targeted with bans on product exports – seem to have been undertaken by the Ahmadinejad government without any serious effort to establish a viable fiscal framework for their operation. "I have no idea what's happening," Iran's oil minister, the longtime technocrat Bijan Namdar Zanganeh, told an industry publication in January 2014. "They made refineries very quickly.... We can't stop supplying them, but how can we get our money?" Zanganeh also raised questions about their operating safety. "They haven't been checked according to schedule, if something has a hole in it and it catches on fire, who is to blame?" Zanganeh queried.[5]

Ultimately, Iran's economy remains caught in the cross fire of the nuclear diplomacy. The sanctions regime erected since 2006 is viciously effective, halving Iran's oil exports, precluding Tehran from repatriating its hard-currency profits from the sales, and impeding Iranian banks from transactions with the rest of the world. The interim nuclear agreement inked in November 2013 by representatives of Iran, America, and five other world powers did not meaningfully alter any of these hurdles. As many predicted at the time, the sanctions relief provided in the November deal has generated little new investment and only modest new avenues of trade for Tehran.

The interim deal provided small benefits for Rouhani's economic challenges: boosting local business confidence and returning a small fraction of Iran's estimated $100 billion in assets that are held in foreign banks. The diplomacy intensified an already-rising arc of petrochemical exports and unofficially facilitated a slight surge in oil exports. Thanks to the deal and the stabilization measures undertaken by Iran's new economic team, some domestic industries, such as the automotive sector, which was exempted from sanctions for the duration of the nuclear talks, have begun to rebound from the precipitous slump experienced since 2012. The currency's value rose consistently higher than prior to Rouhani's election and inflation was reduced to less dire levels. However, Rouhani has not succeeded in

[5] "Euphoria Fades as Oil Sector Faces Sanctions Reality," *Energy Compass*, January 31, 2014.

staunching the ongoing retrenchment in jobs or consumption[6] and the challenges are likely to mount. Moreover, Tehran's inability to deliver a deal by the initial July 2014 deadline, or by its November 2014 extension, only extended the state of limbo for economic planning. The announcement of a revised contract model for oil and gas investment, which was intended to attract new interest from Iran's former partners in the international oil companies, was already deferred multiple times.

While Rouhani has trumpeted the nuclear talks as an avenue to relieving the debilitating restrictions on Iran's ability to interact with the international financial community, he has also insisted that the country's economic rehabilitation cannot be made contingent on the outcome of the talks. In his first official press conference as president, Rouhani promised that his government would "start serious negotiations with the foreign parties and will demonstrate that we are serious about these negotiations. But, at the same time, we will not sit idly to see whether the foreign parties will respond positively or negatively. We have programs for the current condition, and will continue these.... You name it what you may, whether you call it economic resistance or endurance, we will continue this path nonetheless."[7]

Khamenei has branded this the "economy of resistance," and he maintains that strengthening Iran's domestic capabilities can sustain the country without reliance on oil revenues or trade with the West. It is an aspiration that long predates the Islamic Republic; during the 1951–3 British embargo of Iran's newly nationalized oil company, Mosaddeq attempted the same feat. Rouhani and his advisers describe it in slightly more realistic terms; they hope to expand Iran's revenue base by negotiating the end of the sanctions regime or, if negotiations fail, eroding it, while also optimizing Iran's nonoil economy.

One of the key aspects of this strategy is the conviction among the technocrats on the Rouhani team that Iran can avoid some of the pitfalls that undermined its previous attempt to rebuild and restore its economy – notably, the post–Iraq war reconstruction program launched by the then-president (and Rouhani mentor) Ali Akbar Hashemi Rafsanjani in 1989. Then, initial economic improvements were undercut by rapid growth in imports, which contributed to inflation as well

---

[6] Djavad Salehi-Isfahani, "Iran's Economy after One Year of Rouhani," Lobelog, August 4, 2014, www.lobelog.com/irans-economy-after-one-year-of-rouhani/

[7] Rouhani press conference, Islamic Republic of Iran News Network (IRINN), August 6, 2013, from BBC Worldwide Monitoring.

as government difficulties in staying current on the quickly expanding foreign debt burden.

Iran's economic gurus appreciate that even the expeditious lifting of all international sanctions – an unlikely if not impossible prospect – would only create new dilemmas for the country's economy. Masoud Nili, Rouhani's senior economic adviser, who has long experience in devising Iran's economic plans, voiced a key uncertainty in May 2014, questioning,

> If the sanctions are lifted and we get back to having enormous oil revenues again, will we behave again as we did in the years 85 through 90 and go in the same direction? Do we want to impose a new crisis on the nation's economy by increasing imports, or can we use successful international experiences and start national wealth funds with revenues from our natural resources for the improvement of infrastructure and national development? If we take the same path again, in view of the unemployment situation we have, conditions in the economy will become deadly.

Still, it is clear that the initial successful pivot away from the brink will not necessarily ease the Islamic Republic's challenges. The public ebullience for Rouhani and his diplomatic achievements exacerbates the vulnerabilities of Iran's aging revolutionaries. Having raised the expectations of a restless young nation with a popular president and nuclear bargain, Tehran must now deliver. Iranians want to see the fruits of these breakthroughs: the trade that will generate new jobs and economic opportunities, the easing of government repression and social restrictions, a leadership that is accountable to its people and respected abroad.

In other words, the nuclear deal is not a get-out-of-jail-free card for a system confronting epic challenges; rather, Iran's internal reset and the diplomatic breakthroughs that have followed will only exacerbate the pressure from below. The millions of Iranians who thronged to Rouhani's rowdy campaign rallies, who reveled in the streets after he was elected, and who celebrated the nuclear deal are watching and waiting. In case the regime's leadership missed the message, many of those who greeted the nuclear negotiators were chanting slogans in support of the candidates who led the postelection protests in 2009, men who have now endured more than three years of shockingly brutal house arrest.

If Rouhani's government of "hope and prudence" is going to fulfill his people's expectations, then the Islamic Republic's recent embrace of pragmatism must prevail over its well-honed authoritarian impulses and institutions. Nothing in Iran's postrevolutionary history gives reason for optimism about enduring moderation; past attempts by pragmatic presidents to moderate the regime were derailed by hard-liner opposition and intraelite competition. Still, Rouhani has been entrusted with the historic role of engineering the country's first opening to Washington, and he may yet prove able to navigate a path out of the nuclear impasse.

IRAN'S REVOLUTIONARY HISTORY IMPRINTS ITSELF ON TODAY'S ECONOMY

The complexities of Islamic Iran reflect the unintended consequences of its epic 1979 revolution, itself the work of a broad coalition of social forces who shared little beyond their frustration with the monarchy. From the ashes of the revolution they built a state around a unique framework of competing institutions and ingrained elite rivalries. Although the supreme leader nominally wields ultimate authority, no single individual in Iran has complete or uncontested power. This institutional intricacy and reliance on consensus have proven to be a hidden strength of the system, as well as the source of its frequent opacity.

The existential challenges that the Islamic Republic faced during its first decade – civil unrest, tribal insurrections, terrorist attacks, external invasion, protracted war, and leadership transition – mandated a certain rigidity. In the twenty-five years since Khomeini left the scene, Iran has undergone a virtual roller-coaster of political, social, and economic change – first undertaking a massive reconstruction program to mend the scars of its bloody eight-year war with Iraq, later embarking on a heady experiment in liberalizing the revolutionary system, and most recently reinterpreting the regime's radical, populist roots under Ahmadinejad's contentious presidency. Over that period, Iran's economy has boomed along with oil prices and eventually crashed, its boundaries for permissible political speech have burst open and shuttered again, its hemlines and *hejab*s have receded episodically with fluctuating enforcement of Islamic dress codes, and the children of the revolution have begun to assume leadership from its authors.

Along the way, Iranian policies have been forced to adapt in response to a changing context and the country's increasingly youthful population. Occasionally, the shift has been explicit and wholesale, such as Khomeini's belated embrace of family planning after his natalist policies sparked an unsustainable demographic bulge. More often, change has occurred in Iran in gradual but durable fashion, as with the vastly liberalized enforcement of social restrictions that has largely survived the retrenchment of the Ahmadinejad era. And where Iran is concerned, change is a constant; fifteen years after the reversal on birth control, Tehran is now shifting gears once again, retooling its family planning bureaucracy to encourage higher fertility, in hopes of mitigating a dangerously unbalanced population pyramid.

That evolution represents both the precipitant and the product of Iran's much-vaunted reform movement, which moved to the fore during the late 1990s and briefly raised hopes that the revolution's excesses at home and abroad could simply fade into history. Emanating from the disaffection of left-wing politicians and dissident clerics, reformists advocated incremental change and the strengthening of the regime's electoral institutions and constitutional framework. However, the reform movement's restrained ambitions undercut its efficacy and squandered its popular mandate, and orthodox defenders of the revolutionary regime deployed both political savvy and ruthless determination to restore their domination of the levers of power.

The conservatives' restoration culminated with Ahmadinejad's 2005 election, but predictably this milestone only paved the way for new factional infighting. His ascendance began to pass the torch to a younger generation of revolutionaries, but his rabble-rousing rhetoric and disastrous economic policies generated new fissures within the conservative camp. His successor acknowledged in early 2015 that the revolutionary bargain required reconsideration. In an address before an audience of technocrats and economic planners, President Rouhani described Iran's economy as "more political than pure economic" and said:

In our country, as you know all, it has been years and decades that the economy pays subsidies to politics. They say that subsidies cannot be forever and someday it must be stopped. We have to take a decision in this regard. How long can the economy pay subsidies to politics? It pays subsidies both to foreign policy and domestic policy. Let us try the other way round for a decade and pay subsidies from the domestic and foreign policy to economy to see how the lives and incomes of people and the employment of the youth will be like. [8]

IRAN'S FACTIONAL DRAMA REMAINS, BUT ECONOMICS IS NO LONGER THE FLASH POINT

The experience of three and a half decades of revolutionary theocracy has produced a convergence of the once-fierce philosophical debates over

---

[8] Rouhani speech to First National Economy Conference, January 4, 2015, from BBC Worldwide Monitoring.

economic policy. In the earliest days of the revolutionary state, Iran's political elites feuded over the role of the state in the economy and the relationship of Iran's economy to the broader world, with the deepest and most salient cleavage between those who favored state dominance – particularly in foreign trade – and those who sought to protect the traditional sphere of the private sector. These debates paralyzed the bureaucracy and eventually contributed to the reconfiguration of Iran's legislative institutions.

Contrast these ideological debates with Iran today, in which economic policy remains a critical arena for factional dispute. Today, the historic divisions on the basic structure of the economy have nearly evaporated. Despite – or perhaps because of – Ahmadinejad's mismanagement, there is widespread agreement among almost all sectors of the Iran elite on the basic framework for the economy, including support for previously contentious measures such as privatization and international economic integration. Even the epic spender Ahmadinejad himself embraced the sell-off of state-owned enterprises. For his part, Khamenei has given the state's imprimatur to this shift, offering an unusually explicit endorsement of capitalism:

The mere possession of capital and its investment in the progress of the country is not a bad thing. It is an admired thing. It is not contemptible at all. What is contemptible is that capital and capitalism form the basis of all the major decisions made in the country and drag everything toward themselves. This is the problem that the capitalist and the Western block are grappling with. They are reaping the results of that today. The events happening today in Europe, the financial pressure on the people, all emanate from the nature of the capitalist system. This is leech-like capitalism. This is contemptible capitalism. But if some people have capital and they use it to help the country develop - and of course they will also make some profit in this process - then that act [investment] is good, and the profit made is *halal*.[9]

The experience of governing the Islamic Republic has generated an ideological convergence on economic issues. This is largely the function of the disintegration of the leftist Islamic economic discourse, and it suggests that the revolutionary state has absorbed the lessons of history, particularly given how salient the "radical" economics school of thought was during the early years of the revolution. This transformation has reshaped the thinking of the Iranian leadership across the board, as supporters of a traditional interpretation of Islamic jurisprudence feel less constrained by the competition for popular appeal.

[9] Khamenei address to a gathering of students, broadcast on Voice and Vision of the Islamic Republic Channel One, August 7, 2012.

This new consensus does not facilitate more efficient economic policy – or even domestic political comity – in part because Iran's record oil revenues and internal political imperatives provide perverse incentives for rational planning. Still, it is remarkable to appreciate the distinction between the factional infighting of the revolution's first decade and its equally contested situation today. Rather than clashing on the fundamental shape of the economy and scope of state economic management, the most salient divide today within Iran concerns dividing up the spoils of the oil windfalls.

Neither the revolutionary state's modernization of Iran nor the coalescing of factional arguments over the economy mitigates the underlying mismanagement that permeates the Islamic Republic. Nor should these developments be interpreted to suggest that Iran's economy is healthy, as that is by no means the case. Just the opposite: Under- and unemployment are endemic, particularly among the two-thirds of Iranians below the age of twenty-five; epic inflation rates have eroded the pocketbooks of the poor; and power shortages and other daily hardships have deepened the public's alienation from the Islamic regime. In addition, the tendency toward corruption and mismanagement transcends political or ideological identification, suggesting that even a recalibration of the Islamic Republic or shift in its leadership would not end it. Still, the dilution of the salience of socialist economic precepts and the establishment of the strong fundamentals for a competitive capitalist economy give way to legitimate optimism about the future economic and political prospects of Iran, when and if its leadership demonstrates its willingness to adhere to international norms on its treatment of its citizenry and extension of its influence abroad.

POPULISM HAS CREATED COMPETING CLAIMS TO LEGITIMACY

The power struggle and diverse ideological positions within the revolutionary coalition and postrevolutionary elites generated an increasingly prominent embrace of themes surrounding social justice. Before his assumption of political power, Ayatollah Khomeini was a reliably staunch defender of property rights and the role of the private sector, consistent with traditional Shi'a jurisprudence, which generally holds the sanctity of private property to be inviolable. However, to consolidate support for the system and outmaneuver leftist rivals, Khomeini and his allies began articulating a stronger appeal to poor Iranians, or *mostazafan* – the oppressed. Khomeini also softened his defense of private property, tacitly sanctioning the wave of expropriations. All these trends intensified after the Iraqi invasion in September 1980, and for the subsequent eight years the state fully mobilized the nation's resources in support of the war effort.

Mahmoud Ahmadinejad revived these same themes during his original presidential campaign, promising to put the country's oil wealth in the hands of individual citizens and skillfully exploiting popular frustration over elite enrichment by scorning his opponent's notoriously luxurious lifestyle. Ahmadinejad relied on populism as the most reliable tool for stoking the support of his base and intimidating rivals. And his embrace of populist themes extended far beyond rhetoric; during his first term as president, Ahmadinejad spent lavishly, traversing the country incessantly with his full cabinet in tow, taking evident enjoyment in a paternalistic process of doling out funds large and small for picayune provincial projects and even individual appeals.

Iran's oil revenues under Ahmadinejad's first term exceeded eight years of income during both the Khatami and Rafsanjani presidencies; indeed of the more than $700 billion that Iran has earned through oil exports in the past thirty years, nearly 40 percent was during Ahmadinejad's second term. The president's disdain for the state's bureaucrats and technocracy meant the allocations were subject to little transparency. The presumption is that much of it financed epic corruption as well as record consumption, much of it imported, rather than creating jobs, attracting investors, or taking advantage of Iran's large, well-educated baby boom as it comes of age.

Still, what is perhaps most notable about Ahmadinejad's assiduous embrace of populist rhetoric and programs has been the reaction from both the regime's elite and its citizenry. The senselessness of his policies has provoked an intensifying firestorm of criticism from across the political spectrum. At first the critiques were lighthearted. When he once boasted about the bargain price of tomatoes in his low-rent Tehran neighborhood, the president sparked a flurry of popular jokes at his expense and grumbling among the political elite. However, as the ripple effects of the global economic slowdown began to impact Iran and the price of oil crashed to less than one-third of its stratospheric 2008 high, the mood soured among both the regime's veteran personalities and its population at large. In three successive letters, a panoply of the country's most respected economists detailed the dangers of the president's policies. Notably, the critiques were not limited to the president's factional adversaries; much of the disquiet voiced in recent years over the state of the economy emerged from sources ideologically inclined to support Ahmadinejad and his patron the supreme leader, including traditional conservatives with long-standing links to the powerful *bazaar* and the centers of clerical learning.

This criticism, together with the widespread protests and continuing opposition activity that followed Ahmadinejad's hotly disputed reelection in June 2009, suggest that the recurrent reliance on populism by the Iranian regime has inadvertently cultivated a set of public expectations surrounding the performance of their government and its accountability to the people that were never intended by its founders. Khomeini and the other ideologues and political actors who crafted the Islamic Republic consistently made clear that the legitimacy of their authority and the Islamic system is predicated upon ideological and charismatic factors. For the orthodox defenders of the regime, this remains the case today, as is evident in the regime's manipulation of Iran's representative institutions and its unfettered repression of dissenters. They embrace the Islamic Republic precisely because it is a religious state, led by individuals whose credibility is by definition unassailable. The performance of that state is not an issue for the Basijis who have beaten back protesters, and any dissent from the state or the system represents a dissent from Islam.

However, the slogans and agenda of the Iranian opposition suggest that for much of the Iranian population, their support for any government is directly related to its representative institutions and its capacity to perform the normal functions of the state. This sense of political entitlement among a population that has only the most limited experience with democratic government has been fostered by the Islamic regime's persistent reliance on populist promises. Their intent, of course, was to buy off the population – using subsidies on consumer goods to supplant demands for greater political participation and social freedoms. But this strategy backfired. By creating expectations of economic windfalls, greater egalitarianism, and an improvement in the plight of *mostazafan*, Iranian leaders effectively undercut the theocratic basis of their authority and bolstered a competing rationale based on delivery of a better life.

President Rouhani acknowledged the new reality in a speech marking the first anniversary of his election. "The country has no owner except the nation of Iran," he proclaimed, adding that "the government is your individual executor, the performer of your will. The government is the executor of national demands. The government does not dominate national demands but national demands would dominate the government."[10] Iran's recent contention can be understood as a battle between those who continue to assert the divine nature of the Islamic system and those who, in part through the Islamic Republic's own rhetoric and policies, assert that state legitimacy is contingent upon its popular basis and functional performance.

ECONOMIC PRESSURE IS THE NORM, NOT THE EXCEPTION

The Islamic Republic has experienced a number of episodes of severe economic pressure, but none has generated the kind of foreign policy moderation that the authors of the manifold punitive measures against Tehran sanguinely forecast. Rather, past periods of external pressure on Iran during the war with Iraq as well as the 1993 debt crisis and cyclical nadirs in the oil markets have facilitated the coalescence of the regime and the consolidation of its public support. Economic constraint has generated enhanced cooperation among Iran's bickering factions. Tight purse strings have forced moderation of Iran's economic policies but only rarely of its political dynamics or foreign policy. The current political context is, of course, unique, but a review of Iranian history tends to undercut the assumption that Tehran will buckle as soon as it feels the pinch.

The simple reality is that Iran's leadership has been engaged in a dynamic process of economic policy improvisation since the earliest days of the revolution. Sanctions simply feed into these well-established patterns of maneuver and mitigation. The same factors that have shaped Iran's political economy throughout the course of the past thirty-five years – the legacy of its patrimonial economic development, the original sins of a contentious revolutionary coalition and dualistic institutions, the persistence of a resource-based rentier income, and a discordant, ambivalent approach to the world – condition Iranian resilience in the face of even the most strenuous sanctions. Iran's history drives perseverance; mistrust of the international community thwarts compromise; oil revenues avert utter collapse; and the Islamic Republic's fissures and unique institutional arrangements offer endless avenues for mitigation and adaptation. Iran's factional battleground offers greater opportunities and incentives for creative management of a crisis than for questioning the basis of the crisis itself. Any costs-benefits assessment of the options available to Tehran on the nuclear issue that takes into account the

[10] Rouhani speech, Islamic Republic of Iran News Network (IRINN), June 12, 2014, from BBC Worldwide Monitoring.

historical legacy, internal landscape, oil income, and international suspicions makes it clear that submitting to the demands of the international community on the nuclear issue remains an unpalatable trade-off.

This analysis suggests that Iran will continue to subsist under pressure, and that Tehran will continue to accept costs that appear excessive or even unbearable except when they are situated in the context of Iran's political economy. It also underscores how difficult, if not impossible, it may be to ascertain a reliable Iranian "breaking point" on sanctions. It is contextual rather than quantifiable. The only real parallel is the final years of the war with Iraq, and while in retrospect it is clear that there was a shift away from recalcitrance and total war aims, these transformations always appear more striking in retrospect than at the time. Iranian leaders have been persuaded that endurance enhances their leverage, and they can call upon sufficient reserves as well as ongoing income, both barter and cash, to enable the state to sustain the economy for the short term. Still, it seems clear that the wiser heads in the regime appreciate that this standoff cannot persist indefinitely. For much of the policy community in Iran, the specter of 1988 remains quite powerful, as do memories of the 1993 debt crisis and the 1999 oil price collapse.

Moreover, eventually pressure does reshape the political landscape. No one familiar with the history of Iran over the course of the past thirty-five years could argue that the journey from revolution through resistance, reconstruction, reform, recalcitrance, and now a reset has not in fact reflected the economic imperatives of the theocratic experiment. Rafsanjani's pragmatism would not have prevailed over the statist fantasies of the Islamic Left in the absence of the economic devastation of the war. The reform movement might have taken a radically different form if their resistance to the reconstruction agenda had not resulted in their eviction from government in 1992, or if their political ambitions had come to fruition in a time of oil plenty rather than at the height of the Asian economic crisis. Even Ahmadinejad's reckless populism would have played out very differently in any era other than that of the epic oil price escalation and eastward shift in the global economy. And the hyperinflation and self-sustaining crisis also had their impact on Iran's contentious political scene, generating the emergence of a more moderate diplomatic approach by Tehran. Unfortunately the pace of political evolution inevitably moves more slowly than the time line for nuclear diplomacy.

Understanding the context of Iran's political economy is vital to fashioning policies that can be effective in persuading Tehran to alter its course on the nuclear issue, or any of its other policies of profound concern. Without this, the dangers of mutual misinterpretation are quite high. Much as in 1951–3, Iran could find a way to manage the financial and political constraints posed by sanctions. Conditions would remain incredibly adverse, but with relatively limited external debt and an oil price that remains above $100/barrel, the country can sustain itself. Endurance becomes an end in and of itself, and the false god of self-sufficiency persuades even those Iranians who value international engagement that the country's interests are better served by holding out. And Iranians do not seem prepared to return to the streets, certainly not over the price of chicken. That may yet change – 2009 certainly surprised most observers of Iran – but the regime's repressive capacity combined with the sense of cynicism and frustration among Iranians could keep a lid on the street protests.

Absent an understanding of Iran's political economy, it may be tempting to see the decision to muddle through as confirmation of the regime's irrationality and its unshakable determination to acquire a nuclear weapons capability. Just as in 1953, when the British eventually wore down Washington's resistance to dabbling in regime change, it is not difficult to envision a scenario in which the failure of economic pressure to achieve its intended results gives way to military action by the United States, Israel, or a combination of the two.

Even if this disastrous course can be avoided, there is another danger in Iran's copious capacity to manage economic adversity. The constant maneuver and mitigation do not offer an opportunity to acknowledge the manifold missed opportunities and disastrous decisions that have been taken over the course of the past thirty-five years. As many Iranian economists and politicians acknowledge, Iran's latest economic crisis is one that predates sanctions and will survive well beyond them. Iran's economic decline cannot be attributed to a single decision point; there have been a multitude of missed opportunities and turning points that have put Iran in its current predicament. For example, had Iran's revolutionaries retained its gas export contracts with the Soviets, Europeans, and Japanese, Iran might well have emerged as the world's heavyweight gas exporter instead of watching its competitors seize market dominance. Had the Rafsanjani administration managed its debt and its international relations more judiciously, the first postrevolutionary upstream energy deal would have moved forward in 1992, at a time when the end of the Cold War and the newfound American antipathy toward Saddam Hussein might have enabled trade to bridge the U.S.-Iranian estrangement. Had a political figure moved to the fore who could combine

Rafsanjani's recognition of the primacy of pragmatism, Khatami's embrace of holistic solutions and self-reinforcing liberalization, and Ahmadinejad's capacity for risk taking, the Islamic Republic might have navigated its economic policy quandaries more wisely. Some of those opportunities may never be reclaimed. In 2015, Iran was once again facing a critical juncture, and whether the country reclaimed its place in the international community and economy or permitted the forces of factional competition and mistrust of world powers to accelerate its decline rested in the hands of its leadership.

Appendix

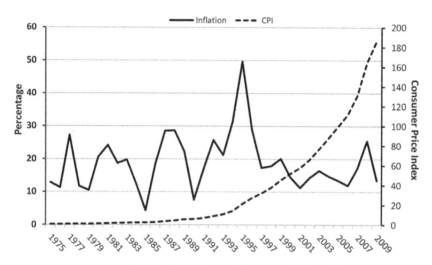

FIGURE APPENDIX 1. Iranian Inflation and Consumer Price Index
Source: Statistical Center of Iran

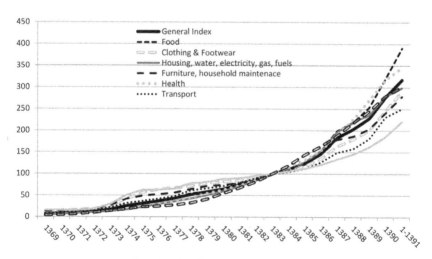

FIGURE APPENDIX 2. Inflation by Category
Source: Statistical Center of Iran

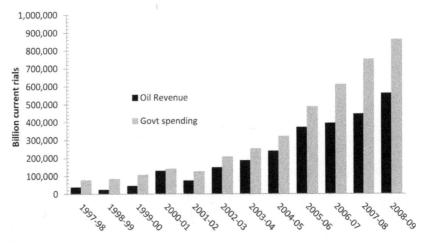

FIGURE APPENDIX 3. Government Spending versus Oil Revenue
Source: Central Bank of Iran, Balance Sheet and Annual Report, and "Islamic
Republic of Iran: Recent Economic Developments," IMF Staff Country Report

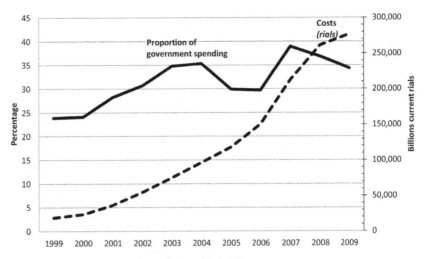

FIGURE APPENDIX 4. Direct Costs of Subsidies
Source: World Bank

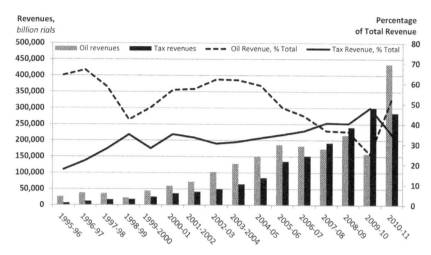

FIGURE APPENDIX 5. Oil Revenue versus Tax Revenue
Source: Annual Reviews of the Central Bank of Iran

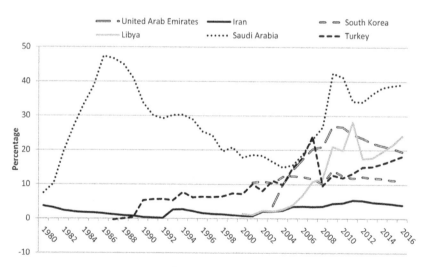

FIGURE APPENDIX 6. FDI Stocks as a Percentage of GDP
Source: UNCTAD

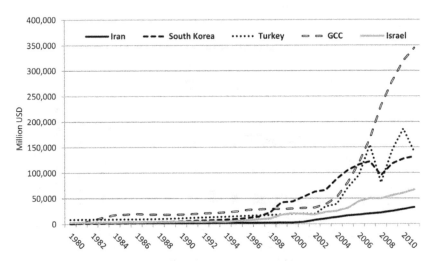

FIGURE APPENDIX 7. Inward FDI Stocks
Source: UNCTAD

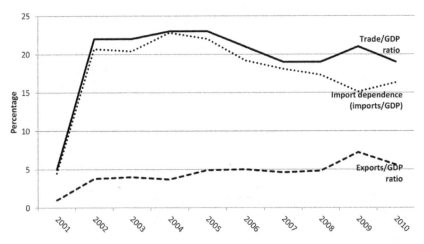

FIGURE APPENDIX 8. Import Dependence
Source: Statistical Center of Iran, "A Summary of Iran Foreign Trade Statistics by
International Classifications," June 12, 2012

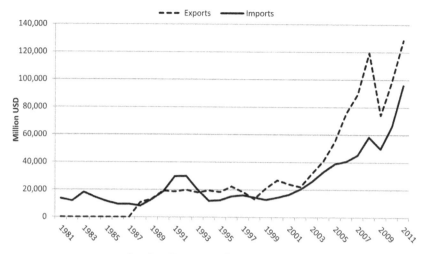

FIGURE APPENDIX 9. Iranian Exports and Imports
Source: IMF Direction of Trade Statistics

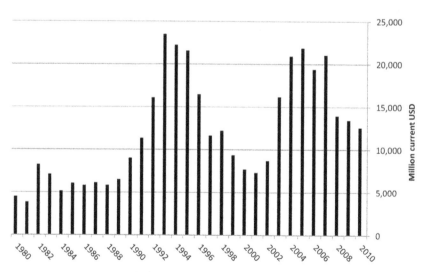

FIGURE APPENDIX 10. Debt
Source: UNCTAD

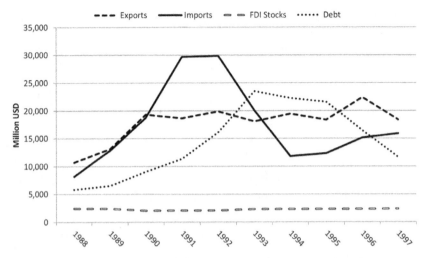

FIGURE APPENDIX 11. Trade and Investment in the Post–Iran-Iraq War Reconstruction Years
Sources: IMF Direction of Trade Statistics; World Bank, World Development Indicators; UNCTAD

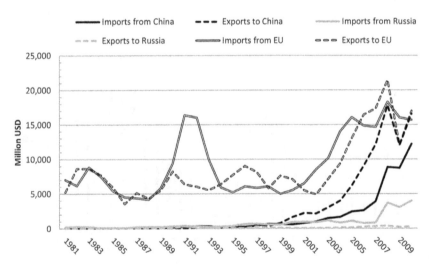

FIGURE APPENDIX 12. Iranian Trade with Russia, China, and the European Union
Source: IMF Direction of Trade Statistics

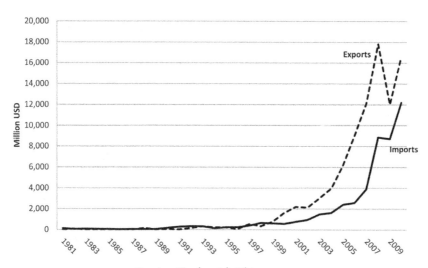

FIGURE APPENDIX 13. Iranian Trade with China
Source: IMF Direction of Trade Statistics

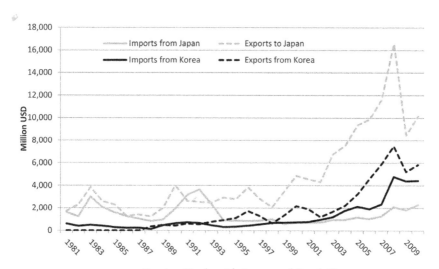

FIGURE APPENDIX 14. Iranian Trade with Japan and South Korea
Source: IMF Direction of Trade Statistics

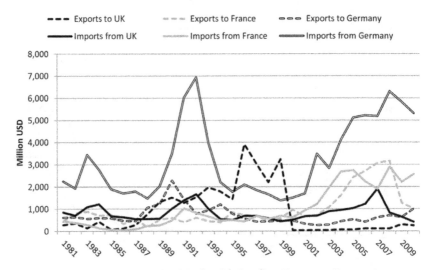

FIGURE APPENDIX 15. Iranian Trade with Leading European Economies
Source: IMF Direction of Trade Statistics

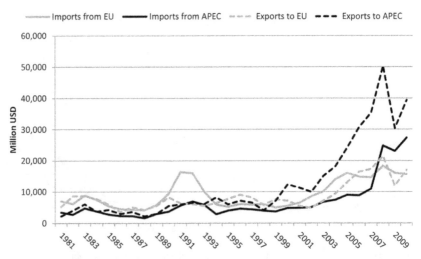

FIGURE APPENDIX 16. Iranian Trade with the EU and the APEC
Source: IMF Direction of Trade Statistics

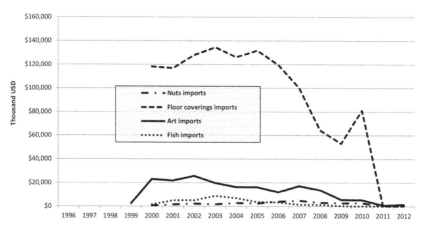

FIGURE APPENDIX 17. US Imports of Iranian products
Source: U.S. Census Bureau

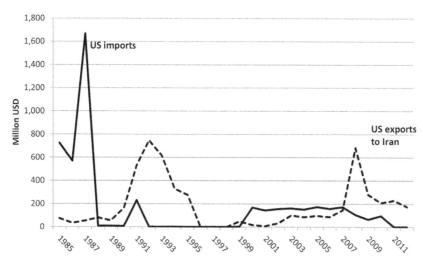

FIGURE APPENDIX 18. Iranian Trade with the United States
Source: U.S. Census Bureau, Foreign Trade Statistics

Appendix

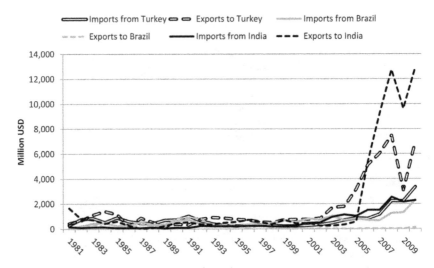

FIGURE APPENDIX 19. Iranian Trade with Major Emerging Economies
Source: IMF Direction of Trade Statistics

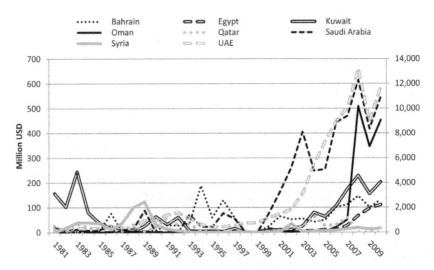

FIGURE APPENDIX 20. Iranian Imports from Middle Eastern Partners
Source: IMF Direction of Trade Statistics

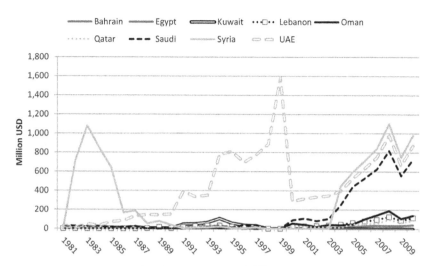

FIGURE APPENDIX 21. Iranian Exports to Middle Eastern Nations
Source: IMF Direction of Trade Statistics

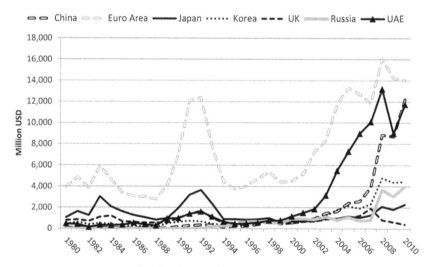

FIGURE APPENDIX 22. Iranian Import Sources
Source: IMF Direction of Trade Statistics

FIGURE APPENDIX 23. Total Iranian Oil Production
Source: BP Statistical Review

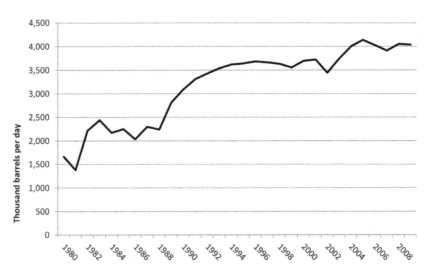

FIGURE APPENDIX 24. Iranian Crude Oil Production
Source: IMF Direction of Trade Statistics

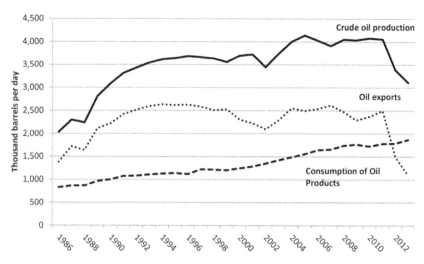

FIGURE APPENDIX 25. Domestic Consumption of Oil versus Exports
Source: U.S. Energy Information Administration

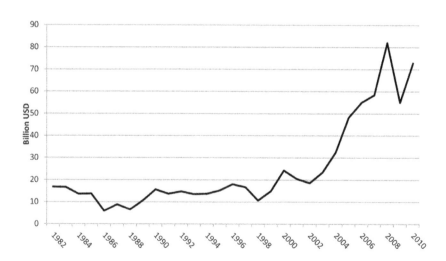

FIGURE APPENDIX 26. Iranian Oil Revenues since the Islamic Revolution
Source: U.S. Energy Information Administration

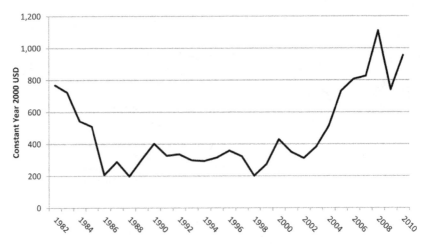

FIGURE APPENDIX 27. Iranian Oil Revenues per Capita
Source: U.S. Energy Information Administration

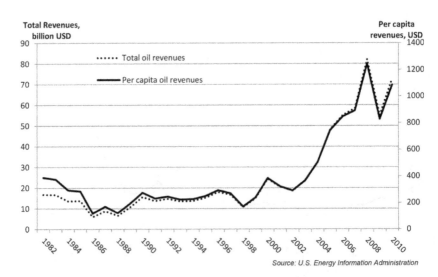

FIGURE APPENDIX 28. Total Iranian Oil Revenues versus per Capita Oil
Revenues
Source: U.S. Energy Information Administration

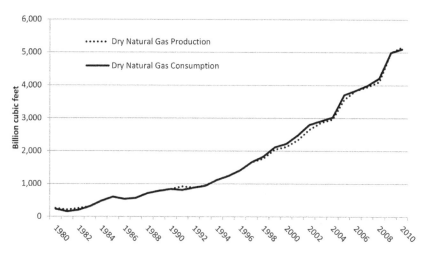

FIGURE APPENDIX 29. Iranian Gas Production and Consumption
Source: U.S. Energy Information Administration

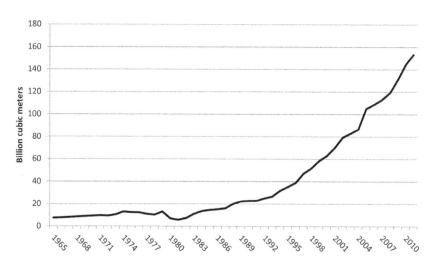

FIGURE APPENDIX 30. Iranian Natural Gas Consumption
Source: BP Statistical Review

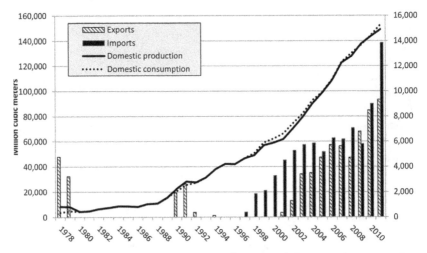

FIGURE APPENDIX 31. Domestic Gas Production and Consumption versus Gas Imports and Exports
Source: International Energy Agency

FIGURE APPENDIX 32. Iranian Gas Exports versus Qatari Gas Exports
Source: International Energy Agency

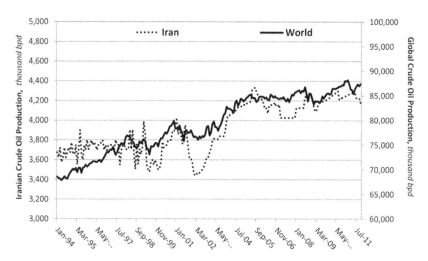

FIGURE APPENDIX 33. Iranian Crude Oil Production versus Global Crude Oil Production
Source: U.S. Energy Information Administration

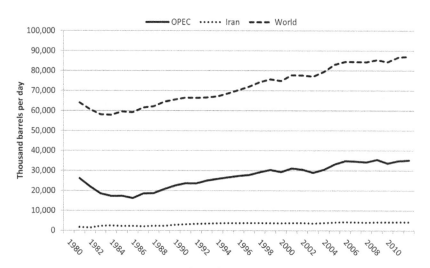

FIGURE APPENDIX 34. Iranian Oil Production versus Total OPEC Oil Production
Source: U.S. Energy Information Administration

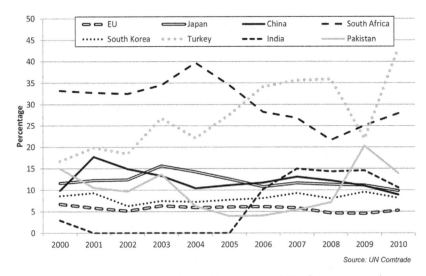

FIGURE APPENDIX 35. Proportion of Nations' Total Crude Import Purchases Originating in Iran
Source: UN Comtrade

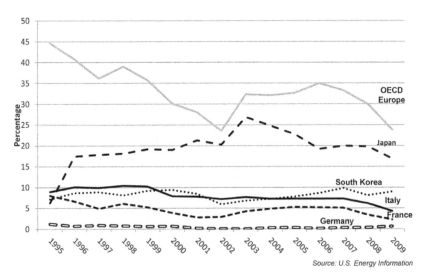

FIGURE APPENDIX 36. Trade Partners' Shares of Total Iranian Crude Oil Exports
Source: U.S. Energy Information Administration

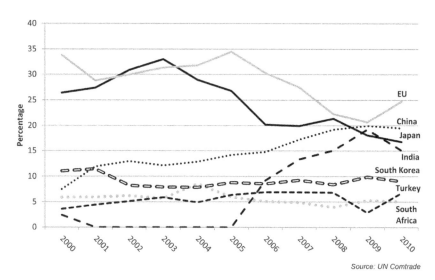

FIGURE APPENDIX 37. Percentage of Iran's Total Crude Export Revenues
Source: UN Comtrade

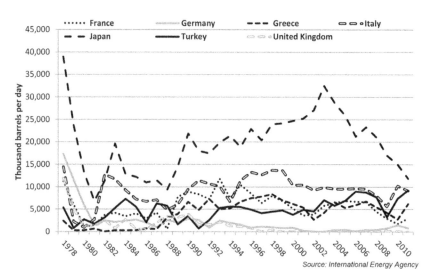

FIGURE APPENDIX 38. OECD Nations' Crude Oil Imports from Iran
Source: International Energy Agency

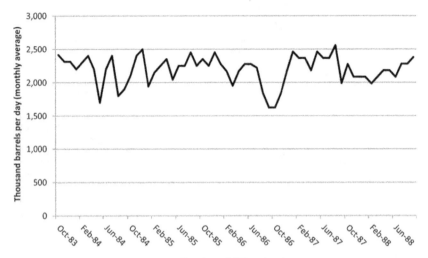

FIGURE APPENDIX 39. Iranian Wartime Oil Production
Source: U.S. Energy Information Administration

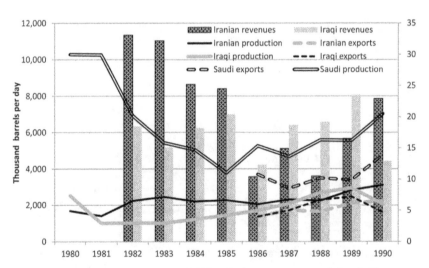

FIGURE APPENDIX 40. Wartime Oil Trends for Iran, Iraq, and the Gulf
Cooperation Council
Source: U.S. Energy Information Administration

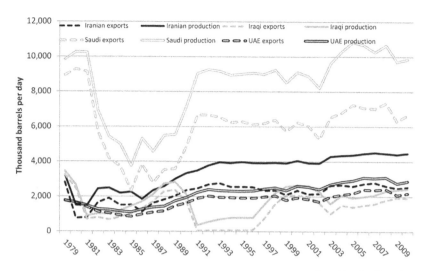

Source: International Energy Agency

FIGURE APPENDIX 41. Oil Production and Exports of Major Middle East
Producers
Source: International Energy Agency

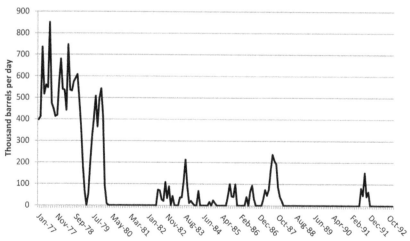

Source: U.S. Energy Information Administration

FIGURE APPENDIX 42. U.S. Imports of Iranian Crude Oil
Source: U.S. Energy Information Administration

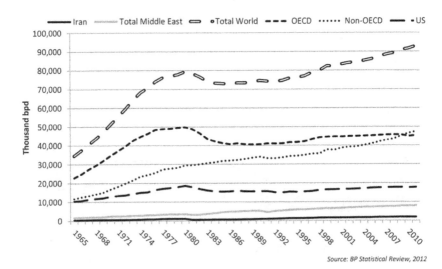

FIGURE APPENDIX 43. Refinery Capacity
Source: *BP Statistical Review*, 2012

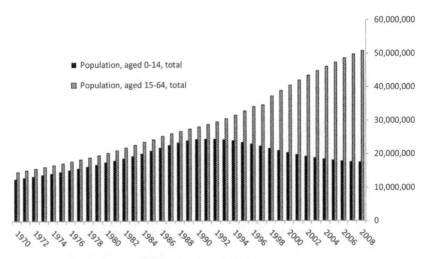

FIGURE APPENDIX 44. The Iranian Youth Bulge
Source: World Bank

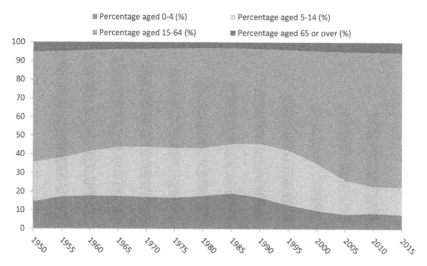

FIGURE APPENDIX 45. Iranian Demographic Shifts
Source: World Bank

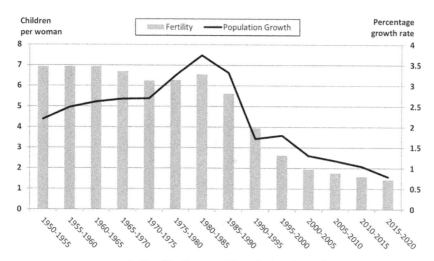

FIGURE APPENDIX 46. Fertility Rate and Population Growth
Source: Population Division of the Department of Economic and Social Affairs of
the United Nations Secretariat, *World Population Prospects: The 2010 Revision*

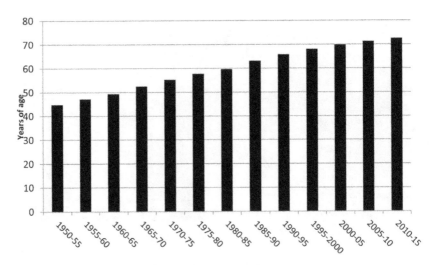

FIGURE APPENDIX 47. Life Expectancy at Birth
Source: UN Population Division, *World Population Prospects: The 2008 Revision*

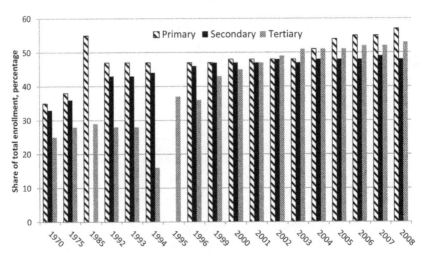

FIGURE APPENDIX 48. Females as a Percentage of Total Students
Source: World Bank

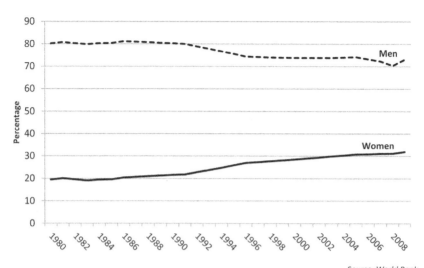

FIGURE APPENDIX 49. Labor Force Participation Rate by Gender
Source: World Bank

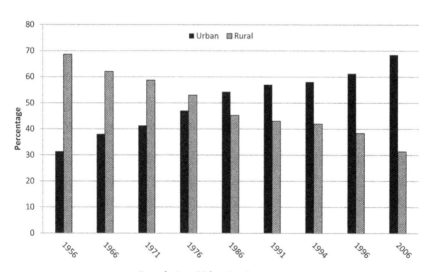

FIGURE APPENDIX 50. Population Urbanization
Source: United Nations Statistics Division Demographics Statistics

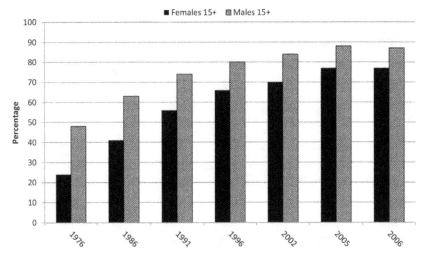

FIGURE APPENDIX 51. Literacy Rate by Gender
Source: World Bank

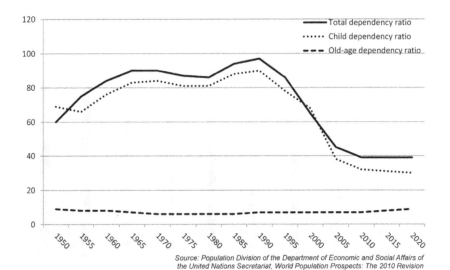

FIGURE APPENDIX 52. Dependency Ratios
Source: Population Division of the Department of Economic and Social Affairs of
the United Nations Secretariat, *World Population Prospects: The 2010 Revision*

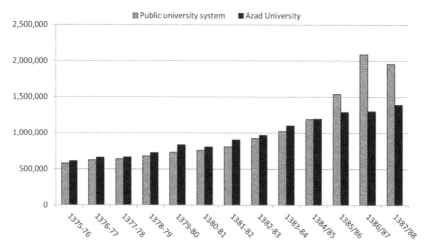

FIGURE APPENDIX 53. University Student Population
Source: Central Bank of Iran, Economic Report and Balance Sheet, Statistical
Appendices, 1379–1389

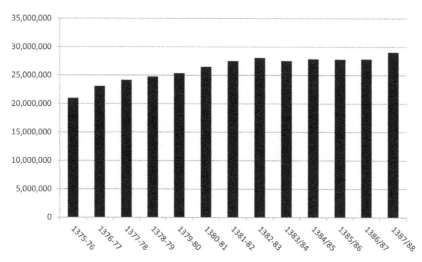

FIGURE APPENDIX 54. Population Served by Social Security Organization
Source: Central Bank of Iran, Economic Report and Balance Sheet, Statistical
Appendices, 1379–1389

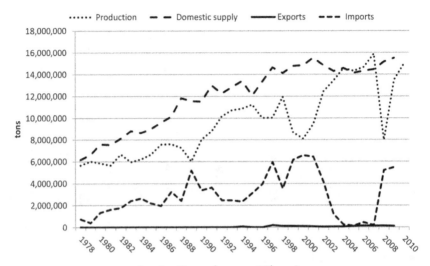

FIGURE APPENDIX 55. Iranian Dependence on Wheat Imports
Source: FAOStat, UN Food and Agriculture Organization

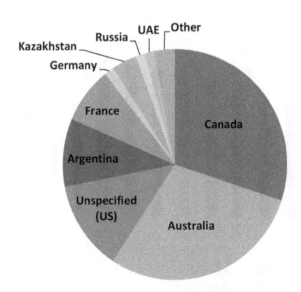

FIGURE APPENDIX 56. Primary Suppliers of Wheat to Iran, 1997–2010
Source: FAOStat, UN Food and Agriculture Organization

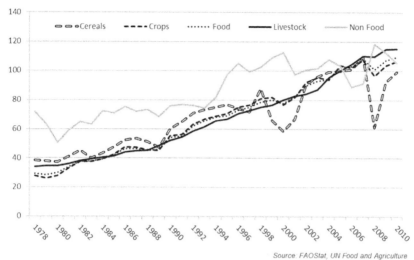

FIGURE APPENDIX 57. Production Indices of Iranian Agriculture
Source: FAOStat, UN Food and Agriculture Organization

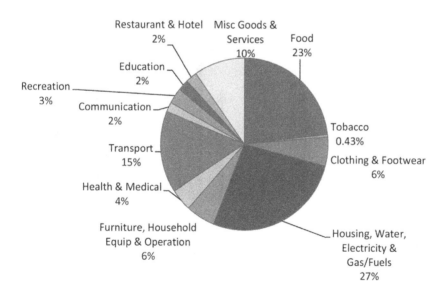

FIGURE APPENDIX 58. Average Urban Household Spending, 2005–06
Source: Central Bank of the Islamic Republic of Iran, General Directorate of
Economic Statistics, Household Budget Survey in Urban Areas in Iran 1384
(March 20, 2005–March 20, 2006)

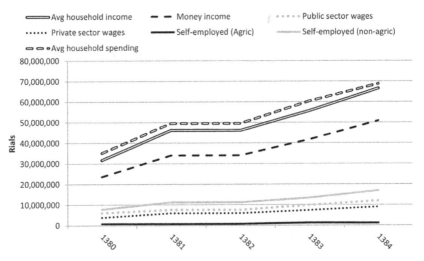

FIGURE APPENDIX 59. Urban Income and Spending
Source: Central Bank of the Islamic Republic of Iran, General Directorate of
Economic Statistics, Household Budget Survey in Urban Areas in Iran

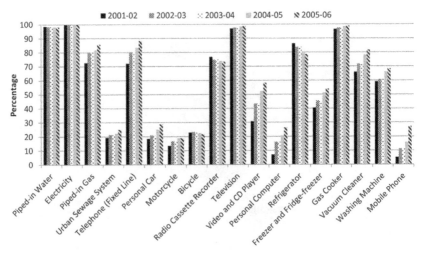

FIGURE APPENDIX 60. Urban Household Access to Amenities
Source: Central Bank of the Islamic Republic of Iran, General Directorate of
Economic Statistics, Household Budget Survey in Urban Areas in Iran

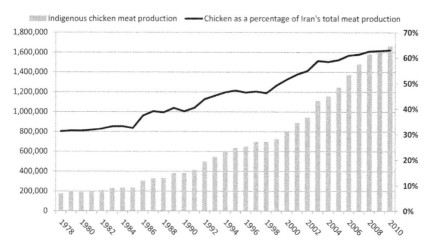

FIGURE APPENDIX 61. Increasing Importance of Chicken Consumption
Source: FAOStat, UN Food and Agriculture Organization

Selected References

Abdi, Abbas. *Power, Law, Culture: Political Editorials from the Newspaper Salaam [Qudrat, Qanun, Farhang: Yaddashtha-ye Siyasi-ye Ruznameh-ye Salaam].* Tehran: 1377 (1998/99).

Abedini, Jamal and Nicolas Peridy. "The Emergence of Iran in the World Car Industry: An Estimation of Its Export Potential." *The World Economy* (2009): 790–817.

Abghari, Siavash. "Political Economy of Political Power of the Islamic Regime in Iran." *Journal of Third World Studies* 24:1 (2007): 247–66.

Abidi, A. "The Iranian Revolution: Its Origins and Dimensions." *International Studies* 18:2 (April-June 1979): 129–61.

Abizadeh, Sohrab and Mahmood Yousefi. "Iran: Tax Structures Changes – a Time Series Analysis." *Bulletin for International Fiscal Documentation* 35:5 (May 1981): 202–6.

Abrahamian, Ervand. "Why the Revolution Survived." *Middle East Report* 250 (Spring 2009): 10–16.

A History of Modern Iran. Cambridge: Cambridge University Press, 2008.

Khomeinism: Essays on the Islamic Republic. Berkeley: University of California Press, 1993.

Iran between Two Revolutions. Princeton, NJ: Princeton University Press, 1987.

"The Crowd in Iranian Politics, 1905–53." In *Iran A Revolution in Turmoil,* ed. Haleh Afshar, 121–48. Basingstoke: Macmillan, 1985.

"Factionalism in Iran: Political Groups in the 14th Parliament (1944–46)." *Middle Eastern Studies* 14:1 (January 1978): 22–55.

Abrashami, Hadid. *The Iranian Economy [Eqtesad-e Iran].* Tehran: Scientific and Cultural, 1375 (1996/97).

Adelkhah, Fariba. "The Political Economy of the Green Movement." In Negin Nabavi, ed., *Iran: From Theocracy to the Green Movement,* 17–38. New York: Palgrave Macmillan, 2012.

Adelkhah, Fariba, Jean-Francois Bayart and Olivier Roy. *Thermidor en Iran.* Brussells: Editions Complexe, 1993.

Adib-Moghaddam, Arshin. "Inventions of the Iran–Iraq War." *Critique: Critical Middle Eastern Studies* 16:1 (Spring 2007): 63–83.

"Reflection on the Emerging Political Economy of Iran." *International Studies Journal* (Winter 2007): 23–37.

Afary, Janet. *The Iranian Constitutional Revolution, 1906–1911: Grassroots Democracy, Social Democracy, and the Origins of Feminism.* New York: Columbia University Press, 1996.

"Peasant Rebellions of the Caspian Region during the Iranian Constitutional Revolution, 1906–1909." *International Journal of Middle East Studies* 23:2 (May 1991): 137–61.

Afkhami, Gholam. *The Iranian Revolution: Thanatos on a National Scale.* Washington, DC: The Middle East Institute, 1985.

Afshar, Haleh. *Islam and Feminisms: An Iranian Case-Study.* New York: St. Martin's Press, 1998.

Afshari, M. Reza. "The Historians of the Constitutional Movement and the Making of the Iranian Populist Tradition." *International Journal of Middle East Studies* 25:3 (August 1993): 477–94.

Afshari, Mohammad Reza. "The Pishivaran and Merchants in Precapitalist Iranian Society: An Essay on the Background and Causes of the Constitutional Revolution." *International Journal of Middle East Studies* 15 (1983): 133–55.

Akhavi, Shahrough. "Elite Factionalism in the Islamic Republic of Iran." *Middle East Journal* 41:2 (Spring 1987): 181–201.

"Institutionalizing the New Order in Iran." *Current History* (February 1987): 53–6, 83–4.

"State Formation and Consolidation in Twentieth-Century Iran." In *The State, Religion, and Ethnic Politics: Afghanistan, Iran, and Pakistan*, eds. Myron Weiner and Ali Banuazizi, 198–226. Syracuse, NY: Syracuse University Press, 1986.

Religion and Politics in Contemporary Iran: Clergy-State Relations in the Pahlavi Period. Albany: State University of New York Press, 1980.

Akhavi-Pour, Hossein and Heidar Azondanloo. "Economic Bases of Political Factions in Iran." *Critique* (Fall 1998): 69–82.

Akhavi-Pour, Hossein. "Privatization in Iran: Analysis of the Process and Methods." In *Islam, Iran, and World Stability*, ed. Hamid Zanganeh, 187–99. New York: St. Martin's Press, 1994.

Alerassool, Mahvash. *Iran Market Structure and Prospects for the 1990s.* London: Middle East Economic Digest, 1993.

Freezing Assets: The USA and the Most Effective Economic Sanctions, New York: St. Martin's Press, 1993.

Alfoneh, Ali. *"How Intertwined Are the Revolutionary Guards in Iran's Economy?"* AEI Middle Eastern Outlook. Washington, DC, October 27, 2007.

Algar, Hamid. "The Oppositional Role of the Ulama in Twentieth-Century Iran." In *Scholars, Saints, and Sufis Muslim Religious Institutions in the Middle East since 1500*, ed. Nikki R. Keddie, 231–55. Berkeley: University of California Press, 1972.

Alizade, Parvin. "Industrial Development in Iran: Recent Changes and Past Experiences." In *Iran's Economy after the Two Wars: Reconstruction and Development*, ed. Anoushiravan Ehteshami, 169–227. London: Institute of Developing Studies, 1992.

Alnasrawi, Abbas. "Oil, Sanctions, Debt and the Future." *Arab Studies Quarterly* 23:4 (Fall 2001): 1–14.

"Economic Consequences of the Iraq-Iran War." *Third World Quarterly* 8:3 (July 1986): 869–95.

Alterman, Jon B. and John W. Garver. *The Vital Triangle: China, the United States, and the Middle East*. Washington, DC: Center for Strategic and International Studies, 2008.

Amid, Javad. "The Dilemma of Cheap Food and Self-Sufficiency: The Case of Wheat in Iran." *Food Policy* 32 (2007): 537–52.

Amin, S. H. "The Iran-Iraq Conflict: Legal Implications." *International and Comparative Law Quarterly* 31:1 (January 1982): 167–88.

Amirahmadi, Hooshang. "Iran's Development: Evaluation and Challenges." *Third World Quarterly* 17:1 (March 1996): 123–47.

"Iranian Recovery from Industrial Devastation During War with Iraq." In *The Long Road to Recovery: Community Responses to Industrial Disaster*, ed. James K. Mitchell. New York: United Nations University, 1996.

"Bunyad." In *Encyclopedia of the Modern Islamic World 1*, ed. John Esposito. New York: Oxford University Press, 1995.

"An Evaluation of Iran's First Development Plan and Challenges Facing the Second Plan." In *Proceedings of a one-day conference: Economic Development in Post-Revolutionary Iran*, March 3, 1995. Upper Montclair, NJ: Montclair State University.

"Towards a Multi-Gap Approach to Medium-Term Economic Growth in Iran." *Orient-Opladen* 33 (1992): 97–118.

"Economic Costs of the War and the Reconstruction in Iran." In *Modern Capitalism and Islamic Ideology in Iran*, eds. Cyrus Bina and Hamid Zaganeh, 257–81. London: MacMillan, 1992.

Revolution and Economic Transition The Iranian Experience. Albany: State University of New York Press, 1990.

"Economic Reconstruction of Iran: Costing the War Damage." *Third World Quarterly* 12:1 (January 1990): 26–47.

"The State and Territorial Social Justice in Postrevolutionary Iran." *International Journal of Urban and Regional Research* 13:1 (March 1989): 92–120.

Amirahmadi, Hooshang and Nader Entessar, eds. *Iran and the Arab World*. New York: St. Martin's Press, 1993.

Amirahmadi, Hooshang and Manoucher Parvin, eds. *Post-Revolutionary Iran*. Boulder, CO: Westview Press, 1988.

Amirahmadi, Hooshang and Hamid Zangeneh. "Iranian Government Budgets: An Analysis." *Journal of Public Budgeting, Accounting and Financial Management* 9:4 (Winter 1998): 572–89.

Amjad, Mohammad. *Iran from Royal Dictatorship to Theocracy*. New York: Greenwood Press, 1989.

Amuzegar, Jahangir. "The Islamic Republic of Iran: Facts and Fiction." *Middle East Policy* 19:1 (Spring 2012): 25–36.

"Iran's Fourth Plan: A Partial Assessment." *Middle East Policy* 17:4 (Winter 2010): 114–30.

"Iran's Twenty-Year Economic Perspective: Promises and Pitfalls." *Middle East Policy* 16:3 (Fall 2009): 41–57.

"Iran's Emerging Economic Threats." *MEES* 51:1 (January 7, 2008).

"Iran's Oil as a Blessing and a Curse." *Brown Journal of World Affairs* 15:1 (Fall/Winter 2008): 47–61.

"Iran Deals with the Oil Windfalls." *MEES* 51:9 (March 3, 2008).

"Iran's Emerging Economic Threats." *MEES* 51:1 (January 7, 2008).

"Islamic Social Justice, Iranian Style." *Middle East Policy* 14:3 (Fall 2007): 60–78.

"Iran's Third Development Plan: An Appraisal." *Middle East Policy* 12:3 (Fall 2005): 46–63.

"Iran's Precarious Public Finance." *MEES* 46:17 (April 28, 2003).

"Iran's Post-Revolution Planning: The Second Try." *Middle East Policy* 8:1 (March 2001): 25–42.

"Khatami and Iranian Economic Policy at Mid-Term." *Middle East Journal* 53:4 (Autumn 1999): 534–52.

"Khatami's Iran, One Year Later." *Middle East Policy* 6:2 (October 1998): 76–94.

"Iran's Economy and the US Sanctions." *Middle East Journal* 51:2 (Spring 1997): 185–99.

"Adjusting to Sanctions." *Foreign Affairs* 76:3 (May/June 1997): 31–41.

Iran's Economy under the Islamic Republic. London: I. B. Tauris, 1993.

The Dynamics of the Iranian Revolution: The Pahlavis' Triumph and Tragedy. Albany: State University of New York Press, 1991.

Amuzegar, Jahangir and Ali Fekrat. *Iran Economic Development under Dualistic Conditions*. Chicago: University of Chicago Press, 1971.

Anderson, Lisa. "Absolutism and the Resilience of Monarchy in the Middle East." *Political Science Quarterly* 106:1 (1991): 1–15.

Araghi, Farshad A. "Land Reform Policies in Iran." *American Journal of Agricultural Economics* 71:4 (November 1989): 1046–9.

Arasteh, Reza. "The Role of Intellectuals in Administrative Development and Social Change in Modern Iran." *International Review of Education* 9:3 (1963): 326–34.

Arjomand, Said Amir. *The Turban for the Crown: The Islamic Revolution in Iran*. New York and Oxford: Oxford University Press, 1988.

"Iran's Islamic Revolution in Comparative Perspective." *World Politics* 38 (April 1986): 383–414.

"Traditionalism in Twentieth-Century Iran." In *From Nationalism to Revolutionary Islam*, ed. Said Amir Arjomand, 195–232. Albany: State University of New York Press, 1984.

The Shadow of God and the Hidden Imam: Religion, Political Order, and Societal Change in Shi'ite Iran from the Beginning to 1980. Chicago: University of Chicago Press, 1984.

"Shi'ite Islam and the Revolution in Iran." *Government and Opposition* 16 (Summer 1981): 293–316.

ed. *Authority and Political Culture in Shi'ism.* Albany: State University of New York Press, 1988.

ed. *From Nationalism to Revolutionary Islam.* Albany: State University of New York Press, 1984.

Arrehchi, Ali. "Iran's Gas Vision: Priorities and Potentials." In *Shia Power: Next Target Iran?* eds. Michel Korinman and John Laughland, 227–233. London: Vallentine Mitchell, 2007.

Aryan, Hossein. "Iran: The Impact of Islamization on the Financial Markets." In *Islamic Financial Markets,* ed. Rodney Wilson, 155–70. London: Routledge, 1990.

Assadzadeh, Ahmad and Satya Paul. "Poverty, Growth and Redistribution: A Case Study of Iran." United Nations University World Institute for Development Economics Research Discussion Paper No. 2001/124 (November 2001).

Ashraf, Ahmad. "Theocracy and Charisma: New Men of Power in Iran." *International Journal of Politics, Culture and Society* 4:1 (1990): 113–52.

"Bazaar-Mosque Alliance: The Social Basis of Revolts and Revolutions." *International Journal of Politics, Culture and Society* 1 (Summer 1988): 538–67.

"The Roots of Emerging Dual Class Structure in Nineteenth-Century Iran." *Iranian Studies* 14:1–2 (1988): 5–27.

"Bazaar and Mosque in Iran's Revolution." *MERIP Reports* 113 (March/April 1983).

"Historical Obstacles to the Development of a Bourgeoisie in Iran." In *Studies in the Economic History of the Middle East,* ed. M. A. Cook, 308–32. Oxford: Oxford University Press, 1970.

Asheghian, Parvaiz. "Comparative Efficiencies of Foreign Firms and Local Firms in Iran." *Journal of International Business Studies* 13:3 (Winter 1982): 113–20.

Ashraf, Ahmad and Ali Banuazizi. "The State, Classes, and Modes of Mobilization in the Iranian Revolution" *State, Culture, and Society* 1 (Spring 1985): 3–39.

Ashraf, Ahmad and H. Hekmat. "Merchants and Artisans and the Developmental Processes of Nineteenth-Century Iran." In *The Islamic Middle East: 700–1900, Studies in Economic and Social History,* ed. A. Udovitch, 725–50. Princeton, NJ: Princeton University Press, 1981.

Askari, Hossein. "Iran's Economic Policy Dilemma." *International Journal* 59:3 (Summer 2004): 655–68.

Askari, Hossein and Noora Arfaa. "Social Safety Net in Islam: The Case of Persian Gulf Oil Exporters." *British Journal of Middle Eastern Studies* 34:2 (August 2007): 177–202.

Avery, Peter, Gavin Hambley and Charles Melville, eds. *Cambridge History of Iran, 7, From Nadir Shah to the Islamic Republic.* Cambridge: Cambridge University Press, 1991.

Ayubi, Nazih H. *Overstating the Arab State Politics and Society in the Middle East.* London: I. B. Tauris, 1995.

Azadi, Raha (pseud.). "Presidential Election and the Struggle for Rights and Civil Society: A Report from Iran." *The Review of Radical Political Economics* 30:2 (Spring 1998): 103–8.

Azimi, Hossein. *Madarha-ye Toseh-ye Niyoftegi dar Etesad-e Iran [Axes of Development in the Iranian Economy]*. Tehran: Nashrani, 1374 (1995/96).

Azkia, Mostafa and Seyed Ahmad Firouzabadi. "The Role of Social Capital in the Creation of Rural Production Associations: A Case Study of the Karkheh Dam Watershed Basin." *Critique* 15:3 (Fall 2006): 295–315.

Bahgat, Gawdat. "Iran's Role in Europe's Energy Security: An Assessment." *Iranian Studies* 43:3 (June 2010): 333–47.

"The Geopolitics of Natural Gas in Asia." *OPEC Review* (September 2001): 273–90.

Bahramitash, Roksana. "Market Fundamentalism versus Religious Fundamentalism: Women's Employment in Iran." *Critique: Critical Middle Eastern Studies* 13:1 (Spring 2004): 33–45.

Bakhash, Shaul. "Iran's Unlikely President." *The New York Review of Books* (November 5, 1998): 47–51.

"Iran's Remarkable Election." *Journal of Democracy* (January 1998): 80–94.

"Iran." *American Historical Review* (December 1991): 1479–96.

"The Politics of Land, Law, and Social Justice in Iran." *Middle East Journal* 43:2 (Spring 1989): 186–201.

The Reign of the Ayatollahs: Iran and the Islamic Revolution. New York: Basic Book, 1984.

"Sermons, Revolutionary Pamphleteering and Mobilisation: Iran, 1978." In *From Nationalism to Revolutionary Islam*, ed. Said Amir Arjomand, 177–94. Albany: State University of New York Press, 1984.

"The Politics of Oil and Revolution in Iran: A Staff Paper." Washington, DC: The Brookings Institution, 1982.

Iran: Monarchy, Bureaucracy and Reform under the Qajars 1858–1896. London: Ithaca Press, 1978.

Bakhshoodeh, M. "Impacts of World Prices Transmission to Domestic Rice Markets in Rural Iran." *Food Policy* 35 (2010): 12–19.

Baktiari, Bahman. *Parliamentary Politics in Revolutionary Iran: The Institutionalization of Factional Politics*. Gainesville: University Press of Florida, 1996.

"Parliamentary Elections in Iran." *Iranian Studies* 26:3–4 (Summer/Fall 1993): 375–89.

Banuazizi, Ali. "Faltering Legitimacy: The Ruling Clerics and Civil Society in Contemporary Iran." *International Journal of Politics, Culture and Society* 8:4 (1995): 563–78.

Bashiriyeh, Hossein. *The State and Revolution in Iran 1962–1982*. London: Croom Helm, 1984.

Bassiry, G. R. and R. H. Dekmejian. "MNCs and the Iranian Revolution: An Empirical Study." *Management International Review* 25:2 (1985): 67–75.

Bausani, Alessandro. *The Persians: From the Earliest Times to the Twentieth Century*. London: Elek Books, 1971.

Bayandor, Darioush. *Iran and the CIA: The Fall of Mosaddeq Revisited*. London: Palgrave Macmillan, 2010.

Bayart, Jean-François. "Republican Trajectories in Iran and Turkey: A Tocque-villian reading." In *Democracy without Democrats? The Renewal of Politics in the Muslim World,* ed. Ghassan Salamé. London: I. B. Tauris, 1994.

Bayat, Asef. *Making Islam Democratic: Social Movements and the Post-Islamist Turn.* Palo Alto, CA: Stanford University Press, 2007.

Street Politics Poor People's Movements in Iran. New York: Columbia University Press, 1997.

Bayat, Mangol. "Shi'a Islam as a Functioning Ideology in Iran: The Cult of the Hidden Imam." In *Iran since the Revolution: Internal Dynamics, Regional Conflict, and the Superpowers,* ed. Barry Rosen, 22–9. New York: Columbia University Press, 1985.

"The Iranian Revolution of 1978–79: Fundamentalist or Modern?" *The Middle East Journal* 37:1 (Winter 1983): 30–42.

Beblawi, Hazem and Giacomo Luciani, eds. *The Rentier State.* New York: Croom Helm, 1987.

Beck, Martin. *Oil-Rent Boom in Iran?* Hamburg: German Institute of Global and Area Studies, October 2009.

Beck. Peter J. "The Anglo-Persian Oil Dispute 1932–33." *Journal of Contemporary History* 9:4 (October 1974): 123–51.

Behdad, Sohrab. "Islamization of Economics in Iranian Universities." *International Journal of Middle East Studies* 27:2 (May 1995): 193–217.

"A Disputed Utopia: Islamic Economics in Revolutionary Iran." *Comparative Studies in Society and History* 36:4 (October 1994): 775–813.

"Property Rights and Islamic Economic Approaches." In *Islamic Economic Alternatives Critical Perspectives and New Directions,* ed. K. S. Jomo, 77–103. London: Macmillan, 1992.

"Winners and Losers of the Iranian Revolution: A Study in Income Distribution." *International Journal of Middle East Studies* 21 (1989): 327–58.

"Foreign Exchange Gap, Structural Constraint, and Political Economy of Exchange Rate Determination in Iran." *International Journal of Middle East Studies* 20 (1988): 1–21.

Behdad, Sohrab and Farhad Nomani. "What a Revolution! Thirty Years of Social Class Reshuffling in Iran." *Comparative Studies of South Asia, Africa and the Middle East* 29:1 (2009): 84–104.

Behnam, M. Reza. *Cultural Foundations of Iranian Politics.* Salt Lake City: University of Utah Press, 1986.

Benard, Cheryl and Zalmay Khalilzad. *"The Government of God" – Iran's Islamic Republic.* New York: Columbia University Press, 1984.

Benard, Cheryl "Secularization, Industrialization, and Khomeini's Islamic Republic." *Political Science Quarterly* 94:2 (Summer 1979): 229–41.

Bialer, Uri. "Fuel Bridge across the Middle East-Israel, Iran, and the Eilat-Ashkelon Oil Pipeline." *Israel Studies* 12:3 (Fall 2007): 29–67.

Bill, James A. "The Challenge of Institutionalization: Revolutionary Iran." *Iranian Studies* 26:3–4 (Summer/Fall 1993): 403–6.

The Eagle and the Lion: The Tragedy of American-Iranian Relations. New Haven, CT: Yale University Press, 1988.

"The Politics of Extremism in Iran." *Current History* (January 1982): 9–13, 36.

"Power and Religion in Revolutionary Iran." *The Middle East Journal* 36:1 (Winter 1982): 22–47.

Bill, James A. and Robert L. Hardgrave, Jr. *Comparative Politics: The Quest for Theory*. Lanham, MD: University Press of America, 1973.

Bina, Cyrus and Hamid Zanganeh, eds. *Modern Capitalism and Islamic Ideology in Iran*. London: MacMillan, 1992.

Bina, Cyrus. "Global Oil and the Oil Policies of the Islamic Republic." In *Modern Capitalism and Islamic Ideology in Iran*, eds. Cyrus Bina and Hamid Zangeneh, 121–57. New York: St. Martin's Press, 1992.

Binder, Leonard. "Iran's Unfinished Revolution: Possible Scenarios." *In Joint Economic Committee of the Congress of the United States, Economic Consequences of the Revolution in Iran*, 22–46. Washington, DC: U.S. Government Printing Office, November 19, 1979.

Bjorvatn, Kjetil and Kjetil Selvik. "Destructive Competition: Oil and Rent Seeking in Iran." Working Paper April 21, 2005.

Bonine, Michael E. and Nikki R. Keddie. *Continuity and Change in Modern Iran*. Albany: State University of New York Press, 1981.

Boroujerdi, Mehrzad. *Iranian Intellectuals and the West: A Study in Orientalism in Reverse*. Albany: State University of New York Press, 1992.

"Iranian Islam and the Faustian Bargain of Western Modernity." *Journal of Peace Research* 34:1 (February 1997): 1–5.

Bosworth, Edmund and Carole Hillenbrand, eds. *Qajar Iran: Political, Social and Cultural Change 1800–1925*. Edinburgh: Edinburgh University Press, 1983.

Bowden, Mark. *Guests of the Ayatollah: The First War in America's Battle with Militant Islam*. New York: Grove Press, 2006.

Brennan, John. "The Conundrum of Iran: Strengthening Moderates without Acquiescing to Belligerence." *Annals of the American Academy of Political and Social Science* 618 (July 2008): 168–79.

Brumberg, Daniel, Jareer Elass, Amy Myers Jaffe and Kenneth B. Medlock III. "Iran, Energy and Geopolitics." Working Paper (May 2008), James A. Baker III Institute for Public Policy at Rice University Energy Forum.

Brun, Thierry and Rene Dumont. "Imperial Pretensions and Agricultural Dependence." *MERIP Reports* 71 (October 1978): 15–20.

Bulloch, John and Harvey Morris. *The Gulf War: Its Origins, History and Consequences*. London: Methuen London, 1989.

Burke, III, Edmund and Paul Lubeck. "Explaining Social Movements in Two Oil-Exporting States: Divergent Outcomes in Nigeria and Iran." *Comparative Studies in Society and History* 29 (October 1987): 643–64.

Calabrese, John. *Revolutionary Horizons: Regional Foreign Policy in Post Khomeini Iran*. New York: St. Martin's Press, 1994.

"Peaceful or Dangerous Collaborators? China's Relations with the Gulf Countries." *Pacific Affairs* 65:4 (Winter 1992–1993): 471–85.

Calder, Kent E. "Coping with Energy Insecurity: China's Response in Global Perspective." *East Asia* 23:3 (Fall 2006): 49–66.

Cann, Rebecca and Constantine Danopoulos. "The Military and Politics in a Theocratic State: Iran as Case Study." *Armed Forces and Society* 24:2 (Winter 1997): 269–88.

Carey, Jane Perry Clark. "Iran and Control of Its Oil Resources." *Political Science Quarterly* 89:1 (March 1974): 147–74.

Carey, Jane Perry Clark and Andrew Galbraith Carey. "Oil and Economic Development in Iran." *Political Science Quarterly* 75:1 (March 1960): 66–86.

Carey, Jane Perry Clark, "Iran and Control of Its Oil Resources." *Political Science Quarterly* 89:1 (March 1974): 147–74.

Caron, David D. "The Nature of the Iran-United States Claims Tribunal and the Evolving Structure of International Dispute Resolution." *The American Journal of International Law* 84:1 (January 1990): 104–56.

Celasun Oya and Goswami Mangal. *An Analysis of Money Demand and Inflation in the Islamic Republic of Iran.* Washington, DC: International Monetary Fund, 2002.

Chaudhry, Kiren Aziz. *The Price of Wealth: Economies and Institutions in the Middle East.* Ithaca, NY: Cornell University Press, 1997.

"The Price of Wealth: Business and State in Labor Remittance and Oil Economies." *International Organization* 43:1 (Winter, 1989): 101–45.

Chehabi, H. E. "Religion and Politics in Iran: How Theocratic Is the Islamic Republic?" *Daedalus* 120 (Summer 1991): 69–91.

Iranian Politics and Religious Modernism: The Liberation Movement of Iran under the Shah and Khomeini. London: I. B. Tauris, 1990.

Chilcote, Ronald H. *Theories of Comparative Politics The Search for a Paradigm.* Boulder, CO: Westview Press, 1981.

Christopher, Warren and Richard M. Mosk. "The Iranian Hostage Crisis and the Iran-U.S. Claims Tribunal: Implications for International Dispute Resolution and Diplomacy." *Pepperdine Dispute Resolution Law Journal* 7:2 (2007): 165–76.

Chubin, Shahram and Charles Tripp. *Iran and Iraq At War.* Boulder, CO: Westview Press, 1988.

Chubin, Shahram. *Iran's National Security Policy: Capabilities, Intentions and Impact.* Washington, DC: The Carnegie Endowment for International Peace, 1994.

"The Last Phase of the Iran-Iraq War: From Stalemate to Ceasefire." *Third World Quarterly* 11:2 (April 1989): 1–14.

Clawson, Patrick, ed. *Iran's Strategic Intentions and Capabilities.* Washington, DC: National Defense University, 1994.

"The Islamic Republic's Economic Failure." *Middle East Quarterly* 15:4 (Fall 2008): 15–26.

"The Impact of the Military on Iran's Economy." In *The Economy of Islamic Iran: Between State and Market,* ed. Thierry Coville, 69–83. Tehran: Institut Français de Recherche en Iran, 1994.

"Knitting Iran Together: The Land Transport Revolution, 1920–1940." *Iranian Studies* 26:3/4 (Summer–Autumn 1993): 235–50.

"La situation économique: perspective et politique." *Les Cahiers de l'Orient* 3:18 (1990): 59–70.

"Islamic Iran's Economic Politics and Prospects." *Middle East Journal* 42:3 (December 1988): 371–89.

"Iran's Economy: Between Crisis and Collapse." *MERIP Reports* 98 (July-August 1981): 11–15.

Cohen, Jean L. and Andrew Arato. *Civil Society and Political Theory*. Cambridge, MA: The MIT Press, 1992.

Cook, M. A. *Studies in the Economic History of the Middle East*. Oxford: Oxford University Press, 1970.

Cooper, Andrew Scott. *The Oil Kings: How the U.S., Iran, and Saudi Arabia Changed the Balance of Power in the Middle East*. New York: Simon & Schuster, 2011.

"Showdown at Doha: The Secret Oil Deal That Helped Sink the Shah of Iran." *The Middle East Journal* 62:4 (Autumn 2008): 567–91.

Cordesman, Anthony H. *Iran's Military Forces in Transition: Conventional Threats and Weapons of Mass Destruction*. Westport, CT: Praeger, 1999.

Cottam, Richard W. *Iran and Iraq: The Threat from the Northern Gulf*. Boulder, CO: Westview Press, 1994.

"Charting Iran's New Course." *Current History* (January 1991): 21–4, 36–7.

The Iran and Iraq War and Western Security 1984–87: Strategic Implications and Policy Options. London: The Royal United Services Institute, 1987.

"The Iran-Iraq War." *Current History* (January 1984): 9–12, 40–1.

"Revolutionary Iran and the War with Iraq." *Current History* (January 1981): 5–9, 38–9.

Cordesman, Anthony H. and Abraham R. Wagner. *The Lessons of Modern War. II. The Iran Iraq War*. Boulder, CO: Westview Press, 1990.

Coulloudon, Virginie. "Privatization in Russia; Catalyst for the Elite." *The Fletcher Forum of World Affairs* 22:2 (Summer/Fall 1998): 43–56.

Coville, Thierry, ed. *The Economy of Islamic Iran: Between State and Market*. Tehran: Institut Français de Recherche en Iran, 1994.

Cronin, Stephanie. "Modernity, Change and Dictatorship in Iran: The New Order and Its Opponents, 1927–29." *Middle Eastern Studies* 39:2 (April 2003): 1–36.

"Modernity, Power and Islam in Iran: Reflections of Some Recent Literature (Review Article)." *Middle Eastern Studies* 37:4 (2001): 237–52.

"Riza Shah and the Disintegration of Bakhtiyari Power in Iran, 1921–1934." *Iranian Studies* 33:3/4 (Summer–Autumn, 2000): 349–76.

The Army and the Creation of the Pahlavi State in Iran, 1910–1926. London: Tauris Academic Studies, 1997.

Dabashi, Hamid. *Theology of Discontent: The Ideological Foundation of the Islamic Revolution in Iran*. New York: New York University Press, 1993.

Dadkhah, Kamran M. "From Global Capital to State Capitalism: The Evolution of Economic Thought in Iran, 1875–1925." *Middle Eastern Studies* 39:4 (October 2003): 140–58.

Dadvar, Faramarz. "Capitalism in Iran." *New Politics* 11:2 (Winter 2007): 135–38.

Daneshvar, Parviz. *Revolution in Iran*. London: MacMillan Press, 1996.

Davidheiser, Evelyn. "Strong States, Weak States: The Role of the State in Revolution." *Comparative Politics* 24 (July 1992): 463–75.

Davies, Graeme A. M. "Inside Out or Inside In: Domestic and International Factors Affecting Iranian Foreign Policy towards the United States 1990–2004." *Foreign Policy Analysis* 4 (2008): 209–25.

Davis, Eric and Nicolas Gavrielides. *Statecraft in the Middle East Oil, Historical Memory and Popular Culture.* Miami: Florida International University Press, 1991.

Denoeux, Guilain. *Urban Unrest in the Middle East: Comparative Study of Informal Networks in Egypt, Iran, and Lebanon.* Albany: State University of New York Press, 1993.

Dessouki, Ali E. Hilal and Alexander S. Cudsi, eds. *Islam and Power.* Baltimore: Johns Hopkins University Press, 1981.

Digard, Jean Pierre, Bernard Hourcade and Yann Richard. *L'Iran au xxe siècle.* Paris: Librairie Artème Fayard, 1996.

Dixon, John, ed. *Social Welfare in the Middle East.* London: Croom Helm, 1987.

Dodson, Michael and Manochehr Dorraj. "Populism and Foreign Policy in Venezuela and Iran." *Whitehead Journal of Diplomacy and International Relations* 9 (2008): 71–87.

Doenecke, Justus D. "Revisionists, Oil and Cold War Diplomacy." *Iranian Studies* 3:1 (Winter 1970): 23–33.

Doessel, D. P. and Abbas Valadkhani. "Economic Development and Institutional Factors Affecting Income Distribution." *International Journal of Social Economics* 25:2/3/4 (1998): 410–23.

Doessel, D. P. "An Analysis of Government Capital Expenditure in Iran, 1963–1993: Using Non-Tested Tests." *The Middle East Business and Economic Review* 10:1,2 (1998): 1–17.

Dominguez, Jorge I. and Christopher N. Mitchell. "The Roads Not Taken: Institutionalization and Political Parties in Cuba and Bolivia." *Comparative Politics* 9 (January 1977): 173–95.

Doner, Richard F. "Limits of State Strength: Toward an Institutionalist View of Economic Development." *World Politics* 44 (April 1992): 398–431.

Dorraj, Manoucher. "Populism and Corporatism in Post-Revolutionary Political Culture." *Political Culture in the Islamic Republic*, eds. Samih K. Farsoun and Mehrdad Mashayekhi, 209–28. London: Routledge, 1992.

From Zarathustra to Khomeini: Populism and Dissent in Iran. Boulder, CO: Lynne Rienner, 1990.

Ehsani, Kaveh. "Rural Society and Agricultural Development in Post-Revolution Iran: The First Two Decades." *Critique: Critical Middle Eastern Studies* 15:1 (2006): 79–96.

"'Tilt but Don't Spill:' Iran's Development and Reconstruction Dilemma." *Middle East Report* 191 (November-December 1994): 16–21.

The Poverty of Revolution The State and the Urban Poor in Mexico. Princeton, NJ: Princeton University Press, 1977.

Ehteshami, Anoushiravan. "Islamic Governance in Post-Khomeini Iran." In *Islamic Fundamentalism*, eds. Anoushiravan Ehteshami and Abdel Salam Sidahmed, 143–62. Boulder, CO: Westview Press, 1996.

After Khomeini: The Iranian Second Republic. London: Routledge, 1995.

The Politics Of Economic Restructuring In Post-Khomeini Iran. University of Durham, Centre for Middle Eastern and Islamic Studies, CMEIS Occasional Paper No. 50, July 1995.

"Iran Boosts Domestic Arms Industry." *International Defense Review* 27:4 (April 1, 1994): 72.

"Iran." In *Economic and Political Liberalisation in the Middle East*, ed. T. Niblock, 214–36. London: British Academic Press, 1993.

Ehteshami, Anoushiravan and Raymond A. Hinnebusch. *Syria and Iran Middle Powers in a Penetrated Regional System*. London and New York: Routledge, 1997.

Ehteshami, Anoushiravan and Abdel Salam Sidahmed, eds. *Islamic Fundamentalism*. Boulder, CO: Westview Press, 1996.

Ehteshami, Anoushiravan, Kamron Mofid (sic), Parvin Alizadeh and Tetsuo Hamauzu. *Iran's Economy after the Two Wars: Reconstruction and Development*. Institute for Developing Economies, 1992.

Eiland III, Murry. "Mixed Messages and Carpet Diplomacy: Opportunities for Détente with Iran." *Middle East Policy* 6:2 (October 1998): 130–9.

Eisenstadt, Michael. *Iranian Military Power: Capabilities and Intentions*. Washington, DC: The Washington Institute for Near East Policy, 1996.

El-Erian, Mohamed A. and Manmohan S. Kumar. *"Mobilization of Saving in Developing Countries: The Case of the Islamic Republic of Iran."* International Monetary Fund Working Paper (WP/96/136), Middle Eastern and Research Departments, December 1996.

Elm, Mostafa. *Oil, Power, and Principle: Iran's Oil Nationalization and Its Aftermath*. Syracuse, NY: Syracuse University Press, 1992.

Emami, Karim, ed. *Rooz-haye atesh, rooz-haye khun: gozaresh-e msavvari az piroozi-ye enquelab-e eslami-ye iran [Days of Fire, Days of Blood: An Illustrated Report of the Islamic Revolution of Iran]*. Tehran: Zamineh, 1979.

Enayat, Hamid. "Iran: Khumayni's Concept of the 'Guardianship of the Juriscon-sult.'" In *Islam in the Political Process*, ed. James Piscatori, 160–80. Cambridge: Cambridge University Press, 1983.

Modern Islamic Political Thought The Response of the Shî'î and Sunnî Muslims to the Twentieth Century. London: MacMillan Education, 1982.

Entessar, Nader. "Factional Politics in Post Khomeini Iran: Domestic and Foreign Policy Implications." *Journal of South Asian and Middle East Studies* 17 (Summer 1994): 21–43.

"The Challenge of Political Reconstruction in Iran." In *Iran and the Arab World*, eds. Hooshang Amirahmadi and Nader Entessar, 217–33. New York: St. Martin's Press, 1993.

Esfandiari, Haleh and A. L. Udovitch, eds. *The Economic Dimensions of Middle Eastern History*. Princeton, NJ: The Darwin Press, 1990.

Esposito, John L., ed. *The Iranian Revolution: Its Global Impact*. Miami: Florida International University Press, 1990.

ed. *Encyclopedia of the Modern Islamic World 1*. New York: Oxford University Press, 1995.

Evans, Peter. "The Eclipse of the State? Reflections on Stateness in an Era of Globalization." *World Politics* 50 (October 1997): 62–87.

Embedded Autonomy: States and Industrial Transformation. Princeton, NJ: Princeton University Press, 1995.

"The State as Problem and Solution: Predation, Embedded Autonomy and Structural Change." In *The Politics of Economic Adjustment: International Constraints, Distributive Conflicts, and the State*, eds. Stephen Haggard and Robert R. Kaufman, 139–81. Princeton, NJ: Princeton University Press, 1992.

Evans, Peter, Dietrich Rueschemeyer and Evelyne Huber Stephens, eds. *States vs. Markets in the World System*. Beverly Hills, CA: Sage, 1985.

Evans, Peter, Dietrich Rueschemeyer and Theda Skocpol, eds. *Bringing the State Back In*. Cambridge: Cambridge University Press, 1985.

Faghfoory, Mohammad H. "The Ulama-State Relations in Iran: 1921–1941." *International Journal of Middle East Studies* 19:4 (November 1987): 413–32.

Fairbanks, Stephen C. "Theocracy versus Democracy: Iran Considers Political Parties." *Middle East Journal* 52:1 (Winter 1998): 17–31.

Farazmand, Ali. *The State, Bureaucracy, and Revolution in Modern Iran: Agrarian Reforms and Regime Politics*. New York: Praeger, 1989.

Farhi, Farideh. *States and Urban-Based Revolutions: Iran and Nicaragua*. Urbana: University of Illinois Press, 1990.

"Class Struggles, the State, and Revolution in Iran." In *Power and Stability in the Middle East*, ed. Berch Berberoglu, 90–113. London: Zed Books, 1989.

"State Disintegration and Urban-Based Revolutionary Crisis." *Comparative Political Studies* 21:2 (July 1988): 321–56.

Farman Farmaian, Sattareh with Dona Munker, *Daughter of Persia: A Woman's Journey from her Father's Harem through the Islamic Revolution*. New York: Doubleday, 1992.

Farmanesh, Amir. *"Regional Dimensions of Economic Development in Iran, a New Economic Geography Approach."* Paper presented at "Iranian Economy at a Crossroads: Domestic and Global Challenges" conference, University of Southern California, September 18–19, 2009.

Farsoun, Samih K. and Mehrdad Mashayekhi, eds. *Political Culture in the Islamic Republic*. London: Routledge, 1992.

Farzanegan, Mohammad Reza and Gunther Markwardt. "The Effects of Oil Price Shocks on the Iranian Economy." *Energy Economics* (2008).

Farzanegan, Mohammad Reza "Illegal Trade in the Iranian Economy: Evidence from a Structural Model." *CESIFO Working Paper No.* 2397 (September 2008).

Farzin, Hossein. "The Political Economy of Foreign Exchange Reform." In *Iran after the Revolution: Crisis of an Islamic State*, eds. Saeed Rahnema and Sohrab Behdad, 174–200. London: I. B. Tauris, 1995.

Farzin, Y. H. "Foreign Exchange Reforms in Iran: Badly Designed, Badly Managed." *World Development* 23:6 (1995): 987–1001.

Fathi, Asghar. "Role of the Traditional Leader in Modernization of Iran, 1890–1910." *International Journal of Middle East Studies* 11:1 (February 1980): 87–98.

Feierabend, Ivo K., with Rosalind L. Feierabend and Betty A. Nesvold. "The Comparative Study of Revolution and Violence." *Comparative Politics* 5:3 (April 1973): 393–424.

Ferdous, Emad. "The Reconstruction Crusade and Class Conflict in Iran." *MERIP Reports* 113 (March-April 1983): 11–15.

Ferrero, Mario and Ronald Wintrobe. *The Political Economy of Theocracy.* New York: Palgrave MacMillan, 2009.

Fesharaki, Fereidun. *Development of the Iranian Oil Industry International and Domestic Aspects.* New York: Praeger, 1976.

Firoozi, Ferydoon. "Income Distribution and Taxation Laws of Iran." *International Journal of Middle East Studies* 9:1 (January 1978): 73–87.

Firouzabadi, Kamal Dehgani. "Analysis on Obstacles to Direct Investment in Iran." *International Studies Journal* 6:3 (2010): 117–35.

Fischer, Michael M. J. "Repetitions in the Iranian Revolution." In *Shi'ism, Resistance, and Revolution*, ed. Martin Kramer. Boulder, CO: Westview Press, 1987.

"Islam and the Revolt of the Petit Bourgeoisie." *Daedalus* 111:1 (1982): 101–25.

Iran: From Religious Dispute to Revolution. Cambridge, MA: Harvard University Press, 1980.

Foran, John, ed. *A Century of Revolution: Social Movements in Iran.* Minneapolis: University of Minnesota Press, 1994.

"The Concept of Dependent Development as a Key to the Political Economy of Qajar Iran (1800–1925)" *Iranian Studies* 22:2/3 (1989): 5–56.

"Theories of Revolution Revisted: Toward a Fourth Generation?" *Sociological Theory* 11:1 (March 1993): 1–20.

Foran, John and Jeff Goodwin. "Revolutionary Outcomes in Iran and Nicaragua: Coalition Fragmentation, War, and the Limits of Social Transformation." *Theory and Society* 22:2 (April 1993): 209–47.

Fossum, John Erik. *Oil, the State, and Federalism: the Rise and Demise of Petro-Canada as a Statist Impulse.* Toronto: University of Toronto, 1997.

Francisco, Ronald A. *The Politics of Regime Transitions.* Boulder, CO: Westview Press, 2000.

Frings-Hessami, Khadija V. "The Islamic Debate about Land Reform in the Iranian Parliament, 1981–86." *Middle Eastern Studies* 37:4 (October 2001): 136–81.

Fuller, Graham E. *The Center of the Universe: The Geopolitics Of Iran.* Boulder, CO: Westview Press, 1991.

"Repairing U.S.-Iranian Relations." *Middle East Policy* 6:2 (October 1998): 140–4.

Gable, Richard. "Electric Utilities and Their Regulation in Iran." *Land Economics* 33:2 (May 1957): 127–38.

Garver, John W. *China and Iran: Ancient Partners in a Post-Imperial World.* Seattle: University of Washington Press, 2006.

Gasiorowski, Mark J. and Malcolm Byrne, eds. *Mohammad Mosaddeq and the 1953 Coup in Iran.* Syracuse, NY: Syracuse University Press, 2004.

Gasiorowski, Mark J. "Economic Crisis and Political Change: An Event History Analysis." *The American Political Review* 89:4 (1995): 882–97.

"The 1953 Coup d'Etat in Iran." *International Journal of Middle East Studies* 19 (August 1987): 261–86.

Gellner, Ernest and John Waterbury, eds. *Patrons and Clients in Mediterranean Societies.* London: Gerald Duckworth, 1977.

Ghamari-Tabrizi, Behrooz. "Memory, Mourning, Memorializing : On the Victims of Iran-Iraq War, 1980–Present." *Radical History Review* 105 (Fall 2009): 106–21.

Ghani, Cyrus. *Iran and the Rise of Reza Shah: From Qajar Collapse to Pahlavi Power*. London: I. B. Tauris, 2000.

Gharehbaghian, Morteza. "Oil Revenues and the Militarisation of Iran: 1960–1978." *Social Scientist* 15:4/5 (May 1987): 87–100.

Ghasimi, M. R. "The Iranian Economy after the Revolution in an Economic Appraisal of the Five Year Plan." *International Journal of Middle Eastern Studies* 24:3 (October 1992): 599–614.

Ghasimi, Reza. "Iran's Oil Nationalization and Mossadegh's Involvement with the World Bank." *Middle East Journal* 65:3 (Summer 2001): 442–56.

Ghods, M. Reza. "Government and Society in Iran, 1926–34." *Middle Eastern Studies* 27:2 (April 1991): 219–30.

Iran in the Twentieth Century A Political History. Boulder, CO: Lynne Rienner, 1989.

Ghoreishi, Ahmad and Dariush Zahedi. "Prospects for Regime Change in Iran." *Middle East Policy* 5:1 (January 1997): 85–101.

Giddens, Anthony. *The Nation-State and Violence*. Berkeley: University of California Press, 1987.

Gieling, Saskia. "The *Marja'iya* in Iran and the Nomination of Khamanei in December 1994." *Middle Eastern Studies* 33:4 (October 1997): 777–87.

Gilbar, Gad G. "The Opening Up of Qājār Iran: Some Economic and Social Aspects." *Bulletin of the School of Oriental and African Studies* 49:1 (1986): 76–89.

"Trends in the Development of Prices in Late Qajar Iran, 1870–1906." *Iranian Studies* 16:3/4 (Summer–Autumn 1983): 177–98.

Gill, Anthony and Arang Keshavarzian. "State Building and Religious Resources: An Institutional Theory of Church-State Relations in Iran and Mexico." *Politics and Society* 27:3 (1999): 431–65.

Gillespie, Kate. "US Corporations and Iran at the Hague." *Middle East Journal* 44:1 (Winter, 1990): 18–36.

Golnar, Mehran. "Social Implications of Literacy in Iran." *Comparative Education Review* 36:2 (May 1992): 194–211.

Goode, James F. *The United States and Iran: In the Shadow of Mussadiq*. New York: St. Martin's Press, 1997.

Gossen, A. Nicholas. "Does the Price of Watermelons Matter? Economic Performance and Political Legitimacy in the Islamic Republic of Iran." *Al Nakhlah* (Fall 2007): 1–12.

Graham, Robert. *Iran: The Illusion of Power*. New York: St. Martin's Press, 1978.

Green, James A. "The Oil Platforms Case: An Error in Judgment?" *Journal of Conflict and Security Law* 9:3 (December 1, 2004): 357–86.

Green, Jerrold D. "Ideology and Pragmatism in Iranian Foreign Policy." *Journal of South Asian and Middle East Studies* 17:1 (Fall 1993): 57–75.

"Iran's Foreign Policy: Between Enmity and Conciliation." *Current History* (January 1983): 12–16.

Griffith, William E. "The Revival of Islamic Fundamentalism: The Case of Iran." *Hamdard Islamicus* 111:1 (Spring 1980): 47–55.

Grummon, Stephen R. *The Iran-Iraq War: Islam Embattled*. Washington, DC: Center for Strategic and International Studies and Praeger, 1982.

Guillaume, Dominique and Roman Zytek. *Islamic Republic of Iran*. Washington, DC: International Monetary Fund, 2010.

Gurdon, Charles. "Iran's Presidential Elections." *Japanese Institute of Middle Eastern Economies Review* 22 (Autumn 1993): 5–17.

Habibi, Nader. *"The Impact of Sanctions on Iran-GCC Economic Relations."* Crown Center for Middle East Studies, Brandeis University, Middle East Brief 45 (November 2010).

Haeri, Shahla. "Women and Fundamentalism and in Iran and Pakistan." In *Fundamentalisms and Society: Reclaiming the Sciences, the Family and Education*, eds. Martin E. Marty and R. Scott Appleby, 181–213. Chicago: University of Chicago Press, 1993.

Haggard, Stephan and Marcus Noland. "Sanctioning North Korea: The Political Economy of Denuclearization and Proliferation." *Asian Survey* 50:3 (2010): 539–68.

Haggard, Stephen and Robert R. Kaufman, eds. *The Politics of Economic Adjustment: International Constraints, Distributive Conflicts, and the State*. Princeton, NJ: Princeton University Press, 1992.

Haghayeghi, Mehrdad. "Agricultural Development Planning under the Islamic Republic of Iran." *Iranian Studies* 23:1/4 (1990): 5–29.

"Agrarian Reform Problems in Post-Revolutionary Iran." *Middle Eastern Studies* 26:1 (January 1990): 35–51.

Hakimian, H. *Labour Transfer and Economic Development: Theoretical Perspectives and Studies from Iran*. Hemel Hempstead: Harvester-Wheatsheaf, 1990.

Hakimian, Hassan and Jeffrey B. Nugent, eds. *Trade Policy and Economic Integration in the Middle East And North Africa: Economic Boundaries in Flux*. London: Routledge, 2005.

Hall, Peter A. and Rosemary C. R. Taylor. "Political Science and the Three Institutionalisms." *Political Studies* 44 (December 1996): 936–57.

Halliday, Fred. "What Does Mohammed Khatami Think? Mohammed and Mill." *The New Republic* (October 5, 1998): 30–4.

"An Elusive Normalization: Western Europe and the Iranian Revolution." *Middle East Journal* 48:2 (Spring 1994): 309–26.

Iran Dictatorship and Development. London: Penguin Books, 1979.

"Theses on the Iranian Revolution." *Race and Class* 11:1 (1979): 81–90.

"Iran: The Economic Contradictions." *MERIP Reports* 69 (1978): 9–8, 23.

Harik, Iliya. "Privatization: The Issue, the Prospects, and the Fears." In *Privatization and Liberalization in the Middle East*, eds. Iliya Harik and Denis J. Sullivan, 1–23. Bloomington: Indiana University Press, 1992.

Harik, Iliya and Denis J. Sullivan, eds. *Privatization and Liberalization in the Middle East*. Bloomington: Indiana University Press, 1992.

Harney, Desmond. "Some Explanations for the Iranian Revolution." *Asian Affairs* 11, (1980): 134–43.

Harold, Scott and Alireza Nader. *"China and Iran: Economic, Political, and Military Relations."* RAND Corporation Center for Middle East Policy Occasional Paper (2012).

Harris, Kevan. "Lineages of the Iranian Welfare State: Dual Instutionalism and Social Policy in the Islamic Republic of Iran." *Social Policy & Administration* 44:6 (December 2010): 727–45.

Hassan, Riaz. "Iran's Islamic Revolutionaries: Before and after the Revolution." *Third World Quarterly* 6:3 (July 1984): 675–88.

Henry, Clement M. and Robert Springborg. *Globalization and the Politics of Development in the Middle East.* Cambridge: Cambridge University Press, 2001.

Hen-Tov, Elliot and Nathan Gonzalez. "The Militarization of Post-Khomeini Iran: Praetorianism 2.0." *The Washington Quarterly* 34:1 (Winter 2011): 45–59.

Hessi, Mary Ann. *Empire and Nationhood: The United States, Great Britain, and Iranian Oil, 1950–1954,* New York: Columbia University Press (1997).

Hetherington, Norriss S. "Industrialization and Revolution in Iran: Forced Progress or Unmet Expectation?" *The Middle East Journal* 36:3 (Summer 1982): 362–73.

Hickman, William F. *Ravaged and Reborn: The Iranian Army, 1982.* Washington, DC: The Brookings Institution, 1982.

Higgins, Patricia J. "Minority-State Relations in Contemporary Iran." In *The State, Religion, and Ethnic Politics: Afghanistan, Iran, and Pakistan*, eds. Myron Weiner and Ali Banuazizi, 167–97. Syracuse, NY: Syracuse University Press, 1986.

Hiro, Dilip. *The Longest War: The Iran-Iraq Conflict.* New York: Routledge, 1991. *Iran under the Ayatollahs.* London: Routledge & Kegan Paul, 1985.

Hoodfar, Homa. "Bargaining with Fundamentalism: Women and the Politics of Population Control in Iran." *Reproductive Health Matters* 4:8 (November 1996): 30–40.

"Devices and Desires: Population Policy and Gender Roles in the Islamic Republic." *Middle East Report* 190 (September–October 1994): 11–17.

Hoodfar, Homa and Samad Assadpour. "The Politics of Population Policy in the Islamic Republic of Iran." *Studies in Family Planning* 31:1 (March 2000): 19–34.

Hooglund, Eric. "Khatami's Iran." *Current History* (February 1999): 59–64.

"Iran 1980–85: Political and Economic Trends." In *The Iranian Revolution and the Islamic Republic*, eds. Nikki R. Keddie and Eric Hooglund, 17–31. Syracuse, NY: Syracuse University Press, 1986.

"Social Origins of the Revolutionary Clergy." In *The Iranian Revolution and the Islamic Republic*, eds. Nikki R. Keddie and Eric Hooglund, 74–83. Syracuse, NY: Syracuse University Press, 1986.

Hosseini, Hamid. "The Change of Economic and Industrial Policy in Iran: President Rafsanjani's Perestroika." In *Islam, Iran, and World Stability*, ed. Hamid Zanganeh, 167–86. New York: St. Martin's Press, 1994.

"From Buchanan to Khomeini: Can Neoclassical Economics Explain the 'Ideal' Islamic State of Iran's Despotic Ayatollah?" *American Journal of Economics and Sociology* 49:2 (April 1990): 167–84.

"Notions of Private Property in Islamic Economics in Contemporary Iran: A Review of Literature." *International Journal of Social Economics* 15:9 (1988): 51–7.

Hourcade, Bernard. *"Post Islamist Iran."* Washington, DC: Working Paper, Institute for National Strategic Studies, National Defense University, January 1997.

Hunter, Shireen T. "Is Iranian Perestroika Possible without Fundamental Change?" *The Washington Quarterly* (Autumn 1998): 23–41.

Iran after Khomeini. Washington, DC: The Center for Strategic and International Studies, 1992.

Iran and The World: Continuity in a Revolutionary Decade. Bloomington: Indiana University Press, 1990.

ed. *Internal Developments in Iran*. Washington, DC: Center for Strategic and International Studies, 1985.

Huntington, Samuel P. *Political Order in Changing Societies*. New Haven, CT: Yale University Press, 1968.

Huntington, Samuel P. and Clement H. Moore, eds. *Authoritarian Politics in Modern Society: The Dynamics of Established One-Party Systems*. New York: Basic Book, 1970.

Huq, Ataul. *Development and Distribution in Islam*. Malaysia: Pelanduk, 1997.

Ibrahimi, Hamid. *Eqtesad-e Iran [The Iranian Economy]*. Tehran: Scientific and Cultural, 1375 (1996–97).

Ikenberry, G. John. "The International Spread of Privatization Policies: Inducements, Learning, and 'Policy Bandwagoning,'" In *The Political Economy of Public Sector Reform and Privatization*, eds. Ezra N. Suleiman and John Waterbury, 88–113. Boulder, CO: Westview Press, 1990.

"The Irony of State Strength: Comparative Responses to the Oil Shocks in the 1970s." *International Organization* 40:1 (Winter 1986): 105–37.

Ilchman, Warren F. and Norman Thomas Uphoff. *The Political Economy of Change*. Berkeley: University of California Press, 1971.

Indyk, Martin, Graham Fuller, Anthony Cordesman and Phebe Marr. "Symposium on Dual Containment: U.S. Policy toward Iran & Iraq." *Middle East Policy* 3:1 (1994): 1–26.

International Monetary Fund, Staff Representatives for the 2008 Consultation with the Islamic Republic of Iran. *Staff Report for the 2008 Article IV Consultation*. Washington, DC: International Monetary Fund, August 2008.

Islamic Republic of Iran: Statistical Appendix. Washington, DC: IMF Publication Services, May 1999.

Islamic Republic of Iran: Recent Economic Developments, IMF Staff Country Report No. 98/27. Washington, DC: IMF Publication Services, April 1998.

Islamic Republic of Iran – Recent Economic Developments, IMF Staff Country Report No. 95/121 Washington, DC: IMF Publication Services, December 1995.

Investment Company of the National Iranian Industrial Organization. *Privatization from Theory to Action [Khasusi-sazi az Teuri ta Aml]*. Tehran: 1374 (1995/96).

Iran Research Group. *Iran Yearbook 1989–1990*. Bonn: MB Medien & Bucher Verlagsgesellschaft mbH, 1989.

"Iran's Islamic Fundamentalism: A View from the Pulpit." *Terrorism* 12 (1989): 401–16.

Issawi, Charles. "Iran's Economic Upsurge." *Middle East Journal* 21:4 (Autumn 1967): 447–61.

ed. *The Economic History of Iran 1800–1914*. Chicago: University of Chicago Press, 1971.

Jacqz, Jane W., ed. *Iran: Past, Present and Future*. New York: Aspen Institute for Humanistic Studies, 1976.

Jalali-Naini, Ahmad R. "Capital Accumulation and Economic Growth in Iran." *Iranian Studies* 38:1 (March 2005): 91–116.

Javanparast, Sara, Fran Baum, Ronald Labonte, David Sanders, Gholamreza Haidari and Sakineh Rezaie. "A Policy Review of the Community Health Worker Programme in Iran." *Journal of Public Health Policy* 32:2: 263–76.

Javidan, Mansour. "Vision and Inspiration: A Study of Iranian Executives." *Journal of Transnational Management Development*: 2:2 (1996): 69–85.

Jomayoun, Assad. "Iran's Administration Persists in Searching for Jihad While Neglecting Its Domestic Base." *Defense & Foreign Affairs Strategic Policy* 21:7 (July 31, 1993): 8–9.

Joyner, Christopher C., ed. *The Persian Gulf War: Lessons for Strategy, Law and Diplomacy*. New York: Greenwood Press, 1990.

Kamali, Masoud. *Revolutionary Iran: Civil Society and State in the Modernization Process*. Aldershot, UK: Ashgate, 1998.

Kaplan, Robert D. *The Ends of the Earth: From Togo to Turkmenistan, from Iran to Cambodia – a Journey to the Frontiers of Anarchy*. New York: Random House, 1996.

"A Bazaari's World." *The Atlantic Monthly* 277:3 (March 1996): 28–31.

Karbassian, Akbar. "Islamic Revolution and the Management of the Iranian Economy." *Social Research* 67:2 (Summer 2000): 622–40.

Karimi, S. "Economic Policies and Structural Changes since the Revolution." In *The Iranian Revolution and the Islamic Republic*, eds. Nikki R. Keddie and Eric Hooglund, 32–54. Syracuse, NY: Syracuse University Press, 1986.

Karimi, Zahra. "Financing Job Guarantee Schemes by Oil Revenue: The Case of Iran." The Levy Economics Institute of Bard College Working Paper 527 (January 2008).

Karl, Terry Lynn. *The Paradox of Plenty: Oil Booms and Petro-States*. Berkeley: University of California Press, 1997.

Karsh, Ephraim, ed. *The Iran-Iraq War Impact and Implications*. New York: St. Martin's Press, 1989.

Karshenas, Massoud. "Structural Adjustment and the Iranian Economy." In *Economic Challenges Facing Middle Eastern and North African Countries: Alternative Futures*, ed. Nemat Shafik, 202–24. New York: St. Martin's Press, 1998.

Oil, State, and Industrialization in Iran. Cambridge: Cambridge University Press, 1990.

Karshenas, Massoud and Hassan Hakimian. "Oil Economic Diversification and the Democratic Process in Iran." *Iranian Studies* 38:1 (March 2005): 67–90.

Karshenas, Massoud and M. Hashem Pesaran. "Economic Reform and the Reconstruction of the Iranian Economy." *Middle East Journal* 49:1 (Winter 1995): 89–111.

Kashani-Sabet, Firoozeh. "Fragile Frontiers: The Diminishing Domains of Qajar Iran." *International Journal of Middle East Studies* 29:2 (May 1997): 205–34.

Katouzian, Homa. "Arbitrary Rule: A Comparative Theory of State, Politics and Society in Iran." *British Journal of Middle Eastern Studies* 24:1 (May 1997): 49–73.

Musaddiq and The Struggle for Power in Iran. New York: St. Martin's Press, 1990.

"The Political Economy of Iran since the Revolution: A Macro-Historical Analysis." *Comparative Economic Studies* 31:3 (1989): 55–66.

The Political Economy of Modern Iranian Despotism and Pseudo-Modernism, 1926–1979. New York: New York University Press, 1981.

Katz, Mark N. "The United States and Iran: Ready for Rapprochement?" *SAIS Review* 18:2 (Summer-Fall 1998): 171–83.

Revolutions and Revolutionary Waves. New York: St. Martin's Press, 1997.

Katzman, Kenneth. "Hamas's Foreign Benefactors." *Middle East Quarterly* (June 1995): 33–8.

The Warriors of Islam: Iran's Revolutionary Guard. Boulder, CO: Westview Press, 1993.

"The Pasdaran: Institutionalization of Revolutionary Armed Force." *Iranian Studies* 26, Nos. 3–4 (Summer/Fall 1993): 389–402.

Kaussler, Bernd. "European Union Construction Engagement with Iran (2000–2004): An Exercise in Conditional Human Rights Diplomacy." *Iranian Studies* 41:3 (June 2008): 269–95.

Kazemi, Farhad. "Civil Society and Iranian Politics." In *Civil Society in the Middle East 2*, ed. Augustus Richard Norton, 119–52. New York: E. J. Brill, 1996.

"Models of Iranian Politics, the Road to the Islamic Revolution, and the Challenge of Civil Society." *World Politics* 47 (July 1995): 555–74.

"The Fada'iyan-e Islam: Fanaticism, Politics and Terror." In *From Nationalism to Revolutionary Islam*, ed. Said Amir Arjomand, 158–73. Albany: State University of New York Press, 1984.

Poverty and Revolution in Iran: The Migrant Poor, Urban Marginality, and Politics. New York: New York University Press, 1980.

Kazemi, Farhad and Ervand Abrahamian. "The Nonrevolutionary Peasantry of Modern Iran." *Iranian Studies* 11:1/4 (1978): 259–304.

Kavoussi, Rostam M. "Trade Policy and Industrialization in an Oil-Exporting Country: The Case of Iran." *The Journal of Developing Areas* (July 1986): 453–72.

"Urban Migrants and the Revolution." *Iranian Studies* 13 (1980): 257–77.

Kazemipur, Abdolmohammad and Ali Rezaei. "Religious Life under Theocracy: The Case of Iran." *Journal for the Scientific Study of Religion* 42:3 (September 2003): 347–61.

Keddie, Nikki R. "The Origins of the Religious-Radical Alliance in Iran." *Past and Present* 34 (July 1996): 70–80.

"Iranian Revolutions in Comparative Perspective." *American Historical Review* 88:3 (June 1983): 579–98.

"The Iranian Revolution and U.S. Policy." *SAIS Review* No. 3 (Winter 1981/1982): 13–26.

Roots of Revolution: An Interpretive History of Modern Iran. New Haven, CT: Yale University Press, 1981.

"Is Shi'ism Revolutionary?" In *The Islamic Revolution and the Islamic Republic*, eds. Nikki R. Keddie and Eric Hooglund, 113–26. Syracuse, NY: Syracuse University Press, 1986.

"The Roots of the Ulama's Power in Modern Iran." In *Scholars, Saints, and Sufis Muslim Religious Institutions in the Middle East since 1500*, ed. Nikki R. Keddie, 211–55. Berkeley: University of California Press, 1972.

"The Economic History of Iran, 1800–1914, and Its Political Impact: An Overview." *Iranian Studies* 5:2/3 (Spring–Summer 1972): 58–78.

"The Iranian Power Structure and Social Change 1800–1969: An Overview." *International Journal of Middle East Studies* 2:1 (January 1971): 3–20.

"Religion and Irreligion in Early Iranian Nationalism." *Comparative Studies in Society and History* 4 (1962): 265–95.

"The Economic History of Iran, 1800–1914, and Its Political Impact: An Overview." *Iranian Studies* (Spring-Summer 1972): 58–78.

ed. *Debating Revolutions.* New York: New York University Press, 1995.

Keddie, Nikki R. and Eric Hooglund, eds. *The Islamic Revolution and the Islamic Republic.* Syracuse, NY: Syracuse University Press, 1986.

Keddie, Nikki R. and Farah Monian. "Militancy and Religion in Contemporary Iran." In *Fundamentalisms and the State: Remaking Polities, Economies, and Militance*, eds. Martin E. Marty and R. Scott Appleby, 511–38. Chicago: University of Chicago Press, 1993.

Kedourie, Elie and Sylvia G. Haim, eds. *Towards a Modern Iran: Studies in Thought, Politics and Society.* London: Frank Cass, 1980.

Kelidar, Abbas. "Ayatollah Khomeini's Concept of Islamic Government." In *Islam and Power*, eds. Ali Dessouki and Alexander S. Cudsi, 75–92. Baltimore: Johns Hopkins University Press, 1981.

Kent, Marian. *Moguls and Mandarins Oil, Imperialism and the Middle East in British Foreign Policy 1900–1940.* London: Frank Cass, 1993.

Keshavarzian, Arang. "Regime Loyalty and Bazari Representation under the Islamic Republic of Iran: Dilemmas of the Society of Islamic Coalition." *International Journal of Middle East Studies* 41 (2009): 225–46.

Khajehpour, Bijan. "Domestic Political Reforms and Private Sector Activity in Iran." *Social Research* 67:2 (Summer 2000): 577–98.

Khalatbari, Firouze. "The Tehran Stock Exchange and Privatisation of Public Sector Enterprises in Iran: A Study of Obstacles to the Private Sector Development." In *The Economy of Islamic Iran: Between State and Market*, ed. Thierry Coville, 177–208. Tehran: Institut Français de Recherche en Iran, 1994.

Khashadourian, Edmund and Abbas P. Grammy. "The Political Economy of Growth-Inflation Transmission: The Case of Iran." *Review of Middle East Economics and Finance* 2:2 (2004): 109–21.

Khatim, Mohammad A. "Structure of the Public and Private Sector in Pre-Revolutionary Iran." In *The Economy of Islamic Iran between State and Market*, ed. Thierry Colville, 29–36. Tehran: Institut Français de Recherche en Iran, 1994.

Kheirabadi, Masoud. *Iranian Cities Formation and Development*. Austin: University of Texas Press, 1991.

Khomeini, Ruhollah. *Topics in Economic Guidance in the Statements of Imam Khomeini [Matalib va mawzu`at va rahnamudha-yi iqtisadi dar bayanat-i Hazrat-i Imam Khumayni]*, Vol. 1. Tehran: Muassasah-i Mutala`at va Pizhuhishha-yi Bazargani, 1985.

*Topics in Economic Guidance in the Statements of Imam Khomeini [Matalib va mawzu`at va rahnamudha-yi iqtisadi dar bayanat-i Hazrat-i Imam Khumayni]*, Vol. 3. Tehran: Muassasah-i Mutala`at va Pizhuhishha-yi Bazargani, 1987.

*Topics in Economic Guidance in the Statements of Imam Khomeini [Matalib va mawzu`at va rahnamudha-yi iqtisadi dar bayanat-i Hazrat-i Imam Khumayni]*, Vol. 4. Tehran: Muassasah-i Mutala`at va Pizhuhishha-yi Bazargani, 1990.

Iman Khomeini's Last Will and Testament. Washington, DC: Interests Section of the Islamic Republic of Iran, Embassy of the Democratic and Popular Republic of Algeria, 1989.

Islam and Revolution: Writings and Declarations of Imam Khomeini, trans. Hamid Algar. Berkeley: Mizan Press, 1981.

Khoshroo, Gholamali. "The Experience of the Islamic Republic of Iran." In *Islamic Perspectives on the New Millennium*, eds. Virginia Matheson Hooker and Amin Saikal, 150–8. Singapore: ISEAS (2004).

Kia, Mehrdad. "Persian Nationalism and the Campaign for Language Purification." *Middle Eastern Studies* 34:2 (April 1998): 9–36.

Kian-Thiébaut, Azadeh. *Secularization of Iran: A Doomed Failure? The New Middle Class and the Making of Modern Iran*. Paris: Peeters, 1998.

Kozhanov, Nikolay A. "U.S. Economic Sanctions against Iran: Undermined by External Factors." *Middle East Policy* 18:3 (Fall 2011): 144–60.

Kramer, Martin, ed. *Shi'ism, Resistance, and Revolution*. Boulder, CO: Westview Press, 1987.

Kuran, Timur. "The Economic Impact of Islamic Fundamentalism." In *Fundamentalisms and the State: Remaking Polities, Economies, and Militance*, eds. Martin E. Marty and R. Scott Appleby, 302–41. Chicago: University of Chicago Press, 1993.

"The Economic System in Contemporary Islamic Thought." In *Islamic Economic Alternatives Critical Perspectives and New Directions*, ed. K. S. Jomo, 9–47. London: Macmillan, 1992.

"Economic Justice in Contemporary Islamic Thought." In *Islamic Economic Alternatives Critical Perspectives and New Directions*, ed. K. S. Jomo, 49–75. London: Macmillan, 1992.

"On the Notion of Economic Justice in Contemporary Islamic Thought." In *The Economic Dimensions of Middle Eastern History*, eds. Haleh Esfandiari and A. L. Udovitch, 93–121. Princeton, NJ: The Darwin Press, 1990.

Ladier-Fouladi, Marie. "Sociodemographic Changes in the Family and Their Impact on the Sociopolitical Behavior of Youth in Postrevolutionary Iran." In *Iran: From Theocracy to the Green Movement* ed. Negin Nabavi, 137–65. (New York: Palgrave Macmillan, 2012).

Lahsaeizadeh, Abdolali. "Contemporary Rural Production Cooperatives in Iran." *Annals of Public and Co-Operative Economy* 61:1 (January 1990): 117–24.

Lai, Hongyi Harry. "China's Oil Diplomacy: Is It a Global Security Threat?" *Third World Quarterly* 28:3 (2007): 519–37.

Lambton, A. K. S. "Some of the Problems Facing Persia." *International Affairs* 22:2 (March 1946): 254–72.

Lawson, Fred H. "Using Positive Sanctions to End International Conflicts: Iran and the Arab Gulf Countries." *Journal of Peace Research* 20:4 (December 1983): 311–28.

Lenczowski, George. "Iran: The Big Debate." *Middle East Policy* 3:2 (June 1994): 52–62.

Russia and the West in Iran, 1918–1948. Ithaca, NY: Cornell University Press, 1949.

Liu, Michael Tien-Lung. "States and Urban Revolutions: Explaining the Revolutionary Outcome in Iran and Poland." *Theory and Society* 17 (1988): 179–209.

Looney, Robert E. *"The Re-Emergence of Iranian Petro-Populism."* *Gulf Yearbook 2006–07* (Dubai, UAE: Gulf Research Center, 2007): 417–26.

"The Role of Military Expenditures in Pre-Revolutionary Iran's Economic Decline." *Iranian Studies* 21:3/4 (1988): 52–83.

The Economic Origins of the Iranian Revolution. New York: Pergamon Press, 1982.

The Economic Development of Iran. New York: Praeger, 1973.

Looney, Robert E. and David Winterford. *Economic Causes and Consequences of Defense Expenditures in the Middle East and South Asia*. Boulder, CO: Westview Press, 1995.

Luhr, Nadia L. "Iran, Social Media, and U.S. Trade Sanctions: The First Amendment Implications of U.S. Foreign Policy." *First Amendment Law Review* 8 (Spring 2010): 500–32.

Luong, Pauline Jones and Erika Weinthal. "Rethinking the Resource Curse: Ownership Structure, Institutional Capacity, and Domestic Constraints." *Annual Review of Political Science* 9 (2006): 241–63.

MacDonald, Charles. "The Kurdish Challenge and Revolutionary Iran." *Journal of South Asian and Middle Eastern Studies* 13:1,2 (Fall/Winter 1989): 52–69.

Mackey, Sandra, *The Iranians: Persia, Islam and the Soul of a Nation*. New York: E. P. Dutton, 1996.

Mafi, Homayoun. "Iran's Concession Agreements and the Role of the National Iranian Oil Company: Economic Development and Sovereign Immunity." *Natural Resources Journal* 48 (Spring 2008): 407–30.

Mahdavy, H. "The Patterns and Problems of Economic Development in Rentier States: The Case of Iran." In *Studies in the Economic History of the Middle East*, ed. M. A. Cook, 428–67. Oxford: Oxford University Press, 1970.

Majd, M. G. "The 1951–53 Oil Nationalization Dispute and the Iranian Economy: A Rejoinder." *Middle Eastern Studies* 31:3 (July 1995): 449–59.

Mahmoudi, Vahid. "Poverty Changes during the Three Recent Development Plans in Iran (1995–2007)." *African and Asian Studies* 10 (2011): 157–79.

Majidpour, Mehdi. "The Unintended Consequences of US-Led Sanctions on Iranian Industries." *Iranian Studies* 46:1 (January 2013): 1–15.

"Land Reform Policies in Iran: Reply." *American Journal of Agricultural Economics* 71:4 (November 1989): 1050–3.

"Land Reform Policies in Iran." *American Journal of Agricultural Economics* 69:4 (November 1987): 843–8.

Makdisi, George. *The Rise of Colleges: Institutions of Learning in Islam and the West*. Edinburgh: Edinburgh University Press, 1981.

Malek, M. "The Impact of Iran's Islamic Revolution on Health Personnel Policy." *World Development*: 19:8 (1991): 1045–54.

Maleki, Abbas. "Energy Supply and Demand in Eurasia: Cooperation between EU and Iran." *China and Eurasia Forum Quarterly* 5:4 (2007): 103–13.

Maljoo, Mohammad. "The Dominant Economic Discourse of Today's Iran in Retrospect." *Oeconomicus* 7 (2004–2005): 25–36.

Mann, Michael. "Nation-States in Europe and Other Continents: Diversifying, Developing, Not Dying." *Daedalus* 122:3 (Summer 1993): 115–40.

Mansur, Abul Kasim, "The Crisis in Iran: Why the US Ignored a Quarter Century of Warning." *Armed Forces Journal* (January 1979): 26.

Marku, Marenglen and Djavad Salehi-Isfahani. "Reversal of Fortunes: A Cohort Analysis of Lifetime Earnings in Iran." Working Paper, January 2008.

Marsh, Steve. "Thirty Years On: Iran's 'Silent Revolution.'" *Iranian Studies* 42:2 (April 2009): 213–29.

"The United States, Iran and Operation 'Ajax': Inverting Interpretative Orthodoxtiy." *Middle Eastern Studies* 39:3 (July 2003): 1–38.

Martin, V. A. "The Anti-Constitutionalist Arguments of Shaikh Fazlallah Nuri." *Middle Eastern Studies* 22:2 (April 1986): 181–96.

"Shaikh Fazlallah Nuri and the Iranian Revolution 1905–09." *Middle Eastern Studies* 23:1 (January 1987): 39–53.

Martin, Vanessa. *The Qajar Pact: Bargaining, Protest and the State in Nineteenth-Century Persia*, London: I. B. Tauris, 2005.

"Mudarris, Republicanism and the Rise to Power of Riza Khan, Sardar-I Sipah." *British Journal of Middle Eastern Studies* 21:2 (1994): 199–210.

"Religion and State in Khumaini's 'Kashf al-asrar'." *Bulletin of the School of Oriental and African Studies* 56:1 (1993): 34–45.

Islam and Modernism: The Iranian Revolution of 1906. Syracuse, NY: Syracuse University Press, 1989.

Mashayekhi, Merhdad. "The Revival of the Student Movement in Post-Revolutionary Iran." *International Journal of Politics, Culture, and Society* 15:2 (Winter 2001): 283–313.

Mather, Yassamine "The Latest Economic Crisis in Iran and the Continued Threat of War." *Critique* 37:1 (February 2009): 67–79.

Matin-asgari, Afshin. "The Causes of Iran's Backwardness." *Critique* (Fall 1998): 103–7.

Maull, Hans W. and Otto Pick, eds. *The Gulf War: Regional and International Dimensions*. New York: St. Martin's Press, 1989.

Mazaheri, Nimah. "An 'Informal' Revolution: State-Business Conflict and Institutional Change in Iran." *Middle Eastern Studies* 44:4 (2008): 585–602.

Mazaheri, Tahmaseb and Mansour Javidan. "HE Tahmaseb Mazaheri, Minister of Economy, on the Iranian Economy." *The Academy of Management Executive* 17:4 (1993): 143–5.

Mazarei, Jr., Adnan. "The Iranian Economy under the Islamic Republic: Institutional Change and Macroeconomic Performance (1979–1990)." *Cambridge Journal of Economics* 20:3 (May 1996): 289–314.

McDaniel, Tim. *Autocracy, Modernization, and Revolution in Russia and Iran.* Princeton, NJ: Princeton University Press, 1991.

McGee, Robert W. and Mahdi Nazemi Ardakani, *The Ethics of Tax Evasion: A Case Study of Opinion In Iran.* Miami: Florida International University Chapman Graduate School of Buisness, January 2009.

McLachlan, K. S. "Food Supply and Agricultural Self-Sufficiency in Contemporary Iran." *Bulletin of the School of Oriental and African Studies, University of London* 49:1 (1986): 148–62.

McNaugher, Thomas and William Quandt. "Oil and the Outome of the Iran-Iraq War." *MERIP Reports* (July–September 1984).

Mehran, Golnar. "Khatami, Political Reform and Education in Iran." *Comparative Education* 39:3 (August 2003): 311–29.

Menashri, David, *Revolution at a Crossroads: Iran's Domestic Politics and Regional Ambitions.* Washington, DC: The Washington Institute for Near East Policy, 1997.

"Strange Bedfellows: The Khomeini Coalition." *Jerusalem Quarterly* (Summer 1979): 38–48.

Metcalf, Gilbert E. and Catherine Wolfram. "Cursed Resources? Political Conditions and Oil Market Outcomes." National Bureau of Economic Research Working Paper 16614, December 2010.

Mir-Hosseini, Ziba. *Islam and Gender: The Religious Debate in Contemporary Iran.* Princeton, NJ: Princeton University Press, 1999.

Mohsen M. Milani. "Political Participation in Revolutionary Iran." In *Political Islam: Revolution, Radicalism, or Reform?* ed. John L. Esposito, 77–93. Boulder, CO: Lynne Rienner, 1997.

The Making of Iran's Islamic Revolution: From Monarchy to Islamic Republic. Boulder, CO: Westview Press, 1994.

"Power Shifts in Revolutionary Iran." *Iranian Studies* 26:3–4 (Summer/Fall 1993): 389–402.

Marriage on Trial: A Study of Islamic Family Law : Iran and Morocco Compared. London: I. B. Tauris, 1993.

"The Ascendance of Shi'i Fundamentalism in Revolutionary Iran." *Journal of South Asian and Middle Eastern Studies* 13:1/2 (Fall/Winter 1989): 5–28.

Moaddel, Mansoor. *Class, Politics, and Ideology in the Iranian Revolution.* New York: Columbia University Press, 1993.

"Shi'i Political Discourse and Class Mobilization in the Tobacco Movement of 1890–1892." *Sociological Forum* 7:3 (September 1992): 447–68.

"Class Struggle in Post-Revolutionary Iran." *IJMES* 23:3 (August 1991): 317–43.

Mofid, Kamran. *The Economic Consequences of the Gulf War*. London: Routledge, 1990.

Development Planning in Iran: From Monarchy to Islamic Republic. Wisbech: Middle East and North African Studies Press, 1987.

Moghadam, Fatemeh E. "State, Political Stability and Property Rights." In *Iran after the Revolution: Crisis of an Islamic State*, eds. Saeed Rahnema and Sohrab Behdad, 45–64. London: I. B. Tauris, 1995.

"Property Rights and Islamic Revolution in Iran." In *The Economic Dimensions of Middle Eastern History*, eds. Haleh Esfandiari and A. L. Udovitch, 147–77. Princeton, NJ: The Darwin Press, 1990.

"An Historical Interpretation of the Iranian Revolution." *Cambridge Journal of Economics* 12:4 (December 1988): 401–18.

Moghadam, Valentine. "Revolution, Religion, and Gender Politics: Iran and Afghanistan Compared." *Journal of Women's History* 10:4 (Winter 1999): 172–95.

"Islamic Populism, Class, and Gender in Post-Revolutionary Iran." In *A Century of Revolution: Social Movements in Iran*, ed. John Foran, 189–222. Minneapolis: University of Minnesota Press, 1994.

Moghissi, Haideh. *Populism and Feminism in Iran: Women's Struggle in a Male-Defined Revolutionary Movement*. New York: St. Martin's Press, 1994.

Mohaddessin, Mohammad, *Islamic Fundamentalism: The New Global Threat*. Washington, DC: Seven Locks Press, 1993.

Moin, Baqer. *Khomeini: Life of the Ayatollah*. London: I. B. Tauris, 1999.

Mojab, Shahrzad, *The State and the University: The 'Islamic Cultural Revolution' in the Institutions of Higher Education of Iran, 1980–1987*. Unpublished doctoral dissertation, University of Illinois at Urbana-Champaign, 1991.

Mokhtari, Fariborz. "Iran's 1953 Coup Revisited: Internal Dynamics versus External Intrigue." *Middle East Journal* 62:3 (Summer 2008): 457–88.

Momeni, Jamshid. "The Roots of Revolution in Iran." *Journal of Political and Military Sociology* 8 (Fall 1980): 287–99.

Monshipouri, Mahmood. "Iran's Search for the New Pragmatism." *Middle East Policy* 6:2 (October 1998): 95–112.

Moore, James W. "An Assessment of the Iranian Military Rearmament Program." *Comparative Strategy* (October–December 1994): 371–87.

Morady, Farhang. "Oil, the State and Industrial Development in Post-Revolutionary Iran." *Amsterdam Middle East Papers* no. 7 (November 1996).

Moshaver, Shahrzad. "Mostazafan and Janbazan Foundation under Majlis Scrutiny." *Payam-e Emrooz* No. 4 (February & March 1995): 22–3.

Moshiri, Farrokh, "Revolutionary Conflict Theory in an Evolutionary Perspective." In *Revolutions of the Late Twentieth Century*, eds. Jack A. Goldstone, Ted Robert Gurr and Farrokh Moshiri, 116–35. Boulder, CO: Westview Press, 1991.

The State and Social Revolution in Iran: A Theoretical Perspective. New York: Peter Lang, 1985.

Mottahedeh, Roy Parviz. "Iran's Foreign Devils." *Foreign Policy* No. 38 (Spring 1980): 19–34.

Mottahedeh, Roy. *The Mantle of the Prophet Religion and Politics in Iran.* New York: Pantheon Books, 1985.

Mottale, Morris M. *Iran: The Political Sociology of the Islamic Revolution.* Lanham, MD: University Press of America, 1995.

Mozaffari, Mehdi. "Changes in the Iranian Political System after Khomeini's Death." *Political Studies* (December 1993): 611–17.

"Why the Bazar Rebels." *Journal of Peace Research* 28:4 (November 1991): 377–91.

Authority in Islam From Muhammad to Khomeini. Armonk, NY: M. E. Sharpe, 1987.

Naghshineh-Pour, Amir. "A Review and Analysis of Iran's Current Economic Status." (October 15, 2008).

Najmabadi, Afsaneh, *Land Reform and Social Change in Iran.* Salt Lake City: University of Utah Press, 1987.

"Depoliticisation of a Rentier State: The Case of Pahlavi Iran." In *The Rentier State*, eds. Hazem Beblawi and Giacomo Luciani, 211–27. New York: Croom Helm, 1987.

"Iran's Turn to Islam: From Modernism to a Moral Order." *Middle East Journal* 41:2 (Spring 1987): 202–17.

"Mystifications of the Past and Illusions of the Future." In *The Islamic Revolution and the Islamic Republic*, eds. Nikki R. Keddie and Eric Hooglund, 147–70. Syracuse, NY: Syracuse University Press, 1986.

Naqvi, S. H. N., H. U. Beg, Rafiq Ahmed and Mian M. Nazeer, "Principles of Islamic Economic Reform." In *Islamic Economic Alternatives Critical Perspectives and New Directions*, ed. K. S. Jomo, 153–87. London: Macmillan, 1992.

Naraghi, Ehsan. Translated by Nilou Mobasser. *From Palace to Prison: Inside the Iranian Revolution.* Chicago: Ivan R. Dee, 1994.

Nash, Manning. "Islam in Iran: Turmoil, Transformation or Transcendence?" *World Development* 8 (July/August 1980): 555–61.

Nashat, Guity. "From Bazaar to Market: Foreign Trade and Economic Development in Nineteenth Century Iran." *Iranian Studies* 14:1–2 (Winter/Spring 1981): 53–85.

National Iranian Investment Organization Investment Company. *Khasusi-sazi az teyuri ta Aml [Privatization From Theory to Implementation].* Tehran: Agah, 1374 (1995/96).

Nejad, Hassan M. "Preconditions and Processes of the Iranian Revolution: A Theoretical and Comparative Analysis." *The Search* 5 (December 1984): 45–71.

Nelson, Joan. "The Politics of Economic Transformation: Is Third World Experience Relevant in Eastern Europe?" *World Politics* 45 (April 1993): 433–63.

ed. *Fragile Coalitions: The Politics of Economic Adjustment.* New Brunswick, NJ: Transaction Books, 1989.

Nettl, J. P. "The State as a Conceptual Variable." *World Politics* 20:4 (July 1968): 559–92.

Nezam-Mafi, Mansoureh E. "Merchants and Government, Tobacco and Trade: The Case of Kordestan, 1333 AH/1919 AD." *Iranian Studies* 20:1 (1987): 1–15.

Niblock, Tim and Emma Murphy, eds. *Economic and Political Liberalization in the Middle East*. London: British Academic Press, 1993.

Nili, Massoud. *Eqtesad-e Iran (The Iranian Economy)*. Tehran: Higher Institute for Research in Planning and Development, 1376 (1997/98).

Norton, Augustus Richard. *Civil Society in the Middle East 2*. Leiden: E. J. Brill, 1996.

ed. *Civil Society in the Middle East 1*. Leiden: E. J. Brill, 1995.

"Reflections on the Dilemma of Reform in the Middle East." *Critique* (Fall 1998): 61–7.

Nourafchian, Nicolo. "Constructive Partner or Menacing Threat? Analyzing China's Role in the Iranian Nuclear Program." *Asian Security* 6:1 (2010): 28–50.

Nourizadeh, Ali. "Editorial." *Al-Moujez an-Iran* 7:6 (February 1998).

Nowshirvani, Vahid F. and Robert Bildner. "Direct Foreign Investment in the Non-Oil Sectors of the Iranian Economy." *Iranian Studies* 6:2/3 (Spring-Summer 1973): 66–103.

Nowshirvani, Vahid F. and Patrick Clawson. "The State and Social Equity in Postrevolutionary Iran." In *The Politics of Social Transformation in Afghanistan, Iran, and Pakistan*, eds. Myron Weiner and Ali Banuazizi, 228–69. Syracuse, NY: Syracuse University Press, 1994.

Okazaki, Shoko. "The Great Persian Famine of 1870–71." *Bulletin of the School of Oriental and African Studies* 49:1 (1986): 183–92.

Omid, Homa. *Islam and the Post-Revolutionary State in Iran*. New York: St. Martin's Press, 1994.

Pahlavi, Mohammad Reza Shah. *Answer to History*. New York: Stein and Day, 1980.

Paidar, Parvin. *Women and the Political Process in Twentieth-Century Iran*. Cambridge: Cambridge University Press, 1995.

Paine, Chris and Erica Schoenberger. "Iranian Nationalism and the Great Powers: 1872–1954." *MERIP Reports* 37 (May 1975): 3–28.

Parsa, Misagh. "State, Class, and Ideology in the Iranian Revolution." *Comparative Studies of South Asia, Africa and the Middle East* 29:1 (2009): 3–17.

"Mosque of Last Resort: State Reform and Social Conflict in the Early 1960s." In *A Century of Revolution: Social Movements in Iran*, ed. John Foran, 135–59. Minneapolis: University of Minnesota Press, 1994.

Social Origins of the Iranian Revolution. New Brunswick, NJ: Rutgers University Press, 1989.

Parsi, Tria. *Treacherous Alliance: The Secret Dealings of Israel, Iran, and the United States*. New Haven, CT: Yale University Press, 2007.

Parsons, Anthony. *The Pride and the Fall: Iran 1974–1979*. London: Jonathan Cape, 1984.

Pelletreau, Robert. "U.S. Policy in the Middle East." *U.S. Department of State Dispatch* 6:33 (1995): 638.

Pesaran, Evaleila. *Iran's Struggle for Economic Independence: Reform and Counter-Reform in the Post-Revolutionary Era*. New York: Routledge, 2011.

"Towards an Anti-Western Stance: The Economic Discourse of Iran's 1979 Revolution." *Iranian Studies* 41:5 (December 2008).

Pesaran, M. H. "Economic Development and Revolutionary Upheavals in Iran." In *Iran: A Revolution in Turmoil*, ed. Haleh Afshar, 15–50. Albany: State University of New York Press, 1990.

"The System of Dependent Capitalism in Pre- and Post-Revolutionary Iran." *International Journal of Middle East Studies* 14 (1982): 501–22.

Peters, F. E. *Jerusalem and Mecca: The Typology of the Holy City in the Near East*. New York: New York University Press, 1986.

Petrossian, Vahe. "Iran Awaits New Confrontation." *Middle East Economic Digest* 40:4 (January 1996): 2–3.

Phillips, James. "The Changing Face of Middle Eastern Terrorism." *Heritage Foundation Reports: 1005* (October 6, 1994).

Piekalkiewicz, Jaroslaw and Alfred Wayne Penn. *Politics of Ideocracy*. Albany: State University of New York Press, 1995.

Piekalkiewicz, Jaroslaw and Christopher Hamilton, eds. *Public Bureaucracies between Reform and Resistance*. New York: Berg., 1991.

Piscatori, James, ed. *Islam in the Political Process*. Cambridge: Cambridge University Press, 1983.

Pontusson, Jonas. "From Comparative Public Policy to Political Economy Putting Political Institutions in Their Place and Taking Interests Seriously." *Comparative Political Studies* 28:1 (April 1995): 117–47.

Postel, Danny, Kaveh Ehsani, Maziar Behrooz and Chris Cutrone. "30 Years of the Islamic Revolution: The Tragedy of the Left." Panel Discussion at University of Chicago, November 5, 2009; Transcript in *Platypus Review* 20: Supplement.

Povey, Elaheh Rostami. "Trade Unions and Women's NGOs: Diverse Civil Society Organisations in Iran." *Development in Practice* 14:1/2 (February 2004): 254–66.

Prigmore, Charles S. "Social Welfare in Iran." In *Social Welfare and Services in an International Context*, eds. Doreen Elliott, Nazneen S. Mayadas and Thomas D. Watts, 171–82. Springfield, IL: Charles C. Thomas, 1990.

Proceedings of a one-day conference: Economic Development in Post-Revolutionary Iran. Upper Montclair, NJ: Montclair State University, March 3, 1995.

Purmoqeyeh, Said Javad. *Eqtesad-e Bakhsh-e Amumi {Private Sector Economics}*. Tehran: Nashrani, 1375 (1996/97).

Rahnema, Ali. *An Islamic Utopian: A Political Biography of Dr. Ali Shariati*. New York: I. B. Tauris, 1998.

Rahnema, Saeed and Sohrab Behdad, eds. *Iran after the Revolution: Crisis of an Islamic State*. London: I. B. Tauris, 1995.

Rahnema, Saeed and Farhad Nomani. *The Secular Miracle: Religion, Politics and Economic Policy in Iran*. London: Zed Press, 1990.

Rahnema, Saeed. "Work Councils in Iran: The Illusion of Worker Control." *Economic and Industrial Democracy* 13:1 (February 1992): 69–94.

Raisdana, Fariborz with Ahmad Gharavi Nakhjavani. "The Drug Market in Iran." *Annals of the American Academy of Political and Social Science* 582 (July 2002): 149–66.

Rajaee, Bahram. "The Politics of Refugee Policy in Post-Revolutionary Iran." *Middle East Journal* 54:1 (Winter 2000): 44–63.

Rajaee, Farhang. "A Thermidor of 'Islamic Yuppies'? Conflict and Compromise in Iran's Politics." *The Middle East Journal* 53:2 (Spring 1999): 217–31.

Rakel, Eva Patricia. "The Political Elite in the Islamic Republic of Iran: From Khomeini to Ahmadinejad." *Comparative Studies of South Asia, Africa and the Middle East* 29:1 (2009).

Ram, Haggay. *Myth and Mobilization in Revolutionary Iran: The Use of the Friday Congregational Sermon.* Washington, DC: American University Press, 1994.

Ramazani, Nesta. "Women in Iran: The Revolutionary Ebb and Flow." *Middle East Journal* 47:3 (Summer 1993): 409–28.

Ramazani, R. K. "Iran's Foreign Policy: Both North and South." *Middle East Journal* 46:3 (Summer 1992): 393–412.

"The Iran-Iraq War and the Persian Gulf Crisis." *Current History* (February 1988): 61–4, 86–8.

"Iran: Burying the Hatchet." *Foreign Policy* (Fall 1985): 52–74.

"Iran's Islamic Revolution and the Persian Gulf." *Current History* (January 1985): 5–8, 40–1.

"Iran's Revolution: Patterns, Problems and Prospects." *International Affairs* 56 (Summer 1980): 443–57.

ed. *Iran's Revolution: The Search for Consensus.* Bloomington: Indiana University Press, 1990.

Ranstorp, Magnus. "Hezbollah's Future?" *Jane's Intelligence Review* 7:2 (February 1, 1995): 81.

"Hizbollah's Command Leadership: Its Structure, Decision Making and Relationship with the Iranian Clergy and Institutions." *Terrorism and Political Violence* 6:3 (Autumn 1994): 303–39.

Rapaczynski, Andrzej. "The Roles of the State and the Market in Establishing Property Rights." *Journal of Economic Perspectives*: 10:2 (Spring 1996): 87–103.

Rashidi, Ali. "De-Privatisation Process and the Iranian Economy after the Revolution of 1979." In *The Economy of Islamic Iran: Between State and Market,* ed. Thierry Colville, 37–67. Tehran: Institut Français de Recherche en Iran, 1994.

"The Political Elite in the Islamic Republic of Iran From Khomeini to Ahmadinejad." *Comparative Studies of South Asia, Africa and the Middle East* 29:1 (2009): 105–25.

Rasler, Karen. "Concessions, Repression, and Political Protest in the Iranian Revolution." *American Sociological Review* 61 (February 1996): 132–52.

Rastegar, Asghar. "Health Policy and Medical Education." In *Iran after the Revolution: Crisis of an Islamic State,* eds. Saeed Rahnema and Sohrab Behdad, 218–28. London: I. B. Tauris, 1995.

Rathmell, Andrew. "Iran's Rearmament – How Much a Threat?" *Jane's Intelligence Review*: 6:7 (July 1, 1994): 317.

Razaqi, Ibrahim. *Funding for Iran's Privatization [Naqdi bar Khasusisazi-ye Iran].* Tehran: Institute of Cultural Service, 1372 (1993/94).

Toseyeh Eqtesadi-ye Iran [Economic Development in Iran]. Tehran: Development, 1369 (1989/90).

Razavi, Hossein and Firouz Vakil. *The Political Environment of Economic Planning in Iran, 1971–1983*. Boulder, CO: Westview Press, 1984.

Razi, G. Hossein. "The Nexus of Legitimacy and Performance: The Lessons of the Iranian Revolution." *Comparative Politics* (July 1987): 453–68.

Reguer, Sara. "Persian Oil and the First Lord: A Chapter in the Career of Winston Churchill." *Military Affairs* 46:3 (October 1982): 134–8.

Reich, Bernard. "The United States and Iran: An Overview." In *Economic Consequences of the Revolution in Iran: A Compendium of Papers*. Submitted to the Joint Economic Committee, Congress of the United States. Washington, DC: US Government Printing Office, 1980.

Reiter, Yitzhak. *Islamic Endowments in Jerusalem under British Mandate*. London: Frank Cass, 1996.

Remmer, Karen L. "Theoretical Decay and Theoretical Development: The Resurgence of Institutional Analysis." *World Politics* 50:1 (October 1997): 34–61.

Rezun, Miron. "Reza Shah's Court Minister: Teymourtash." *International Journal of Middle East Studies* 12:2 (September 1980): 119–37.

Richards, Helmut. "Land Reform and Agribusiness in Iran." *MERIP Reports*: 43 (December 1975): 3–18, 24.

Ricks, Thomas M. "U.S. Military Missions to Iran, 1943–1978: The Political Economy of Military Assistance." *Iranian Studies* 12:3/4 (Summer-Autumn 1979): 163–93.

Riesèbrodt, Martin, transl. Don Reneau. *Pious Passion: The Emergence of Modern Fundamentalism in the United States and Iran*. Berkeley: University of California Press, 1993.

Rinehart, James F. *Revolution and the Millennium China, Mexico, and Iran*. Westport, CT: Praeger, 1997.

Roberson, Barbara Allen. "Iran and the Shia Leadership." *The Gulf States Newsletter* 20:506 (March 1995).

Roniger, Luis and Ayse Gunes-Ayata, eds. *Democracy, Clientelism and Civil Society*. Boulder, CO: Lynne Reinner, 1994.

Roosevelt, Kermit. *Countercoup: The Struggle for the Control of Iran*. New York: McGraw-Hill, 1979.

Rosen, Barry M., ed. *Iran Since the Revolution: Internal Dynamics, Regional Conflict, and the Superpowers*. New York: Columbia University Press, 1985.

Ross, Michael L. "The Political Economy of the Resource Curse." *World Politics* 51 (January 1999): 297–322.

Rouleau, Eric. "Khomeini's Iran." *Foreign Affairs* (Fall 1980): 1–20.

Roy, Olivier. "The Crisis of Religious Legitimacy in Iran." *The Middle East Journal* 53:2 (Spring 1999): 201–16.

"Tensions in Iran: The Future of the Islamic Revolution." *Middle East Report* (Summer 1998): 38–41.

The Failure of Political Islam, transl. Carol Volk. Cambridge, MA: Harvard University Press, 1994.

"Patronage and Solidarity Groups: Survival or Reformation?" In *Democracy without Democrats? The Renewal of Politics in the Muslim World*, ed. Ghassan Salamé, 270–81. London: I. B. Tauris, 1994.

Rubin, Barry. "Iran's Year of Turmoil." *Current History* (January 1983): 28–31, 42.

Paved with Good Intentions The American Experience and Iran. Oxford: Oxford University Press, 1980.

Sadeghi, Mehdi and Sue Wright. "Can FDI Be Encouraged? An Analysis of Iran's Future Economic Prospects." *International Economics and Finance Journal* 2:1–2 (2007): 31–49.

Salamé, Ghassan, ed. *The Foundations of the Arab State*. London: Croom Helm, 1987.

Salami, Habibollah, Naser Shahnooshi and Kenneth J. Thomson. "The Economic Impacts of Drought on the Economy of Iran: An Integration of Linear Programming and Macroeconometric Modeling Approaches." *Ecological Economics* 68 (2009): 1032–9.

Salehi Esfahani, Hadi and Farzad Taheripour, "Hidden Public Expenditures and the Economy in Iran." *International Journal of Middle East Studies* 34:4 (November 2002): 691–718.

Seidi, Ali A. "The Accountability of Para-Governmental Organizations (Bonyads): The Case of Iranian Foundations." *Iranian Studies* 37:3 (2004): 479–98.

"Charismatic Political Authority and Populist Economics in Post Revolutionary Iran." *Third World Quarterly* 22:2 (2001): 219–36.

ed. *Democracy without Democrats? The Renewal of Politics in the Muslim World*. London: I. B. Tauris, 1994.

Salehi-Isfahani, Djavad. "Poverty, Inequality, and Populist Politics in Iran." *Journal of Economic Inequality* 7 (2009): 5–28.

"Growing Up in Iran: Tough Times for the Revolution's Children." *Brown Journal of World Affairs* XV:1 (Fall/Winter 2008): 63–74.

"Human Resources in Iran: Potentials and Challenges." *Iranian Studies* 38:1 (March 2005): 117–47.

"Labor and the Challenge of Economic Restructuring in Iran." *Middle East Report*: 210 (Spring 1999): 34–7.

Salmanzadeh, Cyrus and Gwyn E. Jones. "An Approach to the Micro Analysis of the Land Reform Program in Southwestern Iran." *Land Economics* 55:1 (February 1979): 108–27.

Sarabi, Farzin. "The Post Khomeini Era in Iran: The Elections of the Fourth Islamic Majlis." *Middle East Journal* 48:1 (Winter 1994): 89–107.

Schirazi, Asghar. *The Constitution of Iran Politics and the State in the Islamic Republic*. London: I. B. Tauris, 1997.

Islamic Development Policy: The Agrarian Question in Iran. Boulder, CO: Lynn Rienner, 1993.Schahgaldian, Nikola B. *Iran and the Postwar Security in the Persian Gulf*. Santa Monica, CA: The RAND Corporation, 1994.

"Iran after Khomeini." *Current History* (February 1990): 61–4, 82–4.

The Clerical Establishment in Iran. Santa Monica: The RAND Corporation, 1989.

The Iranian Military under the Islamic Republic. Santa Monica: The RAND Corporation, 1987.

Sciolino, Elaine. "Iran's Durable Revolution." *Foreign Affairs* 61 (Spring 1983): 893–920.

Schulz, Ann T. "Iran: The Descending Monarchy." *Current History* (January 1979): 5, 33–4.

Schwarz, Rolf. "The Political Economy of State-Formation in the Arab Middle East: Rentier States, Economic Reform, and Democratization." *Review of International Political Economy* 15:4 (October 2008): 599–621.

Schwedler, Jillian, ed. *Toward Civil Society in the Middle East? A Primer.* Boulder, CO: Lynne Rienner, 1995.

Scoville, James G. "The Labor Market in the Prerevolutionary Iran." *Economic Development and Cultural Change* 34:1 (1985): 143–55.

Secor, Laura. "The Rationalist." *The New Yorker* 84:47 (February 2, 2009): 31.

Selvik, Kjetil, "From 'Enemies of the Revolution' to Unfulfilled Ideal: Private Industrial Entrepreneurs in the Islamic Republic of Iran." In *Iran: From Theocracy to the Green Movement* ed. Negin Nabavi, 101–19. New York: Palgrave Macmillan, 2012.

Seyf, Ahmad. "Foreign Firms and Local Merchants in Nineteenth-Century Iran." *Middle Eastern Studies* 36:4 (October 2000): 137–55.

Shabiri-Nezhad, Ali Akbar. *Gastreh-ye Mali va Sakhtar-e Budjehi-ye Iran: Algu-ye Manabeh va Masraf [The Expansion of Taxation and Construction of the Iranian Budget: Pattern of Sources and Consumption].* Tehran: Nashrani, 1375 (1996/97).

Shadpour, K. "Primary Health Care Networks in the Islamic Republic of Iran." *La Revue de Sante de la Mediterranee Orientale* 6:4 (2000): 822–5.

Shafik, Nemat, ed. *Economic Challenges Facing Middle Eastern and North African Countries: Alternative Futures.* New York: St. Martin's Press, 1988.

Shahbaz, Seyyed Ali, ed. *Imam Reza (A.S.) and History of the Holy Shrine.* Mashhad: M. M. Ali Khorasani, 1997.

Shahidian, Hammed. "Women and Clandestine Politics in Iran, 1970–1985." *Feminist Studies* 23:1 (Spring 1997): 7–42.

Shahmoradi, Asghar and Afshin Honarvar. "Gasoline Subsidy and Consumer Surplus in the Islamic Republic of Iran." *OPEC Energy Review* (September 2008): 232–45.

Shahri, Nima Nasrollahi. "The Petroleum Legal Framework of Iran: History, Trends and the Way Forward." *China and Eurasia Forum Quarterly* 8:1 (2010): 111–26.

Shambayati, Hootan. "The Rentier State, Interest Groups, and the Paradox of Autonomy: State and Business in Turkey and Iran" *Comparative Politics* (April 1994): 307–31.

Sharbatoghlie, Ahmad. *Urbanization and Regional Disparities in Post-Revolutionary Iran.* Boulder, CO: Westview Press.

Shawcross, William. *The Shah's Last Ride: The Fate of an Ally.* New York: Simon & Schuster, 1988.

Shiravi, Abdolhossein and Seyed Nasrollah Ebrahimi. "Legal and Regulatory Environment of LNG Projects in Iran." *Journal of Energy and Natural Resources Law* 25 (2007): 150–67.

Shiravi, Abdolhossein. "The Legal and Regulatory Framework for BOT Projects in Iran." *International Business Law Journal* 2 (2008): 165–84.

Shirdel, Mohammad-Ali. "Le Changement dans les Stratégies du Développement Economique en Iran, 1980–1988; le Socialism Islamique." *Politique et Sociétés* 26:1 (2007): 97–131.

"La Continuité and le Changement dans les Stratégies du Développement Economique en Iran aprés 1989." *Canadian Journal of Political Science* 40:3 (September 2007): 685–709.

Shugart, Matthew Soberg. "Patterns of Revolution." *Theory and Society* 18 (1989): 249–71.

Siavoshi, Sussan. "Factionalism and Iranian Politics: The Post-Khomeini Experience." *Iranian Studies* 25:3/4 (1992): 27–49.

Sick, Gary. "Iran: The Adolescent Revolution." *Journal of International Affairs* 49:1 (Summer 1995): 145–66.

"Confronting Contradictions: The Revolution in Its Teens." *Iranian Studies* 26:3–4 (Summer/Fall 1993): 407–10.

Sidahmed, Abdel Salam and Anoushiravan Ehteshami, eds. *Islamic Fundamentalism*. Boulder, CO: Westview Press, 1996.

Sigler, John H. "The Iran-Iraq Conflict: The Tragedy of Limited Conventional War." *International Journal* 41:2 (Spring 1986): 424–56.

Skocpol, Theda. "Rentier State and Shi'a Islam in the Iranian Revolution." *Theory and Society* 11 (1982): 265–83.

States and Social Revolutions: Comparative Analysis of France, Russia and China. Cambridge: Cambridge University Press, 1979.

Slavin, Barbara Slavin. "Iran Turns to China, Barter to Survive Sanctions." *Atlantic Council Iran Task Force*, November 2011.

Smith, Benjamin. *Hard Times in the Land of Plenty: Oil Politics in Iran and Indonesia*. Ithaca, NY: Cornell University Press, 2007.

"The Wrong Kind of Crisis: Why Oil Booms and Busts Rarely Lead to Authoritarian Breakdown." *Studies in Comparative Development* 40:4 (Winter 2006): 55–76.

Smith, Pamela Ann. "Rafsanjani's perestroika." *Global Finance* 6 (Fall 1992): 40–3.

Souresfrafil, Omid. *The Islamic Success: The Untold Story of the Islamic Revolution of Iran*. Australia: Wild & Woolley Pty, 1996.

Sreberny-Mohammadi, Annabelle and Ali Mohammadi. *Small Media, Big Revolution: Communication, Culture, and the Iranian Revolution*. Minneapolis: University of Minnesota Press, 1994.

Suleiman, Ezra N. and John Waterbury, eds. *The Political Economy of Public Sector Reform and Privatization*. Boulder, CO: Westview Press, 1990.

"Introduction: Analyzing Privatization in Industrial and Developing Countries" In *The Political Economy of Public Sector Reform and Privatization*, eds. Ezra N. Suleiman and John Waterbury, 1–21. Boulder, CO: Westview Press, 1990.

Tavassoli, Mojgan. "Iran Health Houses Open the Door to Primary Care." *Bulletin of the World Health Organization* 86:8 (August 2008): 585–6.

Teimourian, Hazhir. "Iran's Fifteen Years of Islam." *World Today* 50 (April 1994): 67–70.

Thaiss, Gustav. "Religion and Social Change in Iran: The Bazaar as a Case Study." In *Iran Faces the Seventies*, ed. E. Yarshater: 189–216. New York: Praeger, 1971.

Torbat, Akbar E. "The Brain Drain from Iran to the United States." *Middle East Journal* 56:2 (Spring 2002): 272–95.

Tripp, Charles. "Islam and the Secular Logic of the State in the Middle East." In *Islamic Fundamentalism*, eds. Anoushirvan Ehteshami and Abdel Salam Sidahmed, 51–70. Boulder, CO: Westview Press, 1996.

Turner, Louis and James M. Bedore. *Middle East Industrialisation: A Study of Saudi and Iranian Downstream Investments*. Westmead: Royal Institute for International Affairs, 1979.

UNIDO, *Islamic Republic of Iran: Industrial Revitalization*, London: Economist Intelligence Unit/UNIDO, 1995.

Utvik, Bjørn Olav. "Neo-Cons in Power: End of Reform in Iran?" *Universitetet i Oslo Gulf Studies* 6, 2006.

Vaghefi, M. Reza. "A Micro-Analysis Approach to Modernization Process: A Case Study of Modernity and Traditionalism Conflict." *International Journal of Middle East Studies* 12:2 (September 1980): 181–97.

Vakili-Zad, Cyrus. Collision of Consciousness: Modernization and Development in Iran." *Middle Eastern Studies* 32:3 (July 1996): 139–60

"Continuity and Change: The Structure of Power in Iran." In *Modern Capitalism and Islamic Ideology in Iran*, eds. Cyrus Bina and Hamid Zanganeh, 13–48. London: MacMillan, 1992.

Valadkhani, Abbas. "An Empirical Analysis of the Black Market Exchange Rate in Iran." *Queensland University of Technology, School of Economics and Finance, Discussion Papers in Economics, Finance and International Competitiveness* 144 (May 2003).

Vali, Abbas and Sami Zubaida. "Factionalism and political discourse in the Islamic Republic of Iran: The Case of the Hujjatiyeh Society." *Economy and Society* 14:2 (May 1985): 139–73.

Valibeigi, Mehrdad. "The Private Sector in Iran's Post-Revolutionary Economy." *The Journal of South Asian and Middle Eastern Studies* 17:3 (Spring 1994): 1–18.

"." Iranian Studies 24: 3/4 (1992): 51–65.

"Islamic Economics and Economic Policy Formation in Post-Revolutionary Iran: A Critique." *Journal of Economic Issues* 27 (September 1993): 793–812.

Islamization of the Economy: The Post-Revolutionary Iranian Experience. Unpublished doctoral dissertation, American University, 1991.

Viorst, Milton. "Changing Iran: The Limits of the Revolution." *Foreign Affairs* 74:6 (November/December 1995): 63–76.

Walton, Thomas. "Economic Development and Revolutionary Upheavals in Iran." *Cambridge Journal of Economics* 4 (1980): 271–92.

Waterbury, John. *Exposed to Innumerable Delusions: Public Enterprise and State Power in Egypt, India, Mexico, and Turkey*. Cambridge: Cambridge University Press, 1993.

"The Growth of Public Sector Enterprise in the Middle East." In *The Economic Dimensions of Middle Eastern History*, eds. Haleh Esfandiari and A. L. Udovitch, 239–53. Princeton, NJ: The Darwin Press, 1990.

Waxman, Dov. *The Islamic Republic of Iran: Between Revolution and Realpolitik*. Conflict Studies 308, Research Institute for the Study of Conflict and Terrorism, April 1998.

Weimer, David L., ed. *The Political Economy of Property Rights Institutional Change and Credibility in the Reform of Centrally Planned Economies*. Cambridge: Cambridge University Press, 1997.

Weiner, Allen S. "The Iran-United States Claims Tribunal: What Lies Ahead?" *The Law and Practice of International Courts and Tribunals* 6 (2007): 89–96.

Weiner, Myron and Ali Banuazizi, eds. *The Politics of Social Transformation in Afghanistan, Iran, and Pakistan*. Syracuse, NY: Syracuse University Press, 1994.

eds. *The State, Religion, and Ethnic Politics: Afghanistan, Iran, and Pakistan*. Syracuse, NY: Syracuse University Press, 1986.

Wietfeld, Axel M. "Understanding Middle East Gas Exporting Behavior." *The Energy Journal* 32:2 (2011): 203–28.

Wilkins, Mira. "The Oil Companies in Perspective." *Daedalus* 104:4 (Fall 1975): 159–78.

Wilson, Rodney. *Economic Development in the Middle East*. London: Routledge, 1995.

ed. *Islamic Financial Markets*. London: Routledge, 1990.

Workman, W. Thom. *The Social Origins of the Iran Iraq War*. Boulder, CO: Lynn Rienner, 1994.

Wright, Robin. "Dateline Tehran: A Revolution Implodes." *Foreign Policy* (Summer 1996): 161–74.

Sacred Rage: The Wrath of Militant Islam. New York: Simon & Schuster, 1986.

Wright, Robin and Shaul Bakhash. "The U.S. and Iran: An Offer They Can't Refuse?" *Foreign Policy* (Fall 1997): 124–37.

Xu, Lixin Colin. "Determinants of the Repartitioning of Property Rights between the Government and State Enterprises." *Economic Development and Cultural Change* 46:3 (April 1998): 537–60.

Yarshater, Ehsan, ed. "Bonyad-e Šahid." In *Encyclopaedia Iranica*. Costa Mesa: Mazda Press, 1985.

Yong, William and Alireza Hajihosseini. "Understanding Iran under Sanctions: Oil and the National Budget." *Oxford Energy Comment* (January 2013).

Zabih, Sephr. *The Iranian Military in Revolution and War*. London: Routledge, 1988.

The Mossadegh Era: Roots of the Iranian Revolution. Chicago: Lake View Press, 1982.

Zahedi, Dariush. "What to Do about Iran?" *Harvard Middle Eastern and Islamic Review* 4:1–2 (1997–8): 108–21.

Zahirinejad, Mahnaz. "The Role of Political Structure in Iran's Energy Decision Making Policy." *Journal of Third World Studies* 29:1 (Spring 2012): 231–47.

Zahrani, Mostafa. "Sanctions against Iran." *Iranian Journal of International Affairs* 20:2 (Spring 2008): 23–42.

Zangeneh, Hamid. "Socioeconomic Trends in Iran: Successes and Failures." *The Muslim World* 94 (October 2004): 481–93.

"The Post-Revolutionary Iranian Economy: A Policy Appraisal." *Middle East Policy* 6:2 (October 1998): 113–30.

"International Trade and Investment in Iran: An Appraisal." *Scandinavian Journal of Development Alternatives* 16:2 (1997): 25–42.

ed. *Islam, Iran, and World Stability*. New York: St. Martin's Press, 1994.

Zangeneh, Hamid and Janice M. Moore. "Economic Development and Growth in Iran." In *Islam, Iran, and World Stability*, ed. Hamid Zanganeh, 201–16. New York: St. Martin's Press, 1994.

Zonis, Marvin. "The Rule of the Clerics in the Islamic Republic of Iran." *The Annals of the American Academy of Political and Social Sciences*: 482 (November 1985): 85–108.

"Iran: A Theory of Revolution from Accounts of the Revolution. *World Politics* 35:4 (July 1983): 586–606.

The Political Elite of Iran. Princeton, NJ: Princeton University Press, 1971.

Zonis, Marvin and Daniel Brumberg. "Shi'ism as Interpreted by Khomeini: An Ideology of Revolutionary Violence." In *Shi'ism, Resistance, and Revolution*, ed. Martin Kramer, 47–66. Boulder, CO: Westview Press, 1987.

Zonooz, Behrouz Hady. "Trade Strategies and Industrial Development in Iran: 1979–98." In *Trade Policy and Economic Integration in the Middle East and North Africa: Economic Boundaries in Flux*, eds. Hassan Hakimian and Jeffrey B. Nugent, 138–62. Routledge: 2005.

Zoroofchi, Mahmoud and Nicholas C. Webb. "Iran: The Taxation of Companies and Individuals." *Bulletin of the International Bureau of Fiscal Documentation* (November 1990): 549–57.

Zubaida, Sami. *Islam: The People and the State*. London: Routledge, 1988.

Index

CPSIA information can be obtained
at www.ICGtesting.com
Printed in the USA
BVHW030452030720
582830BV00009B/2

9 780521 738149